# THE ROUTLEDGE COMPANION
# TO FASCISM AND THE FAR RIGHT

*The Routledge Companion to Fascism and the Far Right* is an engaging and accessible guide to the origins of fascism, the main facets of far-right ideology, and the reality of fascist and far-right government around the world. In a clear and concise manner, this book illustrates the main features of the subject using chronologies, maps, glossaries and biographies of key individuals. As well as the key examples of Hitler's Germany and Mussolini's Italy, this book also draws on extreme right-wing movements and regimes in Latin America, Eastern Europe and the Far East.

In a series of original essays, the authors explore the following aspects of fascism and the far right:

- Roots and origins
- Ideology
- Attitudes to nation and race
- Social policy
- Economic thinking
- Diplomacy and foreign policy
- The practice of politics in government and opposition.

**Peter Davies** is Senior Lecturer in European History at the University of Huddersfield. His books include *The National Front in France* (1999), *France and the Second World War* (2001) and *The Extreme Right in France* (2002). **Derek Lynch** is Senior Lecturer in Politics at the University of Huddersfield. He is currently working on a book on radio broadcasting and propaganda in the twentieth century.

# *Routledge Companions*

*Routledge Companions* are the perfect reference guides, providing everything the student or general reader needs to know. Authoritative and accessible, they combine the in-depth expertise of leading specialists with straightforward, jargon-free writing. In each book you'll find what you're looking for, clearly presented – whether through an extended article or an A–Z entry – in ways which the beginner can understand and even the expert will appreciate.

*Routledge Companion to Global Economics*
Edited by Robert Beynon

*Routledge Companion to Feminism and Postfeminism*
Edited by Sarah Gamble

*Routledge Companion to the New Cosmology*
Edited by Peter Coles

*Routledge Companion to Postmodernism*
Edited by Stuart Sim

*Routledge Companion to Russian Literature*
Edited by Neil Cornwell

*Routledge Companion to Semiotics and Linguistics*
Edited by Paul Cobley

*Routledge Companion to Fascism and the Far Right*
By Peter Davies and Derek Lynch

# THE ROUTLEDGE COMPANION TO FASCISM AND THE FAR RIGHT

Peter Davies and Derek Lynch

Routledge
Taylor & Francis Group

LONDON AND NEW YORK

First published 2002
by Routledge
11 New Fetter Lane, London EC4P 4EE

Simultaneously published in the USA and Canada
by Routledge
29 West 35th Street, New York, NY 10001

*Routledge is an imprint of the Taylor & Francis Group*

© 2002 Peter Davies and Derek Lynch

Typeset in Times New Roman by Taylor & Francis Books Ltd
Printed and bound in Great Britain by MPG Books Ltd, Bodmin

*British Library Cataloguing in Publication Data*
A catalogue record for this book is available from the British Library

*Library of Congress Cataloging in Publication Data*
A catalog record for this book has been requested

ISBN 0–415–21494–7 (hbk)
ISBN 0–415–21495–5 (pbk)

# CONTENTS

# MAPS

# ACKNOWLEDGEMENTS

We would like to thank the following people: Gillian Oliver, Lauren Dallinger and Vicky Peters at Routledge for their support and encouragement; Bill Roberts and Rainer Horn at the University of Huddersfield for their help on specific topics.

We are also indebted to the many historians and political scientists who have worked on the subject of fascism before us. It has been a pleasure to explore their writings.

# NOTE

Throughout the book, cross-references will be shown in bold. They aim to help the reader navigate through the book. All names and terms in bold can be found in either the Biography or the Glossary.

# INTRODUCTION

The *Routledge Companion to Fascism and the Far Right* is designed as a reference source and guide for all those with an interest in the phenomenon of fascism and far-right politics. Given a pervasive, and in some respects, unhealthy preoccupation with the **Second World War** and fascism among some sections of the general public, the popular literature on the topic is vast and slightly unhelpful. However, there is also a renewed interest in the serious academic study of fascism and the far right, fuelled by the persistence of extremist ideology in a post-Cold War world in which ideology was meant to wither away.[1] The 1990s witnessed the revived visibility of ethno-nationalism and associated genocidal **violence** (e.g. in Bosnia or Rwanda); the influence of former neo-fascists in the Italian *Alleanza Nazionale* (AN); the prominence of the *Front National* (FN) in France, the *Freiheitliche Partei Österreichs* (FPÖ) in Austria, the *National Demokratische Partei Deutschlands* (NPD) in Germany, and groups like *Pamyat* in Russia. These trends go beyond Europe: we could include the rise of Hindu nationalism in India, as reflected in the ascendancy of the *Bharatiya Janata* Party and the *Rashtriya Swayamsevak Sangh* (RSS), or the prominence of some of the more violent and conspiratorial 'militia' groups in the US. At an instinctive level, all of these are called 'far right', just as fascism is; and yet there is unease about linking them all to Adolf **Hitler** or Benito **Mussolini**. An accurate understanding of these phenomena requires careful study and some effort at dispassionate analysis.

## 'FASCISM' AND 'FASCISMS'

The first problem to be encountered by any observer is that of a definition, or, seen another way, that of too many definitions, not merely of 'the far right' but of 'fascism' itself. A more precise purpose of the *Companion*, therefore, is to help readers understand the location of fascism and the far right on the political landscape, and the boundaries between them and other movements of thought in the twentieth and twenty-first centuries. To this end, readers will find material on rightist parties or personalities that are/were close to fascism, as well as those that are commonly juxtaposed with it.

The *Companion* will provoke readers into asking questions about the nature of these ideologies, as well as providing some answers. One question may already have crossed their minds: why not confine the book to fascism? The most obvious reply is that fascism is seen as a quintessential movement of the far right. It is also evident that some concerns emphasised by fascists were or

1

are still shared by parties of the far right, and the boundary between the two is frequently difficult to define. However, and this is an important point, there are many instances in which the boundary *can* be defined. This is because, on closer inspection, many fascist and fascist-like movements are, or have been, quite revolutionary in their desire to overturn the existing social order or to provoke a kind of permanent revolution. Fascist **populism** has frequently stressed the mobilisation of the masses in ways that scare the more conservative middle classes. While much of fascism's anti-capitalist **propaganda** has merely been rhetorical, some fascisms have exhibited an anti-free market strand inherited from **socialism**, or, indeed, anarchism. Thus, if 'right wing' simply means 'conservative', the question of whether fascism was essentially right wing is not so open and shut. Sternhell, for one, characterised early French fascism as 'neither right nor left'.[2] Ambiguities and paradoxes such as these abound and cannot be dismissed as 'merely academic' preoccupations. They are critical to an understanding of the role of fascism and the far right in modern history and politics, even in the post-Cold War world, and, we hope, are already among the concerns of the curious and inquisitive reader of a book like this one.

Before discussing the 'far right' in general, a few words about fascism itself are in order. The term was most widely used to refer to the movement surrounding Mussolini, although some other right-wing Italian groups in the years after the First World War also employed it. It described the bundle of rods, frequently accompanied by an axe, which was a symbol of discipline and unity, and was associated with the legacy of the Roman Empire. *Fasces* or *fasci* were groups of people bound together in solidarity, like the *Fasci di Combattimento*, the cabal of ex-soldiers grouped around Mussolini and like-minded critics of the Italian state in 1919. Indeed, as early as the 1890s, the term had been used by left-wing peasants who formed a solidarity group called the Sicilian *fasci*.[3] Stressing his unique commitment to truly disciplined struggle and solidarity, Mussolini gradually commandeered the term for his own movement and, eventually, for his system of ideas. It subsequently came to be associated with the Nazi regime in Germany and others that emulated these dictatorships. With a genealogy like that, fascism was never going to be easy to pin down.

Since the end of the Second World War, the problem of definitions has been further complicated by the widespread, but often careless or inaccurate, use of the word as a pejorative term of abuse directed at people who are conservative, right wing or authoritarian in the traditional sense. It can be used even more widely to refer to simply disagreeable people or opinions. Indeed, left-wing political activists have often used it to denigrate one another. Such extremely loose usage does no justice to the historical record and conflates important concepts whose nuances should be of concern to the serious observer of history and politics. On closer inspection, of course, there were even important differences between Mussolini's doctrine and that of Hitler. For many writers, the sheer intensity of Hitler's obsession with **race** and the scale of Nazi terror suggest that the German regime was fundamentally different from that in Italy. According to this perspective, Nazism is a distinct phenomenon and one that is more disagreeable than fascism. Whatever its merits, an excessively narrow focus would miss the bigger picture, namely, the existence of a pattern or cluster of similar political phenomena, especially prevalent in Europe in the first half of the twentieth century. Moreover, when contrasted with other right-wing authoritarian movements of the twentieth century, fascism and Nazism, notwithstanding their differences, are both more systematic and more distinctive, and are therefore classed as 'core fascisms'. (The word 'Fascism', with a capital 'F', is used to refer to the Italian case in particular, while 'fascism' with a lower-case 'f' refers to the concept in general. We adhere to that convention throughout the *Companion*.)

As the reader will soon realise, many movements traditionally characterised as fascist were heavily shaped by national cultures, individual historical experiences and specific timeframes. Each one was different. There is no easy solution to the dilemmas over definitions and boundaries arising from the resulting eclectic mix of ideas and parties. Our approach is to cover a wide range of movements and ideas. As we will explain later, our Glossary entries even extend to some that are anti-fascist and anti-far right, but impinge significantly on our understanding of fascist and far-right politics to such an extent that they cannot be ignored. Their inclusion reflects our central concern that the Glossary should embrace concepts, events and phenomena that, in one way or another, shed light on the nature of fascism and the far right. We aim to identify the similarities and differences among these tendencies. We acknowledge that the boundaries between fascist and non-fascist phenomena are difficult to establish in many cases, though we do point to how these boundaries have been interpreted by others.

Many historians deal with these complexities by invoking a further set of concepts that describe phenomena associated with fascism, some of which are genuine variants of fascism and others merely having word association with it. Of these concepts, the most widely known is '**neo-fascism**', a modification to fascism that arose in post-Second World War conditions (e.g. the *Movimento Sociale Italiano* (MSI) in Italy, especially in the early years). Another is '**para-fascism**', a form of right-wing politics that looks like fascism but is not really all that fascist beneath the surface. Examples here might include the **Antonescu** regime in wartime Romania or **Franco**'s dictatorship in Spain, **Salazar**'s regime in Portugal and the authoritarian rule of **Dollfuss** in Austria. These movements or regimes sought to placate hardcore fascists or to impress Nazi Germany, for instance, but lacked the extremism, the totalitarianism or the 'fire in the belly' of the real thing. Para-fascist regimes were common in Central Europe at the height of Nazi power, as they kept the Germans at bay and avoided the pitfalls of full **Nazification**. For Griffin, they were 'aping fascism' with a poor imitation of fascism itself, frequently with concealed anti-fascist motives.[4] Of course,

3

precisely because they were ambiguous about their real purpose and their true nature, there is scope for debate on which of them were really para-fascist and which were simply traditional conservative dictatorships.

If the nature of fascism and far-right extremism has varied from one country to another, it has also varied over time. Fascism did not just appear like a bolt from the blue: it drew on many aspects of European political culture and society that had been evolving since the mid-nineteenth century, or even since the **French Revolution**. One of the reasons for the many manifestations of fascism is that it represented the coalescence of a broad swathe of opinions, beliefs and political orientations. It borrowed heavily from its rivals and even from its sworn enemies. It is not surprising that Nazism and **Stalinism** produced such intense barbarism on the battlefield as was witnessed in Germany's war on the Soviet Union: two totalitarianisms with such extreme aspirations to remould the world order and even human nature itself could never coexist without a final, cataclysmic showdown. Fascism arose in an intellectual climate when old certainties were under attack and ideas were in flux. **Collectivism** bred hostility to liberal individualism; anarchism challenged and defied alleged 'bourgeois' smugness; **nihilism** had assaulted the centuries-old morality of **Christianity**; and the politics of **identity** was battering at the ramparts of **Enlightenment** rationality. War and new technology created a cult of power and action. The evolution of mass society, and subsequent social dislocation, caused by both demobilisation after the First World War and economic collapse, bred alienation, anger and confusion. The resulting pot-pourri of ideas and half-baked theories generated a fertile spawning ground for all kinds of extremism. Thus, historians explore the intellectual roots of the inter-war far right by looking at the *mélange* of embryonic ideas that formed the many-coloured strands of what eventually crystallised as hardcore fascism.

One concept in particular is used to capture the essence of these ideas: that of **'pre-fascism'**. This is a disputed label pinned retrospectively on thinkers and movements that emerged in the period between approximately 1880 and 1914, and which exhibited signs of embryonic fascism. Historians have detected 'pre-fascism' mainly in France, Italy and Germany. **Barrès**, **Gobineau** and **Sorel**, for example, are commonly viewed as 'pre-fascist' theoreticians, and the nationalist *Associazione Nazionale Italiana* (ANI) in Italy and the *Deutsche National Volks Partei* (DNVP) and *Deutschnationale Handlungsgehilfen-Verband* (DHV) in Germany in the early years of the twentieth century are regarded by some as archetypal 'pre-fascist' organisations. The term **'proto-fascism'** refers to the ideology of political movements that display signs of fascism, but lack the radicalism and populism usually associated with full-blown fascism. In whatever country they appear, proto-fascist movements invariably antedate, and often usher in, genuine fascist organisations. In literal terms, proto-fascism means 'primitive fascism'. The analogy here is with a prototype, an underdeveloped form of the real thing. On the other hand, if these movements do not have the potential for a full transition to fascism, they may simply be called 'semi-fascist'. If their agenda is frustrated by the actions of the wider political **establishment** or by changing political circumstances, they may even be labelled under the heading of '**abortive fascism**'.[5]

So much for the years before 1922. At the other end of the timescale, we find movements that have emerged in post-Second World War conditions. These are usually categorised in terms of the efforts they make either to conceal their fascist or semi-fascist traits, or to disassociate themselves from the inter-war fascist period altogether. 'Neo-fascism' stresses the novelty of its ideas in current conditions (just as neo-Marxists claim to be updating Marxism for twentieth- and twenty-first-century circumstances). Part of the new reality is the consolidation of liberal democracy in West European political culture since the end of the Second World War. Some neo-fascist parties renounce the inter-war experience altogether and try to distance themselves from fascism, ultimately being labelled 'post-fascist', just as the Party of Democratic Socialism in Germany has tried to reinvent itself as 'post-Communist'.[6]

A more contentious category is that of '**crypto-fascism**'. This refers to movements that have adopted broader right-wing or even conservative public images, while concealing a darker and fascist-like mode of operation. Critics charge that this is how **Le Pen**'s FN functions in France. These parties appeal to respectable **middle-class** conservatives with nationalist or traditionalist themes but also show tendencies toward violence, thuggishness and ambiguity about past fascist crimes as a palliative for their more hardcore followers. The key element in crypto-fascism is a concealed allegiance to a more sinister agenda or belief system. On the other hand, by its very nature, a concealed fascist identity can be difficult to prove in a conclusive manner, leaving critics to rely on lurid speculation or conspiracy theories.

## FASCISM AND THE FAR RIGHT

The presumed association between fascism and 'the far right' is based on a rather simplistic and linear view of the political spectrum. This typology places the most militant anarchists and Communists on the far left; socialists and democratic conservatives occupy the mainstream left and right respectively; while the centre is held by 'moderate' social democrats, liberals and Christian Democrats. The placement of Communists and fascists at opposite ends of the spectrum seems justified in view of the rhetorical vehemence of their propaganda against one another. The 'far right' consists of those anti-Communists and anti-socialists who, in the pursuit of their goals, are also either hostile to or indifferent to the values and practices of liberal democracy. However, their view, that the ends justify the means, even if the means include extra-legal violence, terror and **dictatorship**, often echo those of the far left. To that extent, they can be seen as closer to the Communists than they would ever care to admit. This is a theme that appears in much Western writing about fascism, especially that which groups the Soviet and Nazi regimes together. Seen in this way, the political spectrum is shaped like a horseshoe, with the extremes in close proximity but never quite touching.[7]

For those influenced by Marxian traditions, on the other hand, the far right has more in common with the conservative right.[8] Marxians view the world in terms of class struggle, noting the alignment of the middle classes behind the inter-war fascist movements and the anti-socialist and anti-union stance of fascism. There are debates within this camp about the balance of power between the fascists and the capitalists or about the motives of each side; nonetheless, the complete or near-complete convergence of interests between them is central to almost all Marxian approaches. Yet, even the anti-socialism of fascist parties needs to be qualified. Many of the key figures in fascism, and in the far-right movements that contributed to the climate that gave rise to it, were socialists in their youth or claimed that their ideology was a form of socialism peculiar to their own nation and its people. This was true of **Mussolini**, **Hitler**, **Sorel** and **Déat**.[9] Fascist leaders seem to have admired the capacity of socialism to rouse the masses and to challenge the status quo.

While fascism and the far right share many things in common, there is also scope for sharp disagreement. Fascism both inherited and absorbed elements of radicalism, anarchism and populism from its early interaction with anarchism and socialism. Though these were often suppressed in order to maintain alliances with big business or military élites, they were never entirely crushed. The broader 'far right', on the other hand, is often more discernibly conservative in outlook. It sees violence or dictatorship as a means of maintaining the status quo, not building a new society or remoulding human nature. This was true of the Chilean military dictatorship of Augusto **Pinochet** after 1973 and of the right-wing German nationalists who collaborated with Hitler in the 1920s in the belief that his antics and rabble-rousing could be used to restore a Prussian-style authoritarian state or even the German monarchy. Far-right parties often seek to suspend only some democratic freedoms, while making use of others in their own work. Their attitude to fascism can be ambiguous. They fear its radicalism and may oppose much of it as extremist. However, at some point or in some issue areas, they are unwilling to condemn it in its entirety, as democratic conservative parties would normally do. Thus, we see the French FN or Austria's Freedom Party occasionally appearing to belittle the enormity and gravity of the Nazi era or Hitler's crimes against humanity.

Another problem with the left–right spectrum concerns the location of the 'centre'. How far right must a party go to be called 'far right'? The location of the political centre varies over time and from place to place. One has only to look at the impact of Margaret Thatcher, Bill Clinton or Tony Blair to appreciate this fact in the context of US or British politics. How much more salient this point must be in any assessment of the turbulent politics of inter-war Europe. A paternalistic view of African or Asian peoples was less 'extreme' in the 1950s than it is today, because it was a view shared by both left and right at that time. Similarly, what counts as 'mainstream' conservatism in the US

Republican Party might be viewed as 'extreme' in France or Germany. Extremism is relative. While the most outlandish positions are easily identified as such, those that overlap with the concerns of conservatism or other social movements are much more difficult to categorise.

Awareness of these issues is reflected in the organisation and content of the *Companion*. We tackle many of them in various sections but we are cautious about pinning down each and every case. Such ambiguities highlight the richness of the debate rather than a lack of precision on our part. For instance, in selecting entries for the Glossary, we have spread the net quite wide to embrace movements and concepts that shed light on fascism. For the most part, the Biography has a slightly narrower focus – on key figures and personalities of the far right. The inclusion of a movement or a personality in the Biography section does not imply that they are fascist or even neo-fascist in orientation. It only suggests that their politics is or has been seen by others as very far from the centre-right, and, in one respect or another, challenging to the consensus around the norms and values of liberal democracy. This might be because of an ambiguous attitude to political violence, to inter-war fascism or to racial and ethnic hatred and chauvinism. We allow for debate on these points. Movements may be seen as of the far right but may actually be less extreme than suggested by their critics. Inclusion here merely indicates that they are controversial on this score: we are not making a final judgement on their credentials. Our test is simple. Could we avoid commenting on a particular movement in a discussion of far-right politics? If not, we will include it. We discuss these issues again in our description of the individual sections later in the Introduction.

One of the most contentious debates around far-right politics concerns the academic, or, as many would say, pseudo-academic, literature associated with **'Holocaust Denial'**. Writers in this category claim to have evidence that questions the fact of the Holocaust or the guilt of the Nazis for those events. By listing writers associated with this phenomenon in the Biography, we are not dictating an answer to the question of whether Holocaust Denial should be banned, or whether it amounts to fascist propaganda. A writer who intentionally denies the reality of that which he knows to have happened is clearly doing a disservice to history and may well be serving the cause of modern neo-fascism. Indeed, some modern fascist and neo-Nazi groups, as well as some white supremacists in the US or Britain, actually require a credible doctrine of Holocaust Denial to justify their existence, to cast themselves as misunderstood victims of a historical conspiracy. On the other hand, leaving aside the hard-core neo-Nazis and fellow travellers of fascism, there are legitimate arguments about freedom of speech and academic inquiry here. This is not the place to resolve these dilemmas, but no work on fascism can fail to acknowledge them.

In all of this, we are attempting to include concepts, ideas and personalities whose actions, words or very existence shed light on the many manifestations of fascism and far-right politics. It is these, rather than narrowly focused dictionary definitions, that dictate the content of the *Companion*. To see how this works, and how the reader can use this reference work, let us take a brief guided tour.

## ORGANISATION OF THE BOOK

The *Companion* is divided into three sections. Part I provides background and introductory material, in the form of a Chronology and a narrative account of the history of fascist and far-right politics since the late nineteenth century. The events listed in the Chronology highlight key milestones in the evolution of these extremist movements. It is not an open-ended timeline of the early twentieth century, or, still less, of the Second World War. A mere recounting of battles, for instance, would not tell us very much. As with the Glossary, we select items that help the reader grasp the nature of those political phenomena. For example, some battles, like Italy's defeat at **Caporetto** in 1917, acquired symbolic importance in Fascist propaganda and are referred to elsewhere in the book. The associated narrative section gives the reader a broad sweep of history that serves as a general context for the remainder of the *Companion*.

There is also an essay on the historiography of fascism, accompanied by an annotated alphabetical guide to historians who have worked in the area. This is an important addition to the *Companion* because of the intense controversies that surround the study of far-right politics. Almost any claim about historical 'facts' will be challenged from several angles before the ink is dry on the page. The historiography section and the listing of historians maps out the key debates and describes the landscape against which all research on this area is undertaken. Finally, there are maps illustrating the geographical scope of far-right activity, both in Europe and beyond. They also show some of the territorial claims and boundary alterations that shaped the foreign policy concerns of the inter-war movements.

Part II is a series of thematic chapters that introduce the reader to key aspects of fascist and far-right politics. These examine the nuances within the far right and its relationship with other movements of the left and right. Each chapter is accompanied by brief documentary extracts that illustrate the themes under discussion and give the reader a flavour of the tone and mood of far-right discourse. The first two chapters set the scene for more detailed treatment of the modern far right by describing the backdrop against which far-right politics evolved into full-blooded fascism and beyond. The first chapter looks at the roots of fascism, at pre-fascist tendencies in the late nineteenth and early twentieth centuries. Many will no doubt dispute the labels and any word association with the subsequent systems established by Hitler and Mussolini. We are not arguing that the links are absolute, merely that the fascists borrowed from, adapted and, in many cases, misused prior systems of thought. Yet, fascism's engagement with the world of ideas was often quite shallow. Many fascists were hostile to any kind of intellectualising. Hitler's

*Mein Kampf,* is *simultaneously* one of the most powerful or influential texts written by a historical figure, and one of the most vacuous, convoluted and distorted pieces of writing to pass for a philosophical treatise. The second chapter, therefore, explores the ideological evolution of the far right, its effort to use ideas to achieve political ends. The third narrative chapter looks at the varying importance of nationalist, ethnic and racial themes at different times and in different countries. The fourth chapter examines the social policy of fascist and far-right movements. By *social policy*, we mean those areas of public policy beyond the spheres of race and the economy, the latter warranting separate chapters of their own. We will pay particular attention to policies impinging on **gender**, the **family** and **religion**. The fifth chapter focuses on the economy and the sixth examines the implications of far-right politics for diplomacy, national foreign policies and the international system. The seventh chapter draws on many of the points raised in previous chapters to investigate the attitude of the far-right groups to the quest for power, the process of retaining power and their relative powerlessness in opposition. Given that they often define themselves as parties of power and 'action', rather than mere 'talking shops', this topic has more salience for the far right than for any other political tendency. In all of these chapters, the nuances within the far right, as well as the gap between theory and practice, will receive particular attention. Part III is a reference section containing a critical essay on sources, a biographical section, an extended guide to key terms and an exploration of secondary literature.

Entries in the Biography refer to individuals frequently associated with far-right politics. As we pointed out earlier, inclusion does not imply that the person was, or is, fascist or neo-fascist, simply that their stated or perceived opinions are frequently seen as beyond the range of mainstream conservatism. There is a handful of exceptions, usually involving cases where there is a dispute over association with the far right. For example, many of Friedrich **Nietzsche**'s ideas sound quite compatible with the discourse of far-right parties and many claim him as a source of inspiration. Yet, it is difficult to characterise him as 'fascist' or even 'pre-fascist'. The same is true of Georges Sorel, much of whose work was devoted to socialist themes, but whose writings on violence and whose reference to the national context pleased fascists of subsequent decades.

In selecting entries for the Glossary, we go slightly further. To understand far-right politics or fascism, we need a wider set of reference points. We need to appreciate which movements were not fascist or 'far right', as well as those that are, and to know the basis on which such distinctions are made. So here, the mere reference to a concept, organisation or event may not necessarily imply that it belongs to the pantheon of the far right at all. For example, the concept of '**Social Darwinism**' is not exclusive to fascism but has been influential among fascist race theorists. Charles Darwin, on the other hand, was not a political theorist or a pre-fascist. Consequently, 'Social Darwinism' gets an entry in the

Glossary, but Darwin does not feature in the Biography. This rule is a general guide to our practice, though we acknowledge that it is impossible to apply with total precision.

We need to reiterate a point made about the Chronology, since it can be applied more generally to all sections of the *Companion*. Much of the content consists of straightforward factual material. We could obviously expand this publication indefinitely by covering every event in the history of fascism or in its halcyon years (1919–45). However, such an approach would not necessarily enlighten the reader on the nature of fascism itself. Thus, we refer to key events, like battles, when they tell us something about the essence of fascist or far-right ideology or foreign policy. There are countless reference books for those interested in raw historical data about the Second World War. Our focus is on an understanding of political phenomena at the conceptual level. While we have included footnotes with our narrative chapters, we made considerable use of important sources in compiling the Biography and Glossary, especially for checking dates and spellings. By their nature, these sections do not lend themselves to referencing in a standard academic format. Nonetheless, we do wish to acknowledge our use of these sources. Particular use was made of the following:

Anderson, *An Atlas of World Political Flashpoints*;
Avalon Project, Yale Law School;
Bosworth, *The Italian Dictatorship*;
Bracher, *The German Dictatorship*;
Burleigh and Wippermann, *The Racial State: Germany 1933–1945*;
Cheles, Ferguson and Vaughan (eds), *The Far Right in Western and Eastern Europe*;
Cheles, Ferguson and Vaughan (eds), *Neo-fascism in Europe*;
Crampton, *Eastern Europe in the Twentieth Century*;
*Encyclopaedia Britannica* (web edition);
Fry, Tedeschi and Tortorice (eds), 'Italian Life under Fascism' collection at the University of Wisconsin Madison;
Griffin, *Fascism* (Oxford Reader);
Griffin, *The Nature of Fascism*;
Hainsworth (ed.), *The Extreme Right in Europe and the USA*;
Hainsworth (ed.), *The Politics of the Extreme Right*;
Hayes, *Fascism*;
The History Place: World War II;
*The Hutchinson Almanac*;
Internet Modern History Sourcebook website;
Kavanagh, *Dictionary of Political Biography*;
Kedward, *Fascism in Western Europe 1900–45*;
Kitchen, *Fascism*;
Laqueur (ed.), *Fascism: A Reader's Guide*;

Loveman, *For La Patria*;
Lyttelton (ed.), *Italian Fascisms*;
Magnusson, *Chambers Biographical Dictionary*;
Mitchell, *European Historical Statistics, 1750–1970*;
Noakes and Pridham (eds), *Documents on Nazism, 1919–45*;
Nolte, *Three Faces of Fascism*;
Oxford University Press, *Oxford Dictionary of World History*;
Palmer, *Dictionary of Twentieth Century History*;
Preston, *Franco: A Biography*;
Renton, *Fascism, Theory and Practice*;
Roberts and Taylor (eds), *Purnell History of the Twentieth Century*;
Robertson, *Penguin Dictionary of Politics*;
Routledge, *Concise Routledge Encyclopedia of Philosophy*;
Sakwa, *Russian Politics and Society*;
Simon Wiesenthal Centre web gallery;
Snyder, *Encyclopedia of the Third Reich*;
Sternhell, *Neither Right nor Left: Fascist Ideology in France*;
Thurlow, *Fascism*;
Townson, *Dictionary of Modern History, 1789–1945*;
Woolf, *European Fascism*.

(Full details of these works can be found in the Bibliography and other sections of the book.)

Part III ends with a guide to further reading structured around a series of key headings. This supplements the Bibliography at the end of the book, as well as the essay on sources.

The timeframe covered by all of these items can be summarised as follows: the main focus is on the high-point of European fascism from 1919 until 1945, with a secondary emphasis on the social forces and ideological undercurrents that coalesced to produce fascism in the years 1870–1919 and 1945–2002. In the period before 1918, the values of the Enlightenment were systematically discredited in much of European society. In the first thirty years of the twentieth century, economic, cultural, technological and military upheaval mobilised mass publics in an unprecedented climate of fear and frenzy. **Authoritarianism**, war, revolution and 'quick-fix' solutions to age-old problems became attractive at a time of crisis. The collapse of the European order in the First World War, the **Russian Revolution** and the Wall Street Crash appeared to convert a climate of crisis into a reality. Not all of the extreme responses were fascist but each one contributed something to the rejection of liberal democracy that made fascism appear like a viable option. We also look at far-right movements, especially neo-fascist tendencies, in the period from 1945–2002. The focus on inter-war fascism is justified by its development as a globalised phenomenon that made a substantial contribution to systemic war and physical destruction on a massive scale. The wider timeframe provides a picture of continuity and change on the far right. Since the Second World War, extremist

11

movements have re-emerged in Europe and elsewhere. Some have emulated the Nazis; others have borrowed more selectively from them or have tried to reinvent themselves to survive under post-fascist and, indeed, anti-fascist political cultures. Rightist regimes and movements in other parts of the world (e.g. in Latin America or post-Communist Eastern Europe) have often displayed characteristics that are eerily reminiscent of fascism, even if they openly eschew any such association. Like their predecessors, they are as much a product of their own national history as of German or Italian influence.

Notwithstanding all our qualifications, we have based our work on a broad schema that locates various movements relative to a hardcore Nazi–Fascist centre and a periphery where fascist and far-right credentials are blurred or scarcely existent. Entries in the grey area in between are open to debate. There is likely to be ambiguity and disagreement over these cases and we make no claim of finality about our efforts at pinning down movements here. The purpose of this model is to offer an initial framework for our own work, rather than a definitive map. We leave it to the readers to explore the grey zone themselves, using the factual material contained in the *Companion* as a whole as a starting point.

We envisage two likely uses of this book: (1) as a wide-ranging reference source for those already familiar with fascism or far-right movements – such readers will turn to the *Companion* for convenient information or for notes on further sources; (2) as a resource for students and newcomers to this area, who can browse the book in order to get a road map of important themes and concepts before embarking on more detailed research in the academic literature. In the final analysis, however, it is not for us to dictate how anybody might use a reference work of this nature. A good reference source lends itself to a myriad of applications, all dictated by the needs and interests of readers themselves. Readers should feel free to open the *Companion* at any point, to search the index or to read the narratives or historiography. Whether they reach for it as a quick reference or take it down for a lengthier period of reading or browsing, we trust they find it both useful and enjoyable.

Peter Davies, Derek Lynch
Huddersfield
July 2002

# I
# FASCISM AND THE
# FAR RIGHT

## The basics

# CHRONOLOGY

## NOTES

- This section chronicles events of note or interest in the history of fascism and far-right politics.
- Where appropriate, events in, or related to, the same country in the same year are grouped together.

**1870**

**Franco-Prussian War**.

**1871**

Birth of the **Ku Klux Klan**.
Unification of Germany.
Unification of Italy.
US Congressional enquiry into Ku Klux Klan activities.

**1883**

**Mussolini** born in Predappio.

**1886**

Publication of **Drumont**'s *La France Juive* in France; **Boulanger** becomes French Minister of War.

**1889**

**Hitler** born in Braunau, Austria.

**1892**

Hitler's family move to Linz.

**1893**

Founding of **Gobineau Society**.

**1896**

Birth of Oswald **Mosley**.
Italian forces routed at **Adwa**.

**1899**

Formation of *Action Française* (AF) by Charles **Maurras**.

**1900**

H.S. **Chamberlain** publishes *Foundations of the Nineteenth Century*.

**1902**

**British Brothers League** founded.
Mussolini visits Switzerland.

**1903**

Formation of the French National Socialist Movement.
*Wandervogel* movement founded in Germany.
Birth of Italian journal, *Il Leonardo*.

**1904**

Formation of the German Workers' Party in Austria.
*Jaunes* movement founded in France.
Mussolini begins military service.

15

**1906**

Mussolini starts work as a teacher.

**1907**

Hitler moves to Vienna.

**1908**

Birth of the AF newspaper, *L'Action Française*.
Mussolini becomes a journalist.

**1910**

Formation of the *Associazione Nazionale Italiana* (ANI).

**1912**

*Kuomintang* (KMT) leads Chinese Revolution.
Mussolini becomes editor of *Avanti*.

**1914**

Mussolini founds *Il Popolo d'Italia* and leaves *Avanti*; he is expelled from the Italian Socialist Party.
(October) Establishment of *Fasci di Azione Rivoluzionaria* (FAR).

**1915**

Reconstitution of the Ku Klux Klan.
Italy joins the war; Mussolini begins military service.

**1917**

Birth of **German Fatherland Party**.
**National Party** founded in Britain.

**Russian Revolution**.
(November) Italian military defeat at **Caporetto**.

**1918**

**University Reform** movement born in Argentina.
In Austria the **Deutsche Arbeiterpartei** (DAP) evolves into the equivalent of Hitler's National Socialist German Workers' Party and becomes known as the **DNSAP**.
In Germany the **Hohenzollern** Empire collapses and the German Workers' Party (DAP) emerges.
Oswald Mosley elected Coalition Unionist MP for Harrow.
Battle of **Vittorio Veneto**; beginning of *'Biennio Rosso'* in Italy.
*Broederbond* founded in South Africa.
(November) Establishment of **Weimar Republic**.

**1919**

Birth of the *Deutsche National Volks Partei* (DNVP) in Germany.
Founding of *Etelköz* **Association** (EKSZ).
Mussolini hosts **Milan Conference**; Fascist Party programme highlights belief in **corporatism**.
Future Romanian fascists **Codreanu** and **Cuza** meet for first time.
(January) **Drexler** founds German Workers' Party – Munich.
(March) First *Fasci di Combattimento* emerges in Italy.
(June) Treaty of **Versailles**.
(September) **D'Annunzio** captures **Fiume**.
Hitler attends first meeting of German Workers' Party.
(November) Fascist failure in Italian General Election.

**1920**

Oswald Mosley elected Independent MP.
Charter of **Carnaro** published in Italy.
Codreanu launches a range of nationalist movements in Romanian university sector.
Treaty of **Rapallo**.
(February) German Workers' Party becomes known as the National Socialist German Workers' Party (NSDAP) – Hitler announces its new programme.
(March) 'Kapp Putsch' in Berlin. Admiral **Horthy** becomes Hungarian leader.
(December) Ending of D'Annunzio's Fiume occupation.

**1921**

Nazi Storm Troopers (SA) founded in Germany.
Mussolini outlines his 'collective' ideology at **Rome Congress**; he signs 'Pact of Pacification' with the Liberals.
Founding of Society for the Preservation of the National Essence in Japan.
(February) Fascists and Communists clash in Italy.
(May) Fascists win thirty-five seats in Italian General Election.
(July) Hitler becomes Nazi leader.
(November) Mussolini founds Italian Fascist Party.

**1922**

Formation of *Academic Karelia Society* (AKS) in Finland.
**Göbbels** joins Nazi Party.
Collapse of the *Banca Italiana di Sconto*.
Texas sends a Ku Klux Klan representative, Earl Mayfield, to the US Senate.
Second Treaty of Rapallo.
(January) Mussolini sets up syndicates in each sector of the economy.
(August) Italian Fascists clash with left-wing militants.

(October) **March on Rome**; Mussolini becomes Italian Prime Minister and forms government.
(December) Establishment of **Fascist Grand Council**.

**1923**

Treaty of **Lausanne**.
Founding of **British Fascists** (BF).
Italy gains Fiume; Giovanni **Gentile** joins Fascist Party.
**National Christian Defence League** born in Romania.
(January) French and Belgian troops occupy the Ruhr after Germany defaults on reparations payments; German forces offer passive resistance.
(February) Nationalists embrace Mussolini's *Partito Nazionale Fascista* (PNF).
(July) **Acerbo electoral law** passed in Italy.
(August) Captain **Gömbös** founds Racialist Party in Hungary. Unrest in Germany as economic problems increase.
(September) Mussolini involved in Corfu incident. Miguel **Primo de Rivera** becomes Spanish dictator.
(November) Hitler's Munich 'Beer Hall Putsch' – Nazi Party is banned as a consequence.
(December) **Palazzo Chigi Agreement** signed by Mussolini and industrialists; Mussolini founds the *Milizia Volontaria per la Sicurezza Nazionale* (MVSN).

**1924**

*Jeunesses Patriotes* (JP) founded in France.
Oswald Mosley joins the Labour Party but is not elected to parliament in the General Election.
Serpieri begins, and then restarts, 'Battle for Land Reclamation' in Italy.
*Aprismo* movement (**APRA**) founded in Peru.
Formation of National Unity Movement

and National Socialist League of Freedom in Sweden.

(March) Mussolini annexes Fiume.

(April) Fascists gain victory in Italian General Election. Hitler sentenced to five years imprisonment.

(June) Kidnap and assassination of Matteotti by Fascists.

→ (August) **Dawes Plan** outlines Germany's schedule for reparations payments; French troops begin to leave the Ruhr.

(December) Hitler released from prison under general amnesty. Consuls' revolt in Italy.

## 1925

Treaty of **Locarno**.

Founding of *Le Faisceau* in France by Georges **Valois**.

Hitler's ***Mein Kampf*** published in Germany; *Schutzstaffel* (SS) established.

**National Fascists** born in Britain; Mosley publishes *Revolution by Reason*.

Mussolini assumes nickname of *Il Duce*; he disbands the **'Blackshirts'**, places limits on emigration and founds *Opera Nazionale Dopolavoro*.

Birth of Norwegian Patriotic League.

(January) Mussolini announces the beginnings of **dictatorship** and admits responsibility for past Fascist actions; **Farinacci** becomes PNF secretary; European stock exchanges begin to speculate on the fall of the lira.

(February) Nazi Party refounded in Germany.

(April) **Hindenburg** becomes President of Germany.

(June) Mussolini promises to 'make Italy Fascist' in his Augusteo speech; **protectionism** reintroduced and trade unions 'fascistised'.

(July) **Volpi** begins 'Battle for Wheat' in Italy by reintroducing protective tax on wheat.

(October) **Palazzo Vidoni Agreement**

signed by Mussolini, trade unionists and industrialists.

(December) Law gives Mussolini total executive power.

## 1926

Austrian DNSAP changes its name to NSDAP.

Georges Valois publishes *French Fascism* in Italian.

Hitler Youth formed.

Mosley elected Labour MP for Smethwick.

Mussolini guarantees industrialists key public supply contracts; he creates the **Special Tribunal for the Defence of the State** and outlaws all Italian political parties except his own. He also introduces the ***Opera Nazionale Balilla*** and announces a protectorate over Albania.

**Pilsudski** grabs power in Poland.

General Carmona gains power in Portugal.

The Codreanu–Cuza National Christian Defence League wins six parliamentary seats in Romania.

(January) Mussolini's decrees given the power of laws.

(March) Fascist government in Italy tries to discourage peasants from migrating to towns.

(April) **Rocco** Law in Italy paves the way for legal recognition of syndicates; strikes and factory committees banned; collective contracts extended to all labour relations; Mussolini makes unions 'state organisations'; **Turati** becomes PNF secretary.

(July) **Ministry of Corporations** established in Italy; workers' unions combine into National Confederation of Fascist Unions.

(August) Mussolini announces policy of deflation.

(November) Tribunal established in Italy to adjudicate on 'political crimes'.

(December) Gömbös's Racialist Party defeated in Hungarian elections.

## 1927

Mosley elected to the Labour Party NEC.
Valois dissolves his *Faisceau* movement.
**Dinter** expelled from the German Nazi Party.
***Ethnikistiki Enosis Ellados*** (EEE) founded in Greece.
Pilsudski creates *Bezpartyjny Blok Współpracy z Rzadem* (BBWR) in Poland.
**Legion of the Archangel Michael** formed by Romanian fascist Corneliu Codreanu.
(January) Churchill visits Mussolini.
(April) Mussolini establishes Charter of Labour; Italy and Hungary sign friendship pact in Rome.
(December) Lira stabilised at '*Quota 90*' level.

## 1928

KMT government formed in China.
Birth of *Croix de Feu* (CF) in France.
**Imperial Fascist League** founded in Britain.
Mussolini and the Italian King clash over powers of the Grand Council; work starts on several projects: the 'Battle for Wheat', development of public works, land drainage and reclamation; beginning of economic crisis for small/medium-sized industries; **Rossoni** sacked as President of the National Confederation of Fascist Unions; new electoral law introduced; Italy signs friendship treaty with Ethiopia.
**Franco** appointed head of Spanish Military Academy.
Birth of *Anti-Europa*.
(April) **Salazar** becomes Finance Minister in Portugal.
(May) Nazis win twelve seats in Reichstag elections.

(September) Increases in protective tax on wheat announced in Italy. Gömbös rejoins Hungarian government party.

## 1929

Formation of the Estonian *Vaps* movement.
Ultra-nationalist rising in Ostrobothnian, Lapua, Finland; *Lapua* movement founded.
**Himmler** becomes head of SS.
Gömbös becomes Hungarian Minister of Defence.
**Bottai** succeeds Mussolini as Minister of Corporations; **Grandi** becomes Foreign Secretary; the Fascist regime establishes the **Italian Academy**.
Founding of the Swedish National Rural Union.
Wall Street Crash.
(February) Mussolini signs **Lateran Accords** with the Vatican.
(March) First plebiscite elections to the **Chamber of Fasces and Corporations**.
(June) **Young Plan** fixes Germany's reparation payments. Mosley becomes Chancellor of the Duchy of Lancaster in the Labour Government.
(December) Nazis oppose Young Plan in national referendum.

## 1930

Leader of *Ação Integralista Brasileira* (AIB), Plínio **Salgado**, visits Mussolini's Italy.
Birth of the Danish National Socialist Workers' Party.
*Lapua* pressure forces change of Finnish government.
Birth of Mosley's **New Party**.
Agricultural census published in Italy; Turati replaced by Giuriati as PNF secretary.
Founding of the Society of the Cherry in Japan.

Establishment of the *União Nacional* in Portugal – the only legal political movement.

Iron Guard founded in Romania by Codreanu (to work in association with the Legion of the Archangel Michael).

Birth of *Partido Nacionalista Español* (PNE).

Founding of the Swedish Religious People's Party.

(January) Publication of the *Mosley Memorandum*. Dictatorship of Primo de Rivera ends in Spain.

(March) National Council of Corporations set up in Italy. *Lapua*–Communist violence in Finland.

(May) *Korneuburg Oath* of the Austrian *Heimwehr*. Mosley resigns as Chancellor of the Duchy of Lancaster.

(June) Protective tax on wheat increased again in Italy.

(September) Nazis win 107 seats in Reichstag elections. **Starhemberg** becomes leader of the Austrian *Heimwehr* and enters cabinet.

## 1931

**Dollfuss** becomes government minister in Austria.

*Lapua* movement plans coup in Finland.

Establishment of *Istituto Mobiliare Italiano* (IMI) to help banking sector in Italy; **Starace** appointed PNF secretary; Pope issues encyclical in favour of corporatism.

Birth of the Dutch National Socialist Movement (NSB).

**Quisling** establishes Nordic Folk Awakening and becomes Norway's Minister of Defence.

Birth of *La Conquista del Estado* and the **Redondo–Ramos** *JONS* movement in Spain.

(March) Proposal for a German–Austrian customs union. Mosley publishes *A National Policy*.

(June) US President Hoover says there should be a moratorium on Germany's reparation payments. The Vatican condemns Fascist interference in religious freedom.

(July) Young and Strachey resign from Mosley's New Party.

(September) **Putsch** led by Austrian *Heimwehr*. Japan invades **Manchuria**.

(October) New Party fails to win a seat in the British General Election – with Mosley losing in Stoke-on-Trent. Hitler and Nationalist leader **Hugenberg** form alliance.

## 1932

Founding of *Movimiento Nacional Socialista de Chile* (MNS).

Greek *Elefterofronoi* (EL) wins two seats in national parliamentary elections.

Birth of the **Hungarian Hitlerite Movement**.

Formation of *Army Comrades Association* in Ireland.

*Decennale* celebrations in Italy; Mussolini takes over as Foreign Secretary; Gentile writes celebrated entry for 'Fascism' in *Enciclopedia Italiana*.

Birth of **General Dutch Fascist Union**.

Founding of *Nacional Sindicalismo* (NS) movement in Portugal.

Legion of the Archangel Michael wins five seats in the Romanian parliament.

Formation of the Friends of the New Germany movement in the US.

Founding of the *Ustasha* in Yugoslavia.

(January) Mosley visits Rome.

(February) Attempted *Lapua* coup in Finland; the movement is banned and evolves into the People's Patriotic Movement (IKL).

(April) Hitler wins 13,417,460 votes; Hindenburg becomes President; SA and other Nazi paramilitary bodies banned. Austrian Nazis increase their share of the vote in provincial elections. Mosley's New Party is dissolved.

(May) Dollfuss becomes Chancellor of Austria. *by von Paten*

(June) Ban on the Nazi SA overturned; Lausanne Conference discusses the reparations issue.

(July) Nazis win 37 per cent of the vote and 230 seats in parliamentary elections. **Salazar** elected Portuguese leader. Trujillo uprising in Peru.

(October) Mosley founds the **British Union of Fascists** (BUF). **Gömbös** becomes Hungarian Prime Minister.

(November) Nazis gain 196 seats in new elections.

## 1933

Founding of the **Sudeten German Party**.

**Clausen** becomes leader of the DNSAP in Denmark.

Finnish General Election – *Lapua* wins fourteen seats.

Formation of *Franciste* movement in France.

Hitler establishes German Labour Front; **'December Programme'** outlines Germany's remilitarisation plans; **Gestapo** created; Hitler–IG Farben agreement sealed; *Ordensburgen* training schools established; Göbbels becomes Nazi propaganda chief; von **Blomberg** becomes Minister of War.

**Unemployment** goes past the million mark in Italy.

Birth of Mexican Revolutionary Action (ARM).

Formation of *Nasjonal Samling* (NS) movement in Norway by Quisling; Liberal People's Party supports him.

Salazar establishes the **Estado Novo** in Portugal and launches **National Labour Statute**.

*Falange* movement founded in Spain by José Antonio **Primo de Rivera**, who is elected to the Spanish parliament; founding of *Renovación Española*.

Birth of Pelley's **Silver Shirts** in the US.

(January) Hindenburg appoints Hitler Chancellor of Germany in succession to von **Schleicher**.

(February) Hitler's government gains power to make arbitrary arrests; Reichstag fire.

(March) Nazis win 288 seats and 43 per cent of the vote in parliamentary elections; **Enabling Act** gives Hitler the right to rule by decree. Dollfuss suspends parliament in Austria. Birth of Spanish Confederation of Autonomous Rightist Groups (CEDA).

(April) National boycott of Jewish businesses begins in Germany.

(May) Hitler abolishes all trade unions. Dollfuss outlaws Austrian Communist Party.

(June) Banning of Austrian Nazi Party.

(July) Germany becomes a one-party state; Hitler signs **Concordat with the** Vatican. Hungarian leader Gömbös meets Hitler in Berlin.

(September) Dollfuss establishes authoritarian state structure in Austria.

(October) Estonian War of Independence Veterans' League (EVL) win 73 per cent of the vote in the national referendum. Germany leaves the **League of Nations**.

## 1934

Year One of the 'Fourth Humanity', according to the Brazilian AIB.

*Front Paysan* born in France.

Hitler assumes the title **'Führer'**; Himmler becomes head of the Gestapo; Charter of Labour issued; Hitler crushes *Nationalsozialistische Betriebszellenorganisation* (NSBO); von **Fritsch** becomes Commander in Chief of the army.

BUF holds **Olympia Rally**.

Speech by Eoin **O'Duffy** – Ireland's leading fascist – outlining his dream for a 'New Corporate Ireland'.

Mussolini creates mixed corporations;

new economic regulations imposed; start of price rises which ultimately provoke wage increases.

Fascist **Peasant Union** gains power in Latvia; Karlis **Ulmanis** becomes dictator.

**Antonescu** becomes Minister of War in Romania.

Merger of *Falange Española* (FE) and *Juntas de Ofensiva Nacional-Sindicalista* (JONS) in Spain to create *Falange Española de las Juntas de Ofensiva Nacional-Sindicalista* (*FE de las JONS*).

Meeting of **Fascist International** at **Montreux Conference**.

(January) German state parliaments abolished.

(February) The *ligues* riot in Paris. Number of corporations in Italy rises to twenty-two. Austrian Social Democratic Party and trade unions banned.

(March) Estonian Head of State Konstantin **Päts** outlaws *Vaps*. Italy, Austria and Hungary sign the Rome Protocols.

(June) Mussolini and Hitler meet at Venice. '**Röhm Purge**'.

(July) Salazar dissolves rival NS movement in Portugal. Austrian crisis: Dollfuss killed in Nazi putsch; succeeded by **Schuschnigg**; Austrian NSDAP banned; Italian troops moved to border; Mussolini gives his backing to Austrian independence.

(August) Hindenberg dies; plebiscite confirms Hitler as German Führer.

(November) Mussolini creates Council of Corporations.

(December) Ethiopia–Somaliland 'incident'.

## 1935

Birth of the *Falange Socialista Boliviana* (FSB).

**National Fascist Community** scores 8 per cent in Czechoslovakia.

Dutch NSB gains 5 per cent of vote in national elections.

Swastika is integrated into the German national flag.

Gömbös manipulates Hungarian parliamentary elections; formation of **Party of National Will** by Ferenc **Szálasi**; attempted coup by **Scythe Cross** movement.

Death of Polish leader Pilsudski.

Salazar becomes President of the Council of Ministers in Portugal; attempted NS coup.

**National Christian Party** founded in Romania.

Founding of Serb movement, **Zbor**.

(January) Saar votes to be reincorporated into Germany.

(March) Hitler condemns Versailles disarmament articles; compulsory military service introduced in Germany.

(April) Stresa conference – Allies agree on policy towards Germany and Austria.

(June) **National Corporate Party** founded in Ireland by Eoin O'Duffy.

(July) **Popular Front** and CF engage in demonstrations and counter-demonstrations in Paris.

(September) Nuremberg Laws on Citizenship and Race, including the Reich Citizenship Law.

(October) Italian invasion of Ethiopia; League of Nations imposes sanctions on Mussolini.

(December) **Hoare–Laval Pact**.

## 1936

Formation of *Rex* party in Belgium by Léon **Degrelle**.

**Busch** emerges as military dictator in Bolivia.

IKL maintains its parliamentary presence in Finnish elections.

CF becomes a political party in France.

Olympic Games staged in Berlin; **Göring** takes charge of Nazi economic policy.

BUF publishes *The Coming Corporate State*; the movement is defeated in

'Battle of Cable Street'; **Public Order Act** is passed.

Devaluation of the Italian lira.

Revolt of Junior Officers in Japan.

Salazar creates the *Mocidade Portuguesa* and *Legião Portuguesa* – political movements for young people and adults.

Birth of Spanish far-right newspaper, *El Alcázar*.

(February) Beneduce presents special Italian economic development 'masterplan' based on **autarchy**.

(March) Rhineland reoccupied by German troops. Italy, Austria and Hungary consolidate the Rome Protocols. José Antonio imprisoned in Spain.

(May) Austrian government sacks Starhemberg; Abyssinia formally annexed by Mussolini. Degrelle's *Rex* movement wins twenty-one seats in Belgian elections.

(June) Himmler appointed German police chief. **Ciano** becomes Italian Foreign Secretary. French Popular Front bans *ligues*; **Doriot** founds the *Parti Populaire Français* (PPF).

(July) Germany and Austria sign July Agreement. Military revolt in Spain – Redondo killed. Beginning of the **Spanish Civil War** – Mussolini intervenes.

(September) Hitler announces **Four Year Plan for Industry**.

(October) Policy of economic planning launched in Italy. Signing of Rome–Berlin 'Axis'. Hungarian leader Gömbös dies in Munich. Franco emerges as head of government in Spain.

(November) Death of José Antonio and Ramos in Spain. Anti-Comintern agreement signed between Germany and Japan.

**1937**

**Rome–Berlin–Tokyo Axis** established.
**Vargas** puts down the Brazilian AIB.

Rape of Nanking.
**Hossbach** Protocol.
**National Socialist League** born in Britain; Neville **Henderson** appointed Ambassador to Berlin.

Pope condemns Nazi racial policy.

Hungarian Party of National Will is renamed Arrow Cross.

Birth of **Gioventù Italiana del Littorio** (GIL) youth coalition in Italy; **Istituto di Riconstruzione Industriale** (IRI) sets up **Finsider** – large financing body.

China invaded by Japan.

Birth of Mexican **Unión Nacional Sinarquista** (UNS).

*Obóz Zjednoczenia* (OZN) founded in Poland.

Under the slogan 'All for the Fatherland', the Romanian Legion of the Archangel Michael wins 16 per cent of the vote – and sixty seats – in national elections; Antonescu is appointed Chief of General Staff.

(April) **Hedilla** Affair in Spain; Franco merges *FE de las JONS* with the Carlist movement to create Spain's only political party (the *FET de las JONS*). Belgian fascist Degrelle loses out in an electoral battle with his country's Prime Minister; thereafter Degrelle's political ideas radicalise.

(November) Cagoulard conspiracy in France.

**1938**

**Argentinian Fascist Party** founded.

Belgian fascist Degrelle publishes *The Revolution of Souls*.

Failure of MNS coup in Chile; birth of *Falange*.

Finnish government tries to ban IKL movement.

Mussolini scraps Chamber of Deputies; founds Central Corporative Committee.

Introduction of **State of National**

**Renaissance** in Romania; dissolution of Legion of the Archangel Michael.

Great Trek in South Africa and formation of Ox-Wagon Sentinel.

Swedish National Socialist Workers' Party (NSWP) evolves into **Svensk Socialistisk Samling**.

(January) Franco selects his first cabinet.

(March) Seyss-Inquart replaces Schuschnigg as Austrian leader. Hitler annexes Austria (**Anschluss**). Hungarian Prime Minister Darányi announces a range of anti-Semitic measures.

(July) First anti-Semitic measures in Italy (**Manifesto della Razza**).

(August) Hungarian head of state Horthy meets Hitler; Szálasi sent to prison for three years for 'subversion'.

(September) Munich agreement over Czechoslovakian partition.

(October) Hitler occupies **Sudetenland**.

(November) 'Crystal Night': Nazi **Brownshirts** burn down 267 synagogues and 815 Jewish stores.

### 1939

High Court rules that Finnish IKL cannot be outlawed; its number of parliamentary deputies falls to eight.

Walter **Funk** becomes head of the German Central Bank.

Mussolini establishes Inter-Ministerial Committee on **Autarchy**; GIL youth movement made compulsory for young Italians.

Purge of the Legion of the Archangel Michael in Romania – Codreanu killed.

Establishment of Slovak puppet state.

(January) Franco takes Barcelona. Hungary joins **Anti-Comintern Pact**. Hitler announces **Z-Plan**.

(February) Franco's government is recognised by Britain and France.

(March) Prague seized by Germany; Czech **National Confederation** established.

(April) Mussolini annexes Albania. Spain signs Anti-Comintern Pact (already signed by Germany, Italy and Japan). Franco celebrates end of Spanish Civil War.

(May) Arrow Cross Party obtains 37 per cent of the vote in the Hungarian election; the government enacts the 'second Jewish law'. Hitler and Mussolini sign Pact of Steel.

(August) Signing of the **Nazi–Soviet Pact**.

(September) Hitler invades Poland and captures **Danzig**. War starts – Italy stays neutral.

(October) Hitler annexes western Poland.

### 1940

Imprisonment of British fascists.

Hungarian fascist leader Szálasi is released from prison.

Failed Italian invasion of Greece.

Founding of **Imperial Rule Assistance Association** in Japan.

End of Ulmanis's regime in Latvia.

**Mussert** becomes Dutch Head of State.

Salazar's Portugal signs a Concordat with the Vatican.

Antonescu assumes title of '**Conducator**' of Romania; Legion of the Archangel Michael – in the guise of the Iron Guard – is brought into power (led by **Sima**).

Joint meeting between the Ku Klux Klan and the national-socialist German-American Bund.

Zbor outlawed in Yugoslavia.

(April) Germans invade Norway; Quisling sets up NS government.

(May) Nazis invade Belgium; **Rex** movement becomes openly pro-Nazi.

(June) German forces enter Paris; **Pétain** becomes French Head of State; Franco-German Armistice signed, which presages **collaboration**. Italy enters conflict. Hungary and USSR go to war.

(August) Hitler annexes Alsace–Lorraine. **Vichy** decree creates new set of economic organisations for each branch of industry.

(September) Germany, Italy and Japan sign 10-year military pact. Hitler puts NS ministers into office in occupied Norway.

(October) Hitler meets Franco; Hitler meets Mussolini. Montoire meeting between Hitler and Pétain; first anti-Semitic measures enacted by Vichy.

(November) Vichy suppresses unions that cut across trades boundaries, e.g. *Confédération Générale du Patronat*, *Comité des Forges*, *Comité des Houillères*, *Confédération Générale du Travail*, *Confédération Française des Travailleurs Chrétiens*.

(December) Vichy sets up 'Corporation of Agriculture' and bans *Declaration of the Rights of Man*. Hungary goes to war with Britain and US.

## 1941

Founding of **Popular Socialist Vanguard** in Chile.

Ustasha comes to power in Croatia.

Beginning of Finnish–German collaboration.

Round-up of foreign Jews in Occupied France; **Darlan** becomes Pétain's chief minister.

Germany begins extermination of Jews; **Hess** flees to Britain.

Mussolini loses Italian East Africa.

Italy and Germany declare war on the US.

(January) Antonescu destroys Iron Guard-dominated **National Legionary State** on Hitler's advice. Pro-Nazi *Rassemblement National Populaire* formed in France by Marcel **Déat**.

(May) Jews made to wear a yellow star in French Occupied Zone.

(June) Hitler invades Russia, supported by Mussolini.

(September) Jews forced to wear hexagonal star in Nazi Germany.

(October) Vichy promulgates anti-worker Labour Charter.

(December) **Pearl Harbor**. Germany announces declaration of war against US.

## 1942

Franco and Salazar form Iberian Bloc.

El Alamein.

Quisling and Hitler meet.

(January) **Wannsee Conference** – Germany plans 'Final Solution'.

(February) Quisling becomes Norwegian Head of State.

(May/June) Deportation of French Jews to **Auschwitz**.

(June) Vichy sets 'quotas' for employment of Jews. Franco sends 20,000 troops to help the German effort on the Eastern Front. Himmler demands 100,000 Jews from France; **Laval** sends him 10,000 foreign Jews.

(August) French Jewish leaders warn Laval that Jews are being exterminated in Eastern Europe.

(November) German forces move into 'Unoccupied' Zone in France.

## 1943

Poisoning of King **Boris** of Bulgaria.

Danish National Socialist Workers' Party wins 2.1 per cent in elections.

Birth of *Milice* in France – with **Darnand** as head.

Nazis murder 9,000 Jews in northern Italy.

Axis powers defeated in North Africa.

(February) *Service du Travail Obligatoire* (STO) introduced in France, with French workers going to Germany to aid the war effort. Mussolini begins to sack leading Fascists.

(March) Strikes in Italy.

(July) Mussolini voted out of power by Grand Council of Fascism.

(September) Nazis take over Italy after Armistice; surrender of Italy; Mussolini announces establishment of the Fascist Social Republic at Salò and new Fascist Republican Party; publication of the Charter of **Verona**; Mussolini is rescued from Gran Sasso.

(October) Italy declares war against Germany.

(December) Déat and Darnand enter Vichy government after German ultimatum.

## 1944

Birth of *Nouvel Europe Magazine* (*NEM*) magazine in Belgium.

IKL disbanded in Finland.

Dissolution of *Francisme* movement in France.

Nazis outlaw the **Association of Turanian Hunters** in Hungary.

Revolt of Slovak army.

(January) Ciano executed in Italy.

(March) Déat becomes Minister of Labour and National Solidarity at Vichy. Hungary invaded and occupied by German forces; Gestapo rounds up 'enemies'; Sztójay becomes Hungarian Prime Minister on Hitler's demand.

(May) Start of deportation of Jews from Hungary.

(July) Horthy stops deportation of Jews from Hungary. **July Plot** against Hitler.

(August) Liberation of France; Pétain and Laval evacuated to Belfort, then Sigmaringen.

(September): Finnish–Soviet armistice – IKL is dissolved.

(October) Nazis install Hungarian fascist leader Szálasi as Head of State in place of Horthy – whom they arrest.

## 1945

Collapse of German Nazi Party.

*Uomo Qualunque* (UQ) born in Italy; Croce calls for Academy to be disbanded.

Salazar defines the powers of his political police.

*Svensk Socialistisk Samling* dissolved in Sweden.

(February) Death of Doriot, leader of the French PPF.

(April) Hitler kills himself. Partisans murder Mussolini at Dongo.

(May) Unconditional surrender of Germany.

(October) Norwegian Quisling shot as a traitor.

(November) **Nuremberg Trials**.

## 1946

End of the League of Nations.

Argentina elects Juan **Perón** as its President.

Far-right *Deutsche Rechtspartei* (DreP) coalition founded in Germany.

UQ scores over 5 per cent in Italy.

Execution of two key East European fascists: Romania's Antonescu and Hungary's Szálasi.

(December) Founding of the *Movimento Sociale Italiano* (MSI).

## 1947

Birth of Mexican movement, Popular Force.

Spain becomes a monarchy; plebiscite confirms Franco's dictatorship as 'regency' regime.

## 1948

Birth of Ecuadorian fascist movement, *Alianza Revolucionaria Nacionalista Ecuatoriana* (ARNE).

Founding of the *Mouvement Socialiste d'Unité* (MSUF) in France; Bardèche imprisoned.

Mosley establishes **Union Movement** in Britain.

New Italian constitution outlaws any attempts to reconstitute Mussolini's Fascist Party; MSI gains 1.9 per cent and five parliamentary deputies in national elections.

Mexican UNS banned.

**Apartheid** established in South Africa.

## 1949

Founding of the Flemish *Vlaamse Concentratie* (VC).

KMT flees to Taiwan.

Salazar's Portugal enters NATO; electoral irregularities mar the country's presidential election.

**National Party** forms government in South Africa.

Founding of Fellowship of Independent Germany (GUD) in West Germany.

## 1950

Birth of the *Mouvement Social Belge* (MSB).

Greek National Alignment of the Working People (EPEL) scores 2 per cent in national elections.

MSI makes alliance with Italian monarchists.

*Sozialistische Reichspartei* (SRP) founded in West Germany.

*Nation Europa* established.

## 1951

Malmö International; formation of the **European Social Movement**.

**Union of National and Independent Republicans** (UNIR) born in France.

## 1952

Death of Eva **Perón**.

West German courts ban the SRP.

## 1953

Founding of Dutch National European Socialist Movement (NESB).

New West German law states that parties must pass a 5 per cent threshold before they can gain parliamentary representation.

## 1954

Founding of Flemish *Volksunie* (VU).

*Parti Patriotique Révolutionnaire* (PPR) born in France.

**Chesterton** forms **League of Empire Loyalists** in Britain.

## 1955

Outlawing of Dutch NESB.

## 1956

Founding of the Freedom Party of Austria (FPÖ).

Poujadist *Unité et Fraternité Française* (UFF) wins fifty-two seats in French elections.

*Ordine Nuovo* founded in Italy.

Birth of Peruvian coalition, *Acción Popular*.

## 1957

'Papa Doc' becomes President of Haiti.

Birth of the **Liberty Lobby** movement in the US.

## 1958

Pro-Nazi Northern League founded to

promote Teutonic solidarity across Western countries.

**Batista** toppled in Cuba.

*Jeune Nation* banned in France.

**National Labour Party** and **White Defence League** born in Britain.

Founding of Dutch *Boerenpartij* (BP).

Birth of **John Birch Society** and American Nazi Party in the US.

(May) Revolt of army and settlers in Algeria.

## 1960

Birth of Belgian *Mouvement d'Action Civique* (MAC).

Birth of *Europe-Action* and *Societé des Amis de Robert Brasillach* in France.

Founding of the **British National Party** (BNP).

*Avanguardia Nazionale* born in Italy.

(January) 'Barricades Week' in Algeria.

## 1961

**Eichmann** is tried by Israel.

(February) Formation of *Organisation de l'Armée Secrète* (OAS) in French Algeria.

(April) 'Generals' Putsch' against the French Fourth Republic.

(December) 'Anti-OAS Day' in Paris.

## 1962

Formation of **World Union of National Socialists**.

Birth of *Were Di Verbond van Nederlandse Werk-Gemeenschappen* (WD, VNW) in Belgium.

Algeria granted independence by de Gaulle.

**National Socialist Movement** founded in Britain.

## 1963

Birth of *Fédération Ouest-Européene* (FOE).

## 1964

Founding of *Occident* in France.

Birth of the National Democratic Party of Germany (NPD); collapse of the German Reich Party (DRP).

## 1965

**Tixier-Vignancour** wins 5 per cent in the French presidential elections.

Birth of Spanish Circle of Friends of Europe (CEDADE).

## 1966

Founding of Portuguese National Revolutionary Front (FNR).

## 1967

Formation of British **National Front** (NF) – Chesterton becomes Chairman.

'**Colonels' coup'** in Greece.

Assassination of leading US Nazi George Lincoln **Rockwell**; official US government report published – *The Present Day Ku Klux Klan Movement*.

## 1968

Constitution of the German Democratic Republic incorporates 'anti-fascism' article.

Banning of *Occident* in France.

Salazar leaves power in Portugal.

'Racist' campaign of US Presidential candidate George **Wallace**; **National Socialist White People's Party** born.

## 1969

*Ordre Nouveau* born in France.

**Almirante** becomes leader of the Italian MSI; Piazza Fontana bombing – Milan.

*Politica* journal founded in Portugal.

Founding of *Posse Comitatus* in the US.

NPD wins 4.3 per cent of the vote in West German elections; birth of neo-Nazi movement, Friendship Circle for Independent Intelligence (FUN).

## 1970

**Borghese** launches coup attempt in Italy.

Death of American Christian Identity activist Wesley Swift.

## 1971

Chesterton resigns from the British NF.

Son of 'Papa Doc' becomes President of Haiti.

West German *Deutsche Volks Union* (DVU) born.

## 1972

Birth of **Le Pen**'s *Front National* (FN) in France.

Italian MSI scores 8.7 per cent in national elections – its best-ever result.

## 1973

Perón becomes President of Argentina after returning from exile.

Founding of Flemish *Vlaams-Nationale Raad* (VNR).

Danish **Progress Party** scores 16 per cent in national elections.

Founding of *Faire Front* in France.

Birth of *Wehrsportgruppe Hoffmann* in Germany.

Formation of African Resistance Movement (AWB) in South Africa.

Thies **Christophersen** publishes *The Auschwitz Lie*.

## 1974

*Parti des Forces Nouvelles* (PFN) born in France.

Enoch **Powell** leaves the British Conservative Party.

Collapse of Portuguese dictatorship.

## 1975

*Parti des Forces Nouvelles* (PFN) born in Belgium.

Death of Franco; King Juan Carlos I becomes Head of State.

## 1976

Birth of Belgian Nationalist Student Confederation (NSV) and *Voorpost*.

Return of democracy to Portugal.

The Spanish National Front (FNE) is allowed to call itself *FE de las JONS*; birth of *Fuerza Nueva*.

## 1977

Founding of Flemish *Vlaams-Nationale Partij* (VNP) and *Vlaamse Volkspartij* (VVP).

Birth of German neo-Nazi movement, *Aktionsfront Nationaler Sozialisten* (ANS).

National Alignment (EP) founded in Greece.

**Fini** becomes head of the MSI youth movement in Italy.

Founding of *Movimento Independente para a Reconstrucão Nacional* (MIRN) in Portugal.

Birth of **Christian Patriot's Defence League** in US.

## 1978

Founding of *Vlaams Bloc* (VB) and *Union Démocratique pour le Respect du Travail* (UDRT) in Belgium.

Birth of *Légitime Défense* in France; **Duprat** assassinated; de **Benoist** wins *Académie Française* prize.

**Haya de la Torre** becomes President of the Peruvian Assembly.

Publication of William **Pierce**'s *The Turner Diaries*.

Arthur **Butz** publishes *The Hoax of the Twentieth Century*.

## 1979

Austrian FPÖ joins **Liberal International**.

*Khmer Rouge* driven from power in Cambodia.

Founding of *Securité et Liberté* in France.

United Nationalist Movement (ENEK) founded in Greece.

*Unión Nacional* wins 2 per cent in Spanish elections; Blas **Piñar Lopez** elected to parliament.

## 1980

*Oktoberfest* bombing in Germany; founding of **Thule Seminar**; *Wehrsportgruppe Hoffmann* banned.

Founding of **New Order** in Portugal.

US national-socialist Harold **Covington** wins 43 per cent in North Carolina election; David **Duke** founds **National Association for the Advancement of White People**.

(March) **National Democratic Party** (NDP) candidate Norbert **Burger** scores 3.2 per cent in the Austrian presidential election.

## 1981

British **Nationality Act**.

## 1982

Founding of Belgian Nationalist Young Students Association (NJSV).

Re-founding of **British National Party** (BNP).

**Fahd** becomes King of Saudi Arabia.

Banning of the Strasserite German Popular Socialist Movement of Germany/Labour Party (VSBD/PdA).

## 1983

Le Pen's FN gains electoral breakthrough in **Dreux** by-election.

Operation Repatriation-Popular Movement against Foreign Dominance and Destruction of the Environment (AAR) banned in Germany.

Birth of The **Order** in the US.

(November) *Republikaner* party founded in West Germany.

## 1984

Dutch *Centrum Democraten* (CD) established.

Le Pen's FN passes 10 per cent barrier in European elections.

Chabra and Chatilla massacres in Lebanon.

## 1985

Birth of Belgian *Front National-Nationaal Front* (FN-NF).

*Junta Coordinadora de Fuerzas Nacionales* founded in Spain.

## 1986

Controversial presidential election campaign of Kurt **Waldheim** in Austria; Haider takes over the FPÖ; Liberal International carries out enquiry into the politics of the FPÖ.

FN wins thirty-five seats in French parliamentary elections.

*Centrum Partij '86* (CP'86) founded in the Netherlands.

Birth of the Spanish *Frente Nacional*.

*Republikaner* party wins 3 per cent of the vote in Bavarian elections.

Milošević issues **SANU Memorandum** in Yugoslavia.

## 1987

Haider holds 'summit talks' with leading representatives of the Austrian far right.

Banning of French revisionist journal, *Annales d'Histoire Révisionniste*.

Trial of Klaus **Barbie**.

Almirante resigns as leader of the Italian MSI – Fini takes over.

Spanish *Frente Nacional* establishes *Juventades de Frente Nacional* (JFN) youth group.

Turkish Nationalist Labour Party (MCP) wins 3 per cent in elections.

Collapse of US racist group, **Invisible Empire**.

West German DVU evolves into an electoral list.

## 1988

Haider reaffirms his belief in Austria as part of a Greater Germany.

British far-right activists make controversial trip to Libya.

*Alianza Republicana Nacional* (**ARENA**) gains control of the Salvadoran National Assembly.

*Nationale Sammlung* and Homeland Loving Union founded in West Germany.

US scientist, Fred Leuchter, produces *Leuchter Report*, a key revisionist tract on the Nazi gas chambers.

Le Pen wins 14.6 per cent in French presidential election.

## 1989

Birth of Belgian movement, *Agir*.

Le Pen's FN wins parliamentary seat in Dreux by-election.

Birth of Nationalist Youth Front (MEN) in Greece.

Founding of *Força National-Nova Monarquia* (FN-NM) in Portugal.

*Republikaner* party wins 7.5 per cent of the vote in West Berlin (and eleven seats); founding of Kühnen's *Deutsche Alternative* (DA), *Nationale List* and neo-Nazi *Freundeskreis Freiheit für Deutschland* (FFD); banning of *National Sammlung*.

(June) *Republikaner* party wins 7.1 per cent of the vote (and six seats) in European elections.

## 1990

Austrian FPÖ passes 15 per cent barrier in federal elections.

**Party of Well-Being** born in Denmark.

*Republikaner* party loses its eleven Berlin seats.

MSI gains only 4 per cent in local elections: **Rauti** replaces Fini as MSI leader.

Founding of the Romanian Cradle movement.

White supremacist David Duke wins 44 per cent of the vote in a Louisiana election.

(May) **Schönhuber** resigns as *Republikaner* leader in Germany.

(June) Schönhuber re-elected as *Republikaner* leader in Germany.

## 1991

Gulf War.

FPÖ wins 23 per cent in Vienna local elections.

Birth of *Nationaler Bloc*, *Deutsche Liga für Volk und Heimat* (DLVH) and

*Deutscher Kameradschaftsbund* (DKB) in Germany.

Fini restored as leader of the Italian MSI.

Birth of **Movement for Romania** (MPR).

Apartheid ends in South Africa.

Birth of New Democracy in Sweden.

Duke wins 39 per cent share of the vote in election for governor of Louisiana.

(December) Racist incident at **Hoyerswerda**, Germany.

### 1992

Croatian Party of Pure Rights (HCSP) and **Croatian Party of Rights Youth Group** born.

*Republikaner* party wins 11 per cent of the vote in Baden-Württemberg.

**RENAMO** becomes a political party in Mozambique.

Founding of Romanian Party of the National Right (PDN).

(August) Racist incident at **Rostock**, Germany.

### 1993

Dissident members leave Austrian FPÖ to form Liberal Forum; Haider publishes *Freiheitlichen Thesen*; FPÖ withdraws from Liberal International.

Racist incident at **Solingen**, Germany.

Latvian Independence Party wins 13 per cent in national elections.

Party of the National Right founded in Romania – it issues 'Manifesto of the Country'.

Waco siege in the US.

Birth of German *Deutsche Nationalisten* (DN) and *Direkte Aktion/Mittel Deutschland* (DA/MD); banning of *Nationaler Bloc* and FFD.

(September) BNP wins 34 per cent in Isle of Dogs election – and gains its first elected councillor.

(November) Fini stands as MSI candidate for Mayor of Rome; Alessandra Mus-

solini does likewise in Naples; both reach the second round of voting.

### 1994

FPÖ wins 22 per cent in Austrian parliamentary elections.

RENAMO loses Mozambique elections.

(January) MSI leader Fini launches *Alleanza Nazionale* (AN) in Italy.

(March) AN wins 13.5 per cent of the vote in Italian elections; the coalition gains five seats in Berlusconi's cabinet as a result.

(May) Belgian and Danish ministers refuse to shake hands with their Italian AN counterparts.

(June) In European elections, the FN wins 10.5 per cent and the *Republikaner* party wins 3.9 per cent.

(August) Meeting between *Republikaner* and DVU officials in Germany.

(October) Schönhuber sacked as *Republikaner* leader in Germany.

### 1995

Haider makes controversial speech in Austria that praises SS veterans.

Birth of **Danish People's Party**.

Le Pen wins 15 per cent in the French presidential election.

Creation of *Nationale Volkspartij*/CP'86 coalition in the Netherlands.

Rutskoi forms *Derzhava* movement in Russia.

**Oklahoma Bombing**; demise of US **Populist Party**.

(January) MSI dissolves itself.

(June) Le Pen's FN wins municipal power in **Marignane**, **Orange** and **Toulon**.

### 1996

Austrian FPÖ wins 28 per cent in European elections.

(April) AN wins 15.7 per cent in Italian parliamentary poll.

(September) 150,000 Italians attend AN rally in Milan.

## 1997

Catherine **Mégret** wins municipal power in Vitrolles for Le Pen's FN.

Norwegian Progress Party scores 15 per cent in national elections.

## 1998

People's Party scores 7.4 per cent in Danish elections.

*Bharatiya Janata* (BJP) makes electoral breakthrough in India.

(April) German DVU wins 13 per cent of the vote in Saxony elections.

## 1999

Mégret splits from Le Pen's FN and forms the *Front National-Mouvement National* (FN-MN) (later the *Mouvement National Républicain* (MNR)).

(March) Austrian FPÖ wins 43 per cent of the vote in **Carinthia** in provincial elections.

(June) Austrian FPÖ wins 23 per cent and five seats in European elections. In Italy the AN wins almost 10.3 per cent. In Germany the *Republikaner* polls 1.7 per cent and the NPD wins 0.4 per cent. In France the FN gains a 5.7 per cent share of the vote; Mégret's breakaway FN-MN wins 3.5 per cent.

## 2000

Fini becomes Italian Deputy Prime Minister in Berlusconi government.

(Oct) VB wins 33 per cent of the vote in Antwerp local elections.

## 2001

(June) BNP make gains in British parliamentary elections – the party exploits 'race riots' in Oldham, **Burnley** and Bradford.

(August) Scandal involving Edgar Griffin – a Conservative activist with BNP links – rocks Ian Duncan Smith's Tory Party leadership campaign.

(November) Danish People's Party wins 22 seats out of 179 in parliamentary elections.

## 2002

(March) Portuguese Popular Party wins 8.8 per cent in national elections.

(April) Le Pen gains 17 per cent in the first round of the French presidential elections and goes through to the second round run-off.

(May) BNP wins three council seats in Burnley. Le Pen is defeated by Chirac in French presidential run-off. Dutch far-right leader Pim **Fortuyn** is assassinated; his party comes second in national parliamentary elections.

# BACKGROUND

It is impossible to locate a precise point of origin for fascism. To begin with, such a task would require a consensus on the meaning of the term itself. If fascism is seen as a militant, right-wing reaction to radicalism, we could identify such strands in the response to the **French Revolution**, both in France and across Europe. However, much of that was simply a conservative backlash on the part of pre-existing social forces. Nevertheless, the shock of the **Enlightenment** and of the left-wing social movements of the nineteenth century generated new intellectual, cultural and political trends with a life of their own.

## THE SETTING: AN ATMOSPHERE OF EXTREMISM

Industrialisation and **modernisation** caused considerable social dislocation and numerous political realignments. The gradual incorporation of the mass public into the body politic occurred at a time when new emotions and loyalties were coming to the fore. By the late nineteenth century, the countryside was torn apart by industrialisation and the rise of populous cities, the map of Europe had been redrawn by the forces of **nationalism**, and class conflict was intense. The social and political order was shaken and it seemed that there was no endpoint to all this change. Any outcome was possible in the period ahead. Some blamed the Enlightenment for sparking a century-long chain of events that ended in chaos. Others saw **socialism** or a more radical **liberalism** as the next step in the fulfilment of the Enlightenment vision. By the 1890s, radical and extremist ideas were in vogue, with armchair philosophers trying to outdo their rivals or combine apparently contradictory theories into new meta-narratives of the human condition. Of these, nationalist, socialist and hybrid national-socialist paradigms dominated the field of play. It was in this environment that the embryonic ideas that would later coalesce to form fascism emerged.

To justify German unification under Prussian tutelage, the Germans took a keen interest in the cultural, linguistic and ethnic roots of their people. Indeed, to constitute a nation in the first place, a people had to define itself as distinct from others by virtue of a different history and **identity**. The Germanic peoples, once the peripheral 'barbarians' who sacked Rome, would have to deliberately paint a better picture of themselves. Their search for roots, in literature and **language**, was inadvertently aided by Darwinian science. If animals and animal species thrived through competition and the survival of the fittest, perhaps ethnic and cultural groups did too. Issues such as these were absorbed into some strands in German nationalism so as to give it a preoccupation with the themes of race and culture. Those same elements were to be exaggerated and abused by **Hitler** several decades later, to the great detriment of German nationalism and the German people.

The Italians were also shaken by the new politics of the nineteenth century. The process of unification (the *Risorgimento*) brought the otherwise independent Italian-speaking states on the peninsula into a single entity that needed to justify its existence. Some Italians did so using a liberal democratic discourse. Others pointed to race and language. Of course, Italy did have a glorious past in the form of Rome. If the Germans felt that their meteoric modernisation was lacking a great story of origins, the Italians had the opposite problem. The new republic was obviously less significant or impressive on the world stage than its ancient ancestor. Thus was born an Italian inferiority complex that affected the character of its politics from 1870 until at least 1945. Italian nationalism needed to impress the home audience and the world at large, but the weak Italian state was unable to muster the power and resources that this required. As a result, both the late nineteenth-century liberal or nationalist élites, and the Fascists who succeeded them, were constantly strutting and asserting themselves but achieving little in comparison to the great powers. The *Risorgimento* produced a united Italy but one that was always going to be a disappointment, a source of frustration. Italian social scientists and writers belittled and attacked their own state and its government, always dreaming of something more powerful and glorious.

## CHALLENGING THE STATE: FROM WORDS TO ACTION

The First World War seemed to bring this ferment to a head. The Russian, Austrian and Ottoman Empires, fixtures of European politics for half a millennium and beyond, came crashing down. The whole of Eastern Europe was now a chaotic vacuum, a fertile place for both military and philosophical adventurism. Would it be socialist, liberal or nationalist? Would it be Prussian or Russian? In 1918, as in the late nineteenth century, anything was again possible. The establishment of a totalitarian Communist state after the 1917 **Russian Revolution** confirmed this. Here, or so it seemed to many, was a philosophy previously confined to paper, now enthroned as the basis of a new order, not just for Russia but for the world. There was certainly a workers' uprising. However, what was really noticeable was how a small and committed group, the Bolsheviks, struck a decisive blow and changed the course of history. With the systematic use of modern instruments of terror and **propaganda**, this committed élite was apparently remaking the world. Suddenly, any one of the strange concoctions of ideas floating about in Europe since the 1890s could be the basis for a new order. All it required was the right circumstances, effective and determined leadership, and a **will** to action.

The First World War, the peace settlements and the post-war economic crisis took care of the circumstances. The 'war to end all wars' produced mass suffering on a scale never experienced before. It also showed the destructive potential of modern weaponry. Hundreds of thousands had been mobilised; now demobilised, they were disappointed in the peace. The disappointment might have been avoided. US President Woodrow Wilson announced his famous fourteen-point plan. The centrepiece was the principle that the big European empires were to be broken up and the constituent nationalities were to be given their own states. However, because of the complex patchwork of ethnic groups in East Central Europe, the carve-up could never be accurate and many peoples were to be disappointed with their new state boundaries. The principle was not applied to the Germans, many of whom were now to live as minorities in states like Czechoslovakia and Poland. The Hungarians lost much of their territory to Romania and many of them lived as a minority in the Slovak areas of Czechoslovakia. Italy and Japan, which had been backing the Allies by war's end, were not granted the territory or the free hand they demanded in their respective backyards. So the Treaty of **Versailles** and its associated documents and agreements were much resented by many Europeans.

The resentment was also fuelled by the punitive tone of the post-war settlement. Germany had to pay crippling war reparations, limit the size of her army, and grant territorial concessions to neighbours. She was formally blamed for the war and its consequences. Extremist movements offered militant nationalism as a solution to these problems. As a mobilising **ideology**, revolutionary socialism had been commandeered by the Bolsheviks. It was not proving influential among European workers. Moreover, it seemed to serve either Russian or even more nebulous 'internationalist' purposes. Following the lead of their late-nineteenth-century precursors, the new movements advocated what they characterised as 'national' forms of socialism as the answer to economic crisis and **unemployment**. Their anti-**Communism** and hostility to left-wing trade unions appealed to those who feared that the nation or its traditions would be swept away in a tide of Bolshevik-inspired world socialist revolution. After all, socialists had tried to stage such revolutions in Bavaria and in Hungary immediately after the First World War. An undercurrent of anarchism prevailed in some parts of Spain, frequently erupting in anti-government **violence**.

By the early 1920s, Italian Fascism was beginning to look like a distinctive movement with a yearning for power. It settled on nationalism as its rallying cry. In Germany, Hitler rose to become leader of the *Deutsche Arbeiterpartei*, the German Workers' Party. He renamed it the German National Socialist Workers' Party and turned it into a fighting machine with a mission to seize power.

The fascists had a few false starts: **Mussolini** was outmanoeuvred for a while by other right-wing extremists like the poet, Gabriele **D'Annunzio**, whose illegal militia seized control of the disputed city of **Fiume** (Rijeka) in Croatia in 1919. In 1923, in the 'Munich **Beer-Hall Putsch**', Hitler unsuccessfully tried to hijack a nationalist conspiracy against the democratic **Weimar Republic**. He was arrested and jailed. The fascists, it appeared, could look like fools. Nonetheless, they showed the real instincts of the predator, adapting their tactics to changing circumstances. These tactics included street violence, back-street thuggery, assassination, threats of coups and putsches, and ostentatious shows of bluff and swagger at dramatic mass rallies. Mussolini's armed militias confronted striking workers and seized control of provincial centres. In 1922, a major show of force, hyped up by the Fascists as a '**March on Rome**', terrified the Italian political **establishment** into accepting him in government.

However, both Hitler and Mussolini also realised the need to obtain the tacit support, or at least the silence, of existing establishment figures. Hitler cultivated key individuals like President von **Hindenburg**, persuading him to use his constitutional discretion in ways that helped the far right. He played party politics in the *Reichstag*. Both Hitler and Mussolini made themselves sound traditional, conservative or moderate to broaden their appeal along the way. In both Germany and Italy, nationalists and conservatives were agitated, angry at the post-war settlement and fearful of Communism. They thought the fascists could be useful allies, though essentially a passing phenomenon that needed to be tamed or neutralised. They played along with the fascists, believing that they could be domesticated or marginalised. Yet, they also feared fascism's street mobs or the intemperate and unpredictable leaders it seemed to throw up. Weighing up the options, they gambled on giving power to the fascists.

Sensing the need to keep the establishment on-side, or at least indifferent to a fascist threat, Hitler, Mussolini and **Franco** were even prepared to crack down on their own more militant activists to ensure that this process of change and consolidation would always be under their control. Thus, once in the corridors of power, Hitler reduced the power of his militant Storm Trooper militia and Mussolini reined in his *squadrista* street-fighters. The focus had shifted to the consolidation of power.

## CHALLENGING THE WORLD: FASCIST REGIMES AT HOME AND ABROAD

The period from 1922–45 was the high-point of fascism and far-right politics. Once in office, the new dictators lost no time in consolidating their hold on key institutions. From 1925, Italy became a one-party and one-man **dictatorship**. Through the **Enabling Act** and subsequent legislation, as well as by means of plebiscites, the Nazis created an even more formidable dictatorship. Hitler fused the Presidency with the Chancellorship, making the latter the centre of power but actually establishing a leadership institution of his own in the person of the **Führer.** State terror and domestic campaigns against the Jews and opponents of the regime ensued.

In foreign policy, this period was marked by **militarism**, expansionism and **war**. The phenomenon of far-right politics became internationalised, even globalised, as Germany, Italy and Japan concluded a series of bilateral and multilateral treaties that resulted in the **Rome–Berlin–Tokyo Axis**. Fascist militarism and extreme nationalism brought conflict both in Europe and East Asia. Initially, the fascists focused attention on irredentist attacks on contiguous areas across national frontiers inhabited by people of their own nationality. Germany merged with Austria under the *Anschluss* and then occupied German-speaking **Sudetenland**. Earlier, in March 1936, it had reoccupied the Rhineland. To some, this was just a case of correcting Versailles, which had neglected the status of German minorities outside the Reich. However, there were signs that there was more to fascist expansionism than met the eye. In the mid-1930s, for instance, Mussolini occupied Ethiopia (known then as Abyssinia). Japan occupied **Manchuria** and launched a vicious war against China. Hitler finally moved against the rest of the Czech lands and encouraged the creation of a separate, right-wing authoritarian state in Slovakia. While Britain and France had appeased Hitler in his revisionist moves on Germany's periphery, they realised too late that his occupation of Czechoslovakia was part of a more ambitious plan. Their ultimatum to him – not to invade Poland – was ignored. Secure from attack in the east, following a pact with Stalin, Hitler invaded Poland in 1939 and the **Second World War** had begun.

The history of that war is well known. It expanded the fascist sphere of influence. Occupation forces brought Nazi policies, including the campaign for the extermination of the Jews, to all corners of Europe. The Germans established puppet states or forced non-fascist right-wing dictators to ape their style of leadership, propaganda and **pageantry**. They intervened in Spain's civil war to consolidate the power of General Franco and his extreme right-wing military regime.

Apart from Hitler, Mussolini and Franco, the climate of the inter-war period had legitimated right-wing authoritarian movements, parties and governments all over Europe. Many were more traditionalist than fascist, but they all saw democracy as a fool's game, an experiment of the past. Most had revisionist aims, wishing to alter the boundaries of Europe, and they were persuaded, coaxed or pressurised into facilitating Hitler and Mussolini, albeit with varying degrees of enthusiasm.

So far, we have described how fascism was transformed from a loose set of idiosyncratic ideas into a globalised system of government, war and terror. One of the worst aspects of this transformation was the translation of latent **racism** and **anti-Semitism** into what became known as the **Holocaust**. Anti-Semitism and racial prejudice can be traced back over several centuries. They were a key part of the late nineteenth-century intellectual ferment described earlier. Hitler's *Mein Kampf* was driven by this line of thought. Until about halfway into the war, however, it had only manifested itself in violent persecution of Jews and in discrimination against them. Once Germany had a free hand in the East, however, Hitler moved to translate the hatred of Jews, and of Slavic peoples like the Russians and the Poles, into something more macabre. The killing of Jews in urban pogroms was not enough: the entire Jewish population of Europe was to be eliminated. Those who did not die through slave labour were to be gassed to death and have their bodies destroyed in the furnaces at concentration camps, like that at **Auschwitz** in south-western Poland.

Despite the great variety of new far-right movements and currents that have emerged in the period since 1945, the high-point of fascism, the great crisis of 1922–45, still has a significant impact. Koreans argue with Japan over school texts that play down Japanese war crimes. Germany enforces a ban on **Holocaust Denial**. Mussolini's granddaughter is a focal point for controversy in Italian politics. There are still monuments to General Franco in Tenerife. Most countries that were victims of fascism are determined never to forget.

## MARGINALISED EXTREMISM: THE POST-WAR FAR RIGHT

The defeat of the Axis Powers in 1945 appeared to bring an end to the fascist nightmare. Those leaders who had not committed suicide were tried and either executed or imprisoned. Fascism was discredited and became a term of abuse. Western Germany, Italy and Japan were democratised under US and Western control, while the Soviet Union created an East European Communist satellite state in East Germany. By the late 1940s, all of Eastern Europe, the *Lebensraum* sought by the Nazis for a 'one thousand year Reich', was ruled by the Slavic and Communist Soviet Union. That was a striking outcome of Hitler's war.

Initially there were a few extreme right groups on the fringe, like the *Movimento Sociale Italiano* (MSI) in Italy. However, there was no public demand for the rebirth of Italian Fascism or hardcore German National-Socialism. On the other hand, there were new motivations for anti-democratic politics on the right. In Latin America and Greece, for instance, many conservatives, especially those in the security forces, concluded that right-wing dictatorship was an appropriate response to Communist subversion or insurgency. Indeed, the US appeared to endorse this view from time to time by turning a blind eye to such regimes or by supporting them against left-wing rebels.

Some manifestations of far-right politics had pre-dated core fascism and survived well into the twentieth century. One such focal point for violent far-right politics was the struggle to preserve racial supremacy in the face of change or reform. By the late nineteenth century, anti-black violence and discrimination were already established as part of the backlash against the Republican victory in the US Civil War. This was especially true in the old Democratic South, where groups like the **Ku Klux Klan** came to the fore. Similarly, racially motivated far-right extremism was also a feature of South African politics, where the ruling party tried to operate an enforced system of racial separation or **Apartheid**, using discrimination and violence. Although these racist movements gave solace to post-war German Nazis, they had deeper roots in US and South African history.

The 1980s and 1990s saw three further manifestations of far-right activity. First, the increases in **immigration** and multi-ethnic societies in Western Europe led to **xenophobia** and anti-immigrant feeling. Various parties exploited this:

some, like the National Democratic Party of Germany (NPD), openly used Nazi symbolism and had been around since the 1960s; others, like the French *Front National* (FN), were not explicitly fascist but rather extreme nationalists driven by opportunism and prejudice. The issue of immigration also allowed the neo-fascist Italian MSI to come in from the cold and gain more respectable conservative allies. Many of these organisations have distanced themselves from the inter-war fascist period: some go further in this respect than others. **Fini**'s *Alleanza Nazionale* (AN) in Italy, for instance, has moved further and further from its post-war neo-fascist MSI roots, embraced democracy and, in 1994, entered a 'Freedom Alliance' coalition with Silvio Berlusconi's reformist, conservative *Forza Italia*.

Similarly, Jörg **Haider**'s Freedom Party has entered a coalition with Austria's Christian Democrats, to the irritation of Europe's liberal and left-wing governments. Much of Haider's agenda is about free markets and restricting immigration, and is not vastly different from that of mainstream conservatives. On the other hand, he has made complimentary remarks about some features of the Nazi Reich and many fear that his party conceals an uglier side to its nature.

War and social dislocation following the collapse of Communism have produced a large number of ethnic and nationalist movements whose behaviour, discourse and attitudes bear an uncanny resemblance to those of the fascists or far right in the past. Though they claim to be righting past wrongs, these groups have been responsible for promoting ethnic hatred and endorsing genocidal mass killings in south-eastern Europe and the Caucasus. In the early 1990s, authoritarian regimes in Croatia and in Serb-controlled regions of Bosnia-Herzegovina, in particular, used systematic terror and **ethnic cleansing** to 'purify' their territories of 'enemy' peoples. Economic collapse, complex border disputes and unfamiliarity with liberal democracy are fuelling xenophobic, irredentist and anti-democratic organisations like Russia's *Pamyat* or the extremist Greater Romania Party. Much of this is accompanied by renewed anti-Semitism. Meanwhile, in Rwanda, an ideology founded on élitism and inter-ethnic hatred led to the deaths of half a million Tutsis at the hands of a Hutu-dominated *Interhamwe* militia in 1994.

The principal feature of post-war far-right politics is its eclectic nature and, in many cases, its lack of continuity with hardcore fascism. There is a blurring of the lines between the new movements and other tendencies such as **conservatism**. There are also violent and terrorist variants. On the other hand, the combination of **totalitarianism**, militarism, nationalism, nationalised forms of socialism and ritual that characterised fascism can be seen in many nationalist movements in the Third World or even in the more radical forms of Islamic fundamentalism. Mu'ammar **Qaddafi**, for instance, talks much about socialism and **Islam**. Looking more closely, however, one can see a rather bombastic showman who plays a role of Arab leader, whose 'Green Book' ideology is a combination of a Libyan form of socialism, tradition, personality cult, Islam and mystical Arab nationalism. Libyan state ideology is not Italian

Fascism. However, the character of the Great Socialist People's Libyan Arab *Jamahiriyah* owes more to it than either Italian neo-fascists or the 'Leader of the Revolution' would care to admit.

Whether in the echoes from its violent past, in the inter-ethnic wars of the post-**Cold War** years, or in the efforts of esoteric revolutionaries to create new syntheses of nationalism and socialism, fascist and far-right politics have an enduring impact on our modern world.

# HISTORIOGRAPHY

For all the enterprise, for all the time and critical intelligence devoted to the under-
taking, we really have very little purchase on 'understanding' 'fascism'.[1]

How should we interpret fascism? This puzzle has detained scholars for the
best part of a century. Historians, social scientists, sociologists, political scientists and social psychologists have all struggled to comprehend the essential
nature of the **ideology**. The 'consensus' view is that fascism represented **middle-
class** rebellion against the established **Enlightenment**-influenced order; it was
invariably irrational and anti-Communist, and sought to impose a new age, a
new civilisation. However, the fact is that the study of fascism has become a
battleground, an arena where competing ideologies have taken centre stage.
There is no *single* interpretation of fascism; moreover, at certain junctures, the
plethora of explanations that do exist merge and overlap.

As Payne suggests, the debate about fascism began as soon as the **March on
Rome** had finished.[2] The first attempts at historiography were made during the
1920s and 1930s when **Mussolini**'s regime, and then **Hitler**'s, came under in-
depth scrutiny. However, studies of fascism penned before 1945 are not regarded in a very positive light, with Gregor, for one, arguing that they are 'full
of generalisations'.[3] Following the **Second World War**, not unexpectedly, fascism suffered a period of 'moral condemnation' and 'extra-terrestrial exile'.[4]
The overall effect was that it was not taken seriously as historical subject
matter.

Things began to change in the 1950s and 1960s. Arendt's study of **totalitarianism** (1951) appeared to rescue fascism from scholarly oblivion, and thereafter a range of studies appeared.[5] Nolte states:

It is perhaps permissible to regard the years 1959 and 1960 as the beginning of a
change, a change that was certainly related to an alteration in the world situation
characterised by a relaxation in the Cold War, the onset of polycentrism in the
East, and a renewed readiness for self-criticism in the West. In 1959, after a long
hiatus, the concept of fascism once again appeared in the title of a book.[6]

He cites the works of Dante Germino, Seymour Lipset and Ralf Dahrendorf as
representative of this new trend.

By the end of the 1960s, it would be fair to say that fascism had acquired
some respectability as a historical topic. More survey texts, detailed national
histories and comparative studies began to appear.[7] By the beginning of the
twenty-first century, 'fascism studies' had established itself as a specific discipline, with historians such as Griffin, Eatwell and Payne primarily interested in

the ideological richness and variety of the genus. **Neo-fascism** and other forms of right-wing extremism also gained their historians: such as Cheles, Ferguson and Vaughan *et al.*, Hainsworth *et al.*, and Eatwell.

Over the decades historians have debated a wide range of issues. Should we talk about fascism in the singular or plural? Is it a homogenous or heterogeneous phenomenon? Should the emphasis be placed on varieties or commonalities? To what extent were Italian Fascism and German Nazism 'peas from the same pod'? Is there a generic fascism? And can 'ideal type' theory, checklists, typologies and the notion of a 'fascist minimum' help us to understand the subject at a deeper level?[8]

Furthermore, is fascism new or old, revolutionary or reactionary? Is it merely a radicalised **conservatism** or an entirely novel phenomenon? Is there a post-1945 fascism as well as a pre-1945 fascism? Similarly, is there an extra-European fascism in addition to a European fascism? Would it be true to say that national disintegration in the years after 1918 was the root cause of fascism? Or were there other factors? What does the fact that fascist parties were able to forge alliances with conservative movements and ruling élites tell us?

Observers of fascism have faced a major quandary over whether to rationalise it or treat it with the utmost scepticism. Most commentators, with the notable exception of Allardyce,[9] have taken the former approach, as evidenced by the wide array of 'theories of fascism' that have emerged.

Payne, for instance, identifies eight main interpretations: fascism as a product of **capitalism**, moral breakdown, pathological neuroticism, the 'amorphous masses', economic development, totalitarianism, resistance to **modernisation**, and middle-class radicalism.[10] Hagtvet *et al.* go further and suggest eleven distinct perspectives: those associated with 'demonic' personality, moral disease, national development, capitalism as an agent, totalitarianism, the 'revolt against transcendence', social structure outgrowth, modernisation, an 'aesthetic aberration', cultural tradition, and **counter-revolution**.[11] De Felice, who devotes much of his study to theorising about the Italian experience, also makes a range of more general observations. He locates psychosocial, sociological and socio-economic explanations as well as a range of other 'classical' explanations.[12] Thurlow, meanwhile, refers to a 'new consensus' on fascism – connected to the writings of Payne, Griffin and Eatwell. Nevertheless, he is still able to identify five 'standard' views from the pre-consensus era: the Marxist approach, the thesis of Ernst Nolte, and the notions of fascism as 'extremism of the centre', 'totalitarianism' and 'a function of modernisation'.[13]

By way of synthesis, we can classify these 'paradigms' by theme (socio-economic, moral/psychological, political) and ideological orientation (Marxist, nationalist, conservative, liberal, idealist, Christian, Jewish).[14] To clarify things still further, these different theories will be outlined and explained separately. However, we should be aware that, clearly, someone who holds a Marxist viewpoint, for example, does so on the basis of certain assumptions about the socio-economic and political nature of fascism. Thus there will be much cross-over between the two main sub-sections.

## INTERPRETATIONS BY THEME

Let us start with what we may choose to call the more 'thematic' interpretations. Moral and psychological theories hold that fascism was an 'aberration'. The moral interpretation, advanced by both pro- and anti-fascist commentators alike, says that fascism was a product of crisis and disease in society.[15] Pro-fascist authors take a romantic line. They talk about 'young and heroic idealists' revolting against 'a superannuated and materialistic social order', and argue that fascism was a remedy for 'moral crisis', a spiritual reawakening, an ethical, heroic response to all that was wrong in liberal society.[16] The anti-fascist view, on the other hand, puts the emphasis on despair. According to this interpretation, fascism was an 'aesthetic aberration', a product of perversity and corruption, a return to absolutism, an escape from disillusionment.[17] As Drucker has stated:

> Armaments, the totalitarian organisation of society, the suppression of freedom and liberties, the persecution of the Jews, and the war against religion are all signs of weakness, not of strength. They have their roots in blackest, unfathomable despair. The more desperate the masses become, the more strongly entrenched will totalitarianism appear to be. The further they push on the totalitarian road, the greater will be their despair.[18]

Summing up, Gregor says that this view sees fascism as 'a consequence of moral failure, the advent of a new irrational and unethical conception of life that ruthlessly imposed itself upon the nation'.[19] However, he also argues that it could never be a causal explanation because it is difficult, if not impossible, to ascribe 'moral motives' to human beings. He also casts doubt on the quality of the scholarship that supports this view.[20]

Moral and psychological interpretations of fascism are related in the sense that they both revolve around the notion of a 'sick society' or a world that has gone 'mad'.[21] Kedward says that psychological approaches to fascism have always been controversial:

> How does a knowledge of Hitler's infancy help one to understand the rise of Nazism? Doesn't psychology tend to excuse and explain away the evils of fascist rule? How can psychologists analyse people who are dead? These are some of the familiar questions which stem from a suspicion of psychology as soon as it is applied to recent history. In fact they indicate more than suspicion. There is also a fear that psychology will upset the black-and-white view of fascism which has been prevalent since 1945; that it will demand a more generous understanding than we are prepared to give or that it will find fascism to be less abnormal than we have assumed. In short, it may make us reconsider well-established judgements.[22]

However, he goes on:

> If we want to know why Hitler was so fanatically anti-Semitic or why violence is
> so recurrent in all fascisms or why so many people welcomed authoritarianism,
> then the approach of the psychologist will be as important as that of the political
> historian or the economist.[23]

So it is possible to rationalise the merits of psychological enquiry on an
individual and collective level. Kitchen goes further:

> The sadistic behaviour of fascist gangs, the extraordinary mass hysteria generated
> by fascist rallies, and the apparently pathological conduct of many fascist leaders
> seemed to be such striking characteristics of fascist regimes that it was widely
> assumed that psychology was the only discipline capable of providing an adequate
> explanation of fascism. Social psychologists saw fascism and anti-semitism as a
> fruitful area for fresh research and speculation, or as confirmation of their fondly
> held theories.[24]

Psychological interpretations suggest that fascism was attractive to certain
personality types and tapped into people's inner psyches. Carsten argues that
certain aspects of fascism had particular appeal – the 'lust for power' and the
'hatred of weakness'. It is also manifest that fascism catered for those who
wished for strong, charismatic leadership and authority.[25] Here the work of
Freudian Marxists Adorno and Fromm is important. Both men emerged from
the **Frankfurt School** to cast important psychological light on fascism.

Adorno likens fascism to 'neurosis' and 'delinquency', and claims that the
anti-democrat is 'anti-semitic, ethnocentric, an economic conservative, holds
rather rigid beliefs, condones violence against opponents, uses stereotypes,
distinguishes sharply between "in-group" and "out-group" and admires strong
men'. This is the 'prejudiced personality' that, in Adorno's view, is attracted to
fascism.[26] Fromm takes a similar line, arguing that fascism aims at 'the
annihilation of the individual self and its utter submission to a higher power'.
The underlying contention in his work is that 'modern democratic man' cannot
cope with unlimited freedom because it brings wholesale insecurity.[27] Kedward
says that:

> [Fromm] saw the problem of man's freedom as a psychological one: how far does
> man want to be free? Can he face the difficulties of freedom? Is he prepared to act
> alone? Will he value freedom when it is new, strange and uncomfortable? In short,
> does freedom breed as many fears as hopes?

And he adds: 'Psychologically Nazism had much to offer those who wanted
both security and sadistic power in place of the freedom they were unable to
face.'[28] It is in this sense that Fromm identifies the 'sado-masochistic character'
and the 'authoritarian character', arguing that human beings have an innate
desire to submit to authority. Kitchen, reflecting on these issues, claims that

45

**authoritarianism** 'is part of the search for new secondary bonds to replace the primary bonds which have been lost'.[29]

Over time, scholars have emphasised other psychological dimensions to fascism. Freud has spoken of the 'frustration, insecurity and failure' of the young Hitler and the 'psychosexual' problems he faced as a young child; Platt has described fascist ideology as a 'new way of making sense of the world'; Theweleit has referred to the distinctive 'inner world' of fascists; and Jung has equated fascism to an 'upsurge of the dark forces of mankind'.[30]

As regards leaders and led, there are a series of psychological hypotheses. In the German context, 'Hitler-centric' theories are commonplace, though not particularly well regarded. Saussure and Erikson have utilised the model of the 'madman' in their enquiries into the leadership of fascist groups, while those historians interested in the 'rank and file' of such movements have built upon Le Bon's interest in 'the crowd' in history. Trotter, for instance, has talked about the 'instincts of the herd'.[31]

Payne argues that psychological interpretations are 'speculative'; Gregor says they are unprovable and able to explain 'too much'.[32] Whatever the case, they certainly do not impress Marxists, the majority of whom feel duty-bound to stick to a strict economic determinism. However, it would be wrong to dismiss all psycho-theories. It is stating the obvious to say that the rise of an ideological creed like fascism must tell us something quite profound about people and their psychological needs.

In the socio-economic sphere there are a range of would-be explanations. On one level fascism has been interpreted as 'extremism of the middle classes' or 'extremism of the centre', a theory associated with the sociological model developed by Seymour Lipset in 1959. He stated:

> The classic fascist movements have represented the extremism of the centre. Fascist ideology, though anti-liberal in its glorification of the state, has been similar to liberalism in its opposition to big business, trade-unions, and the socialist state. It has also resembled liberalism in its distaste for religion and other forms of traditionalism.[33]

In Italy particularly, where the middle classes were petrified of 'Red Revolution', fascism thrived on the fear of social change. Kitchen states that the membership figures of fascist parties supports the 'middle-class' thesis, while Turner identifies a 'middle-class core' to fascism.[34]

On the surface it might appear that Lipset's notion of 'middle-class extremism' is not too far removed from the idea of capitalism and high finance as the 'lackeys' of fascism (the Orthodox Marxist view). However, we should guard against categorising these two interpretations in the same bracket. It is true that those on the left depict fascism as the ultimate product of class struggle, of a middle-class offensive against the working class,[35] but whereas Marxists view matters in a deterministic light – as rigid and somehow inevitable – those who buy into Lipset's interpretation are less mechanical in their thinking and allow for an independent relationship. This is what Kitchen is alluding to when he contrasts 'heteronomic' theories of fascism with 'autonomic' theories.[36] In a totally different manner, some historians have depicted fascism as a mass movement, with an innate ability to appeal to 'the crowd'.[37] Commentators refer to the new psyche of the people – their 'mass mind' and common purpose.[38]

Historians and sociologists have also debated the connection between fascism and modernisation. The most commonly held view is that the two phenomena went hand in hand. It has been argued that fascism was the product of advanced, industrial society and a key staging-post in the modernisation process, and also that fascism was a 'modernising force' in itself; but if fascism and modernisation are intrinsically related, as many commentators say they are, why did fascism not take root in all industrial societies? This is the conundrum that exponents of the 'modernisation' thesis have to deal with.

However, not all observers are convinced by the 'modernisation' thesis. Some prefer to view fascism as nostalgic and reactionary, as an anti-modern, anti-modernisation revolt. Kitchen, for instance, argues that fascism was in essence the 'reverse image' of modernisation;[39] and Turner, focusing on the German experience, says that Hitler wished to create an 'anti-modern utopia'.[40] Hence Cassels's contention that there were actually two types of fascism: one that emerged in industrial societies and another that came to the fore in under-industrialised societies.[41]

On the whole historians have tended to accept the argument that sees fascism as an agent of, or accompaniment to, modernisation, but what is the relationship between fascism and development in a more general sense? Structuralist theories suggest that fascism is the product of 'delayed industrialisation'. Gregor, for example, depicts fascism as a 'developmental' regime, one that in the Italian context helped the country through to economic maturity.[42]

It is also possible to view fascism in terms of national political development. Griffin talks about a 'development sequence' and emphasises the fact that Germany and Italy shared similar histories.[43] It is easy to sketch out the commonalities: conquest by Napoleon, unification in the 1860s and 1870s, weak liberal governments in the early twentieth century, and national humiliation in 1918. In both countries the post-war settlement became a cause of resentment and frustration – a state of affairs that was exploited mercilessly by Mussolini and Hitler.

Payne argues that 'developmental' interpretations are too 'suggestive';[44] others argue they are too general and vague. However, it is a fact that the emergence of Italian Fascism and German Nazism cannot be separated out from the economic and political context. Nonetheless, it would be prudent to take account of the general point made by Drucker. From a liberal perspective he contends that the socio-economic dimension to fascism has been grossly exaggerated, claiming the emergence of Mussolini and Hitler had nothing to do with their economic agendas and dismissing the notion that fascism came to power on the back of one particular class or group.[45] He goes on to state that the defeat of the ideology will come when the liberal-democratic nations establish 'a new non-economic concept of a free and equal society'.[46] It could be argued that this line of thought is not just novel but a refreshing antidote to Marxist and sociological interpretations.

. It could be argued that there are three mainstream 'political' interpretations of fascism. First, according to Mosse, Sternhell and Eatwell (among others), fascism was a radical new political solution. While Mosse, a historian of Germany, depicts Nazism as a 'Third Way' between Marxism and capitalism,[47] Sternhell, a scholar with French interests, interprets fascism as a revolutionary synthesis, declaring that fascism was at the same time a *fusion of* left and right, and an ideological creed that was *beyond* left and right. His main thesis is that the roots of fascism lay in 1880s and 1890s France in the writings of **Barrès** and that in full bloom the ideology stood as a violent revolt against positivism and **liberalism**.[48]

British historian Eatwell takes a similar view, depicting fascism as 'elusive because it drew from both the right and left, seeking to create a radical "Third Way" which was neither capitalist nor communist'.[49] Elsewhere he has stated:

> The pioneer French fascist Georges Valois (1878–1945) held that nationalism + socialism = fascism. This formulation helps illustrate the vital mutations at the heart of fascism, but is in crucial ways misleading .... Although still misleading, it would be more accurate to say that nationalism $\pm$ conservatism = fascism.[50]

These synthetic interpretations have a lot going for them. They take account of fascism's roots – in the late nineteenth century when new political ideologies had to make an appeal to the masses – and also help to highlight the cross-class appeal, and some would say ambiguity, of fascism.

Second, fascism has been viewed as counter-revolution, particularly by those on the left. In 1928, the **Comintern** announced that 'Fascism's chief function is to annihilate the revolutionary vanguard of the working class i.e. the communist strata of the proletariat and their leading cadres.'[51] Five years earlier, the same body had stated:

> Although fascism by its origin and its exponents ... includes revolutionary tendencies which might turn against capitalism and its State, it is nevertheless becoming a dangerous counter-revolutionary force. That is shown where it triumphed in Italy .... The working classes of the entire world are threatened with the fate of their Italian brothers.[52]

It is not that fascism championed monarchism or wished to restore traditional élites – far from it – but that, through organised state terror, it was ready to clamp down on all symptoms of dissent and opposition. In this sense fascism can be viewed as counter-revolution 'from above'.[53] In Italy, fascism was perceived to be a response to fears of Socialist Revolution; likewise in France the *ligues* can be interpreted as a response to radicalism and the electoral rise of the left (the two 'waves' of French fascism relate directly to the arrival of the *Cartel des Gauches* and **Popular Front** in government (1924 and 1936 respectively). And it is also a fact that in 1940 the **Vichy** regime – regarded by many as the only example of genuine French fascism – styled itself as the ultimate in counter-revolutionary forces, banning the 1789 Declaration and replacing the revolutionary triptych, 'Liberty, Equality, Fraternity', with the new slogan, 'Work, Family, Country'.

That said, the equation of 'fascism' with 'counter-revolution' raises as many questions as it answers. For instance, we should be aware that fascism is often portrayed as a 'revolutionary', rather than a counter-revolutionary, ideology. Clearly there is much evidence to suggest that fascism was overtly radical – its populism, economic dynamism and belief in a 'new age'. Perhaps the best way to think about it is as an ideology that was able to embrace *both* revolutionary and counter-revolutionary ideas. Carsten rationalises things in the following way: he says there *was* a 'fascist revolution', but that all fascist movements included counter-revolutionary elements.[54]

Third, fascism has been interpreted as totalitarianism. This explanation dominated the 1950s and 1960s, and was heavily influenced by **Cold War** attitudes. (Griffin says it had waned by the 1980s.) Associated in particular with the work of Hannah Arendt, this explanation depicts fascism and Communism, controversially, as symptoms of an all-embracing totalitarianism. Liberals in particular favour this view.[55]

Here it is argued that fascism amounts to a totalitarian attack on the liberty of the individual, that it identifies an 'enemy within' (the Jews), and puts its faith, additionally, in 'permanent terror' and 'ideological rigidity'.[56] In the view of Friedrich, 'fascist totalitarianism' incorporates six main features: an over-reaching ideology, a single political party, a state terror apparatus, a government-controlled media, a monopoly on arms and a centrally directed economy.[57] For their part Neumann and the Frankfurt School focused on economics, suggesting that the relationship between capitalism and fascism was close, and that fascism stood ultimately for 'totalitarian monopoly capitalism'.[58]

For liberals the ramifications of this interpretation are clear: a war on fascism and its totalitarian 'brother', Communism. For others the theory is of only partial merit. Gregor suggests that it is a helpful aid but does not really add to our general understanding of fascism.[59] Kitchen, reflecting Marxist concerns, is equally sceptical:

> Although the theories of totalitarianism have raised many important issues and set off a lively debate on the nature of fascism and communism, they have been far from satisfactory as theories of fascism. Only when the insistence on the essential identity of fascism and communism is denied is the theory capable of producing valid insights into the nature of fascism, but when this occurs 'totalitarianism' is given a different meaning and the original premises of the theory are abandoned. Liberal society is indeed challenged by the left and by the right, but

the assumption that left and right must therefore be essentially similar is a severe hindrance to the understanding of either alternative.[60]

Finally, we must note the contribution of Nolte to the historiography of fascism. His 'phenomenology' thesis has a curious reputation: it is acclaimed as a major contribution to the debate about fascism, is regularly referred to and is one of the best-known individual theories, but few scholars are enthusiastic about its content. In addition, it fits into no neat categories and claims to be politically neutral – although Kitchen depicts Nolte as a historian who is attached to 'liberal-bourgeois society'.[61]

Chapter 1 of Nolte's keynote study – published in 1965 – is entitled 'Fascism as characteristic of an era', and this sets the tone for his 561-page enquiry.[62] In general he argues that fascism 'was a specifically inter-war phenomenon, linked to the unique combination of historical circumstances that characterised the period'.[63] In a sense this position is uncontroversial but it does have its significance. It means that Nolte has broken away from Arendt's 1951 'totalitarian' thesis and also encourages him to think of fascism in comparative terms – hence his interest in three European countries (France, Italy and Germany).[64] In fascist historiography these were interesting and novel developments.

Nolte went further and interpreted fascism as 'resistance to transcendence', a fairly vague description but taken to imply that the ideology embraced by Mussolini and Hitler was, in his view, a reaction against **modernity**. Again, this is a fairly uncontroversial assertion but it is dressed up in such jargon that it perhaps appears more impressive than it actually is – and the same could also be said for many other parts of Nolte's thesis.

Kitchen depicts the 'phenomenology' thesis as 'limited and confusing',[65] but it is an important landmark in the historiography of fascism and a useful reference point for students. Moreover, in taking fascism 'seriously' as a political ideology, Nolte can rightly claim to have encouraged and provoked further historical enquiry.

So, 'thematic' perspectives cover the full spectrum – psychology, sociology, economics, politics – but how do they juxtapose with polemical interpretations?

## INTERPRETATIONS BY POLITICAL ORIENTATION

Over time, fascism, predictably, has become a great source of polemical debate. Commentators from across the political spectrum have elaborated their own specific approach to the subject, and in this section we will explore the full range of perspectives. It should be noted that considerable space will be devoted to the Marxist interpretation because, arguably, it is the most stark and controversial of all theories. It has also become a battleground and reference point that no polemicist or historian can ignore.

On the left it is difficult for some commentators to remain neutral about fascism. Take, for example, the following passage:

When writing about any political ideology, the historian is obliged to be critical. It would be a mistake to take the language of political figures at face value. The formal pronouncements of any leaders should be weighed against their practice. It is enough to assume that because a politician used words like 'freedom' or 'democracy', that these terms were meant in the way that a different audience might understand them. There is a need to analyse all ideologies critically, and this is especially true of fascism, a political tradition which from its inception set out to kill millions. Indeed, how can a historian, in all conscience, approach the study of fascism with neutrality? What is the meaning of objectivity when writing about a political system that plunged the world into a war in which at least forty million people died? How can the historian provide a neutral account of a system of politics which turned continental Europe into one gigantic prison camp? One cannot be balanced when writing about fascism, there is nothing positive to be said of it. Fascism is wholly unacceptable, as a method of political mobilisation, as a series of ideas, and as a system of rule.[66]

Notwithstanding the fact that Renton has located three Marxist strands – 'right', 'left' and 'dialectical'[67] it is standard practice to talk in terms of two broad theses: 'Orthodox' and 'non-Orthodox'. The following two passages are representative of the Orthodox Marxist line:

Fascism is the open, terrorist dictatorship of the most reactionary, most chauvinist and most imperialist elements of finance capital. Fascism tries to secure a mass basis for monopolist capital among the petty bourgeoisie, appealing to the peasantry, artisans, office employees and civil servants who have been thrown out of their normal course of life, and particularly to the declassed elements in the big cities, also trying to penetrate into the working class.[68]

Fascism, a political trend which emerged in capitalist countries in the period of the *general crisis of capitalism* and which expresses the interests of the most reactionary and aggressive forces of the imperialistic *bourgeoisie*. *F. in power is an openly terroristic* dictatorship of these forces. F. is characterised by extreme *chauvinism, racism* and *anti-communism*, by the destruction of democratic freedoms, the wide practice of social demagogy and the strictest control over the public and private life of citizens.[69]

So, Orthodox Marxists (like Dimitrov, Palme Dutt and Togliatti before the war, and Petzold after it) took their line from Stalin and the Communist International in the 1930s and referred to fascism as the 'agent' of monopoly capitalism and high finance. Griffin states:

In November 1922, only weeks after Mussolini's March on Rome, the Fourth Congress of the Communist International held in Moscow debated how Fascism was to be explained within a Marxist–Leninist perspective. One interpretation which resulted predictably saw it as an essentially reactionary movement which had been forced into existence when the attempted proletarian revolution of the so-called 'red biennium' (1919–20) threatened the bourgeois-liberal order. Like colonialism, imperialism and the First World War before it, fascism was thus accommodated without too much soul-searching (or 'self-criticism') within the teleological scheme of revolutionary socialism which predicted the imminent collapse of capitalism.[70]

Orthodox Marxists went on to make strong connections between the rise of fascism and industrial and imperialistic expansion; in this regard fascists are viewed as the 'lackeys' of big business and full-blown fascism is viewed exclusively in economistic terms.[71] It is also argued that fascist leaders duped the proletariat into thinking that fascism would help to build a 'new and better world'.[72]

Although the Comintern stated that on occasions fascist leaders resorted to 'anti-capitalist phraseology', it is self-evident that in leftist strictures fascism is simply viewed as being synonymous with capitalism.[73] Kitchen labels the Orthodox Marxist theory 'heteronomic' because implicit in it is the belief that fascism thrived on external factors (e.g. capitalism) and adds: 'Central to all socialist theories of fascism is the insistence on the close relationship between fascism and industry.'[74] Accordingly, Marxist orthodoxy demands the overthrow of capitalism as the only way to rid modern society of fascism.

On the whole, the Orthodox Marxist interpretation has been ridiculed by commentators. Turner, for example, refers to an 'ideological straitjacket' and states:

> Almost without exception, these (Marxist) writings suffer from … over-reliance on questionable, if not fraudulent scholarship, and from egregious misrepresentation of factual information. Until such independent Marxists who write about fascism acquaint themselves with the most recent findings of empirical scholarship and develop more scrupulous habits in their use of factual data, they cannot expect their position to receive a full hearing in the forum of international scholarship.[75]

In the light of these comments it is not difficult to point to the defects of the 'standard' Marxist line. It is not just crude, simplistic and over-focused on economic matters, but there is a tendency to identify fascists and fascism in every nook and cranny – in Spain, Poland, Greece, Portugal, Chile, Argentina, South Africa and even within the British Conservative Party.[76] Furthermore, the notion of **'social fascism'** implies that even Social Democrats are fascists![77] The fact of the matter is that traditional Marxists are undiscerning, unenthusiastic about nuanced analysis and always on the lookout for 'new permutations'.[78]

Orthodox Marxists are invariably blinkered by the political dimension to fascism. In dogmatic terms, they affirm Horkheimer's dictum that 'whoever is not prepared to talk about capitalism should also remain silent about fascism' (and would also agree with Togliatti's reworking of this: 'You can't know what fascism is if you don't know imperialism').[79] However, in doing so, they overestimate the grip that industrialists had on fascists and the links that existed between bourgeois society and fascism, automatically viewing the latter as a 'reactionary' response to the left and a form of 'anti-proletarian hysteria'.[80] Similarly, as Payne notes, they do not distinguish between the fascist right and conservative right.[81] In addition, old-style Marxists do not like to give the impression that fascism was in any way progressive or revolutionary. And to cap it all, Mosse and Nolte claim that Marxist theoreticians are simply misinformed. The former argues that they lack evidence to substantiate their theories, while the latter claims they failed to legislate for the growth of a political phenomenon outside of 'the dictatorship of the proletariat' or 'bourgeois democracy' (even though Marxists would argue that fascism was an innately bourgeois phenomenon).[82]

Thus, although the Orthodox Marxist view has little credibility among modern commentators, it is of crucial historiographical importance, and also helps us to comprehend three 'thematic' interpretations: those that see fascism as a product of 'extremism of the middle classes', as a function of modernisation and as a counter-revolutionary force.[83]

Needless to say, Orthodox Marxists view all interpretations that do not emanate from the Orthodox fold as a product of 'bourgeois' historiography.[84] But it is a fact that a range of non-Orthodox Marxist interpretations emerged in the 1930s and the post-war period as a response to 'changed circumstances'.[85] Thalheimer, Horkheimer, Vajda, Bauer, Galkin, Kühnl, Gramsci, Kitchen and Renton could all be labelled 'neo-Marxist' theoreticians, and all are viewed with suspicion by Orthodox Marxists.[86]

On the whole, 'neo-Marxist' theoreticians do not diverge radically from the Orthodox line, but do present their ideas differently (Gregor talks about a 'Revised Standard Version').[87] They still place significant emphasis on economic factors but are less crude and more synthetic. Kitchen, for example, has made a distinction between fascist regimes and military dictatorships, while others have differentiated between Italian and German experiences.[88] These might seem small advances, but given the rigidity of the Orthodox view we should probably interpret them as a radical departure! It is also a fact that East European and West European Marxists have advanced different theories of fascism:

> Academics within the Soviet empire had little option but to apply to pre-war Comintern orthodoxy to demonstrate empirically the nexus formed by capitalism and state power in Mussolini's Italy, the Third Reich, and what were assumed to be 'weaker' fascist regimes such as Franco's Spain or Perón's Argentina. Their limited perspective produced a steady flow of data-cum-propaganda about how such regimes functioned as socio-economic systems of production and destruction at the expense of the 'people'. Western Marxists, on the other hand, were free to elaborate their own conceptual framework, drawing on the significant modifications to historical materialism pioneered by Gramsci, the Frankfurt School, or structuralists, which have allowed the power of ideology and the irrational to be recognised as well as the complexity of class relations under fascism. All were spurred on by the conviction that fascism cannot be safely consigned to 'history', but is a latent tendency in all modern states.[89]

By the early 1970s, Western Marxists were further watering down the Orthodox line and adding nuances to the traditional view of fascism as a function of the rise of the middle classes and big business.[90] Fascism was now interpreted by some as 'progressive' and 'revolutionary', rather than simply reactionary.[91] Griffin reflects on the upsurge in neo-Marxist theorising:

> It is hardly surprising if some highly nuanced Marxist interpretations of fascism came into being outside the hegemony of the Comintern even before the Second World War. The most significant of these were the elaborations of Marx's concept of Bonapartism by Thalheimer and Bauer, and the sophisticated explanatory model of Fascism which Gramsci constructed on the basis of his concept of ideological hegemony and of Lenin's theory of a 'Prussian' path to capitalism, both of which influenced post-war Marxist theorists. By the 1980s, crude equations of fascism with monopoly capitalism had become largely a thing of the past outside the East bloc.[92]

At times it appeared that a *non*-Marxist theory with strong socio-economic underpinnings had emerged. However, we should not exaggerate the amount of political space that separates non-Orthodox from Orthodox Marxists. Non-Orthodox Marxists still have a tendency to see fascism 'everywhere' and to campaign for stringent 'anti-fascist' measures, and in many ways neo-fascism is viewed as just as dangerous as Italian or German fascism in the inter-war years. The argument is that fascism is alive and not yet consigned to history.[93]

Likewise, some non-Orthodox Marxists still hold that fascism was 'a specific form of reactionary mass movement', and economic factors are still viewed as being of pivotal importance.[94] And, as Petzold has argued, this marks *all* Marxists out as different: 'The question of what relationship the Nazi movement and fascist activism have at all to monopoly capital has become the main focus of the controversy between Marxist and non-Marxist historians in the field of fascist studies.'[95] This leads us on nicely to a consideration of other, non-Marxist interpretations.

In general terms conservatives are mistrustful of fascism. Although some admire the ideology of Mussolini and Hitler – reflecting the fact that many 'mainstream' conservatives made alliances with the two dictators – most focus on its 'plebeian traits' and denounce its radical and revolutionary tendencies. In nostalgic fashion conservatives such as Hermann Rauschning align themselves with 'traditional values' and the 'good old days' that preceded wholesale social and economic change.[96] Proponents of the nationalist view tend to see fascism as either the zenith or nadir of nation-based politics: they either support fascism on the basis that it places enormous emphasis on the nation, or yearn for better, earlier times.[97] The Christian interpretation, put forward by Luigi Sturzo (among others), sees fascism as a 'secular' phenomenon. Accordingly the Mussolini and Hitler regimes are viewed as the embodiment of a new 'godless' era, but the credibility of this perspective is placed in doubt by the pro-fascist leanings of some religious organisations in Germany and Italy.[98] The idealist interpretation emphasises the mythical character of fascism, while the Jewish perspective on the phenomenon 'is based on the most appalling of all human experiences. Nothing is more natural than that this conception should bring the whole weight of ... experience to bear in favour of a distinction between National Socialism and fascism.'[99]

Aside from Marxist and neo-Marxist views, and notwithstanding the significance of the theses just outlined, it is liberal thinking on fascism that has gained most prominence. The first point to make here is that there are many shades of liberal opinion and not just one widely held view. Indeed, at times, liberals would agree with Marxist analyses and buy into many of the 'thematic' theories discussed earlier. It would be fair to say, though, that liberal theses are not as contentious or disputed as leftist interpretations:

> The debate over the nature of fascism within Marxism was pursued more energetically than in the liberal camp. There are several reasons for this: (1) in the inter-war period fascism was a rival revolutionary (or as Marxists would have it, counter-revolutionary) creed; (2) fascism displayed a degree of activist violence towards revolutionary Marxism which far surpassed the animosity of liberalism; (3) Marxist orthodoxy suggested that a precondition for fighting fascism was the scientific analysis of its dynamics; (4) the debate reflected deep cleavages both between factions of revolutionary Marxists and between these and reformist socialists, especially social democrats.[100]

Furthermore, it has been argued that, in the early twentieth century, liberals found it difficult to adapt their version of history to 'a new form of political energy which sought to use nationalist myths to mobilise the masses in a spirit which was both reactionary and revolutionary, traditionalist and modernising, elitist and populist'.[101] However, a liberal interpretation of fascism soon emerged, associated in the main with Salvatorelli and Borgese, and embraced later by others.[102]

The liberal view depicts fascism as a specifically European ideology and a political creed responsible for the **Holocaust** and the worst excesses of the twentieth century (and which was also implicated in Cold War antagonisms). Hence, many liberals point to the intellectual bankruptcy of fascism and its lack of ideological coherence.[103] And as with many other interpretations, they also lump fascism and Communism together as symptoms of the same totalitarian phenomenon – a strategy that annoys Marxists intensely![104]

Another perspective on the liberal thesis can be gleaned from the writings of Mosse. Ledeen, commenting on the ideas of the noted German historian, has stated:

> [Mosse] rightly condemns several attempts to over-simplify the question of fascism, pointing out that the traditional liberal explanation – that fascism was some sort of temporary aberration – does not explain the great success of fascism everywhere in Europe, or that it finally fell only because of military defeat. Liberals who wish to believe that fascism was simply imposed on Europeans have great difficulty in explaining the virtual non-existence of opposition to fascism from within, and they generally ignore the fact that fascism came to power by legitimate means, not via *coups d'état*.[105]

So, the thesis is vulnerable to attack on a range of scores and it could be argued that liberals have a lot of explaining to do.

The analyses of Salvatorelli were informed by the liberal values of Italian unification and he ultimately coined the term 'Anti-*Risorgimento*' to describe the essence of fascist politics.[106] At the same time he anticipated the theses of Parsons and Lipset when, in 1923, he put forward the 'middle-class theory', arguing that fascism was the product of the 'humanistic petty bourgeoisie'.[107] Borgese, on the other hand, 'recognised the universal implications of fascism' but 'interpreted it within the context of the historical development of the Italian spirit since the Middle Ages'. He could appreciate fascism's 'positive and creative elements', but was also aware of its threat; hence the title of his book, *Goliath: The March of Fascism*.[108]

However, Renton, a neo-Marxist, depicts liberal historians in a different light. He says that even though they portray fascism as a 'totalitarian political system', commentators like Griffin, Payne and Eatwell – key names in the modern liberal school of 'fascism studies' – are guilty of detachment, neutrality and near-apologetic analysis. Renton holds that a 'comfortable' liberal consensus exists today and argues that historians should be 'taking sides' on the issue of fascism rather than viewing it in an almost apolitical light. He contends that the 'Age of Fascism' is not over, that the ideology conceived by Mussolini and adapted by Hitler is still a threat in the contemporary world, and thus believes that liberals should not just dismiss the theses of anti-fascist historians. Overall Renton argues that through their enthusiastic interest in fascist ideas, liberal observers flatter and legitimise a 'dangerous' creed.[109]

As such, the liberal thesis can be viewed in two contrasting ways: as an interpretation that demonises 'totalitarian' fascism, or, if we take Renton's argument into account, as an approach that is not critical enough, which is interested in the ideas rather than the actions of fascists.

Thus, fascism is disputed territory. Historians have adopted a range of thematic and polemical perspectives, and have invariably juxtaposed ideas and theories. And, whatever historians like Renton might say about the 'detachment' of modern liberal thinkers, all the scholars we have encountered so far are in no doubt as to the scale and gravity of fascism's impact, especially 'in power' in Germany and Italy.

However, this cannot be said of 'Historical Revisionists'. These people, who have gained significant notoriety in recent years, offer pseudo-academic arguments in support of the claim that fascism was an 'innocent' ideology. They do not offer interpretations of fascism, but denials. David Irving, the most notorious of this school, argues that 'no documentary evidence exists that Hitler was aware of what was befalling the Jews', and further, that 'the extermination programme had gained a momentum of its own'.[110] As a result of such statements, Irving has acquired the status of a pariah in the intellectual community.

Eatwell suggests that **Holocaust Denial** theses rest on four main types of evidence – 'confessional', 'scientific', 'statistical' and 'survivor testimony' – plus an assessment of who 'benefits' from the Holocaust 'myth'.[111] And Griffin, reflecting on the arguments of Irving and others, says that revisionism has engaged in the 'conscious minimilisation, relativisation or juggling away' of fascism's excesses. He goes on:

> Taking advantage of the more poorly educated strata of post-1945 generations concerning the realities of the Second World War, 'vulgar' revisionism boils down to a point-blank denial that six million Jews died as victims of the Nazis' genocidal anti-Semitic campaign, dismissing the idea as a historical myth put about by the Jews themselves or their backers.[112]

In conclusion, it would appear that the revisionist phenomenon – however unpleasant – is an indication that the debate about fascism shows no sign of abating.

As we have seen, there is a range of competing interpretations. Several are associated with specific eras, or themes, or polemical positions. None is universally accepted and the majority are highly contentious. In locating political, cultural, economic, psychological, aesthetic and social interpretations, Hagtvet *et al.* talk about 'theoretical discord'.[113] Clearly, the debate continues.

# A–Z OF HISTORIANS

## NOTES

- Hundreds of historians have examined and analysed fascism so it has been difficult to choose just a selection. We have tried to illustrate the richness of debate, and, in this sense, we have endeavoured to diversify our coverage.
- The task is made more complex by the fact that not just historians, but also social scientists, sociologists, political scientists and social psychologists, have dissected fascism.
- In addition there is sometimes a fine dividing line between 'academics' and 'political activists'. This is particularly the case on the left where Marxist historians blend together with Communist and dissident Communist theoreticians.
- There is also the case of individuals like Trotsky, Gramsci and Bauer, who warranted a place in the Biography section. We have included these people, and other historians/ political activists, in the A–Z of Historians.
- This A–Z is by necessity selective but also, hopefully, accessible and user-friendly.

**THEODOR ADORNO** Freudian Marxist and researcher at the Frankfurt Institute whose most significant work was *The Authoritarian Personality* (1950). He argued that 'the psychologist should have a voice' in any discussion about the origins of fascism. Although Adorno has his critics, even on the left, he produced an original analysis that likened fascism to a kind of social disease, claiming that certain personality types – inflexible and prejudiced 'authoritarians' – would invariably see an attraction in fascism. However, he was confident that democracy would triumph over fascism, even though significant sections of the European **middle class** had been taken in by it.

**GILBERT ALLARDYCE** US scholar who views the term 'fascism' with extreme scepticism. He feels it is acceptable to use the word in the Italian context but does not believe in fascism as a generic concept. Writing in 1979, he argued that historians 'have the responsibility to confess how truly inadequate the term fascism has become: put simply, we have agreed to use the word without agreeing on how to define it'. Allardyce calls fascism a 'mullish concept' and ridicules the notion of fascism as an international phenomenon. He put forward his thesis in 'What fascism is not: Thoughts on the deflation of a concept', *American Historical Review*, 84(2). He has also explored the political ideas of the French fascist, Jacques **Doriot**.

**HANNAH ARENDT** Her 1951 study, *The Origins of Totalitarianism*, which described fascism in terms of 'terror and ideological rigidity', is a landmark in the historiography of fascism. It was one of the first analyses to appear after the war and held that the growth of **totalitarianism** was linked to individuals' increasing tendency to see themselves as part of a group. Arendt also placed particular emphasis on the availability of 'mobilisable masses'

– in her view, a key determining factor in the success of fascism in achieving and maintaining power. But her study – published against the backdrop of intense **Cold War** tension – alienated many Marxists who did not appreciate the fact that fascism and Communism had been bracketed together as crude and almost indistinguishable totalitarian systems. Others have also criticised her interpretation, saying that it does not get to the heart of what fascism is and is not.

**OTTO BAUER** Austrian Marxist whose thinking was shaped by political events in his own country: in particular the conflict between the **Dollfuss** regime and the workers. A First World War veteran, he edited the political journal, *Der Kampf*, and served as a parliamentary deputy until 1934. In his writings he makes a number of telling observations: he describes fascism in power as a '**dictatorship** of armed gangs', as an organised attempt to destroy the achievements of reformist **socialism**, and as Bonapartist in character (here he agrees with Thalheimer). Bauer also refined Marxist thinking on the fascism–**capitalism** relationship, arguing that the two 'systems' had common interests but that the alliance was merely 'temporary'. He escaped Austria for Czechoslovakia and France, and died in 1938.

**ERWIN VON BECKERATH** Leading German specialist on fascism who established his reputation with *Essence and Development of the Fascist State* (1927). In this study he depicts **Mussolini**'s regime as an authoritarian state that was part eighteenth- and part twentieth-century 'neo-absolutism', as he calls it. His expertise was recognised in 1931 when he was asked to write an essay on fascism for the *American Encyclopedia of Social Sciences*. A non-Marxist, von Beckerath looked upon fascism as a fascinating political experiment and held that 'the authoritarian state' would always be an option in times of political and economic change.

**MARTIN BLINKHORN** British historian who has investigated the intriguing relationship between the radical and non-radical right in inter-war Europe. The book he edited, *Fascists and Conservatives* (1990), adopts a country-by-country approach and the overall conclusion is that the relationship between the two political currents was 'complex, fluid and subtle'. He and his associates depict situations in which fascism and **conservatism** coexisted, where the former radicalised the latter, and where there was outright hostility between the two. Not unexpectedly, increasing numbers of scholars are now interested in this vital relationship. Blinkhorn is a specialist in nineteenth- and twentieth-century Spanish history, is the author of the introductory text, *Mussolini and Fascist Italy* (1991), and is also interested in the contrasting methodologies of historians and social scientists.

**GIUSEPPE BORGESE** Italian cultural historian who moved to the University of Chicago in 1931. He published a study of **D'Annunzio** – the man who paved the way for Mussolini's rise to power – and went on to produce an in-depth work on Italy under *Il Duce* (*Goliath: The March of Fascism* (1936)). As a liberal he knew that fascism was a profound threat to civilised society, but he could not help identifying its attributes: most notably, energy, discipline and **modernity**. Borgese also empathised with fascist leaders' critique of **democracy** – although he did not condone their would-be solutions.

**KARL DIETRICH BRACHER** Author of one of the most acclaimed studies of Nazism, *The German Dictatorship: The Origins, Structure and Consequences of National Socialism* (1969). He deals with all aspects of the **Hitler** regime. In his introduction to the English translation, Peter Gay talks about the intensity of the book and says it 'offers a difficult but wholly successful amalgam of long-range and short-range history, structural and narrative history, intellectual, sociological, economic and political history. With its obvious, authoritative control over a vast array of material, the book debunks myths with its very sobriety.' In his other writings, Bracher has examined the **Weimar Republic** and other aspects of German and European history.

**ALAN BULLOCK** British historian and author of the classic biography, *Hitler: A Study in Tyranny* (1952). In one sense this is a standard narrative account of the Führer's life; in another it is a distinctive and highly controversial attempt to understand the essence of Nazism. Bullock's focus is the dictator rather than the dictatorship, and his conclusion is that Hitler was not just a 'frontman' or 'symbol'. Instead he argues that 'no other man played a role in the Nazi revolution or in the history of the Third Reich remotely comparable with that of Adolf Hitler'. In identifying the 'egotism' of the Führer and the political 'gifts' he possessed, Bullock announces that he has 'no axe to grind' and no desire to either indict or rehabilitate Hitler as Nazi leader. Critics argue that his 'explanation' of Nazism is one-dimensional and far too Hitler-centric.

**WILLIAM CARR** One of the biggest names in the field of modern German history. He was Emeritus Professor at the University of Sheffield and died in 1991. His writings covered all aspects of nineteenth- and twentieth-century German history. On Nazism his most celebrated works were *Arms, Autarchy and Aggression: German Foreign Policy* (1972), *Poland to Pearl Harbor: The Making of the Second World War* (1985) and *Hitler: A Study in Personality and Propaganda* (1978). He introduces this last study by saying: 'In this

book I have attempted to present Hitler in the light of modern historical science which embraces the totality of historical experience – political, social, economic, and cultural history, the investigation of individual pathology and, what is more significant for the historian, the study of the collective psychology of people.'

**FRANCIS CARSTEN** Professor of Central European History and a prolific author on German and Austrian fascism. 'How could fascism conquer civilised countries?' This is the question that has fascinated him, and much of his work is conditioned by the fact that he was a resident of Berlin during the 1930s. Carsten argues that 'classic' fascism was a unique ideology, radical at first but less so later on. He claims that anti-Communism was a vital defining characteristic, but not the only one. His most noted works are *The Rise of Fascism* (1967) and *Fascist Movements in Austria: From Schönerer to Hitler* (1997). On Germany he has written in-depth studies on the *Reichswehr* and the workers.

**GEORGI DIMITROV** Marxist thinker who provided one of the most famous definitions of fascism in 1935. At the Seventh **Comintern** Congress he announced that it amounted to 'the openly terroristic dictatorship of the most reactionary, most chauvinistic and most imperialistic elements of finance-capital'. As such he equated fascism to the 'last stage' of capitalism and to a concerted attack on the European proletariat. At the same time Dimitrov stood opposed to the notion of **'social fascism'**, arguing in favour of a united left-wing front against right-wing dictatorship. Although the 1935 interpretation has little credibility among liberal scholars, it has stood the test of time in Orthodox Marxist circles. As late as 1980 it was still being cited in official Soviet publications.

**PETER DRUCKER** Viennese political scientist whose key work, *The End of Economic Man*, was published in 1939. He had first-hand experience of fascism – he was forced to flee Nazi Austria – and in his writings he likens the ideology to a 'moral malaise'. Drucker claimed that Hitler and Mussolini thrived on disillusionment and despair, and that ordinary people were primarily attracted to fascism because it offered 'security'. In addition he argued strongly that the rise of European fascism should be interpreted in cultural rather than socio-economic terms, maintaining that totalitarianism would only be defeated when a new liberal and egalitarian order was established. He dismissed the notion of man as an 'economic unit'.

**RAJANI PALME DUTT** Stalinist theorist who argued that fascism was a 'terroristic tool of finance capital'. Moreover he stated that fascism was a product of 'capitalism in its decay' and linked to the 'winding down' of productive processes. Writing in the 1930s and 1940s he argued that the European situation was desperate and that any kind of delay in combating the right-wing ideology was unacceptable. In his view the only way to effectively oppose 'reactionary' fascism was through 'social revolution'. His two most famous works are *Fascism and Social Revolution* (1934) and *Fascism: An Analysis* (1943).

**ROGER EATWELL** Contemporary British liberal historian who has written extensively on the modern far right and fascism as a generic concept. Part of the 'fascist studies' school, he argues that 'classic' fascism should be taken seriously as a political ideology; and in his view it was a synthesis of **nationalism** and conservatism rather than nationalism and socialism. Eatwell has also written a general-survey history of fascism – focusing on Britain, France, Germany and Italy – and a variety of specialist studies on subjects such as

**Poujadism, Holocaust Denial** and the modern British far right. With O'Sullivan, he has produced a theoretical introduction to the US and European right; more recently he has appeared on BBC TV offering an academic perspective on the 2001 'race riots' in northern England.

**GEOFFREY ELEY** Modern historian who is particularly interested in the historical continuities at play on the German right at the end of the nineteenth century and the start of the twentieth century. He argues that fascism was, simultaneously, a 'counter-revolutionary ideological project' and a 'new kind of popular coalition'. Moreover he contends that in the European context it was the product of long-term trends and specific short-term circumstances. His key works are *Reshaping the German Right: Radical Nationalism and Political Change after Bismarck* (1980) and *From Unification to Nazism* (1990). Eley says his aim is to 'develop a particular way of approaching the German past between Bismarck and Hitler, which is at some variance with how German history has mainly been written since the Second World War'.

**RENZO DE FELICE** Italian historian of international renown who has produced several important studies of the Mussolini regime. In addition to a multi-volume biography of *Il Duce* (1966), he has examined, among other things, the conflicting interpretations of Italian Fascism, Mussolini's conquest of power and the organisation of the Fascist state. In general, de Felice identifies Italian Fascism with the lower middle classes and depicts the Mussolini era as a progressive one. As a result of this – and his 'apologetic' portrayal of Fascist foreign policy – he has attracted his critics, especially on the left. In broader terms he has explored the 'check-list' approach to defining and understanding generic fascism.

**CARL FRIEDRICH** One of the leading theorists of totalitarianism. In association with Brzezinski, Curtis and Barber, he has created a model of totalitarian dictatorships, arguing that such systems are characterised by an all-embracing **ideology**, state terror, media censorship, a monopoly of arms, central economic control and one-party government. His schema applies to Communist regimes as well as fascist regimes – much to the chagrin of Marxist theorists. The consensus among scholars is that Friedrich's definition of totalitarianism is a useful descriptive tool, but lacking in analytical and theoretical content.

**ERICH FROMM** German scholar who was based at the Institute of Social Research. His major work, *The Fear of Freedom* (1942), was a milestone in the historiography of fascism for it interpreted the appeal of Nazism exclusively in psychological terms. Fromm, a Freudian Marxist, argued that 'democratic man' felt ill at ease with an excess of freedom and thus resorted to the 'security' and 'authority' of fascism. Although noted primarily for his psychological theses – they were hugely influential and encouraged others to take a similar path – he also demonstrated his interest in structural perspectives, class relations and sociological analysis.

**ALEXANDER GALKIN** Post-war writer who crafted what one commentator has called the 'Revised Standard Version' of the Marxist interpretation of fascism. In *Capitalist Society and Fascism* (1970), he reiterated a number of Orthodox Marxist ideas but made a number of significant amendments, arguing that fascism was: (1) a modernising movement; (2) a product of capitalist crisis, but not necessarily the final one; and (3) not an inevitability. In general terms he argued that capitalism and fascism were not synonymous and, moreover, that capitalists and fascists did not automatically see eye to eye on every-thing. Even allowing for the new post-war context, Galkin's theory was a radical departure.

**ANTONIO GRAMSCI** Marxist writer and opponent of Italian Fascism. His *Prison Notebooks* (1928–37) and other works emphasised the importance of ideology as an instrument used by the capitalist class to create a consensus favourable to their agenda. These approaches to hegemony and dominant ideology were an important element in subsequent critical theory and implied a shift away from crude Marxist thought and the rehabilitation of the Marxist 'superstructure'. Gramsci started out as a socialist but become a hugely influential figure in the Italian Communist Party. In *On Fascism* (1921) he described Mussolini's ideology as 'an attempt to resolve the problems of production and exchange with machine-guns and pistol-shots'. He went on to call fascism a violent and irrational 'scourge' that was the ultimate product of cultural and civil decay.

**ALEXANDER DE GRAND** US-based academic who has authored several books on fascism: *Italian Fascism* (1982), *The Italian Nationalist Association and the Rise of Fascism in Italy* (1978) and *Fascist Italy and Nazi Germany: The 'Fascist' Style* (1995). The last volume is a comparative study that examines the two regimes in a range of key areas: most notably, origins and development, leadership, economic policy and military outlook. De Grand states: 'This account does not pretend to search for deep ideological affinities or establish parallel psychological or intellectual profiles of the two supreme leaders .... I would like to concentrate on connections and differences between the two regimes that arose out of practice from 1919 to the outbreak of the Second World War.'

**JAMES GREGOR** US scholar whose work has focused on ideology, theories of fascism and the Italian experience. In more specific terms he has demonstrated an interest in interpretations of fascism, whether political, economic, sociological, moral or psychological. Noted for his portrayal of fascism as a 'developmental dictatorship' – in effect a response to delayed industrialisation – he is particularly aware of the contribution that social and behavioural sciences can make to the study of political phenomena. Gregor views Italian Fascism as a coherent ideological system, emphasises its innate modernity and is critical of Marxist theory. His enquiries into the nature, origins and development of the ideology lead him to conclude that it is first and foremost a totalitarian system.

**ROGER GRIFFIN** British academic and the author of several recent studies on fascism. A representative of the 'fascism studies' school, he has written on the British experience and on the relationship between fascism and theatre, but his most notable work is on generic fascism. In the 1990s he produced an in-depth survey of the ideology and also edited a topical anthology of texts (covering 'Fascism in Italy', 'Fascism in Germany', 'Abortive fascisms 1922–45', 'Theories of fascism' and 'Post-war fascisms'). Griffin's most important contribution to the historiography of fascism is to locate a 'palingenetic myth' at the heart of the ideology; he argues that this belief in national rebirth and regeneration acts as the defining feature of all movements and regimes that are genuinely fascist.

**BERNT HAGTVET** Oslo-born political scientist who worked with colleagues Larsen and Myklebust to produce *Who Were the Fascists* (1980), an enormous and eclectic volume that examines fascism in all its richness and variety. Hagtvet has a range of academic interests: **nation-building**, intellectuals in politics and theories of fascism. With Stein Rokkan,

he asked, 'was there a core concept of fascism and how could this essence be identified in the welter of complex interactions in each concrete development?' On this question, the two scholars conclude that in the inter-war years several European countries witnessed 'a series of competitive elections under multi-party systems' and 'the victory of a monolithic alliance and the abolition of pluralist opposition'.

**PAUL HAINSWORTH** Modern British scholar who specialises in the French far right and European **neo-fascism**. He has edited two volumes on the contemporary extreme right. Highly contemporary, these studies have depicted the ultra-nationalist right in all its richness – from America and Austria to Spain and Serbia. The books are particularly strong on the post-Communist experience in Eastern Europe, and Hainsworth's thesis is that the modern far right is varied and complex but gathering momentum all the time. 'From the Margins to the Mainstream' is the sub-title of his 2000 work – and this would appear to reflect his overall conclusion as regards the current trajectory of the contemporary far right.

**MAX HORKHEIMER** Jewish scholar who studied at the Institute of Social Research in Frankfurt, then in the US, when the Nazis banned it, and then in Frankfurt again after 1950. Before the war he posed as a traditional Marxist, coining the famous dictum, 'Whoever is not prepared to talk about capitalism should also remain silent about fascism.' However, in the years after 1940 he moved towards a neo-Marxist position, insisting that fascism could be separated from capitalism after all, and that Nazi Germany and Communist Russia shared similar authoritarian features. As a result he gradually lost favour with 'old guard' Marxist theoreticians.

**IAN KERSHAW** Prolific British author on twentieth-century German history. He is particularly interested in competing interpretations of Nazism; here his major works include *The Nazi Dictatorship: Problems and Perspectives of Interpretation* (1985) and *Popular Opinion and Political Dissent in the Third Reich* (1983). He has also explored the **myth**-making surrounding Hitler. His conclusion is that the image of the Führer was of far more significance than the person and was a key factor in the longevity of the Nazi system; here his key work is *The Hitler Myth* (1987). He has also written two authoritative biographies of Hitler. Kershaw is based at the University of Sheffield.

**MARTIN KITCHEN** Neo-Marxist historian who has gained plaudits for his work in updating, improving and developing left-wing thinking on fascism. Unafraid to criticise the 'standard' **Third International** line, he has brought elements of synthesis and sophistication to the Marxist fold, something it severely lacked in the early days. The Canada-based scholar – who has also produced more mainstream work on inter-war European history – argues that historians should not just concentrate on Germany and Italy but acknowledge fascism's chameleon-like qualities and the profound danger posed by 'civilised' neo-fascists. In Kitchen's view, all anti-fascist activity must begin with analysis and understanding.

**WILLIAM KORNHAUSER** Author of *The Politics of Mass Society* (1959), a highly significant contribution to the post-war debate about fascism. He argued that totalitarian systems – like fascism – take the form of mass organisations, rather than class-based organisations. As he says: 'Although fascism tends to recruit a disproportionate number of its adherents from the middle class, and communism attracts more of its adherents from the working class, these movements cannot be understood merely as political expressions of the middle class and working class, respectively.' Kornhauser was also fascinated by the 'rural masses', arguing that these people were prone to 'emotional nationalism', and thus were more likely to have affinities with fascism than communism.

**REINHARD KÜHNL** German theorist who emerged as one of the leading neo-Marxist theorists in the post-war period. The author of several influential works in the late 1960s and early 1970s, he depicted fascism as a new political structure and devoted particular attention to 'left fascism' (although he concludes that this could never succeed). In trying to refine the old Stalinist orthodoxy, Kühnl helped to formulate a 'Revised Standard Version', not dissimilar to the accounts put forward by Galkin and Vajda. Professor of Political Science, Kühnl studied in both Germany and Austria, and his scholarly writings focus on inter-war fascism and post-war neo-fascism.

**WALTER LAQUEUR** Former editor of the *Journal of Contemporary History* and director of the Institute of Contemporary History. The editor of a collection of specialist essays on the Second World War, he has published on a wide variety of subjects, including European history, Russia and **Zionism**. He has also produced an in-depth study of Weimar culture. However, in the specific context of far-right politics, he is best known for the volume he edited in 1976, *Fascism: A Reader's Guide*. Laqueur takes the reader through the history of the ideology and the literature it has spawned, and, in his preface, he is right to imply that it is a path-breaking study. In 1966, he published *International Fascism* (with Mosse), and, in 1993, *Black Hundred: The Rise of the Extreme Right in Russia*.

**MICHAEL LEDEEN** Scholar of Italian Fascism. His major works include *The First Duce: D'Annunzio at Fiume* (1977) and, in association with de Felice, *Fascism: An Informal Introduction to its Theory and Practice* (1976). However, he is most noted for *Universal Fascism: The Theory and Practice of the Fascist International, 1928–1936* (1972), a book that unravels the meaning and significance of the revisionist brand of Fascism known as *Fascismo Universale*. He traces the history of the movement and argues that Mussolini saw it as his destiny to evangelise. He quotes *Il Duce* in 1930: 'Today I affirm that Fascism is Italian in its particular institutions, and universal in spirit.' Ledeen has also worked with fellow historian Mosse on a study of Nazism.

**JUAN LINZ** Contemporary specialist in political science and sociology. Across a variety of publications he has demonstrated concern over the term 'fascism' and discussed the heterogeneity of the concept. He defines it as a 'latecomer' to the political landscape and emphasises its **anti-dimension** ('anti-parliamentary, anti-liberal, anti-Communist, anti-proletarian, partly anti-capitalist and anti-bourgeois, anti-clerical, or at least, non-clerical'). In addition, he labels fascism 'hypernationalist, often pan-nationalist'. More broadly, Linz – a US-based academic – is interested in the 'political space' that fascism inhabits and, more specifically, the relationship, and overlap, between movements of the radical and conservative right.

**SEYMOUR MARTIN LIPSET** US scholar whose post-war enquiries into the sociological basis of political movements have been hugely influential. His primary finding was that fascism equated to 'extremism of the centre' or 'middle-class extremism', and although some commentators have questioned his analysis, the notion of a sociological explanation has gained many adherents. Lipset argues that in the inter-war period the liberal middle classes were threatened from a variety of directions and thus sought solace in fascism – an ideology that in its hostility to trade unions and socialism (among other things) had genuine appeal.

**ADRIAN LYTTELTON** Scholar of Italian Fascism with an international reputation. In addition to editing *Italian Fascisms from Pareto to Gentile* (1973) – a well-crafted collection of texts – he has written *The Seizure of Power: Fascism in Italy 1919–1929* (1973) and 'Fascism in Italy: The second wave' (1966). He is interested in a number of significant issues: the relationship between Fascism and capitalism, the mechanics of oligarchic **corporatism** in power and the nature of the ideology – both revolutionary *and* reactionary. He also argues that 'Fascism cannot be reduced to an expression of Mussolini's personality, nor can Mussolini's personality be identified entirely with fascism. But certainly one cannot conceive of the fascist regime in Italy without Mussolini.'

**DENNIS MACK SMITH** By common consent, the most famous non-Italian historian of Italy. He has published on many aspects of Italy's nineteenth- and twentieth-century history. In addition to *Italy: A Modern History* (1959), he has explored the history of Sicily and the relationship between the nation and its monarchy. On the Fascist era his most noted work is a much acclaimed biography of *Il Duce*, *Mussolini* (1981). In it he states: 'Mussolini was neither born great nor had greatness thrust upon him but had to fight his way out of obscurity by his own ambition and talents .... By the time of his death in 1945 he left to his successors an Italy destroyed by military defeat and civil war; he was, by his own admission, the most hated person in the country; and having once been praised to excess, was now being blamed for doing more harm to Italy than anyone else had ever done before.'

TIM MASON Oxford-based scholar who died in 1990. He was at the forefront of research into class and **gender** in Nazi Germany, and his posthumously published work, *Nazism, Fascism and the Working Class* (1995), was a collection of ten of his most provocative essays. In the words of Jane Caplan, who wrote the introduction to the book, Mason was especially interested in 'the relationship between politics and class, the sources and limits of individual and collective agency, the ferocity and destructiveness of Nazi power, and, most controversially, the domestic sources of Nazi aggression in 1939'. She argued that the volume was 'a pious memorial to a talented historian who died too young. Mason's work on the history of Nazi Germany was pathbreaking.'

BARRINGTON MOORE A key name in the world of development theories. His 1966 work, *The Social Origins of Dictatorship and Democracy*, has had an enormous impact on the debate about fascism. He identifies a correlation between industrial and political development. Thus, 'fascism developed most fully in Germany where capitalist industrial growth had gone the furthest within the framework of a conservative revolution from above. It came to light only as a weak secondary trend in such backward areas as Russia, China and India.' However, it is easy to criticise Moore's thesis: it is over-generalised, unconvincing in the way it tries to explain the non-existence of fascism in Britain and the US, and very much a 'fashionable' response to the academic climate of the 1960s.

GEORGE MOSSE An internationally renowned historian of fascism, and German Nazism in particular. In general terms he has likened fascism to a 'scavenger', moulding bits of old ideologies into a new whole. He puts particular emphasis on the notion of 'new fascist man' and argues that Mussolini, Hitler and other leaders were aiming to steer a '**Third Way**' between **Marxism** and capitalism. Mosse is especially insightful in the German context, arguing that Nazism was not just '**propaganda**' but an organised mass movement that tried to 'nationalise' the **working class** and was successful in creating an almost neo-religious style of politics. Although he rejects some attempts at historical 'linkage', he is happy to interpret Nazism as the culmination of more than a century of ***Volk***-centred discourse in Germany.

FRANZ NEUMANN **Frankfurt School** theorist who produced one of the most influential studies of Hitler's Reich, *Behemoth* (1942). From a leftist perspective, he explained fascism in totalitarian terms but did so in a way that did not threaten or refute the Orthodox Marxist interpretation. He saw fascism and capitalism as being intimately connected and actually argued that fascism was 'the final stage' in the history of capitalism (hence his notion of 'totalitarian monopoly capitalism'). Critics would say that Neumann's work is dated, but he provided a range of important insights, most notably into the common outlook of industrialists and Nazi leaders.

ERNST NOLTE German philosopher-historian and author of *Three Faces of Fascism* (1965) – an in-depth study of French, Italian and Nazi variants – who argued that the ideology was characteristic of the inter-war period. His 'phenomenological' approach has its critics – one commentator has called it 'historicism in fancy dress' – but there is no doubt about its central importance in historiographical circles. Nolte, who was at the centre of the

'Historians' Debate' in Germany during the mid-1980s, is particularly interested in fascism's relationship to the left and places great emphasis on its 'anti-Marxism'; although he rejected the 'totalitarian' interpretation, he does conclude that fascism and Communism had similar properties. Some have questioned his portrayal of the *Action Française* as a prime example of 'early fascism', but for most observers he remains the undisputed expert in the subject area.

CIARÁN O'MAOLAIN Author of *Latin American Political Movements* (1986) and *The Radical Right: A World Directory* (1987). The latter, a 500-page compendium, is a Keesing's Reference Publication and a highly valuable work. It is organised on a country-by-country basis and includes entries for over 3,000 movements. O'Maolain was aided in his research by *Searchlight* and other anti-fascist organisations, and used a range of practical strategies. In defining the political orientation of political movements, he identifies three general strands within the radical right – 'ultra-conservatism', 'antiCommunism', 'right-wing extremism' – and argues that the terms 'Nazi' and 'fascist' should be utilised in a restricted fashion.

TALCOTT PARSONS US sociologist who died in 1979. Heavily influenced by the writings of Max Weber, Durkheim, **Pareto** and **Le Bon**, he developed a range of novel socio-psychological perspectives on the origins and nature of fascism (especially in Germany). He argued that capitalism and **modernisation** inevitably brought tensions and change; that this created a sense of '**anomie**'; and that fascism emerged into the 'void' that this produced. In general terms he depicted fascism as a romantic revolt against the 'rationalisation of society', and thus in effect a 'substitute religion'. Critics have alleged that Parsons's analysis was too ambitious and underplayed conventional economic factors.

STANLEY PAYNE A specialist in Spanish fascism – the *Falange* in particular – he has also worked on defining and explaining fascism as a generic concept. Scholars have been especially impressed with his helpful checklist-style 'typological' description of fascism that focuses on the ideology's 'negations', 'ideology and goals' and 'style and organisation'. Furthermore, Payne, a US academic, has produced comparative analyses and explored the historiography of West European fascism. One of his most interesting assertions is that Nazism and Communism are closely related.

JOACHIM PETZOLD East German Orthodox Marxist whose ideas became highly representative of Eastern bloc thinking on fascism. Indeed he was strongly critical of 'bourgeois historians' and 'Western' Marxist analyses. His most famous work, *The Demagogy of Hitler-Fascism* (1983), reiterates his belief that fascism and capitalism are closely intertwined and that the former is a non-autonomous and anti-proletarian force. He stays loyal to the Comintern description of fascism as 'the open terrorist dictatorship of the most reactionary, most chauvinist, and most imperialist elements of finance capital', and in doing so dismisses any notion that fascism was the product of local factors or individual personalities.

NICOS POULANTZAS Greek scholar who produced the first major post-war examination of the Hitler and Mussolini regimes from a Marxist perspective, *Fascism and Dictatorship* (1970). Throughout, the author is aware that he is assessing a hugely important subject and argues that fascism *could* repeat itself, but only if a fresh set of 'unique' circumstances arise. Poulantzas – an academic who has taught in universities all around Europe – produces an original Marxist synthesis. He describes fascist dictatorship as a particular type of capitalist state, an 'exceptional regime', and is especially interested in the relationship between fascism and the middle classes. He restricts his analysis to the Axis powers and points to delayed industrialisation as a key commonality.

**WILHELM REICH** Austrian writer whose most famous work, *The Mass Psychology of Fascism* (1933), was banned by the Nazis. Approaching the subject from a Marxist–Freudian perspective, he argued that the origins and nature of fascism were best explained in psychoanalytical, rather than political or economic, terms. Reich blamed bourgeois society for the rise of fascism, arguing that it was 'the basic emotional attitude of the suppressed man of our authoritarian machine civilisation'. He placed significant emphasis on the sexually inhibited and sexually repressed nature of twentieth-century society, concluding that fascism was some kind of 'compensation' for this state of affairs. Commentators tend to view his thesis as both brilliant and highly unorthodox. He left Austria for the US in 1939.

**DAVE RENTON** Modern neo-Marxist historian whose *Fascism: Theory and Practice* (1999) is a useful guide to leftist interpretations of fascism. A member of the **Anti-Nazi League**, he is extremely critical of the new consensus that has emerged through 'fascism studies', arguing that fascism was a 'reactionary mass movement' and not just an ideology of the past. Renton says that historians must 'take sides' on the issue not least because, in his view, fascism and neo-fascism are still a threatening force today. He claims that his ideas amount to a 'radically different and critical theory of fascism'. Associated with *Socialist Review*, he has also written on British fascism in the 1930s and 1950s.

**GAETANO SALVEMINI** Liberal historian and polemicist who wrote *The Origins of Fascism in Italy* (1942), one of the most celebrated anti-regime histories. A former member of the Italian Socialist Party, he viewed Mussolini's doctrine as 'irrational' and 'absurd'; hence his attempts to counter Fascist propaganda by warning the people of Italy about the inherent 'danger' of *Il Duce*. His own stance was interesting: he was an interventionist (like Mussolini) and interpreted Fascism as a self-serving oligarchy that made life worse rather than better for the working class. One of the many intellectuals who fled Italy during the Mussolini era, Salvemini became noted for his gloomy prognoses. His significance lies in the fact that he was one of the first anti-Fascist historians.

**LUIGI SALVATORELLI** Liberal Italian scholar who became one of the leading experts on the Mussolini regime. Editor of the anti-fascist publication, *La Stampa*, he is noted for three in-depth historical studies: *Nazionalfascismo* (1923), *Sotta la Scure del Fascismo* (1948) and *La Storia d'Italia nel Periodo Fascista* (1952 – with Mira). He was one of the first writers to put forward the 'middle-class theory' of fascism, an interpretation subsequently developed by sociologists. In addition Salvatorelli was heavily influenced by the values of the ***Risorgimento***, and as such equated the ideology of Mussolini to the Anti-*Risorgimento*. This was meant as a criticism – he was depicting Fascism as a form of totalitarianism – but Mussolini actually utilised the term for positive advantage.

**IGNAZIO SILONE** Italian political activist who spent his early years in the Socialist Party. He was a founder member of the

Communist Party in 1921 and edited the organisation's weekly paper, *L'Avanguardia*. He became an influential figure in Comintern circles but left the organisation in 1930. In his writings he depicts fascism as a unique form of reaction that thrives on economic crisis; he also argues that new nation-states are especially vulnerable to it. In Silone's view, fascism is a contradiction: as a movement it had mass appeal but as a regime it was synonymous with high finance (he describes corporatism as '**state capitalism**'). He fought against Mussolini's forces in the Second World War and served as a Socialist deputy after 1945. He died in 1978.

**ROBERT SOUCY** US scholar who has made a highly original contribution to the debate about fascism and '**pre-fascism**' in France. His thesis centres on writer and politician Maurice **Barrès** who, he claims, underwent a 'conversion to rootedness' in his philosophical life, and thus jettisoned **individualism** for nationalism. Soucy goes on to label him the 'first French fascist' on account of his sophisticated fusing of nationalist and socialist ideas in the 1880s and 1890s. In this regard Soucy's key works are *French Fascism: The Case of Maurice Barrès* (1972) and 'Barrès and fascism' (1967). He has also written a seminal article, 'The nature of fascism in France' (1966), and several studies on the inter-war *ligues* and the broader phenomenon of 'veterans' politics'.

**ZEEV STERNHELL** Israeli scholar who has written extensively on the intellectual origins of fascism. He argues that it developed in embryonic form in France in the 1880s and 1890s, and identifies novelist-turned-politician Maurice Barrès as the key figure in this process. Sternhell also places great emphasis on the ability of **Boulanger** and others to ingratiate themselves with the masses – hence his view that the late nineteenth century in France

witnessed the emergence of 'pre-fascism'. He argues that this new intellectual climate was ushered in by the cataclysmic military defeat of 1870–1 by Prussia. In broader terms he portrays full-blown French fascism as a revolutionary synthesis of 'right and left'.

**A.J.P. TAYLOR** Controversial British historian whose book, *The Origins of the Second Word War* (1961), postulated that Hitler, and Europe, 'blundered' into war in 1939, Elsewhere he depicts the Nazi leader and Mussolini as 'Napoleons of the twentieth century, the heroes of our time. Both were pure-hero types, without any of the adventitious aids of their predecessors. Frederick the Great inherited his crown; Napoleon had a background of military success; Cromwell and Lenin rested on a compact revolutionary class. Hitler and Mussolini made themselves. Except as heroes, they were nobodies ... They invented their uniforms and their methods of address – *Duce* and *Fuehrer*, titles never heard before.'

**AUGUST THALHEIMER** Dissident member of the German Communist Party during the 1920s and 1930s who emerged as a leading neo-Marxist theoretician. An Austrian by nationality, he viewed fascism as an 'autonomous' political force and watered down several key aspects of Marxist orthodoxy, especially as regards its relationship with the bourgeoisie. Most notably, he used Marx's writings on Napoleon III to help craft a novel thesis that likened fascism to **Bonapartism** on a variety of levels, including hostility to the working class. Thalheimer's work was hugely influential – particularly for Trotsky – but critics have argued that his analyses are slightly remote and do not reflect the reality of Nazi Germany. He died in 1948.

**RICHARD THURLOW** One of the leading experts on the **British Union of Fascists** and other British fascist movements. He is author of *Fascism in Britain: A History 1918–85* (1987) and co-editor of *British Fascism: Essays on the Radical Right in Inter-war Britain* (1980). He explores a number of interesting aspects of British fascism: its high anti-Semitic content, Nazi connections and leftist tendencies. He says that Mosley's ideas contained 'rational and metaphysical elements'; they were not embedded in **anti-Semitism** and **racism**, but simply 'alternative' beliefs. Thurlow is also fascinated by the failure of fascism in Britain and puts this down to two factors: (1) the movement's own internal weaknesses; and (2) the reaction of the state. He maintains that, for significant periods, British fascism was nothing more than a 'public order irritant'.

**PALMIRO TOGLIATTI** Former socialist who became general secretary of the Italian Communist Party in 1922. Within years he had become a major figure in the Comintern and by 1935 was lecturing on Marxist theory in the USSR. He argued that fascism was a unique form of reaction: in opposition it took the form of a mass movement, but in power it evolved into an oligarchy – of major industrialists, financial experts and large landowners. He also stated that fascist regimes retained their unity through terror and **imperialism**. After 1945 Togliatti returned to Italy and held governmental posts in various Communist administrations. Interestingly, he claimed that Britain would never succumb to fascism because the working class was already subjected to 'reactionary' rule.

**LEON TROTSKY** Russian revolutionary whose theorising on the nature of fascism took place in the early 1930s when the Hitler phenomenon was most vivid. In dialectical fashion he concluded that fascism was a reactionary ideology *and* a mass movement; that it was synonymous with a dominant petty bourgeoisie (work-ing in the interests of capital); and that in Germany the proletariat would inevitably be crushed by the overpowering force of Nazism. He located the origins of fascism in the aftermath of war, rather than the inherent properties of capitalism, and in this sense diverged from the Orthodox Marxist line (as he did in his view of fascism as a modern form of Bonapartism). He believed that a 'United Front' strategy (Communist–socialist co-operation) could counter Hitler's system effectively, but critics argue that he underestimated the durability of fascism. For various political reasons, Trotsky's analysis of fascism has been slightly neglected in left-wing circles.

**HENRY TURNER** Post-war US scholar with a specialism in German and European history. The editor of *Reappraisals of Fascism* (1975), he has demonstrated a particular interest in the relationship between fascism and modernisation, arguing that there was a 'utopian anti-modernism' at the heart of German Nazism and, to a lesser extent, Mussolini's ideology. He states that the issue is still unresolved, but that, whatever the outcome, it has significant implications for the debate about generic fascism. In broader terms Turner is fascinated by the problems of interpretation that surround fascism, and distinctly unimpressed by 'impressionistic and non-empirical' Marxist theorising on the subject.

**MIHALY VAJDA** Hungarian scholar who has emerged as a leading neo-Marxist thinker. In *Fascism as a Mass Movement* (1976) and 'The rise of fascism in Italy and Germany' (1972), he has expounded a revised, anti-Stalinist interpretation. He accepts that fascism and capitalism are inter-related, but depicts them as independent and autonomous forces. Vajda does not view fascism as 'inevitable' in any sense, but rather the product of specific circumstances. His theoretical ideas were directed not just against Stalin, but Trotsky and the Comintern as a whole; in general terms they are not dissimilar to those of Thalheimer, Galkin, Kühnl and Kitchen.

**EUGEN WEBER** Post-war historian with an interest in many right-wing subjects including fascism and comparative fascism. He established his reputation through *Varieties of Fascism* (1964) and *The European Right* (1966 – co-edited with Hans Rogger) and throughout puts forward the view that fascism is a dynamic but vague ideology, with few specific, predetermined objectives. Weber is particularly intrigued by Romanian and French variants, and in 1962 penned what is commonly viewed as the ultimate work on *Action Française*. Although critics argue that he overplays the importance of the organisation – and the intellectual influence of its leader **Maurras** – it is an impressive study. Its sub-title, *Royalism and Reaction in Twentieth Century France*, hints at its main focus.

**STUART WOOLF** Specialist in Italian history who has branched out into the economics of fascism. He has edited two important University of Reading collections: one that investigates the varieties of European fascism – from Italy and Germany to Poland, Finland and Norway – and another that explores the social and economic significance of the ideology. Woolf is fascinated by the notion of a fascist economic 'system', claiming there were both similarities and differences between individual fascist economies (he notes in particular the contrasting rates of development). In the end he calls fascism a 'mass movement of reaction' and a doctrine that was able to exploit the 'Red Peril' for its own benefit. In 1968 he also claimed that the word 'fascism' should be banned on account of its constant misuse!

# MAPS

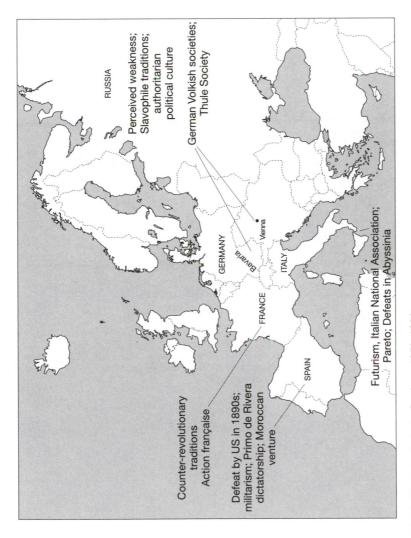

*Map 1* Anxiety and rebellion: prelude to fascism, 1870–1920

*Note:* This map shows a selection of the ideological, intellectual and political trends that marked a Europe-wide revolt against the Enlightenment and nineteenth-century social reform. In Spain and Russia, the tensions were serious enough to provoke bouts of violence and revolution. In Central Europe, they produced a renewed interest in cultural identity and an obsession with *Volk*. In France, there was much intellectualising about the relationships between socialism, nationalism, violence and myth. However, the map shows, most of all, that this ferment was not confined to any one country or region.

Counter-revolutionary traditions
Action française

Defeat by US in 1890s; militarism; Primo de Rivera dictatorship; Moroccan venture

Perceived weakness; Slavophile traditions; authoritarian political culture

German Volkish societies; Thule Society

Futurism, Italian National Association; Pareto; Defeats in Abyssinia

RUSSIA

GERMANY

Bavaria

Vienna

FRANCE

ITALY

SPAIN

*Map 2* Flashpoints in Central Europe, 1918–39

*Note*: This map shows the 'unfinished business' of Versailles, Locarno and the other post-war treaties, especially on Germany's eastern border. The Danzig Corridor gave the Poles access to the sea but also split East Prussia from the rest of Germany. Meanwhile, Hungarian and German territorial losses after the First World War provided ammunition for irredentist policies in Romania, Czechoslovakia and Poland.

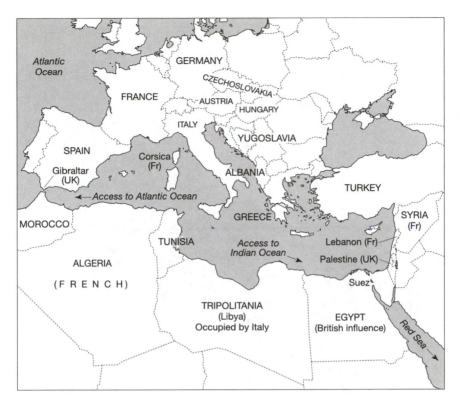

Labels on map:
Atlantic Ocean — GERMANY — CZECHOSLOVAKIA — FRANCE — AUSTRIA — HUNGARY — ITALY — YUGOSLAVIA — SPAIN — Corsica (Fr) — ALBANIA — Gibraltar (UK) — TURKEY — ←—Access to Atlantic Ocean — GREECE — SYRIA (Fr) — MOROCCO — Lebanon (Fr) — TUNISIA — Access to Indian Ocean — Palestine (UK) — ALGERIA — (FRENCH) — Suez — TRIPOLITANIA (Libya) Occupied by Italy — EGYPT (British influence) — Red Sea →

*Map 3* Mussolini's cage

*Note*: Mussolini's geo-political dream, of reaching out to the Atlantic and Indian oceans, was blocked, in his view, by British and French colonial outposts at either end of the Mediterranean. A more serious obstacle, though, was Italy's lack of military power or other resources needed to pursue a truly global strategy. The map shows how the Mediterranean looked to the Italians.

*Map 4* Japanese ambitions: from continentalism to the Greater East Asia Co-Prosperity
  Sphere

*Note*: The map illustrates two phases of Japanese expansion. The inner line shows territories Japan
gained from its League mandate and from its earlier imperialist attacks on Korea and China.
The outer line shows the maximum extent of Japanese power in the Second World War. It is
clear that Japan's goal was to be master of the western Pacific. This would give her control
over shipping routes and access to the resources of Indonesia and China.

*Map 5* Some right-wing dictatorships in Europe, 1920–45

*Note*: This map shows how most of Europe succumbed to right-wing dictatorships in the years 1922–45. These were not simply a consequence of Nazi occupation, important though that was, but of home-grown far-right nationalisms as well.

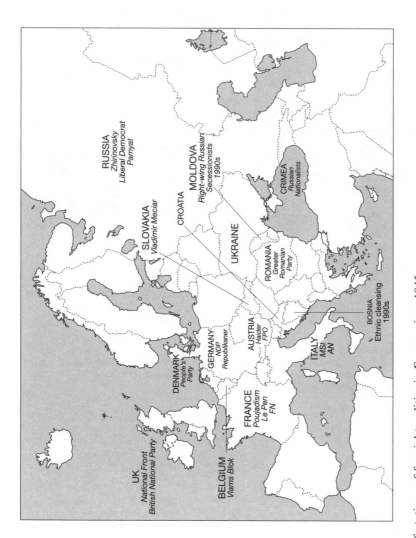

*Map 6* Some manifestations of far-right politics in Europe since 1945

*Note*: This map charts a sample of the political phenomena, parties and movements associated with the far right in Europe since the Second World War. It is not intended to be comprehensive but rather to demonstrate the geographical spread of these activities.

*Map 7* Some manifestations of right-wing dictatorship and violence in Africa since 1965

*Note*: This map shows some of the prominent movements and events associated with right-wing dictatorship or violence, as well as ethnic and racial hatred, in Africa since 1965. Some of this, as in South Africa or Rwanda, was motivated by prejudice. Other instances of right-wing activity were motivated by Cold War concerns or were responses to similar activities on the left.

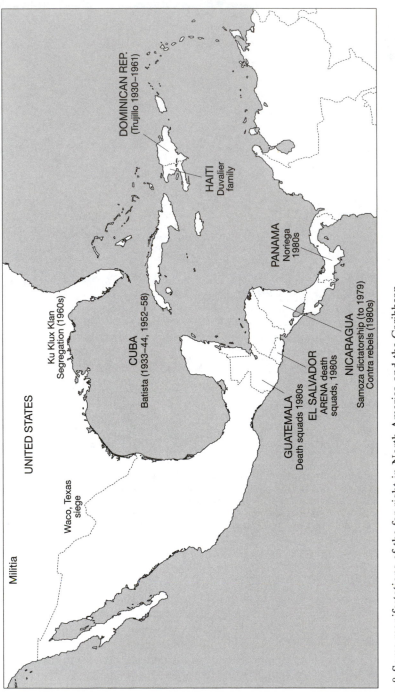

*Map 8* Some manifestations of the far right in North America and the Caribbean

*Note:* Although some were populist and others were traditional Latin dictatorships, this map shows that most of this region was ruled by authoritarian regimes at various points throughout the twentieth century. The map does not show every dictatorship, since there were so many, but it does illustrate the extent to which a culture of right-wing authoritarianism and violence affected most countries south of the Rio Grande. The map also shows some focal points for far-right activities in the USA itself.

COLOMBIA
Death squads
Drug cartels

EQUADOR
Intermittent
military
dictatorship
until 1979

BRAZIL
Vargas 1930–45, 1951–54

PERU
Alberto Fujimori
dictatorship, 1990s

BOLIVIA
intermittent
dictatorship

PARAGUAY
Stroessner/
Nazi refuge,
1954–89

CHILE
Pinochet, 1973–89,
IBANEZ, flirtation
with fascism, 1930s

ARGENTINA
Perónism,
1946–55, 1973–74,
Military regimes,
death squads in
1970s, 1980s

URUGUAY
dictatorship,
1970s–80s

*Map 9* Some manifestations of right-wing dictatorship in South America, 1930–90
*Note*: This map shows the geographical scope of military rule and dictatorship in Latin America for
most of the twentieth century. Again, almost every country was affected at some point,
though liberal democracy has been the norm since the late 1980s.

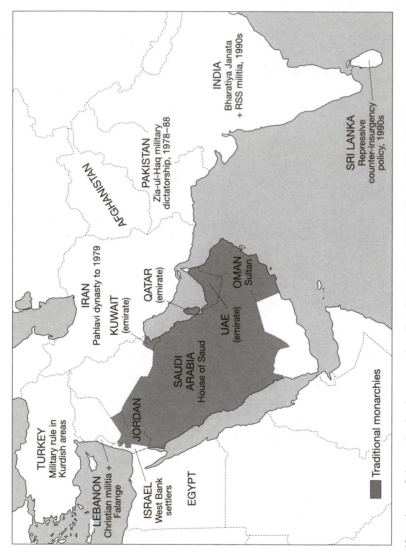

*Map 10* Some manifestations of the authoritarian or nationalist right in the Middle East and South Asia

*Note:* A notable feature of the Middle East is the persistence of traditional autocracies and conservative monarchies in the Arabian Peninsula and the southern half of the region. However, it should be noted that there is some tentative liberalisation under way in Jordan and Qatar. The northern belt of states, from Syria to Afghanistan, has been ruled by left-wing or Islamist dictatorships. Egypt and Turkey are difficult to categorise, since they are experimenting with democracy while using military muscle and repressive measures against Islamic groups and, in Turkey's case, minorities like the Kurds. In both South Asia and the Middle East, right-wing authoritarianism is directed as much against Islamic fundamentalism as against left-wing opponents of the existing regimes.

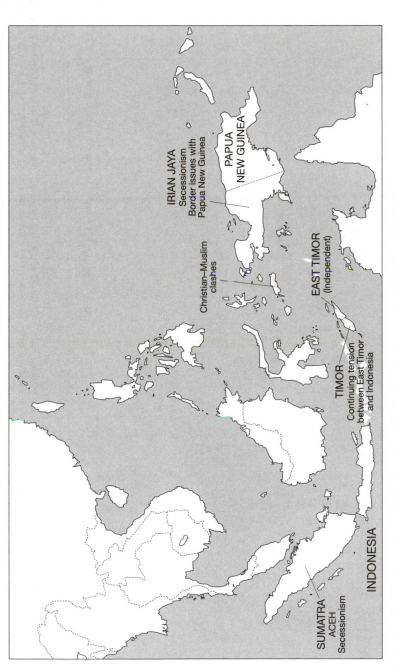

*Map 11* The break-up of a nation? Flashpoints for secessionism and repression in Indonesia, 2002

*Note:* Pro-Army elements in Indonesia wreaked havoc in East Timor as the territory broke free of Indonesian control at the end of the twentieth century. With a population of 180 million and many regions demanding autonomy or independence, the Indonesian military and the more extreme paramilitary groups may well be tempted to prevent the break-up of the state. This map shows some of the flashpoints that would provoke a crackdown on regional groups and political reformists. Some of these regions were subjected to heavy repression in the Suharto years.

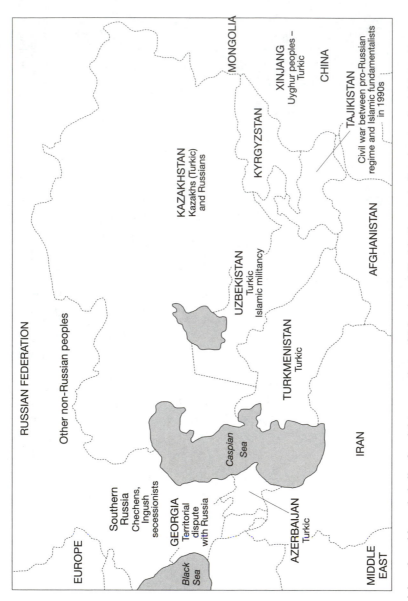

*Map 12* Russia's vulnerable underbelly: far-right perceptions of Islamic and Turkic threats to Russian territorial integrity

*Note:* The region from Xinjang in western China to the borderlands of South European Russia is inhabited by many peoples. Many are of Turkic origin and of the Islamic faith. Some live within the borders of the Russian federation itself. The Russian far right recalls Russia's historic struggle with these peoples in Siberia and Central Asia, and portray this region as a zone of instability and danger. The same theme was adopted by Vladimir Putin on his rise to power, although Putin phrases it in a less simplistic and less alarmist way. This map shows the area that is the focus of concern for many on the Russian right, and especially for the extreme right.

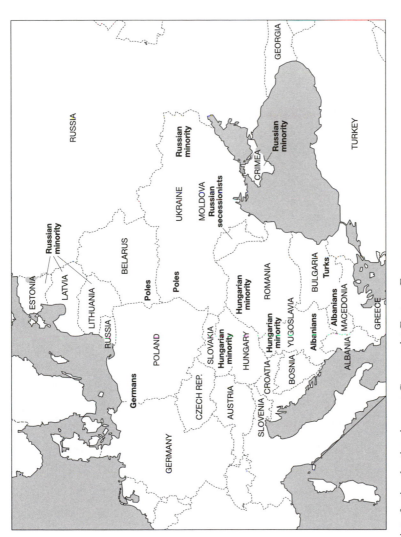

*Map 13* Flashpoints for irredentism in post-Communist Eastern Europe

*Note*: This map shows some of the ethnic groups that live just outside the states normally associated with their respective nations. Such groups are the target of irredentist propaganda from extreme nationalists. Their present status may be a consequence of boundary alterations arising from the two world wars or of the collapse of Soviet power in Europe after 1989. Note especially the location of Russian, Hungarian and Albanian minorities in the Baltic Sea region and in the Balkans.

# II
# FASCISM AND THE
# FAR RIGHT

## Themes

# ROOTS AND ORIGINS

In its mystical patterns a new cellular-structure of the German *Volk*-soul is developing. Present and past are suddenly appearing in a new light, and as a result we have a new mission for the future.

(Alfred Rosenberg, *Myth of the Twentieth Century*, taken from R. Pois [ed.], *A. Rosenberg: Selected Writings*, London, Jonathan Cape, 1970)

In 1922 **Mussolini** emerged as Italian leader and in 1933 **Hitler** became German dictator. In their wake, a range of fascist and national-socialist movements developed in Western Europe, Eastern Europe, South America and elsewhere. And ever since, the issue of 'causation' has been a battleground. Are the origins of fascism to be located in the nineteenth century or the twentieth?[1] From the left, right and centre, polemics flowed. Anybody who was anybody developed their own 'general theory of fascism'. Sociologists, psychologists and political scientists were all brought into the debate. Most contentiously, Marxists argued that fascism was a 'product of **capitalism**' and, moreover, an 'agent of capitalism and high finance'. At another extreme, it was argued that fascist **totalitarianism** could be traced back to Plato.[2]

The onus, therefore, has been on historians to produce a balanced and informed appraisal of fascism's origins; for fascism has roots just like a phenomenon of the natural world has roots. We can actually view the roots of fascism on two related planes: on the level of ideas and **ideology** and on the level of politics and elections. In the last decades of the nineteenth century and the first years of the twentieth century, 'the age of revolt', the same assumption was made on both levels: society was in decline and there was an urgent need for renaissance and resurrection.

## IDEAS AND IDEOLOGY

On the plane of ideas we have to be careful. Hayes is in no doubt that fascism is a difficult phenomenon to analyse:

The intellectual basis of fascism is a strange mixture of theories, ranging from the radical to the reactionary and encompassing ideas about race, religion, economics, social welfare and morality which are at the very least dissonant .... Fascist theory is not a tightly-knit bundle of ideas, interdependent and interrelated. It is, in fact, rather untidy and inchoate. It is composed of a large number of diverse ideas, drawn from different cultures.[3]

Italian Fascism and German Nazism, in particular, were home to many influences and had a variety of 'ideological precursors'. It is necessary to distinguish, on the one hand, between direct linkages and random connections, and, on the other, between nascent fascism and twentieth-century fascists' ability to identify, co-opt and then pervert ideas and concepts for their own use and for purposes of credibility. In this context, it is interesting to note the way in which twentieth-century fascists have used, or rather misused, Hegel's ideas on the state for their own ends.[4]

It is in this context that we encounter the problematic concept of '**pre-fascism**', a term so controversial and contentious that it is often accompanied by quotation marks. In the opinion of some historians, 'pre-fascism' was discernible in the period 1880–1900, the 'incubation years of fascism', as Sternhell has put it. It was not so much a movement of ideas or even a coalition of forces but, rather, a 'mood', a set of attitudes that, together, anticipated and pre-dated the emergence of 'fascism' as both dictionary term and authentic political ideology. Sternhell goes on:

> On the eve of the First World War, the essentials of fascist ideology were already well defined. The word did not exist yet, but the phenomenon it would eventually designate had its own autonomous existence, and thenceforward awaited only a favourable combination of circumstances in which to hatch into a political force.[5]

'Pre-fascism', or fascism in embryonic form, was, further, a cross-national phenomenon. Prototype fascist organisations began to emerge in the first two decades of the twentieth century, the *Associazione Nazionale Italiana* (ANI) in Italy and the **German *Völkisch* Defensive and Offensive League** (DVSuTB) in Germany, for instance, but in terms of ideas, France, in the opinion of Soucy and Sternhell, was the key country.[6] **Sorel**, **Le Bon**, **Gobineau**, **Barrès** and **Bergson** all made telling contributions to the ferment in France, and their thinking was to influence a range of late nineteenth-century movements: the *Ligue des Patriotes*, **Boulangism**, the anti-Dreyfusard Movement and the *Action Française*. It could be argued that, as a consequence, France travelled from 'pre-fascism' via '**proto-fascism**' to 'early fascism' in rapid time. It is impossible to attach dates to this evolution, but the whole journey probably took place between 1880 and 1910.

Perhaps the key factor was the war of 1870–1, which ended in catastrophe for the French. The first governments of the Third Republic showed themselves to be particularly uninterested in standing up to the new Germany; however, on the nationalist right the annexation of Alsace and Lorraine was viewed as an enormous humiliation. In due course this issue was to propel a range of political activity; and, because most of this was based around anti-German **xenophobia** and a revolutionary 'national-socialist' agenda, historians have turned to the phrase 'proto-fascism' to describe it.[7]

However, what exactly was 'pre-fascism'? In essence, it was an eclectic mix of **Social Darwinism**, élitism, **Futurism** and irrationalism, but if one attitude stood out, it was revolt, against reason, rationality and the wholesale legacy of the **Enlightenment** and the **French Revolution**. If 'pre-fascism' was targeted at anything in particular, it was **egalitarianism** and **individualism**. Thus, there was a strong emphasis on 'superiority' and 'inequality'; and on **collectivism** and the ultimate collective unit, the nation. It was also imbued with an almost romantic whiff of *fin de siècle* flamboyance and hope: hence the emergence of the term 'Generation of 1890'. This was a label pinned on the sociologists, philosophers and scientists who were at the forefront of revolt, individuals like **Nietzsche**, Sorel, Bergson, Spencer and Gobineau.

On the plane of ideas, the driving force behind fascism was 'Social Darwinism'. This notion was, in effect, a reworking of Darwin's most celebrated scientific theory, which said that species survive in accordance with their strength. Darwin postulated that strength equated to 'success' and weakness to 'failure'; the logical corollary of this was that a species' least healthy elements should be rooted out and eliminated. Darwin had applied the theory to the natural world but, in the later years of the nineteenth century, thinkers and writers started to adapt this theory to the social world as well. Sternhell says that living organisms were likened to social organisms and natural selection in nature to natural selection in human society.[8] Notions of selective breeding, **eugenics** and natural selection emerged. In short, this meant 'the **survival of the fittest**'. And, of course, this notion could be manipulated and used politically. Heywood argues that Social Darwinism was an integral part of both Fascism and Nazism.[9]

Social Darwinism combined with, and also had much in common with, **élitism** and Futurism. Vilfredo **Pareto** was the leading theorist of élitism and, in the opinion of Sternhell, replicated Social Darwinist assumptions in his élite theory.[10] Pareto held that society was a pyramid, with the talented rising to the top and the 'ordinary' staying at the bottom. As such, society was equated to a living organism. Pareto argued that in both contexts natural selection took place; social conflict was not class-based but, rather, a contest between élites or 'aristocracies'. **Mosca** and **Michels** shared many of Pareto's assumptions. Élitism helped early fascists justify their aversion to the institutions of liberal democracy, especially parliament, and also gave fascism a much-needed dose of intellectual respectability. It was extremely convenient for fascist leaders to be able to rationalise their belief in the *Führerprinzip*, the division of society into 'leader', 'élite' and 'masses', via the theories of recognised sociological thinkers.

Futurism was also a significant influence on early fascism. In its original form, it was an artistic movement, but it soon developed a political agenda of its own. **Marinetti**, a leading Futurist, talked about war and the 'cult of Italy' as driving forces of a new era. In true Futurist vein, he talked about the disease of 'pastism' (a near obsession with the past) – a disease, he said, from which Italy was dying. In the immediate post-war period, when Mussolini was drawing up plans to form his movement, the Futurists were advertising their own programme. The Political Futurist Party, formed in 1918, stressed the value of youth and war, and pleaded for renaissance and a new sense of

**patriotism**. Griffin describes their 1918 programme as a manifesto aimed at national renewal. He goes on:

> Significant too are several aspects of the programme which, quite independently of Mussolini, adumbrate aspects both of Fascism and generic fascism: the concern with the nation's strength, special destiny, and need for autonomy, the emphasis on the need for the Italians to become a rejuvenated and physically healthy race, the fusion of élitism with a concern for the people (populism), the call for nationalism to become a 'political religion', the embracing of technology and the radical thrust towards a (nebulously defined) future.[11]

Political Futurism evolved independently from, but parallel to, fascism. Many Futurist concerns were fascist concerns too. In this sense, Futurism was a tributary that fed into fascism.[12]

It could be argued that the final ingredient in the fascist 'cocktail' was irrationalism or anti-rationalism. This brand of thinking is associated with Nietzsche in particular. Although commentators have argued that he would have been sceptical about the methods of a Hitler or a Mussolini in action, it is clear nevertheless that Nietzsche had a profound impact on the ideological development of fascism, especially in the *fin de siècle* period. Nietzsche's emphasis on the importance of emotion and **will** epitomised the intellectual revolt of the late nineteenth century. Heywood explains:

> The emphasis in fascism upon action and movement reflects a rejection of human reason and intellectual life in general. Conventional political ideas were based upon a belief in rationalism, for example liberals and socialists both believe that the world can be understood and transformed through the exercise of rational analysis. In the late nineteenth century, however, thinkers had started to reflect upon the limits of human reason and draw attention to other, perhaps more powerful, drives and impulses.[13]

This is where Nietzsche comes in. He advanced the concept of the 'heroic superman' ('overman' or '*Ubermensch*'). This acted as a blueprint or model for fascist strongmen of the twentieth century. Eatwell describes as crucial the 'developments in psychology which stressed the subconscious and irrational'.[14] Nietzsche also shared many of the assumptions held by the élitists. He conceived of history as a never-ending struggle and believed that the 'strong' would always overpower the 'weak'. Wilford states that Nietzsche, Pareto and Michels all helped to foster 'what has been described as the "baleful creed" of permanent struggle, élitism and unreason'. He adds:

> They were key contributors to the climate of irrationalism that characterised the intellectual turmoil of the later nineteenth century. The cult of élitism, the emphasis on power, struggle and authoritarianism, the stress on feeling and instinct, were all pitted against the rational individualism of the liberal world.[15]

However, there were other intellectual strands to irrationalism. Sorel wrote extensively about the importance of political 'myths' and how they could be used to 'capture' the working class; Bergson's **vitalism** stressed the 'life force' at work within all organisms; and Darré idolised the notion of '**blood** and soil'.[16] However, in the nature of their irrationalism, and in the way they articulated their irrationalist ideas, Barrès and Gobineau stand out as of fundamental importance to any discussion of 'pre-fascism'.

Barrès was a novelist and politician who supplied the French radical right of the 1880s and 1890s with its intellectual backbone. In 1889, he stood for election as a Boulangist and described his manifesto as 'national socialist'. As such, he mixed economic xenophobia with **protectionism** and pro-worker proposals in the spheres of training and welfare. His **socialism** came with a caveat: he was only interested in it as long as it benefited French workers, and French workers alone. Barrès was also a key player in the **Dreyfus Affair** that dominated French domestic politics in the 1890s and the first decade of the twentieth century. Captain Alfred Dreyfus had been convicted of selling secrets to the German army; almost immediately, the republican left put the case for Dreyfus's defence and the forces of **conservatism** and **nationalism** coalesced to form the Anti-Dreyfusard Movement. Barrès, a leading anti-Dreyfusard, argued:

> The campaign mounted by a certain group of people which is called 'the Dreyfus Affair' is an example of the disassociation and decerebralisation of France. At the same time, it widens the division amongst us and troubles the spirit of the nation. Déroulède's formula is really striking. He states: 'It is highly improbable that Dreyfus is innocent, but it is absolutely certain that France herself is innocent.'[17]

Thus, the ultra-pragmatic Barrès paid very little attention to the concept of 'absolute truth'; in his opinion, justice was malleable. Weiss states: 'There could be no international standards of abstract truth. For the French, there could only be French truth, French reason and French justice .... Truth was always relative to a situation and forged by emotional needs.'[18] As such, Barrès stood as the epitome of irrationalism.

There was another layer to Barrès as well. Away from the demands of practical day-to-day politics, he spent a lot of his time wandering around the graveyards of north-eastern France. As a Lorrainer, he felt the 1871 annexation badly and put a particular premium on the life and death of French soldiers. This explains his obsession with military cemeteries and their significance. He thus couched his nationalism in a mystical, neo-religious language and put great emphasis on the power of 'unconscious forces'. It is no surprise, therefore, that Soucy has identified Barrès as the 'first French fascist'.[19]

Gobineau's work reflected the same general 'mood', but he was associated with only one issue: **race**. The title of his main tract, *Essai sur l'inegalité des races humaines* (1855),[20] indicates the main thrust of his writing, and Hayes confirms that it was Gobineau's 'view of the hierarchical structure of races' that held most sway with later thinkers. Overall, Wilford argues that he was one of the earliest exponents of racial theory, while Epstein suggests that, together with Vachter de Lapouge and Chamberlain, Gobineau was part of an important international anti-Semitic tradition that influenced Nazism.[21]

This emerging intellectual climate gave rise to new political thinking. Revolutionary **syndicalism** gained its adherents, **anti-Semitism** was reinvigorated and the ideology of nationalism was given a contemporary makeover. All these currents found a home in Fascism and Nazism. Everything crystallised in the concept of '*Volk*', an almost untranslatable German term that denoted 'fatherland' or 'spiritual homeland' and had both nationalist and racialist overtones.[22] Wilford argues that **Fichte** and **Herder** were two of the earliest exponents of *Völkisch* doctrine; in the nineteenth century Richard **Wagner** espoused a similar discourse and, even though we must take Griffin's scepticism seriously,[23] it is abundantly clear that in the 1920s and 1930s Hitler and the Nazis placed the German *Volk* at the centre of their political discourse. There were linked developments elsewhere. In the three decades before 1914, Barrès had established his own type of mystical French nationalism and Italian nationalists had formulated a post-*Risorgimento*, pre-Mussolini brand of 'Italian-ness'. In time, **ultra-nationalism** would become the 'engine' of fascism.

## WAR, REVOLUTION AND CRISIS

In the same way that the 'Generation of 1890' offered a philosophical critique of society, the first fascist activists prepared a political argument. There was a slight difference in emphasis. Whereas the sociologists and philosophers were reacting, primarily, to abstract concepts such as reason, rationality, equality and individualism, fascists in Italy, Germany and elsewhere had more 'concrete' enemies, chief among which were parliament, **liberalism** and democracy.

Before the arrival of fully-fledged fascism, however, a range of 'proto-fascist' movements emerged in the first two decades of the new century: most notably the ANI in Italy and the ***Deutsche National Volks Partei*** (DNVP) in Germany.[24] However, we should not just assume that 'proto-fascism' evolved automatically into 'fascism' either. Griffin states: '"Proto-fascism" in pre-war Germany, far from being an irresistible force, was only the most radical element within a highly fractious political sub-culture of the right.'[25] In this period, would-be fascist leaders seized upon a variety of evidence to substantiate their claims that society was in a state of malaise and in need of rejuvenation; at the same time, they were aided by circumstances that, in time, proved to be highly conducive to the growth of a new ideology. However, we must be aware that individual factors were at work in particular countries. Eatwell writes:

> The first self-styled 'fascist' movement was founded in Italy in 1919. Within the space of a few years, most European countries witnessed the creation of their own fascist parties .... To understand why they took different forms, and why some prospered and others failed, it is necessary to begin the story well before the First World War, and to examine specific national traditions.[26]

94

Eatwell goes on to depict the 'national roots of fascist movements' and argues that in Britain, France, Germany and Italy, the four countries he focuses on, there was a variety of parochial factors at play.[27]

For the most part, however, historians have been happy to talk in terms of 'generic roots'. And in this respect we must acknowledge the enormous impact of the Great War and its legacy. Epstein is clear:

> What were the historical prerequisites of Europe's Age of Fascism ...? First and foremost was the pulverising impact of the First World War upon the predominantly liberal society of nineteenth-century Europe. The war caused not only untold suffering but shook the moorings of a still largely intact traditionalism; both effects intensified the demand of the broad masses for a higher material and psychological stake in the community.[28]

Italy and Germany, and other countries, suffered profoundly in the immediate post-war years. There was wholesale social dislocation to overcome, economic catastrophe to deal with, and hundreds of thousands of dead to bury. Sheridan Allen states:

> Defeat and unilateral disarmament left Germans with a sense of being preyed upon by hostile neighbours, a conviction reinforced by Polish incursions into Silesia, the French seizure of the Ruhr, the seeming despoliation of reparations, and frequent international humiliation. For Italy the war culminated in what was widely seen as a 'mutilated victory', an attitude understandable only in light of the extensively held belief among Italians that they had won the war for the Allies.[29]

Even more potently perhaps, Italy and Germany had to come to terms with a range of unfulfilled nationalist aspirations and expectations. It was the **Versailles** Treaty of 1919 (and some of its smaller sister treaties) that was to 'blame' for this. In Italy **D'Annunzio** orchestrated a 'dress rehearsal' for a fascist coup at **Fiume** in 1919. This was the direct product of post-war bitterness, a symptom of what Griffin calls '*combattentismo*'.[30]

However, the experience of 'total war' did something else: it gave Italians and Germans a taste of national solidarity. At the time, Mussolini called it 'trenchocracy' and Sheridan Allen, assessing the phenomenon with hindsight, has described it as a 'fleeting but unforgettable experience ... of what national integration felt like'.[31] In the 1920s and 1930s fascist groups in both countries tried to exploit this feeling. It was inevitable that, on the fringes of power, and then in government, Mussolini and Hitler would play heavily on the post-Versailles climate; in reality, neither leader could afford to ignore it. However, this tends to underplay their political instincts, for both made post-1918 discontent and bitterness a central plank of their manifestos.

At the same time, fear of the left was emerging as a stimulant to fascist activity. It is almost impossible to underplay the significance of anti-**Communism** as a unifying theme in fascist ideology. It is probably the one political attitude that connects all pre-fascist, fascist and neo-fascist groupings. In the aftermath of the First World War, when fascist ideas were appearing in embryo, fear of Communism was a determining factor.

The **Russian Revolution** was particularly demonised. Early fascists played on the 'dangers' inherent in **Bolshevism** and the contrasts, as they perceived them, between Communism and fascism. Epstein writes:

> The *international* character of the Communist challenge suggested the advantage of a *national* response in an age when nationalism was still burning .... The 'scientific rationalism' of communism provoked a counter-appeal to the 'irrational currents' that had played an influential role in European culture since the turn of the century.[32]

However, it was the rise of the left in a broader sense that was provocative. In France the emergence of the *Cartel des Gauches* government in 1924 triggered a discernible 'wave' of fresh fascist, or semi-fascist, activity.

There was also a crucial economic undercurrent to fascism's emergence. Mussolini and Hitler thrived on the devastating economic consequences of the First World War and the international crisis that followed on from the Wall Street Crash of 1929. They made promises to everyone: jobs for the workers, land for the peasants and stability for the middle classes. **Corporatism** and national-socialism were heralded as antidotes to the 'tired' workings of capitalism.

So, economic issues were vital. There was huge **propaganda** potential in the 'collapse' of international capitalism, but Eatwell is sceptical. He writes: 'Socio-economic crisis was a necessary precondition for the emergence of mass fascist movements in the inter-war years. But it is a set of political factors which provides the real key to how potential was turned into reality'.[33] It is difficult to disagree with this comment. Economic factors played their part, of course, but the essence of fascism, in opposition and in power, was its ultra-nationalism and its powerful critique of liberal **democracy**.

In this context, it would seem to be no coincidence that Italy and Germany, the two countries where fascism first established itself, were new nations and inexperienced democracies. The *Risorgimento* had finally produced Italian unity in 1870, while in Germany full-scale unification was the immediate consequence of the **Franco-Prussian War** in 1871.

Thus, the argument goes that in the early decades of the twentieth century, Italy and Germany were infant nations.[34] Mussolini denounced the weakness of Giolitti's liberal administration and Hitler ridiculed the impotence of the **Weimar Republic**. The two countries were naïve and inexperienced, relatively speaking. National impulses had been instrumental in their creation, and commentators suggest that in the immediate post-1918 period some of these impulses were still unfulfilled. This, it is argued, opened the door to fascism.

However, whichever angle we take, we should not be too mechanistic about the question of roots; nor should we ignore other, more nebulous factors. In relation to Italy, Eatwell argues:

[Fascism] had not succeeded simply because of the economic crisis or a threat from the left: if anything, these were receding by October 1922. Success had come more from a form of syncretic legitimation. Mussolini had managed to give his party a dual appeal: one side played to specific economic grievances, while a more affective veneer of respectability was achieved by portraying fascism not so much as a radical break with the past as a vital force for the completion of the *Risorgimento*.[35]

The same kind of point could be made about the rise of fascism in more general terms. As an ideology, it was a synthesis of various intellectual developments and no doubt fascist leaders felt that this added to their credibility. It also thrived on events, on the 'crisis' afflicting liberal democracy in the first half of the twentieth century. Historians will forever debate whether fascism was a 'radical break' or a 'revelation of the national past'.[36] What our discussion of 'roots' demonstrates is that fascism had a variety of origins and as an ideology was, at one and the same time, both new and old.

## EXTRACTS

### Document 1

*Fichte: an early expression of national sentiment*

This is an early acknowledgement of German national feeling, with a strong element of cultural nationalism contained within it as well. Later nineteenth-century writers developed these ideas and pushed them in a more extreme direction.

> Freedom to them meant ... remaining Germans and continuing to settle their own affairs independently and in accordance with the original spirit of their race, going on with their development in accordance with the same spirit, and propagating this independence in their posterity. All these blessings which the Romans offered them meant slavery to them, because then they would have to become something that was not German; they would have to become half-Roman. They assumed, as a matter of course, that every man would rather die than become half a Roman, and a true German could only want to live in order to be, and to remain, just a German, and to bring up his children as Germans.

(Source: J. Fichte, 'Love of fatherland entails a willingness to fight for it', *Addresses To The German Nation,* 1804, reprinted in E. Luard (ed.) *Basic Texts in International Relations: The Evolution of Ideas about International Society,* London, Macmillan, 1992, pp. 61–4)

### Document 2

*The Futurist Manifesto*

*The Futurist Manifesto,* published in 1913, was an audacious and very controversial document. It was calculated to offend liberal middle-class sensibilities, but also to point to the youth, speed and action that Futurists thought would characterise the new century. Futurism was absorbed into Fascism at a later date and made a significant contribution to its cult of action.

> No.1 We want to sing the love of danger, the habit of energy and rashness.
> No.2 The essential elements of our poetry will be courage, audacity and revolt.
> No.3 We want to exult movements of aggression, feverish sleeplessness, the double march, the perilous leap, the slap and the blow with the fist.
> No.4 We declare that the splendour of the world has been enriched by a new beauty: the beauty of speed. The racing automobile, with its bonnet adorned with great tubes like serpents with explosive breath ... a roaring motor car which seems to run on machine-gun fire, is more beautiful than the Victory of Samothrace.
> No.8 ... Time and space died yesterday. We are already living in the absolute, since we have already created eternal, omnipotent speed.
> No.9 We want to glorify war, the only cure for the world, militarism, patriotism, the destructive gesture of the anarchists, the beautiful ideas which kill, and contempt for woman.
> No.10 We want to demolish museums and libraries, fight morality, feminism and all opportunist and utilitarian cowardice.
> We will sing of great crowds agitated by work, pleasure and revolt; the multi-coloured and polyphonic surf of revolutions in modern capitals:
> It is in Italy that we are issuing this manifesto of ruinous and incendiary violence, by which we today are founding Futurism, because we want to deliver Italy from its gangrene of professors, archaeologists, tourist guides and antiquaries .... Standing on the world's summit we launch once again our insolent challenge to the stars.

> (Source: A. Lyttelton (ed.) *Italian Fascisms, From Pareto to Gentile*, London, Jonathan Cape, 1973, pp. 209–15)

## Document 3

*F. Nietzsche: 'The Anti-Christ'*

This extract illustrates the revolt against 'polite bourgeois morality' that emerged in the late nineteenth century and found its way into some strands of violent syndicalism, anarchism and fascism.

> What is good? – Whatever augments the feeling of power, the will to power, power itself, in man.
> What is evil? – Whatever springs from weakness.
> What is happiness? – The feeling that power increases – that resistance is overcome.
> Not contentment, but more power; not peace at any price, but war; not virtue, but efficiency (virtue in the Renaissance sense, *virtu*, virtue free of moral acid).
> The weak and the botched shall perish: first principle of our charity. And one should help them to it.
> What is more harmful than any vice? – Practical sympathy for the botched and the weak – Christianity ....

Wherever the will to power begins to decline, in whatever form, there is always an accompanying decline physiologically, decadence. The divinity of this decadence, shorn of its masculine virtues and passions, is converted perforce into a god of the physiologically degraded, of the weak. Of course, they do not call themselves the weak; they call themselves 'the good' ....

(Source: F. Nietzsche, 'The Anti-Christ', reprinted in Racial Nationalist Library (far-right site). Available online at http://netjunk.com/users/library/christ_1.htm)

## Document 4

*Sorel expounds on myth*

In his *Reflections on Violence*, first published in 1907, Georges Sorel commented on the value of myth in social mobilisation.

These results could not be produced in any very certain manner by the use of ordinary language; use must be made of a body of images, which, by intuition alone, and before any considered analyses are made, is capable of evoking as an undivided whole the mass of sentiments which corresponds to the different manifestations of the war undertaken by Socialism against modern society. The Syndicalists solve the problem perfectly by concentrating the whole of Socialism in the drama of the general strike; there is thus no longer any place for the reconciliation of contraries in the equivocations of the professors; everything is clearly mapped out, so that only one interpretation of Socialism is possible ....

Experience shows that the framing of a future, in some indeterminate time, may, when it is done in a certain way, be very effective and have very few inconveniences; this happens when the anticipations of the future take the form of those myths, which enclose with them, all the strongest inclinations of a people, of a party or of a class; inclinations which recur to the mind with the insistence of instincts in all the circumstances of life.

(Source: Georges Sorel, *Reflections on Violence*, New York, The Free Press/Macmillan, 1950, pp. 122–5)

# EVOLUTION OF IDEOLOGY

Italians! Here is the national programme of a solidly Italian movement. Revolutionary, because it is opposed to dogma and demagogy; robustly innovating because it rejects preconceived opinions.
(Programme of the Italian Fascists, 6 June 1919, taken from J. Whittam, *Fascist Italy*, Manchester, Manchester University Press, 1995, pp. 145–6)

This chapter examines the engagement of fascist and far-right movements with the world of ideas. It discusses the concept of **ideology**, the composition of fascist and far-right ideologies, and the role played by those ideologies in their quest for and exercise of political power. The balance between continuity and change will be a key theme throughout.

There is almost as much debate about the study of ideology in history and political science as there is about fascism itself. Brendan Evans, citing Seliger, distinguishes between a loose and inclusive concept of ideology.[1] The term can refer broadly to ideas and beliefs that underpin political action, both by way of explanation and rationalisation. This interpretation makes no judgement about the validity or moral rectitude of the ideology concerned: the study of ideology is the study of a more or less ordered set of ideas. An alternative, 'restrictive', concept of ideology is used by those who wish to contrast what they see as 'false' ideas with their own supposedly 'scientific' view of human relations. For Evans, this is to be found among positivist social scientists, among practitioners of the natural sciences and frequently among Marxian writers. The last see ideology as a powerful instrument in the hands of the dominant classes in their efforts to foster false consciousness among their victims. Gramsci, for instance, characterised this 'dominant ideology' or 'hegemony' as the key to capitalist domination of politics and society.[2] In another sense altogether, ideology is described in terms of irrational or extremist discourse. All of these interpretations can be applied to the ideas that were propagated by, or had an impact on, fascist leaders.

On the other hand, it is perhaps ironic to discuss the concept of 'fascist ideology' at all. Fascists and far-right leaders, especially **Mussolini** and **Franco**, saw their movements as driven by a thirst for action rather than by abstract intellectual fashions. Of the principal right-wing dictators, only **Hitler** attempted to pen a general self-authored tome, *Mein Kampf*, as a would-be intellectual justification for his regime. Nonetheless, on their way to power and beyond, many far-right movements did court theorists and intellectuals to add *gravitas* to their public identities. Mussolini appointed the philosopher, Giovanni **Gentile**, as his Education Minister. We can only speculate on the reasons for this; many of the earliest supporters of fascism came from the ranks

100

of demobilised soldiers embittered at civilian politics. Moreover, in their endorsement of frequently unpopular liberal and socialist causes, much of Europe's intellectual élite was an easy target for fascist **populism**.

Nonetheless, much of fascism's bid for greatness depended on a battle of ideas, not only with **Communism** but with liberal **democracy** as well. This was especially evident in the claim that fascist movements represented a new '**Third Way**' between left and right, between Marxian **socialism** and **capitalism**. Despite his own dislike of intellectuals, Mussolini himself had, of course, started his political career as a sort of ideologist, as a journalist working for the polemical socialist paper, *Avanti*. In his own mind, it was his words that would spark the revolution for which he was working. Whatever his disdain for liberal or left-wing intellectuals, Mussolini was conscious of the battle of ideas and the power of the pen.

The same was true of the Nazis. Hitler's conception of the world of ideas was even cruder than Mussolini's but he had a compensation in the person of **Göbbels**. The latter's **propaganda** campaigns became so important to the Nazis that he was, with **Himmler**, the real Deputy-**Führer**. When Hitler himself took a prominent role in the German Workers' Party (DAP), the forerunner to the Nazi Party, he put most of his effort into organisation and propaganda.

The obsessions with domestic propaganda, and the control of education and the arts, were means of ensuring that the people followed their leader. In *Mein Kampf*, Hitler was explicit about the need to reduce propaganda to the simplest message that would trigger the right psychological response among the masses.[3] So whatever sophistication fascists claimed for their ideology, the masses could do with crude propaganda.

## THE COMPONENTS OF FASCIST IDEOLOGY

Despite the claim of innovation, fascists borrowed heavily from other ideologies of the left and the right. The founders brought ideas into the movements at their very inception. **Middle-class** anti-Communists brought arguments against the **materialism** of socialism, while the socialist background of men like Mussolini himself helped them to hone a powerful anti-capitalist discourse. Capitalism was based on a **plutocracy**, with privileged minorities pulling the strings and holding national economies to ransom. The early party rallies passed anti-capitalist resolutions, including some urging the death penalty for 'usurers and profiteers'.[4] For Hitler, Jewish bankers and financiers fitted the bill quite well. Faced with enemies such as these, the 'ordinary' person or the small shopkeeper was helpless. Great national industries were also vulnerable to shifts in the international economy, shifts driven by the unseen corporate leaders of the Anglo-Saxon powers. This message had a two-pronged effect: to suggest an anti-élitist and anti-capitalist agenda, while simultaneously reassuring 'patriotic' capitalists that their victimisation by foreign forces was near an end.

Beyond this, pinning down a shared set of 'core' beliefs in all the various fascisms is especially difficult. Not only was there a different fascist doctrine in every country, but even individual fascisms, like that in Italy, were so multi-dimensional that they could easily be characterised as incoherent. Griffin argues that a 'palingenetic and populist ultra-nationalism' was their lowest common denominator.[5] The 'people', victims of **liberalism**, **decadence** and socialism, would be reborn. However, unlike **traditionalism** and **conservatism**, this fascist reincarnation would not replicate the past but transcend it, taking it to a higher level. Thus, it gave the aspect of being both forward-looking and modernist but simultaneously responsive to its primordial roots.

The bridge between past and future was what historians call the element of 'myth' in fascist ideology. For Griffin, the common myth that unites all fascisms is the simple story behind palingenetic **ultra-nationalism** that constitutes the lowest common denominator in these movements.[6] Fascism borrowed the use of myth from **Sorel**, who emphasised the importance of concentrating the intuitions and emotions of the masses in a powerful idea, such as a show-down between capital and labour in a momentous general strike, as a means of sparking revolutionary action. Mussolini himself used the term 'myth' to describe a driving belief that could motivate people to work toward a common future. The myth did not have to be true but could be sensed to be real nonetheless, on account of its effects.[7] The myths of fascism were a means of linking the past to the future and of mobilising many disparate people in a common movement. The myth was partially an ideological construct but also, as we will see again in 'Fascism and the Far Right in Government and Opposition', a tactic designed to generate action. In the Italian case, the myth of *romanitá* was the key. Fascist Italy was to be the new Rome. Like its predecessor, it would extol order and discipline, but it would also be modern and revolutionary. For Hitler, world history would be conflated into that great struggle between the Aryan or Nordic race and the lesser races, especially the Slavs and the Jews. The Germans had an Aryan past and they would have an Aryan future. The Nazis employed anthropology, biology, history and linguistics, even classical music, to 'confirm' this racial myth and its relevance. Ironically, the regime's ideologist on race, Alfred **Rosenberg**, was not a 'pure' German at all, but of Lithuanian and Estonian background. Rosenberg was useful in the elaboration of a 'rationale' for racial policy at first, but, when 'implementation' took priority, he seemed to take a back seat to Reinhard **Heydrich** and Heinrich Himmler. Himmler's final 'rationalisation' for the **Holocaust** was not even ideological at all: he simply suggested that, due to their brutal record, the Nazis could simply not afford to allow Jewish women to bear children who would surely wreak horrible revenge on all the German people.

Of course, the relationship between religious traditions and national cultural myths, on the one hand, and the national state, on the other, vary from case to case. The Japanese militarists had a relatively easy task, in that large parts of the population already believed in the divinity of Emperor **Hirohito** and Japanese society was already heavily imbued with mythic traditions. Religion and tradition are also important in India. However, in this case, the official state ideology is secularist. Thus, if the Indian far right, as represented by the *Bharatiya Janata* Party (BJP) or its militia-like affiliate, the ***Rashtriya Swayam-sevak Sangh*** (RSS), want to use Hindu chauvinism as a political tool, the central state apparatus will not be an ally. Nonetheless, the antiquity of Hindu traditions, the multiplicity of gods and the richness of its epics provide an attractive basis for a powerful myth to accompany any far-right movement that chooses to exploit them to the full. Indeed, Hindu fundamentalist movements in the 1920s and 1930s did precisely that, and it is from this period of ideological ferment and communal tension that the RSS gained its original impetus.[8]

Rhetorical anti-materialism is another notable feature of both fascist and far-right movements. For those in Southern Europe, Catholic social doctrine may have played a role here. Of course, in practice, the fascists also believed in material wealth and power; that was a large part of their purpose. However, their rhetoric traditionally emphasised the notion of 'spirit'. The nation, the people or the race represented a spiritual force that was above the greedy inclinations of capitalism. Anti-materialism also cast the fascists in opposition to socialism and Communism, both of which were firmly rooted in the scientific materialism of Marx and Engels.

Even the Japanese used the anti-materialist tradition in East Asian cultures as part of their rhetorical armoury. The Asian spirit was contrasted with Western materialism. This was a genuine concern of many in the region (e.g. in Chinese variants of Buddhism and Taoism) and remains so even today; witness the current debate over 'Asian values' and a 'clash of civilisations'.[9] However, it was an important ideological current in the Japanese wartime regime, which stressed that Japanese spiritual power was a match for and even superior to US technological and military prowess. This power could produce victory against the odds: hence the willingness of Japanese soldiers and aviators to fight to the end and undertake kamikaze suicide missions. Fascists and far-right movements were certainly nationalist but they took their **nationalism** to new extremes. The nation was defined in cultural and frequently in racial terms. It became a quasi-spiritual force for which other values of civilisation could be sacrificed (see 'Nation and Race' and 'Diplomacy and International Relations').

Fascist ideologies were also collectivist. Individual freedom could only have meaning through the community or the group; in this case, the people or the nation, as embodied in the state and party. This obviously distinguished them from liberal individualists but also from traditional rightist authoritarians. The latter were not particularly concerned with the role of individuals or groups in society, provided they did not challenge authority or threaten the dictatorship. Fascist regimes, on the other hand, were interested in representing, or appearing to represent, the masses and in mass adulation. The individual German, frustrated by the 'capitulations' of liberal élites, could find a voice as part of the *Volk*. Hitler's press chief, Dr Dietrich, argued that 'only those who feel the community thought or endeavour to comprehend it can understand National Socialism'.[10] Similarly, Mussolini's fusion of the individual and the nation into a spiritual unity is captured in one neat sentence: 'The man of Fascism is an individual who is nation and fatherland, which is a moral law, binding together individuals and the generations into a tradition and a mission.'[11]

One of the most contentious issues that arises in characterising these movements and regimes is the debate over the concept of **totalitarianism**. As used by Zbigniew Brzezinski and Carl Friedrich, this refers to a political system with a dominant mass party, a secret police, state terror and an all-encompassing ideology. That description refers, in the first place, to the *practice* of totalitarianism.[12] Critics allege, however, that the concept was misused by US political scientists in the **Cold War** years as a means of artificially lumping Communism with fascism together in order to discredit the Soviet Union. It is, of course, true, that in the real world very few regimes are fully totalitarian. They do not control society in all aspects and at all times. Communist Party control of the Soviet Union, for instance, was never complete and state power was certainly less invasive of other areas of society from Khrushchev's time onwards than under Stalin. Nonetheless, the USSR was more than a simple autocracy. The ideology behind the Party aspired to a total fusion of party, state and society, even if it had difficulty in achieving this in practice. On the other hand, the Soviets shied away from the word 'totalitarian' itself, seeing it as a term of abuse.

Mussolini had no such qualms: he explicitly used the expression to describe his model state.[13] Like the Communists, however, the Italian Fascists found totalitarianism difficult to implement in practice. As we will see in 'Fascism and Civil Society', they were effectively unable to control independent institutions like the Catholic Church. Indeed, the philosopher-apologist for Italian Fascism, Giovanni Gentile, in setting out the doctrine of Fascism, conceded that the task of bringing the whole mass of the people to the same consciousness as a 'progressive' party was very difficult, since such a people might take centuries to elevate to that level.[14]

For the purposes of this chapter, however, totalitarianism as a description of an ideology is more important than the nature of a totalitarian political system in practice. Regardless of how much control the fascists actually exercised, it is very clear that they wished to control more issue-areas in society and more aspects of life than traditional autocracies. Totalitarian movements have a policy on many issue-areas; they have an opinion on everything because, for them, everything is political. Everything is defined in terms of the nation and its mysterious 'spirit'. Thus, Germany would have socialism, according to Hitler, but it would be a German socialism. The idea that socialism, essentially a cosmopolitan ideology, could be 'nationalised' in this way was also a feature of extremist discourse in early twentieth-century France.[15] Similarly, art and culture would be 'nationalised' in the true sense of the term: not simply taken over by the state but redefined to serve the purposes of the fascist nation. **Wagner**'s description of his German nationalism was one such example.

> Now it is me no one grasps: I am the most German being, I am the German spirit. Question the incomparable magic of my works, compare them with the rest: and you can, for the present, say no differently than that – it is German. But what is this German? It must be something wonderful, mustn't it, for it is humanly finer than all else? – Oh heavens! It should have a soil, this German! I should be able to find my people! What a glorious people it ought to become. But to this people only could I belong.[16]

This was not an unusual sentiment. For the Germans, unlike the English or the French, were newcomers to nationhood. They had to define the boundaries of the nation: what constituted 'German-ness' was not plain from history but had to be elaborated by means of an ideology. Such cultural nationalism has to grasp at whatever morsels of history, soil and **race** that it can find: hence the link between nostalgic **romanticism**, linguistics and anthropology in nineteenth-century Europe. As Hannah Arendt has argued, the rootless peoples of Eastern Europe had even less of a fixed historical identity and homeland.[17] The brashness of the cultural revival in Europe masked deep cultural insecurity.

Fascism, however, went beyond romantic nationalism. Insecurity was to be overcome by systematic **modernisation**, taking all forces to their extreme. Arendt argues that, for the fascists, this meant becoming the master race, systematically defining new subordinate classes (in the form of racial groups) below them, as the Afrikaners had done in Southern Africa. Success required racial prejudice and romantic nationalism as starting blocks but ultimately demanded the will to smash existing taboos and conventions as well. It was not enough to silence critics and dissenters. The aim was not to depoliticise society and culture, but to actively 'encourage' them to sing from the leader's song sheet with gusto and passion.

One contributor to fascist anti-intellectualism may have been the cult of action. This existed in almost all the movements and was usually fused with the cult of the leader. In the case of Italy and Germany, for example, it may have been influenced by the presence in the movements of large numbers of demobilised soldiers. Hitler and Mussolini empathised with these people. For them, action spoke louder than words. Similarly, the place of 'action', high up on the fascist value system, was emphasised by association with other values like manliness, virility, strength and power. These values were not only conveyed in words but through art, culture and the symbolism of great events. Italian success in sport, for instance, was attributed not only to Fascism but to some quality of 'Italian-ness'. Taking their cue from the phenomenon of 'vitalism' in philosophy, the Fascists spoke as if this quality ran in the veins, or, in some other way, inhabited the mind and body of each Italian, from one generation to the next. The great events, the 'spectacles', were both products of the ideology and showcases for it. This was especially true of the 1936 Berlin Olympics. Since the inception of the modern Olympics, the Games were supposed to be based on the premise that participation counted more than winning. From the very beginning, nations interpreted victories in a political way (and still do). The Nazis in particular surrounded the Games with all the chauvinist and nationalist symbolism they could muster, even if they did try to conceal the worst excesses of **anti-Semitism**.[18]

An important contribution to the cult of action came from one of the sub-groups that had joined Italian Fascism at the beginning: the Futurists. Futurists extolled the value of force, speed and power. These were to be the characteristics of the machines and processes of the twentieth century. They believed themselves to be challenging 'reactionary', 'bourgeois' society. They defied tradition, very often in a deliberately offensive way. Rather than talk about philosophies and theories, the Futurists would make their agenda known through the propaganda of the deed, a most aggressive form of self-assertion.[19] This, of course, was a central component in both the ideology and tactics of archetypal terrorist organisations, of both the far left and the far right, in the second half of the twentieth century.

The street violence that accompanied Fascism's rise to power served to reinforce the idea that it was about action, not words. Like subsequent extra-parliamentary movements, the Fascists believed that if their objectives could not be achieved within the constraints of the liberal democratic political system, it was necessary to work outside or even against it. Some employers took advantage of this culture of violence to have Fascist gangs attack strikers or trade union officials. While post-war Italian liberal governments made concessions to demonstrating workers and appeared unable to deal with lawlessness and chaos in the countryside, Fascism confronted the strikers and protesters in a very direct way. The extra-parliamentary action from the left and right raised the spectre of civil war, but this risk factor became not a source of fear, but a source of power for the Fascists.

The sense that different ideological currents have their own time in history was also an important theme for the far right. The nineteenth century had seen the increasing power of liberalism and liberal states like the US and Britain. The twentieth century would be dominated by an ideology that could mobilise people in more powerful ways and on a more systematic basis than liberal democracy. With all the tools of technology and propaganda, they could mobilise the entire society to achieve the collective purpose. Lenin and the Bolsheviks demonstrated how this approach could apparently work in Russia. Liberalism, in contrast, appeared to be in decline. Capitalism appeared to be afflicted by economic depression and collapse, and liberals were war-weary. If totalitarianism and power were to be the arbiters of the new century, fascists and Communists were determined to paint as stark a choice as possible for those who doubted the effectiveness of liberalism or social democracy. Many supported the Republicans or the Nationalists in the **Spanish Civil War** precisely because they accepted the idea of a stark choice between competing totalitarianisms. Similarly, the Finnish 'White' or anti-Communist forces – many with authoritarian and proto-fascist leanings – represented their struggle with the left as a zero-sum game in which there could be no middle position.[20] A doctrine of inevitability was as important to fascism as determinism had been to **Marxism**.

Since action was so important to fascists, ideology was about preparing the ground for action, about uniting the past and present, worker and employer, tradition and **modernity**. Failure in the practical sphere could undermine that ideology. Because fascist movements were so internally incoherent, contradictions and setbacks were inevitable. The purpose of education, propaganda and censorship was to mask those contradictions. The real irony is that the fascists believed that war, action *in extremis,* would ultimately separate sheep from goats and reveal the weaknesses of their enemies. Instead, it was their call to action that failed, and that failure showed the hollowness of their ideology.

## IDEOLOGY FOR THE SAKE OF EXISTENCE

Post-war neo-fascist and far-right movements are a much more eclectic group. Some, like those involved in **terrorism** or in football hooliganism, have taken to the politics of action again, rather than pamphleteering. Others have devoted their thinking and writing skills to electioneering. Nonetheless, ideology has taken on a new urgency. It is no longer there simply to rationalise action but to explain the need for such movements in the first place. In the pre-fascist period, ideological ferment was all the rage. Hegel, Marx and others had set off a train of pamphleteering. The years 1870–1914 were rich in syntheses, many quite paradoxical and bizarre.[21] In contrast, the Cold War environment of 1946–65 was strictly bi-polar, in ideological as much as in structural terms. The anti-Communist movement was to be led by the US, the leader of the liberal democratic and capitalist order in Europe. The left was social democratic, democratic socialist or Communist. The scope for paradox was gone.

The 1960s opened up new possibilities for ideological ferment. On the left, Marxists and those close to Communism began to disassociate themselves, to varying degrees, from the Soviet model, while remaining critical of what they termed 'bourgeois democracy'. With the anti-war movements of the 1970s, anti-Americanism became fashionable and universities were often at the forefront of the protests. The far right began a metamorphosis into something more than a throwback to Fascism and Nazism. It exploited the backlash against the left among many conservative elements in society. However, it also copied the left and claimed to be searching for newer forms of political and social order fit for the late twentieth century. Like the nation, far-right ideology was apparently capable of rebirth and regeneration on a higher plane than before.

We have already noted the many differences among inter-war far-right groups and even between the core movements in Germany and Italy. The other main feature of the far right since the mid-1960s has been a further ideological diversification. Some claimed to occupy a 'Third Position', neither left nor right but, also, no longer crudely nostalgic for wartime fascism. New names proliferated, often without the words 'right' or 'fascist' anywhere to be seen. There was a sense in which these groups jumped on bandwagons, as, for instance, with the trend of associating themselves with heavy metal, youth culture or ecology, just as the New Left had done.[22]

Stealing the name, and parts of the agenda, of other conservative trends was always a tactic of the far right. Perhaps some of the greatest confusion of all comes in their attempted capture of the mantle 'New Right'. The **New Right** was primarily an Anglo-American phenomenon associated with neo-conservatism and free market ideology, especially under Ronald Reagan and Margaret Thatcher. While some would characterise its social conservatism as authoritarian, its roots are firmly in the liberal and conservative traditions of the democratic right. It was not a development of **neo-fascism**. However, the term is also used to refer to racist and extremist forms of neo-fascism that mask their philosophy in a critique of liberalism and **egalitarianism** that sounds similar to that of the socially conservative wing of neo-conservatism.[23] The difference between the two is fundamental: social neo-conservatives attack 'political correctness' because they believe it to be replacing one form of discrimination with an equally unsatisfactory and loaded system, while the neo-fascist New Right use similar arguments to explain the decline of racial or cultural purity. Thus, the neo-fascist New Right actually owes more to classic fascism, even if that is concealed. This can be seen in themes such as love of **élitism**, heroism and beauty, anti-materialism, vitalism, '**blood** and soil', 'the regeneration of history' and, in some cases, a tendency to dabble in paganism and the occult.[24]

However, the confusion does not end there. The neo-fascist New Right has frequently adopted neo-conservative New Right positions, especially on the economy or social welfare reform, in order to appear to be swimming 'with the tide'. In France, **Le Pen**'s *Front National* (FN) went through such a phase in the 1980s and **Haider**'s Freedom Party (FPÖ) in Austria has done likewise since the 1990s. This is really a tactical move, designed to avoid isolation and to steal voters from more mainstream parties of the right. The resulting picture is quite complex, but it can be summarised by reference to the following categories:

• Neo-fascist New Right positions that owe their origin to fascism (e.g. **racism**, ultra-nationalism).
• Positions shared by the neo-fascist and neo-conservative New Right (e.g. social conservatism on **gender** issues).
• Neo-conservative New Right positions stolen or adopted by the neo-fascist New Right (e.g. rhetorical anti-statism, free market economics).

If this is confusing, perhaps that is as it is intended to be. Ambiguity permits flexibility and tactical repositioning. In this, at least, the far right remains true to its past.

Perhaps one of the greatest fears of the far right is the realisation of an end to ideological conflict as a result of a new global consensus around liberal democracy and capitalism. For the liberal writer, Francis Fukuyama, the end of ideology is nothing less than the end of history itself.[25] Given the far right's need to oppose and to challenge, this would spell disaster. Thus, the constant regeneration of their ideology now thrives on diversity and eclecticism, just as it did in the pre-fascist years. What an ironic fate, though, for ideological currents, whose roots lie in anti-intellectualism and the privileging of action above all else, to be reduced to little more than obscurantist debating clubs on the margins of political life.

## EXTRACTS

### Document 1

*Anti-materialism in Japanese militarist propaganda*

The evocation of spirits and the mystical has two aspects to it: it resonates with the deeper traditions of the people but it also suggests that the ruling regime has a spiritual force that gives it advantages over its enemies.

> A number of miraculous and mysterious events, transcending the existing limits of science, are reported to have occurred in the Kiska area, which many soldiers on the spot believe to this day had been worked by the souls of the heroes, who went down fighting to the last man at Attu. Miracles, mysterious occurrences have been reported as occurring on the battlefield. There are no longer any Japanese forces at Kiska, but it seems in that, in their place, the heroic spirits of Attu landed. Foreign reports reveal that the American forces fought intensely and bitterly against this army of spirits over a period of three weeks. In the South Pacific too, spirits of the Japanese troops have got hold of the enemy.
>
> (Source: *Nippon Times*, 24 August 1943, quoted in B. Shillony, *Politics and Culture in Wartime Japan*, Oxford, Clarendon Press, 1981, p. 136)

### Document 2

*Adolf Hitler on 'nationalising' the masses*

For the far right, nationalisation is a process whereby a group or a phenomenon is rendered 'national' or brought to a high level of national consciousness. Here, Hitler insists that the process be absolute and that there should be no half-measures.

> The nationalisation of the broad masses can never be achieved by half-measures,

109

that is to say, by feebly insisting on what is called the objective side of the question, but only by a ruthless and devoted insistence on the one aim which must be achieved. This means that a people cannot be made 'national' according to the signification attached to that word by our bourgeois class today – that is to say, nationalism with many reservations – but national in the vehement and extreme sense. Poison can be overcome only by a counter-poison, and only the supine bourgeois mind could think that the Kingdom of Heaven can be attained by a compromise.

> (Source: A. Hitler, *Mein Kampf*, Chapter 12. Reprinted at Stormfront.org
> (far-right site). Available online at http://www.stormfront.org)

## Document 3

*Iron Guard veteran on the ideology of the Iron Guard*

With its hints of ruralism and Christian zeal, this is typical of the near-spiritual tone of Iron Guard and inter-war Romanian far-right discourse

*N.N.* – Could you tell us why you joined the Legionary Movement and what has kept you active on its behalf ever since?

*J.D.* – The innermost folds of my soul drew me irresistibly to it. I sensed intuitively that the Legionary Movement was, at long last, the organisation really meaning to clean the stables of the political pestilence fouling up the country; to do away with the corruption and moral decadence of the body politic; to end the exploitation of the long suffering peasantry and improve the lot of the worker. And I have stuck to the same faith in these endeavours for I have believed the Legionary Movement to be one of a spiritual regeneration gifted by God to a people perhaps once in a millennium through its predestined leader, Corneliu Z. Codreanu, the 'Captain'.

*N.N.* – What were the principal ideals of the Iron Guard?

*J.D.* – Perfection through virtue, respecting life's original harmony; sub-ordination of matter to spirit; installing 'a forceful Christian faith, an unlimited love of country, correctitude of soul as the expression of honour, and unity as the premise for success'. These are the pillars of Codreanu's school which were based on the foundation of 'the rule of the spirit and moral value'. The Legion endeavoured to create a national elite of character leading to an aristocracy of virtue sustained by love of country and permanent sacrifice for the Fatherland, on justice for the peasantry and the workingman, on order, discipline, work, honest dealing, and honour.

(Source: Jianu Dianieleau, interviewed in *New Nation* (UK National Front maga-zine), No. 7, Summer 1985. Reprinted on site devoted to the Romanian far right. Available online at http://www.netcolony.com/members/legiunea/iron-guard.html)

## Document 4

*About Pamyat*

This is publicity material about the Russian far-right organisation from its website. The tone highlights its use of traditionalism and nostalgia, as well as its opposition to democracy and its anti-Semitism.

> The National-Patriotic Front 'Pamyat' is the Orthodox, monarchistic and national union of loyal citizens of Russian power. The leader of 'Pamyat' is Dimitry Vasiliev ....
>
> The aim of 'Pamyat' is the restoration of the monarchy and rightful succession of autocratic power in Russia. 'Pamyat' does not recognise ... the myth about the right of succession to the throne of so-called Prince Georgy, who doesn't have any rights to the Russian throne according to the basic rules of Russian Empire. The monarch is the anointed sovereign and only God can decide who will be monarch.
>
> 'Pamyat' rejects such concepts as 'class' or 'class struggle' and affirms as principle the division of society into open estate-groups, the association into Assembly of the Land. 'Pamyat' also affirms consiliarism [*sic*] as a mental principle of decision about most important state problems.
>
> 'Pamyat' affirms personal, collective, and national property. 'Pamyat' holds Russian raw materials for the national property and appeals against the transformation of Russia into a raw material appendage of international capital. 'Pamyat' holds the right for soil property as the basis of property and appeals for free delivery with the right of inheritance of soil to all people who want to till it.
>
> 'Pamyat' does not recognise the legality of incumbent power because this power has succession to the illegal revolution of 1917 .... 'Pamyat' takes the overthrow of monarchy for an act of realisation of the Zionistic and freemasonic conspiracy against Russia – the bulwark of Christianity. 'Pamyat' has been fighting against Zionistic ideology, which is the theory of apartheid. 'Pamyat' regards Communistic ideology as the doctrine of Talmud. 'Pamyat' regards democracy as a part of the preparation for the coming of Jewish emperor, which was described in the *The Protocols of the Meetings of The Learned Elders of Zion*! Front 'Pamyat' appeals to all patriots to unite and be guided by the idea of restoration of the Autocratic Monarchy in Russia. You understand only too well – our strength in unity. Victory by Zionists in Russia is a pledge for victory in all countries!
>
> (Source: *Pamyat* website, 2001. Available online at
> http://www.pamyat.org/about.html [accessed 1 May 2001])

## Document 5

*The spiritual dimension to Japan's war effort*

This extract, although from an earlier time, echoes the anti-materialist theme of the foregoing *Pamyat* document, but contrasts spiritualism with individualism, suggesting that a spiritual nation is more likely to be successful.

> The key to final victory lies not in the material fighting strength of the nation, but in the spirit which infuses strength in all directions. There are some who are

pessimistic in view of the enormous national resources of the US. However, material wealth does not decide the outcome of war. The side with a great productive power can be compared to a bulky adversary in a duel. It is not difficult to recognise a difference in spirit between the Anglo-Americans and the Japanese. They have been brought up with the ideology of individualism and democracy, while we, the Japanese, have been raised in sacred spiritual ideas. Should we be determined to sink every enemy ship, then we have nothing to fear, regardless of great number of enemy warships. The mightier the enemy forces are, the greater Japan's victory will be.

(Source: Reserve General Suzuki Teiichi, quoted in B. Shillony, *Politics and Culture in Wartime Japan*, Oxford, Clarendon Press, 1981, pp. 134–5)

# NATION AND RACE

Austria is not a country of immigration.

(Freedom Party website – www.fpoe.or.at)

If we are looking for a pivot around which fascist doctrine revolves, we must look no further than 'nation' and 'race'. Sternhell's depiction of fascism as 'supremely nationalistic and therefore above all exclusive' is particularly pertinent.[1] Before we go on to examine the terms in detail, and also examine a range of tangential concepts and ideas, we must make several introductory points about fascism, nation and race.

First, within many variants of fascism there is an implicit assumption that the terms 'nation' and 'race' are synonymous. Hayes refers to the concept of 'folk-nation', while Wilford traces the historical development of the link between the two terms. He argues that 'by the end of the nineteenth century the distorted equation of race with nation [was] solidly grounded in the European intellectual soil'.[2] He says 'distorted' because, in reality, 'nation' and 'race' are not, and cannot be, interchangeable terms. No pseudo-scientific theory can prove otherwise (hence the triumph of 'open' **nationalism** over 'closed' nationalism in most periods of modern history).

Second, not unnaturally given the previous point, there is a powerful belief within fascist ideology that the nation is of overwhelming importance relative to the individual. There is something fundamentally communal and collectivist about fascism. We must remember here that the *'fasces'*, the ancient Roman symbol that came to be adopted by **Mussolini**, consisted of several individual sticks bound together. This is highly significant. It indicates the fascist belief in corporate power: individuals only become important if they are bound together in solidarity. Pearson, a racial theorist, uses an adjacent kind of language. He contrasts the strength of the 'tribe' with the weakness of the 'individual'.[3] So, the veneration of 'nation' and 'race' by fascists has a corollary: a muscular anti-**individualism**.

Third, it is important to comprehend that nationalism is just one element within fascism, albeit the most explicit. Some historians refer to fascism as a 'cocktail'. Eatwell, for example, muses on the contention that fascism is simply an aggregate of nationalism and **socialism**. In the end, however, he concludes that it is more accurate to assert that fascism is the combined effect of nationalism and **conservatism**.[4] This is particularly interesting because it is usually just assumed that fascism equates, in a general sense, to 'national-socialism' (a term that **Hitler** in Germany, **Mosley** in Britain and **Corradini** in Italy, among others, were happy to utilise in the interest of self-definition;

Barrès in France preferred the phrase 'Socialist Nationalism'). Others, however, assert that fascism is essentially a fusion of nationalism and syndicalism, and emphasise the contribution of Sorel's anti-bourgeois discourse to the development of fascist thought. Whatever the exact verdict, it is clear that, in general terms, fascism takes its social values from the left and its political values from the right.[5]

Perhaps the best preliminary conclusion to draw is this: nationalism is fundamental to fascism in a way that socialism and conservatism are not. This, in turn, explains why historians are more likely to place fascism on the right of the political spectrum than on the left.

Fourth, it must be acknowledged that fascism is an overtly anti-intellectual creed and, as such, puts a premium on emotion rather than reason. This is important to understand because, in the context of 'nation' and 'race', fascism resorts (not infrequently) to myth-making, to belief in the irrational and even to spiritual, neo-religious language (like, for example, *Volk*). Mussolini talked about the nation as an 'immense reservoir of knowledge' and regarded national feeling as the moving force of history.[6] The nation is the central 'myth' of fascism in the same way that 'class' is the crux of socialism. Fascism, however, is devoid of any real theory and also lacks a Marx-like figure that could be viewed as its undisputed theoretician. Mussolini made great play of his dislike of manifestos, yet more evidence of fascists' suspicion of words and rationality.

Likewise, fascism places a huge emphasis on 'war'. In foreign policy terms, fascist regimes can be bellicose in the extreme. In another way, however, 'war' is a rhetorical tool. 'War' and other similar words can be used to rouse the masses and inspire patriotism in the domestic arena. Mussolini, for instance, launched a **'Battle for Grain'** and a **'Battle for Births'**. Predictably, fascism is damning on pacifism. Pacifists are viewed as weak and spineless; in the same way, fascists look upon **'liberalism'** as a byword for 'weakness'. The glorification of 'war' is an undercurrent to all fascist strictures on nation and race.

Finally, as a prelude to the forthcoming discussion, we should be aware that 'fascism' is not at all a homogenous ideology. There are significant regional variations and these are more evident perhaps in this chapter than in any of the others. For example, whereas anti-Semitism in Nazi Germany reached the proportions of genocide, in Italy it could be argued that it was an after-thought (more specifically, an attempt by Mussolini to ape Hitler). As Krejčí argues:

> Fascist nationalism aimed at absorption, not extermination, of ethnic minorities and, above all, did not share the anti-Semitic fury of the Nazis. As racial policy was in fact the cornerstone of what was hailed as the National Socialist revolution there was, in matters of domestic policy, less common ground between the Fascists and the Nazis than is widely believed.[7]

The case of anti-Semitism is just one example, albeit a significant one.

It is obvious from the above that nationalism has an extremely high profile in fascist ideology. As Hayes has written: 'The influence of nationalism upon fascist doctrine and practice has been so strong that fascist and nationalist have on occasion been regarded as virtually interchangeable terms.' Griffin puts it in a different way. He says: 'Nationalism ... is practically the only common denominator of all previous accounts of fascism's definitional characteristics, whether proposed by Marxists ... or non-Marxists.' Here it is significant that fascist/neo-fascist movements often use the name '**National Front**'. This has been the case in Britain where, in the post-war years, the NF has published two poignantly titled journals: *The **British Nationalist*** and *The Young Nationalist*.[8]

There is, thus, a strong intrinsic connection between 'fascism' and 'nationalism'. However, we cannot leave it that. The relationship is complex and defies easy explanation. Perhaps the best way to approach this matter is as follows. At the heart of fascism is a core belief in the nation as a fundamental social and political entity. This belief can evolve into patriotism and nationalism, or what Griffin calls 'populist ultra-nationalism'.[9] And sometimes it can evolve into **xenophobia**. Some 'fascisms' would stop here.

The most notorious types of fascism have, however, gone even further; in such cases 'nation' has been directly equated with 'race'. Hence, we find the incorporation of racialist language and attitudes into some 'fascisms'. Here there is a belief in racial 'superiority' with human beings neatly split up into 'Aryans' and 'Jews'. At its extreme, in Nazi Germany and in the former Yugoslavia, fascism and fascist-style philosophies can countenance genocide and **ethnic cleansing**.

Thus, there is something of a 'sliding scale'. At its most 'moderate', fascism can be viewed as a form of nationalism; at its 'worst', it can evolve into a brutal form of **totalitarianism**. Let us look at the key concepts in depth.

## NATION, PATRIOTISM AND NATIONALISM

Fascism begins and ends with the nation. Eatwell writes: 'The nation is seen as the "natural" unit of state organisation by fascists, and is central to fascist ideology.'[10] Even though he goes on to argue that there is, within fascism, a discernible pan-Europeanism, the point is made that nation and nationhood stand as the central, defining features of the ideology. The best way to illustrate this is to highlight the concept of *Volk*.

*Volk* is a German term. The nearest literal translation in English would be '**Fatherland**'. The fact is that *Volk* has almost spiritual and religious connotations; as Hayes argues, in the early nineteenth century when the German lands were threatened and disunited, the German people's sense of *Volk* actually increased.[11] This is of profound significance: it illustrates how 'suffering' can strengthen individuals' attachment to their nation. Wilford states: '*Volk* was represented as a romantic concept that emphasised the wholeness of the national community.'[12] In the 1920s and 1930s, *Volk*, a notion closely associated with the writings of **Fichte**, became a central concept in Nazi discourse.

115

In France the same trend can be witnessed in the aftermath of the 1870–1 war against Prussia. The traumatic and humiliating French defeat was acutely symbolised by the Prussian annexation of Alsace and Lorraine. By the 1880s, French politics had changed out of all recognition. Individuals like **Boulanger** and **Barrès**, and movements like the *Ligue des Patriotes*, were subsumed by the idea of France gaining 'revenge' for her territorial loss. The spiritual, pseudo-religious side to this phenomenon was explicit. Barrès, for one, split his time between conventional political activity and starry-eyed graveyard pilgrimages. He was in awe of the men and women of France who had sacrificed themselves while fighting for their nation and felt it was his duty to pay homage to them:

> The bodies of young men of twenty and twenty-five are piled together under the stones of this captured country. Their lives would have had no meaning had one refused to look for it in the idea of the homeland. But now, today, they will live again .... We are the sum of a collective life that speaks in us. May the influence of our ancestors be permanent, the sons of the soil vital and upstanding, the nation one.[13]

It is in this context that we can see, despite the origins of the term itself, the existence of a powerful *Völkisch* tradition in countries other than Germany.

As has already been stated, the nation is not viewed by fascists as a 'living space', open, humane and welcoming. Rather, it is viewed as an exclusive 'club' for people of a certain birthright. This, in essence, is the 'ethnic' conception of the nation, a conception that stresses the destiny of a specific, 'chosen' people ('*the* People'). In all of this, the task of the state is to protect the nation and its specific make-up.[14] Griffin points to this in his account of the uniqueness of fascism:

> The idea that a 'nation' is an entity which can 'decay' and be 'regenerated' implies something diametrically opposed to what liberals understand by it. It connotes an organism with its own life-cycle, collective psyche, and communal destiny, embracing in principle the whole people ... and in practice all those who ethnically or culturally are 'natural' members of it, and are not contaminated by forces hostile to nationhood.[15]

Indeed, within fascist rhetoric there is, and always has been, a major emphasis on 'decline' and 'renaissance'. The two themes are intrinsically linked: liberals and others bring on national weakness, and it is the job of fascists to put a stop to crisis and chaos, and restore national strength.

South America offers us two graphic examples of regeneration-centred discourse. In the 1930s the *Movimiento Nacional Socialista de Chile* (MNS) talked constantly about the '**decadence**', 'moral anarchy' and 'disintegration' afflicting Chile, and thus the need for 'spiritual reconstruction'. In the same era the *Ação Integralista Brasileira* (AIB) in Brazil referred to the dawn of a 'Fourth Humanity' that would help resurrect a 'Dead Nation'. As if summing up the essence of fascist nationalism around the world, the Brazilian **Salgado** declared: 'The soul

116

of a people ... can only awaken through sacrifice and pain'. The title of his book, *Let's Wake up the Nation* (1935), was also indicative of his philosophy.[16]

In modern times, neo-fascists have used **AIDS** as a metaphor for national malaise. In the 1980s and 1990s, the ***Front National*** (FN) declared that France was suffering from a political form of '*SIDA*' and that there were four main symptoms: '*Socialisme*', '*Immigration*', '*Delinquence*' and '*Affairisme*' (Socialism, Immigration, Crime and Corruption).[17] Likewise, veteran British far-right activist, John **Tyndall**, coined the phrase 'spiritual AIDS' to describe what he perceived to be the decadence-induced illness from which Britain was suffering in the post-war period. This kind of rhetoric implies that far-right activists have a duty to act as 'midwives' in the rebirth of their nation and the creation of 'new fascist man'.[18]

At the heart of fascist discourse on the nation is an exaggerated sense of patriotism. Paul **Déroulède**, a key figure at the heart of French **'pre-fascism'**, has been described as a 'super-patriot'. It is no surprise, therefore, that the movement he founded was christened '*La Ligue des Patriotes*', nor that one of the most high-profile fascist groups in inter-war France was named *Jeunesses Patriotes*.

The case of Marshal **Pétain** is also interesting in this context. He became French leader in 1940 and was responsible for instigating the policy of **collaboration** with the Nazis. His patriotic credentials were unquestionable (he had acquired national fame as the 'Victor of Verdun' in 1916) but many contemporaries accused him of being a closet fascist and selling out to the Germans. France had been split in two, a German occupation force had stationed itself in the north, and Hitler was exploiting French labour for the good of the German war effort. Nevertheless, Pétain still asserted his patriotism and challenged others to follow his lead. On one **propaganda** poster, a picture of the Marshal was accompanied by the words: *Êtes-vous plus Français que lui?*[19]

Whether or not Pétain's patriotic claims had validity is a question that we can sidestep. The key point to note is that Pétain, a man branded as a 'fascist' and a 'traitor', maintained a powerful sense of his own patriotism. This helps us understand the driving force behind fascist ideology (if we are happy to equate *Pétainiste* politics with fascism, which some historians are happy to do).

More often than not, the patriotism of fascists and fascism evolves into nationalism. In Pétain's case, of course, he could claim to be *patriotic* (loyally serving and supporting his country, in his own individual way), but he had certainly betrayed his *nationalist* credentials by collaborating with the Nazis (though, naturally, he would not have seen it this way).

Full-blown, fascist nationalism has several key features. On the most basic of levels, fascists emphasise the integrity and *grandeur* of the nation. Hitler believed that Germany had the right to dominate Europe; Mussolini wished to create a 'new Roman empire'. Other fascisms attach high importance to elucidating, and perhaps embroidering, national greatness. Take, for example,

'**Hungarism**' in 1940s Hungary and **neo-fascism** in Portugal, which played on the Discoveries and the country's 'Atlantic calling'.[20]

In more theoretical terms, fascism harbours the belief that nationality is determined and defined by specific factors. The narrowest definitions stress **blood** and descent; slightly less strict definitions highlight **language** and culture. However, they all point to an ideology based on a 'closed' conception of nationalism, rather than an 'open' interpretation. This means that far-right movements have invariably stressed the importance of nationality law.

In more conceptual terms, fascism has important connections with '**integral nationalism**'. **Maurras** is the link. His movement, the *Action Française* (AF), has been described by Nolte as one of the 'three faces' of inter-war fascism. This is a contentious viewpoint. McClelland prefers to see Maurras as the high priest of integral nationalism, which basically amounted to a 'France first' philosophy.[21] Other ideas follow on; most notably, the need for a protectionist trade policy and a national economy based on a corporatist model.

It is in the light of this that Sheridan Allen has described fascist movements as 'hyper-nationalistic' and Kitchen has identified the 'rabid nationalism' at the heart of the ideology.[22] Furthermore, if we conceive of fascist nationalism as a 'religion', the nation, most certainly, is its god.

## XENOPHOBIA, RACISM AND RACIALISM

It is difficult to pinpoint at exactly what stage 'nationalism' evolves into 'xenophobia', but on the fascist right this is a common occurrence. In the 1980s and 1990s, **Le Pen in France** and **Schönhuber** in Germany were continually skating on thin ice. They talked constantly of their 'national pride' and always stressed the fact that they 'were not against foreigners'. Yet, however much they tried, they could not totally shake off accusations of xenophobia and **racism**.

In a sense this is inevitable because the exaggerated emphasis that fascists and neo-fascists place on the concept of nation and nationhood has a natural corollary: people and things 'outside' the nation are viewed not just as 'foreign' and 'of the other', but as 'threats'. So when Le Pen established 'France for the French!' as his party's main slogan, and when Schönhuber touted the idea of a 'rotation system' for foreign workers in Germany, the dominant perception was that the 'race' card was being played quite explicitly.[23]

Thus, there is, within far-right discourse, a stark insularity and a fundamental lack of tolerance. This xenophobia is evident in every fascist movement and every fascist regime. Just as Portuguese fascism has thrived on the 'Spanish threat', German neo-Nazism has picked on immigrant Turks and the FN in France has scapegoated North African Arabs. In the 1880s and 1890s Barrès stigmatised Germany and Germans. He also likened immigrant workers to parasites. Within a decade or so, Charles Maurras, founder and leader of the AF, had coined the term 'anti-France' to describe the 'four confederate states' that, in his view, were poised to destabilise the French nation: Jews, Protestants, socialists and stateless people.

This pseudo-conceptualisation is interesting on two counts. First, it has become a mantra of the radical right in France and still has currency today. In particular Pétain and Le Pen have both utilised the phrase 'anti-France' and exploited it for political capital. Second, it is significant that the 'anti-France' term does not pick out 'foreigners' as such but, rather, four groups of people whose national loyalty is 'questionable'. After all, Jews, Protestants, socialists and stateless people could all hold French nationality. Thus, 'anti-France' discourse is concerned not so much about 'territory', 'national borders' and 'foreigners' as about 'Fifth Column' threats to national integrity. In recent times, politicians on the French far right have added 'Americanisation' to their list of national perils. Mickey Mouse, Coca-Cola, the Internet: they are all seen as symbols of invasion. This indicates a deep paranoia about anti-national 'plots' and 'conspiracies'.

Commenting on the nature of Portuguese fascism, Pinto has written: 'Catholic dogmatism, anti-cosmopolitanism and nationalist isolationism against a "world in chaos": these central values of the Salazarist universe, were asserted against the "enemies within" and the pernicious influence of fashions from outside.'[24] These words could in fact have been written about any variant of fascism in any era.

Fundamental to much of fascist nationalism and xenophobia is a latent belief in 'superiority' and 'inequality'. This, usually, translates itself into a language of **imperialism** (*Lebensraum*, expansionism, **colonialism**, etc.). In extreme cases, it breeds, in quite explicit terms, racism (the belief that human abilities are the product of race), racialism (the conviction that some races are 'superior' to others) and anti-Semitism (a specific hostility to Jews). In Germany, of course, Nazi strictures about 'superior' Aryans and 'sub-human' Jews[25] led to the **Holocaust**, genocide as a policy of state. It would be accurate in fact to talk in terms of a German anti-Semitic tradition; Hayes argues that, back in the nineteenth century, the ideas of Fichte were not just nationalist, but racialist. Wilford traces anti-Semitism back to the notion of *Volk*. Naturally, the discourse of '**Holocaust Denial**' adds another layer of intensity to the phenomenon of Nazi anti-Semitism.[26]

Anti-Semitic attitudes have been prevalent on the far right for more than a century. They have infected South-Eastern Europe as much as any other region. In the late nineteenth century **Drumont** published *La France Juive* (1886), a vivid tract that stimulated a torrent of anti-Semitic activity; in the late twentieth century *Circulo Español de Amigos de Europa* (CEDADE) peddled a particularly vulgar brand of anti-Jewish hatred in Spain.[27] In between times, both countries have witnessed the birth of their own genuine and indigenous anti-Semitic traditions.

In other countries, racism has taken a different form. In Italy, for example, Mussolini and **D'Annunzio** boasted about their 'Latinness', and *Il Duce* only really engaged in anti-Semitic rhetoric when he felt that it would be politic to ape Hitler. Griffin sums things up neatly: 'Fascism is essentially racist, but not intrinsically anti-Semitic or genocidal, and it is nationalistic but not necessarily imperialistic.'[28]

Throughout fascist discourse on nation and race, 'blood' is utilised as a symbol. It signifies an ethnic 'people' and, thus, a 'nation'. As Fichte stated: 'Like cannot dissociate itself from like, nor can blood of the same mixture belie itself, even though it may have branched off from the main stream into smaller vessels.'[29] In Nazi vocabulary, blood is a barometer of 'purity' and 'impurity'. There are ordinary races and 'chosen' races.

## NATION, RACE AND THE ORIGINS OF FASCISM

'Nation' and 'race' are not just keynote ideas *within* fascism: the two terms can also help us understand the *emergence of* fascism as a governmental system and an ideology.

It is clear, first, that the rise of early fascist movements was linked, intrinsically, to national humiliation and frustration. We have already seen how the defeat of 1871 propelled France into a period of collective soul-searching, and how the demand for 'revenge' against the new Germany was fundamental to the leaders of the new right of the 1880s and 1890s, and the political philosophy associated with this phenomenon.

Likewise, in Italy and Germany after 1918, national frustrations of an intensely bitter kind acted as a stimulus to political protest and, ultimately, to the emergence of Mussolini and Hitler as central personalities. Italy may have emerged from the war on the winning side, but the rhetoric of the two leaders was not dissimilar: their respective nations had been let down and humiliated by **Versailles**; traditional liberalism had 'failed'; and a charismatic 'saviour' figure was urgently required.

The fact that both Mussolini and Hitler could appeal to a wide range of social groups was not unconnected to their hardcore nationalist stance. *Il Duce* had a particular attraction to Italian soldiers who had fought in the Great War and who, afterwards, had nothing to show for it. As Sternhell writes: 'In Italy D'Annunzio and Corradini were the best known spokesmen for a nationalist movement which reached far and deep, feeding on external defeat, as it had done in France in the aftermath of 1870.'[30]

In Germany the situation was comparable. As Sternhell argues:

> In the years preceding the First World War Europe experienced an extraordinary revival of nationalism. Well before 1914 *Völkisch* ideology, the set of ideas which are crucial to the understanding of Nazism, had found a widespread acceptance in society. As Professor George Mosse has pointed out, the Nazis found their greatest support among respectable and educated people. Their ideas were eminently respectable in Germany after the First World War, and indeed had been current among large segments of the population even before the war.[31]

At the level of ideas, fascism is deeply indebted to a range of nationalist thinkers and racial theorists. We have already referred to D'Annunzio and his influence on fascist ideas in Italy. In addition, we must acknowledge the impact of **Gobineau** and **Sorel** in France and **Rosenberg** in Germany. Needless to say, the intellectual influence of these individuals was profound and wide-ranging.

If one body of thought impacted upon fascism more than any other, and perhaps even heralded the emergence of racialist politics in the late nineteenth and early twentieth century, it was **Social Darwinism**. This notion, which placed great emphasis on the reality of 'struggle' and 'the **survival of the fittest**', was implicit in much of fascist doctrine. Hayes calls Social Darwinism 'a new and more powerful form of racialism' while Sternhell argues that it 'played a large part in the evolution of nationalism and the growth of modern racialism'.[32]

Finally, we should be aware of two other important points about fascist discourse on nation and race. First, fascist movements have a noticeable tendency to glorify the past; in particular, a 'Golden Age' in the history of their nation or civilisation. Of course, this does not negate the radical, revolutionary dimension to fascism, but it does cloud it. For Mussolini, nostalgia meant Ancient Rome; for Vichy it meant Ancient Gaul. In essence, this strategy is all about myth-making, in the true Sorelian sense. Second, we must qualify a point we made earlier. Granted, the nation and nationalism are intrinsic to fascism, but this does not preclude fascists and neo-fascists having other loyalties. Le Pen, a Breton, has emphasised the importance of regionalism to a 'healthy' nation and has argued that belief in regional identities is entirely compatible with belief in the nation. By contrast, Le Pen's 'brothers' in the Spanish National Front have talked in terms of 'unity' between the countries of South-Western Europe[33], again, something that is viewed as not inconsistent with nationalism.

It is also a fact that numerous far-right movements have glorified the concept of 'Europe'. Here, however, we must distinguish between the glorification of Europe as a continent and civilisation, and the use of Europe as a lever to bind like-minded fascist organisations together. Griffin weaves these two threads together:

> Fascism, though anti-internationalist in the sense of regarding national distinctiveness and identity as primordial values, is quite capable of generating its own form of universalism or internationalism by fostering a kindred spirit and bond with fascists in other countries engaged in an equivalent struggle for their own nation's palingenesis, often against common enemies .... In Europe this may well lead to a sense of fighting for a common European homeland on the basis of Europe's alleged cultural, historical, or even genetic unity in contrast to non-Christian, non-Indo-European/Aryan peoples .... Within such a Europe, national or ethnic identities would, according to the fascist blueprint, be strengthened, not diluted.[34]

In this context, Linz offers us the best summary. He says that fascism was 'hyper-nationalist, often pan-nationalist'.[35]

Concepts of nation and race are fundamental to any understanding of fascist nationalism. In turn we must conclude that <u>nationalism is fascism's main ingredient and conditions many aspects of fascist policy, especially diplomatic and economic</u>. Fascist nationalism can also evolve into ugly forms of racism. Hence the view of Hayes:

> Because of the particular forms racial theory took during the period of Nazi ascendancy on the continent of Europe, the campaigns for the systematic elimination of the Jews and the Slavs, the myth of race is perhaps the most widely known fascist theory.[36]

## EXTRACTS

## Document 1

*Nazis prepare the Holocaust: Wannsee Protocol, 20 January 1942*

The **Wannsee Conference** was a major meeting of Reich officials to discuss the 'final solution' to the Jewish problem, on the basis that routine persecution, random killing and mass expulsions were not sufficient to eliminate the Jews from German and European life. This document was used in the case against the Nazis at the Nuremberg Holocaust trials. (Note the expression 'dealt with accordingly' – a euphemism for killing.)

> Under proper guidance, in the course of the final solution the Jews are to be allocated for appropriate labor in the East. Able-bodied Jews, separated according to sex, will be taken in large work columns to these areas for work on roads, in the course of which action doubtless a large portion will be eliminated by natural causes. The possible final remnant will, since it will undoubtedly consist of the most resistant portion, have to be treated accordingly, because it is the product of natural selection and would, if released, act as the seed of a new Jewish revival (see the experience of history). In the course of the practical execution of the final solution, Europe will be combed through from west to east. Germany proper, including the Protectorate of Bohemia and Moravia, will have to be handled first due to the housing problem and additional social and political necessities. The evacuated Jews will first be sent, group by group, to so-called transit ghettos, from which they will be transported to the East . . . .
>     State Secretary Dr Bühler stated further that the solution to the Jewish question in the General Government is the responsibility of the Chief of the Security Police and the SD (Security Service) and that his efforts would be supported by the officials of the General Government. He had only one request, to solve the Jewish question in this area as quickly as possible. In conclusion the different types of possible solutions were discussed, during which discussion both Gauleiter Dr Meyer and State Secretary Dr Bühler took the position that certain preparatory activities for the final solution should be carried out immediately in the territories in question, in which process alarming the populace must be avoided.

> (Source: Wannsee Protocol, 20 January 1942; from US Government files. Reprinted at Eurodocs (Brigham Young University), April 1995. Available online at http://library.byu.edu/ rdh/eurodocs/germ/wanneng.html [accessed 16 August 2001])

## Document 2

*Incitement to genocide in Rwanda*

This is a description of overt incitement to ethnic killing in Rwanda during the civil war of the 1990s. It is based on a transcription of a broadcast from neighbouring Zaire, but Rwandan radio stations, especially Radio Milles Collines, were quite explicit in their advocacy of genocide.

> People must bring a machete, a spear, an arrow, a hoe, spades, rakes, nails, truncheons … barbed wire, stones … and the like, in order, dear listeners, to kill the Rwandan Tutsis …. They must attack them …. Wherever you see a Rwandan Tutsi, regard him as your enemy …. Those of you who live along the road, jump on the people with long noses, who are tall and slim and want to dominate us.
>
> (Source: M. Fachot, 'Counteracting hate radio', Radio Netherlands, Media Network Dossier (Revision 2). Available online at http://www.rnw.nl/realradio/dossiers/html [accessed 1 January 2001])

## Document 3

*A Hindu nationalist prayer to the motherland*

This prayer illustrates the use of religious and traditional symbolism as a means of mobilising and retaining support. It is easy to see that a myth of 'Mother India' is being used here to create an exclusive concept of nationhood. The extract is from the **Rashtriya Swayamsevak Sangh** (RSS), the most prominent far-right militia group in India.

### Bharat Mata Ki Jay

> Forever I bow to thee, O Loving motherland! O Motherland of us Hindus, Thou has brought me up in happiness. May my life, O great and blessed Holy land, be laid down in Thy cause. I bow to Thee, again and again.
>
> We, the children of the Hindu Nation, bow to Thee in reverence, O Almighty God. We have girded up our loins to carry on Thy work. Give us Thy holy blessings for its fulfilment. O Lord! Grant us such might as no power on earth can ever challenge, such purity of character as would command the respect of the whole world and such knowledge as would make easy the thorny path that we have voluntarily chosen.
>
> May we be inspired with the spirit of stern heroism, which is the sole and ultimate means of attaining the highest spiritual bliss with the greatest temporal prosperity. May intense and everlasting devotion to our Ideal ever inspire our hearts. May our victorious organised power of action, by Thy Grace, fully protect our dharma and lead this nation of ours to the highest pinnacle of glory.
>
> VICTORY TO MOTHER INDIA!
>
> (Source: RSS (Indian far-right) website. Available online at http://www.rss.org [accessed 20 August 2001])

## Document 4

*One Nation immigration policy*

This right-wing Australian party emphasises an 'Australia first' policy. Critics charge its policy toward immigrants is motivated by racial prejudice, especially toward Asians. One Nation denies that charge but their policy is very harsh and shows hints of the preferential approach favoured by most far-right parties. The following is a summary of the main points:

Abolition of the policy of multiculturalism.

Immigration levels based on zero nett gain – that is to essentially cap the population with the exception of the births/deaths ratio by replacing the 30,000 or so people per year who permanently leave Australia. The policy is non-discriminatory.

Skilled migration will consist of 20% of the programme and must be directly related to the needs, which cannot be addressed by existing Australian workers.

20% of the programme will be allocated to business migrants who will be carefully assessed as to the benefit they would bring to Australia.

Family reunion has been an important part of Australia's history and will continue but for dependant immediate family only.

The Citizenship oath will be strengthened to included a pledge of commitment and loyalty to Australia and its people above all others. Five years of permanent residence will be necessary before being eligible for citizenship.

Deportation of non-citizens for criminal offences that result in a gaol term. These offenders will be, by negotiated treaty, returned to their country of origin to serve their sentence – where necessary we will contribute to the cost of their gaoling in their own country. In most cases this will be cheaper than the same costs in Australia.

Genuine refugee numbers will be maintained at the current level, but there must be no expectation of automatic permanent residence. If possible, they will return to their own country when the unrest in their homeland has been resolved.

(Source: One Nation Immigration Policy Summary Sheet, 1998.
Available online at http://www.gwb.com.au/onenation/press/020798.html
[accessed 25 August, 2001])

## Document 5

*Translation of a property confiscation order*

This was typical of the type of ordinances issued by the Nazi authorities in Germany and in occupied Europe. Notice the insensitivity implied in the policy of informing the victim that their pleas for leniency will be ignored

The Military Commander
of Belgium and Northern France
Military Administration Chief

Group: XII Az: GA21n.

Concerning: an order about the termination of the property and possessions of the Jews in favour of the German Reich on April 22, 1942.

According to paragraph one and paragraph two of the ... order, your property will be confiscated by the German Reich. Through the administration and utilisation of the German Reich, the confiscated property will be in the commission of the Brussels Trusteeship Company SPRL, located on 47 Cantersteen Street in Brussels.

The confiscated possessions will be reported to the Military Commander of Belgium and Northern France, Military Administration Chief.

The enclosed form includes the registration which should be filled out in four copies and sent within eight days to:

The Registration Office for Jewish Possessions
47 Canterseen Street, Brussels.

Those who send an unlawful order to the German Reich that is not properly or correctly filled out and not punctually registered will be punished.

Should you protest the confiscation of your property, fill out a separate clause in two copies, and it will be added at the same time to your possession announcement. Later your protests will be disregarded.

For the Military Commander of Belgium and Northern France.
The Military Chief –
On behalf:
REINKE

(Source: The Holocaust Education Program Resource Guide, undated. Available online at http://www.holocaust-trc.org/wmp16.htm [accessed 19 August 2001])

# CIVIL SOCIETY

Work, Family, Country

(Slogan of the Vichy regime in France, 1940–4)

The concept of 'society', as used in social and political analysis, has generated its own share of controversy. The term refers to the wider setting for historical action beyond the formal institutions of **state** and politics. The term 'civil society' is now widely used to refer to the arenas for civic action and political activity outside the narrow framework of parliaments, bureaucracies and parties. Two important aspects of the wider social setting of fascism are covered elsewhere: its attitude to **race** has already been examined in 'Nation and Race', and its approach to class politics will be explored in 'The Economy'. Of the remaining players in the wider society, we will cover here the **family**, **gender** relations, youth and the elderly, and religious communities and institutions.

The attitude of fascist, as opposed to conservative, regimes to any or all of these social forces is shaped, first and foremost, by the aspiration to **totalitarianism**. A totalitarian society fuses the nation, the state and the ruling movement with key social institutions. Faced with pre-existing and powerful institutions, a would-be totalitarian regime faces a choice:

- to destroy them without replacement,
- to destroy them but then rebuild them in its own image, or
- to accommodate them as an awkward or partially convenient fact of life.

Many fascist regimes sought to do the second but had to settle for the third option. The first was not even on the table. Unlike mainstream rightist authoritarians, fascists wanted a model society, not just an empty **dictatorship**. Besides, institutions like the family could never be merely removed in one fell swoop.

The twin instruments of fascist social policy were mobilisaton and coercion. The construction of an artificial civil society was designed to link these social forces to the regime. However, totalitarian mobilisation cannot rely on persuasion or spontaneity. Consequently, we will need to take account of the other interface between regime and society, the instruments of state terror. However, first, we must examine the processes of mobilisation and social engineering, the key to understanding fascism's view of social relations and politics.

## FASCISM, THE FAMILY AND GENDER RELATIONS

In some respects, fascist thinking on the family merely reflected the social **conservatism** of the early twentieth century. In Catholic countries, for instance, it frequently echoed that of official Church doctrine. Marriage was the bedrock of a stable society. Within marriage, there was to be a functional division of labour, with women largely performing traditional roles and the men acting as soldiers and breadwinners. Abortion, divorce and homosexuality were frowned upon, since they were seen as incompatible with both the cultural and physical reproduction of this kind of society through marriage, childbirth and direct parental rearing of the young.

Fascist support for what feminists would characterise as a 'patriarchal' society was not solely a response to social conservatism, however. Griffin has argued that fascism drew an analogy between the courageous warrior in struggle and the struggle of the **nation**. The result was a **myth** by analogy, which glorified perceived male virtues:

> The nation, as the sum of all its fascistised individuals, must behave like a warrior-male. It must be disciplined, proud, courageous, well-equipped and trained, ready to fight, bent on conquest, and supplied with the human means to do this by the reproductive and caring qualities of woman.[1]

As in other areas, however, the fascists went beyond conventional conservatives in the pursuit of these goals. Homosexuals, for instance, were ultimately included among those sent to **concentration camps**.[2] Physical attacks, literary censorship and discrimination were encouraged. These policies intensified after the embarrassing revelation that Ernst **Röhm**, a *Sturm Abteilung* (SA) leader, was a leading homosexual activist before the curtailment of the SA in the '**Night of the Long Knives**'. The more orthodox SA members subsequently called for the death penalty as a punishment for homosexual practices, although this never became official regime policy. Despite their widespread maltreatment and the deaths of many as a result of appalling labour camp conditions, the policy did not match the scale or ruthlessness of the systematic strategy of genocide directed against the Jews.

For the rest of society, reproduction became a kind of national duty, especially for those fascists preoccupied with racial 'purity'. **Mussolini**'s campaign for Italian fertility was given the grandiose title of the '**Battle for Births**'. This programme was backed up with campaigns against prostitution, abortion and family planning, as well as state support for marriage, themes shared with traditional conservative movements. A state agency, the *Opera Nazionale di Maternita e Infanzia*, managed unmarried mothers.[3] In more recent times, Jean-Marie **Le Pen**'s *Front National* (FN) in France has used postcard images of white babies to encourage the maternal instinct among Frenchwomen, clearly suggesting that large numbers of French babies are preferable to a big influx of Arab or non-French immigrants. Far-right nationalists in general equate increasing the national population with enhancing the power and security of the nation itself.[4] In power, or in their bid for power, they commit the state to the promotion of fertility. Whereas traditionalists and social conservatives value maternity and delight in the birth of every child, for the far right, this becomes a quantifiable policy target, like an indicator of industrial productivity. Whereas the social conservative sees childbirth as good for society, the far right characterises it as a specific duty to the nation. The difference between far-right movements like the French FN and outright fascists lies in the latter's use of the full coercive power of the state to mobilise society for reproduction. Modern far-right parties are content to restrict themselves to vocal campaigns and socially conservative legislation.

Despite their relatively passive role in the far-right scheme of things, women can occasionally be used as role models or heroines. A classic case is the cult of Joan of Arc used by Le Pen. In a movement that often associates itself with the ultra-**Catholicism** of Archbishop **Lefebvre**'s Tridentine Church, this cult combines the iconography of Joan as war heroine with that of Joan the virgin defender of the Faith.[5]

The socialisation of women into a caring and supportive role for the warrior male was taken to a new level in Germany. Women were organised by public institutions like the *Frauenwerk* and the Women's Labour Service. They were drafted to provide social support to the poor or to small farmer communities, as well as general social work. This provided a substitute for a welfare state, and, indeed, support for the work of building a new Nazi society. There has been some debate over the extent to which this involvement in the Nazi project constituted victimisation and exploitation of women or whether it also implied a certain level of complicity with the regime.[6] Given the violent and totalitarian nature of the system, however, many women had little choice. The dilemma was similar to that faced by most citizens of the Reich who could not participate in active resistance. Pursuing everyday activities and surviving might have facilitated the normalisation of society under Nazi rules but the dangers of precipitous resistance were enormous.

## THE CULT OF YOUTH: FROM EDUCATION TO EUTHANASIA

The cultural reproduction of the nation and its national society is done through education and the mobilisation of youth. Reference has already been made to the cult of action among fascists (see 'The Evolution of Fascist Ideology'). Who better to represent the inevitability of the fascist future and the potential for speed and action than the young! Of course, this tactic was not confined to fascists: it was used by more moderate liberal nationalists in the nineteenth century (e.g. in the 'Young Italy' or 'Young Ireland' movements). The fascist mobilisation of youth, however, was more than a spontaneous appeal to the young for the purposes of a passing protest or electoral advantage. Fascist movements organised youth rallies and organisations, replete with pomp, drill and **pageantry**. Such activities 'got them young' and were designed to leave a lasting impression. To the adult world, the spectre of the nation's youth rallying to fascism would only confirm the inevitability of a fascist future. Once in power, the enthusiasm of youth was increasingly orchestrated as spontaneity gave way to regimentation: mobilisation blended with marshalling.

In Italy, the *Opera Nazionale Balilla* (ONB) served as an umbrella for youth and sports organisations tolerated by the regime. Those not affiliated to the ONB were harassed or banned. The management of youth activities by the ONB was extended to the sporting and leisure activities of the population as a whole through another Fascist Party body, the *Opera Nazionale Dopolavoro* (OND). The OND often used commandeered socialist sports centres or meeting halls. However, since it enabled many poor Italians to expand their horizons a little or to travel to the seaside, it was relatively popular.[7] By 1937, its importance to the process of social mobilisation was underlined by the decision to make it a state rather than a party institution. In Germany, the Hitler Youth educated teenage boys in military drill and Nazi ideology, as well as organising sports events. The parallel League of German Girls catered for those between fourteen and twenty-one years of age. They were trained to care for soldiers or peasant workers rather than to be soldiers themselves. Observers at the time noted the sparse attention paid to this organisation in contrast with its male counterpart.[8]

In their zeal to manipulate the young, the fascists came up against more traditional social institutions with a deep interest in the youth, especially the Catholic Church in Italy. As we will see below, this exposed the limits of the totalitarian project and revealed how far Mussolini had still to go to fascistise Italian society as a whole.

Other para-fascist movements had similar institutions for mobilising the young. However, in many cases, as for example among the Irish **Blueshirts**, youth activities were not taken very seriously. The fun element often predominated at the expense of **ideology** and many participants had only a vague idea of their true political purpose.

Yet, in the most seriously totalitarian regime, the cult of youth had a darker corollary: a dismissive and often cruel approach to those who did not meet the youthful ideal. Attitudes to the old were generally ambiguous in all of the core fascist movements. The older generation was a repository of tradition and conservatism that could be counted on to oppose **liberalism** and **socialism**. On the other hand, the cult of youth and action favoured the young. Once in power, the Nazis in particular worked toward the perfection of the 'Aryan race'. This ultimately led to the desire to weed out those who had genetically transmitted diseases, those suffering from mental illness and the physically unfit. Frailty became a mark of personal failure: the **survival of the fittest** became a literal programme for action, as well as an explanation for social development.[9] While **eugenics** is normally discussed in the context of race, it was also seen as a way of removing the 'unfit' from the population and encouraging a higher proportion of 'fit' persons. Of course, the social planning behind eugenics was also endorsed at various times between the 1930s and the 1970s by some feminists and social democrats on the left, especially in Scandinavia, where it was believed that forced sterilisation of 'the unfit' would prevent future pressure on the welfare state.[10] The climate of the first half of the twentieth century put a premium on macro-social engineering of all kinds at the expense of individual rights. Again, the Nazis took things a stage further by advocating the outright killing of the targeted groups. **Euthanasia** was actively employed against the old and the handicapped under the secret T4 Programme from as early as 1939. Whereas enforced sterilisation was a favoured topic of discussion in peacetime, the Nazis believed that wartime conditions would provide a better cover for a more widespread euthanasia initiative.[11]

## FASCISM AND RELIGION

Fascist and far-right movements had an ambivalent attitude to **religion** in general, and to organised religion in particular. The more traditionalist and less fascist or non-fascist among them genuinely shared much of the religious culture of the wider society. **Franco** and many of his supporters were devout Catholics. This was also true of the more conservative-minded elements in the **Vichy** regime. In Romania, Orthodox priests actively participated in the ceremonies of the **Legion of the Archangel Michael**. The defence of the Russian Orthodox Church against competitor churches, as well as against secular **modernity**, is still an important aspect of far-right Russian nationalism. The identification with a religious institution is easiest when it is one that is historically intrinsic to a given society, like the Greek or Russian Orthodox Churches. In these cases, religion is already partially nationalised, in the sense of 'rendered national' rather than 'taken over' by the state. Though the Italians would lay claim to it, the Catholic Church had a separate existence from the state and is largely transnational in scope. The Protestant Churches in Western Europe have a similar network of transnational connections going back to the Reformation. Fascist regimes had the challenge of capturing these elusive institutions for the nation or creating their own substitute for them.

In Spain, Franco portrayed himself as the 'Defender of the Faith' and was keen to have his regime legitimated by a conservative Church. Typical of this was his elaborate parade and ceremony devoted to the official dedication of Spain to the Eucharist in 1952.[12] Yet, even in a country where tradition was a key theme of regime ideology, there were tensions over the militancy of the ruling movement. In the late 1930s and the 1940s, for example, Cardinal Pedro Segura actively protested Franco's flirtation with the Nazis and the violence of the Falangists, and the latter's attempt to desecrate cathedrals with *Falange* graffiti.[13]

A similar tension existed between the Catholic Church and the Perónist regime in Argentina. Initially, Juan **Perón** saw the Church as an ally. It had influence over education and social policy. It also shared some of his corporatist views about overcoming class politics, as well as his anti-**Communism**. However, by the 1950s, the Church was more critical of Perón and especially of his restrictions on Christian Democrat parties. As in Italy, Church and state disagreed on the boundaries of autonomous Christian social action.[14]

On the other side of the equation, religious movements often gave tacit support to fascism or far-right movements, either to protect themselves from fascist violence or as a lesser of two evils in what they saw as an especially menacing century for religion. Religious conservatives shared the fascists' declared abhorrence of **materialism**, social disorder, sexual promiscuity and atheistic Communism, all of which appeared to flood Europe from every direction after the 1890s and the **Russian Revolution**. In the Spanish case, Francoist atrocities against the left during the Civil War were matched by the persecution and killing of clergy and nuns, as well as the closure and destruction of churches.[15] This had the effect of rallying traditional and rural Catholics to Franco for decades afterwards. However, that pattern was not followed everywhere: Basque Catholics largely opposed the regime.

Where traditional religious communities felt pressurised by competition from neighbouring religious and ethnic groups, they often rallied to fascism and the far right, which, in turn, sometimes incorporated those religious traditions into its own definition of the nation. This was true of **Tiso's** clerical fascism in pre-war Slovakia. It was even more critical to the character of the wartime Croatian Ustasha, headed by Ante **Pavelić**. The Ustasha wanted to purify Croatian society, not only of Jews and gypsies, but of Orthodox Serbs as well. Catholic religious purity was a driving force behind their brutality.

In the late twentieth century, Tridentine Catholics under Archbishop Lefebvre have given explicit endorsement to the French FN, including its anti-Islamic rhetoric. Under the influence of Integrist Catholicism, the FN has also sought to associate itself with mainstream Catholicism, using Catholic heroes and heroines (Clovis and Joan of Arc), religious ceremonies and a conservative policy programme on family issues.[16] However, there is a significant contradiction here. One of the centrepieces of mainstream Catholicism is loyalty to the Pope and the indivisibility of the Church. However conservative its views on family issues, the Holy See has been quite explicit in its renunciation of the Tridentine rebellion against Rome. Lefebvre's agenda looks like a procedural one (e.g. the use of the Tridentine Mass) but the form of his rebellion has implicit doctrinal consequences as well.[17] There is a further contradiction in Le Pen's interpretation of the Church position on **Islam**. The mainstream Church, while critical of violent fundamentalism, generally endorses a dialogue with Islam. Indeed, in key United Nations (UN) conferences on population and women's issues, the Vatican has frequently aligned itself with some Islamic states against socially liberal policies advocated by the UN majority.

A key impetus for a drift to the right in Catholic countries in the early part of the twentieth century was the rise of secularising socialist parties and their likely influence in government. This threatened the traditional primacy of the Church in social policy and education. There was a polarisation around education because both radical secularists and religious activists saw each other as an evil force preying on the young through indoctrination and therefore seizing control of the nation's destiny. This, of course, can be traced to the Reformation and to the conflicts over religion during the **French Revolution**. The secular–clerical cleavage affected much of Europe but was especially powerful in France's Third Republic. It was therefore inevitable that when movements of the far right and far left turned totalitarian in the twentieth century, they would take the struggle over education to new heights.

Church–state relationships in Italy were particularly complex. Because the Papacy originally constituted a state, as well as a bishopric, Mussolini's relationship with the Pope was as much a matter of diplomacy as of internal social policy. With all Catholics looking to Rome, every action would have global significance. Il Duce must have loved this opportunity to strut on the world stage, but these factors also constrained his behaviour. It must be remembered that the Italian state, of which Mussolini urged his people to be so proud, was established in a conflict with the Papacy over its own territories in central Italy. *Risorgimento* nationalists, especially the more irreligious among them, gloried in the notion of putting the Pope in his place. The association of the Italian state itself with rabid anti-clericalism undermined its legitimacy in the eyes of many conservative Catholics. Mussolini's latter-day nationalists wanted to appeal to Italian traditionalists, many of whom were likely to be loyal Catholics. Mussolini needed to assert Italian nationhood in a way that did not mobilise Catholic opinion against the state. This would require a *modus vivendi* with the Church. The Fascists made positive references to the role of Catholicism in Italian culture.[18] The accommodation culminated in the 1929 Lateran Treaty, by which the Church regained formal statehood in the Vatican.

The other problematic issue in Church–state relations was, as we have seen, the pastoral care of the young. Both the Church and the Fascists had youth organisations and they were often working at cross-purposes. Many Catholics were critical of the violence, brutality and corruption of the Fascist regime. In the countryside, some Church communities supported the co-operative movement. As tensions mounted, Fascist leaders called for tightening control over autonomous Church agencies that competed with those of the state, especially those in the youth sector. The Church position in schools was also questioned. However, both sides feared the consequences of a really intense showdown. Hard-line Fascists might actually move against the Church, provoking more violence and a Catholic backlash. For Mussolini, a confrontation could also dent his legitimacy. The two sides agreed on a formula by which the Church would be free to teach as it liked on spiritual matters, while its youth organisations would not dabble in politics. Church marriages would have the sanction of the state. Nonetheless, despite the accords at the top, conflict persisted at lower levels, as it was never easy to divorce the spiritual from the practical.

Mussolini's forced accommodation with the Church left its scars. Many Fascists found it troubling for a long time afterward. It meant that the Fascist state could not be fully totalitarian and any social revolution among the young would be incomplete. Catholic Action, a key Church umbrella for mobilising the young and the laity, would stand in glaring defiance as one of the few such independent organisations not fully subsumed into Fascist structures. Although the Church was forced to prevent former PPI personnel (inter-war Christian Democrats) from playing a role in Catholic Action, the ban on politicisation was difficult to enforce in practice.

As in other areas, Hitler went much further than Mussolini. He was more overtly hostile to organised religion and wanted to create a National-Socialist church (the German Christians) that would legitimate his policies and draw some Christians from other denominations. The 'German Christian Church' was supported by a National-Socialist Theological Seminary. Nazis propagated the idea that, whatever the nature of the afterlife, there could be no question of conflicts of loyalty between faith and the **Führer** in this life.[19] The effort was largely unsuccessful but it did serve to expose the totalitarian character of Nazism and the shallowness of its declared conservatism, with which it wooed centre-right **middle-class** Christians in the inter-war years. There were particularly sharp conflicts with religious groups whose value system directly challenged Nazi militarism. Christian pacifists, conscientious objectors and Jehovah Witnesses were harassed for refusing to commit themselves to the regime.

There is much debate over the role of Pope Pius XII in these developments, and especially over the Church's attitude to the worst crimes of fascism. The desire of the Church to reach a *modus vivendi* with fascism against the backdrop of repression and the **Holocaust** led some to denounce it as an agent of **collaboration**, or at least as morally compromised. Some say it could have done more to save Jews from deportation to the death camps.[20] Alternatively, it could be argued that the Church was concerned with maximising its own freedom of action in extremely dangerous circumstances. It did speak out against fascist crimes even though the Pope's own pronouncements were relatively muted. Still, Church figures throughout Europe played a key role in rescuing Jews and others from the certainty of labour camp death.

In addition to the conflicts and compromise with organised religion, fascist and far-right movements also compete with mainstream religion at the level of ideas. Fascism's anti-materialism (see 'The Evolution of Fascist Ideology') led many of its followers into a language, and even cults of, transcendence. The most extreme consequence of this was the tendency of a minority of fascists to dabble with the occult. That, of course, was not specific to fascism and cannot be seen as an important characteristic of the movement. On the other hand, fascist rituals and language frequently hinted at a mysticism echoing that of religious ceremonies in the mainstream churches. Romanian legionaries used ritual **blood** signatures and oaths that go back into the deeper traditions of the Balkans. In a notorious example, a pro-Fascist fashion magazine published in Milan in the 1930s showed a nativity scene in which the Biblical characters were visited by boys and girls wearing caps or shirts reflecting the colours and symbols of the Fascist youth movement.[21] A Fascist 'Decalogue' published in

1934 and again in 1938 had ten commandments stressing obedience and such principles as 'the *Duce* is always right'.[22]

Today, the Russian *Pamyat* movement compares the relationship between Church and state to that of body and soul.[23] The conspiracy against Russia, spearheaded by Jews and Freemasons, is also linked to demonic and anti-Christian forces. Indeed, *Pamyat* also encourages hostility to what it sees as foreign churches that compete with Russian Orthodoxy. On the other hand, there is some evidence that the Nazis dabbled in, or were influenced by, non-Christian and even occultist value systems.[24] This was encouraged by their interest in Aryanism. In one of the most bizarre aspects of fascist mysticism, Maximiani Portas, a woman of mixed European background, took the Hindu name Savitri Devi after becoming interested in Eastern religions and culture. She rejected the Judeo-Christian tradition and sought the spiritual, as well as the racial, roots of Aryanism. As a result, she became a focus of interest for both Nazis and Indian Hindu fundamentalists. Dubbed 'Hitler's priestess', she continued to support neo-Nazi groups after the war and they continued to extol her work.[25]

Such symbolism amounted to an effort to compete with established religions at a subliminal level. It could be interpreted either as Fascist endorsement of religion and tradition in general or as part of a more sinister totalitarian fascistisation of society, in which even the realm of individual faith would not go untouched and unexplored by the regime.


## MOBILISATION AND COERCION: A TWO-SIDED COIN

Education, **propaganda** and mass mobilisation were key instruments of regime power. The other side of the coin was the apparatus of state repression. In authoritarian regimes, and in Mussolini's Italy, this was relatively narrowly focused on political and trade union dissent. For these regimes, existing police and military institutions were often quite adequate, with some support from a limited secret police. As we approach a more thoroughly fascist system, on the other hand, the party's own terror apparatus becomes very important and the range of issues monitored by the secret police widens. Such party machinery is usually inherited from the paramilitary and street-fighting groups that facilitate fascists' rise to power through the intimidation of opponents. The relationship between these entities and state institutions is often quite tense, in part, because the paramilitaries often represent the radical and revolutionary end of fascism, while established security services are essentially more conservative and order-driven. In Germany, Hitler suppressed his revolutionary vanguard, the SA **Brownshirts**, on the 'Night of the Long Knives' (29 June 1934) by killing many of its top leaders and reining in the movement. In 1921, Mussolini fused his own Blackshirt militia with the Fascist Party. Franco acted against the fascist-style *Falange* **militia** to preserve the dominance of the military in his regime, essentially incorporating the movement into his regime but silencing its earlier radical message.

Even after such upheavals, party institutions continued to rival those of the state. The German secret police, the *Gestapo*, was taken under the wings of the core security organ of the Nazi Party, the *Schutzstaffel* (SS). The notion of a parallel mirror image of state institutions operating within a dominant party has been common in many forms of totalitarianism, including Soviet Communism. In some respects, however, the primacy of the leader in the core fascist regimes worked against a total fusion of party and state. Bracher, for instance, notes how Hitler left much of the army and the civil service intact and partially autonomous. The resulting competition among centres of power only heightened his role as the final arbiter of policy.[26] Yet, his contemptuous attitude to the army at critical points at the height of the **Second World War** emphasises the point that he ultimately wanted the subordination of state institutions, if not to the party, then at least to his own will.

On paper at least, the marshalling of youth, women and the management of religious groups was all part of a choreographed direction of society as a whole. While old social institutions would be crushed, there would not be a vacuum. Instead, their place would be taken by 'fascistised' or 'Nazified' counterparts or clones that would respond to the agenda of the leader. In practice, each regime was different and operated in a different societal context. Hitler was most ruthless in his drive at social engineering but even he was not entirely successful at replacing what his violence had vandalised. Mussolini was weaker still and had to paper over the cracks and compromises. The more authoritarian and less fascist regimes, like those in Lithuania or even Spain, did not aim at social transformation in the first place. They were content if independent institutions went their own way but simply refrained from open challenges to the authorities. For all these dictatorships, the complex dynamics of human society proved just as problematic as the turbulent global economy. Their attempts at macro-social engineering were as ineffective and their claims of social knowledge were exaggerated. What was really important was that they believed they could play God with both history and with human evolution That gave them the arrogance and ruthlessness to proceed regardless of the outcome.

## EXTRACTS

### Document 1

*Hitler on the 'feminine' character of nations*

These critical observations about German weakness and British propaganda reveal Hitler's dichotomous view of the sexes and a negative opinion of women, as well as a cynical view of public opinion.

The great majority of a nation is so feminine in its character and outlook that its thought and conduct are ruled by sentiment rather than by sober reasoning. This sentiment, however, is not complex, but simple and consistent. It is not highly differentiated, but has only the negative and positive notions of love and hatred, right and wrong, truth and falsehood. Its notions are never partly this and partly that. English propaganda especially understood this in a marvellous way and put what they understood into practice. They allowed no half-measures which might have given rise to some doubt.

(Source: A. Hitler, *Mein Kampf*, Chapter 6, reproduced at Stormfront.org
(far-right site). Available online at http://www.stormfront.org
[accessed 20 August 2001])

## Document 2

*Hitler on a woman's battle for the existence of her people*

Hitler's claim that a woman's life is a battle to reproduce for the nation echoes Mussolini's 'Battle for Births' campaign for large families. The analogy with military struggle also reflects the tendency among fascists to see combat as the essential metaphor for a wide range of social phenomena.

The sacrifices which the man makes in the struggle of his nation, the woman makes in the preservation of that nation in individual cases. What the man gives in courage on the battlefield, the woman gives in eternal self-sacrifice, in eternal pain and suffering. Every child that a woman brings into the world is a battle; a battle waged for the existence of her people ....

Whereas previously, the programmes of liberal, intellectualist women's movements contained many points, the programme of our National Socialist women's movement has, in reality, but one single point, and that point is the child, that tiny creature which must be born and grow strong and which alone gives meaning to the whole life-struggle.

(Source: A. Hitler, Speech to National Socialist Women's Organisation,
September 1934; reprinted in J. Noakes and G. Pridham (eds)
*Documents on Nazism, 1919–45*, London, Jonathan Cape, pp. 364–5)

## Document 3

*The Aryan female*

This poem by 'Grayson' illustrates a common theme in most far-right discourse: the function of women as bearers of a new generation of children of the chosen race. It appears on a current-active far-right site in the US.

The Aryan female how graceful she sings
Brings life to us and beauty she clings
She is the most needed, the most beautiful
Expands our race and does it so well

Without her we'd be in perilous strife
She gives birth and nurses our pure white life
So thank and love and think why you're here.

(Source: Stormfront.org (far-right site). Available online at
http://www.stormfront.org [accessed 20 August 2001])

## Document 4

*Initiation into Hitler Youth*

A formulaic speech by the local Hitler Youth leader to be made on the
admission of new members of the official youth organisations emphasises the
desire to control young people and to organise society around values of
discipline and absolute loyalty to the Führer.

Dear Boy!/Dear Girl!

Today, for the first time, you swear allegiance to the *Führer*, which will bind you
to him for all time.

And every one of you, my young comrades, enters at this moment into the
community of all German boys and girls. With your vow and your commitment,
you now become bearers of the German spirit and German honour. Every one,
every single one, now becomes the foundation for an eternal Reich of all Germans ....

And the *Führer* demands of you and of us all that we train ourselves to a life of
service and duty, loyalty and comradeship. You, ten-year-old cub, and you, lass,
are not too young nor too small to practice obedience and discipline, to integrate
yourself into the community and show yourself to be a comrade. Like you,
millions of young Germans are today swearing allegiance to the *Führer* and it is
a proud picture of unity, which German youth today presents to the whole world.
So today, you make a vow to your *Führer* and here, before your parents, the Party
and your comrades, we now receive you into a great community of loyalty. Your
motto will always be, '*Führer*, command: we follow!' Now say after me: 'I promise
always to do my duty in the Hitler Youth in love and loyalty to the *Führer* and to
our flag'.

(Source: 'Ceremony of admission into the cubs of the *Deutsches Jüngvölk*',
document dated 1940, reprinted in J. Noakes and G. Pridham (eds),
*Documents on Nazism, 1919–45*, London, Jonathan Cape, p. 357)

## Document 5

*The political mission of German education*

This was set out in a speech by the Reich Interior Minister, Wilhelm **Frick**, and
it reflects the totalitarian character of the Nazi state. The Nazis wanted to turn
the education system into a form of high-powered propaganda machine that
would create model Nazi citizens.

137

Liberal notions of education have totally destroyed both the *raison d'être* of education and our educational institutions in line with these notions. Our schools have schooled rather than nurtured. They have failed to develop the strengths of the pupils for the benefit of nation and state, but rather have communicated knowledge for the benefit of the individual. They have not helped to shape German people, rooted in the nation and duty-bound to the state, but rather free individuals. The national revolution lays down a new law for German schools and their educational duties.

(Source: Speech by Interior Minister, Wilhelm Frick, on 9 May 1935; reprinted in M. Burleigh and W. Wippermann, *The Racial State: Germany, 1933–1945*, Cambridge, Cambridge University Press, 1991, pp. 232–3)

# THE ECONOMY

There will be no room in Britain for those who do not accept the principle, 'All for the State and the State for All'.
(Oswald Mosley, quoted in R. Wilford, 'Fascism', in R. Eccleshall, V. Geoghegan, R. Jay and R. Wilford, *Political Ideologies*, London, Hutchinson, 1986, pp. 237–8)

It is not an easy task to comprehend, or explain, the essence of fascist economics. In certain aspects and phases fascism is, and was, both pro-worker and anti-worker; both pro-capitalist and anti-capitalist; and also left-wing, centrist and right-wing in matters of political economy. There is therefore much ambiguity in the way that fascist regimes in power, and fascist movements that never achieved power, approached economic matters. Woolf suggests that, in reality, fascist economics amounted more to 'a series of improvisations' than to a 'system'. He raises the possibility that the economic actions of any single fascist regime (such as in Italy or Spain) could have been 'so contradictory as to make it difficult to speak of a coherent and consistent economic policy in one country, let alone of a more general system'. Furthermore, Childs has argued that Nazism was, among other things, both anti-Marxist and anti-capitalist.[1] Still, it is possible to identify a number of undercurrents to fascist economics and to locate a range of other significant themes.

## RECURRING MOTIFS

First of all, it would be true to say that economic 'calamity' actually heralded the arrival of fascism in power in several countries.[2] This in itself is of significance. In Italy and Germany there is a clear relationship between post-First World War economic malaise and the rise of fascist ideas. It is possible to argue that individuals like **Mussolini** and **Hitler** actually thrived on, and exploited for political gain, the economic problems their countries experienced in the period after 1918. Hitler declared in 1921:

At the end of the World War, Germany was burdened with her own debt of some 7 or 8 milliards of marks .... Therefore, in the economic sphere, November 1918 was in truth no achievement, but it was the beginning of our collapse.

Hitler and Mussolini both placed particular emphasis on the economic dimension to **Versailles** and, in addition, Hitler took advantage of the 1929 Crash and the Depression to stake a claim for power. Renton argues that the same historical pattern can be detected in both Germany and Italy: 'Economic backwardness and war led to revolution and then counter-revolution.'[3]

Similarly, in the post-war world, movements labelled as 'neo-fascist', like the *Front National* (FN) in France and various far-right parties in Germany, have exploited economic conditions for political advantage. They have highlighted the damaging effects of depression and dependency on immigrant labour.[4]

Indeed, as Chiarini has argued, post-war groups have thrived on what they have seen as the failure of the free-enterprise economy.[5] In the same way, earlier in the century fascist regimes and fascist movements around Europe had railed against free trade, 'liberal capitalism' and the 'liberal–bourgeois order'. Even the new post-Communist parties of the far right in Eastern Europe, especially in Russia, have exploited the growing pains of transition economies to their advantage. They have attacked the alleged oligarchies and the new business élites, and linked them to what they characterise as Western and Jewish 'parasitic **capitalism**'. The rise in **unemployment** and economic dislocation following the collapse of **Communism** and the mismanagement of early post-Communist capitalism has left many people disillusioned. Former Communist apparatchiks, ex-factory managers and corrupt politicians have often stripped the assets of privatised firms and engaged in the worst excesses of crony capitalism, as if straight out of a Marxist song sheet. However, since **socialism** itself is discredited as an alternative, many frustrated and impoverished East Europeans, like Germans in the inter-war years, are willing to turn to the eccentric fringe with its promises of a native and 'patriotic' way out of the morass.

It is perhaps strange then that, in power, Mussolini and Hitler, and other fascist leaders, never put huge stress on the economy or on a distinctive economic policy. Obviously, every fascist regime had its economic programme and executed a range of economic policies. Mussolini's government also tended to hype up its economic campaigns; hence **'The Battle for Grain'**, 'The Battle for the Lira', etc. However, the truth is that other areas of government tended to excite fascist leaders more.

So, in contrast with, say, their foreign policy, fascists' management of the economy was often low-profile and quite flexible. Instead of a coherent fascist economic philosophy, what emerged amounted to a pragmatic mix of ideas: some revolutionary, some conservative; some associated with the left, some associated with the right; some that hint at a strong commitment to **modernisation** and some that suggest a strong belief in ecology and **ruralism**, or what Whittam calls 'ruralisation'.[6] Not surprisingly then, it is also a fact that fascist movements have recruited from left and right of the political spectrum.

One of the most bizarre juxtapositions of policy came at **Vichy**, home to the French collaborationist regime during the **Second World War**. Marshal **Pétain**, the Vichy leader, illustrated his **traditionalism** and nostalgia for 'Golden Age' France by launching a 'back to the land' policy and emphasising the nation's agricultural roots; at the same time, however, his regime was also at the forefront of a technocratic and planning revolution that had a significant legacy for post-war governments. Thus, no doubt for political reasons, Vichy economic policy was a strange cocktail. As regards fascism's support base,

Milward argues that in the inter-war period it was a combination of the urban and the rural. Hitler, we must recall, had a huge following in the countryside, and his policy emphases duly reflected this.[7]

Fascism is also associated with economic modernisation, with many fascists arguing that the **nation**, and people's **patriotism**, could be invigorated by economic dynamism. Left-wing critics of fascism certainly saw things this way and declared that economic modernisation and monopoly capitalism led invariably to war. Lenin famously stated that fascism was synonymous with the 'final stage' of **imperialism** and monopoly capitalism, and in 1935 the **Third International** reiterated this thesis.

Woolf argues that fascist economies 'are certainly capitalist economies',[8] but we must take Lenin's exaggerated polemical statements with a pinch of salt. In practice, what we see is a system that emerges in different phases and presents itself in different guises. Eatwell has written: 'Economic policy in fascist regimes, therefore, tends to be seen as something which owed much to circumstance.'[9]

At root, the political economy of fascism – as far as there is such a thing – is based around two central concepts: nation and state. The main belief is that the state is the instrument of the nation, and has a duty to protect it. As Mussolini wrote in 1932: 'If the nineteenth century was a century of individualism, it may be expected that this will be the century of collectivism and hence the century of the State.'

This core assumption gives rise to other beliefs. First, it is the role of the state, by means of a giant bureaucratic machine, to control, direct and 'plan' the nation's economy. This does not imply ownership, as in the Communist model, but does imply intervention in a broad sense. Thus, there was a sizeable gulf between the fascist conception of '**state capitalism**' and the traditional liberal–capitalist belief in the free market and free trade. Fascist officials held that state intervention in the economy speeded up economic development, whatever 'level' the economy was at to begin with. As such, Mussolini's regime imposed protective tariffs, regulated credit and co-ordinated a structured wages and prices policy. It also launched a series of Four Year Plans. However, as Kitchen writes:

> It would be quite mistaken to believe that this state intervention resulted in either nationalisation or 'state capitalism' ... 99 per cent of the coal, 80 per cent of iron, 65 per cent of steel and 36.8 per cent of transport was controlled by the state, but the private form of these industries was maintained.[10]

State involvement in the economy, and the belief in large units of production, had another significant consequence: at times it became difficult for fascist governments to protect the '**small man**', except in the countryside.

Whatever the level of state intervention, it could be argued quite forcefully that belief in private property was central to fascist ideology. As Eatwell states:

> The sympathetic reference to socialism did not mean that fascists accepted the abolition of private property. This was seen as a law of nature. The point was

more to mould in a suitable way the value system and institutional structure which accompanied private property.[11]

Krejčí contends that fascist regimes demanded political rather than economic power and were quite happy to let private ownership exist alongside state planning.[12] In reality both systems tended to benefit the same socio-economic groups; namely, those on the right and in business. The belief in control also leads, at times, to calls for **protectionism**, and protective import duties in particular. In the modern era, movements like the **British National Party** (BNP) and FN have made economic nationalism a central pillar of their programmes. And as a result, they have both indicated their hostility to the European Union (EU) and the policy of recruiting immigrant workers.

And it is a short step from economic protectionism to **autarchy**, a policy aimed at national self-sufficiency and insulation in the economic sphere. This brand of economic nationalism (or economic isolationism) is a defining feature of fascism in power. Hayes has traced the history of autarchy back to the middle of the nineteenth-century.[13] It is often associated with periods of diplomatic and military tension, but he adds that we should not assume that autarchy was always advanced in an 'aggressive' form: it could have a defensive rationale as well. Autarchy also featured strongly in fascist **propaganda** campaigns, with slogans such as 'HELP US DEFEND YOU!', 'GERMAN JOBS FOR GERMAN WORKERS!', 'BUY ITALIAN GOODS!' On the whole though, as Milward argues, it is clear that Italy under Mussolini was slightly more open to the outside world than Germany was; an indication perhaps that, as in many other spheres, the Italian regime was less efficient and less disciplined than the Nazis.[14]

Fascist economic policy also shifted over time. Kitchen argues that in Italy there was, initially, some tension between 'Manchester liberalism' and autarchy.[15] In due course, however, autarchy became a fundamental principle of the regime, a particularly radical and utopian goal, for in the modern interdependent world economy, isolationism and economic self-sufficiency were never going to be attainable in practice.

It is also clear that the **anti-Semitism** inherent in fascism has had, and can have, a significant economic rationale. In much of fascist discourse 'parasitic' Jews are strongly associated with 'exploitation' and 'money-making'. Most notoriously, the Nazi regime sought to identify, and then scapegoat, the Jewish population. In Mussolini's Italy, no Jew was allowed 'to own a large business or a large estate', and in Britain and Spain, inter-war fascist activists also railed against the 'financial masterdom' and 'parasitic' behaviour of the Jewish community.

Not unrelated to this is the tendency of fascist governments to detect potent 'anti-regime' conspiracies. For most of the time, these 'conspiracies' are more imaginary than real, the product of deep paranoia, but they do help us to understand the essence of the nation–state relationship. For example, many fascist governments pinpointed the Jews as a threat to the nation because of their alleged financial 'crimes' and their apparent hegemony within the capitalist system; the regimes in question then utilised the full force of the state to victimise the Jewish community in a pre-planned and organised fashion.

## CORPORATISM: A CLAIM TO INNOVATION?

However, it is with the fascist concept of **corporatism** that the role of the state, in the economic context, becomes abundantly clear. As a concept, corporatism has a variety of origins and applications, and is closely linked to that of **syndicalism**. There are also many forms of corporatism but in general terms it refers to the collective management of the economy by employers, workers' representatives and state officials using formal mechanisms at national level. This need not take a coercive or anti-worker form. Many Catholic and centrist parties in inter-war Europe saw collective arrangements and the formal representation of interest groups in the political system as a means of softening the **violence** of class conflict, which was a feature of politics at that time. The 1937 Irish constitution, influenced by corporatist and Catholic social doctrine, provided for the formal representation of interest groups organised into 'panels' in the Senate. Collective bargaining and consensus economic management in its non-authoritarian, or 'neo-corporatist', form re-emerged as a strong current in policies of the post-war Christian Democrat parties. The Church supported these trends throughout the inter-war period and beyond. It based its teaching on the Papal utterances of the late nineteenth century, as well as the 1931 encyclical, *Quadragessimo Anno*. In addition to its abhorrence of class warfare, the Vatican no doubt saw corporatism and **neo-corporatism** as antidotes to Communism.

Therefore, the ideas that went to make fascist-style corporatism were around for some time before. However, the way that the corporate ideal was implemented robbed it of its spontaneity. Just as plebiscites and elections became exercises in rubber-stamping, the representatives of labour and industry were forced into corporations, as the Fascists saw it, 'in the public interest'. The resulting 'consensus' was a fake or a forced one, with the workers' representatives losing more autonomy than the employers. As Hayes makes plain: 'Fascism, through corporativism, sought to concentrate all power and direction in the hands of the state .... [It] became a doctrine of absolutism, the repression of dissent, the abolition of bargaining power and of aggressive economic expansion.'[16] So, essentially, corporatism was about control and is fundamental to understanding how authoritarian right-wing governments in Italy, Germany, Spain and France managed economic life, and how inter-war fascist movements like the **British Union of Fascists** (BUF) and the **Blueshirts** in Ireland wished to control economic life. Some regimes adhered to a 'pure' corporatist ideology; others like **Salazar**'s in Portugal 'tempered' the corporate system with a strong dose of 'Social Catholicism'. Woolf is in no doubt that corporatism 'was utilised in one manner or another by all the fascist regimes'.[17]

The philosophy that lies behind the corporate state is clear: the nation needs to be strong and united; class conflict is bad for a country and its ruling élite; therefore, everything must be done to foster class collaboration and establish a stable community. In essence, it is an economic idea with significant ramifications in both the political and social spheres. Thus, in putting corporatism into practice, and in bringing employers and employees together to discuss matters of mutual concern, fascist governments tried to foster real national unity. The centrality of corporatism to fascist economic thinking is unquestionable, and in many ways the associated emphases on 'consensus' and 'social harmony' add up to a powerful rebuke to Marxists, who argue for the inevitability of the class struggle. In 1921 Hitler declared: 'There are no such things as classes', and in 1932 Mussolini stated that in a variety of ways fascism was the antithesis of **Marxism**, not least in its attitude to class relationships. Nevertheless it is a fact that the corporatist idea was far more engrained in Italy than in Germany, probably because, as Eatwell notes, Mussolini was more statist in his thinking than Hitler, but also because of the influence of Catholic social teaching. Overall, however, Whittam is convinced that in Italy the fascist regime came to govern in the interests of the *Confindustria*, a business organisation that was always on the lookout for friends in high places.[18]

## INDUSTRIALISTS AND WORKERS

In Italy the Fascists' alignment with the top industrialists, evident especially in the 1930s, was particularly interesting because during the period 1919–22, when Mussolini and his new political party were fighting to gain power, they made numerous pledges in support of the **working class**. In Germany and Japan as well, 'early' fascist activity was marked by left-wing declarations (in favour of nationalisation, for example). This appeal to the masses is not unusual; rather it is the very trademark of fascism. However, this populism is fundamentally pragmatic – and based on acquiring the necessary political support. As Eatwell has argued: 'Some reactionaries sought to turn the clock back, but the most perceptive right-wing politicians and theorists realised that the task was more how to attract the newly, or about to be, enfranchised working classes.'[19]

This is fine, but as Woolf argues: 'The corollary to this anti-capitalism was not undue affection for the industrial worker (indeed Kita **Ikki** expressed the widespread Japanese contempt for the urban proletariat), but strong concern for the small man, the petty bourgeois and peasant landholder.'[20] Even though fascism took on board many left-wing ideas, it remained, in fundamental terms, both anti-socialist and anti-Communist. It also believed in class collaboration rather than class conflict, so there was never any need for fascism to idolise and exalt the working class in the way that socialism and Communism did.

Pierre **Poujade**'s *Union de Défense des Commerçants et Artisans* (UDCA), which came and went in 1950s France, was a good example of a far-right movement that incarnated strong anti-capitalist attitudes, but idolised the 'small man' rather than the 'worker'. Poujade was a small-town stationer and founded the UDCA to represent the nation's shopkeepers. His movement was as much a lobby group as a political party, and sought to give a voice to all those people threatened by post-war French modernisation (it was hostile, in particular, to the move towards supermarkets and hypermarkets). Poujade was demonised in the French press as a would-be Hitler and depicted as a threat to democracy. He was no socialist, but he did incarnate an extremely significant brand of extreme-right politics that viewed monopoly capitalism as the main enemy.

In a different but related way, Nazism appealed to the 'small men' in German society: small businessmen, artisans and the self-employed. Hitler's attitude to these people was one of admiration: they had shown themselves to be hard working and upwardly mobile. It is in this sense that fascism is viewed as having a significant constituency among what Marxian sociologists term the 'petty bourgeoisie'.

It is also relevant here to refer to the writings of Turner. He has examined the relationship between fascism and modernisation, and concluded that both German and Italian variants of fascism exhibited both modernist and anti-modernist tendencies. He is in no doubt that both Hitler and Mussolini oversaw impressive industrial achievements, but he also detects an anti-modernist flavour to much of their rhetoric. He cites, for example, Nazism's attachment to 'folk culture' and 'simple agrarian life', and its belief that **Lebensraum** would give Germany access to 'arable soil in Eastern Europe'; he also refers to Mussolini's desire to 'ruralise' Italy. His general point is that fascism, in all its guises, does not necessarily equate, pure and simply, to a belief in modernisation; in fact, he argues, the contrary is just as likely to be true.[21]

In the years immediately after 1918, Hitler and Mussolini, in their 'socialist' phases, put a lot of emphasis on capitalism's inadequacies. Hitler's colleagues, **Feder** and the **Strasser** brothers, also railed against 'finance capital', 'anonymous financial powers' and 'today's capitalist economic system'. However, it would not be accepting the Orthodox Marxist interpretation of fascism uncritically to say that most fascist regimes fall under the spell of big business eventually. So, in turn, fascism can be both anti-capitalist and pro-capitalist. Schweitzer identifies this characteristic, and argues that this is a feature of **'partial fascism'**. This, for him, is a definite stage in fascism's development, when it still harbours grievances against both socialism and capitalism. He goes on to argue that **'total fascism'**, the final stage in the evolution of fascism, equates to the emergence of fascist capitalism.[22]

It is, therefore, easy to understand those people on the left who argue that fascism, like imperialism, is merely capitalism in disguise or in an overgrown form. Trotsky, for instance, talked about fascism as 'a plebeian movement in origin, directed and financed by big capitalist powers'. But he went on to characterise fascism as a product of 'the petty bourgeoisie, the slum proletariat, and even to a certain extent ... the proletarian masses'; he argued that the Nazi movement in Germany employed 'a great deal of Socialist demagogy'. So, in one sense, Trotsky was determined to connect fascism with capitalism, but in another sense, even he was aware that both German and Italian 'brands' possess not insignificant 'plebeian', 'socialist' characteristics.[23]

However, despite fascist officials' claims to the contrary, appeals to the workers have always been pretty half-hearted; in the end, fascist regimes have found it much easier to cosy up to vested interests and the traditional authorities. And conversely, it has often been in the interest of industrialists to support fascist regimes financially (good examples of this come in Italy and Germany). Kitchen, a neo-Marxist, states:

> The fascists destroyed the labour movement, actively helped the further exploitation of labour, pursued an aggressive trading policy, worked for autarchy, gave the order for massive re-armament, and finally unleashed a world war. All this enabled heavy industry to achieve maximum production at minimum cost, and thus ensured vast profits .... Fascism and big business thus had essentially identical interests. The fascists consolidated and increased their power. Industry extracted additional profits. One hand washed the other.[24]

In a sense, autarchy and corporatism can be viewed as artificial and coercive, nothing more than state-sponsored capitalism. This is why those on the left have demonised fascism to such a degree. The corporate idea has also lasted into the twenty-first century, with both the BNP and the FN still loyal to the concept (although the latter, it should be pointed out, maintains an eclectic and inconsistent economic policy that is, simultaneously, both free-market and corporatist).[25] Fascist regimes, and movements, may believe passionately in the idea of class collaboration rather than class conflict but we must conclude that, overall, corporatism has always looked better on paper than in practice.


## 'THE THIRD WAY'

It would not be too controversial to argue that, together, the emphases on nation, state, autarchy and corporatism do add up to a distinct economic philosophy, however vague. Many fascist leaders have concluded that fascist regimes tried to steer a '**Third Way**' in economic policy. In Spain José Antonio **Primo de Rivera** stated in 1935: 'We will impose a new order of things .... Neither right, nor left! Neither communism nor capitalism! A national regime. The National Syndicalist regime! Long live Spain!'

On reflection, historians have also identified a unique economic philosophy. Eatwell states: 'The goal was to create what was sometimes referred to as a "third way" (neither socialism nor capitalism), a term first popularised by German "conservative revolutionaries" after 1918. In particular, the emphasis was on making man less money-centred, more co-operative.'[26] In the post-1945 period neo-fascist groups have also shown loyalty to this idea. Chiarini has studied the ***Movimento Sociale Italiano*** (MSI) in Italy and has concluded that:

146

The rejection of the guiding role which the two victorious super-powers had taken upon themselves offered [the MSI] the chance to argue in favour of an unlikely 'third way', a way that was allegedly different from, and superior to, both capitalism and Communism, because it was capable of avoiding their shortcomings: extreme individualism in one case, and out-and-out State control in the other.[27]

This is a sound point. However, for Whittam, planning rather than private enterprise has been central to fascist economic thinking; likewise for Hayes, who argues that 'state direction and the need for living space' were the prime characteristics of inter-war fascist economies.[28] And even if fascist regimes did steer the 'Third Way' they claimed to, they were certainly not immunised from the normal economic cycle, as they claimed to be. Italy and Germany both suffered enormously in the Depression of the early 1930s.

Perhaps the last word on the economy should be left to Gramsci, who said that fascist economic policy aimed to nationalise losses, but not profits, a neat summary of its essence and uniqueness.[29] This, therefore, is one conclusion. Four others would also seem to be apparent. First, it is clear that fascist economies are often subordinated to the demands of war, or preparing for war. Likewise, it is obvious that the level of state control required for the policies of autarchy and corporatism to work effectively means that, by necessity, fascist governments have invariably evolved into totalitarian structures. Second, it would probably be accurate to point out that, on the whole, fascist governments have a poor economic record, and that several fascist economies collapsed under the strain of world war.

Third, in the post-war era, with a totally new economic context, fascist and neo-fascist movements have not broken totally with 'inter-war' economic policies, though refinements have been made to take account of changed circumstances. On the other hand, we must also acknowledge the fact that many post-war movements on the extreme right have embraced libertarian or 'new right' economics in an attempt to reinvent themselves and to compete with mainstream conservative parties. Fourth, fascism was, and still is, a broad church. As Hayes says, the economic policies pursued by Hitler and Mussolini were 'a compound of pragmatism and mysticism'. There was always the possibility too that the mix of positions and attitudes could cause problems. Milward has commented:

Fascist parties ... inherited a revolutionary syndicalist anti-capitalist ideology and a small segment of 'working-class' support. On all this was superimposed the attempt by the business community to harness fascism to its own interests. What economic policies could possibly keep such an alliance together?[30]

So, as **Mosley** in Britain and Juan **Perón** in Argentina both indicated, fascism combined a 'sensible' economic outlook with a highly spiritual vision of the world.[31]

**EXTRACTS**

**Document 1**

*Economic nationalism*

This extract does not emanate from anyone on the far right but from a social scientist. However, the summary of economic nationalism captures the essence of mercantilist economic policy. When that policy is used for aggressive state ends, we have what Robert Gilpin termed 'malevolent mercantilism', a term he specifically applied to Nazi Germany's economic exploitation of Eastern Europe.

> I believe that practically all mercantilists, whatever the period, country, or status of the particular individual, would have subscribed to all of the following propositions:
> Wealth is an absolutely essential means to power, whether for security or for aggression.
> Power is essential ... as a means to the acquisition or retention of wealth.
> Wealth and power are each proper ultimate ends of national policy.
> There is long-run harmony between these ends, although in particular circumstances it may be necessary for a time to make economic sacrifices in the interest of military security and therefore also of long-run prosperity.

> (Source: J. Viner, quoted in R. Gilpin, *The Political Economy of International Relations*, Oxford, Princeton University Press, 1987, p. 32)

**Document 2**

*Alfredo Rocco: report on the Corporations Bill*

This is a strong defence of the corporatist system by one of its leading proponents. Note how the Fascists equated any tendency for autonomy among social or economic institutions with selfishness and greed. In practice, however, employers had more autonomy than workers in the actual operation of the corporations.

> The modern corporation is thus very different from the medieval corporation or guild. The latter was indeed a completely self-governing body of producers but it regulated production only in their own selfish interests. The guild existed outside the state and sometimes in opposition to it, and it was natural that, being thus enclosed in the narrow circle of its own interests, it ended by stifling productive activity and arousing the hatred of the mass of consumers .... The Fascist corporation, on the contrary, regulates production through the producers, not only in their interest but primarily in the interests of all concerned, under the effective guidance of the state. The modern corporation is thus not organised outside but within the state, as a state body.

> (Source: J. Whittam, *Fascist Italy*, Manchester, Manchester University Press, 1995, pp. 158–9)

## Document 3

*BNP economic policies*

The policy positions of the BNP in the 1990s reflected the traditional concerns of protectionists and economic nationalists but paid less attention to corporatism than did other far-right parties. They suggest that, rather than allowing state policy to be dictated by economics, the BNP would prefer economic policy to be driven by state interests and nationalist ideology.

> British ownership and control of British industry and resources.
> Protection of British industry by the selective exclusion of foreign manufactured goods from the British market.
> An end to the financial swindle that causes inflation and slump, and its replacement by a sane and fair financial system that will give the people the purchasing power to buy the goods they produce.
> The subordination of the power of the City to the power of government, and harnessing of the City to the needs of British industry.
> The regeneration of British farming, with the object of achieving the maximum possible self-sufficiency in food production.
> An end to overseas aid and the allocation of the money saved to the financing of repatriation and greater help for the needy at home.

> (Source: 'What we stand for', *British Nationalist* (BNP publication), May 1993; reprinted in R. Griffin (ed.) *Fascism*, Oxford Readers series, Oxford, Oxford University Press, 1995, pp. 384–5)

## Document 4

*Quadragessimo Anno: corporatism and Catholic social teaching*

The Catholic Church issued Papal encyclicals on labour issues in the late nineteenth century, and again in the 1930s. While the latter were very hostile to left-wing trade unions and strikes, there was a constant thread of concern about workers' rights as well. The Church position dovetailed with that of the Fascists in its rejection of class conflict in favour of institutions that would bring both sides of industry together.

> 28. A new branch of law, wholly unknown to the earlier time, has arisen from this continuous and unwearied labour to protect vigorously the sacred rights of the workers that flow from their dignity as men and as Christians. These laws undertake the protection of life, health, strength, family, homes, workshops, wages and labour hazards ... everything which pertains to the condition of wage workers, with special concern for women and children. Even though these laws do not conform exactly everywhere and in all respects to Leo's recommendations, still it is undeniable that much in them savours [*sic*] of the Encyclical, *On the Condition of Workers*, to which great credit must be given for whatever improvement has been achieved in the workers' condition.
> 29. Finally, the wise Pontiff showed that 'employers and workers themselves

can accomplish much in this matter, manifestly through those institutions by the help of which the poor are opportunely assisted and the two classes of society are brought closer to each other.' First place among these institutions, he declares, must be assigned to associations that embrace either workers alone or workers and employers together. He goes into considerable detail in explaining and commending these associations and expounds with a truly wonderful wisdom their nature, purpose, timeliness, rights, duties, and regulations.

30. These teachings were issued indeed most opportunely. For at that time in many nations those at the helm of State, plainly imbued with Liberalism, were showing little favour to workers' associations of this type; nay, rather they openly opposed them, and while going out of their way to recognise similar organisations of other classes and show favour to them, they were with criminal injustice denying the natural right to form associations to those who needed it most to defend themselves from ill treatment at the hands of the powerful. There were even some Catholics who looked askance at the efforts of workers to form associations of this type as if they smacked of a socialistic or revolutionary spirit.

(Source: *Quadragessimo Anno* (Papal Encyclical), 1931; reproduced at Vatican State website. Available online at http://www.vatican.va/holy_father/pius_xi/encyclicals/documents/hf_p-xi_enc_19310515_quadragesimo-anno_en.html [accessed 10 August 2001])

## Document 5

*Austria Freedom Party programme: ruralist tendencies*

The pro-countryside and pro-farmer policies of the Freedom Party reflect its appeal to traditional voters. At the same time, it represents a challenge to the more left-wing tendencies of Europe's Green and environmentalist parties. As far-right parties attempt to remould their image, they are increasingly inclined to poach voters from other parties using vague but populist themes.

The preservation of fertile soil, thriving forests and pure water forms the basis for the production of quality food when agriculture and forestry can be close to nature. Domestic agriculture contributes substantially to ensure the supply of quality foodstuffs to the Austrian population.

For centuries the Austrian landscape has been cultivated and shaped by the work of its farmers. The Austrian landscape, the village settlements, animal species, agriculture and rural customs form the scenic culture which in its regional diversity contributes to the cultural richness of Austria.

The rural countryside has additionally to provide for recreation and to act as a natural refuge in the interests of the general public. Only efficient, productive and independent farmers can maintain the natural basis for this existence in the country. Thus it is in the public interest to safeguard the existence of Austrian farmers and their communities.

(Source: Austrian Freedom Party website. Available online at http://www.fpoe.or.at/ [accessed 1 August 2001])

# DIPLOMACY AND INTERNATIONAL RELATIONS

Russia and Germany together will be able to ensure the violent end of the United States and the establishment of a healthier racial balance on the continent of Europe.

> (Taken from Liberal Democratic Party (LDP) party newspaper, *Sokol Zhirinovskogo*, 1992, quoted in R. Griffin (ed.), *Fascism*, Oxford, Oxford University Press, 1995, pp. 387–9)

Most people associate fascism with a violent, expansionist and aggressive foreign policy. However, as with other policy areas, the distinctiveness of fascist diplomacy and strategy cannot be taken for granted. It is even more doubtful that the non-fascist far right has a distinctive foreign policy agenda, apart from prioritising the national interest and asserting it wherever possible. If a claim for distinctiveness is to be made, it is not to be found in the warlike behaviour of fascists but in their attitude to the importance of **war** itself.

Inter-war fascism was, in many senses, a mobilisation of society and human existence for war. Nationhood, **identity** and survival became bound up with a cult of combat. As we have seen in 'The Evolution of Fascist Ideology' and 'Nation and Race', this required a fundamental transformation of domestic politics. It also had profound implications for the traditional European states system and even complicated relationships among the fascists themselves. Ultimately, the fascist experiment in macro-political engineering failed as miserably on the world stage as it did at home, but not without unleashing the most dreadful war in human history. This chapter looks at the attempted fascist assault on the international system, as well as the legacy of those policies for both neo-fascist and non-fascist far-right parties ever since.

What lay behind this disaster? Was there a fascist style of foreign policy? At face value, the answer is 'yes'. Fascist states pursued militaristic, aggressive and expansionist policies, driven in part by racial hatreds and prejudice. However, that does not tell us very much. Almost every powerful state is accused of expansionism and aggression. The European colonial powers sought outright territorial conquest for centuries. **Race** was a key factor in European **colonialism**, much of which was premised on the idea that 'backward' non-Europeans could be enslaved, killed or, later, remoulded by 'civilised' Europeans. Looked at from some perspectives, the fascists merely exploited pre-existing foreign policy concerns and magnified them, taking them to extremes that still made sense in terms of the game of power politics. At another level, some of their policies suggested a potential threat to the underlying norms of the inter-state system that had developed over the centuries. On closer inspection, we find a range of motives behind the foreign policies of fascist and far-right movements. There were many driving forces behind fascist aggression and the relative strength or significance of each factor varied from case to case. In general terms, five broad motivators were particularly noticeable:

- Radical impulses which had the most profound implications for how the international system as a whole would function, e.g. **Hitler**'s racial obsessions.
- The consequences of fascist and far-right **nationalism**.
- The consequences of fascist **totalitarianism**.
- Moderate **revisionism** of defeated states.
- Moderate revisionism of frustrated rising powers.

Let us now look at these phenomena in more detail.

## RADICAL IMPULSES

The most common understanding of Hitler's foreign policy was that it was the product of a madman and of a very evil person. In this view, it was the man himself who made the regime and its aggressive policies what they were. Hitler's racial theories took Germany's ambitions and her conduct of international conflict far beyond those of previous power players. The Nazis treated Russians and European **Slavs** as *untermenschen* or 'sub-human'. This was partly an ideological response to **Bolshevism**, but race was clearly a factor in its own right. Indeed this whole racial ideology demanded the total destruction of the Westphalian system of sovereign equality that had existed in theory, if not always in practice, for three centuries. Under these arrangements, Europe was to be divided into sovereign states, with no over-arching power. Conflicts and wars would still occur, but these would merely result in adjustments to the existing balance of power, a balance based on interests, not **ideology** or race. The elimination of Ottoman Turkey and the Austro-Hungarian Empire after the First World War certainly implied a weakening of the Westphalian order but the idea of a Europe of sovereign states and strong powers was still intact. Though his ambitions were confined to the Mediterranean and Africa, **Mussolini** was prepared to play with fire by aligning himself with Hitler's unmistakably anti-Westphalian campaign.

The radicalism of Hitler's agenda was evident in his reaction to the Treaty of **Versailles** that had taken territory from Germany and restricted her military power. For him, the correction of the treaty could not be brought about by diplomacy. Moreover, in *Mein Kampf*, he argued that German survival depended on world power status. This, in turn, required it to have the 'magnitude' of a world power, and, thus, more than a refinement of the Versailles map.[1] Hence, we must consider the more far-reaching interpretation of fascist diplomacy and strategy as directed at a revolutionary assault on the deep-rooted norms of the international system itself.

In line with this, fascists were not just interested in any war: at certain points, they sought to bring to fruition **von Clausewitz**'s concept of absolute war, 'an act of **violence** pushed to its utmost bounds'.[2] The French revolutionary armies suggested a possible model, although neither the technology nor the methods of social organisation to carry it off were available at the turn of the nineteenth century. In Erich **Ludendorff**, a military leader in the First World War, and a participant with Hitler in the 1923 '**Beer Hall Putsch**', the Germans had a military thinker who claimed to know better than von Clausewitz. Von Clausewitz had concluded that 'real war' involved compromises with the complex realities of politics. Absolute or total war, a war of annihilation, would be difficult, if not impossible.[3]

The energy invested in the national project made the fascist experiment look like a cross between a religious movement and a scientific approach to society and politics. This energy, characterised by the Italians as 'dynamism', was contrasted with Italy's lack of military and diplomatic success under the old Liberal governments. In their article for the **Enciclopedia Italiana** in 1932, Mussolini and **Gentile** stressed the '**will to power**' and the importance of action and the offensive. Whereas states did not have to conquer others to build an empire (empires could be spiritual), an outward-looking policy was favoured over staying at home. The tendency to 'the expansion of nations' was thus 'a manifestation of vitality'. It could be used to make total war a viable possibility at last.[4]

The lethal mixture of anti-**Communism** and racial hatred, as well as the intensity of the zero-sum struggle between Nazism and Communism (see 'The Evolution of Fascist Ideology'), made Hitler's campaign against the Soviet Union all the more extreme and led him to defy his generals and geo-strategists, like Haushoffer. Facing possible defeat at **Stalingrad**, he chose to fight on. In this sense, Hitler's foreign policy ceased to be based on power politics and became more and more ideological or even irrational.[5]

The totalitarian character of fascist states gave a particular flavour and impetus to their aggression. Morgan argues that we can only understand fascist **militarism** by looking at the unusual way in which fascist and Communist regimes fused **state** and society, as well as domestic and foreign policy. A similar mobilising impetus existed in the Soviet Union. However, the Russians were increasingly preoccupied with consolidation at home and their strategy was essentially a long-term one. Though they were to be more aggressive in a later phase, the Soviets initially shifted from revolutionary subversion to a pragmatic realism that served Moscow's own purpose. The attempted fusion of state and society was indeed undertaken in part for the purposes of a mobilisation for war. Commenting on the links between foreign policy and domestic agitation at the time of Mussolini's aggression against Ethiopia, Morgan captures the essence of Fascist **totalitarianism** by noting that 'Fascism's new order was the nation in a perpetual state of mobilisation for war.'[6]

The concept of the **nation** used by far-right movements also impels them toward expansionism. This is not the same as saying that nationalism causes fascism. National pride among the Czechs, the Indians or the Icelandic peoples has not had this effect. Indeed, national heritage can be defined in terms of democratic values or tolerance. Even **cultural nationalism** need not take a violent turn. The fascists, however, seized existing national sentiments and married them to the glorification of force, disdain for the systemic consequences of their actions and a racial hatred based on their own supposed superiority over others. It was this combination, and not any single component, which translated fascist cultural and racial ideologies into bellicist military doctrines.

The Japanese military leaders who prosecuted the **Second World War** also added race to their armoury. They interpreted Western caution about acknowledging Japanese power as a product of **racism** directed against Asians in general, and Japan in particular.[7] They used this motif in their **propaganda** campaigns, in much the same way that the Soviet Union and its allies tried to persuade non-aligned countries that the Communist bloc was the 'natural ally' of the **Third World** in international affairs.

Ironically, when they needed to form alliances, fascist ultra-nationalists faced a grave dilemma in Central Europe: that same **ultra-nationalism** posed the risk of a conflict among the fascist states or right-wing regimes themselves. It was easy to ally with distant Japan: their officials only needed to conceal their racism or other hatred while visiting Asia. It was much more difficult in the close proximity of European neighbours. Italy and Austria, for example, had an uneasy relationship dating back to the days of the Austro-Hungarian Empire. The frontier was never fully agreed and the fate of German and Italian minorities on either side was a constant source of tension. As German pressure on Austria mounted, Mussolini was unsure about what to do. In the early stages, he even endorsed restrictive measures against Austrian Nazis.[8]

The same problem arose when Nazi Germany became involved in the tangled relationships among Hungary, Romania and the Soviet Union. The right-wing **Horthy** regime in Budapest was inclined towards co-operation with Berlin, since both states wanted to change international boundaries. However, it had claims on the territories of the pro-German Slovaks and of Romania, a key source of oil for the Germans. At the time of the **Nazi–Soviet Pact**, when Hitler and Stalin were supposed to be on the same side, the Russians advanced on **Bessarabia** (now Moldova), a Romanian-speaking region between Romania and Ukraine. Romanian nationalists blamed the pact for allowing the Russians too much of a free hand.[9]

Taking advantage of the strategic environment to pursue irredentist claims was also the game-plan of the Croatian fascists, the Ustasha. They were less traditionalist than the Hungarians and modelled themselves on the Italian Fascists, gaining a reputation for atrocities in their drive to capture large areas of Bosnia-Herzegovina. Once Germany saw the strategic situation in Romania begin to weaken, it intervened heavily in Yugoslavia, even though that complicated relations with Italy, Hungary and Bulgaria, all of whom hoped to feast on a dismembered Yugoslavia torn apart by inter-ethnic rivalry. So, leadership of the Axis could be a politically perilous task. On the other hand, the sheer weight of German power and the ferocity of its terror machine kept the other European nationalist dictatorships in line. They all needed the protection of Germany but dared not disrupt Hitler's plans too much lest they be occupied and subjected to full-blown Nazi rule.

What fascists themselves believed is also a matter of debate that complicated the picture. For example, was Hitler's racial obsession with Slavs a primary motive throughout his period in power? Did he always plan the outright physical extermination of the Jews? Or, was his aim to persecute them and ultimately expel them? The policies clearly became more extreme as the war dragged on, especially once the Nazis met even limited resistance in the East. That would suggest that the agenda evolved over time. On the other hand, the vehemence of Nazi racism was always evident in its propaganda literature, especially in *Mein Kampf* (see 'Nation and Race'). The racial theories he absorbed and propagated saw European Jewry as a virus that had to be stamped out permanently. There has also been controversy over Hitler's intentions with regard to a world war. The historian, A.J.P. Taylor, for one, argued that Hitler may have intended to use military force on the German periphery but that he blundered his way into a full-scale war with the other European powers. Much of Hitler's rhetoric suggested that he thought he could get away with creeping expansion of German territory through a policy of bluff and swagger, on the basis that Britain and France would grudgingly accept new 'facts on the ground' rather than risk a new war so soon after the First World War.[10] He may have been aided in this belief by the appeasement of his moves on Austria, the **Sudetenland** and Czechoslovakia, as well as by the weak response of the **League of Nations** to Italian aggression in Africa and Japan's war in China. On the other hand, the **Hossbach** Memorandum, a document describing a top-level Nazi military strategy meeting in 1937, clearly shows that Hitler envisaged war at some stage and certainly before 1943–5. He was aware of growing resistance ('counter-measures') to his policies and the likely consequences of that opposition. He also spoke openly about more *Lebensraum* (or 'living space') for the Germans in Central Europe.

## SUB-SYSTEMIC REVISIONISM

All of the above arguments point to specific features of fascism and far-right ideology, many of which threatened the very foundations of the international system. A more cautious view suggests that fascist regimes wanted to complete the work of nationalists who had dominated European politics since the mid-nineteenth century. The Nazis and the Fascists were not the only ones unhappy with the outcome of the First World War. The widespread desire to revise

European territorial boundaries after 1919 was based on three factors: (1) **irredentism**, or the aim of regaining 'national' territories lost to others as a result of the war and subsequent treaties, (2) disappointment at failure to effectively exploit the war to enhance national prestige, and (3) frustration at the inability to translate rapid national demographic and economic growth into Great-Power status, often resulting in an inflated sense of national potential. Although these reactions to world events could be particularly violent, they were not specific to fascists alone.

As frustration and disappointment bred nationalist irredentism, the inter-war far right also used, and misused, academic theory to give an air of legitimacy to their policies. In this connection, there is much speculation on whether the German tradition of *geopolitik* was a development in international relations theory with a wider application, or merely an intellectual cover for Nazi expansionism. For some, it was an expansionist, imperialist doctrine. **Haushofer** argued that control of the Eurasian–African land mass required control over its heartland, East Central Europe. This fitted the Nazi preoccupation with *Lebensraum*. On the other hand, an area of weak states constituting a vacuum between a rising Prussia–Germany and Russia was inevitably going to become an arena for competition and territorial expansion. Even in post-**Cold War** circumstances, Russian, US and German economic and cultural forces are still competing in this region. Haushofer's *geopolitik* is as useful as a warning against expansionism, or as a guide about how to thwart it, as it is a cookbook for **imperialism**. He denied that he was an apologist for German militarism. Indeed, the possibilities that he would oppose the conquest of the Asian USSR contributed to his imprisonment in Dachau near the end of the war.[11] Whatever his intentions, his theories were certainly used and misused by the Nazis. Hitler's case against Versailles was based in part on Haushofer's argument that the post-1918 borders were unfair in granting national self-determination to other nations but dividing Germans and restricting them. This 'correction' of the Versailles map was supported by many Germans and attracted sympathy among revisionists elsewhere in Europe, e.g. in Hungary and Ireland.[12]

The first phase of Hitler's aggression has frequently been interpreted, or misinterpreted, as merely the release of anger and frustration at a particularly harsh Versailles peace settlement, a limited form of irredentism. Whereas the Allies proclaimed their belief in national self-determination, and granted national states to, for instance, the Poles and the Romanians, they left millions of Germans outside the **Weimar Republic**, as minorities in other countries. All the right-wing parties and even many on the left saw this as unjust. Gustav Stresemann, the moderate German foreign minister before the rise of Hitler and fêted as a 'good European', used diplomacy to advance German national goals and effectively undermine the treaties.[13] Part of the rationale behind early appeasement of Hitler was that he would stop his expansionism once he had acquired Austria and the German-speaking areas of western Czechoslovakia (the Sudetenland). While his policies threatened the European order, he appeared to want to deal with Britain in the power politics tradition. He would weaken, though not dismantle, the Empire and force a humbled UK to acknowledge German hegemony in Europe.[14] He did not appear to want to conquer and subjugate Britain but launched the final assault when Churchill refused to see a new world order based on a carve-up between London and Berlin. When he moved to take control of the rest of Czechoslovakia, many leaders who had previously given him the benefit of the doubt belatedly realised his real game-plan and adopted a more robust stance.

As already noted, the Hungarian far right also played a revisionist card. For the last half-century of its existence, the Habsburg Empire had operated on the basis of a Dual Monarchy. Hungary exercised imperial power in the eastern half of the Empire, especially over the Slovaks and in the northern half of what is now Romania. Under the Treaty of Trianon, Hungary lost Slovakia and **Transylvania**. The latter retained a substantial Hungarian population.[15] The Horthy dictatorship in Hungary echoed popular resentment at the loss of Hungarian territory. Alignment with revisionist Germany, it was hoped, might bring an answer to Hungarian irredentist demands. However, since Horthy was of royal lineage, and also looked back to Hungarian royal traditions, he was no Nazi radical. Like **Pétain** in France, he was simultaneously joining the Axis (as he did in 1940) and asserting Hungarian national autonomy, while keeping the Nazis themselves at bay. The alignment was completed when Horthy assisted the Nazi invasion of the Soviet Union. Horthy emphasised both **authoritarianism** and anti-Communism but, in other respects, appeared hostile or indifferent to Nazism. He ultimately abandoned Hitler and was rewarded with his freedom by the Allies. **Göbbels** complained bitterly about his lack of enthusiasm for the anti-Semitic campaigns of the Reich and said he was all 'tangled up with the Jews through his family'.[16]

In Spain, the right-wing resentment at liberal politics that gave rise to **Franco**'s drive for power could be traced to Spain's humiliating defeat by the US in 1898. The loss of Cuba signalled the final disintegration of Spain's once great empire in Asia and the Americas. She tried to hold tenaciously to some lesser outposts in Morocco and, even here, she was frustrated by the French and by Arab resistance. Franco constructed a powerful history of his own military exploits in defence of Spanish Morocco.[17] The shared anger and military camaraderie among his fellow soldiers in Morocco, not to mention the brutalising effects of the violence used against the local population, had a lasting effect on both the man and a substantial segment of his age cohort in Spanish society, especially in the military.[18] This bred right-wing dictatorship under **Primo de Rivera** (1923–30), and, later, under Franco himself. Military heroism and national assertion were his preferred antidotes to historical shocks and national depression.

These assertive responses to international disappointment are not unusual, even in democracies. The popularity of Ronald Reagan, for instance, was the

US's answer to the Vietnam Syndrome. Similarly, Vladimir Putin, while professing no desire to terminate the liberal democratic political system, began his period in office with calls for a 'strong state' and a more vigorous foreign policy. In the case of the fascists and the far right, however, it was **democracy** itself, a peaceful, process-driven political order, that was blamed for the malaise. Democratic norms encouraged too much diversity and deliberation. In this view, weakling politicians, whether Italian Liberals under Giolitti or German Social Democrats in the Weimar Republic, produced capitulatory foreign policies.

This current of 'anti-politics' has also been a common theme in what Brian Loveman has called the 'militarylore' [sic] sustaining rule by the armed forces in Latin American countries in the nineteenth and twentieth centuries. Military putschists claimed that their actions were designed to save the nation, *la patria*, from subversion. While intervention prior to the 1930s was often based on conservative motives, military leaders in the inter-war years linked their repressive measures with **populism** and some social reform. Major Germán **Busch**, a hero of the **Chaco War** with Paraguay (1932–5), instituted what he called 'military socialism' in Bolivia from 1936–9. The aim was to strengthen Bolivia's defences and modernise the economy.[19] Bolivians had suffered a double blow to national pride: the loss of access to the Pacific in their contest with Chile in the nineteenth and early twentieth centuries, and failure to secure territorial gains in the Chaco War with Paraguay in the 1930s. The populist and nationalist **dictatorship** echoed the themes we have seen elsewhere, even if it was unable to engage in any further military expansionism.

The same thinking can be found today on the post-Communist far right in Russia. Vladimir **Zhirinovsky**, leader of the far-right Liberal Democratic Party, characterises the politicians of the Yeltsin years as weak and corrupt, as poodles of the CIA and of the US. Moreover, Zhirinovsky has spoken of a renewed Russian Empire, embracing the old Soviet Union, one that might even include Poland and Alaska.[20]

In one respect, Italy presented a slightly different picture from some of the other revisionist states. Its disappointment after the First World War was all the more bitter because they had reason to expect substantial gains, on account of their alignment with Britain, France and the US in the First World War. Since the 1880s, Italian Liberals and nationalists had sought Great-Power status through expansionist schemes. In particular, they wanted to move southwards into Africa and to participate in the carve-up of a declining Ottoman Empire. After the First World War, Italy felt that it did not get enough of Austrian territory in Europe or of ex-Ottoman land in the Middle East. It had occupied Albania from 1914–20, so Mussolini's meddling there in the late 1920s was not seen as a great departure. This interest culminated in occupation in 1939, when the major powers were fixated on German aggression in Central Europe. Mussolini pursued the same agenda. His forays in Corfu (1923) and Ethiopia (1935–6) were particularly aggressive but could still be understood in terms of the traditional goals of Italian foreign policy. They also showed his bombastic side: he was actually forced to leave Corfu after a brief occupation but he still trumpeted his 'victory'.[21] If he outdid his predecessors, it was in his more deliberate equation of this south-easterly drive with the conquest of Mediterranean lands by Ancient Rome.

However, there was still an important contrast between Liberal foreign policy and that of Mussolini. The old élites did use power politics and the threat of war to advance their aims, especially in Africa. They also sought to achieve their objectives using conference diplomacy. This was clearly within the confines of a Great-Power System. Mussolini was prepared go further to break out of what he perceived as a geo-strategic straitjacket arising from the bastions of Anglo-French power at both ends of the Mediterranean.

Britain held Gibraltar and Egypt, as well as Palestine. France had much of North-West Africa and Syria under its control. Mark Robson notes that Mussolini correlated independence with maritime access and this was blocked by this Anglo-French power base that controlled an area bounded by Tunis, Corsica, Malta and Cyprus.[22] A south-easterly thrust into the Balkans and a tightening of Italian control over Libya (Tripolitania) were the only avenues for power projection. Like a bull in a China shop, Mussolini had no qualms about such a drive, regardless of the consequences for European order. For him, this was escaping from what he termed 'the cage'. In setting out this geo-strategic picture of the Mediterranean, however, Mussolini revealed a more ambitious goal, to march towards 'the Ocean', by which he meant the Indian Ocean and/ or the Atlantic. This could only be done by challenging British power in East Africa and Egypt, and French power in the Maghreb.[23] Clearly, the Italians fancied themselves as a world sea power. The most amusing aspect of this, of course, was that Mussolini did not have, and had no prospects of acquiring, a world-class navy.

Because Italy shifted sides in the course of the First World War, eventually fighting on the Allied side, Rome expected significant territorial gains as a reward. That these were not granted, or granted in only limited measure, angered many Italians. Mussolini felt this anger, especially among many in the working classes who had joined the war for love of country. From this emotional cocktail, he coined his theme of a 'mutilated victory'.[24] Alongside the glorious myth of a new Rome, he constructed a tragic myth around the Battle of **Caporetto** in 1917. Gaetano Salvemini has argued that, although it was a major defeat for Italy, it was only one among many significant defeats suffered by major powers in the war. The Fascists turned it into a symbol of failure and treachery, and gave it a meaning that poured shame on the entire Italian political and military **establishment**.[25] The betrayal by the establishment was matched, in Mussolini's eyes, by the betrayal of Italy on the part of the Allies. Despite the terms of the 1915 Treaty of London, hinting at Italian gains in western Croatia, the major powers were slow to grant Italy a free hand in Yugoslavia and the eastern Mediterranean.

Like the Italians, the Japanese had been pursuing a regional imperial policy since the 1890s. By defeating China in 1895, and Russia, a European power, in 1905, Japanese modernising élites had demonstrated that the strategy of importing Western technologies and administrative methods would serve Japan well. The 1911 Anglo-Japanese pact was interpreted as recognition of Japan's status as the first modern Asian world power. Initial success, however, gave the Japanese a set of false expectations. The US opposed a regional hegemony in the north-west Pacific. In the aftermath of the First World War, US liberals also drew uncomfortable parallels between their naval rivalry with Japan and the Dreadnought race before 1914. The result was a series of naval disarmament agreements at the Washington Disarmament Conferences in 1920–1. These agreements also attempted to restrain territorial expansion in China. By the 1930s, some Japanese military circles and far-right forces reinterpreted these agreements as aimed at preventing Japan from achieving full equality as a Great Power. Optimism turned to anger, frustration and violence, both at home and in China. The US was charged with racism and envy, and Japan became a victim of injustice.

Another possible explanation of aggressive revisionism is the problem of adjustment to rapid structural changes in a regional balance of power. This has consequences for the system as a whole and for the expanding state. One could argue that the rapid rise in German power after 1870, and perhaps even after unification in 1990 as well, might have produced a perceived 'German problem', regardless of the nature of the German polity itself. Other states have difficulty coming to terms with the rapid pace of change and this generates tension. Thus, the First World War, the Second World War and even the current sensitivities of states in the EU are all manifestations of the same phenomenon. Of course, such a structuralist interpretation does not account for the vastly different outcomes of this 'German problem' and the ways in which it was resolved.

Japanese expansionism in the early twentieth century has a similar origin to that of Italy: a rapid growth in relative power that is unrecognised by the major powers. Since the partially coerced opening of Japan to the world in the mid-nineteenth century, the Japanese Empire copied Western patterns of technical **modernisation** to a much greater extent than China or its other neighbours. By 1905, it could defeat the Russian Empire, the first significant defeat of a European power by a non-Western state for centuries. The Japanese conquest of Korea and Taiwan in earlier wars with China confirmed the wisdom of this course. By forming an alliance with Britain in 1911, Japanese leaders sought recognition as a world power. Despite formal neutrality in the First World War, Japan thought that the local Asian power, namely herself, could take some of the spoils of the crumbling German Empire in the western Pacific (e.g. the Solomon Islands and New Guinea).

For all their ferocity, even the Nazis were constrained by politics and circumstance, the side of Clausewitz they would probably choose to ignore in their rhetoric. They were compelled to engage in pragmatic diplomacy and tactical retreats, to make concessions to the untidy environment around them. Hitler signed agreements, like the Nazi–Soviet Pact, with the erstwhile Bolshevik devil, simply to deny Britain and France an important ally if they dared to intervene against his planned move on Poland.[26] He also held doggedly, even well into the war, to the hope of a *modus vivendi* with the relatively racially pure Anglo-Saxons in Britain, until it became abundantly clear that Churchill was determined to oppose permanent Nazi hegemony in Continental Europe.

Mussolini sought territorial rights in the eastern Mediterranean in a secret dialogue with Britain and France. Meanwhile, he acted as a co-guarantor of the **Locarno** Treaties, designed to consolidate Europe's post-war borders in the West. Given their absolute commitment to an extensive revision of the international system, these policies were most likely tactical, designed to buy time. Italy was also a less than reliable Axis partner. When the right-wing Austrian Chancellor, Engelbert **Dollfuss**, was assassinated, Mussolini called Hitler 'a horrible sexual degenerate'.[27] In the early years, Italy seemed wary of German power, even though that same menacing power was an important means of extracting revisionist territorial concessions out of the Allies. This tactical manœuvring was, in some respects, a continuation of the old regime strategy of the 'decisive weight', under which Italy would pick the winner from the table of world powers and gain accordingly.[28] The jury is still out on this, though British concessions to Italy, including the cautious response to its aggression in Ethiopia, suggest that extensive appeasement failed to bring the intended effects.[29]

The fascist states seized opportunities; in this, they were little different from other powers. However, because they were emboldened by what they perceived to be a scientific approach to military mobilisation, by the novelty of ideology and commitment, as well as by vehement racial hatred, they acted without regard to the consequences for the international system. They presented a stark contrast with a war and Depression-weary Europe or Russia. Thus, the arrogance of fascist assertiveness was itself a form of diplomatic *Blitzkrieg* that threw the rest of the world into a temporary state of shock and confusion.

## THE FAR RIGHT AFTER THE SECOND WORLD WAR

The post-Second World War far right was not in any position to implement foreign policy, let alone military strategy. Besides, the Cold War was so all-encompassing as to overshadow everything else. Here, **neo-fascism** had competition from the anti-Communism of mainstream **conservatism** and the US. Neo-fascists could only join in calls for the defence of 'the West', with ambiguity over whether that meant the racially 'pure' white nations or the 'plutocracies' that dominated NATO and other manifestations of 'the West' as defined by the Americans. The ambiguity actually suited the post-war far right in that it allowed them to preach two foreign policy doctrines: the first to their thuggish and neo-fascist core, and the second to the mass public and other right-wing parties.

A second theme in post-war far-right discourse was opposition to **decolonisation**. Here, right-wing extremists came close to having a real impact, as when they appealed to imperialist die-hards in France as the country encountered major defeats in Algeria and Indo-China. Discontent in the military and among French settlers in the Maghreb, especially Algeria, contributed to the collapse of the Fourth Republic and the constitutional crisis that brought General de Gaulle to power.

The end of the Cold War brought new opportunities for far-right foreign policy initiatives, but also more scope for contradictions and confusion. Thus, Jean-Marie **Le Pen** appeared to back the erstwhile socialist Arab, Saddam **Hussein**, while opposing Arab **immigration** into France. Hussein was at least a nationalist.[30] Le Pen has frequently joined the rest of the French establishment in a chorus of anti-Americanism, especially focused on alleged US cultural imperialism directed at Francophone culture and identity. However, while Europe was one bulwark against the Americans, it was also a potential threat to individual nations. Likewise, far-right groups in Russia have increasingly aligned themselves with ex-Communists in mourning the country's alleged humiliation at the hands of the West since 1991, leaving much ambiguity over whether the Russia they long to restore is Tsarist or socialist.

The absence of a Communist enemy has somewhat disoriented far-right parties all over Europe. Some have sought to shift the focus to **Islam** and the Arab world. This can be useful if it reinforces the 'threat' to national cohesion that they associate with immigration from Turkey or North Africa. Furthermore, this theme also draws in some support from mainstream conservatives who may wish to restrict immigration for logistical as opposed to racial or cultural reasons, as well as among those who are genuinely concerned about the proliferation of weapons of mass destruction and associated delivery systems in states like Iran, Iraq, Libya or Algeria. The ability of the far right to 'cosy up' to other conservative parties, and to 'steal' and distort their policies, poses a serious dilemma for the centre-right, both in terms of ideological identity and electoral strategy.

Fortunately, however, the relative prosperity of most Western countries has deflected public attention from foreign policy. Only the campaign against 'globalisation' seems capable of generating anything remotely like a destabilising current on the streets. The exception to this rule is Russia. There, economic collapse is systematically linked to the fall of the Soviet Empire, the loss of Russian prestige and the redrawing of the maps in Europe and Central Asia. Many of the driving forces behind inter-war fascist aggression are present in the Russian body politic. The fate of Russians in the 'Near Abroad', former republics of the USSR, continues to animate many people. Some suffer discrimination in their new homes; in other cases, as in Kazakhstan, they constitute almost half the population. The Russian military has transit rights across Lithuania to link with the base at Kaliningrad on the Baltic. Lithuania is also a very anti-Russian state of the 'Near Abroad'. Just as Hitler wanted to link German East Prussia with the German Heartland, by occupying the **'Danzig**/Polish Corridor' in-between, Lithuania's security is precarious. All of these issues feature strongly in the discourse of the new Russian far right. The feeling of bitterness and humiliation is so strong in some quarters that a *de facto* anti-Western alliance has emerged, embracing Communists and extreme right-wing nationalists. Russia's democracy totters on the verge of a coup and Vladimir Putin's faction is increasingly influenced by hard-liners from the old regime.

Of course, the international setting is different. Russia has not suffered military occupation. We live in a nuclear-armed world. And Russians have also suffered at the hands of authoritarian rule. The crisis of 1918–39 occurred at a time when democracy was under threat all over Europe. Today, despite the disillusionment, democracy remains the preferred option of most Europeans. Still, there are some parallels with Weimar and these are being ruthlessly exploited by movements whose priorities display some parallels with the fascist right of the inter-war years. In foreign affairs, as in much else, far-right movements pursue the policies of their predecessors to extremes, but their own themes seem unlikely to go away.


**EXTRACTS**


**Document 1**

*Fascism and war*

This extract from Mussolini's own definition of Fascism shows the importance accorded to war and militarism. It explains how writers like Morgan have viewed Fascism as a sort of permanent national mobilisation for war.

> Fascism, the more it considers and observes the future and the development of humanity quite apart from political considerations of the moment, believes neither in the possibility nor the utility of perpetual peace. It thus repudiates the doctrine of Pacifism – born of a renunciation of the struggle and an act of cowardice in the face of sacrifice. War alone brings up to its highest tension all human energy and puts the stamp of nobility upon the peoples who have courage to meet it. All other trials are substitutes, which never really put men into the position where they have to make the great decision – the alternative of life or death.

> (Source: B. Mussolini and G. Gentile, 'What is Fascism?', *Enciclopedia Italiana* (1932), reprinted in Internet Modern History Sourcebook, Fordham University. Available online at http://www.fordham.edu/halsall/mod/mussolini-fascism.html [Accessed 17 August 2001])

**Document 2**

*Hitler's war plans*

The Hossbach Memorandum was part of the Nazi leadership's efforts to plan for worst-case scenarios in the diplomatic and military contest of Europe around the start of the Second World War. It shows that Hitler had always envisaged war, not least because of European resistance to his policies. The timing and scale were at issue and he thought that bluff and appeasement could buy him time. In this selection, Hitler links his foreign policy and the urgency he attaches to expansion to his race policies and the desire for *Lebensraum.*

Memorandum

BERLIN, November 10, 1937

Minutes of a Conference in the Reich Chancellery, Berlin, November 5, 1937, from 4.15 to 8.30 P.M.

Present: The *Führer* and Chancellor, Field Marshal von Blomberg, War Minister, Colonel General Baron von Fritsch, Commander in Chief, Army, Admiral Dr Raeder, Commander in Chief, Navy, Colonel General Göring, Commander in Chief, Luftwaffe, Baron von Neurath, Foreign Minister, Colonel Hossbach.

The *Führer* then continued:
    The aim of German policy was to make secure and to preserve the racial community (*Volksmasse*) and to enlarge it. It was therefore a question of space.
    The German racial community comprised over 85 million people and, because of their number and the narrow limits of habitable space in Europe, constituted a tightly packed racial core such as was not to be met in any other country and such as implied the right to a greater living space than in the case of other peoples. If, territorially speaking, there existed no political result corresponding to this German racial core, that was a consequence of centuries of historical development, and in the continuance of these political conditions lay the greatest danger to the preservation of the German race at its present peak. To arrest the decline of Germanism (*Deutschtum*) in Austria and Czechoslovakia was as little possible as to maintain the present level in Germany itself. Instead of increase, sterility was setting in, and in its train disorders of a social character must arise in course of time, since political and ideological ideas remain effective only so long as they furnish the basis for the realisation of the essential vital demands of a people. Germany's future was therefore wholly conditional upon the solving of the need for space, and such a solution could be sought, of course, only for a foreseeable period of about one to three generations.

(Source: 'The Hossbach Memorandum', minutes of a conference in the Reich Chancellery, Berlin, 5 November 1937, reprinted at Avalon website. Available online at http://www.yale.edu/lawweb/avalon/imt/hossbach.htm, 1996 [accessed 2001]).

## Document 3

*Italy's glory in Abyssinia*

Mussolini explains the significance of his conquest.

> I entered Addis Ababa at the head of the victorious troops. During the thirty centuries of her history Italy has lived many memorable hours. This is certainly the most solemn. I announce to the world that the war is finished and peace is re-established. It is necessary, I should add [*sic*], that it is our peace, a Roman peace, which is expressed in these terms, the final and definite terms: 'Ethiopia is Italian'. The people of the Lion of Judah have shown clearly that they wish to live under the tutelage of the Italian people.

> (Source: Mussolini speech on 5 May 1936, announcing a victory telegram from Marshal Badoglio, on the occasion of the annexation of Ethiopia (Abyssinia); *Manchester Guardian*, 6 May 1936)

## Document 4

*Göbbels on Japanese war motives*

Göbbels supports Japan's war effort, not because it is resisting Western aggression, but because it is going on the offensive. This underscores the bellicist attitude of the Nazis to war.

> Japan has shown once again the enormous power in a people's national dynamics. One is deeply moved by the accounts of the heroic deeds of Japan's death-defying naval airmen. Japan knows that, like Germany and Italy, it is fighting for its future, for its very life. The alliance of these three Great Powers that despite their millennia of history retain youthful vitality is natural, the result of the inescapable power of a bitter historical logic. They see in this war their best chance at national existence. Their leadership and their peoples know what is at stake. It is true that they were forced into this war, but they are fighting it offensively, not defensively. Their young men at the front burn with passion to solve the life problems of their nations with weapons. Never before have they had such an opportunity to test their courage, their strength, their manly readiness. They see themselves affronted and insulted by plutocracy's leaders in a way that rules out any possibility of surrender. Mr. Churchill and Mr. Roosevelt still have no idea what they have got themselves into. They may have envisioned a pleasant war in which they would stroll to Berlin, Rome and Tokyo, supported by the people of countries who had been seduced by their leaders. They overlooked the fact that these governments are only saying and doing what their people want, even insist on or demand.

> (Source: P. Göbbels, *Das eherne Herz* [A Different World], Munich, Zentralverlag der NSDAP, 1943; reprinted in A. Furst von Urach, *Das Geheimnis Japanischer Kraft*, Berlin, Zentralverlag der NSDAP, 1943. Reprinted on Japanese Nazi Organisation website. Available online at http://www.nsjap.com/axis/english.html [accessed 17 August 2001])

**Document 5**

*Mussolini's foray into geo-politics*

Mussolini often promoted grandiose plans for which he did not have the talent or the resources. Here, echoing theories of naval strategy that emphasise oceanic power, he talks of reaching for the Indian and Atlantic Oceans. However, to do this, he would have to break British and French power at both ends of the Mediterranean. In his terms, Italy would have to escape the prison or cage represented by British and French bases in the region, although the Italian navy was in no position to do this.

> The bars of this prison are Corsica, Tunisia, Malta, Cyprus: the guardians of this prison are Gibraltar and Suez. Corsica is a pistol pointed at the heart of Italy; Tunisia at Sicily, while Malta and Cyprus are a menace to all our positions in the central and eastern Mediterranean
>
> And from this situation we must draw the following conclusions: It is the aim of Italian policy, which cannot have and does not have territorial ambitions in continental Europe, except for Albania, to begin by breaking the bars of the prison.
>
> Having broken the bars, Italian policy has just one basic aim: to march towards the ocean. Which ocean? The Indian Ocean, through linking up the Sudan, Libya and Ethiopia, or the Atlantic Ocean through French North Africa. In either case, we find ourselves confronted by the French and the British.

(Source: Mussolini, foreign policy address to Fascist Grand Council, 4–5 February 1939, in R. de Felice, *Mussolini il Duce ii*, Turin, 1981, pp. 321–2; reprinted in J. Whittam, *Fascist Italy*, Manchester, Manchester University Press, 1995, pp. 164–5)

# THE PRACTICE OF POLITICS IN GOVERNMENT AND OPPOSITION

> The French people no longer have a say. The *Front National* wants to win power in order to give it back to the people of France.
>
> (*Front National* (FN) website – www.front-national.com)

From its roots in the 1880s and 1890s to the dawn of the twenty-first century, far-right discourse has always placed a premium on action and power. Ideas mattered little if they could not catapult these movements to the centre of public attention or into the great citadels of state. Indeed, a group like *Action Française* (AF) in 1930s France, which romanticised the good old days of royalist absolutism, but did nothing to restore it in practice, could be seen as non-fascist precisely because of its lack of interest in political action. However, the potential for action also depends on the circumstances and environment in which it is to occur. This chapter examines how far-right movements conducted the struggle for power under vastly different conditions, especially at the high-point of fascist rule and in their wilderness years. The strategies involved have varied from street-fighting to 'respectable' electoral politics. Nonetheless, more than in any other political movement, success and failure have been defined by the correlation between action and power.

Almost every political movement that rises to power undergoes a transition along the way. Fascist movements often had humble beginnings that betrayed little of the prominence they would achieve many years later. At the same time, post-war far-right movements have had fewer opportunities for the kind of street action enjoyed by **Mussolini**'s **'Blackshirts'**, and elections, rather than coups, have become the principal avenue to power, even for erstwhile Latin American dictators. Some have retrenched into internecine debates about obscure concepts or now revel in metaphorical allusions to the past that are unintelligible to all but the party faithful. As Cheles observed of Italian *Movimento Sociale Italiano* (MSI) **propaganda** in recent decades, 'This emphasis on the message aimed at the initiated suggests that the MSI's attempt to appeal to a wider electorate is half-hearted, and that, in fact, the party prefers to talk to itself'.[1] On the far right, the story of the transition from revolutionary movements and gods of war to powerless ideologues and spin-doctors is truly breath-taking. However, it also highlights the limits of the quest for absolute power, as well as the flexibility and diversity of the tactics.

## FROM THEORIES TO TACTICS: REVOLUTIONARY ACTION

In the years 1870–1922, fringe groups and the currents of thought that subsequently crystallised to form fascism and the modern far right offered a rumbling critique of the reformist and revolutionary trends that had gained ground in nineteenth-century Europe. As discontent and alienation spread in the wake of the First World War, these ideas held out a vague promise of something different. For many, they offered a chance to restore an old order and presaged a backlash against change. To others, they suggested the possibility of revolutionary transformation, using modern instruments of state power, a revolutionary change to compete with anything the left might offer. The mystique of these movements, and especially of fascism itself, lay in their ability to hint at all these promises simultaneously, to be all things to all people. Without a record in power, the promise was all the more alluring.

Revolutionary **syndicalism**, heavily influenced by Georges **Sorel**'s *Reflections on Violence*, emphasised the importance of tactics for translating such abstract ideas into action. First, there had to be a case for violence, or at least for dramatic action. That meant challenging the violence of the state against its enemies and the centrality of parliamentary methods. Second, it was necessary to focus attention on what Sorel called '**myth**'. He was not referring to just any old myth: it had to be one that could reduce politics to a simple, but powerful, formula that would mobilise the masses by its sheer force of emotion or intuition, rather than by reason. Sorel saw both of these conditions fulfilled in the socialist or syndicalist myth of a great confrontation, the general strike. This could embody all the hopes of those aspiring to revolution and to action. For **Rosenberg**, **Hitler** and the race theorists of Nazism, the coming apocalyptic confrontation between the Nordic race and the Jews could fit the same role. Futuristic apocalypses are also in vogue among some of the more exotic Christian fundamentalists on the contemporary US far right. Of course, the myth could also draw on the past, such as the myth of a new Rome or of a return to cultural roots.[2] By simplifying and distilling abstract concepts so as to play on human emotions, myth could be the tool that translates abstract theory into a recipe for action.

Beyond the mythology and the promises, however, these extremists faced a practical problem. The path to power would not be as smooth as many had hoped. Mussolini was acutely conscious of this. Part of the reason for his disenchantment with revolutionary **socialism** was the realisation that the masses would not spontaneously follow a movement just because its pamphleteers expressed the case with eloquence or passion. The public was fickle and Socialist Party activists could also be treacherous. The workers might not even constitute the revolutionary class.[3] Hitler came to the same conclusion, albeit independently. Both understood that the achievement of power required a viable conspiracy, not just dreams and rhetoric. Ironically, Lenin's strategy for party leadership and decisive action followed the same logic. Although he retained a rhetorical commitment to the workers, he too believed that a vanguard party of action was central to the hope of revolution.

The practical conspiracies planned by Hitler and Mussolini ultimately involved supping with the 'bourgeois' and 'plutocratic' devil, dividing the forces that might get in the way. For all their militancy and violence, Nazi paramilitaries like the **Sturm Abteilung** (SA) were no substitute for the German army. It was the Army that would fight Hitler's wars. Similarly, the bureaucracy and élite of the Prussian–German state were deeply entrenched. They might eventually be Nazified, but that could not happen overnight. The state could not be smashed with one blow. Indeed, Hitler decided that the state and the old **establishment** would have to be used as key instruments in his conquest of power.

Mussolini was also an early learner in the skills of tactical **pragmatism**. After several years of anti-capitalist tirades in the Socialist newspaper, *Avanti*, he started taking money from business concerns and using his violent gangs as strike-breakers. Whereas, previously, all capitalists were demonised, there would now be 'national' or 'patriotic' firms that could be spared the criticism directed at other hostile plutocratic forces. Mussolini's Blackshirts and *squadristi* worked outside the law and threatened the state. Yet, initially at least, they were also aware of the danger of going too far. An establishment backlash could result in a pre-emptive crackdown. This caution was especially important at the very moment when the Fascists entered power. Thus, once Mussolini was in government for the first time, he backed away from further action. This was most evident in his reaction to the Matteotti Crisis in 1924, when the murder of a Socialist politician, Giacomo Matteotti, threatened a premature end to the Fascist experiment.[4] Mussolini ordered his 'dogs of war' and his most militant supporters to retrench. The monarchy would be by-passed, not deposed. The Church, as already noted in 'Fascism and Civil Society', would have to be appeased. The emphasis on normality and legality lasted only a year, and Fascist controls were tightened still further in 1925. Nevertheless, Mussolini did clamp down on the more autonomous elements of Fascism. The Matteotti affair marked a transition: thereafter, the Fascist Party was no longer half-government, half-rebel movement, but an establishment in power that had to look grave and responsible, whatever its activists felt.

It is not easy to ascertain how much of this was part of a gradualist takeover of power, a hard-headed but longer-term strategy. It is clear, on the other hand, that Mussolini, in particular, was in a relatively weak position. Despite his rhetoric, he appeared to lack Hitler's extremist lust for the brutality required for full-blooded **totalitarianism**. Some compromises were tactical and some were forced on him by the logic of circumstances. Maintaining power against this backdrop was not an easy proposition in political terms either. Excessive zeal could scupper the best-laid plans if the old establishment balked too soon. On the other hand, insufficient militancy could leave party leaders vulnerable to opposition from within their own rank and file. Hitler's leadership style prevented this from the beginning. From his earliest days in the **Deutsche**

*Arbeiterpartei* (DAP), the forerunner to the Nazi Party, he centralised power and demanded absolute loyalty.[5] Despite the dominant role of *Il Duce*, the Italian Fascist Party (PNF) was more diverse and factionalised. Figures like **Gentile** and **Rocco** were influential in their own right. Earlier, even before the Fascist movement reached full fruition, Mussolini was almost eclipsed by the nationalist leader, Gabriele **D'Annunzio**, whose paramilitary forces occupied **Fiume** (Rijeka), a disputed Croatian city at the heart of Italian discontent after the First World War. The road to power was not only a struggle with your enemies but a contest with your rivals as well.

## INTERNECINE STRUGGLES: FROM IDEOLOGICAL CONTRADICTIONS TO PARTY PURGES

In 'The Evolution of Fascist Ideology', we saw how the inter-war fascist movements were a maze of ideological contradictions. These ambiguities and tensions had practical implications as well. They were tolerable when the movement was on the fringe of society, debating the occult or *romanitá*. However, they were much more problematic when the movement was on the threshold of real power. Both Fascism and Nazism experienced critical showdowns in which party militants were brought to heel. In Italy, this occurred after the aforementioned Matteotti Crisis. In Germany, it manifested itself in the **'Night of the Long Knives'**, in which the Storm Troopers were smashed and the *Schutzstaffel* (SS), a party-controlled élite guard, and the *Gestapo*, a Nazified state secret police, emerged more powerful. The suppression of the SA in 1934 was accompanied by action against the left wing of the Nazi movement and there were even suggestions that Nazi Party organs might be merged with those of the state.[6]

The earliest manifestation of Spain's *Falange* movement was seen as less than loyal to the military and traditionalist elements. Later, even when it had been brought under the control of **Franco** supporters, some of its activists were seen as excessively pro-German. It survived in a mutilated form. Though it appeared to be the ruling party in post-war Spain, it was the military that really held power.[7]

From a Marxian perspective, all these events signify the suppression of radicalism and the consolidation of the alliance between fascism and conservative elements. However, they can also be interpreted as a necessary requirement for stable government, regardless of the vested interests involved. As Maoist China realised decades later, permanent revolution is not sustainable for very long.

Even the cult of leadership and the *Führerprinzip* had their limits. A dictator could not be involved in every decision. Power had to be devolved. In Hitler's case, senior figures were set against one another. Competition and envy were encouraged as a means of increasing performance and keeping threats at bay. Still, some figures did amass more than their share of power: **Göbbels** used his propaganda role to become a chief ideologue of the Nazi regime. By sidestepping von **Ribbentrop**, he even emerged as its second best-known voice overseas. Meanwhile, having contributed to the neutralisation of **Röhm** and **Göring**, **Himmler** became its master of terror.

The militancy and violence of extremist movements can haunt them in other ways once they achieve power. A noticeable feature of many dictatorships is their tendency for violent power transitions. While the bureaucratic lethargy of the Soviet system generated a paradoxical stability, the most extreme and violent dictators have often lived in fear of assassination plots. Hitler, Stalin and Saddam **Hussein** are testimony to this. Indeed, their fears were not ungrounded. In Hitler's case, the **July Plot** in 1944 revealed that elements of the German Army and the old establishment could still conspire against him. When the tide turned on Mussolini, the **Fascist Grand Council**, including his son-in-law and foreign minister, Count **Ciano**, proved treacherous. Totalitarian cults of leadership can produce fantastic displays of lights, banners, parades and jubilant crowds; behind the scenes, they are invariably accompanied by the darker forces of paranoia and the most lurid conspiracies. These, in turn, fuel the violence and sadism necessary to strike fear into the hearts of their enemies, real or imagined.

Far-right movements after the **Second World War** faced a different scenario altogether. To begin with, they now had a record and it was an unenviable one. Indeed, it was so horrible that **anti-fascism** became an official ideology of the new political élites, not only on the left but on the right as well. Some critics, notably Renzo de Felice, complained that this distorted the work of historians in the immediate post-war period. He questioned the motives of those who glorified the Resistance, especially of the Communists.[8] In East Germany, anti-fascism became a sort of cult that went beyond mere rejection of Nazism. It required condemnation of anything that the ruling Socialist Unity Party of Germany defined as fascist or remotely associated with fascism. Communist rhetoric routinely accused the West German Christian Democrats of 'revanchism' and linked mainstream conservative ideas with softness on fascism.

There is a legitimate debate on the effects of this culture of denunciation. All democratic parties, of the right, left and centre, agree that it is good to warn our young against the evils of fascism and to teach the history of the **Holocaust**. On the other hand, far-right movements also benefit from continuous demonisation. They can cast themselves in the role of persecuted outsiders whose views cannot be heard and are therefore all the more mysterious to the younger generation, or to naïve and disaffected people in difficult economic circumstances. Thus, as real memories of fascism in power faded and new generations grew up, the far right began to appear as just another alternative to the mainstream. It accentuated this sense of novelty by engaging in very overt exercises in renewal, reform or reinvention.

## FRINGE MOVEMENTS

As fringe movements, fascist parties are often treated with contempt. This leads their egotistical leaders and agitated followers to feel even greater frustration and tension. When Mussolini broke with his radical socialist counterparts and Hitler was treated as a second-rate player after the 1923 **Munich Putsch**, both men chose a new strategy based on engagement with the old establishment. Embittered as a result of the experience, they became much more flexible and pragmatic. The same humiliation befell the Italian MSI movement after the war. The dominance of the Christian Democrats and the consensus around anti-Fascist thinking meant that they were marginalised for a very long time, forcing them to come to terms with the new Italian republic and its political system.

So, once brazen radicalism is recognised as inadequate to the task, the next stage on the road to power involved compromising with the establishment. In the case of Mussolini, this involved taking money from big Italian corporations. The original link with big business was not so much out of love for **capitalism** but because some Italian and foreign business interests shared Mussolini's belief in Italian intervention in the First World War.[9] He had, after all, been expelled from the Italian Socialist Party (PSI) in 1914 precisely over this issue. He had realised that **nationalism** had a broader cross-class appeal than socialism.

Much of Mussolini's dealings with the existing order had to do with a search for respectability. However, he was always acutely conscious of his weakness. On the eve of his dramatic **March on Rome**, he was negotiating with the Liberals lest they should move precipitously to ban him, while simultaneously promising revolutionary positions to followers of his rival, D'Annunzio.[10] Once in power, Mussolini pursued a twin-track strategy: he participated in a broad, multi-party coalition, in which the Fascist Party was a minority. However, on the streets, Fascists cultivated a climate of terror and near-civil war.[11]

Hitler thought that his involvement in the 1923 Munich Putsch could simultaneously outsmart his right-wing rivals but also impress them with his determination and sense of initiative. He realised that some aspects of Nazism scared traditional conservatives. Consequently, as he toyed with the parties in the *Reichstag* and sought to influence the President, Hitler tried to present himself as a good German and as somebody who was not hostile to the Catholic traditions of Bavaria. He also emphasised the need to achieve power by apparently using legitimate means. To this end, he took full advantage of the weaknesses in the German Constitution. Article 48 gave the German president powers to dissolve the *Reichstag* and to appoint the Chancellor. Right-wing authoritarians urged the president to use his emergency powers and his ability to rule by decree to move the state in an authoritarian direction. They cited the alleged Bolshevist sympathies of the left, the economic crisis and Germany's weak and chaotic political situation. Hitler supported this broad strategy, emphasising its constitutionality.[12] Finally, having been made Chancellor, Hitler ensured the fusion of the posts of Chancellor and President by using a plebiscite, an inherently democratic appeal to the people to endorse his leadership. Thus, he could crave respectability, not because he believed in it, but because he needed to get endorsement from other quarters to facilitate his rise to power.

This game also involved electoral politics. The more the right-wing parties parleyed with Hitler, the more their own voters saw him as potentially respectable rather than menacing. As Weimar progressed, the far right had little support in the 1920s, even though nationalist and conservative groups were an increasingly vocal opposition to the centre-left Weimar establishment. After the collapse of a pro-Weimar coalition in 1930, the party system fragmented and support for the Nazis and Communists increased. By 1932, the Communists and the Nazis had a combined vote of over 50 per cent. The Nazi gains were accounted for by substantial defections from the right-wing nationalist parties.[13] In this fluid situation, President von **Hindenburg**, himself an old-style authoritarian nationalist, dismissed the Centre Party Chancellor, Brüning, replacing him with a weak non-party figure, Franz von **Papen**. Von Papen had little support among the mainstream parties in the *Reichstag* but used the President's powers of decree to enact legislation. He was open to influence from all directions, especially the far right. Ultimately, he persuaded the President to appoint Hitler as Chancellor, with him as deputy. Although the *Reichstag* could overturn Presidential decrees, the fragmentation of the party system and the strength of the anti-system factions meant that the *Reichstag* was no protection for constitutional safeguards.

Once in the Chancellery, Hitler immediately took advantage of a new election to gain a far-right majority in the *Reichstag*, albeit with the help of right-wing nationalists. He also began the orchestration of a campaign of violence against opponents and started to undermine regional state governments. Adding to this climate of crisis, the *Reichstag* was set on fire and left-wing agitators, including a future Bulgarian Communist leader, were blamed. Against this backdrop, the *Reichstag* passed an Enabling Decree in 1933 that effectively secured the Hitler dictatorship. As deputies voted, the SA and SS cordoned off the streets around the building where these momentous decisions were taken.[14] Thus, the violence, intimidation and crisis environment was matched at all stages by a plethora of apparently democratic and constitutional measures designed to legitimate the Nazi coup. In this way, Hitler was answering those who had dismissed him as both a criminal and an amateur after the failure of the Munich Putsch ten years earlier.

Franco also mixed opposition politics with a desire to be part of the establishment. He was proud of his membership of the Spanish armed forces. He wanted to achieve his objectives through the official Spanish Army. Franco was distrustful of the *Falange* because of its potential militancy.[15] For him, the Army, an instrument of the establishment, was very much the place to be and it was the centre of attention, the focal point of his interests. Franco wanted to portray his left-wing opponents as the rebels who were undermining Spain, and the Spanish Army as intervening to save the nation. At the same time, Franco and his closest supporters felt themselves in opposition to the whole liberal–left establishment élite that had ruled as a partner of the Republic.

The same mixture of establishment and opposition politics can be seen elsewhere. In Japan, the establishment was at the heart of right-wing politics. The drift to the extreme right came from within: it was not the result of an attack from the streets like Mussolini's March on Rome. The militarists argued that Japan had been betrayed by the liberal politicians, but the right-wing authoritarian governments of the 1930s had paved the way for **Tōjō**'s military takeover. At no stage, however, did the Japanese militarists attempt to topple the Emperor. Indeed, they presented themselves as doing the work of the Emperor and saving the Japanese Empire.

In general terms, then, it can be said that fascists and far-right extremists often perceive the need for co-operation with establishment forces because they lack the necessary public appeal. They also realise that it could take a long time to fascistise or 'co-ordinate' the state and all its institutions. Consequently, they must focus on getting their hands on the levers of power. This was a key element in the fascist road to power.

Getting the institutions of state to do what they wanted was the first challenge facing fascists in power. Initially, they seemed to get along quite well. The establishment civil servants might have been suspicious but they also preferred the fascists to Communists or socialists, and many of them believed that their own societies were on the verge of social breakdown. In some cases, as, for example, in Germany, the establishment pre-dated the democratic experiment and the relationship was hostile anyway. Much of the German nationalist right distrusted a **Weimar Republic** dominated, as they saw it, by social democrats. They echoed the widespread view that Germany was unfairly treated at **Versailles** and had been betrayed by liberal and socialist politicians at the end of the First World War. Thus, some of the Nazi message fell on fertile ground. Despite their radical intentions, the Nazis appeared to acknowledge the links with the old order. Even the concept of a **'Third Reich'** suggested taking up where the Second Reich (or Empire) had left off at the point of its defeat.

More generally, the non-fascist but authoritarian right in inter-war Europe may have welcomed aspects of fascist rule while fearing others. This particular difficulty arose once the fascist leadership wanted to go beyond that purely conservative backlash against the status quo and institute more radical changes. There was also the problem of fascist party institutions. The fascist and Communist parties believed in setting up a parallel set of institutions to rival those of the state. This was all very fine in opposition. These institutions could shadow, challenge or reveal the weaknesses of officialdom. However, once the fascists were in power, the question arose as to the relative importance of party and state institutions. In Communist systems, the answer to this was often quite clear: the aim was to substitute party rule for state power. Thus, in the Soviet Union, Communist Party bodies were the real centres of power, and state institutions, like the Supreme Soviet, were often nominal and powerless bodies. Yet, it was easier for the Bolsheviks to put their party at the heart of the state: the old Tsarist establishment and the Provisional Government of

Alexander Kerensky had fled or crumbled, whereas in Germany and Italy the old establishment was very much in government, in the form of the army and bureaucracy. It would not go away anytime soon. It had to be placated. The problem for the fascists was how soon to open another front against the old establishment: whether to continue to co-operate with them for a long time or to institute a permanent revolution at the earliest possible opportunity.

## LOSING POWER

The loss of power was especially hard for the first generation of fascists. Going back into parliamentary opposition was not in their game plan: Hitler planned a 'One Thousand Year Reich', and he meant a National Socialist Reich. Fascists portrayed themselves as the party of action and of brute force. It was the pursuit and exercise of power, not the elaboration of new philosophies or theories, that gave them their *raison d'être*. Hence, defeat was characterised as someone else's fault, as an act of betrayal. Disappointments and setbacks were signs of treachery. The absolutist nature of fascist ideology and its obsession with struggle also made defeat harder to bear. The struggle with the enemy was a battle unto death. When it came to the deathblow, it had to be 'either them or us'. In such a climate of frustration, the fascist élite besieged in the lair turns in on itself and becomes ever more fanatical. Since it is already focused on the person of the leader, it can do little else. An open or pluralistically structured organisation could deliberate at such a point; a frustrated individual can only despair or descend into a psychotic state. From his *Führerbunker* under the Berlin Chancellery, Hitler denounced many of his closest associates and accused them of treason. While Nazi leaders scrambled to find some diplomatic escape route, they were ultimately powerless as long as Hitler was alive. The **leadership cult** meant that he and the Reich were synonymous to the end.

A similar scenario arose in the Italian end-game. As the Allies closed in, leading Fascists tried to disassociate themselves from Mussolini. Here, we see that the Fascist Party and its Grand Council had a more meaningful independent existence than the ***National Sozialistische Deutsche Arbeiterpartei*** (NSDAP). Among those leading the 'treachery' was Count Ciano, the son-in-law of Il Duce. A coup against the Fascist state, involving the King, Victor Emmanuel, resulted in Mussolini's capture and detention. Given his own penchant for dramatic gestures and feats of action, what happened next must have appeared as if in one of Mussolini's wildest fantasies: he was 'rescued' by the Germans in the chaos that ensued as Italy was divided in three. However, Hitler did not really trust Mussolini at this stage. After all, he had only joined the Germans at the last minute. Italy had vacillated and switched positions in the First World War as well. Mussolini could establish a new Italian Social Republic, the so-called **Salò Republic**. However, it would be a German puppet state.[16] It was occupied by German troops and the Fascists did, or were forced to do, all the things that had separated them from the Nazis. As Hitler became more extreme toward the end, so did the Salò Republic, as illustrated in its radical and militant Verona Manifesto of 1943. It was as if the original Fascist 'revolution' was in full spring again. However, it was an eerie revolution this time, proclaiming heroism but surrounded by the ruins of war, and all of this under German occupation and tutelage. The scene was more reminiscent of the fall of the Roman Empire, (ironically, to the Germanic 'barbarians' once again) than Mussolini's vision of a new Rome basking in glory.

The Japanese denouement was just as dramatic. Here though, the militarists were actually off-stage. It was Emperor **Hirohito** and the citizens of Hiroshima and Nagasaki who felt the burden. Hirohito, who was portrayed as a deity, was revealed to be human and capable of being humiliated. He who could never be seen was forced to appear in public. As for the two southern cities, their fate suggested that Japan itself was following its kamikaze pilots, suffering death and destruction for an indefinable cause. However, Japanese **militarism** and extremism were harder to pin down. Tōjō's policy was to some extent a continuation or extension of that pursued by his predecessors. The beginnings of Japanese 'fascism' (if it really was fascism) were hard to identify. The military chiefs were like passing military chiefs anywhere: pinning blame on the Emperor was deemed both difficult and politically dangerous in view of his formerly 'divine' status. Though individuals were tried and punished, the real source of Japan's nightmare was never identified and appeared to slip away into history like a malign spirit.

For the next twenty years, alleged collaborationists and puppets tried to disassociate themselves from the inter-war and wartime regimes. Some failed and were executed or imprisoned; others managed to hide or to excuse themselves. The **Cold War** was an inadvertent bonus. Western countries soon became preoccupied with a new threat from the Soviet Union. **Denazification** continued but took second place to fighting **Communism**. In France and Italy, insipient political instability raised a particularly strong fear of Communist subversion or even of its electoral success.

### JUSTIFY YOURSELF: THE RETURN TO IDEOLOGY

The post-war far right has come in three manifestations. The first are neo-fascist groups seeking a return to fascism, albeit with refinements to take account of new circumstances. These parties are prepared to risk connections with the inter-war period, as when the Republican Party in the Germany of the late 1980s named a leader who was a former member of the SS.[17] The second are neo-fascist and post-fascist groups whose agenda emphasised a new beginning and a break with the inter-war years. The third are violent or extremist right-wing protest politics with no links to past fascisms, often responding to local circumstances.

At the beginning of this chapter, we noted how easy it was for fascists and pre-fascists to make dramatic claims: they had no record. Now the fascists had a record and the far right as a whole had been tarnished by it. The principal task of the far right is to deal with that record and shift the focus to their current agenda. This is done in either of two ways: by questioning the record of fascism through **Historical Revisionism**, or by distancing themselves from it altogether or even denouncing old-style fascism.

New far-right protest politics is heavily influenced by the experience of the US. Here, there is a danger in dismissing very conservative opinions on the right of the US Republican Party that would seem too conservative for Gaullists or Christian Democrats. Such views may be too right wing for Europeans, but they are well within the US conservative mainstream. Of relevance to our consideration of the far right here are movements that endorse or engage in violence and that are beyond the *US* conservative fringe. These include opponents of abortion who are prepared to bomb clinics or kill doctors, as well as paramilitary 'militias' and extremist groups (like, for instance, the **Order**) that specifically prepare for war with the United Nations or against the US Federal Government and its agencies.[18] Ironically, many of these groups are copying the 'direct action' tactics and even the discourse used by anarchists and the far left in the 1960s.[19] Some of these groups also borrow from Protestant **Christian Fundamentalism** an obsession with Biblical exegesis, e.g. with claims that the US is the 'new Promised Land' or that God-fearing Americans can look forward to a forthcoming clash between the Christ and anti-Christ on Mount Lebanon or elsewhere in the Middle East. Because of its obscurity and prophetic content, the Book of Daniel is a particular favourite. Such prophecies are not simply spiritual exercises but guides to domestic and foreign policy positions that must be adopted in preparation for the Apocalypse.

In addition to the new manifestations of far-right politics in local circumstances, there are far-right phenomena that pre-date fascism and appear endemic to certain regions. Military dictatorships tied to landowners or powerful élites have been a factor in Latin American politics since the nineteenth century. Some adopted a proto-fascist or para-fascist hue in the 1930s, notably under Ibañez in Chile, **Péron** in Argentina and, to a lesser extent, **Vargas** in Brazil.[20] However, when fascism disappeared, they reverted to classic Latin dictatorships. Interestingly, the left-wing military dictatorships in Peru in the 1960s and 1970s used **populism** and radicalism in the same way, as a sugar coating for their otherwise oppressive regimes. Indeed, there was a tendency for traditional authoritarians everywhere to adopt fascist features or forms at that time, almost as if it was a fad. Thus, Fairbank describes the paramilitary 'Blueshirts' associated with Chiang Kai-Shek in China in the 1930s as fascist, but if they were, it was only a passing phase.[21] He too reverted to traditional autocracy once it was clear that fascism was a non-starter. Racist extremism in the southern US is the other continuous far-right phenomenon that can be traced back to the immediate aftermath of the US Civil War. Though greatly diminished since the 1960s, organisations like the **Ku Klux Klan** do make an appearance from time to time and their outlook is often evident in the propaganda of newer groups.

For a period after the war, responses to fascism were polarised but overwhelmingly negative. Under these circumstances, groups promoting neo-fascist doctrines could either hide, or present their case as an act of nostalgia, defiance or both. In Italy, the MSI was the principal voice of **neo-fascism**. When war memories had faded and many **middle-class** people were again anxious over leftist violence and agitation during the 1960s, the extremists on the right appear to have become even braver. Bracher argues that the leading neo-Nazi party in post-war Germany, the *National Demokratische Partei Deutschlands* (NPD), was not really 'new' when it appeared on the political stage in 1964: it was an extension of the *Deutsche Reichspartei* that had been active in the 1950s. The NPD claimed to be democratic but was also 'anti-system'. It made reference to what it considered 'good' in National Socialism.[22] For Bracher, one of the worrying aspects of this party was its ability to pick up votes in areas that had been Nazi strongholds in the past, as well as the number of ex-Nazis in its ranks. The NPD had competition from the *Republikaner* party in the late 1980s and early 1990s. Though still relatively ambivalent on Nazism itself, the *Republikaner* made even fewer references to the Nazi past, focusing instead on **immigration**. As the effort to distance the far right from National Socialism becomes ever more complex, these parties craft different messages for different audiences. Among hardcore supporters or even the thuggish or 'skinhead' element that are part of their membership, they can be quite crude and explicit about violence, **racism** and the 'virtues' of Nazism. However, when addressing the public at large or conservative traditionalists worried about immigration or **unemployment**, they stick to a single-issue line and appear to echo old right themes. For some of the new arrivals on the far-right scene, there is little glorification of inter-war fascism at all, just a silence on the issue. Critics charge such parties with '**crypto-fascism**', concealing their neo-fascism beneath a veneer of respectability.

The development of **post-fascism**, akin to post-Communism on the left, makes the task of analysing the far right still more difficult. The best example here is the *Alleanza Nazionale* (AN) led by **Fini** in Italy. This party has cleansed itself so much of violence, thuggery and reminders of Fascism that it looks like another entity altogether. It was able to enter the Berlusconi government in 2001 without much difficulty; allegations about Berlusconi's business empire provoked more controversy. And yet, the AN and many of its leaders are a product of the MSI. The ex-MSI elements in the AN, with their air of respectability, are still, to some extent, heirs of the post-war MSI, which, in turn, came out of the Fascist experience. This can be interpreted as an evolutionary process but more cynical observers might prefer to see a cyclical pattern. Does the emergence of post-fascism mean that the centre-right has finally succeeded in taming fascism? Or are Italian political élites headed for humiliation once again, as the Giolittian Liberals were in the past? Whatever the answer, the practice and study of far-right politics, at least in Italy, has entered uncharted territory.

Elsewhere, the route to power still follows a traditional path. Critics of the Japanese political system allege that the extreme right exercises influence from within the establishment, as it did in the past, although to a much lesser extent. The Education Ministry, for instance, is constantly embroiled in disputes over nationalist textbooks. The Imperial Family is slow to acknowledge the full extent of its complicity in the actions of the Tōjō regime. Ministers from Japan's mainstream centre-right Liberal Democratic Party often issue vague statements about the war. However, this failure to come to terms with 1945 may be a cultural problem, part of a desire to leave well enough alone. Few take seriously the prospect of Japan being seized by a militarist clique. On the other hand, the conspiracies of the *Aum Shin Rikyo* sect in the early 1990s came as a surprise to outside observers. They not only planted a nerve gas bomb in the Tokyo subway but also were negotiating substantial arms purchases overseas. Could they have attacked the Japanese cabinet or killed large numbers of civilians? Who knows what effect such a 'success' could have had, or the impact of such a shock, on the otherwise plodding and calm demeanour of Japanese politics. Their doctrines were equally mysterious: outwardly, their radio broadcasts were about 'the Eternal Truth in Holy Heaven' and 'Heavenly Peace', a synthesis of Buddhism and **Christianity**. Yet, their followers were preparing for a violent apocalypse.

The democratic consensus in Latin America since the 1980s, coupled with the end of the Cold War, the crisis of Cuban Communism and exhaustion of both sides in the region's guerrilla wars, have made military coups especially unpopular in Latin America. Even the Péronists became US-style neo-liberal free marketers. On the other hand, if capitalist liberal democracy falters and there is no socialist alternative, right-wing populism may still constitute a familiar '**Third Way**' for some Latin generals. The experience of Peru, when an elected President, Alberto Fujimori, converted himself overnight into a dictator, suggests that a coup need not be led by a general. The region's right-wing regimes have always shown a flair for innovation when it comes to style and form: even those who appeared to copy the European dictators did it their way.

Faced with the difficulties of a world in which liberal democracy is more triumphalist than ever, far-right groups are following the lead of the left and co-operating across frontiers. As argued in 'Diplomacy and International Relations', this was also a goal of the inter-war movements, but one frustrated by their own rivalries. This time, the leaders are in opposition and they are not at war. The impetus for co-operation is greater. Thus, the European extreme right works together, in the European Parliament and elsewhere, in transnational groupings. There is also a more narrowly focused '**Eurofascism**' involving German and Nordic groups with a common interest in European **civilisation** and the Nordic races. Co-operation among extremist groups beyond Europe raises the prospect of 'universal' movements, including '**Universal Fascism**'. This kind of globalisation of solidarity is not new. After all, the Chilean dictator, Augusto **Pinochet**, was the only foreign dignitary at General Franco's funeral.[23] Given the existence of military dictatorships all over Latin America when he was in power, Franco could have turned the concept of Latin solidarity or *Hispanidad* into a celebration of solidarity among dictators. On the other hand, the diversity of far-right movements and their roots in local and national cultures makes a globalisation of rightist extremism very difficult to realise. The best they could hope for is tactical co-operation on a case-by-case basis. A 'universal' fascism is another convenient myth but little more.

Despite the lust for power shown by Hitler and Mussolini, it is possible that some of the more recent far-right groups are coming to enjoy the role of permanent opposition, just as 'New Left' campaigners did in the 1960s. They know they will never rule but their task is not to play the parliamentary system, anyway, but to frustrate it. Permanent opposition allows them to gain public attention, support and perhaps even influence without the responsibility of power. Campaigns and struggles are like the hunter's chase, more exciting than the catch itself. As ethnic rioting spreads or mainstream parties flurry to compete with their policies, they can sit back and observe the impact. When things go wrong, the 'establishment', the government or their political enemies can always get the blame.

This 'permanent campaigning opposition' model is, ironically, partly influenced by the campaigning groups of the New Left in the 1960s and 1970s. They, like far-right campaigners, stressed the futility of formal democratic politics and urged 'direct action' or 'extra-parliamentary opposition' instead. There is also an element of old-style syndicalism and street-fighting 'action' in this, with echoes of the 1930s.

## POWER OR INFLUENCE?

So what does the far right want today? As in the past, they would ideally like to hold the reins of power in government. This can be achieved by going down the route of respectability, by playing the parliamentary game, as Fini has done in Italy. However, the record of fascism is too heavy a burden to carry, even for the non-fascist far right. They have realised that the door to national government is closed to them in most Western democracies. The mode of struggle must change accordingly.

Many will settle for power at local level. The FN gloried for a while in its 1995 victories in **Toulon**, **Marignane** and **Orange**, and a later success in **Vitrolles**.[24] Earlier, Germany's *Republikaner* party had fared particularly well in the 1989 local elections in Berlin. However, the greatest change since the Second World War is the realisation by the far right, like the far left, that extra-parliamentary opposition can be fun, and, moreover, that it is another avenue to publicity and influence, and, hence, to power, under conditions of mature liberal democracy. It is a slower process but no less corrosive for that. The fabric of democracy is weakened by each manifestation of ethnic or racial hatred or by tolerance of violence. It is also weakened when democrats stoop to the fascists' level by abandoning norms like freedom of expression in the interests of preserving democracy. Reading the propaganda of Göbbels or Mussolini, it is clear that the most effective lines of fascist propaganda are written by well-meaning people whose actions or utterances make democratic systems themselves look chaotic, incompetent, oppressive or hypocritical. In liberal democracy's tragic crisis of confidence between 1890 and 1922, the fascists and their predecessors persuaded many well-meaning people that democratic values themselves were insufficient to fight the threat of Communist dictatorship. Must we now admit that those same values are insufficient to protect us from neo-fascism? And what are the consequences of our answer? Studying the far-right quest for power will tell us much about these movements, as well as about the stability and security of existing democratic institutions in yet another period of great social change.

## EXTRACTS

### Document 1

*Reining in the fascist revolution*

After many years of radical street action and anti-capitalist agitation, the Fascist Party used the second half of the 1920s to consolidate its power and build relationships with the Italian establishment. The party called for an end to spontaneous Fascist activity.

> The party and its members, from the highest to the lowest, now that the revolution is complete, are only a conscious instrument of the will of the state, whether at the centre or at the periphery. Now that the state is equipped with all its own methods of prevention and repression, there are some 'residues' that must disappear. I am speaking of *squadrismo*, which, in 1927, is simply anachronistic, sporadic, but which reappears in an undisciplined fashion during periods of public commotion. These illegal activities must stop, the era of reprisals, destruction and violence is over.
>
> The prefects must prevent this happening by using all means at their disposal.

(Source: *Partito Nazionale Fascista* (PNF) circular to prefects on 5 January 1927, reprinted in J. Whittam, *Fascist Italy*, Manchester, Manchester University Press, 1995, p. 153)

### Document 2

*Austria's Freedom Party programme: an endorsement of plebiscites*

This could simply be an Alpine phenomenon, copying Switzerland, but it also echoes the hostility to parliamentary representation of the Nazis and of the pre-war authoritarian regimes in Austria.

> Parliamentarianism has to be complemented by the development of instruments of direct democracy. The legislative bodies – the National Assembly and the

Federal Council – must be strengthened in comparison with the executive power. The National Assembly should be elected on the basis of a genuine electoral law. The Federal Council must be inter-linked with those sent from the provincial legislatures. In all fields of federal and provincial legislation, plebiscitary rights should be guaranteed and extended. Thus it is necessary to ... reduce bureaucratic obstacles in conducting public questionnaires.

(Source: Austrian Freedom Party website. Available online at
http://www.fpoe.or.at/ [accessed 20 August 2001])

## Document 3

*Jean-Marie Le Pen: a man of action*

On its official website, the French FN highlights the heroic and active character of its leader.

With a diploma in Political Science and a degree in Law, he was president of the Paris Law Students Association. He was a sportsman who played rugby and was vice-president of the Pierre de Coubertin Committee. In January 1953, when the Netherlands were submerged by devastating floods, he took the initiative to organise a rescue group made up of student volunteers who went up to Holland to help the afflicted people. He had no hesitation in directly contacting the President of the Republic, Vincent Auriol, to obtain the support of the authorities, which was granted. In 1955 he was the delegate of the Union for the Defence of French Youth. In January 1956 he was elected Member of Parliament for Paris, and at the age of 27 became the youngest parliamentary leader in the National Assembly. In 1957 he became General Secretary of the National Servicemen's Front (FNC). The next year, after being re-elected Member of Parliament for the 5th *Arrondissement* of Paris, he joined the parliamentary group of the self-employed and Farmers National Centre Party whose chairman was Antoine Pinay. He was war budget speaker for parliament and speaker on defence for the Senate. In 1972, Jean-Marie Le Pen set up the *Front National* in spite of difficulties. In business life, he still runs a publishing and record company specialising in historical novels. His collection 'Men and Deeds of the 20th Century' has received the *Grand Prix du Disque* on several occasions. Jean-Marie Le Pen has written three works: *Les Français d'Abord* (Carrère-Lafon, 1984), *La France est de Retour* (Carrère-Lafon 1985) and *L'Éspoir* (Albatros, 1989). He wrote the preface to *Droite et Démocratie Économique* (1978) and *Pour la France* (1986). Jean-Marie Le Pen is one the few contemporary politicians who has risked his life for his country and for his ideas. He served as an officer in the Foreign Parachute Battalion in Indo-China and in the glorious 1st Foreign Parachute Regiment in Algeria. During his command of the Foreign Legion in Algeria, he took part in the Franco-British Suez operation. His political commitment is based on love of his people and his homeland together with a lofty and noble idea of politics. A man of faith, he believes that decadence is not inevitable and that it is not true that our country must stop making history and submit itself to the history of other nations.

(Source: *Front National* (France), Home Page (English): Party Publicity, 20 August 2001. Available online at http://www.front-national.com/ [accessed 20 August 2001])

**Document 4**

*Austrian Freedom Party programme: ideological competition with liberal and conservative parties*

This extract demonstrates the evolution of far-right party programmes away from totalitarianism in line with the post-Communist environment. It also illustrates the use of obscure language and competition with other right-wing or liberal tendencies.

> Government indoctrination, tutelage and state-induced dependency are funda-mentally in contradiction to human dignity and deny human diversity. The recognition of human diversity, however, does not justify any discriminatory evaluation of the dignity of the individual. Imposed benevolence and totalitarian transformation to new beings to fit a present mould and ideological concept are not compatible with human dignity.

(Source: Austrian Freedom Party website. Available online at<br>http://www.fpoe.or.at/ [accessed 15 August 2001])

**Document 5**

*Hitler on propaganda*

Writing in *Mein Kampf*, Hitler stresses the limited reasoning powers of the mass public and urges a systematic dumbing down of propaganda in response.

> [N]ot by any means to dispense individual instructions to those who already have an educated opinion on things or who wish to form such an opinion on grounds of objective study – because that is not the purpose of propaganda, it must appeal to the feelings of the public rather than to their reasoning powers. All propaganda must be presented in a popular form and must fix its intellectual level so as not to be above the heads of the least intellectual of those to whom it is directed. Thus its purely intellectual level will have to be that of the lowest mental common denominator among the public it is desired to reach. When there is question of bringing a whole nation within the circle of its influence, as happens in the case of war propaganda, then too much attention cannot be paid to the necessity of avoiding a high level, which presupposes a relatively high degree of intelligence among the public.

(Source: A. Hitler, *Mein Kampf*, Chapter 6. Reprinted at<br>www.stormfront.org (far-right site))

# III
# FASCISM AND THE
# FAR RIGHT

## Sources, names and terms

# GUIDE TO SOURCES

## NOTES

- This annotated guide to primary sources is designed to pinpoint a variety of key texts, document collections and websites.
- Everything listed is fascism- or far right-related in some sense but there are exceptions to this rule. The running commentary will help the reader in this respect.

## GENERAL

R. Griffin (ed.), *Fascism* (Oxford, Oxford University Press, 1995) is a broad-ranging and highly authoritative anthology of texts and covers fascist movements and interpretations. E. Weber, *Varieties of Fascism: Doctrines of Revolution in the Twentieth Century* (New York, Van Nostrund, 1964) is part analysis and part anthology of documents. It includes texts from Belgium, Romania and Hungary, as well as from core fascist states. See also N. Greene, *Fascism: An Anthology* (New York, Crowell, 1968), M. Blinkhorn, *Fascism and the Right in Europe 1919–1945* (London, Longman, 2000), a book that includes a range of key documents, and D. Smith, *Left and Right in Twentieth-Century Europe* (London, Longman, 1970), a comparative study that weighs up Communism, Fascism and Nazism in the same analysis, and includes connected extracts.

## ROOTS OF FASCISM

M.D. Biddiss (ed.), *A. de Gobineau: Selected Political Writings* (London, Jonathan Cape, 1970) brings to life the 'Father of Racism' and organises his writings around key themes – racial inequality, élite morality and national/international crisis. Refer also to A. de Gobineau, *Sons of Kings* (London, Oxford Library of French Classics, 1966). To understand the impetus behind Social Darwinism – a key current within early fascism – see C. Darwin, *The Origin of Species* (Oxford, Oxford University Press, 1951).

R. Pois (ed.), *A. Rosenberg: Selected Writings* (London, Jonathan Cape, 1970) is a collection of racial treatises that had a significant influence on the Nazis (Rosenberg's most famous work, *The Myth of the Twentieth Century*, is quoted extensively). Refer also to G. **Sorel**, *Reflections on Violence* (London, Collier-Macmillan, 1961), a book that puts great emphasis on '**myth**' as a political tool, a way of thinking that appealed to the syndicalists and neo syndicalists who were crucial to the development of Fascism in Italy. On a different tack, see S.E. Finer (ed.), *V. Pareto: Sociological Writings* (London, Pall Mall Press, 1966) and G. Hegel, *The Philosophy of Right* (London, Oxford University Press, 1978). This latter work contains sections and passages that would have appealed to Fascist theoreticians who, on the whole, used Hegel very selectively.

## ITALY

A. Lyttelton (ed.), *Italian Fascisms: From Pareto to Gentile* (London, Jonathan Cape, 1973) is an excellent introduction to the various strands and includes extracts from the writings of **Mussolini**, **Pareto**, **Prezzolini**, **Corradini**, **Soffici**, **D'Annunzio**, **Lanzillo**, **Marinetti**, **Malaparte**, **Rocco** and **Gentile**.

Mussolini's own ideas can be gleaned from *The Corporate State* (New York, Howard Fertig, 1975 [1936]) – a collection of speeches and documents – and M. Ascoli (ed.), *The Fall of Mussolini 1942–44* (New York, Farrar, Straus & Co., 1948), a well-packaged guide to *Il Duce*'s verdict on events. See his wife's reflections – R. Mussolini, *The Real Mussolini* (London, Saxon, 1973) – and refer also to the curious work by Cassius, *The Trial of Mussolini* (London, Victor Gollancz, 1943), a make-believe version of Mussolini's visit to court!

On foreign policy and diplomacy there is nowhere to go but A. Mayer (ed.), *Ciano's Diary 1937–38* (London, Methuen, 1952) – which lifts the lid on the **Anschluss**, Munich, Czechoslovakia and the **Anti-Comintern Pact** – and H. Gibson (ed.), *The Ciano Diaries 1939–1943* (New York, Doubleday, 1946). See also M. Muggeridge (ed.), *Ciano's Diplomatic Papers* (London, Odhams, 1948), an intriguing collection of conversations, letters and reports from the period 1936–42.

In addition, G. Ferrero, *Four Years of Fascism* (London, King, 1973 [1924]), is a vivid portrayal of the last years of the 'old regime' and the first years of Fascism.

For Mussolini nostalgia, go to the *Movimento Fascismo e Liberta* website at www.geocities.com.Capitol Hill/Lobby/5552.

More on the two main far-right electoral forces of today can be gleaned from www.msifiammatric.it, the official website of the *Movimento Sociale Italiano* (MSI), and www.alleanzanazionale.it, the official website of the *Alleanza Nazionale* (AF) – very organised and professional looking.

## GERMANY

The obvious starting point is A. **Hitler**, *Mein Kampf* (London, Heinemann, 1969). H.R. Trevor-Roper (ed.), *Hitler's Table Talk* (London, Weidenfeld & Nicolson, 1973) is a summary of private conversations involving the **Führer**, 1941–4; W. Maser (ed.), *Hitler's Letters and Notes* (London, Heinemann, 1973) is a collection of transcribed correspondence; and H. Rauschning, *Hitler*

*Speaks* (London, Thornton Butterworth, 1939) is verbatim notes of the author's discussions with the Nazi leader.

See also A. Hitler, *Secret Book* (New York, Grove Press, 1962), N.H. Baynes (ed.), *The Speeches of Adolf Hitler* (Oxford, Oxford University Press, 1942) and G.W. Prange (ed.), *Hitler's Words* (Washington, American Council on Public Affairs, 1944).

Away from Hitler there are several significant memoirs: H. Heiber (ed.), *The Early Goebbels Diaries* (London, Weidenfeld & Nicolson, 1962) and L.P. Lochner (ed.), *The Goebbels Diaries 1942–1943* (New York, Doubleday, 1948). See also W.A. Boelcke, *The Secret Conferences of Dr Goebbels* (London, Weidenfeld & Nicolson, 1967), a collection of conference minutes.

A. **Speer**, *Inside the Third Reich* (London, 1970) is the most celebrated account of Nazism, and narrates the story right up to Nuremberg. F. von **Papen**, *Memoirs* (London, Deutsch, 1952) is a very personal story that begins in the late nineteenth century. Less notorious figures also penned their testimonies: Ambassador U. von Hassell, *The von Hassell Diaries 1938–1944* (Connecticut, Greenwood, 1977) narrates the period 1938–43; ex-Gauleiter A. Krebs, *The Infancy of Nazism* (London, New Viewpoints, 1976), concentrates on the psychology of Nazism as a system and the psyche of individual Nazis like **Hess**, **Göbbels** and **Strasser**; W.E. Dodd and M. Dodd (eds), *Ambassador Dodd's Diary* (London, Victor Gollancz, 1941) tells the story of the period 1933–8 through the US Ambassador in Berlin (and also includes a helpful scene-setting introduction by C.A. Beard). See also F. Thyssen, *I Paid Hitler* (London, Hodder & Stoughton, 1941) and H. Schacht, *Account Settled* (London, 1948).

To understand a key influence on Nazism, see O. **Spengler**, *The Decline of the West* (London, 1971) and *The Hour of Decision* (London, 1963).

The best collection of texts is J. Noakes and G. Pridham (eds), *Documents on Nazism* (London, Jonathan Cape, 1974). B. Lane and L. Rupp (eds), *Nazi Ideology before 1933* (Manchester, Manchester University Press, 1978) is also a useful selection of extracts on **race**, economics and society, and contains key excerpts from the Nazis' political programme.

On Nazi foreign policy, see *Documents on German Foreign Policy 1918–45* (London, HMSO, 1983 – Vols C and D) and *Hitler's War Directives* (London, Sidgwick & Jackson, 1964), a collection of military documents from the period 1939–45.

Other angles on Nazism come courtesy of W. Shirer, *Berlin Diary* (London, Hamish Hamilton, 1941), the 1939–40 journal of a German news correspondent; H.K. Smith, *Last Train from Berlin* (London, Hollen Street Press), a US newsman's view of the late 1930s and early 1940s in Germany; H. Metelmann, *A Hitler Youth* (London, Caliban, 1922), the memoirs of a once enthusiastic member of the Hitler Youth; *Dimitroff's Letters from Prison* (London, Victor Gollancz, 1935), a selection of correspondence that casts interesting light on the Reichstag fire. On the denouement, see International Military Tribunal, *Proceedings* (Nuremberg, 1948).

On Weimar, see A. Kaes, M. Jay and E. Dimendberg, *The Weimar Republic Sourcebook* (Berkeley, University of California, 1994), a very thorough collection, and M.P. Price, *Dispatches from the Weimar Republic* (London, Pluto, 1999), an interesting selection of *Daily Herald* reportage from the period 1918–23.

On the modern-day far right, go to www.rep.de, the official website of the **Republikaner** movement, and also www.rep-berlin.de (the party in Berlin) and www.rep-landtagbw.de (the party in Baden Württtenberg).

## FRANCE

J.S. McClelland, *The French Right from de Maistre to Maurras* (London, Jonathan Cape, 1971) is an excellent survey of writings. In tracing the history of the radical right, McClelland takes extracts from the work of de Maistre, Taine, **Drumont**, Sorel, **Le Bon**, **Barrès** and **Maurras**. Claudel D. Thomson, (ed.), *Empire and Republic* (London, Macmillan, 1968) is a collection of primary extracts and includes many that are related to fascism (or varieties of fascism).

For a taster of Barrès's writings, see 'The Panama scandal', *Cosmopolitan* XVII (June 1894); *The Soul of France: Visits to Invaded Districts* (London, T. Fisher & Unwin, 1915) and 'Young soldiers of France', *The Atlantic Monthly* CXX (July 1917). The works of 1915 and 1917 are particularly stirring and evocative.

For a first-hand account of February 1934, see L. Ducloux, *From Blackmail to Treason* (London, Deutsch, 1958). For excellent insights into the workings of **Vichy** and **collaboration**, refer to *France during the German Occupation, 1940–44* (California, Hoover Institution, *c*. 1947 – 2 vols) – a gigantic collection of post-1945 recollections – and P. **Laval**, *The Unpublished Diary of Pierre Laval* (London, The Falcon Press, 1948), a fantastic *cri de coeur* from a man about to die. Meanwhile, P. Tissier, *The Government of Vichy* (London, Harrap, 1942) is a hostile but illuminating account.

The **Front National**'s (FN) official website, www.front-national.com, is an impressive site with English-language options available. **Mégret**'s new party can be found at www.m-n-r.com – again, modern and professionally designed.

## GREAT BRITAIN

**Mosley**'s political ideas emerge in a variety of publications: most notably, *My Life* (London, Nelson, 1968), which tells the tale of his political odyssey, and *Mosley – Right or Wrong?* (London, Lion, 1961), which incorporates his in-depth answers to 316 questions emanating from journalists and ordinary people; See also: O. Mosley, *Fascism: 100 Questions Asked and Answered* (London, 1936); O. Mosley, *The Greater Britain* (London, BUF, 1932), and O. Mosley and J. Strachey, *Revolution by Reason* (London, 1925). W.A. Rudlin, *The Growth of Fascism in Great Britain* (London, Allen & Unwin, 1935) stands as a fairly predictable '**democracy** in crisis' account and includes a series of intriguing documents relating to the Olympia episode.

The modern British **National Front** can be explored via www.natfront.com, its official website. The **British National Party** can be located at www.bnp.org.uk, an official website that is strong on topical news.

## THE NETHERLANDS AND BELGIUM

### The Netherlands

The best way to understand the Dutch experience of fascism is to dip into one of several diaries. *The Diary of Anne Frank* (London, Hutchinson, 1947) is obviously the most famous wartime account but there are others. P. Mechanicus, *Waiting for Death* (London, Calder & Boyars, 1968) and Etty, *A Diary 1941–43* (London, Jonathan Cape, 1983) are both compelling depictions of Nazi invasion from a Jewish perspective. Dutch Foreign Minister E.N. van Kleffers offers his first-hand version of events in *The Rape of the Netherlands* (London, Hodder & Stoughton, 1940), as does newspaper editor L. De Jong in *Holland Fights the Nazis* (London, Drummond), written during the war.

### Belgium

To understand the mentality of the country's twenty-first century far right, see http://ubj.org, the regularly updated site of the *Vlaams Bloc Jongeren*; www.frontnational.be, the official website of the Belgian Front National; www.fnb.to, the official website of the *Front Nouveau de Belge/Front Nieuw België*; and www.chez.com, the official website of the *Alliance Nationale*.

## SCANDINAVIA

### Norway

On the **Quisling** episode, refer to P.M. Hayes, *Quisling* (Newton Abbot, David & Charles, 1971), an in-depth political biography that unearths a variety of new documents relating to Quisling's trial. See also T. Myklebost, *They Came as Friends* (London, Victor Gollancz, 1943), a highly emotive commentary on Norway's wartime relationship with Germany; and M. Wright, *Norwegian Diary 1940–1945* (London, Friends Peace and International Relations Committee, 1974), a very personal account of the non-violent campaign against the Quisling regime. As regards contemporary politics, see www.frp.no (**Progress Party**).

### Sweden

See www.nydemokrati.se for more on the New Democracy movement.

## Denmark

The country's 'First Patriotic Homepage' can be located at www.patriot.dk. Freedom 2000 (formerly known as the Progress Party) can be located at www.frp.dk, and the **Danish People's Party** at www.danskfolkeparti.dk.

## Finland

Go to http://kauhajoki.fi for the official website of the *Isänmaallinen Kansanliike* (IKL), complete with stirring medieval imagery.

## EASTERN EUROPE

### Hungary

On the inter-war experience, see H. **Horthy**, *Memoirs* (London, Hutchinson, 1956).

### Romania

The official website of the Iron Cross can be found at http://pages.prodigy.net. See also www.geocities.com/CapitolHill/Senate/1268 for some serious **Codreanu** nostalgia.

### Russia

The bizarre world of Vladimir **Zhirinovsky** can be explored at www.ldpr.ru, the official website of his Liberal Democratic Party. See also www.geocities.com/Colosseum/Loge/8461, the official website of the *Pamyat* movement.

## SPAIN AND PORTUGAL

C.F. Delzell (ed.), *Mediterranean Fascism 1919–1945* (London, Macmillan, 1971), incorporates documentary evidence from Spain and Portugal (and Italy).

### Spain

H. Thomas (ed.), *The Selected Writings of José Antonio Primo de Rivera* (London, Jonathan Cape, 1972) is an excellent introduction to the ideas that lay behind Falangism. It forms part of the 'Roots of the Right' series and includes a wide array of documents from the 1930s.

On the Civil War, refer to F. Morrow, *Revolution and Counter-Revolution in Spain* (London, Pathfinder, 1996), a classic left-wing view of events. As regards modern-day political organisations, see:

- www.falange.es – official website of the *Falange Española de las Jons.*
- www.geocities.com/dnbcn2001/wmDN.html – website of *Democracia Nacional* (Barcelona).
- http://mens-es.com – official website of the *Movimiento Europeo Nacional Sindicalista* (MENS/CENS/FENS)

And for the General **Franco** Museum, go to www.geocities.com/Eureka/Park/3167/, where you will discover an array of Franco-related information.

## Portugal

For **Salazar** nostalgia go to www.geocities.com/CapitolHill/Lobby/6559/, and click on the image of the dictator for more details. There are links to biographical information and ***Estado Novo*** – and some evocative music.

## CENTRAL EUROPE

### Austria

G.-K. Kindermann, *Hitler's Defeat in Austria 1933–1934* (London, Hurst, 1988) includes a selection of interesting documents. On modern-day politics, go to www.fpoe.or.at, the official website of **Haider**'s Freedom Party (and click through to the English-language version).

### Switzerland

On the modern far right, see www.schweizer-demokraten.ch, the official website of the Swiss SD, and www.udc.ch, the official website of the Swiss *Union Démocratique du Centre.*

### US

See P.B. Levy, *The Civil Rights Movement* (London, Greenwood, 1998) for a selection of primary sources and an extensive bibliography. On the modern-day far right, see www.davidduke.com for an archive of **Duke**'s writings and other resources. There are also David Duke .org and .net sites. Refer also to www.buchanan.org, Pat **Buchanan**'s official website.

### JAPAN

The phenomenon of inter-war **ultra-nationalism** is covered in two useful collections of documents: R. Tsunoda, W.M.T. de Berry and D. Keene, *Sources of Japanese Tradition, Volume II* (New York, Columbia University Press, 1964) and D. John Lu, *Sources of Japanese History, Volume II* (New York, McGraw-

Hillbrook, 1974). On the modern far right, see www.nsjap.com/axis/english.html.

## AFRICA

### South Africa

See www.lantic.co.za, the official website of the *Afrikaner Weerstandsbeweging* (AWB).

## CONTEMPORARY REPORTS

See De Piccoli Report (European Parliament, Strasbourg, 1993); G. Ford, *Fascist Europe: The Rise of Racism and Xenophobia* (London, Pluto Press, 1992); D. Evrigenis (ed.), *European Parliament Working Documents: Report Drawn up on Behalf of the Committee of Inquiry into the Rise of Fascism and Racism, Report No.2–160/85* (European Parliament, Strasbourg, 2 vols, 1986); *The Extreme Right in Europe and the United States* (Amsterdam, Anne Frank Foundation, 1985); A. Bell, *Against Racism and Fascism in Europe* (Socialist Group of the European Parliament, Brussels, 1986); Commission of the European Community, 'Racism and xenophobia', *Eurobarometer* (special), November 1989. See also http://europa.eu.int/comm/dg10/epo/eb.html for more *Eurobarometer* poll information and http://www.eumc.eu.int for the home page of the European Monitoring Centre on Racism and Xenophobia.

## ADDITIONAL WEB LINKS

- http://netjunk.com/users/library/christ_1.htm: Racial Nationalist Library.
- www.stormfront.org: apart from giving an insight into contemporary neo-Nazi activities, this site is a useful source of documents and texts.
- www.unification.net: Sun Myung **Moon** home page.

# BIOGRAPHY

**NOTES**

- The net has been spread far and wide, dictionary-like, rather than over-concentrating on the main figures.
- Where possible we have included the dates of key individuals.
- The main scholars of fascism are included in the 'A–Z of Historians' rather than this section.
- Inclusion of a name in this section does not necessarily imply that the individual concerned is a 'fascist' or 'of the far right'. For the majority of entries, this is the case. However, we have also included some individuals on the right of the political spectrum who are not 'fascists' or 'of the far right' but who are directly linked to one or the other or both; some individuals (unrelated to fascism and the far right) whose philosophical outlook or political ideas have nevertheless influenced, or been co-opted by, fascist and/or far-right leaders; and some individuals who are actually opponents of fascism and the far right. The guiding rationale throughout has been to include individuals whose actions and/or words help to shed light on the nature of fascism and the far right.

**THORVALD AADAHL (1882–1962)** Norwegian journalist and politician with a background in agrarian party politics who supported **Quisling**'s *Nasjonal Samling*. He was editor of far-right publication *Nationen*.

**HERMANN HARRIS AALL (1871–1952)** Norwegian theorist and philosopher who was **Quisling**'s political mentor. He was author of *Social Imperialism* and acted as go-between for Quisling and the Nazis.

**GIACOMO ACERBO** Junior government minister under **Mussolini** who drafted a key piece of legislation consolidating the Fascist dictatorship. The law, enacted in 1923 and known as the **'Acerbo electoral law'**, stated that any party gaining more than 25 per cent of the total vote (or the largest party in terms of votes) would acquire two-thirds of all seats. It was replaced by a new law in 1928. Acerbo also served as Minister of Agriculture under Mussolini and was heavily involved in the regime's 'battle for land reclamation'.

**LUIGI ALBERTINI (1871–1941)** Italian senator and editor of *Corriere della Sera* between 1900 and 1925. He was in favour of **Mussolini** seizing power in the summer of 1922.

**DR JOSÉ MARÍA ALBIÑANA Y SANZ (1883–1936)** Fanatical Spanish Catholic–nationalist who founded the proto-fascist *Partido Nacionalista Español* in 1930.

**GIORGIO ALMIRANTE (d. 1988)** Founding father of the Italian *Movimento Sociale*

*Italiano* (MSI) and party leader, 1946–51 and 1969–88. During the **Second World War**, he criticised fellow Fascists who questioned the anti-Semitic race laws introduced to impress the Germans. He went on to work for the **Salò Republic** and always regarded its legacy as a positive one. As MSI supremo, he sought to minimise internal-faction fighting, modernise the party's image and deradicalise its political programme. He was a fanatical anti-Communist and an effective street agitator.

**GASTON-ARMAND AMAUDRUZ** Militant Swiss Eurofascist.

**ALCESTE DE AMBRIS** Neo-syndicalist thinker who helped to draft the Charter of **Carnaro** of 1920, an important document in the history of Italian **'pre-Fascism'**.

**IDI AMIN DADA (b. 1925)** Ugandan military dictator responsible for major human rights violations, and persecution and exclusion of his country's Asian community. Amin made little effort at mass mobilisation. His philosophy was not very well developed and could not be called fascist; neither was he particularly opposed to Marxist regimes in Africa. However, his campaign against the Asians and the brutality of his rule marked him out as a notorious dictator. He fled following the toppling of his regime by an invading Tanzanian army in 1979 and settled in Saudi Arabia.

**IAN ANDERSON** Leader of the British **National Front** (NF) during the 1980s.

**VILHO ANNALA** Influential figure in the Finnish *Isänmaallinen Kansanliike* (IKL) who was heavily influenced by Italian-style **corporatism**.

**BERNARD ANTHONY (ALIAS ROMAIN MARIE)** Influential figure on the integrist Catholic wing of the *Front National* (FN). He has represented **Le Pen**'s party in the French National Assembly and the European Parliament.

**GENERAL ION ANTONESCU (1882–1946)** Romanian soldier who led a para-fascist government in Romania during the **Second World War**. After a high-profile military career – during which he served as Minister of War (1934–8) and Chief of General Staff (1937) – Antonescu succeeded King **Carol** as Head of State in 1940 as a result of Nazi ascendancy in Europe. In power, he established the **National Legionary State**, which outlawed all political parties except the fascist Iron Guard (he actually appointed its leader, Horia **Sima**, as Deputy Prime Minister). Antonescu is generally regarded as an authoritarian conservative – a leader who incorporated fascism into his regime, in the shape of the Iron Guard, rather than embodying fascism himself. In 1941, under the strong influence of Hitler, Antonescu turned on the Iron Guard and liquidated the movement. In so doing he turned Romania into a Nazi puppet state; he was overthrown in 1944 and found guilty of war crimes in 1946.

**MAJOR ROBERT D'AUBUISSON** Much feared founder of the far-right *Alianza Republicana Nacionalista* (**ARENA**) party in El Salvador in 1981. He was a rival of Christian Democrat and US-backed President, José Napoleon Duarte, who ruled for most of the civil war against the Marxist *Farabundo Marti* rebels during the 1980s.

# B

**SERGEI BABURIN** Ultra-patriotic activist in modern-day Russia.

**MARSHAL PIETRO BADOGLIO (1871–1956)** Italian soldier associated with his country's military defeat at **Caporetto** in October 1917. Subsequently supportive of **Mussolini**, he made his name as conqueror of Abyssinia, for which he won the nickname 'Duke of Addis Ababa'. He signed the armistice with the Allies in 1943 and emerged as post-Mussolini head of state.

**ITALO BALBO (1896–1940)** High-profile Italian fascist leader who led the **Blackshirts** during the **March on Rome** in 1922. He was killed by the Italian Air Force in June 1940 after losing favour with **Mussolini**.

**OLIVER BALDWIN (1899–1958)** English politician and son of Stanley. He supported Oswald **Mosley** over the formation of the **New Party** in 1930.

**EWALD BANSE (1883–1953)** Geo-politician who helped to spread fascist ideas in the German Army.

**KLAUS BARBIE (1919–91)** Leader of **Gestapo** units in Lyon from 1942–4. Nicknamed 'the Butcher of Lyon', Barbie was tried as an old man in 1987 for his alleged role in the torture, death and/or deportation of thousands of **Holocaust** victims. The case highlighted the sensitivities of sections of the French public to the country's wartime record of **collaboration**.

**MARCEL BARBIER** Belgian activist prominent in the outlawed *Front de la Jeunesse* and the WNP.

**MAURICE BARDÈCHE (b. 1907)** Right-wing agitator in the 1930s and the first French fascist intellectual of note to emerge out of hiding after 1945. In the immediate post-war period he was critical of **Hitler** and **Mussolini**, and determined to create a radical pan-European neo-fascist movement. He was imprisoned in 1948 for trying to justify **collaboration** and the **Holocaust**. In 1951 he founded the **Union** of **National and Independent Republicans**, and won four seats. His dream was a racially pure national-socialist France (and, by extension, Europe). His idol was literary fascist Robert **Brasillach**, whose sister he married.

**ALEXANDER BARKASHOV** Leader of the neo-Nazi **Russian National Union**.

**MAJOR JOHN STRACHEY BARNES** High-profile British enthusiast for **Mussolini**- and **Hitler**-style fascism. He was a member of the Royal Institute of International Affairs.

**ENRICO BARONE (1859–1924)** Italian economist and writer who was a noted follower of **Pareto**. He did not approve of the policy of **autarchy**.

**MAURICE BARRÈS (1862–1923)** French novelist and politician, and viewed by some as France's first genuine national-socialist. He was fundamental to the 'pre-fascist' era in late nineteenth-century France. He placed particular emphasis on enfranchising the masses, expelling immigrants and introducing training, education and union rights for workers. He was a key figure in **Boulangism** and the Anti-Dreyfusard Movement.

**JEAN-MARIE BASTIEN-THIRY** French colonel who became a leading member of the *Organisation de l'Armée Secrète* (OAS). He was put on trial and executed for plotting an assassination attempt on de Gaulle.

**FULGENCIO BATISTA (1901–73)** Cuban leader from 1933–44 and again from 1952–9. His second period in office was marked by a corrupt and oppressive dictatorship along traditional Latin American lines but characterised by **conservatism** and crony capitalism rather than any form of fascism. He was toppled by Fidel Castro's forces in 1959.

**DEREK BEACKON** The **British National Party**'s first elected councillor – Tower Hamlets, September 1993. He won 34 per cent of the vote.

**LOUIS BEAM** Prominent member of the modern-day **Ku Klux Klan**.

**HENRY HAMILTON BEAMISH** British anti-Semite who founded the **Britons** publishing house in the inter-war years.

**JOHN BECKETT** Former socialist who rose to prominence in the **British Union of Fascists**. A vehement anti-Semite, Beckett was appointed Director of Publications by **Mosley** but did not particularly see eye to eye with him. After leaving the movement he founded the **National Socialist League** (with William **Joyce**) and later became associated with the Duke of Bedford's pro-German **British People's Party**.

**RENÉ BELIN** Minister of Industrial Production and Labour under the **Vichy** regime. He had special responsibility for French economic planning during the war.

**RICHARD BELLAMY** Author of the unpublished official history of the **British Union of Fascists**.

**GOTTFRIED BENN (1886–1956)** German poet who viewed Nazism as the answer to **decadence** and social malaise. A medic by training, he was particularly interested in issues of race and **eugenics**, but eventually fell out with **Hitler**. Nevertheless, representatives of the post-war New Right view him as an important conservative revolutionary.

**ALAIN DE BENOIST (b. 1943)** Doyen of the French **New Right** (*Nouvelle Droite*). He spent his formative years in **Europe-Action** and *Fedération des Etudiants Nationalistes* (FEN), but made his mark in the *Groupe-ment de Recherche et d'Étude pour la Civilisation Européennes* (GRECE). Winner of an *Académie Française* prize in 1978, de Benoist is the chief architect of *Nouvelle Droite* thinking. The terrain he has chosen to fight on is cultural and intellectual, but his ideas have infiltrated both the mainstream right and the *Front National* (FN). His political philosophy centres on the need for ethnic and national distinctiveness, and a powerful critique of liberal **egalitarianism**. It also incorporates anti-Communist, anti-capitalist and pagan strands.

**RUDOLF BERAN** Czech fascist leader who headed the **National Confederation** – the pro-Nazi Protectorate administration of 1939.

**FRIEDRICH VON BERNHARDI (1849–1930)** Senior German general whose philosophy of military expansionism gained favour with both **Hitler** and **Mussolini**. Von Bernhardi viewed **militarism** as natural – hence his notion of *Machtpolitik* ('the politics of might').

**PAUL BIYA** Aging Cameroon dictator with close links to France. The regime is more of an authoritarian fiefdom for Bia himself than a mobilised fascist state. He has survived several coups.

**MICHELE BIANCHI** Revolutionary syndicalist who became Fascist Party secretary in Italy between 1921 and 1922. He emerged as a key advisor to **Mussolini** on labour issues.

**PIERRE BIÉTRY** Founder of the French *Parti Socialiste National* in 1903. He went on to join the *Jaunes* movement and in 1906 was elected to parliament.

**RENÉ BINET** Militant French activist who became a prominent figure in post-war **Eurofascism**.

**ADMIRAL LUIS CARRERO BLANCO (d. 1973)** Influential **Franco**-era politician assassinated by Basque terrorists.

**THOMAS BLANTON JNR Ku Klux Klan** activist who was sentenced to life imprisonment in 2001 for involvement in the murder of four black girls in Alabama in 1963.

**FIELD-MARSHALL WERNER VON BLOMBERG (1878–1946)** German Minister of War between 1933 and 1938. He was very loyal to **Hitler** and helped in the suppression of the *Sturm Abteilung* (SA). Hitler eventually got rid of his office.

**COLONEL BO HI PAK** Korean CIA official associated with the **World Anti-Communist League**.

**FÉLIX HOUPHOUËT BOIGNY (1905–93)** Authoritarian dictator in the Ivory Coast (now Côte d'Ivoire). He dabbled with the notion of a one-party state but did little by way of fascist-style mass mobilisation. His regime was more of a personal **dictatorship** and was quite oppressive, although it was also relatively successful in economic terms. While its neighbour, Ghana, was a showcase for **socialism** under Kwane Nkrumah, Houphouët-Boigny's capitalist experiment was ultimately more effective. He was broadly pro-US but was especially close to France.

**EMILIO DE BONO (1866–1944)** Military leader in Fascist Italy. He participated in the **March on Rome** and made his mark on the battlefield during the Abyssinia war. He was executed in January 1944 for his role in the anti-**Mussolini Fascist Grand Council** meeting of July 1943.

**MASSIMO BONTEMPELLI (1878–1960)** Italian poet and Fascist theoretician who was heavily influenced by **Futurism**.

**PRINCE VÁLERIO BORGHESE** Italian naval hero who emerged as a key military figure under the **Salò Republic**, establishing his own independent armed force in an effort to combat the Italian Resistance. After the war he was put on trial but was let off. He went on to join the *Movimento Sociale Italiano* (MSI) and the Italian *Fronte Nazionale*, and even launched an unsuccessful coup attempt in 1970. He ended up exiled in Spain.

**KING BORIS III (1894–1943)** Autocratic Bulgarian monarch who presided over a dictatorial regime between 1935 and 1943. His government had fascist traits but there was no revolutionary or paramilitary impetus behind it. He joined the Axis in March 1941 – helping the Nazis against Greece – but had an uneasy relationship with **Hitler**, in part because of Bulgaria's traditional ties with Russia. Boris was fatally poisoned soon after Hitler criticised Bulgaria's neutral position during the **Second World War**.

**UMBERTO BOSSI** Charismatic and controversial leader of the 'anti-system' *Lega Nord* movement. His organisation campaigns for a federal state and an end to **immigration** and multi-culturalism in modern Italy. Bossi is a populist rather than a fascist or neo-fascist.

**ZOLTÁN BÖSZÖRMÉNY** Leader of the Hungarian **Scythe Cross** movement in the 1930s.

**GIUSEPPE BOTTAI** Radical and enthusiastic Corporate State theorist during the Fascist era in Italy. He was appointed Under-Secretary at the **Ministry of Corporations** in 1926 and later became Minister of Corporations. A powerful critic of the liberal state, he was especially interested in the relationship between political and economic spheres.

**GENERAL GEORGES BOULANGER (1837–91)** Charismatic French soldier appointed Minister of War in 1886. He ultimately formed his own one-man political movement and was on the verge of staging a coup when he lost his nerve and committed suicide. Some historians view Boulanger as 'pre-fascist' in the sense that he attempted to create his own personality cult, engaged with the newly enfranchised urban masses, and put forward a radical action-based doctrine.

**PIERRE BOUSQUET** French far-right activist. In the post-war period he was leader of the small *Mouvement Nationaliste de Progrès* and a prolific writer on the extreme-right journal, *Militant*.

**CORNEL BRAHAŞ** Romanian ultra-nationalist, formerly a member of the *Partidul Unitati Nationale Române* (PUNR).

**ROBERT BRASILLACH (1909–45)** Ex-*Action Française* member who emerged as one of the most notorious intellectual collaborators during the **Second World War**. A writer and journalist, he edited far-right publication *Je Suis Partout* and believed in a radical, élitist brand of fascism. He was killed by firing squad at the end of the war as France sought to erase the memory of **collaboration** and **collaborationism**. His brother-in-law, Maurice **Bardèche**, founded the *Société des Amis de Robert Brasillach* in 1960.

**EVA BRAUN (1912–45) Hitler**'s mistress. She played no major role in his public or political life and married him the day before committing suicide by poisoning.

**FRANÇOIS BRIGNEAU** French far-right activist who has belonged to both *Ordre Nouveau* and the *Front National* (FN) in the post-war period. He is famed particularly for his aggressive writing.

**ANDREW BRONS** Prominent British **National Front** activist.

**MARCEL BUCARD (1895–1946)** Founder and leader of inter-war French grouping, the *Francistes*. He was inspired by a meeting with **Mussolini** and went on to represent France at the 1934 Fascist International. The editor of *Le Nouveau Siècle*, he collaborated with the Germans during the Occupation and emerged as a passionate pro-Nazi figure. He was shot in 1946 as part of the post-war purge conducted by the new French authorities.

**PAT BUCHANAN** US ultra-right politician and religious broadcaster. A presidential hopeful on more than one occasion, Buchanan is the ultimate conspiracy theorist, believing that modern-day America is mortally threatened by international finance. He has been accused of anti-semitism.

**NORBERT BURGER** Far-right Austrian politician who gained 3.2 per cent of the vote in the 1980 presidential elections. He has been associated with both the *Ring Freilicher Studenten* (RFS) and the **National Democratic Party**.

**GERMÁN BUSCH** Bolivian military dictator who oversaw a 'military socialist' regime between 1936 and 1939. His policies combined right-wing **nationalism** and populist reform. He also played a part in the 1932–5 **Chaco War** against Paraguay.

**FRIEDHEIM BUSSE (b. 1928)** Veteran German far-right activist who became leader of the *Aktionsfront Nationaler Sozialisten/ Nationale Aktivisten* (ANS/NA) after **Kühnen**'s death. He has suffered imprisonment as a consequence of his political activity and has also led the *Freiheitliche Deutsche Arbeiterpartei* (FAP).

'REVEREND' R. BUTLER US far-right leader active in the Identity Church and **Aryan** Nations World Congress.

ARTHUR BUTZ Historical Revisionist who published *The Hoax of the Twentieth Century* in 1978. Butz is a US academic.

MARCELO CAETANO **Salazar**'s successor as Portuguese leader in 1968. He ruled until 1974.

GENERAL CARMONA Portuguese military dictator who appointed **Salazar** to the posts of Finance Minister (in 1928) and Prime Minister (in 1932). He then served as figurehead President as Salazar established his authoritarian dictatorship.

KING CAROL II (1893–1953) Romanian monarch (1930–40) who established his own **Mussolini**-inspired dictatorship in 1938. At first he tried to destroy **Codreanu's Legion of the Archangel Michael**, but in 1940 set about wooing it in an effort to 'fascistise' his **State of National Renaissance** (the name he gave to his own parafascist movement). After a diplomatic setback in September 1940, Carol was deposed and General **Antonescu**, backed by **Hitler**, became Romania's new leader.

WILLIS CARTO American political activist who has been associated with several far-right groupings in the US: the **Liberty Lobby**, **Patriot Movement** and **Populist Party**.

PIERRE CAZIOT (b. 1876) Minister of Agriculture under the **Vichy** regime in France.

EMILIO CECCHI Italian writer who was elected to the **Italian Academy** during the Fascist period.

LOUIS-FERDINAND CÉLINE Hysterical French anti-Semite who emerged as one of the most notorious ideological collaborators of the Occupation period. A novelist by trade, he was a frequent contributor to *L'Action Française*.

GUSTAVS CELMIŠ Leader of the Latvian *Pērkonkrust* in the 1930s.

HOUSTON STEWART CHAMBERLAIN (1855–1927) British-born race theorist and propagandist who became a naturalised German in 1916. Chamberlain, heavily influenced by Richard **Wagner**, offered a scientific justification of **racism** that underpinned much early fascist discourse. He published *Foundations of the Nineteenth Century* in 1900; his second wife was Wagner's daughter Eva.

FRANÇOIS CHASSEIGNE Secretary of State for Food under **Vichy** in wartime France.

A.K. CHESTERTON (1899–1973) Anti-Semitic activist involved with the **British Union of Fascists** between 1933 and 1938. He was editor of the party's newspaper, *Blackshirt*, and its chief propagandist. After leaving the British Union of Fascists, Chesterton founded the **League of Empire Loyalists** in 1954; and then became the first chairman of the National Front (NF) in 1967. He did not approve of the NF's **neo-Nazism** and resigned in 1971. Throughout his varied career he stressed the same themes: the importance of the British Empire, the threat of **decadence** and the conspiratorial nature of the Jews. He wrote *The New Unhappy Lords* in 1965.

STEFANO DELLE CHIAIE (b. 1936) Former New Order and *Movimento Sociale Italiano* (MSI) activist and founder of the neo-fascist *Avanguardia Nazionale* in 1960. He was a supporter of political **violence** – hence his nickname 'The Black Bombadier'. His political doctrine revolved around anti-Communism and anti-democratic subversion.

**THIES CHRISTOPHERSEN (b. 1918)** German Historical Revisionist who published *Die Auschwitz Lüge* in 1973. He was involved in the post-war *Bürger-und Bauerninitiative* (BBI) movement, but fled to Denmark in 1986.

**COUNT GALEAZZO CIANO (1903–44)** Key figure in the conduct of Italian foreign policy under **Mussolini**. He married *Il Duce*'s daughter at the age of twenty-seven and, after a spell in the diplomatic service, became Italian Foreign Minister in the mid-1930s. He participated in the July 1943 **Fascist Grand Council** meeting that sought Mussolini's resignation but was subsequently caught by Mussolini loyalists and executed in January 1944.

**LODE CLAES** Belgian far-right activist. In the inter-war years he was a youth member of the VERDINASO movement; in the post-war period he was elected a *Volksunie* senator and founded the *Vlaamse Volkspartij* (VPP).

**HEINRICH CLASS (1868–1953)** Pan-German League propagandist. Editor of *Odin* and author of *If I Were the Kaiser* (1912), he advanced an explicitly *Völkisch* doctrine, arguing that Germany was endangered by an array of threatening forces. He believed that the answer to his country's problems lay in strong right-wing parliamentary government, rather than a coup, and an expansionist foreign policy.

**FRITS CLAUSEN** Danish doctor who became leader of the pro-Nazi *Danmarks Nationalsocialistiske Arbeider Parti* (DN-SAP) in 1933. After 1940 he supported the German occupiers.

**CARL VON CLAUSEWITZ (b. 1780)** Prussian soldier and military theorist whose *On War* is a classic text. It described total war as an extreme struggle of annihilation. Later German military leaders, like the pro-Nazi **Ludendorff**, sought to achieve this ideal but ignored von Clausewitz's warning that war is usually constrained by politics and diplomacy; war becomes the 'pursuit of politics by other means' and, in practice, is subservient to political (i.e. more ambiguous civilian) goals.

**STAF DE CLERQ (1902–42)** Pro-German Flemish nationalist who founded the *Vlaamsch Nationaal Verbond* (VNV) movement.

**CORNELIU ZELEA CODREANU (1899–1938)** Romanian fascist who founded the **Legion of the Archangel Michael** in 1927 after a period in the **National Christian Defence League**. Codreanu's movement became a significant player in Romanian politics but King **Carol** II's government was constantly trying to crush it. Codreanu – a fervent nationalist and anti-Semite – was murdered by the monarch's forces in the year his movement was disbanded.

**ION COJA** Far-right activist in modern-day Romania. He has flirted with a number of ultra-nationalist movements – Agrarian Democratic Party of Romania (PDAR), **National Salvation Front**, **Vatra Românească**, *Partidul Unitati Nationale Române* (PUNR) – and come close to standing as a presidential candidate. Coja is an apologist for the inter-war Iron Guard movement.

**ENRICO CORRADINI (1865–1931)** Right-wing Italian nationalist who was particularly interested in the concept of Italy as a 'proletarian nation'. He was influential mainly in the period before 1914.

**FILIPPO CORRIDONI** Interventionist and radical neo-syndicalist theoretician in early twentieth-century Italy.

**CARLO COSTAMAGNA (1881–1965)** Italian Corporate State theorist who was heavily influenced by Hegelian ideas.

**FATHER CHARLES E. COUGHLIN (1891–1979)** Michigan priest and broadcaster who preached an extreme brand of **populism** and **anti-Semitism** in the late 1930s. By the late 1930s, his broadcasts verged on the expression of sympathy for European fascism and he was eventually gagged by the Catholic Church.

**HAROLD COVINGTON** Leader of the National Socialist Party of America.

**BENEDETTO CROCE** Arguably Italy's most famous philosopher. Even though he was a liberal, he came to accept and admire **Mussolini**'s regime, particularly the strong leadership that Fascism brought. In the end, however, he turned against it and in 1945 called for the **Italian Academy** to be disbanded.

**ISTVAN CSURKA** Modern-day Hungarian nationalist associated with the *Magyar Demokrata Fórum* (MDF), which is a conservative, but not far-right, party. He was also associated with the **Hungarian Justice Party** and is loyal to the notion of a **Greater Hungary**.

**ALEXANDRU CUZA** Co-founder of the Romanian **National Christian Defence League** in 1923. Cuza held government office at one point and stood for a populist brand of **ultra-nationalism** and **anti-Semitism**. He acted as mentor to fellow Romanian fascist, **Codreanu**.

**WERNER DAITZ** Nazi ideologue associated with 'soldierly economics' and the regime's policy of **autarchy**.

**GABRIELE D'ANNUNZIO (1863–1938)** A First World War hero and leading figure in Italian literary circles, he emerged as an arch-nationalist precursor to **Mussolini**. His dramatic seizure of **Fiume** (Rijeka) in Croatia, with the help of an unofficial **militia**, was a dress rehearsal for Mussolini's subsequent takeover of Italian cities. Though they shared a similar rightist and nationalist outlook, as well as a taste for melodramatic and flamboyant action, Mussolini saw D'Annunzio as a dangerous rival. He was sidestepped once the Fascists consolidated their power.

**ADMIRAL JEAN LOUIS XAVIER FRANÇOIS DARLAN (1881–1942)** French politician who was head of the Navy between 1933 and 1939. He held several governmental positions at **Vichy** – Minister of Marine, Minister of National Defence and Foreign Minister – and was **Pétain**'s Chief Minister between February 1941 and April 1942. He was assassinated at the end of the war.

**AIMÉ-JOSEPH DARNAND (1897–1945)** Former *Action Française* member and Cagoulard who became one of France's most famous collaborationists. He won a bravery medal in the First World War and expounded a passionate anti-German line during most of his early life. In 1940 he was quick to demonstrate loyalty to Marshal **Pétain** and became head of the notorious paramilitary *Milice* organisation in 1943. A year later he swore an oath of loyalty to **Hitler**.

**RICHARD WALTHER DARRÉ** Peasant leader in Germany who was appointed Minister of Food and Agriculture by **Hitler**. His role was to spread Nazi **propaganda** among the country's farming community.

**MARCEL DÉAT (1894–1955)** French fascist with a neo-socialist background. He split from the *Section Française de l'Internationale Ouvrière* (SFIO) to pursue a nationalist-corporatist agenda, and genuinely believed that the masses could be seduced by the idea of the **nation**. As such, he stood for a type of **'left fascism'**. In 1941 he formed the collaborationist *Rassemblement National Populaire* (RNP) in the hope that it would become France's vanguard fascist party and he would emerge as the Nazis' puppet leader. The RNP was a flop – but the ambitious Déat gained the respect of the Germans and the **Vichy** leadership. He became **Pétain**'s Minister of Labour when the Germans started to call the shots in the Southern Zone. He fled after the war and underwent a bizarre religious conversion in Italy.

**LÉON DEGRELLE (1906–94)** Charismatic Belgian fascist leader whose influence straddles both pre-1945 and post-1945 eras. A hardline integral Catholic, Degrelle was eventually excommunicated by the Vatican for wearing a fascist uniform in church. He founded the *Rex* movement in 1936 and suffered a disastrous by-election defeat in April 1937; following this, *Rex* underwent a process of **Nazification** and during the war he led the SS Walloon Brigade on the Eastern Front. In 1938 Degrelle published *The Revolution of Souls*.

**EUGÈNE DELONCLE** Paranoid French plotter who founded the *Cagoule* and led an unsuccessful coup attempt in 1937. A military hero during the First World War, he was a *Camelots du Roi* activist before establishing his own highly conspiratorial and ritualistic movement. Paradoxically, he was an admirer of Lenin's revolution-

ary strategy and also a fierce anti-Communist. He worked for the Germans between 1940 and 1943, and was eventually killed by a **Gestapo** bullet.

**PAUL DÉROULÈDE (1846–1914)** Leader of the nationalist pressure group, *Ligue des Patriotes*, in late nineteenth-century France. A veteran of the **Franco-Prussian War** and a poet by training, he was dominated by the need to reconquer the 'lost territories' of Alsace and Lorraine. Déroulède was a key figure in French **'pre-fascism'** and placed enormous emphasis on the 'physical fitness' of a **nation**. He eventually threw in his lot with **Boulangism**.

**FILIP DEWINTER** Leader of the Belgian *Vlaams Bloc* (VB). He rose through the movement's youth wing and is a key party organiser.

**DR OTTO DICKEL** *Völkisch* agitator during the Weimar period in Germany. Although his doctrine was national-socialist in character he was never a Nazi and fell out with **Hitler**.

**RUDOLF DIELS** German Nazi Party official appointed by **Göring** to oversee the persecution of Communist activists.

**GEORGE DIETZ** Former Hitler Youth member who emigrated to the US in the late 1950s. There he set up far-right publishing house, **Liberty Bell** publications.

**KAREL DILLEN (b. 1925)** High-profile Flemish nationalist and neo-fascist activist. Since 1945 he has been involved in a variety of Belgian far-right movements: JNP, *Volksunie* (VU), *Vlaams-Nationale Raad* (VNR) and *Were Di Verbond van Nederlandse Werk-Gemeenschappen* (WD, VNR). He founded the *Vlaams-Nationale Partij* (VNP) in 1977 and then helped mastermind the ultra-right merger that created the *Vlaams Bloc* (VB) in 1978. He eventually became VB leader and won election to the Belgian parliament and Senate, and to the European Parliament where he joined the Euro-Right group. His dream is Flemish independence, with Brussels as capital of the new state.

**ARTHUR DINTER** Nazi Party member whose notion of 'German Christianity' – blending **nationalism** with **religion** – led to his expulsion from the movement in 1927.

**FRANÇOISE DIOR** Daughter of French designer Christian and ex-wife of British far-right activist Colin **Jordan**. She was active in the post-war West European Federation and **Our Nation**.

**ROMAN DMOWSKI (d. 1939)** Inter-war Polish anti-Semite associated with the National Democratic Movement. Although he was hostile to the parliamentary system he was cautious about advocating **violence**. His influence carried over into the post-war period.

**ENGELBERT DOLLFUSS (1892–1934)** Para-fascist Austrian leader in the 1930s. Dollfuss had a military background but made a career out of politics. He joined the Christian Social Party as a young man, became a government minister in 1931 and was appointed Chancellor in May 1932. A corporatist and fanatical anti-socialist, he took on dictatorial powers in 1933 and introduced a fascist-style state structure in 1934. In power, he had understandings with the *Heimwehr* at home and **Mussolini** abroad. Austrian socialists disliked Dollfuss on account of his savage campaigns against them and national-socialists despised his para-fascist tendencies. He was assassinated by the Nazis in July 1934.

**'POPE' CLEMENTE DOMÍNGUEZ** Spanish priest and leader of the fanatical religious

movement, *Palmar de Troya*. He has links with the *Fuerza Nueva*.

**IAN STUART DONALDSON** Activist on the modern British far right. He was associated with rock band **Skrewdriver** and the *Blood and Honour* magazine.

**ADMIRAL KARL DÖNITZ (b. 1891)** German naval commander and, later, successor to **Hitler**, pending final German surrender in 1945. He oversaw the U-Boat campaign in the **Second World War**, and was sentenced to ten years at Nuremburg for his role in the regime.

**HENRI DORGÈRES** Leader of the *Front Paysan* in inter-war France. He personified the phenomenon of 'peasant fascism' and gained more than 10,000 followers, mainly in western regions.

**JACQUES DORIOT (1898–1945)** Thuggish French revolutionary agitator who moved from extreme left to extreme right in the inter-war years. Even though he had been elected Communist deputy-mayor for the Paris district of Saint-Denis, he had become disillusioned with the Communist Party. In 1936 he founded the fascist – and passionately anti-Communist – *Parti Populaire Français*. The Berlin-sponsored party quickly acquired a youthful mass following. Doriot posed as the 'French **Führer**' and *Doriotistes* loved the sheer arrogance of their leader. In 1940 Doriot glorified **Pétain** but was soon put off by **Vichy**'s 'soft' **conservatism**. He turned towards **Hitler** and was regarded as the ultimate German 'agent'. During the war he established the *Légion des Voluntaires Français* (LVF) and fought in German uniform on the Eastern Front. He died in Germany in 1945 after an Allied attack.

**GIULIO DOUHET (1869–1930)** Italian advocate of the use of air power and its role in devastating enemy society. He led Italian experiments in military aviation during the **Second World War** and urged a greater role for an independent Air Force during the inter-war years. Douhet wrote of the effects of air power on civilian populations and the use of gas as a weapon. Though his relevance extends beyond fascism, Italian use of gas and air power in Abyssinia reflected his theories.

**ANTON DREXLER** Founder of the German Workers' Party, forerunner to the Nazi Party. An Austrian locksmith, he had little time to devote to party organisation and faded into the background as **Hitler** pushed his way to the top of the *Deutsche Arbeiterpartei* (DAP) and transformed its character.

**PIERRE DRIEU LA ROCHELLE (1893–1945)** French fascist intellectual who committed suicide in the aftermath of Liberation. He was the last editor of *Nouvelle Revue Française* – a Nazi-censored literary journal – and displayed sympathy for **Doriot**'s *Parti Populaire Français*.

**EDOUARD DRUMONT (1844–1917)** Scurrilous French anti-Semite who published *La France Juive* in 1886. Although some commentators argue that he was a figure of the left, his crude biological **racism** eerily anticipated Nazi ideas. A journalist by training, Drumont was a leading player in the Dreyfus controversy. He also founded the anti-Semitic newspaper, *La Libre Parole*.

**A.I. DUBROVIN** First chairman of the **Union of Russian People** (URP) in early twentieth-century Russia.

**DAVID DUKE** Key figure on the American extreme right. He was a **Ku Klux Klan** member in the 1970s and founded the **National Association for the Advancement of White People** in 1980. In the 1980s and 1990s he achieved some staggering election results – winning a seat in the Louisiana House of Representatives. A champion of 'Rights for Whites', Duke has scapegoated the 'black underclass' and opposed the **Civil Rights Movement**.

**AMERIGO DUMINI** Worked in **Mussolini**'s Press Office in the 1920s. He was associated with the murder of reformist socialist party figure, Giacomo Matteotti, in 1924.

**FRANÇOIS DUPRAT (d. 1978)** Anti-Semitic leader of *Ordre Nouveau* and one of the *Front National*'s early ideologues. He was associated with 'revolutionary nationalist' and '**Third Way**' factions within **Le Pen**'s movement. He died in suspicious circumstances in a car accident in 1978.

**FRANÇOIS ('PAPA DOC') DUVALIER (b. 1907)** Right-wing Haitian dictator. He was elected President in 1957 after years of service as health minister and opposition leader to the military regime. His supporters combined Haitian **cultural nationalism** and voodoo; however, his presidency degenerated into one of nepotism and oppression, spearheaded by a private army, the *Tontons Macoutes*. Excommunicated for attacks on Catholic clergy, 'Papa Doc' had himself declared 'President for Life'; his son, Jean-Claude 'Baby Doc', succeeded him after his death in April 1971. The Duvalier regimes made attempts at nationalist mobilisation and **mysticism** but were too corrupt and unfocused to count as fascist. They were criticised and intermittently subjected to US sanctions but tolerated in preference to the Communist regime in neighbouring Cuba.

E

**ADOLF EICHMANN (1906–62)** Responsible for the Final Solution in Hungary. He was a member of the Nazi Party from 1932 and the *Schutzstaffel* (SS) from 1933. As head of the Department for Jewish Affairs in the Security Service of the SS, he organised record-keeping, movement of Jews and key logistics behind the Final Solution. He participated in the **Wannsee Conference** in 1942, which discussed the details of the Final Solution. He fled to Argentina in the 1950s but was kidnapped by Israeli agents in 1960. He was tried by Israel in 1961 and executed in the following year.

**FRANZ VON EPP (1868–1947)** Disillusioned First World War veteran who served as **Hitler**'s Minister for Colonies between 1941 and 1945.

**ELOF ERIKSSON** Swedish fascist who helped to found the National Unity Movement in 1924. He was inspired by **Mussolini**'s Italian regime.

**JULIUS EVOLA (1898–1974)** Highly original fascist thinker influential in both inter-war and post-war eras. He was an acquaintance of many leading Nazis; **Mussolini**, however, arrested him for being 'too extreme'. His aristocratic background led to a passionate belief in **hierarchy** and **élitism** and he was hostile to both bourgeoisie and **working class**. Evola looked enviously towards 'warrior-priest' societies in other parts of the world (and in other epochs), and in Europe foresaw the emergence of 'Political Soldiers' who would lead the war against **decadence** and decline. He was involved in the *Nuclei Armati Rivoluzionari* (NAR) but generally saw himself as 'above' conventional politics. His thinking had an immense impact on European **neofascism**, '**Third Positionism**' and **New Right** politics, and he is now viewed as a key reference-point for all modern far-right thinkers.

**F**

**FAHD BIN ABDUL AZIZ BIN SAUD, KING** Ruler of Saudi Arabia since 1982, he is typical of a class of traditional right-wing rulers in the Arabian Peninsula. The Saud family rules an autocratic state based on tribal tradition and the Qu'ran, albeit with considerable industrialisation and development in parts of the country dominated by oil exploration. The system is a polar opposite of fascism in that such regimes make virtually no effort to encourage mass participation in politics: their assemblies have only a consultative role and there are no political parties. This kind of traditional Arab monarchy has also been characteristic of politics in Oman, the UAE, Qatar, Bahrain and Kuwait, although partial democratisation is underway in Qatar.

**ROBERTO FARINACCI (1892–1945)** Radical neo-syndicalist and Italian National Association activist who became a key figure in Italian Fascism. An ex-socialist, he was noted for his notion of '**left fascism**'. He served as Fascist Party secretary (1925–6) and Grand Council member (1935–43). He ended up at Salò – and was executed by partisans in 1945.

**LOUIS FARRAKHAN (b. 1933)** US black separatist who founded the Nation of **Islam** in 1985, basing it on a prior movement of the same name. He was originally a supporter of Malcolm X. He is controversial because of his socially conservative views on **family** issues and **homosexuality**, and his critics have charged him with **anti-Semitism**. These controversies were partly behind the non-involvement of key black leaders in Farrakhan's 'Million Man March' on Washington DC in 1995, a massive rally in which African American men committed themselves to moral regeneration and cultural pride. He was also banned from visiting the UK and Israel in the 1980s and 1990s because of his perceived extremism.

**ROBERT FAURISSON** Senior Lecturer in Literary Criticism at University of Lyon-2 and a prominent Historical Revisionist. His studies have focused on scientific controversies, legal documentation and secondary historical sources.

**GOTTFRIED FEDER (1883–1941)** German critic of **capitalism** and the role of Jews within the economy. He also argued that women should be servile to men; and, as a member of the *Deutsche Arbeiterpartei* (DAP), was a significant influence on **Hitler**.

**LUIGI FEDERZONI** Founding father of the Italian National Association (ANI). He was an early theorist of Italian national malaise and emerged as a key figure under Fascism.

**DR DANIEL FÉRET** Leading figure in the Belgian *Front National-Nationaal Front* (FN-NF).

**COUNT FESTETICS** Leader of the proto-fascist **Hungarian National Socialist Party** during the inter-war period.

**JOHANN FICHTE (1762–1814)** German critic of **liberalism**. The Nazis laid particular emphasis on his view that the Germans constituted a strong *Volk* because they avoided inter-mixing **language** or racial stock. He stressed the importance of fighting for one's **nation** (*Address to the German Nation* [1807]) and the significance of culture, ethnicity and language. An advocate of a planned economy, regulation and a more isolated economy, he also wanted Germany to expand her national boundaries. His nation-based, **race**-based thinking inspired many brands of German **nationalism**.

**GIANFRANCO FINI (b. 1952)** Leader of the right-wing *Alleanza Nazionale* (AN), a right-of-centre group incorporating former members of the neo-fascist *Movimento Sociale Italiano* (MSI). This suave, ultra-modern political operator was originally elected leader of the neo-fascist MSI in 1987. He became head of the party's youth movement in 1977 and in his formative years viewed **Almirante** as his chief mentor. He was secretary of the MSI from the late 1980s and a former candidate for Mayor of Rome. He helped to incorporate the bulk of the MSI into the AN, which won 109 seats in the 1994 parliamentary elections (although he himself chose to stay out of government). He acted as an ally of Silvio Berlusconi in the 1990s and became Deputy Prime Minister in Berlusconi's government of June 2001. Although Fini has targeted the **immigration** issue as vital to the AN, he sees himself as a 'post-fascist' and has disassociated himself from the more radical and vulgar elements on the Italian right. Fini intended the fusion with the AN to signify the end of the MSI, although a hardcore of MSI supporters remained behind. Ideologically, Fini champions free-market ideas and traditional Catholic values. He is committed to constitutional change and wants Italy to become a presidential republic.

**DOMENICO FISICHELLA** Member of the *Alleanza Nazionale* coalition in 1990s Italy who has experience of government and acted as special adviser to **Fini**.

**PIM FORTUYN (d. 2002)** Maverick gay politician whose movement emerged as an influential force in Dutch politics in the early months of 2002. He resisted the 'extreme right' label, but in one infamous remark declared that the Netherlands was 'full' – thus illustrating his strong anti-immigration stance. He was assassinated in May 2002.

**FRANÇOIS-MARIE-CHARLES FOURIER (1772–1837)** French writer who believed in organising society into communities of producers called phalanges. His views were a precursor to **corporatism** and he was particularly admired by French fascist **Déat**.

**GENERAL FRANCISCO FRANCO BAHMONDE (1892–1975)** Authoritarian leader of Spain between 1939 and 1975. He was born in El Ferrol, Galicia, and worked his way up through the Spanish Army. In 1926, at the age of thirty-three, he became the youngest general in Europe; in 1928 he took charge of Spain's Military Academy; and in 1935 he was appointed Chief of Staff. Onlookers were rightly wary of his political ambitions. During the Civil War he emerged as the leading military figure on the Nationalist side. In October 1936, Franco spearheaded a full-scale military assault on the Spanish state and the republican government, and in April 1939 celebrated victory in the war. In the meantime, he had managed to bring unity to the Nationalist coalition by merging the *Falange* with the Carlists. Franco kept Spain neutral during the **Second World War** but had strong Axis sympathies. In power, his political agenda was founded on **corporatism**, **Catholicism** and anti-democratic repression. 'The Caudillo', as he became known, was more a strict conservative than a fascist. Diminutive in stature – he was only 5'3" – Franco was famed for his survival instincts rather than his political charisma.

**HANS FRANK (1900–46)** Nazi Minister of Justice who argued that **Hitler** had been invested with God-like qualities.

**FRANCO (GIORGIO) FREDA** Italian lawyer who became a high-profile *Ordine Nuovo* activist.

**DR GERHARD FREY (b. 1933)** Munich-based neo-Nazi activist who founded the *Deutsche Volks Union* (DVU) pressure group in 1971 and *Deutsche Volks Union/ Liste D* political movement in 1987. Frey believes in direct-action tactics and owns the Druckschriften und Zeitungsverlag publishing house. He is also the publisher of three extreme-right publications and editor of *Deutsche Nationalzeitung*.

**WILHELM FRICK (1877–1946)** Interior Minister under the **Third Reich**, one of only two Nazis in Hitler's first cabinet. He participated in the **Munich Putsch** of 1923 and played a key role in the preparation of domestic legislation between 1933 and 1943, especially the anti-Semitic Nuremberg Laws. He lost influence to Himmler's *Schutzstaffel* (SS) and was executed for 'crimes against humanity' after the **Nuremberg Trials**.

**THEODOR FRITSCH** One of the founders of the German Anti-Semitic League and a key *Völkisch* writer. He was a significant influence on **Hitler**'s personal doctrine, but he stayed outside the Nazi fold.

**GENERAL WERNER FREIHERR VON FRITSCH (1880–1939)** Commander in Chief of the German army between 1934 and 1938. A conservative figure, he was hostile to the *Schutzstaffel* (SS) and opposed **Hitler**'s military plans.

**KONOE FUMIMARO (1891–1945)** Japanese Prime Minister at intermittent periods between 1937 and 1941. He represented civilian factions in the Japanese élite but was also a member of the Imperial Family. He tried to restrain the military but pursued more nationalist and authoritarian policies as Japan's domestic crisis and military entanglements deepened.

**GHEORGHE FUNAR** Leading figure in the modern Romanian *Partidul Unitati Nationale Române* (PUNR) movement and mayor of Cluj. As mayor, he showed hostility to local ethnic Hungarians.

**WALTER FUNK (1830–1960)** Briefly German Economics Minister and then Chairman of the Central Bank from 1939. He helped implement Nazi racial discrimination and war planning but was less central to economic policy than **Göring**. He was sentenced to life at the War Crimes Tribunals but freed in 1957.

**BIRGER FURUGÅRD** Sweden's first Nazi leader. A vet by training, he founded the Swedish National Socialist League of Freedom in 1924.

**SIGURD FURUGÅRD** Influential member of the inter-war Swedish National Socialist League of Freedom. **Hitler** and **Quisling** were among his contacts.

# G

**JACK GABRIËLS** Belgian cabinet minister at the centre of political scandal in May 2001. He was accused by the media and opposition MPs of having links with a *Schutzstaffel* (SS) **veterans'** support group.

**GENERAL RADOLA GAJDA** Leader of the **National Fascist Community** – Czechoslovakia's only indigenous fascist movement in the inter-war period.

**LEOPOLDO GALTIERI** Traditional authoritarian military leader and member of the military **junta** that ruled Argentina during the 1982 Falkland–Malvinas War with Britain. He was widely seen as having used the war to distract attention from domestic economic problems and political opposition. He was ousted following Argentina's humiliating defeat.

**PETROS GAROUFALIAS** Former Minister of Defence who emerged as leader of the shortlived *Ethniki Demokratiki Enosis* (EDE) movement in 1970s Greece. His ideology was a blend of **ultra-nationalism** and anti-leftism.

**PASCAL GAUCHON** Supporter of **Tixier-Vignancour** and leader of the French *Parti des Forces Nouvelles*.

**GIOVANNI GENTILE (1875–1944)** Prominent Italian philosopher who became **Mussolini**'s Minister of Education. He joined the Fascist Party in 1923 and wrote numerous articles and pamphlets on the nature of Fascism and its supposed debt to Hegel. Gentile's role as apologist for Italian Fascism gave an otherwise anti-intellectual movement some gravitas. He edited the journal, *La Critica*.

**STEFAN GEORGE (1868–1933)** German poet whose *Völkisch*, anti-liberal writings anticipated a 'new age' and gained plaudits from Nazi leaders. The *Georgekreis* was the name given to the group of writers who congregated around him.

**GUGLIELMO GIANNINI** Italian writer who in 1945 founded a political movement on the back of a newspaper of the same name. *Uomo Qualunque* was one of the first far-right parties to emerge in post-**Mussolini** Italy.

**JOSÉ MARÍA GIL ROBLES (b. 1898)** Catholic, counter-revolutionary Spanish politician. As leader of the inter-war *Confederación Española de Derechas Autónomas* (CEDA) movement, he advanced a strongly anti-socialist, anti-republican and authoritarian–corporatist doctrine; so much so that some observers viewed him as a fascist-in-waiting. He was said to have some admiration for German Nazism.

**ERNESTO CABELLERO GIMÉNEZ (b. 1899)** Widely acknowledged as the first champion of fascist ideas in Spain. A staunch Catholic, Giménez idolised **Mussolini** and the cult of 'latinity'.

**GIOVANNI GIURATI (1876–1970)** Ex-Blackshirt who became president of the Chamber of Deputies and then secretary of **Mussolini**'s *Partito Nazionale Fascista* (PNF) (1930–1).

**JOOP GLIMMERVEEN** Leading figure in the Dutch *Nederlandse Volksunie* (NVU). In the mid-1970s he made his name as an outspoken opponent of **immigration**.

**MOGENS GLISTRUP** Founding father of the 'anti-system' Danish **Progress Party**. Anti-tax and anti-immigration, he left the movement in 1990 to form the **Party of Well-Being**. Although he has warned his followers against illegal anti-tax protest, he himself served a prison sentence in the mid-1980s for tax evasion.

**PAUL JOSEPH GÖBBELS [ALSO, GOEBBELS]** (1897–1945) Head of the powerful Reich Ministry for Public Enlightenment and Propaganda under the Nazi regime. His name became synonymous with 'the big lie' and with distortion and information control on a grand scale. One of **Hitler**'s closest friends, he joined the Nazi Party in 1922 and remained fiercely loyal to the end. His wife and children were also in Hitler's circle of friends. By 1924 he was involved in party journalism and **propaganda**. After holding a succession of posts, notably in Berlin, he became the Reich's propaganda chief after Hitler's accession to power in 1933. Göbbels criticised other Nazis and the Italian Fascists for lack of zeal or commitment. He competed with von **Ribbentrop** in the presentation of German foreign policy and also showed an unrelenting hatred of the Jews that seemed to surpass that of Hitler himself. Against Hitler's wishes, he stayed in Berlin as the Soviets closed in and committed suicide rather than surrender.

**COUNT ARTHUR GOBINEAU (1816–82)** French diplomat and author of *Essai sur l'Inégalité des Races Humaines* (*Essay on the Inequality of the Human Races*) in 1853. Gobineau believed in a permanent **hierarchy** of races and linked the political and economic success of a nation to its status in that hierarchy, as well as to its racial 'purity'. Of his three principal racial groups (white, Asian–Mongol and black), whites were cast as superior. Similarly, he linked **language** groups to **race** and believed in the existence of a superior **Aryan** race. These views found support among right-wing and anti-Semitic circles in early twentieth-century Europe.

**OCTAVIAN GOGA** Key political figure in inter-war Romania. He led the **National Christian Party** and served in government. His background was in agrarian politics.

**CAPTAIN GYULA GÖMBÖS (d. 1936)** Pro-fascist Hungarian Prime Minister between 1932 and 1936, and leading member of the ultra-nationalist **Party of Racial Defence**. He tried to 'fascistise' **Horthy**'s conservative–authoritarian regime and ally Hungary with Germany and Italy.

**JORGE GONZÁLEZ** Zealous Chilean fascist with a Hispano-German background. He set up the *Movimiento Nacional Socialista de Chile* (MNS) in 1932, attempted to seize power in 1938 and was accused of 'insanity' in 1940.

**HERMANN GÖRING (1893–1946)** **Hitler**'s Air Force chief and would-be successor. In his capacity as head of the **Gestapo**, he competed with Heinrich **Himmler** as *Schutzstaffel* (SS) Chief. Göring lost out to

Himmler, who eventually gained control of both organisations. Earlier, Göring was a First World War hero in the fledgling Air Force. From 1936, he was in charge of German economic policy. In the early part of the war, he enjoyed success as head of the Luftwaffe but fell out of favour as Germany lost the Battle of Britain. Hitler accused him of disloyalty on several occasions as the war neared its end. Though sentenced to death at Nuremberg, Göring managed to commit suicide before the sentence could be carried out.

**DINO GRANDI** Originally a radical agrarian agitator, Grandi eventually became Italian Ambassador to London. He was critical of **Mussolini**'s attempted engagement with the Liberals under the 'Pact of Pacification' in 1921 (which was designed to allow the Fascists to enter normal party politics and to reduce random violence in the countryside). He was among the Fascists who abandoned Mussolini as Italian positions fell after the Allied invasion of Italy.

**ASVERO GRAVELLI** Early believer in '**Universal Fascism**'. He was director of *Anti-Europa*, an evangelising body with a radical European vision, founded in 1928.

**EDGAR GRIFFIN** In August 2001 he was caught up in political controversy when he was forced to resign from Ian Duncan Smith's Conservative Party leadership campaign team after being accused of involvement with the **British National Party** through his son, Nick.

**NICK GRIFFIN** Cambridge graduate who spearheaded the **British National Party**'s renaissance in the General Election of June 2001. In the Oldham West constituency he won 6,552 votes, a result that sent shockwaves through British politics. He also masterminded the BNP's 2002 local election campaign, which resulted in the party winning three council seats in Burnley.

**WALTER GROSS (1904–45)** Nazi official who held special responsibility in the area of education. He attempted to justify the **Holocaust** and **euthanasia** as practical policies.

**JEAN-STÉPHANE GUILLE** Secretary-General of the National Fund for Agricultural Credit under **Vichy**.

**HANS F.K. GÜNTHER (1891–1968)** Leading **race** theorist in Nazi Germany. He was a key figure in the pseudo-academic field of race research promoted by the regime. Günther propagated the idea of history as a contest between the Nordic–German race on the one hand and the Jews on the other.

**H**

**THEO HABICHT** Emissary sent by **Hitler** to 'sort out' the Austrian Nazi Party in 1931.

**ERNST HEINRICH HÄCKEL (1834–1919)** German racial theorist who transposed his biological findings into the human and philosophical world. Appointed Professor of Zoology at the University of Jena, he was especially interested in Darwinism and **élitism**. He emerged as a significant influence on the policies of state **racism** and **eugenics** practised by the Nazis.

**CARL I. HAGEN** Chairman and leader of the Norwegian **Progress Party**. Throughout the 1970s, 1980s and 1990s he tried to foster a moderate image, particularly on the issue of **immigration**.

**JÖRG HAIDER** Former leader of the Austrian *Freiheitliche Partei Österreichs*

(FPÖ) and one of the most significant figures on the European far right today. In the mid-1980s his party jettisoned **liberalism** and moved towards a particularly virulent form of right-wing **populism**. Haider has tried to foster a moderate political image but on occasions the mask has slipped. He has demonstrated admiration and affection for some aspects of the **Third Reich**, snubbed wartime resisters in a very public fashion and publicised his loyalty to the notion of a Greater Germany (including Austria). He cuts a smart figure in his double-breasted suits but some sections of domestic and international opinion now view his approach as crypto-fascist and a danger to Austrian democracy. Haider – who retains a strong power base in the **Carinthia** region – is hardline on **immigration** and, critics say, is equivocal in his attitude to liberal democracy.

**FRANZ HAISER** German thinker who anticipated Nazi themes in his ideas about the 'racial stock' of a **nation** and the need for strong, charismatic leadership. In a different context, he also argued in favour of slavery.

**LIEUTENANT K.O. HALLGREN** Key figure in the inter-war Swedish Fascist People's Party.

**JEFFREY HAMM** Welshman who emerged as one of Oswald **Mosley**'s closest lieutenants. Fiercely anti-Semitic and anti-leftist, he made his name as a street-level rabble-rouser and stood as a candidate for Mosley's unsuccessful post-war **Union Movement**. Hamm was a teacher by profession.

**JOHN R. HARRELL** Founder of the US **Christian Patriot's Defence League**. An Illinois-based millionaire, his involvement in far-right politics began in the 1950s.

**KARL HARRER** German political activist who helped **Drexler** found the **Deutsche Arbeiterpartei** (DAP) – the movement **Hitler** embraced in his formative years. A journalist by trade, Harrer was an arch-exponent of racial ideas and was eventually expelled from the organisation by Hitler in 1920.

**E. HASSE** Influential member of the **Alldeutscher Verband** in the early twentieth century. In his autarchic, racialist and expansionist thinking he anticipated key elements of Nazi **ideology**.

**KAUL HAUSHOFER (1869–1946)** German scholar whose geopolitical thinking had a significant impact on the Nazi leadership. He was particularly interested in the issue of territorial expansionism and argued that Germany had a right to expand to her 'natural boundaries' in the east and west. A half-hearted national-socialist, he turned against **Hitler** after what he saw as the 'misapplication' of his ideas.

**VÍCTOR RAÚL HAYA DE LA TORRE (1895–1979)** Founder and leader of the Peruvian **APRA** movement between 1924 and his death. Authoritarian but pragmatic, Torre advanced a unique brand of leftist, populist fascism. He contested the 1931 elections but soon turned to **violence**. The Trujillo Uprising of July 1932 was a seminal moment in Torre's life, creating as it did several hundred APRA martyrs. His party gained significant electoral success in the post-war period and he became President of the Peruvian Assembly in 1978.

**S. HEDENGREN** Artillery officer who became a key figure in the inter-war Swedish Fascist People's Party.

**MANUEL HEDILLA** Radical Nazi-inspired *Falangist*. A fierce critic of both liberal **democracy** and **Marxism**, he made his name as a leading member of the Spanish *Falange* in the mid-1930s. He fell out with **Franco** in 1937.

**MARTIN HEIDEGGER (1889–1976)** German philosopher who supported the Nazis. His existentialist philosophy had an important impact after the **Second World War** but he was noted chiefly for his efforts to align university faculties with the policies and interests of the Nazis during the 1930s.

**NEVILLE HENDERSON (1882–1942)** British diplomat who gained few plaudits as Ambassador to Berlin between 1937 and 1939.

**KARL HENLEIN** Leader of the **Sudeten German Party** in inter-war Czechoslovakia.

**JOHANN HERDER (1744–1803)** Theorist of **nationalism** who emphasised the value of a compact cultural community or *Volk*, whose members had a shared history. He saw relatively small but culturally homogeneous nations as the natural units and disliked expansive, multi-national empires. He had a considerable influence on the development of cultural nationalism and in this sense is a key name in the ancestry of fascism.

**ANGEL HERRERA (1886–1968)** Key *Confederación Española Derechas Autónomas* (CEDA) ideologue.

**RUDOLF HESS (1894–1987) Hitler** confidante who was accused of treason after an unexpected flight to Britain in May 1941. It is unclear whether he was acting on his own initiative or flying a kite for the Nazi regime or factions within it. He was tried for **war crimes** and sentenced to life imprisonment at Spandau Prison near Berlin. Despite the willingness of Western states to free him in his old age, the Soviet Union was insistent that he serve his full term.

**REINHARD HEYDRICH (1904–42)** *Schutzstaffel* (SS) leader with specific responsibility for implementing the Final Solution and the mass killing of Jews. He gained a reputation for brutality and cold-bloodedness. He administered the death camps and drove Polish Jews into rat-infested ghettos. Heydrich was finally killed in a bomb attack by Czech resistance fighters.

**HEINRICH HIMMLER (1900–45)** Ambitious and brutal head of the *Schutzstaffel* (SS) who was ultimately responsible for the management of the logistics associated with the transportation of Jews to the death camps. Himmler participated in the Munich **Beer Hall Putsch** (1923) and headed the SS from 1929. He also had his own security agency and enjoyed spying on fellow Nazis. In 1936 he gained control over the **Gestapo**, thus commanding the entire terror apparatus of the Reich. In 1945 he tried to gain concessions from the Allies by promising to help the Jews. As a result, he was disowned by **Hitler**. Himmler was tried at Nuremberg but committed suicide.

**FIELD-MARSHALL PAUL VON HINDENBURG (1847–1934)** German President (1925–33) who facilitated **Hitler's** rise to power. Previously a renowned military leader who fought in the **Franco-Prussian War** and the First World War, he used his connections on the nationalist right, his links with the military and his powers of decree to subvert the democratic intent of the Weimar constitution. He appointed Hitler as Chancellor in 1933 but his influence declined and the latter had no need of a presidency with the emergence of his Führer state and von Hindenburg's death.

**EMPEROR HIROHITO (1901–89)** Japanese leader whose role as a god-like figure saved him from both his own army and the post-war Allied forces. There is considerable debate over the scale of his complicity with, or manipulation by, the military, though he used his relative autonomy to authorise a Japanese surrender after the atom bombing of Hiroshima and Nagasaki. Militarists justified their action and encouraged the Japanese to fight for the sake of the Emperor. Hirohito survived as a constitutional monarch under post-war democracy until his death but renounced god-like status and adopted a slightly more public role. He was not strictly a fascist or right-wing figure but was invested with such symbolism by the Japanese far right, both during and after the war.

**ADOLF/ADOLPH HITLER (1889–1945)** Leader (**Führer**) of the Nazi Party between 1921 and 1945, and of Nazi Germany (the self-styled **'Third Reich'**) between 1933 and 1945. He was the central figure in **National-Socialism** and the instigator of the **Second World War** and the **Holocaust** against six million European Jews. Son of Alois Hitler, a customs official, he was born and educated in Austria. His family moved from a small border town to Linz in 1892, after a brief stay in Bavaria. He left school at sixteen after a mediocre performance and the death of his father. After 1907 he was based in Vienna, having failed to make headway in the art world. While drifting in the city's underworld he came across, and was excited by, various pamphlets and magazines extolling **race** and conspiracy theories. At twenty-four he fled to Munich to avoid Austrian military service but then joined the German Army. He fought in the First World War – and was a victim of gas poisoning – and joined the German Workers' Party in 1919. He showed a flair for **propaganda**, organisation and politicking, rather than theory, and urged the party to change its name to the National Socialist German Worker's Party, with centralised leadership structures. Hitler assumed full leadership of the party in 1921 and, amid tensions between right-wing nationalists and the Berlin Government, attempted a **putsch** in Bavaria in 1923, with plans to hijack a projected nationalist march on Berlin. However, the old right and the military were unsure of Hitler's intentions and capabilities, and abandoned him. He was arrested and subsequently changed tactics, taking a less strident approach and building relationships with the **establishment**, while continuing his violent and subversive activities in the background. However, he also used the early part of this interval, while imprisoned for his part in the putsch, to write *Mein Kampf*, in which he laid out his programme of arch-**nationalism**, **anti-Semitism** and totalitarian dictatorship. Between 1929 and 1932, his Nazi Party scored significant gains in electoral terms, having persuaded the nationalist right to back it. After considerable manoeuvring in parliament and with the use and abuse of the powers of decree on the part of President von **Hindenburg**, Hitler became Chancellor in 1933. He quickly assumed full powers and established a one-party state. The remainder of his life story is also the history of Nazi Germany itself. By 1941, having instigated the Second World War in 1939, he was master of Europe, with the exception of Russia, Britain and a handful of neutral states. However, he narrowly escaped an assassination bid in 1941 and both his mental and physical health deteriorated after reverses on the battlefield in Russia from 1942 onwards. As Soviet forces closed in, he committed suicide with his mistress, Eva **Braun**, in a bunker under government buildings in 1945. His body was burned by the advancing Red Army. Subsequent German regimes in both East and West have obliterated all traces of Hitler's life and death in order to deny neo-Nazis an opportunity for provocative ceremonies and demonstrations.

**MSGR ANDREJ HLINKA** Slovak cleric who

headed the inter-war People's Catholic Party – a movement that gradually shifted from a separatist to a fascist agenda. He had such an influence on his organisation that it became known as the **Hlinka Guard** (and its student arm, Hlinka Youth). He was succeeded by **Tiso**.

**KARL-HEINZ HOFFMANN** Leader of the German *Wehrsportgruppe Hoffmann* in the 1970s and 1980s.

**ROGER HOLEINDRE** *Algérie Française* veteran who emerged as a leading figure in **Le Pen**'s *Front National* (FN) during the 1980s and 1990s. He co-ordinated the movement's ex-servicemen's association.

**ADMIRAL MIKLÓS HORTHY DE NAGYBA-NYA (1868–1957)** Hungarian Head of State between 1920 and 1944. He had an aristocratic, military background and helped put down left-wing revolts in 1919–20. The regime he established in 1920 was conservative–authoritarian. It was both anti-Communist and anti-Semitic, but historians are agreed that any fascist features were purely cosmetic. He was eventually deposed by the Germans in 1944, sent to a concentration camp and replaced by **Szálasi**.

**ALFRED HUGENBERG (1865–1951)** German businessman, publisher and conservative politician who provided funding and **propaganda** outlets for the Nazis in their electoral and parliamentary manœuvres of the early 1930s. He was leader of the *Deutsche National Volks Partei* (DNVP), which gave critical support to **Hitler** in the Reichstag coalition deals of 1932–3. Though not enthusiastic about Nazism *per se*, Hugenberg preferred an authoritarian, conservative solution to Weimar's problems and shared Hitler's arch-nationalist revisionism in foreign policy. He advocated national-front tactics to unite the nationalist right and became Minister of Finance in Hitler's

cabinet of 1933. However, his DNVP was ultimately wound up and he was sidelined once Hitler consolidated his power.

**SADDAM HUSSEIN (b. 1937)** President of Iraq and leader of the Iraqi wing of the Ba'ath Arab Socialist Party. Saddam was part of a Ba'athist **junta** that ruled the country after a coup in 1968 but he seized power for himself in 1979. He modelled Iraq as a one-party state, partly on Soviet Stalinist lines, but with a strong military and tribal element to the ruling élite. He has always exhibited an intense hostility to Israel (which he calls 'the Zionist Entity'), verging on **anti-Semitism**. In some respects, he is more of a Marxist nationalist revolutionary than a fascist, but is capable of shifting ideological focus as circumstances require. Since the collapse of **Communism**, for instance, he has rediscovered his Islamic credentials. Iraq waged and lost both an irredentist war against Kuwait in 1991 and an opportunistic war against an Iran weakened by revolutionary turmoil (1980–8). Hussein is often likened to **Hitler**. However, his philosophy owes as much to **Stalinism** and regional Arab concerns as to anything approaching fascism. While his foreign policy is aggressive, it lacks the global reach of **Hitler**'s plan for a **New Order**. Nonetheless, his conception of himself as a Saladin, restoring Arab power and greatness, coupled with **socialism** and **militarism**, have echoes of the palingenetic nationalism associated with fascism. The debate over the character of his regime remains wide open.

I

**KITA IKKI (d. 1937)** Ultra-nationalist Japanese leader noted for his hatred of the **working class** and his belief in a new national order. He yearned for a military coup, believed that Japan should take the leading role in Far East diplomacy and, in his *General Outline of Measures for the Reconstruction of Japan* (1919), put forward policies such as nationalisation and land reform. He was an authoritarian revolutionary and also a loose canon whose ego often got the better of him. Nevertheless, he had a significant influence on nationalists and military personnel in the 1920s and 1930s. He was executed in 1937.

**BÉLA IMRÉDY (1891–1946)** Hungarian Prime Minister between 1938 and 1939. He collaborated with the Nazis and enacted anti-Semitic legislation in Hungary. He was executed for **war crimes** in 1946.

**DAVID IRVING** Highly controversial British historian who has become the most notorious advocate of Historical Revisionist theses. He is the author of *Hitler's War* (1977).

**JACQUES ISORNI** Marshal **Pétain**'s lawyer during his 1945 trial. In 1951 Isorni was elected to the National Assembly as a representative of **Bardèche**'s *Union of National and Independent Republicans* (UNIR) party.

**J**

**KIRSTEN JACOBSEN** Leader of the Danish **Progress Party** in the 1990s.

**HANS JANMAAT** The man who personified the Dutch extreme right during the 1980s. He was associated with a variety of movements (Centre Party, *Centrum Democraten* [CD]), and was renowned for his hardline attitude to immigrants. He founded the CD in 1984 and became its undisputed driving force. In the early 1980s he represented the CD in the Dutch Second Chamber. Jamaat and the CD lost further support during the 1990s.

**PHILIP JENNINGER** Parliamentary speaker in West Germany who resigned his post in 1988 after publicly empathising with **Hitler**'s Nazi programme in a keynote speech.

**COLIN JORDAN** Cambridge graduate who emerged as an influential figure on the British post-war far right. He was involved in a succession of organisations – the **White Defence League**, the **British Movement**, *Fédération Ouest-Européene* and **British National Party**. Jordan helped establish his own anti-Semitic publication (*Gothic Ripples*). He was a protégé of veteran British anti-Semite Arnold **Leese** and was married to the daughter of Christian **Dior**, Françoise.

**WILLIAM JOYCE (1906–46)** Anti-Semitic agitator involved first with the **British Fascists** and then the **British Union of Fascists**. He was appointed Director of Propaganda by **Mosley** but left the movement after a conflict with the leadership. With John **Beckett** he founded the **National Socialist League**, but this movement was banned in 1939. During the war he defected to Germany and gained infamy as 'Lord Haw-Haw' on **Göbbels**'s English-language radio service (his catchphrase was 'Germany calling'). He was arrested by British troops in 1945 and hanged for treason in 1946.

**EDGAR JUNG (1894–1934)** German veteran of the First World War who believed in a unique blend of **nationalism**, **Christianity** and monarchism. In pinpointing the **decadence** at the heart of early twentieth-century society he believed that he was 'preparing the way' for a new, rejuvenated Germany. Although his ideas were tangential to fascism in many ways, his brand of 'organic' nationalism was far removed from the Nazi doctrine of biological **racism**. As such he identified with von **Papen** and the *Konservative Volkspartei* rather than **Hitler**; and in the end he suffered for his political beliefs, killed in the **Röhm Purge** of 1934.

**ERNST JÜNGER (b. 1895)** Conservative revolutionary who evolved from soldier to writer. The watershed nature of the First World War was a particularly strong influence on Jünger and he is now seen as representative of the brand of fascism known as **'soldierly nationalism'**. In his writings he played on many Nazi themes – *Völkisch* **nationalism**, strong leadership and the need for a new 'warrior' people – but was appalled at some aspects of the **Hitler** regime. After 1945 he became an icon for European neo-fascist groups and in 1982 won the Goethe Prize – an important sign that Germany was coming to terms with its past and making an effort to rehabilitate great right-wing thinkers.

# K

**GORDON KAHL** Notorious member of US group, **Posse Comitatus**. In 1983 he killed two federal officials in North Dakota and emerged as a hero in the eyes of far-right activists.

**GUSTAV VON KAHR** Bavarian Minister-President in 1920–1. As a right-wing authoritarian conservative he had some sympathy with **Hitler**'s political agenda but hindered his plans at the time of the **Beer Hall Putsch**. The Führer did not forget and had him executed in 1934.

**WOLFGANG KAPP (1858–1922)** Right-wing German politician who led the attempted 1920 **putsch** against the **Weimar Republic** that bears his name. The Kapp putschists wanted to replace the Weimar state with a right-wing dictatorship or to restore the monarchy. Despite giving birth to a rebel 'government', the coup collapsed in a general strike. Kapp died in detention while awaiting trial for his role in the affair. The putschists had the support of **Hitler** and his followers who became increasingly convinced that they could gain political advantage by joining conspiracies against Weimar from within the system, notably by exploiting dissension in the Army and among the **middle class**.

**RADOVAN KARADŽIĆ (b. 1945)** Bosnian Serb psychiatrist, turned political leader, accused of promoting human rights violations and **ethnic cleansing** in Bosnia-Herzegovina in the early 1990s. Karadžić was leader of the autonomous Serb entity in Bosnia, *Republika Srpska*, at various times between 1992 and 1996. In 1995, he lost the support of the Yugoslav government in Belgrade and was forced to sign the Dayton Peace Accord, which created separate autonomous states in a single Bosnian state. Karadžić has been indicted by the Yugoslavia War Crimes Tribunal.

**BERT KARLSSON** Businessman who co-founded the relatively unsuccessful Swedish New Democracy movement in 1990.

**GENERAL KAÚLZA DE ARRIAGA** Senior Portuguese military figure who founded *Movimento Independente para a Reconstrução Nacional* (MIRN) in the mid-1970s. Although opponents viewed him as a light-weight, he was a key personality on the extreme right. Hostile to **democracy** and nostalgic for the Portuguese Empire, he served a prison term for his political beliefs.

**GENERAL WILHELM KEITEL** Senior military figure who was appointed Chief of Staff of the High Command by **Hitler** in 1938. At the end of the war he signed Germany's surrender papers and was executed after the **Nuremberg Trials**.

**CARLOS KELLER** Hispano-German who became a leading ideologue in the Chilean *Movimiento Nacional Socialista de Chile* (MSN).

**WILHELM KEPPLER** Key economic adviser to **Hitler**. Between 1936 and 1938 he worked on the Nazis' Four Year Plan and was then appointed to the Foreign Office. In general terms he acted as an intermediary between the Nazi Party and the community of German industrialists.

**AYATOLLAH RUHOLLAH KHOMEINI (1900–89)** Founder of the Islamic Republic of Iran and leader of the 1979 Islamic Revolution. Khomeini's regime emphasized anti-Americanism and anti-**imperialism**; it also imposed curbs on women and intellectuals in Iranian society. Its economic policy was anti-socialist and anti-Marxist but, until the late 1990s, was still quite *dirigiste*. The regime encouraged mass participation in politics, but this was only permitted in accordance with the narrow guidelines of the Muslim clergy. The institutions of state were also quite complex, with militant 'Revolutionary Guards' acting as a parallel force to the army and police, and the Islamic clergy shadowing the President. Since the late 1990s, liberal clerics and politicians have put less emphasis on the details of Khomeini's doctrines and there is more domestic pluralism and foreign policy moderation than before.

**EMIL KIRDORF (1847–1938)** German coal tycoon who helped to finance **Hitler**'s 1929 election campaign.

**PIA KJAERSGAARD** Leader of the Danish People's Party. She is noted for her moderate discourse, but this has not stopped her from denouncing immigration in strong terms.

**RUDOLF KJELLÉN (1864–1922)** Swedish biologist and political thinker who presaged the main ideological thrust of fascism in his glorification of the state and fierce anti-**individualism**. He was particularly pro-German in outlook.

**SERGE KLARSFELD (b. 1935)** Romanian-born writer and attorney who emerged as a key figure in the hunt for, and trial of, Nazi and **Vichy** war criminals, including Klaus **Barbie**.

**VIHTORI KOSOLA** Farmer who became leader of the *Lapua* and *Isänmaallinen Kansanliike* (IKL) movements in inter-war Finland.

**KARL KRAUCH** Influential industrialist in Nazi Germany. A director of *IG Farben*, he was put in charge of chemical production in the years preceding the outbreak of war.

**BRUNO KREISKY** Austrian socialist leader who made an electoral pact with the Austrian Freedom Party (and the emerging **Haider**) in the mid-1970s. Kreisky's Jewish origins provoked significant outside interest in the deal.

**GUSTAV KRUPP (1870–1950)** German industrialist who offered **Hitler** significant economic and political support. He ignored the terms of the **Versailles** Treaty and was a key player in Germany's rearmament efforts after 1933.

**FRITZ KUHN (1896–1951)** American-German who irritated **Hitler**'s Nazi Party intensely with his posturing as the 'American **Führer**' during the 1930s.

**MICHAEL KÜHNEN (1955–91)** Militant neo-Nazi activist involved in a variety of post-war German groups including *Aktionsfront Nationaler Sozialisten* (ANS) (founded by Kühnen in 1977 and banned two years later) and *Aktionsfront Nationaler Sozialisten/Nationale Aktivisten* (ANS/NA). Throughout his political career he displayed intense admiration for **Hitler** and always dreamed of formally reconstituting the Nazi Party. Although he made some concessions to **Strasserism**, his ideology was consistently hardline: élitist, anti-Semitic, anti-Communist and anti-capitalist. He was heavily influenced by **Nietzsche** and believed strongly in **violence** – hence his regular prison sentences. He died of AIDS.

**ARTURO LABRIOLA** Italian national-syndicalist and ex-trade unionist who was a noted contributor to *La Lupa*. He eventually gave his full backing to the **Mussolini** regime.

**PAUL DE LAGARDE (1827–91)** German anti-Semite who had a significant influence on the *Völkisch* movement that developed at the start of the twentieth century. His philosophical position was a unique blend of '**blood' nationalism**, anti-liberalism and 'German Christianity'. An academic by training, he was a key figure in the revolt of the 'Generation of 1890'.

**HUBERT LAGARDELLE** French Marxist and editor of *Le Mouvement Socialiste* who ended up as **Pétain**'s Minister of Labour at **Vichy**.

**KARL LAMPRECHT (1856–1915)** German polemicist who championed the cause of na-

tional and economic expansionism at the turn of the century. He believed that Germany needed a 'hero' leader to help restore national greatness.

**AUGUST JULIUS LANGBEHN (1851–1907)** 'Pre-Nazi' German writer whose most famous work, *Rembrandt as Educator* (1890), was highly regarded by **Third Reich** leaders (and ran to over forty editions). A protégé of de **Lagarde**, he stood for an irrational, 'blood and soil' **nationalism** that looked forward to the rebirth of Germany as leader of a new, rejuvenated Europe. Langbehn was a key figure in the 'Generation of 1890' and moved away from Aryanism towards **Catholicism** in his later life. His highly spiritual brand of nationalism was complemented by a strong belief in **ruralism**.

**ANDERS LANGE (d. 1974)** Founding father of the Norwegian **Progress Party** in 1973. A veteran right-wing operator, he was involved in fascist activity during the inter-war years but was opposed to **Hitler**'s regime and the Nazi occupation of Norway. In the post-war years he was associated mainly with anti-tax protests.

**HELMUT LANGENBUCHER** German poet who was looked on with favour by Nazi leaders.

**AGOSTINO LANZILLO** Italian neo-syndicalist and interventionist who followed the teachings of **Sorel**. The author of *The Post-War Revolution* (1922), he believed that Italy was in need of social, political and spiritual transformation. Lanzillo emerged as a key Fascist supporter.

**PAUL LATINUS (d. 1984)** Ex-leader of the Belgian *Front de la Jeunesse* (FJ), and founder member of the neo-Nazi **Westland New Post** organisation.

**PIERRE LAVAL (1883–1945)** French politician who began his career on the left and ended it as France's most notorious pro-Nazi collaborator. He was a lawyer by trade and rose swiftly to prominence in the Socialist Party (becoming Mayor of Aubervilliers, a district of Paris). He gradually moved to the right and was appointed Prime Minister in 1930 and 1935. In the mid-1930s he put the case for appeasement and a Franco-Italian alliance. In 1940 **Pétain** appointed him Premier. Laval quickly absorbed himself in Franco-German diplomacy and gained notoriety as the chief architect of **Vichy**'s policy of **collaboration**. He was famed for his wheeler-dealer qualities and his cynical **pragmatism**. He initiated 'industrial conscription' via the *Service du Travail Obligatoire* and '*Réleve*', and was proactive in sending Jews to their death in Nazi Germany. At the end of the war he fled to Spain. He tried to commit suicide, but was tried for treason and executed.

**T.E. LAWRENCE (LAWRENCE OF ARABIA)** Friend of Henry **Williamson** who supported the idea of Anglo-German *rapprochement* in the 1930s and, in tandem with Williamson, wished to set up a special meeting with **Hitler**.

**GUSTAVE LE BON** Influential French right-wing thinker whose *Psychology of Crowds* (1895) likened history to biological evolution. His 'natural selection' ideas helped to shape early fascist ideology and he became a fervent admirer of **Mussolini**.

**ARNOLD LEESE** Anti-Semite who began his political career in the **British Fascists** (BF) but left to found the **Imperial Fascist League** (IFL) in 1929. A vet by trade, Leese was jailed for six months in the late 1930s for making inflammatory anti-Jewish remarks. He believed passionately that Britain should not go to war with Nazi Germany.

**MGR MARCEL LEFEBVRE (d. 1991)** Controversial French Catholic archbishop who emerged in the 1980s as a keynote supporter of **Le Pen**'s *Front National*. Lefebvre, who continued to celebrate Mass in the traditional Latin rite, broke with the Vatican in the 1960s over its reform programme and was deemed to be excommunicated by the Church in 1988.

**FRITZ LENZ (1887–1946)** German geneticist who anticipated Nazi thinking on **eugenics**.

**LEO XIII (1810–1903)** Pope whose 1891 *Rerum Novarum* encyclical contained corporatist ideas.

**JEAN-MARIE LE PEN (b. 1928)** Founded the *Front National* (FN) in 1972 and has been its leader ever since. In the 1950s he was a supporter of *Algérie Française* (he served as a paratrooper) and the *Union de Défense des Commerçants et Artisans* (UDCA) (in 1956 he was elected the youngest ever French deputy on the Poujadist ticket). A colourful, charismatic and scandal-hit politician, Le Pen emerged as a key player in French politics in the mid-1980s. He has served as a Euro-MP, polled 15 per cent in the 1995 French presidential elections and for the first time entered the second round of a presidential poll in 2002 on the back of a 17 per cent score. (He was easily beaten by Jacques Chirac in the run-off.) He is probably the most famous far-right politician in post-war Europe.

**ANDRZEJ LEPPER** Leader of the modern Polish Self Defence movement. A political maverick, he was strongly opposed to government agricultural policy and sought a 'Third Way' between **capitalism** and **socialism**. With his party devoid of parliamentary representation, Lepper concentrated on street-level agitation and was fiercely opposed to the sale of Polish farmland to foreigners.

**JACQUES LEROY-LADURIE** Minister of Food under **Vichy**.

**KID LEWIS** Jew who stood as a candidate for **Mosley**'s **New Party** in the early 1930s. Later he helped coach the **British Union of Fascist**'s paramilitary squads.

**ROBERT LEY (1890–1945)** Loyal Cologne-based follower of **Hitler** who succeeded Gregor **Strasser** as leader of the *Deutsche Arbeits Front* (DAF) in 1932. Ley was uncharismatic but efficient: banning all trade unions, constantly reiterating the Nazi work ethic and turning the *Front* into the biggest organisation in the **Third Reich** with over 25 million members. In 1939 he launched a series of special welfare reforms.

**MICHAEL LIBERT** Belgian far-right activist. An influential member of the **Front de la Jeunesse** (FJ), he also played a key role in the emergence of the WNP in the late 1970s.

**LANZ VON LIEBENFELS** Early twentieth-century Austrian nationalist thinker who specialised in Occult-based **Aryan racism**. His dream was the spiritual rebirth of the whole German people.

**S.O. LINDHOLM** Army sergeant who became a significant figure in the inter-war Swedish Fascist People's Party.

**ROTHA LINTORN ORMAN (d. 1935)** Founder of the British **Fascisti** in 1923. She was fairly ignorant of European fascism, but was provoked into political activity by her experiences during the First World War and her powerful anti-Communism.

**FRIEDRICH LIST (1789–1846)** German writer who advocated imperial expansion, a planned economy and the regulation of capital and labour in the interests of the state. He wrote *Das Nationale System der* *Politischer Ökonomie* in 1904. In retrospect, his ideas can be seen as anticipating fascism.

**DIMITRIJE LJOTIĆ** Leader of the *Zbor* movement in 1930s Yugoslavia. He was a former member of the Serbian Radical Party and was appointed Minister of Justice in 1931. He was arrested in 1940 and his movement outlawed.

**GENERAL GIOVANNI DE LORENZO** Italian military figure who was co-opted onto the *Movimento Sociale Italiano* (MSI) ticket for the 1972 elections.

**AGOSTINHO LOURENÇO** Head of **Salazar**'s *Policia de Vigilancia e Defesa do Estado* (PVDE) secret police force.

**FIELD-MARSHALL ERICH LUDENDORFF (1865–1937)** German military commander in the First World War who favoured using modern military transport and armoured divisions to wage total war on the enemy. He subsequently supported **Hitler**. Ludendorff largely ignored **Clausewitz**'s warning that real war has a moderating political framework. He participated in nationalist and far-right conspiracies against Weimar, including the Kapp and Munich putsches. He was a Nazi Party member and a Reichstag deputy from 1924–8.

**KARL LUEGER** Leader of the Austrian *Christlich-Soziale Partei*. Lueger's organisation moved in the direction of fascism as the inter-war period progressed.

**MINO MACCARI (1898–1989)** Editor of anti-modern Italian newspaper, *Il Selvaggio*. He emerged as a committed racist during the Fascist era and argued that Italy had to be purged of all 'decadent' elements.

**HJALMAR MÄE** Head of Propaganda for the *Eesti Vabadussõjalaste Liit* (EVL). He became Estonian leader during the period of collaboration with the Nazis.

**BOB MAES** Founder and head of the Belgian *Vlaamse Militanten Orde* (VMO). He wound up the movement in 1971.

**ALBERT MAKASHOV** Neo-Stalinist who was a candidate in the Russian presidential elections of 1991.

**CURZIO MALAPARTE** Florence-based intellectual who emerged as a key **myth**-maker inside **Mussolini**'s party. He joined the Fascists in 1921, took part in the **March on Rome** and argued that the spirit of the *squadrismo* was the essence of Italian Fascism. His populist **ruralism** took him in the direction of the anti-modern *Strapaese* movement and *Il Selvaggio*. He was also associated with *La Conquista dello Stato*, an influential political journal founded in 1924.

**HENRI DE MAN** Belgian intellectual who wrote *Beyond Marxism* in 1926. As a theoretician he was on the left but the experience of the First World War taught him that the **nation** was more important than class as a driving force in history. He attempted to blend conservative and revolutionary ideas, and, significantly, **Mussolini** admired his work.

**THOMAS MANN (1875–1955)** Arguably, the most famous German novelist of the twentieth century. He became one of the fiercest critics of Nazism and a key figure in anti-fascist circles. He emigrated to Switzerland and was eventually disowned by **Hitler**'s Germany.

**GRAAF DE MARCHANT ET D'ANSEMBOURG** Important figure in the inter-war Dutch national-socialist movement, *Nationaal Socialistische Beweging* (NSB). He collaborated with the Germans during the war and was sentenced to a 15-year prison term as a result.

**FERDINAND MARCOS (1917–89)** Filipino dictator who ruled the country from 1965 to 1986. Though initially reformist and pro-American, his regime became more nationalist and authoritarian in the 1970s. Marcos was not a fascist but his blend of right-wing crony capitalism and corruption were matched by spasms of anti-US **nationalism** and by proclaiming solidarity with the poor. The latter was a theme in the public image cultivated by his wife, Isabella, despite her own profligacy and excess (symbolised by her extensive collection of shoes). This mixture of right-wing and populist politics was vaguely similar to that found in **Perónism**. However, Marcos became more conservative and pro-American again in his later years and was eventually toppled in 1986 in a US-backed popular revolution led by centrist and conservative reformers.

**FILIPPO TOMMASO MARINETTI (1876–1944)** Influential representative of the Italian Futurist Movement who believed in the 'Cult of Italy'.

**SPYROS MARKEZINIS** Veteran Greek politician who refounded the far-right Progressive Party (Komma Proodeftikon) in 1979.

**N.E. MARKOV** Leader of the **Union of Russian People** (URP) movement in succession to **Dubrovin**.

**MIHAILO MARKOVIĆ** Modern ethnic Serb nationalist and formerly philosopher and party ideologue in the Serbian Socialist Party (SPS).

**ADRIEN MARQUET (1884–1955)** Close ally of French fascist **Déat**. In the inter-war period Marquet was at the forefront of the revolt against **socialism** – a revolt that was instrumental in the growth of fascism in France. In 1940 he shared the defeatist attitudes of **Laval**.

**AUGUSTO DE MARSANICH** Appointed leader of the Italian *Movimento Sociale Italiano* (MSI) in 1951. His main aim was to moderate the image of the party.

**ELIO MASSAGRANDE** Founder member and deputy leader of the Spanish *Ordine Nuovo*.

**ROBERT MATHEWS** Founder of The **Order**, a pro-white movement in post-war America. He was previously involved in the **National Alliance** and the Church of Jesus Christ Christian. He was killed in a street shoot-out, and thereby emerged as a far-right hero and martyr.

**CHARLES MAURRAS (1868–1952)** Founder and leader of the *Action Française* (AF), a movement generally regarded as representative of 'early' French fascism. He came from an archetypal right-wing background: he was hostile to all forms of equality and **egalitarianism**, and loyal instead to notions of **hierarchy** and tradition. A vociferous critic of the Third Republic, he established the AF in 1899 to carry on the fight against Dreyfus. Maurras believed that the restoration of the monarchy would solve all France's problems and it was to this cause that he devoted his whole life. A thinker rather than a doer, he saw himself as 'above' party politics and did not take part in elections. In 1940 when Marshal **Pétain** emerged as French leader he believed that the nation's saviour had at last arrived. He idolised the Marshal and the Marshal came to view him as his chief ideologue. But Maurras's influence extends further than **Vichy**. He is not only regarded as the founding father of the modern French right but as one of the greatest French intellects of the twentieth century. The Pope once described him as 'a very fine brain, but alas, only a brain'.

**JOSEPH MCCARTHY** Zealous anti-Communist US senator of the 1950s.

**VLADIMIR MECIAR (b. 1942)** Communist-turned-nationalist who led independent Slovakia for most of the period 1993–8. Critics questioned the commitment of his Movement for a Democratic Slovakia to **democracy**, in part because of its association with nationalist hostility to Hungarian and gypsy minorities.

**BRUNO MÉGRET** Apostle of new-style liberal *Front National* economics in the 1980s and 1990s. He became **Le Pen**'s right-hand man but left the movement in 1999 to form the *Front National-Mouvement National*, later known as the *Mouvement National Républicain* (MNR). He scored 2.4 per cent in the 2002 presidential elections. He is the husband of Catherine.

**CATHERINE MÉGRET** Novice political operator who became *Front National* Mayor of **Vitrolles**, Marseilles, in 1997. She only stood in the election because her husband, Bruno, had been banned from taking part on a technical matter. Madame Mégret made no secret of her political naïvety and most onlookers assumed that her spouse was the 'real mayor' of Vitrolles after 1997.

**ZOLTÁN MESKÓ** Founded the green-shirted **Hungarian Hitlerite Movement** in 1932.

**GENERAL IONNIS METAXAS (1871–1941)** Greek army officer who founded the nationalist Free Believers Party in 1920 and rose to become military dictator between 1936 and 1941. He became Prime Minister in 1936 and was allowed by the King to take on a dictatorial role. In power Metaxas's 'Regime of the 4th of August' pursued a range of illiberal policies: strikes were banned, political parties were outlawed and Communists were demonised. His efforts to establish 'fascism from above' led him in a variety of directions. He created a massive youth movement, dreamt of a **'Third Hellenic Civilisation'** and adopted **Hitler**-style ritual. However, whatever the trappings, his regime always lacked genuine mass support.

**TOM METZGER Ku Klux Klan** activist who founded the White American Political Association, later known as the White Aryan Resistance. He maintained that a skinhead army would be at the forefront of the 'revolution' against liberal democracy.

**GENERAL VITO MICELI** Former head of the Italian Secret Service. He went on to represent the *Movimento Sociale Italiano* (MSI).

**ARTURO MICHELINI (d. 1969)** Accountant and former secretary of the Rome Fascist Party. He emerged as *Movimento Sociale Italiano* (MSI) leader in the early 1950s and championed a particularly moderate brand of **neo-fascism**, which bore only minor resemblance to **Mussolini**'s interwar ideology. He aimed to integrate the MSI into the Italian political system, but never really achieved this. He led the movement up to his death.

**ROBERT/ROBERTO MICHELS (1876–1936)** Social scientist famous for his 'iron law of oligarchy'. This suggests that organisations competing for power, such as political parties in a democracy, will tend to develop centralised and oligarchic internal power structures dominated by a tight nucleus of leaders. This is necessary for the discipline and organisation required for effective struggle with its rivals. Michels's work was devoted to oligarchic tendencies in the German Social Democratic Party but one could easily see its attraction for fascists. If the 'iron law' was applied to states in competition with one another in the international system, for example, it could be used to justify dictatorship at home in order to mobilise for war. Though born in Germany, he worked in Italy and eventually became sympathetic to Fascism.

**ROBERT MILES** Michigan-based activist with links to the US Mountain Church and the United Klans.

**GLENN MILLER** US far-right activist with links to both the Knights of the **Ku Klux Klan** and the White Patriot Party.

**YUKIO MISHIMA (1925–70)** Japanese novelist and right-wing agitator in the interwar period. He eventually committed suicide.

**PRESIDENT JOSEPH MOBUTO SESE SEKO (KOKO NGBENDU WA ZA BANGA) (1930–97)** Zairean-Congolese President between 1965 and 1997 who was installed with US support. He initially brought stability to the former Belgian Congo after civil war and emphasised African authenticity (renaming his country 'Zaire', for example). His regime degenerated into one of the most corrupt in Africa, with the President siphoning off most of the country's wealth and suppressing opposition. He supported conservative African governments against Soviet or Cuban-instigated Marxist rebellions and served as an agent of US influence. He was a target of Soviet-, Angolan- and Cuban-backed insurgency, notably in Shaba province. He fled to Morocco in 1997 after a period of instability dating from 1994. Mobuto's Zaire also competed with the neighbouring Marxist People's

Republic of the Congo. The fall of the regime led to the implosion of the state and civil war. Though oppressive, and despite superficial efforts at mass mobilisation by means of a political party, the *Mouvement Populaire de la Révolution*, Mobuto's regime was mostly a personalised fiefdom rather than a proper fascist state. The translation of his full name from Lingala reads: 'The all-powerful warrior who, because of his endurance and inflexible will to win, will go from conquest to conquest, leaving fire in his wake.'

**ARTHUR MOELLER VAN DEN BRUCK (1876–1925)** Influential theorist of conservative revolution who anticipated Nazi ideas. A key figure in the 'Generation of 1890', he mixed pessimistic analysis with the genuine hope that a charismatic saviour figure could save Germany from national decay and establish a new political order. Antiliberal and anti-democratic, he put enormous emphasis on culture and **conservatism**. Moeller van den Bruck was associated with the *Juni-Klub* and *Das Wissen*, and his 1923 work, *The Third Reich*, presented the Nazis with an important piece of nomenclature. Many neofascists and **New Right** thinkers look upon him as a highly significant figure in the history of right-wing thought.

**DANIEL ARAP MOI (b. 1924)** Leader of the Kenyan African National Union, the ruling party in Kenya's one-party state between 1978 and 1991. Moi grudgingly introduced multi-party democratic reforms during the 1990s but remained Prime Minister. Unlike most other one-party regimes, Moi's was conservative rather than Marxist. Though an ally of the US in the **Cold War**, Moi turned against the US during the 1990s over its criticism of his human rights record.

**GENERAL BAUTISTA MOLINA** Senior Argentine military figure who headed the parmilitary movement, *Alianza de la Juventud Nacionalista*, between 1937 and 1943. He was an admirer of **Hitler**.

**'REV.' SUN MYUNG MOON** Wealthy head of the **Moon Organisation** and **Unification Church**. A fanatical anti-Communist, he developed close links with the **World Anti-Communist League** and subsidised the organisation's 1970 conference to the tune of $1 million. At the height of the **Cold War** he viewed himself as potential 'world leader' against Moscow.

**GAETAMO MOSCA (1857–1941)** Italian social scientist who propagated the élite theory of social systems in which a minority ruling class is seen as an inevitable feature of social and political development. For fascists this approach to politics appeared to vindicate their critique of liberal democracy as a fraud and justify their own emergence as a ruling élite. However, as an Italian legislator, Mosca was a vocal critic of **Mussolini**.

**JÜRGEN MOSLER** German militant associated with *Die Bewegung*.

**SIR OSWALD MOSLEY (1896–1980)** Maverick politician of aristocratic background who founded the **British Union of Fascists** in 1931. In the immediate aftermath of the First World War, Mosley sat as an MP for the Conservatives and Labour, and as an Independent. He was Chancellor of the Duchy of Lancaster in Ramsay McDonald's 1929–31 government, but left over a row about economic policy. Mosley founded the **New Party** soon after but this movement had a very short lifespan. On a trip to Italy he had been hugely impressed by **Mussolini**, and the British Union of Fascists took on many Fascist/Nazi-style trappings. However, his views were deemed to be 'unpatriotic' during the war and he spent the years 1940–3 in prison. He founded the **Union Movement** in 1948 but it had minimal electoral impact. He spent most of his later life in exile.

**ION MOTA (d. 1937)** Mystical Romanian fascist who led the **Brotherhood of the Cross** in the 1920s. He became a key figure in **Codreanu**'s **Legion of the Archangel Michael** and represented the movement at the 1934 Fascist International in Montreux. He died fighting for the Nationalists in the **Spanish Civil War**.

**ANTON MUSSERT (1894–1946)** An engineer by trade, he founded the Dutch *Nationaal Socialistische Beweging* (NSB) in 1931.

**ALESSANDRA MUSSOLINI** Granddaughter of Benito **Mussolini**. A former film star, she was elected to the Italian Chamber of Deputies and only just missed out on becoming Mayor of Naples in the early 1990s.

**ARNALDO MUSSOLINI** Brother of Benito **Mussolini** and one of his few close confidantes.

**BENITO MUSSOLINI (1883–1945)** Italian dictator between 1922 and 1943 who was originally a radical anarcho-socialist and a member of the revolutionary Socialist Party of Italy. He delighted in polemic journalism and pamphleteering. Seeking to maximise social disorder and create revolutionary conditions, he initially opposed intervention in the First World War, then backed it. He sought a leadership role in any revolution that might ensue but lost faith in the ability of the **working class** to create such conditions. He turned to **nationalism** as a source of mass mobilisation and began to collaborate with industrialists after 1918. He founded the Fascist Party in 1919, combining nationalist, right-wing and socialist themes in his political doctrine. He sought notoriety and fame on the right, in competition with nationalists and militarists like **D'Annunzio**, and emerged as Fascist leader with support from anti-liberal forces on the extreme right and left. He viewed militant activity and street violence as a counter to left-wing radical revolution but also as a threat of further disorder. After the **March on Rome** in 1922, Mussolini bullied the political élite and the King into accepting him as head of government. In power his policies involved a similar reliance on threats, bluffs, dramatic gestures (like his **Abyssinian invasion** or the attack on Corfu). On the other hand, he could be indecisive, as when he did not know how to handle radical fascism in the 1920s or the possible alliance with **Hitler** in the late 1930s. His domestic policy was dominated by the establishment of a Corporate State and complex relations with the Church. In 1929 he established a **Concordat**, effectively giving the Church some autonomy in education and youth affairs, and re-establishing an independent papal state. His foreign policy was preoccupied with expansion in Africa, the Mediterranean and South-Eastern Europe. He also invaded and conquered Abyssinia in 1936. He entered the war on the Axis side in 1940, despite misgivings about Germany's role in Austria. He directed his forces southwards in North Africa and eastwards into Greece but played a secondary role to that of Hitler. Following Allied gains, the Italian regime fled and the **Fascist Grand Council** voted to topple Mussolini in 1943. *Il Duce* – as he came to be known – was subsequently kidnapped out of Allied detention and reinstalled under tight German control as puppet head of the **Salò Republic**, a new fascist statelet with more extreme and more pro-German policies. In the end he was identified by Communist partisans and shot as Salò collapsed in the face of advancing Allied armies. His daughter, Edda, married Count **Ciano**, his Foreign Minister, while his granddaughter, Alessandra, was active in far-right Italian politics during the 1990s.

**EDDA MUSSOLINI** Favourite daughter of Benito **Mussolini**. She married Count **Ciano**, his Foreign Minister.

**NARSULTAN NAZARBAYEV** President of Kazakhstan for life. He used a 1995 referendum to grant himself extensive and arbitrary power. He was formerly the Communist ruler of Kazakhstan and a representative of Moscow's interests when the republic was part of the Soviet Union. Nazarbayev pursues a Bonapartist strategy, ensuring his own election and replacing **socialism** with **secularism** and **nationalism** as official ideologies. His regime is more of an authoritarian and personalised dictatorship than a totalitarian system.

**MILAN NEDIĆ** Serb puppet leader under the Germans between 1941 and 1944.

**KONSTANTIN VON NEURATH** Nazi Foreign Minister during the 1930s.

**ERNST NIEKISCH (1889–1967)** Influential theorist of 'National Bolshevik' fascism. He looked towards the Communist USSR rather than Nazi Germany for an example of national renaissance. Some of his ideas would impact on post-war **neo-fascism**.

**FRIEDRICH NIETZSCHE (1844–1900)** German philosopher famous for describing the rise of **nihilism** in nineteenth-century Europe. Nietzsche saw the decline of **religion** and tradition as the source of a wider challenge to accepted morality. He predicted that secular ideologies like **nationalism** would be posited as new sources of truth. This emphasis on questioning existing 'bourgeois' norms was a powerful impetus for the rebellious streak in **Futurism**,

Fascism and anarchism, though his philosophy was often misapplied by the ideologists of those movements.

**BORIS NIKOL'SKI** Key intellectual in the Union of Russian People (URP).

**FRANCO NOGUEIRA** Former Minister of Foreign Affairs who became a pillar of **Salazar**'s regime and, later, biographer of the Portuguese dictator.

**ROGER NOLS** Controversial Belgian mayor famous for his anti-immigrant campaigns in Schaerbeek, a suburb of Brussels.

**MANUEL NORIEGA** Panamanian military strongman and dictator who was deposed and captured by US forces following the US invasion of Panama in 1989. He seized outright power in a military coup in 1988. During the 1980s, Noriega had supported US-backed right-wing forces in the Central American civil wars. However, his involvement with the inter-American drugs trade and new concerns about his human rights record were factors in a US policy reversal that led to his downfall. He was convicted of drug trafficking in 1992 and imprisoned in the US.

**LORD NUFFIELD (WILLIAM MORRIS)** Morris cars entrepreneur who helped finance the **British Union of Fascists** in the 1930s.

**EOIN O'DUFFY** Irish fascist involved in various inter-war movements. A former policeman, he began his political career in the **League of Youth** and in 1933 became leader of the **Blueshirts**. In 1935 he founded the **National Corporate Party** (or **Greenshirts**). Throughout the 1930s

228

O'Duffy posed as the 'Irish Mussolini'. He put forward a corporatist, nationalist vision but none of the organisations he was involved in gained much influence. He attended **Fascist International** meetings and led the Irish Brigade during the **Spanish Civil War**. He left the political fray in 1937.

**OLIVIER D'ORMESSON** French politician elected to the European Parliament in 1984 on a *Front National* ticket. He resigned his seat when **Le Pen** refused to withdraw controversial comments he made about the **Holocaust**.

**THEODOROS PANGALOS (1878–1952)** Greek dictator whose short-lived inter-war regime has been labelled fascist by some observers. He banned elections and displayed vague totalitarian ambitions, but was politically confused more than anything else. In 1932 he left Greece for exile in Corfu, and a decade later was accused of collaborating with the Axis powers.

**SERGIO PANUNZIO (1886–1944)** Italian neo-syndicalist thinker whose political ideas anticipated those of **Mussolini**. A political scientist by training, he championed Italian interventionism in the Great War, a leftist brand of **corporatism** and, in general terms, the notion of irrational revolt against the liberal **establishment**. A fervent nationalist, he was a great admirer of *Il Duce*.

**COLONEL GEORGE PAPADOPOULOS** One of 'The **Colonels**' who executed a military coup against the Greek civil authorities in 1967. He became the first leader of the Greek National Political Union (EPEN) in 1984, even though he was serving a prison sentence at the time. His ideology was a mixture of anti-**Marxism**, **nationalism** and **xenophobia**. Most observers view Papadopoulos as a paternalistic military man rather than any kind of radical political figure.

**MARTIN PAPE (b. 1928)** Founder of the German *Freiheitliche Deutsche Arbeiterpartei* (FAP) in 1979 and leader of the movement until 1988.

**FRANZ VON PAPEN (1879–1969)** Right-wing German politician who facilitated **Hitler**'s rise to power and the German–Austrian *Anschluss* (Union). Originally from the largely Catholic Centre Party, he became more and more authoritarian and nationalist. By the early 1930s, he was operating above party politics but had significant influence with the President and the nationalist right. As Chancellor in 1932, he undermined the Weimar constitution and placated the Nazis. When Hitler came to power, partly as a result of his connections with the President and the Reichstag parties, he was named Vice-Chancellor. Though he claimed he could moderate Hitler's policies, the violent suppression of the *Sturm Abteilung* (SA) and attempts on his own life led to his resignation. He escaped with a light sentence from the post-war trials.

**GIOVANNI PAPINI (1881–1956)** One of the most important right-wing intellectuals in pre-Fascist Italy. He was the brains behind the 1904 *Nationalist Programme* and became editor of the radical *Lacerba* in 1913. Widely read and boasting a sizeable entourage, Papini was an ardent nationalist, interventionist and imperialist who was heavily influenced by Futurist, Nietzschean and Social Darwinist ideas. He played on the memory of Ancient Rome, believed in the regenerationist function of war and became associated with both the *Associazione Nazionale Italiana* (ANI) and **Mussolini**. Under the Fascist regime he gained major prominence: he was appointed to the Royal Academy, edited the cultural periodical, *Il Frontespizio*, and became a university professor. He was particularly interested in racial matters but was uncomfortable with Nazi policies in this area.

**DOBROSLAV PARAGA** Leading figure on the modern Croatian far right. A former dissident in Communist Yugoslavia, he founded the *Hrvatska Stranka Prava* (HSP) in 1990 and demands an ethnically homogenous Great Croatia. A solid rather than spectacular political operator, Paraga has demonstrated nostalgia for the wartime *Ustasha* administration and nineteenth-century Croat nationalism.

**VILFREDO PARETO (1848–1923)** Leading sociologist and élite theorist, and a major influence on Italian Fascism. Pareto believed in the inevitability of élite and hierarchical rule. He was a fierce critic of the alleged double standards of liberal democracy.

**KONSTANTIN PÄTS** Estonian Head of State who ruled by decree and banned the fascist *Eesti Vabadussõjalaste Liit* (EVL) in March 1934. His hostility to the EVL did not stop him from pursuing a policy of **fascistisation** in power.

**DR ANTE PAVELIĆ** Zealous Croatian nationalist and leader of the terrorist *Ustasha* movement. Pavelić had a lot of enemies – Jews, Communists and democrats – but he was first and foremost anti-Serb. In 1941 he was installed by the Nazis as leader of the independent state of Croatia.

**ALESSANDRO PAVOLINI** Former Blackshirt who rose to become **Mussolini**'s Minister of Popular Culture in 1939. At Salò in 1943 he emerged as leader of the new Fascist Republican Party and a year later established the Black Brigades, an élite terror group highly reminiscent of the

*squadristi* of the 1920s. He eventually set up his own post-Salò political movement.

**ROGER PEARSON (b. 1927)** Far-right sympathiser associated with the **World Anti-Communist League** and the **Northern League**.

**EVA PERÓN (1919–52)** Known as 'Évita' – the second wife of Juan **Perón**. She tried to cultivate the left-wing and populist strand in **Perónism** but could not shake off her own élite status. She was forced by the Army to abandon a bid for the Vice-Presidency in 1951.

**JUAN DOMINGO PERÓN (1895–1974)** Right-wing populist military dictator in Argentina. He came to power in a **junta** in 1943. Although the country was neutral in the **Second World War**, many Perónists admired **Mussolini** and the regime had good relations with Germany. Perónist military leaders also facilitated the escape of many Nazi figures to Latin America after the war. Perón's own domestic policies combined right-wing **authoritarianism** and anti-Communism with support for pro-regime labour unions, public investment and expanded welfare provision. Perón won the 1946 election but ruled as a dictator until 1955. By then, his regime had become more like a traditional, conservative Latin American military dictatorship. He returned to Argentina in 1973 and won a free election but died in office.

**CLARA PETACCI Mussolini**'s long-time mistress. *Il Duce* had to fight off accusations of corruption when her family gained favours as a result of the liaison. She was shot, with him, in April 1945.

**MARSHAL PHILIPPE PÉTAIN (1856–1951)** France's most famous soldier and the man who decided to collaborate with **Hitler** in 1940. His military career was glittering. He became a Colonel in 1912, won mythical status as the 'Victor of Verdun' in 1916 and was appointed Minister of War in 1934. In 1939 he was sent to Madrid as French Ambassador to the new **Franco** state. Politically, Pétain was always on the right. Because of his military prowess, and high patriotic credentials, he was the ideal man to 'save' France in the aftermath of humiliating defeat in 1940. He signed the Franco-German Armistice and became leader of the Unoccupied (Southern) Zone. As head of the puppet **Vichy** state, Pétain launched the **National Revolution** – a conservative and ultra-traditionalist policy agenda. His Vichy regime collaborated closely with the Nazis; and, as a result, in July 1945, he was tried for treason and found guilty. His punishment was life imprisonment on the Île de Yeu, where he died.

**WALTER PFRIMER (1881–1940)** Leader of the Austrian *Heimwehr*. His country, he argued, could only be saved through fascism and to this end he co-ordinated an ultimately unsuccessful coup attempt in 1931.

**BOLESLAW PIASECKI** Maverick leader of the *Obóz Narodowo-Radykalny* (ONR) breakaway movement, *Falanga*, in inter-war Poland. His doctrine was a blend of **nationalism**, **anti-Semitism** and **militarism**, and he made himself available to collaborate with the Nazis during the **Second World War**. Under Communist rule he led the Catholic *Pax* movement.

**MARIO PIAZZESI** Florence-based Fascist who was actively involved in the **March on Rome**, the **Abyssinian invasion** and the **Salò Republic**. After the war he went into exile but in 1980 published a controversial account of his political career.

**WILLIAM PIERCE** Author of *The Turner Diaries* (1978), a utopian novel that in-

spired the emergence of American far-right coalition movement, The **Order**.

**JOSEPH PILSUDSKI** Inter-war Polish dictator whose military regime has variously been described as 'pre-fascist' and 'semi-fascist'.

**BLAS PIÑAR LÓPEZ** Charismatic leader of the Spanish *Fuerza Nueva*. He idolised **Franco** and José Antonio, and based his whole political programme around **traditionalism** and nostalgia. Between 1979 and 1982 he was the only parliamentary representative of the *Frente Nacional* (FN).

**GIORGIO PINI** A journalist by trade, he held ministerial office at Salò and emerged as a key player in the early history of the *Movimento Sociale Italiano* (MSI). In the 1950s he left the party, unhappy with the way it had veered away from the ideas contained in the Charter of **Verona**. He went on to found a rival neo-fascist movement.

**GENERAL AUGUSTO PINOCHET (b. 1915)** Right-wing Chilean military dictator who came to power in a coup against the democratically elected Marxist regime of Salvador Allende in 1973. The coup also won the tentative support of centre-right parties in Chile, partly to protect economic and business élites but also in response to the activities of the radical and pro-Castro wing of Allende's Socialist Party. Pinochet's economic policies were liberal and free market-oriented, rather than corporatist. The regime was guilty of a large-scale campaign of killings and torture directed against the Chilean left. In economic terms, however, Chile was a Latin success story. The dictatorship became less repressive in its latter years and Pinochet permitted a democratic transition after a referendum in 1988 and a free election in 1990. Fearing a military backlash, the new democratic governments in

Chile accepted terms under which key military leaders won immunity from prosecution and Pinochet was made Senator for life. He had earlier attended **Franco's** funeral but Spanish judges sought his extradition from Britain in 2000–1 in connection with the deaths of foreigners in Santiago de Chile during his initial reign of terror. He was ultimately deemed unfit for trial on medical grounds. While opponents hoped for legal action against him in Chile, he was also deemed unfit for trial there in 2001.

**POPE PIUS XI/ACHILLE RATTI (1857–1939)** Pope from 1922 to 1939. Pius XI authored the famous encyclical *Quadragessimo Anno* that condemned class conflict and urged institutionalised cross-class collaboration in the running of the economy. The document was a partial endorsement of **corporatism** and was a basis for much of the social policy promoted by Catholic parties like the Italian *Partito Populare Italiano* (PPI). Tensions with the Fascists and the Nazis led to a condemnation of fascism in another encyclical, *Mit Brennender Sorge*, in 1931.

**POPE PIUS XII/EUGENIO PACELLI (1876–1958)** Pope for the bulk of the **Second World War**. Although critical of the worst excesses of fascism, he was attacked for not saying enough in defence of Jews and other victims of the **Holocaust**. The Vatican attempted to strike a delicate balance between protecting human rights and its own survival in a Europe dominated by fascist regimes.

**ADOLPHE POINTIER** National President of the Farm Corporation under **Vichy**.

**PAULO PORTAS** Leader of the modern-day Portuguese Popular Party. He has recently entered government as a minister.

**BERNARD POSTMA** Leader of the Dutch

*Nederlandse Volksunie* (NVU) until 1974. He left the movement in 1976.

**POL POT/SALOTH SAR (1925–98)** Fanatical Communist dictator whose 1975–9 regime in Cambodia was responsible for the death of 2 million of his countrymen. His ultra-**Marxism** was combined with *Khmer* **nationalism**. Following Vietnam's occupation of Cambodia, he led the *Khmer Rouge* from the hills with a collective leadership. However, he became more reclusive with time and was reported dead in 1998. Pol Pot's system had some fascist-like features but was essentially an extreme form of **Communism**. It was opposed to modern money and it re-educated intellectuals in rural labour camps. Its campaign of mass murder has erroneously been called genocide: it was not, in fact, aimed at killing off a particular race but, rather, political and ideological opponents from among his own people.

**PIERRE POUJADE** Maverick right-winger who belonged to the *Parti Populaire Français* (PPF) and Vichy Youth in his early years. At the start of the 1950s he founded the *Union de Défense des Commerçants et Artisans* (UDCA), a boisterous pressure group that spoke for shopkeepers and artisans in a period of rapid economic change. Poujade's party won fifty-two seats in the 1956 elections – a stunning flash-in-the-pan result. The French press christened him *Poujadolf* on account of his Hitler-esque direct-action tactics.

**EZRA POUND (1885–1972)** American poet who became one of the most famous 'celebrity fascists'. An Italian resident during the inter-war years, he was a passionate anti-Semite and contributed literary material to **Mosley**'s *European Journal*. Pound was a supporter of the 1943 **Salò Republic**.

**ENOCH POWELL (1912–98)** British Conservative MP and government minister

(1960–3). He caused outrage in 1968 with his 'Rivers of Blood' speech that warned against the perils of Commonwealth **immigration** for the UK. He left the Tory Party in 1974 and became an Ulster Unionist MP.

**VICTOR PRADERA** The chief ideologue of Spanish Carlism. He was also author of *El Estado Nuevo* (1934), a key corporatist tract.

**ROLÃO PRETO** Founder of the fascist *Nacional Sindicalismo* (NS) movement in Portugal in 1932. Preto's party – heavily influenced by Lusitanian **integralism, syndicalism** and Nazism – was constantly at loggerheads with **Salazar**'s para-fascist regime. In 1934 the dictator outlawed the NS and sent Preto into Spanish exile. Preto, lacking in genuine political charisma, attempted a coup in 1935 but Salazar was able to survive and consolidate his conservative dictatorship.

**GIUSEPPE PREZZOLINI** Italian nationalist and interventionist who, in the early years of the twentieth century, yearned for a 'new Italy'. He was scathing in his criticisms of the 'old' liberal establishment and believed that some kind of national revolution was the only option for his country. The editor of *La Voce*, Prezzolini also worked on *Il Leonardo* and helped **Papini** draft *The Nationalist Programme*. His political ideas bore the hallmark of Nietzschean influence.

**JOSÉ ANTONIO PRIMO DE RIVERA (1903– 36)** Son of Miguel – and known simply as José Antonio – he made his name as leader of the Spanish *Falange*. He began his political career in the authoritarian *Unión Monárquica Española* (1930–1) but became a leading light in the newly formed *Falange*. His political vision was infused with a range of values: Catholic, corpora-

tist and national syndicalist. He idolised the rural poor and resented big-business capitalism. Although José Antonio represented the *Falange* at the 1934 **Fascist International** in Montreux, and admired many aspects of **Mussolini**'s regime, it is debatable whether his radical 'neither right nor left' Hispanic ideology amounted to fascism. His *Falange* party merged with the **Juntas de Ofensiva Nacional-Sindicalista** (JONS) movement in 1934 to form the **FE de la JONS**. He was executed by left-wing militants in November 1936 but his memory lived on for those on the Spanish right.

**GENERAL MIGUEL PRIMO DE RIVERA (1870–1930)** Spanish dictator who seized power in 1923 after overthrowing King Alfonso XIII. As an authoritarian paternalist he had little time for **democracy** and political parties. Although he admired **Mussolini**, and aped some aspects of his Italian regime, he always shunned the fascist label. Indeed, Primo de Rivera was content simply to peddle a fairly traditional Catholic–corporatist doctrine. He created a single party – *Unión Patriótica* – in an effort to seduce the masses, but his regime never acquired a popular base. Losing popularity, he left power in 1930. Historians tend to view him as a transitional figure in Spain's slide towards Falangism, Francoism and dictatorship.

**PIERRE-JOSEPH PROUDHON (1809–65)** French thinker and a leading light in the history of anarchism who considered private property to be symptomatic of 'theft'. Subsequent anarcho-syndicalists brought the cult of direct action, as opposed to parliamentarianism, into the embryonic currents of fascism that developed in Europe before 1918. However, much of Proudhon's work was also libertarian and opposed to statism; these aspects were ignored by fascist movements, especially when they were in power. He was particularly admired by inter-war French fascist, **Déat**.

**V.M. PURISHKEVICH** Leading figure in the **Union of Russian People** (URP) at the beginning of the twentieth century.

Q

**COLONEL MU'AMMAR AL QADDAFI (GADDAFI) (b. 1942)** Military dictator and self-styled 'Leader of the Revolution' in Libya after 1969. He came to power in a military coup and his regime embraces elements of **totalitarianism**, **socialism**, **Islam** and Arab nationalism (the combination varies over time, as does the Colonel's focus on Africa or the Arab World). Though not explicitly fascist, the **Socialist People's Libyan Arab Jamahiriya** combines fanatical nationalism, extreme anti-Israeli positions, support for violent groups overseas and radical **populism**. Qaddafi spends much of Libya's oil wealth on health and welfare, and puts considerable effort into mass mobilisation, spectacular public rallies, grassroots agitation and **propaganda**.

**VIDKUN QUISLING (1887–1945)** Infamous Norwegian collaborator. A soldier by trade, he was appointed Minister of Defence in 1931 and in the same year established the regenerationist Nordic Folk Awakening movement. In 1933 he founded the anti-democratic and ultra-nationalist *Nasjonal Samling* (NS). At first it championed a very Nordic brand of fascism but gradually Quisling moved towards the German Nazis and Hitlerite ideology. In 1939 he considered a coup attempt; by 1942 he had been installed as Norway's puppet prime minister by **Hitler**. NS was the only political party not to be outlawed. He was executed on a charge of high treason in October 1945 and ever

since his surname has become a by-word for high-level deception and betrayal.

R

**ADMIRAL ERICH RAEDER (1876–1960)** Commander in Chief of the German Navy between 1928 and 1943. He was found guilty of **war crimes** at Nuremberg as a consequence of German naval attacks on civilian shipping. He favoured maritime strategy over land-based warfare, such as that required for **Hitler**'s 'Operation **Barbarossa**' against the Soviet Union.

**RAMIRO LEDESMA RAMOS (1905–36)** Fascist intellectual and co-founder of Spanish movement *Juntas de Ofensiva Nacional-Sindicalista* in 1931.

**WILLIAM MAULE RAMSAY** Anti-Semitic Conservative MP who founded the anti-Communist, pro-German **Right Club** in the inter-war period.

**E.D. RANDELL British Union of Fascists** member and poet who penned the movement's battle-cry anthem, 'A Marching Song'.

**WALTER RATHENAU (1867–1922)** Industrialist who became German Foreign Minister in 1922 and was assassinated soon after. His views on élitist rule had a significant impact on **Drexler** and the early Nazi Party.

**FRIEDRICH RATZEL (1844–1904)** German writer on geopolitics who emphasised the importance of territorial expansionism. A Leipzig professor, he emerged as a key pan-German theorist and a major influence on Karl von Haushoffer.

**GIUSEPPI (PINO) RAUTI (b. 1926)** A key figure in the history of Italian **neo-fascism**.

In his early years he joined the Spanish Foreign Legion and took up arms on behalf of the **Salò Republic**. He joined the *Movimento Sociale Italiano* (MSI) in 1948 but did not approve of its 'moderate' political stance, leaving to form the conspiratorial *Ordine Nuovo*. However, he made up with the MSI in 1969 and went on to become an important party figure and was elected to both the Italian and European parliaments. Rauti stayed loyal to **Evola**'s political teachings and was touted as a possible leader of the MSI.

**JOHN KINGSLEY READ (d. 1984)** Former Chairman of the British **National Front**.

**LUCIEN REBATET** Ex-*Action Française* member and fanatical French Germanophile. A senior journalist on the far-right newspaper, *Je Suis Partout*, he was a passionate anti-Semite and became one of the most notorious Paris-based Nazis during the Occupation.

**WALTER REDER** Convicted war criminal at the centre of political controversy in Austria in the mid-1980s. There was a public outcry when a *Freiheitliche Partei Österreichs* (FPÖ) government minister gave Reder an official welcome.

**ONÉSIMA REDONDO Y ORTEGA (1905–36)** Co-founder of the *Juntas de Ofensiva Nacional-Sindicalista* in inter-war Spain. An admirer of Nazism, Redondo emerged as one of the main leaders of the *Falange*.

**THAON DE REVEL** Italian Minister of Finance in the mid-1930s.

**JOACHIM VON RIBBENTROP (1893–1946)** Foreign policy adviser to **Hitler** and subsequently foreign minister. Despite his status, Ribbentrop had to compete for influence with Göbbels and others in the foreign-policy sphere. He was seen as responsible for Germany's miscalculation of British resolve and motives in the early phases of the war. He was an author of the Molotov–Ribbentrop/Nazi–Soviet Pacts, partitioning Poland and confirming the Soviet takeover of the Baltic states. He was executed for **war crimes** after the **Nuremberg Trials**.

**RENATO RICCI** Pro-Nazi Italian Fascist who was a key figure in the **Salò Republic**.

**DIOISIO RIDRUEJO** Head of **propaganda** under the **Franco** regime. He was known as the 'Spanish Göbbels' but moved over to the social-democratic left later in life.

**LENI RIEFENSTAHL** Notorious Nazi filmmaker. Her most famous work, *Triumph of the Will*, was an evocative profile of **Hitler** and the 1934 Nuremberg party rally.

**SUSANNE RIESS-PASSER** Leader of the *Freiheitliche Partei Österreichs* (FPÖ). Known as '**Haider**'s puppet', she joined the party in 1987 and caused embarrassment for the British Royal Family when she was photographed with the Earl and Countess of Wessex at a drinks reception in 2001. She has experience of government.

**PAUL RITTER** Nazi minister who was particularly enthusiastic about colonial expansion into Africa.

**ALAIN ROBERT** Leader of post-war French movement, *Ordre Nouveau* (ON). He is also associated with the far-right *Parti des Forces Nouvelles* (PFN).

**ALFREDO ROCCO (1875–1935)** Italian nationalist who became Minister of Justice under **Mussolini**. He drew up the regime's 1926 legislation on trade unions and strikes, which restricted union activity and outlawed industrial disputes. A strong believer in an organic, élitist state, he helped to devise the 1927 Charter of Labour. He held that a hierarchical economic structure was the necessary counterpart to the Fascist political hierarchy.

**GEORGE LINCOLN ROCKWELL (d. 1967)** Founding father of the American Nazi Party in 1958. A provocative and controversial politician, he was murdered by a disaffected former member of his organisation.

**COLONEL FRANÇOIS DE LA ROCQUE** President of inter-war French movement, *Croix de Feu* (CF). He saw it as his personal mission to 'save' France from disorder and left-wing anarchy, and turned the CF into one of the biggest and most intimidating political organisations in France. De la Rocque had an unremarkable military record during the Great War but his authoritarian style and zealous **patriotism** had an enormous appeal for France's community of disgruntled ex-servicemen. In 1936 he transformed the CF into a slightly more orthodox political party, the *Parti Social Français* (PSF). He is often pigeon-holed on the far right, but he never considered himself to be a fascist.

**ERNST RÖHM (1887–1934)** Leader of the *Sturm Abteilung* (SA) and a prominent figure on the left of the German Nazi Party. He lost power in 1934 when **Hitler** decided to silence his more militant supporters and the SA. He was detained and murdered by the Nazis following a personal confrontation with Hitler. Röhm was also a homosexual and this was a factor in his loss of influence. **Himmler**'s *Schutzstaffel* (SS) was the main beneficiary of Röhm's downfall.

**RICARDO ROJAS** Influential Argentine writer. His brand of **cultural nationalism** put significant emphasis on *Völkisch* themes and was both anti-immigrant and anti-cosmopolitan in tone. However, he remained a liberal in political terms.

**FIELD MARSHALL ERWIN ROMMEL (1891–1944)** German military leader famed for his obstinate struggle with the Allies in the North African Desert – hence his nickname, 'Desert Rat'. He reportedly supported a conspiracy to topple **Hitler** but did not take part in the **July Plot** of 1944. He committed suicide after being named as a conspirator by one of the participants in that incident and being detained by the Nazis.

**ALFRED ROSENBERG (1893–1946)** German race theorist who is generally viewed as the godfather of Nazi racial policy. He participated in the **Munich Putsch**, and, during the **Second World War**, he took an active part in the **Holocaust** and the repression of Slavic communities in Eastern Europe. Rosenberg was hanged after the **Nuremberg Trials**.

**EDMONDO ROSSONI** Aide to **Mussolini** and radical Corporate State theorist. He became President of the National Confederation of Fascist Unions but was sacked in 1928 after upsetting Italian employers. The organisation was eventually dissolved.

**LORD ROTHERMERE (HARMSWORTH, HAROLD (SYDNEY), 1ST VISCOUNT) (1868–1940)** Press baron whose newspapers, notably the *Daily Mail*, backed the **British Union of Fascists** in 1933. By the late 1930s, however, support for the fascists was less popular and Lord Rothermere distanced himself from them.

**HANS-ULRICH RUDEL** Maverick figure on the German far right. He made his name as the 'Eagle of the Eastern Front' during the **Second World War**, was imprisoned by US forces and also lost a leg. He became a significant figure in the post-war *Deutsche Reichspartei* (DRP).

**JOSÉ MARÍA RUIZ-MATEOS** Unorthodox 'anti-system' campaigner who scored an electoral success for the Spanish far right in the 1989 European elections. Fiercely anti-leftist, he had a powerful appeal for ex-Francoists and other far-right voters. He announced that he was not interested in electoral pacts with other extremist movements on the right.

**ALEXANDER RUTSKOI** Former Vice-President of Russia; ultra-nationalist who has also aligned himself with the Communists. Noted for involvement in the hard-line Russian parliament that sparked a violent confrontation with President Yeltsin in 1993 by rejecting Yeltsin's efforts to have it dissolved. However, in 1991 Rutskoi, a former soldier, was on the side of the liberals during the failed Communist coup. He was associated with **Derzhava**, a loose alliance of neo-Communist and far-right parties in the Russian parliament. His own platform emphasised the unification of the eastern Slavs and the restoration of Russia as a great power. From the mid-1990s, Rutskoi focused his energies on the governorship of Kursk and threw his weight behind the Communists.

**S**

**GENERAL RAOUL ALBIN LOUIS SALAN (1899–1984)** Senior French military figure who became one of the leading figures in the *Algérie Française* movement. He served in the **Second World War** and the Indo-China conflict, and in 1958 was appointed Commander in Chief of the French army in Algeria. At this point he was pro-de Gaulle but when, as President, de Gaulle announced his intention to grant Algeria its independence, Salan took up arms against the Republic. He was branded a fascist on account of his anti-democratic, imperialist and ultra-nationalistic ideology. As a leading player in the terrorist *Organisation de l'Armée Secrète* (OAS), he was involved in various anti-Paris rebellions between 1960 and 1962. He was arrested, sentenced to life for treason, but only served six years. He was pardoned by de Gaulle in 1968.

**DR ANTÓNIO DE OLIVEIRA SALAZAR (1889–1970)** Portuguese dictator between 1932 and 1968. After a spell as Professor of Economics at the University of Coimbra, he was appointed Minister of Finance in 1928, and then Prime Minister in 1932. He was austere and lacking in charisma, but swiftly established a personal dictatorship. Salazar's Portugal revolved around the corporate *Estado Novo* (New State) and *União Nacional* (the 'artificial' movement set up to give the new regime an aura of legitimacy). In power, he put heavy emphasis on **hierarchy**, economic stability and social harmony, and used the slogan 'God, Country and Family' to sum up his guiding philosophy. He also took on extra roles: Foreign Minister between 1936 and 1947 and War Minister during the period 1936–44. He supported the Nationalists in the **Spanish Civil War** but purposefully did not get close to **Hitler** or **Mussolini**. He left power as a result of a medical condition in 1968. Historians tend to view Salazar's regime as para-fascist in nature.

**PLÍNIO SALGADO (b. 1901)** Founder and leader of the Brazilian *Ação Integralista Brasileira* (AIB). He was 'converted' to fascism after a 1930 visit to Italy and formed his party two years later. He was inspired by **Mussolini**'s example and integralist Catholic ideas, but was unable to topple **Vargas**, Brazil's para-fascist leader. Salgado eventually went into exile.

**ERNST VON SALOMON** Early Nazi terrorist who published a book, *The Questionnaire* (1950), about his political exploits.

He also became a noted exponent of '**soldierly nationalism**'.

**FRANZ PFEFFER VON SALOMON** Aristocratic figure who made his name as leader of the Westphalian *Freikorps* and went on to become Supreme Commander of the *Sturm Abteilung* (SA) between 1926 and 1930. His background was thoroughly right wing: he took part in the 1920 **Kapp Putsch**, was powerfully anti-leftist and during the Nazi years became intrigued by issues of biology and **eugenics**. He was very aware of the race issue and preferred being called 'Pfeffer' rather than 'Salomon' because he thought the latter sounded too Jewish. He eventually fell out with **Hitler**.

**FRITZ SAUCKEL** Appointed Minister for Labour under the Nazis in 1942. At the end of the war he went on trial at Nuremberg and was found guilty of crimes against humanity.

**JONAS SAVIMBI (1934–2002)** Anti-Communist guerrilla and leader of the Union for the Total Independence of Angola. He fought Portuguese colonial rulers until independence in 1975, and then the Marxist Popular Movement for the Liberation of Angola and its Cuban backers. His anti-Communism and pro-democracy rhetoric, as well as Cuban involvement on the opposite side, won US support in the 1980s and 1990s. However, his failure to take advantage of a democratic opening, despite a creditable showing by his own party in internationally monitored elections, coupled with his violation of ceasefires negotiated under US, Russian and **United Nations** auspices, later alienated Washington. Savimbi's forces have been accused of human rights violations and of plundering mineral wealth to fund their campaign. Though his tactics in the bush and his rejection of MPLA reforms and peace overtures justify his categorisation on the far right, Savimbi was not a fascist and it is difficult to say if he would have operated a pluralist democracy if he had won power at an earlier stage. He was killed by MPLA forces in 2002, after which UNITA abandoned its violent campaign.

**HJALMAR SCHACHT (1877–1970)** President of the *Reichsbank* (1933), Minister of Economics under **Hitler** (1934–7) and general adviser to the Nazis on economic policy. A banker by trade and a close ally of industrialist **Thyssen**, he was a confident and pragmatic operator who in government argued against non-stop expansion of Germany's arms programme. He escaped punishment at the **Nuremberg Trials**.

**FRANZ SCHAUWECKER** Influential theorist of '**soldierly nationalism**'.

**RONALD SCHILL** Won 19.4 per cent of the vote for the Law and Order Party in Hamburg in 2001. He believes in the death penalty and castration for perpetrators of sexual crime.

**GENERAL KURT VON SCHLEICHER (1882–1934)** Authoritarian conservative politician known as the 'grave-digger of the **Weimar Republic**'. He was an intriguer and behind-the-scenes plotter, with his own political ambitions, who eventually paved the way for **Hitler**'s emergence. He served as Defence Minister and also as the last Chancellor of the Republic. Bonapartist by political temperament, he had sympathies for the Nazis and argued against a legal ban on the *Sturm Abteilung* (SA) in the years before Hitler gained power. However, the Nazi regime deemed him a conservative 'enemy' and he was shot in 1934.

**RUDOLF SCHLIERER** 'Moderate' intellectual who succeeded **Schönhuber** as *Republikaner* leader in December 1994. Schlierer is opposed to any electoral pact with the **Deutsche Volks Union** (DVU).

**CARL SCHMITT (1888–1985)** Known as the 'Crown Jurist of the **Third Reich**' – the man who attempted to justify and vindicate the Nazi regime in legal terms. A professor in Law, Schmitt converted to **National-Socialism** in 1933 and became closely associated with the notion of 'Conservative Revolution'. In the end he was outmanœuvred by the movement's racist wing, but his ideas have served as an inspiration to many on the post-war right. He is regarded as one of the greatest thinkers in modern German history.

**GEORG RITTER VON SCHÖNERER** Leader of the *Völkisch* and anti-Semitic Austrian pan-German movement in the early twentieth century.

**FRANZ SCHÖNHUBER** Ex-member of the *Schutzstaffel* (SS) who became leader of the far-right German Republican Party in the 1980s. He was originally associated with the left and then the CSU cause. Though he subsequently denounced the Nazis, he advocated a nuclear-armed Germany. His movement's 7 per cent score in the June 1989 European elections surpassed that of the liberal FDP.

**ARTHUR SCHOPENHAUER** Racial theorist whose ideas influenced **Hitler**'s early political doctrine, as expounded in *Mein Kampf*.

**KURT VON SCHUSCHNIGG** Authoritarian Austrian leader who ruled in tandem with **Dollfuss** and then succeeded him. He put forward a corporatist ideology but was more para-fascist than fascist. The 1938 *Anschluss* put an end to his rule.

**NAKANO SEIGŌ (1886–1943)** Japanese politician and overt advocate of European-style fascism in inter-war and wartime Japan. He headed a movement called *Tōhōkai*, which held fascist-style rallies. However, the **Tōjō** regime was too conservative for full-blown fascism. After several clashes with the authorities, Seigō died by ritual disembowelment.

**ARRIGO SERPIERI** Italian agronomist who became Under-Secretary of State for National Economy. He began the 'battle for land reclamation' in 1924.

**SERBAN SURU** Romanian teacher who founded a series of far-right political organisations in the early 1990s in honour of the 1930s Iron Guard. This initiative was deemed to be extremely provocative and he was forced to back down.

**VOJISLAV ŠEŠELJ** Charismatic leader of the ultra-nationalist Serbian Radical Party. Throughout the 1990s he articulated his belief in the notion of a **Greater Serbia**, the defence of the state and the undesirability of inter-ethnic mixing. An ex-Communist, he talks about the Serbs as a 'warrior people', even though he has sworn himself to non-violent political action. Šešelj's relationship with Milošević has had its ups and downs, but it is significant that the ex-Yugoslav President once called him his 'favourite opposition leader'.

**JORIS VAN SEVEREN (1894–1940)** Leader of the Nazi-style Verdinaso – founded in Belgium in 1931.

**OKAWA SHUMEI** Ultra-nationalist Japanese plotter with militarist instincts. In 1921 he co-founded the Society for the Preservation of the National Essence with Kita **Ikki**.

**PIERRE SIDOS** Post-war French far-right activist who founded *Jeune Nation*. His father was murdered by the *Milice* during the wartime Nazi Occupation.

**HORIA SIMA** Post-**Codreanu** leader of the Romanian Iron Guard. He became Deputy Prime Minister under **Antonescu**'s **National Legionary State** during the **Second World War**.

**REV. ELIAS SIMOJOKI** One of the co-founders of the Finnish **Academic Karelia Society** (AKS). Later he was also involved in the *Isänmaallinen Kansanliike* (IKL) and the **Blue Blacks**.

**JOHN K. SINGLAUB** Ex-CIA official who became head of the **World Anti-Communist League** (WACL) in 1985.

**OTTO SKORZENY (1908–75)** Co-founder of the Austrian Nazi Party in 1935 who went on to join the *Schutzstaffel* (SS). After 1945 he co-ordinated a worldwide organisation for ex-Nazis and became involved in the international arms trade.

**IAN SMITH (b. 1919)** Leader of the white minority government of Rhodesia (now Zimbabwe). He declared unilateral independence from Britain in 1965 in order to resist demands for black majority rule and an end to the government policy of systematic racial discrimination. His government and its guerrilla opponents were guilty of serious human rights violations in the 1970s. He eventually surrendered power in 1979 after years of sanctions and civil war. In the 1990s, Smith was a sharp critic of Zimbabwean President, Robert Mugabe, and a vocal defender of white landowners.

**ARDEGNO SOFFICI** Florence-based poet and intellectual who emerged as a key player in pre-Fascist Italy. Influenced heavily by Nietzschean ideas, he became a close associate of **Papini** and argued for an end to **liberalism** and the emergence of a strong new élite. When that arrived in the shape of **Mussolini** and the Fascists, Soffici became a prominent figure. He was at the heart of the pro-**ruralism** *Strapaese* movement – even though he had a Futurist background – and worked on both *Lacerba* and *Il Selvaggio*.

**GEORGES SOREL (1847–1922)** French Marxist who glorified violence and the power of the proletariat. His notion of 'the myth' in history came to inspire many twentieth-century fascists and he had a significant influence on **Mussolini** and his Corporate State philosophy.

**RADU SORESCU** Leader of the Romanian Party of the National Right and editor of the movement's journal, *Noua Dreaptá*.

**JOSÉ CALVO SOTELO (1893–1936)** Radical and ruthless Spanish counter-revolutionary who was a government minister under the **Primo de Rivera** dictatorship. He founded the anti-parliamentary *Bloque Nacional* in 1934 and pushed for a military rising. One historian has described his right-wing **ideology** as 'monarcho-fascist'. He was assassinated by state police.

**JULES SOURY** 'Pre-fascist' theorist of psychological determinism.

**OTHMAR SPANN (1878–1950)** Austrian academic responsible for a range of semi-fascist writings during the inter-war years. He went on to become a *Heimwehr* leader.

**ALBERT SPEER (1905–81)** Nazi official and author of a best-selling account of the regime, *Inside the Third Reich* (1970). Speer constructed grandiose and classical looking buildings in Berlin – which the Nazis thought would befit the 'Thousand Year Reich' – and was imprisoned for his role as Armaments Minister and in managing the war economy.

**OSWALD SPENGLER (1880–1938)** Influential German theorist of conservative revolution whose keynote work, *The Decline of the West* (1918–22), depicted a **civilisation** in terminal decay and in need of cultural and nationalist regeneration. Although commentators portray him as a prophet of pessimism and gloom, Spengler claimed to have a more optimistic vision of a heroic race, a powerful élite and a new sense of 'Prussiandom' (to include an explicit socialist element). Although he saw himself as 'outside' **Hitler**'s system, he had a significant impact on Nazi thinking. He was also read by **Mussolini** and many neo-fascists.

**GASTONE SPINETTI** Italian theorist of **Universal Fascism**. He was associated with CINEF and *La Sapienza*, and believed that Italy would be at the vanguard of a new fascist **civilisation**. He wrote *Fascismo Universale* in 1934.

**GENERAL ANTÓNIO DE SPÍNOLA** Portuguese military leader who served in the transitionary military regimes in the early 1970s following **Salazar**'s departure from politics. He purged the military and state apparatus of Salazar followers and neo-fascists but was cautious about surrendering power himself. After being toppled in a coup, he led various right-wing groups from abroad and played an important role in opposing the left-wing politicians and military officers who almost succeeded in achieving a Communist military coup during the crisis of 1974–5. Following the emergence of centrist parties, supported by the US, both Communists and far-right military leaders were marginalised. He fled the country in 1975.

**UGO SPIRITO** Radical Corporate State theorist whose belief in **integral corporatism** was equated by some to a belief in common ownership. Branded a 'leftist' by some, and

'anti-property' by others, he was eventually sacked as a minister by **Mussolini**.

**ACHILLE STARACE (1889–1945)** Veteran of the First World War and national secretary of **Mussolini**'s Fascist Party between 1931 and 1939. He was appointed head of the *Opera Nazionale Dopolavoro* (OND) leisure organisation in 1925 and went on to become a leading propagandist. As a populist and someone who valued style over substance, he was fascinated by the symbolism of uniform and ritual, and in the notion of Fascism as a 'civic religion'. An accountant by trade, Starace ended up at Salò.

**PRINCE ERNST VON STARHEMBERG** Austrian anti-Nazi who was dismissed from government in May 1936. He was a key figure in the *Heimwehr* movement and co-operated with the **Dollfuss–Schuschnigg** regime. He was a key exponent of '**soldierly nationalism**'.

**KLAUS VON STAUFFENBERG** Ring-leader of the anti-**Hitler** '**July Plot**' of 1944.

**CHRISTOPH STEDING** Inter-war German theorist whose analysis of European society, and conception of a Greater Germanic Empire, impressed both **Heydrich** and **Himmler**.

**ALBERTO DE STEFANI** Italian Finance Minister up to 1925, when he was dismissed after the currency crisis. In office he co-ordinated a liberal economic policy, championing free trade and pushing up taxes.

**NORBERT STEGER** Jörg **Haider**'s predecessor as leader of the Austrian *Freiheitliche Partei Österreichs* (FPÖ). Steger comes from the liberal wing of the party and consequently the two men are political rivals.

**RICHARD STEIDLE (1881–1938)** Austrian lawyer who became part of the *Heimwehr* leadership and a consistent opponent of **Dollfuss**, the country's para-fascist leader in the 1930s.

**STEPHANOS STEPHANOPOULOS** Veteran Greek politician and leader of the ultra-nationalist *Ethniki Parataxis* (EP) movement in the 1970s.

**JEAN-PIERRE STIRBOIS** Influential figure in the early history of the French *Front National* (FN). He was secretary of the movement in the early 1980s and the party's election candidate in **Dreux** (1983) when it made its national political breakthrough. He died in a car crash soon after, but left his wife, Marie-France, to carry his political torch.

**MARIE-FRANCE STIRBOIS** Leading personality in **Le Pen**'s *Front National* (FN) and the party's sole parliamentary *député* for a period after her **Dreux** by-election victory in 1989. She is the widow of Jean-Pierre.

**GREGOR STRASSER (1892–1934)** Left-wing Nazi extremist. A powerful critic of **capitalism**, he was murdered in the 1934 **Night of Long Knives** when **Hitler** ordered the killing of some of his most radical rivals. He was the brother of Otto.

**OTTO STRASSER (1897–1974)** Radical Nazi whose influence helped shift the Nazis' manifesto further to the left. He was the brother of Gregor.

**JOSÉ STREEL** Key ideologue in the Belgian fascist movement, *Rex*. He wrote *The Revolution of the Twentieth Century* (1942).

**JULIUS STREICHER** Tub-thumping Nazi propagandist associated with *Der Stürmer*.

**ALFREDO STROESSNER (b. 1912)** Paraguayan military dictator between 1954 and 1989. His regime was not specifically fascist but Stroessner (from a German background himself) cultivated the German community in South America and was noted for giving refuge to Nazi fugitives in the post-war years. He was exiled to Brazil when Paraguay was democratised in the 1990s.

**RADEN SUHARTO (b. 1921)** Right-wing Indonesian dictator from 1967 until 1998. He came to prominence in a military crackdown on Communists in 1966. He toppled the left-wing regime of Sukarno in 1967. Suharto tried to balance a pro-American foreign policy with Indonesia's Non-Aligned credentials. Domestically, he gave prominence to the Army, to a nominal ruling party (*Golcar*) and the state bureaucracy. He occupied East Timor after the Portuguese withdrawal in the mid-1970s. Suharto's **authoritarianism** and his tendency to centralise power brought conflict with peripheral regions such as Aceh, Irian Jaya and East Timor in the 1990s. This, coupled with economic crises, brought pressure for democratisation and he was forced from power in 1998.

**FERENC SZÁLASI (d. 1946)** Hungarian fascist who founded the **Party of National Will** in 1935. His movement, renamed Arrow Cross in 1937, gained **Hitler**'s backing and won more than 30 per cent of votes in pre-war elections. He was feared by **Horthy**'s authoritarian regime – hence his arrest in 1938. In 1944 he was helped into power by the Nazis as Horthy's successor. As puppet leader Szálasi was a willing accomplice in the Final Solution and dreamt of creating a **Greater Hungary**.

T

**PIERRE TAITTINGER** Former conservative *député* who made his name as leader of French fascist group, the *Jeunesses Patri-*

*otes* (JP), in the 1920s. A fervent admirer of **Mussolini**'s regime, Taittinger's doctrine was a fairly unradical blend of Bonapartist **nationalism** and anti-socialism.

**MARCO TARCHI** Influential representative of the Italian New Right.

**EUGENE TERRE'BLANCHE/TERBLANCHE** Founded the *Afrikaner Weerstandsbeweging* (AWB) in South Africa in 1973. He is white supremacist in political orientation and incorporates elements of Nazi Christian Socialist doctrine into his outlook. He opposed any form of compromise with the ANC. After the collapse of **Apartheid**, Terre'Blanche and his armed supporters took up a militant position in favour of white secessionism or autonomy. He was imprisoned for assault in 1997.

**ADOLF VON THADDEN (b. 1921)** Former *Deutsche Reichspartei* (DRP) parliamentary deputy who helped to found the neo-Nazi National Democratic Party (NPD) in the early 1960s and became its leader in 1967. He fought in the **Second World War** and was an admirer of **Hitler**, even though his stepsister had been executed for treason by the Nazi regime. A charismatic speaker, his spell as NPD supremo ended in 1972 amid internal divisions.

**SPYROS THEOTAKIS** Veteran Greek right-winger who emerged as an important figure in the royalist *Ethniki Parataxis* (EP) movement of the 1970s.

**A. RAVEN THOMSON** Author of *The Coming Corporate State* (1935) – a key element of the **British Union of Fascists**' political programme.

**FRITZ THYSSEN (1873–1951)** German steel manufacturer who gained the reputation of 'Hitler's favourite industrialist'. A committed supporter of the Nazi Party long before it gained power, he helped finance the movement's 1929 election campaign. He shared Hitler's dislike of the **Young Plan**, but eventually broke with him over the conduct of German economic policy.

**ALFRED VON TIRPITZ (1849–1930)** German admiral who was responsible for the 1898 and 1900 Naval Laws and who, in the inter-war years, emerged as leader of the nationalist and anti-Semitic Fatherland Party.

**MSGR JÓSEF TISO (1887–1947)** Co-founder of the separatist Slovak People's Party in the inter-war period. In October 1938 he became head of the newly independent Slovak state and was named President in March 1939. During the war he collaborated with **Hitler** and advanced a Slovakian brand of **national-socialism**. Communist pressure led to his execution in April 1947.

**JEAN-LOUIS TIXIER-VIGNANCOUR** Minister in the **Vichy** government. He was also a fervent supporter of *Algérie Française* – he acted as lawyer to **Salan** – and stood as the extreme right's presidential candidate in 1965.

**DR ROBERT TOBLER** Leader of the Swiss National Front from the late 1930s onwards.

**GENERAL HIDEKI TŌJŌ (1884–1948)** Military strongman in wartime Japan, especially from 1941 to 1944. Though he copied some elements of fascism, his regime was more of a coalition of generals and authoritarian politicians. He was tried for **war crimes** and executed after the defeat of Japan and was largely responsible for Japanese aggression in China and South-East Asia. He headed the **Kwantung** Army in **Manchuria** in 1937.

**MEINOUD MARINUS VAN TONNINGEN** Key figure in the inter-war Dutch *Nationaal Socialistische Beweging* (NSB). He collaborated with the Nazis during the war and committed suicide (allegedly) soon after it.

**GERHARD TOPFER** Post-war German political activist who championed **Third Positionism**.

**RAFAEL TRUJILLO (1891–1961)** Traditional Latin-style authoritarian dictator in the Dominican Republic (1930–38 and 1942–52). He came to power claiming a desire to modernise the country. His regime was marked by corruption, repression and violent conflict with neighbouring states, notably Haiti. Trujillo was assassinated in 1961.

**ALEKSANDÛR TSANKOV** Professor who became leader of the Bulgarian National Socialist Movement in the 1930s.

**FRANJO TUDJMAN (d. 1999)** Modern Croatian leader whose political strategy was to both crush and befriend extreme-right forces. He demonstrated some nostalgia for the wartime *Ustasha* regime.

**CORNELIU VADIM TUDOR** Ultra-nationalist writer in modern-day Romania. A member of the Greater Romania Party, he has identified both Jews and gypsies as 'anti-national' threats. He was also connected to the Ceauşescu regime. He has argued that 'Romania can only be ruled through the barrel of a machine gun.'

**AUGUSTO TURATI (1888–1955)** Brescia-based Fascist activist who was appointed secretary of the Fascist Party in 1926. Six years later he was expelled from the organisation.

**ALPARSLAN TURKES** Leader of Turkish neo-fascist movement, **Nationalist Action Party** (MHP). During the war he took a pro-**Hitler** position and was imprisoned after a 1960 coup attempt against his country's rulers. He stood on the margins of Turkish politics during the 1980s.

**JOHN TYNDALL** Veteran activist on the modern British far right. He was a key player in the **National Front** (NF), but left to resurrect the **British National Party** (BNP) in 1982. He was also involved in the **Greater Britain Movement** (GBM) and several other political organisations. He has links with the far-right journal, *Spearhead*.

**KARLIS ULMANIS** Leader of the Latvian **Peasant Union** that staged a successful coup in 1934. He was heavily influenced by **Mussolini** and some commentators have described his regime as 'para-fascist'. The main opposition to his government came from the fascist Thunder Cross movement.

**XAVIER VALLAT** Commissioner of Jewish Affairs under the **Vichy** regime. He went on to edit the *Action Française* journal, *Aspects de France*, after the war.

**GEORGES VALOIS (d. 1945)** French fascist who left the *Action Française* (AF) to form his own more radical movement, the *Faisceau*. Strongly attached to syndicalist ideas, Valois held that fascism was a compound of **nationalism** and **socialism**.

**GETÚILIO VARGAS (1882–1954)** Gifted politician who ruled Brazil as President during the periods 1930–45 and 1950–4. In power his political agenda revolved around **nationalism**, **corporatism** and welfarism. He was elected democratically but established an authoritarian state structure. Onlookers have described him variously as populist, Perónist and para-fascist. If anything, Vargas was anti-fascist – outwitting and then in 1938 destroying the overtly fascist *Ação Integralista Brasileira* (AIB). He committed suicide in August 1954.

**CAPTAIN FERRUCCIO VECCHI** Member of the Italian Fascist *Arditi* force. Vecchi helped to burn down the headquarters of the left-wing *Avanti* newspaper – a publication edited previously by **Mussolini**.

**IVAN VEKIĆ** Leader of far-right Croatian *Nacionalna Demokratska Liga* (NDL) in the 1990s.

**MAÎTRE JACQUES VERGES** Lawyer who defended Nazi war criminal Klaus **Barbie** in his controversial 1987 trial.

**GUY VERHOFSTADT** Chairman of the post-war Belgian *Vlaams Bloc* (VB).

**RICHARD VERRALL** Influential **National Front** member in the 1970s and editor of far-right journal, *Spearhead*.

**GENERAL JÖRGE RAFAËL VIDELA (b. 1925)** Argentine military dictator between 1978 and 1981. His regime was associated with the worst excesses of the 'dirty war' against left-wing opponents, many of whom died at the hands of army death squads. He was opposed to Perónist influence in the military and sought to restructure it along traditional Latin American lines. In the late 1990s, Argentine legislators moved to rescind pardons for military leaders issued in the 1980s, raising the possibility of legal action against Videla. He also had links with the **World Anti-Communist League** (WACL).

**EMANUELE VITTORIO/VICTOR EMMANUEL III** Monarch who invited **Mussolini** to become Italian prime minister in October 1922.

**ALBERT VÖGLER** German steel tycoon who very publicly supported the **Hitler** regime.

**AUGUSTINAS VOLDEMARAS** Far-right Lithuanian intellectual and poet.

**COUNT GIUSEPPE VOLPI** Important Venitian industrialist and financier who became President of the *Confindustria*. Appointed Minister of Finance in 1925, he quickly gained the trust of the Italian business community. He pursued a tax-cutting policy in office, indicated his dislike of **Mussolini**'s autarchic policy and its consequences, and launched the **'Battle for Grain'**. He was succeeded as Minister of Finance by Mosconi.

**HANS VONWY** Founding father of the Swiss National Front in 1930.

**IAN WACHMEISTER** Co-founder of the Swedish Progress Party in 1990.

**RICHARD WAGNER (1813–83)** German composer with chauvinist, anti-Semitic and nationalist views whose music was greatly admired by **Hitler**. As a result, Wagner's work has long suffered from its association with the Nazis and was banned for a time in Israel.

**KURT WALDHEIM (b. 1918) United Nations** Secretary General between 1972 and 1982, and President of Austria, 1986–92. During the **Second World War** he was a member of the German Army and won the War Merit Cross. Waldheim's 1986 presidential campaign was dogged by allegations that he had a Nazi past and had helped to deport Jews during the war. The case against him was never proved but Austria was ostracised during his period as president.

**MICHAEL WALKER** Former **National Front** organiser and **New Right** ideologue who in 1981 founded the journal, *Scorpion.*

**GEORGE WALLACE** US presidential candidate in 1968. A 'populist conservative', he polled 10 million votes and played significantly on the race issue.

**MARTIN WEBSTER** Leading member of the British **National Front**. He has also been associated with the **Greater Britain Movement** (GBM), the **British Movement** (BM) and far-right journal, *Spearhead*. He set up the **Our Nation** (ON) grouping.

**ROBERT H.W. WELCH** Founding father of the **John Birch Society** in post-war America. The conspiratorial Welch became noted for his radical anti-Communism. ——

**WILLIAM II (1859–1941)** Last Kaiser in the old German Empire from 1888, and the man who led his country into the First World War and defeat (1914–18). He represented the old authoritarian right in German politics, and was motivated by a globalist foreign policy (*Weltpolitik*) that Germany was unable to match with adequate power or resources. Though the Nazis paid tribute to his Second Reich, they promised that theirs would regenerate the German nation in a more radical and revolutionary form. Monarchist supporters of the Kaiser gave tentative support to

**Hitler** in the false belief that he might restore the old regime.

**HENRY WILLIAMSON** Author of *Tarka the Otter* who joined the **British Union of Fascists** in 1937. He took a pro-German/anti-war position and emerged as a high-profile enthusiast for **Mosley**'s party.

**GENERAL KARL WOLFF** German military leader who formally surrendered in April 1945.

---

# Z

**VLADIMIR ZHIRINOVSKY** Kazakh-born leader of the far-right *Liberalno-Demokraticheskaya Partiya Rossii* (LDPR) in post-Communist Russia. He ran for the Presidency in 1992 but only won 8 per cent of the vote. However, for a brief period, polls showed him to be the second most popular figure in Russia. His party's fortunes have declined since the emergence of Vladimir Putin and his more assertive nationalist agenda in 2000. Zhirinovsky has called for the restoration of Russia's borders as they were under the Soviet Union or the Tsarist Empire and has questioned the existing frontiers of former Soviet republics and newly independent East European states. He openly advocates dictatorship but also frequently strikes a popular chord by campaigning for cheaper vodka.

**MOHAMMED ZIA UL-HAQ (1924–88)** Authoritarian military leader of Pakistan, 1978–88. He combined an Islamic agenda with military autocracy, and his regime was noted for human rights violations, including the execution of former President, Zulfikar Ali Bhutto, after a controversial trial. Zia's foreign policy was broadly pro-American. Under his rule, Pakistan was a front-line state in the Afghan war against the Soviet Union, a conduit for Western arms to the Mujahadeen and a haven for refugees.

**ERNEST ZÜNDEL** Canadian-based far-right broadcaster and publicist who emigrated from Germany in 1958. Jewish groups in Canada have sought legal action against him for website material that questioned accepted facts about the **Holocaust**. He has produced material for conservative short-wave radio evangelical stations in the US. In 1993, the Canadian Government denied his citizenship requests, calling him a threat to national security.

**GENNADY ZYUGANOV** Leader of the Communist Party of the Russian Federation whose anti-Yeltsin discourse took on an extremist bent in the mid-1990s when he embraced right-wing ultra-nationalist ideas. Given his shifting ideological stances, Zyuganov's switch to 'motherland in danger' rhetoric may merely be a tactical manoeuvre.

# GLOSSARY

**NOTES**

- This section lists and defines a broad range of terms relating to fascism and the far right.
- With organisations, we have tried to include their 'native' title, the English translation and initials (where appropriate). We have listed them according to 'original' or 'native' title, but where only the English title or initials are known we have listed them according to these.
- The net has been spread far and wide, dictionary-like, rather than just concentrating on the most obvious terms.
- Where a term has more than one application (e.g. 'Blueshirts') we have listed all cases in one entry.
- Inclusion of a term in this section does not necessarily imply that it is, or was, associated with fascism and the far right. For the most part this is the case, but where appropriate we have also included terms that shed light on the phenomenon of fascism and the far right in a more general sense.

**ABORTIVE FASCISM** Label used by Griffin to denote inter-war fascist movements that were either marginalised or crushed by regimes in power.

**ABYSSINIAN INVASION** Major overseas military venture by **Mussolini** in 1936 that challenged the authority of the **League of Nations** and the principles of **collective security**. It was designed to consolidate Italy's position in East Africa and pressurise British outposts in the region. The failure of other states to act against the Italians seemed to embolden Axis leaders. Abyssinia (Ethiopia) had been the object of Italian expansionist aims since the 1890s but Mussolini's action, and the weak response to it, were portrayed in

Fascist **propaganda** as confirmation of the success of *Il Duce*'s foreign policy.

**ACADEMIC KARELIA SOCIETY (AKS)** Finnish proto-fascist movement founded by military personnel in 1922. Anti-Russian and anti-Swedish, it built upon traditional Finnish mythology and dreamed of creating a Finnish 'super race'. It drew much support from students.

**AÇÃO INTEGRALISTA BRASILEIRA (BRAZILIAN INTEGRALIST ACTION) (AIB)** Formed in 1932, the AIB is generally regarded as the nearest Latin America ever came to a genuine fascist movement. Its leader, Plínio **Salgado**, was converted to fascism by a trip to **Mussolini**'s Italy in 1930; he took on board Maurrasian-style **Catholicism** and also aped Nazism in the way he created a 'shadow' state structure. The AIB was a genuine mass movement, holding huge rallies, boasting a membership of almost

200,000 in 1934, and utilising an array of ritual (salutes, armbands, anthems). It deemed 1934 to be Year One of the 'Fourth Humanity'. In 1937 Brazil's para-fascist leader **Vargas** put down the movement.

**AÇÃO ESCOLAR VANGUARDA** Voluntary youth movement created by **Salazar** to rival **Preto**'s *Nacional Sindicalismo* (NS) **Blueshirts** in inter-war Portugal.

**ACCIÓN ESPAÑOLA (SPANISH ACTION)** Faction of the Alfonsine neo-monarchist movement in inter-war Spain. It acted as a kind of royalist think-tank, heavily influenced by the reactionary, counter-revolutionary ideas of **Maurras** and the *Action Française* (AF) in France. It had some influence on **Franco**.

**ACCIÓN POPULAR (POPULAR ACTION)** Peruvian coalition born in 1956 that stood on a militarist and populist agenda. Its discourse was dominated by **cultural nationalism**.

**ACCIÓN REVOLUCIONARIA MEXICANA (MEXICAN REVOLUTIONARY ACTION) (ARM)** Small opposition movement founded in 1933 and known as the *Dorados* on account of the gold-shirted uniform worn by members. Led by General Nicolás Rodríguez, ARM displayed counter-revolutionary and anti-Semitic tendencies, and employed violent terror tactics. It was devoid of real fascist characteristics but was strongly authoritarian and anti-Communist.

**ACERBO ELECTORAL LAW** Passed by **Mussolini**'s Fascist regime in 1923. It stated that any party gaining 25 per cent of votes would automatically acquire two-thirds of seats, and thus be able to form a government. This decree was obviously intended to benefit the Fascists and consolidate their grip on power.

**ACHAIOI (ACHAEANS)** Greek far-right movement of the mid-1970s. Led by Brigadier Dimitri Ioannides, it had strong connections with the military regime that lost power in 1974. The *Achaioi* evolved into the *Pneumatiki Ananeotiki Ormi* (PAO).

**ACTION FRANÇAISE (FRENCH ACTION) (AF)** Influential movement founded by Charles **Maurras** in 1899 to maintain the offensive against Dreyfus and the Third Republic. In 1908 the AF launched a newspaper, *L'Action Française*, which acquired huge notoriety; by the 1920s and 1930s it was the most important far-right organisation in France. Its main slogan was **'Conservative Revolution'** and it sought to create a climate favourable to a royalist restoration. Although its doctrine was highly xenophobic and Maurras displayed great admiration for **Mussolini**'s Italy, most historians are sceptical about its fascist credentials. Maurras showed little interest in seizing power and his movement was content to exist as an upmarket talking shop (hence its nickname among satirists – 'French Inaction'). The AF has had a profound influence on the twentieth-century French right; it still exists today and still dreams of a monarchical renaissance.

**ADWA/ADOWA** Site of the defeat of the Italian army by Ethiopian forces in 1896. For **Mussolini** Adwa symbolised the incompetence of liberal and nationalist Italian governments even when they were pursuing an imperialist foreign policy. Defeat of a European power by Africans was also portrayed as a blow to Italian pride.

**AESTHETICS** The philosophy of beauty, especially in art. It is concerned with the criteria by which people attach value to artistic products. For fascists, aesthetics could not be divorced from politics and ideology. On the other hand, Fascist Italy and Francoist Spain relied so heavily on past cultural successes that the aesthetic values of the regimes were not peculiar to fascism *per se*.

**AFIRMACIÓN DE UNA NUEVA ARGENTINA (ADUNA)** Ultra-rightist coalition led by Lugones during the years 1933–8. It is regarded by some as an example of **proto-fascism**.

**AFIRMACIÓN ESPAÑOLA (SPANISH STATEMENT) (AE)** Modern ultra-right group led by Alberto Vasallo de Number and home to many ex-military figures.

**AFRIKANER WEERSTANDSBEWEGING (AFRICAN RESISTANCE MOVEMENT) (AWB)** Pro-**Apartheid** movement in modern South Africa. Formed in 1973 and led by Eugene **Terre'Blanche**, the AWB fiercely upholds the Boer identity of South Africa and is, in effect, a political movement that has only dallied with the idea of trying to attain power legally. Its anti-liberal programme singles out blacks, Jews and Communists as enemies of the Boer nation. The AWB boasts a high profile, even though its active membership is small. It is probably the most famous post-war fascist movement on any continent.

**AGENT THEORY** In essence, the belief that monopoly **capitalism** is the 'agent' of fascism – an article of faith for all Orthodox Marxists. Over time this interpretation, developed by Stalin and the **Comintern** in the 1930s, gradually lost credibility, even in left-wing circles; hence the emergence of a range of neo-Marxist theories of fascism.

**AGIP** Italian chemical firm that particularly benefited from the **autarchy** policy pursued by **Mussolini**.

**AGIR (ACT)** The only significant far-right grouping to emerge in modern Wallonia (Belgium). It was founded in 1989 and in its early days put forward a pagan, anti-American message, viewing itself as the French-speaking counterpart to the *Vlaams Bloc* (VB).

**AGORA** Pro-**Salazar** journal of the post-war Portuguese radical right.

**AGRARIAN LEAGUE** Key ally of **Dollfuss**'s para-fascist regime in Austria.

**AIDS** Metaphor for national decline employed by several neo-fascist groups, including the French *Front National* (FN). For **Le Pen** *SIDA* stands for '*Socialisme, Immigration, Delinquence, Affairisme*'.

**AKTIEFRONT NATIONAAL SOCIALISTEN (NATIONAL SOCIALIST ACTION FRONT) (ANS)** Outlawed Dutch neo-Nazi movement.

**AKTION AUSLÄNDERRÜCKFÜHRUNG – VOLKSBEWEGUNG GEGEN ÜBERFREMDUNG UND UMWELTZERSTÖRUNG (OPERATION REPATRIATION – POPULAR MOVEMENT AGAINST FOREIGN DOMINANCE AND DESTRUCTION OF THE ENVIRONMENT) (AAR)** Modern German neo-Nazi movement that never passed the 0.5 per cent barrier in national elections. It was outlawed in 1983.

**AKTIONSFRONT NATIONALER SOZIALISTEN (NATIONAL SOCIALIST ACTION FRONT) (ANS)** German neo-Nazi movement founded in 1977. Under the leadership of Michael **Kühnen** the ANS specialised in provocative acts. It was banned in 1983 but still remained active.

**AKTIONSFRONT NATIONALER SOZIALISTEN/NATIONALE AKTIVISTEN (ANS/NA)** German neo-Nazi grouping – heir to the *Aktionsfront Nationaler Sozialisten* (ANS).

ALARM Belgian neo-Nazi publication of the 1970s.

ALBERTO POLLIO INSTITUTE FOR HISTORICAL AND MILITARY STUDIES Post-war Italian think-tank that planned for 'revolutionary war' against the extreme left.

ALCÁZAR, EL Spanish far-right newspaper founded in 1936.

ALGÉRIE FRANÇAISE Slogan around which opponents of Algerian independence gathered in the mid-1950s. The French Army, European settlers in Algeria and various ultra-right elements in Paris all upheld the colonial cause and despised the idea of the French government 'selling out' to the *Front de Libération Nationale* (FLN) nationalist movement. In 1958, 1960 and 1961 anti-Paris coups were launched, but none ultimately succeeded in preventing Algerian independence (sealed in 1962). Not only did French neo-fascists support the *Algérie Française* cause in the late-1950s, but the Army and settlers were labelled fascist on account of their intransigent, terroristic and ultra-nationalist agenda.

ALIANZA DE LA JUVENTUD NACIONA-LISTA Pro-**Hitler** paramilitary group active in Argentina in the 1930s and 1940s. It was led by General Bautista **Molina**.

ALIANZA REVOLUCIONARIA NACIONA-LISTA ECUATORIANA (ARNE) Ecuadorian fascist-style group founded in 1948.

ALLDEUTSCHER VERBAND (PAN-GERMAN LEAGUE) Powerful lobby group in early twentieth-century Germany. Some observers argue that it anticipated Nazism in its doctrine – particularly its aggressive, expansionist stance on foreign policy – and thus label it 'proto-fascist'. Its Aus-trian sister movement was led by **Schönerer**.

ALLEANZA NAZIONALE (NATIONAL ALLIANCE) (AN) Populist Italian right-wing coalition of which **Fini**'s neo-fascist *Movimento Sociale Italiano* (MSI) is a part. In two separate 1994 polls – legislative and European – it gained 5 million votes (12 per cent), and improved on this in the parliamentary elections of 1996 (13.5 per cent). The AN portrayed itself as both 'moderate' and 'respectable', and in 2001 entered government.

ALLGEMEINE ELEKTRIZITÄTS GESELL-SCHAFT (AEG) Industrial manufacturer that profited greatly from **Hitler**'s policy of **autarchy**.

ALLIANCE RÉPUBLICAINE POUR LA LIB-ERTÉ ET LE PROGRÈS (REPUBLICAN ALLI-ANCE FOR FREEDOM AND PROGRESS) (ARLP) Political movement that sponsored **Tixier-Vignancour**'s bid for the French presidency in 1965. Through its discourse, and its title, it attempted to place itself within the orbit of mainstream republican politics.

ALLIANZA NACIONAL 18 DE JULIO (18 JULY NATIONAL ALLIANCE) Pro-**Franco** movement that scored 0.36 per cent in the 1977 Spanish elections.

ALLOCATION FAMILIALE **Family** allow-ance-type payment instituted by the **Vichy** administration in wartime France. It varied according to the size of the wage earner's family and is a good example of the kind of 'welfarist' measures that regimes of a fascist or far-rightist character were implementing in the 1930s and 1940s.

AMANECER (DAWN) Far-right journal in inter-war Spain.

**AMERICAN DISSIDENT VOICES** Far-right US organisation of the 1980s. It perceived itself to be at the vanguard of 'Aryan Resistance'.

**AMERICAN INSTITUTE FOR HISTORICAL REVIEW** Pseudo-academic body that promotes **Historical Revisionism**.

**ANARCHO-SYNDICALISM** Revolutionary political movement that provided Italian Fascism with much of its political programme; hence the notion of syndicalist–corporative ideology. Influenced by **socialism**, anarchism and the thought-system of Georges **Sorel**, it saw a key role for workers in the political process.

**ANGST** Term used to convey the 'fear' associated with fascism and the appeal of fascist ideology. The word originates in the writings of **Heidegger**. In the context of the early twentieth century it relates to the crisis of **liberalism** in which the effects of war, uncertainty over European boundaries, economic and social dislocation caused by the **Great Depression**, and pessimism about liberal democracy, combined to produce a climate of tension and unease. This was exploited by fascists, especially in their offer of simplistic solutions to national problems and reassurance for the disaffected.

**ANNALES D'HISTOIRE RÉVISIONNISTE** French journal that has peddled Historical Revisionist ideas.

**ANNE FRANK STICHTING** Post-war 'fascism-watch' group based in the Netherlands.

**ANOMIE** Feeling of powerlessness leading to a breakdown of social norms and standards, and a term often associated with sociologist Emile Durkheim. The economic, political and social dislocation caused by rapid **modernisation** and the consequences of war left many young people atomised and alone in an unfamiliar world; in this sense they became fodder for the paramilitary street-fighting groups and new far-right political parties that emerged after the First World War.

**ANSALDO** Italian munitions company that backed **Mussolini** financially – and in return expected that *Il Duce*'s policies at home and abroad would help keep it occupied and in profit.

**ANSCHLUSS** Union of Austria and Germany in 1938. It was resisted – even by right-wing Austrians under Kurt von **Schüschnigg** and, to a lesser extent, under Engelbert **Dollfuss** – but following the murder of Dollfuss it was brought about through a combination of external pressure and threats from Berlin, as well as Nazi agitation and paramilitary posturing within Austria itself. The policy of *Anschluss* was based upon **Hitler**'s concept of a Greater Germany and the lack of an independent Austrian national identity following the fall of the Austro-Hungarian Empire.

**ANTI-COMINTERN PACT** 1936 agreement between Germany and Japan to oppose Communist and Soviet influence in Europe and elsewhere. It was part of the process of consolidating the **Rome–Berlin–Tokyo Axis**. Italy joined in 1937.

**ANTI-DIMENSION** Term used to denote the many 'negations' at the heart of fascist ideology. Payne's checklist approach to defining fascism highlights this aspect in particular.

**ANTI-FASCISM** Loosely defined, this simply refers to opposition to fascism. However, it acquired the status of a national creed in many countries after the war. In Italy, it assumed that all the main parties had come out of the wartime **resistance**.

Elsewhere, anti-fascist bodies organised militant counter-demonstrations to those orchestrated by far-right groups. Critics charge that militant anti-fascism and far-right extremism feed off each other; defenders claim it is merely a necessary form of consciousness-raising, lest future generations forget the crimes of the past. In Communist East Germany, the cult of anti-fascism was used to brand all anti-socialist tendencies, especially in West Germany, as fascist or 'revanchist'.

**ANTI-FRANCE** Term used by French fascists to describe the full spectrum of 'anti-national' threats (whether real or imaginary). Jews, Communists, socialists, immigrants, homosexuals and **gypsies** have all fallen into this category.

**ANTI-NAZI LEAGUE (ANL)** British coalition movement that emerged in the 1970s as a response to the rise of the **National Front** (NF). Dominated by left-wing movements and pressure groups – especially the Socialist Workers Party – its campaigns against fascism revolve around special events, leaflet campaigns and other forms of **propaganda**. It claims to be responsible, at least in part, for the decline of the NF in the 1980s.

**ANTI-RACISM** Overt campaign against racial prejudice and racial discrimination. Loosely interpreted, it could simply mean opposition to **racism**; however, in recent decades it has become associated with a specific commitment to broadening the definition of racism in particular ways (e.g. by including indirect and unintended offence in the definition). Critics, including some who also oppose racial prejudice, see the more zealous aspects of the anti-racism campaign as a form of 'political correctness' that is counter-productive and needlessly controversial.

**ANTI-SEMITISM** Loosely interpreted, it covers hatred of Jews and Jewish religion and culture (even though Arabs are also a Semitic people). It has many roots, from early Christian association of Jews with the persecution of Christ to class envy at Jewish success in business and finance in nineteenth-century Europe. As a group of non-European origin, Jews were an easy target for such prejudice (take, for example, the pogroms in Russia and the **Dreyfus Affair** in France). Much anti-Semitism was based on false or selective stereotyping: fascists pointed to wealthy Jewish business leaders, but ignored the poverty of many East European Jews, or highlighted the minority of Jews who were socialist intellectuals, while ignoring the persecution of Jews by Soviet Communists. Anti-Semitism was central to **Hitler**'s philosophy and enormously important in numerous far-right movements. *Mein Kampf* singled out the Jews as the source of most evils in modern society. Anti-Semitism was of lesser importance in Italian Fascism, or under Japanese militarists, but was used by these regimes to impress the Nazis. It was also a feature of post-war **neo-Nazism** and **Aryan** race supremacists. Under Nazism, it reached a zenith in the 'Final Solution', in which 6 million Jews perished at death camps in Germany and Poland.

**APARTHEID** Afrikaans word for separation or separateness. It describes the social system established by the South African **National Party** between 1948 and 1991. Proponents denied it was racist, arguing that it was simply a reflection of the difficulty of integrating black, mixed-race and white South Africans. In practice, it amounted to a hierarchical and structured system in which the black majority was discriminated against in almost all areas of life. Inter-marriage and even movement was carefully restricted to keep the races apart. Some restrictions were eased in 1986 but the system was not entirely dismantled until 1991. Some early Afrikaans Nationalists in the 1940s and opponents of the easing of Apartheid in the 1980s also flirted with Nazi racial supremacy doctrines. This element can trace its roots to the influence of **race** theories under German rule in Namibia in the inter-war years.

**APRA** Populist, anti-democratic Peruvian movement founded in 1926 and led by veteran activist Víctor Raúl **Haya de la Torre**. The Apristas' brand of **corporatism**, **mysticism** and pan-Latin Americanism – *Aprismo* – acquired a mass following, but the party never gained power. In the inter-war period, the APRA leadership displayed great admiration for Nazism.

**ARBEITSGEMEINSCHAFT NATIONALER VERBÄNDE VÖLKISCHER BUND (WORKING COMMUNITY OF NATIONAL ORGANISATIONS POPULIST LEAGUE) (ANV/VB)** German far-right coalition of the 1980s.

**ARDITI** Early black-shirted paramilitary arm of **Mussolini**'s fascist movement. Most members were First World War **veterans**.

**ARENA** (1) National Renewal Alliance – post-war far-right Brazilian coalition that lacked genuine fascist credentials, particularly mass appeal; (2) *Alianza Republicana Nacional* (National Republican Alliance) (ARENA) – far-right Salvadoran political party sometimes associated with the country's notorious death squads during the 1980s civil war. ARENA was a rival to the US-backed centre-right Christian Democrats and gained control of the National Assembly in 1988.

**ARGENTINIAN FASCIST PARTY** Short-lived movement, founded in 1938, which tried to ape the European model.

**ARMED FORCES** Key institution in many rightist dictatorships where national defence and **war** are valued. In European fascism, however, the military was traditionally seen as a rival to the ruling fascist party; thus, the history and strategic culture of the military were often viewed with suspicion. In Latin America, Spain and Japan, on the other hand, the impetus for far-rightist politics came from within the military itself. In such cases, military institutions were important and camaraderie among the officer corps was a key instrument of élite socialisation. This was especially true of the formative years of Francisco **Franco**, for instance. Strong military leaders either suppressed radical fascist movements or incorporated them into dummy fascist-like institutions in order to tame them. In Latin America, rightist regimes like that of Perónist Argentina were gradually defascistised and evolved into conservative military dictatorships.

**ARMÉE RÉVOLUTIONNAIRE (REVOLUTIONARY ARMY) (AR)** Pro-*Algérie Française* movement founded, and outlawed, towards the end of the Algerian War.

**ARMY COMRADES ASSOCIATION** A non-partisan welfare association for **veterans** of the Irish War of Independence and the Civil War, which ultimately became a recruiting ground for the Blueshirt movement after opening its ranks to non-veterans in the mid-1930s. It became politicised, with a strong emphasis on law and order, but was not as overt about its politics as **O'Duffy**'s organisation.

**ARRIBA ESPAÑA** Far-right journal in inter-war Spain.

**ARYAN** Term associated with the peoples who speak languages descended from **Indo-European**. Though there may have been a single **language** root, it is less certain that there was a single racial origin. Nazis used the term to refer to Caucasians, but excluding Jews. They tried to argue there was a direct link between the Germans and proto-Indo-Europeans, and some even took up the theme of a link between the German language and **race**, and the languages and races of the Indian sub-continent. In US and South African white supremacist **propaganda**, Aryan is shorthand for 'white'.

**ARYAN NATIONS CONGRESS** Annual gathering of America's community of white supremacists.

**ASPECTS DE FRANCE** Newspaper of the *Action Française*.

**ASSOCIATION OF TURANIAN HUNTERS** Anti-German paramilitary grouping active in inter-war Hungary. Led by Miklós Kállay, it played up its 'Turanian' rather than '**Aryan**' ancestry – and was eventually outlawed by the Nazis in 1944.

**ASSOCIAZIONE FRA LE SOCIETÀ PER AZIONI** Coalition of businessmen that helped finance **Mussolini**'s Fascist Party via a special election-time levy.

**ASSOCIAZIONE NAZIONALE ITALIANA (ITALIAN NATIONALIST ASSOCIATION) (ANI)** High-brow political formation established by **Federzoni** in Florence in 1910. In its **corporatism**, **ultra-nationalism** and anti-**liberalism**, it anticipated themes that were to underpin full-blown Fascism. In 1914 the ANI campaigned for Italian involvement in the First World War, seeing military intervention as a first step on the road to national regeneration. **Rocco** and **D'Annunzio** were both members.

**AUSCHWITZ** Polish concentration camp associated with the gassing to death of Jews and forced labour regimes.

**AUSGRENZUNG** Name given to the mainstream parties' 'policy of exclusion' aimed

at **Haider** and the *Freiheitliche Partei Österreichs* (FPÖ) in modern Austria.

**AUSTRIAN CRISIS** Period of tension between Germany and Austria marked by the murder of Engelbert **Dollfuss** by Nazi putschists in 1934 and the forced union of Austria and Germany in 1938. Dollfuss's successor, Kurt von **Schuschnigg**, tried to negotiate with Hitler but ultimately decided to assert Austrian independence by means of a plebiscite. Hitler's response was to step up his threats and to intensify Nazi agitation and subversion within Austria, paving the way for a forced merger of the two states and German military occupation. Outside powers refused to support Austria and **Mussolini** dropped his earlier opposition to German influence there, as his alignment with Hitler grew stronger.

**AUSTRIAN IDEOLOGY** Catholic, tradition-based creed that was at the base of **Dollfuss**'s inter-war *Standestaat* dictatorship.

**AUSTROFASCISM** Controversial umbrella term that groups together the various flowerings of **semi-fascism** and **para-fascism** in 1930s Austria.

**AUTARCHY/AUTARKY** A concept denoting economic self-sufficiency. It gained currency particularly in Nazi Germany in the years preceding the **Second World War** when large-scale military conflict was on the horizon – a period in which **Hitler**'s regime placed a large premium on self-sufficiency and the country's preparedness for war. **Mussolini** also attached great importance to autarchy: his '**Battle for Grain**' was aimed directly at lessening Italy's reliance on imports. The concept has non-fascist ancestry – it was popularised by Saint-Simon, **List** and Naumann – but was used in the twentieth century by a range of fascist movements.

**AUTHORITARIANISM** Tendency to value the importance of authority rather than pluralism and diversity as a basis for social order. Rightist authoritarian regimes typically controlled society in specific issue-areas (e.g. in framing rules governing public order or sexual conduct) but, unlike totalitarian regimes, did not attempt comprehensive control in all sectors. Political leaders in democratic systems can also exhibit an authoritarian style of leadership in which they assume the mantle of national leadership and act as authority figures, e.g. de Valera in Ireland and de Gaulle in France. Authoritarianism, involving restrictions on some key democratic freedoms, was a feature of right-wing governments in the inter-war years but was viewed by fascists as a half-baked form of dictatorship.

**AUTOBAHNEN** German motorways – one of the most notable areas of capital investment under **Hitler**.

**AVANGUARDIA NAZIONALE (NATIONAL VANGUARD)** *Movimento Sociale Italiano* (MSI) offshoot movement founded in 1960 by Stefano Delle **Chiaie**. Fiercely anti-Communist and anti-Semitic, it specialised in anti-system political violence.

**AVANGUARDIA SOCIALISTE (SOCIALIST VANGUARD)** Italian neo-syndicalist journal in the period before 1914.

**AVANTI** Socialist newspaper edited by **Mussolini** prior to 1914.

**AWAKENING HUNGARIANS** Nationalist group that liaised with **Hitler** in an attempt to overthrow the inter-war **Horthy** regime.

**AZIONE CATTOLICA (CATHOLIC ACTION)** Lay organisation whose youth groups rivalled **Mussolini**'s in the 1920s and 1930s.

The Fascist regime was suspicious of *Azione Cattolica* but eventually recognised the movement – on condition that it stayed out of politics. In time it became the only non-fascist organisation able to operate legally under Mussolini.

**BA'ATH PARTY/BA'ATH ARAB SOCIALIST (RENAISSANCE) PARTY** Dominant political organisation in the one-party states of Syria and Iraq, combining **nationalism** with Stalinist **Marxism** and anti-Israeli stridency. Nationalism can be Arab nationalism, aiming to create a single Arab entity with an anti-Western orientation, or state nationalism, stressing Syrian or Iraqi interests. The original Ba'ath Party had Arab nationalist and socialist credentials but the leadership cults and rivalries of Saddam **Hussein** and Hafez al Assad led to increasing divergence, culminating in Syria's participation in the Gulf War of 1991 on the Allied side against Iraq. The combination of distorted **socialism**, nationalism and **totalitarianism** is reminiscent of fascism. Saddam Hussein's alleged personal interest in **Hitler** and his militantly anti-Israeli stance have added to this impression, though the precise contours of Ba'athism are hard to pin down.

**BAJUVARIAN LIBERATION ARMY** Violent and secretive far-right group active in 1990s Austria.

**BANCA ITALIANA DI SCONTO** Major Italian bank that collapsed in 1922 – one feature of the post-war economic crisis eventually exploited by **Mussolini**.

**BANCO AMBROSIANO** Italian bank associated with post-war crime.

**BANCO DI ROMA** Italian bank that **Mussolini** helped to save in 1923.

**BARBAROSSA, OPERATION** Nazi attack on the Soviet Union in 1941. It represented an outright reversal of the German policy of collaboration with the Russians, as announced under the **Nazi–Soviet Pact**.

**BARDOLFF CIRCLE** Early twentieth-century pan-German study group. Future Austrian leader **Dollfuss** was a member.

**BASES AUTÓNOMAS (AUTONOMOUS GRASSROOTS GROUPS)** Anarchic far-right movement active in late-1980s Spain.

**BATTALION OF LEGIONARY COMMERCE** A chain of shops and restaurants run by the Romanian **Legion/League of the Archangel Gabriel**. The nomenclature was indicative of the flamboyant and bombastic tenor of the League's activities.

**BATTLE FOR BIRTHS** Name given to **Mussolini**'s high-profile campaign to expand Italy's demographic rates. Celibate people were taxed, **family** allowances introduced and abortion and **homosexuality** outlawed – all in an effort to make the nation stronger and more formidable on the world stage. Mussolini wanted to double the Italian population, but failed miserably.

**BATTLE FOR GRAIN** Mussolini's grand plan in the agricultural sector. He aimed to make Italy self-sufficient in grain and, in so doing, help the nation's balance of trade figures. To publicise the 'Battle for Grain', *Il Duce* posed for a series of famous photos driving a tractor. One estimate has it that grain production doubled between 1922 and 1939.

**BECCO GIALLO (YELLOW BEAK)** Irreverent anti-Fascist newspaper in 1920s Italy. Estimates suggest it had a six-figure circulation.

**BEER HALL PUTSCH** Name given to **Hitler**'s first abortive bid for power – November 1923, Munich.

**BELGISCHE NATIONALE PARTIJ (BNP)** Flemish translation of *Parti National Belge*.

**BELLICISM** Belief in the virtues of war for its own sake – not to be confused with endorsement of war as an instrument of policy. Fascist and Nazi obsession with the concepts of *combattimento* and 'struggle' lend credence to the proposition that their philosophy was bellicist. Struggle was not just an ideological phenomenon: one interpretation of fascist **totalitarianism** and regimentation stated that it was nothing more than mass social mobilisation for a permanent military campaign. The role of war **veterans** and the influence of military defeat in the First World War also point to an excessive preoccupation with war among fascists in the 1920s and 1930s. In Germany, one key **Hitler** supporter, Erich **Ludendorff**, misinterpreted von **Clausewitz** to preach a doctrine of 'total war'. Modern fascists and neo-fascists are more likely to share conventional conservatives' beliefs in strong national defence than to espouse blatantly bellicist doctrines.

**BERLINER LOKALANZEIGER** Pro-Nazi/nationalist newspaper in inter-war Germany.

**BESSARABIA** Also known as Moldova or Moldavia. A Romanian-populated region lying between Romania and Ukraine. It was ceded to the Soviet Union by the Romanian dictator, **Antonescu**, as a response to German pressure to keep Stalin happy with the **Nazi–Soviet Pact**. It was briefly reoccupied by Romanians in 1941 and subsequently became part of the USSR, but the surrender of Bessarabia has been a sore point for Romanian nationalists ever since. As Moldova it acquired independence in the 1990s but it is now torn between far-right Russian nationalists, advocates of Moldovan independence and Romanian irredentists. Some regions of the original Bessarabia are also part of Ukraine.

**BEWEGUNG, DIE (MOVEMENT, THE)** Tiny, internally divided West German neofascist group that wanted to refound the Nazi Party.

**BEZPARTYJNY BLOK WSPÓŁPRACY Z RZADEM (NON-PARTY BLOC OF CO-OPERATION WITH THE GOVERNMENT) (BBWR)** Government party created by semi-fascist Polish dictator **Pilsudski** in 1927. It tried to create an understanding with the *Falanga*.

**BIENNIO ROSSO (TWO RED YEARS)** Name given to the period 1919–21 in Italy. These years witnessed widespread economic instability and serious fears of a Bolshevik takeover – a situation that turned many employers and much of the **middle class** towards Fascism.

**BINDING RECHTS (BR)** Short-lived far-right grouping that emerged from the 1968 split within the Dutch *Boerenpartij* (BP).

**BLACK FRONT** Embryonic Dutch fascist organisation – 1935.

**BLACKSHIRT** Newspaper of the **British Union of Fascists**.

**BLACKSHIRTS** Nickname given to **Mussolini**'s hardline *squadristi*. Most Blackshirts were either ex-servicemen, students or members of the **middle class**. They were organised in squads and were responsible for the assassination of socialist politician Matteotti; they gradually became more

and more anarchic and were eventually disbanded in 1925.

**BLITZKRIEG** Literally, 'lightning warfare' (from the German). *Blitzkrieg* denoted a lightning strike with tanks and armoured vehicles, and was popularised by **Hitler**'s forces in the **Second World War**.

**BLOOD** Key theme in the nation-orientated discourse of fascists and far-right activists. It is a consistent element in their rhetoric, particularly where they address issues such as **patriotism**, nationality law and **ruralism**.

**BLOOD AND HONOUR** Post-war British far-right magazine and music cult associated with Ian Stuart **Donaldson**.

**BLOQUE NACIONAL (NATIONAL BLOC)** Alliance of authoritarian, anti-democratic Spanish movements formed in December 1934 by Calvo **Sotelo**. The aim of the coalition was to execute some kind of coup.

**BLUE BLACKS** Youth movement of the *Isänmaallinen Kansanliike* (IKL) fascist movement in inter-war Finland. Members wore black shirts and blue ties.

**BLUESHIRTS** (1) Far-right **militia** or vigilante-type movement active in inter-war Ireland. It became involved in vigilante protection work for *Cumann na nGaedhal* candidates at election rallies, and membership was originally drawn from the veteran-based Army Comrades Association. The 'blue shirt' was in the colour of Saint Patrick (this blue was the original colour associated with Ireland before green was appropriated by Irish nationalists). Though they tried to ape Italian Fascism, most Blueshirts treated their organisation as a vehicle for parades and entertainment or as a means of settling local scores with *Fianna Fáil* or old civil war opponents. Although it was ultimately banned, the movement was not taken seriously as a fascist threat. It was incorporated as a minor faction in **Fine Gael**, the successor party to *Cumann na nGaedhal* founded by the Blueshirt leader, Eoin **O'Duffy**. The term 'Blueshirt' is still used as a derogatory name for the more conservative *Fine Gael* supporters; (2) Alternative name of the *Nacional Sindicalismo* (NS) in 1930s Portugal; (3) Romanian paramilitary group associated with the National Christian League of Alexandru **Cuza**. It engaged in anti-Semitic attacks in the mid-1930s and competed for influence with Corneliu **Codreanu**'s green-shirted Iron Guard activists; (4) Alternative name of the *Francistes* – **Bucard**'s fascist group in inter-war France; (5) Movement associated with **Franco**'s Spanish *Falange*.

**BOERENPARTIJ (BP)** The first significant far-right movement to emerge in the Netherlands after the **Second World War**. Founded in 1958, it was led by Henrik Koekoek and boasted a predominantly urban clientele. It cultivated a moderate image and at its peak won seven seats in the Dutch parliament. It disappeared in the early 1980s.

**BOLSHEVISM** Name given to Soviet **Communism** in its early years, based on the title of the ruling party. It is used in fascist **propaganda** as pejorative shorthand for Communism, though Nazis also linked it, without much reason, to Jewish conspiracies.

**BONAPARTISM** Authoritarian political style associated with Emperors Napoleon I and III that came to characterise a variety of pre-fascist and fascist movements in France (for instance, **Boulangism** in the late nineteenth century and the *Jeunesses Patriotes* in the inter-war period). Following Napoleon I's claim to be carrying on the legacy of the 1789 Revolution, Bonapartists attempted to legitimate authoritarian dictatorship by claiming, or appealing to, mass popular support. The use of plebiscites to consolidate dictatorship is a typically Bonapartist tactic.

**BORUSSENFRONT** Modern German extreme-right movement led by Siegfried Borchardt. Fiercely anti-immigrant, it was linked in organisational terms to football hooligan groups.

**BOULANGISM** Set of ideas associated with the Boulangist movement in late nineteenth-century France. Boulangism was an amalgam of fierce anti-German **nationalism**, progressive socio-economic ideas and vehement anti-parliamentary rhetoric. It sought to adapt itself to the new democratic context in France after 1871 and, as such, aimed to attract and enfranchise the urban masses. Boulangism is variously described as 'neo-Bonapartist' and 'pre-fascist'.

**BRANDENBERGISCHE VOLKSPARTEI (BRANDENBERG PEOPLE'S PARTY) (BVP)** German far-right group of the 1990s. It was home to many ex-*Deutsche Alternative* (DA) members after their movement had been outlawed.

**BRANDWAG** Vigilante group attached to the South African *Afrikaner Weerstandsbeweging* (AWB).

**BRASILIDADE (BRAZILIANNESS)** Indigenous ideology of the inter-war *Ação Integralista Brasileira* (AIB). It was an original mixture of native culture, multi-ethnic values and **anti-Semitism**.

**BRITAIN FIRST National Front** newspaper of the 1970s.

**BRITISH BROTHERS LEAGUE** Small xenophobic movement that emerged in Edwardian Britain.

**BRITISH FASCISTS (BF)** Small-scale British movement founded in 1923 by Rotha **Lintorn Orman**. The BF had some fascist traits – a paramilitary arm and a blue-shirted uniform, for example – but was slightly ignorant of what fascism actually was. It was fiercely patriotic and anti-Communist, but its political impact was minimal. It had died away by the mid-1930s.

**BRITISH MOVEMENT (BM)** Body founded in 1968 and formerly known as the **National Socialist Movement** – led by Colin **Jordan**.

**BRITISH NATIONAL PARTY (BNP)** Far-right movement formed by John Bean in 1960 and re-founded by John **Tyndall** in 1982. Its programme is based primarily on hostility to **immigration**. In September 1993 it won a local by-election victory in Tower Hamlets on the Isle of Dogs with 34 per cent of the vote; a year later it did not field any candidates in the 1994 European elections. Estimates put its membership at around 3,000 in the mid-1990s. It achieved significant success in the 2001 British General Election – particularly in northern England – and won three council seats in Burnley in local government elections in May 2002.

**BRITISH NATIONAL SOCIALIST MOVEMENT** Political organisation formed in the 1980s. It was home to many former **British Movement** activists.

**BRITISH NATIONALIST, THE** Monthly newspaper of the **British National Party**.

**BRITISH PEOPLE'S PARTY** 1930s far-right movement associated with the Duke of Bedford and John **Beckett**.

**BRITISH UNION OF FASCISTS (BUF)** Movement formed in October 1932 and led by Oswald **Mosley**. Members wore black shirts, engaged in paramilitary violence and talked a racial language. It staged a huge rally at Olympia in 1934, took part in mass riots in 1936 and was comfortably the most significant British fascist organisation of the inter-war period. Mosley's group claimed to have more than 50,000 members at its peak.

**BRITONS** Anti-Semitic publishing house founded by Henry Hamilton **Beamish** in the aftermath of the First World War.

**BROEDERBOND (BROTHERS ASSOCIATION)** Secretive proto-fascist South African movement founded in 1918. Heavily anti-Semitic, it championed a particularly virulent brand of *Völkisch* **nationalism** and pro-Afrikaner **racism**. It was representative of the ideology known as **Christian Nationalism**.

**BROTHERHOOD OF THE CROSS** Romanian fascist movement of the 1920s led by Ion **Moţa**. It was a forerunner of **Codreanu**'s **Legion of the Archangel Michael**.

**BROTHERS' LEAGUE** Small British anti-immigrant movement founded in 1902.

**BROWNSHIRTS** Nickname given to the Nazi *Sturm Abteilung* (SA) because of the colour of their uniform.

**BÚFALOS** Name of the **APRA** paramilitary force in inter-war Peru.

**BULLDOG** Youth journal of the modern British **National Front**.

**BUND DEUTSCHER FRAUENVEREINE** Women's organisation in Weimar Germany. It was nominally feminist but kowtowed to **Hitler**'s agenda.

**BUND DEUTSCHER MADEL (BDM)** Nazi organisation for girls over the age of fourteen.

**BUND HAMBURGER MADEL (LEAGUE OF HAMBURG GIRLS) (BHM)** Neo-Nazi group connected to the *Aktionsfront Nationaler Sozialisten* (ANS) – a rare all-female association.

**BUNDES MINISTERIUM DES INNEM (FEDERAL MINISTRY FOR THE INTERIOR) (BMI)** Government department with ultimate responsibility for monitoring right-wing (and left-wing) extremism in modern-day Germany.

**BUNDESAMT FÜR VERFASSUNGSSCHUTZ (FEDERAL OFFICE FOR THE PROTECTION OF THE CONSTITUTION) (BFV)** Government body charged with monitoring far-right extremism in modern-day Germany.

**BUNDESKRIMINALAMT (FEDERAL CRIME OFFICE) (BKA)** German governmental body set up to counter the extreme-right threat in the 1990s.

**BÜRGER- UND BAUERNINITIATIVE (CITIZENS' AND FARMERS' INITIATIVE) (BBI)** Neo-Nazi support group linked to Thies **Christophersen**.

**BURNLEY** Lancashire town in which the **British National Party** (BNP) won 11.3 per cent of the vote in the 2001 General Election, and which only days later was the scene of violent **race** riots. In May 2002 the BNP won three council seats in the town.

C

**CAMELOTS DU ROI** Thuggish group of street-fighters attached to the *Action Fran-*

*çaise* during the inter-war period and after.

**CAMERE DEL LAVARO (CHAMBERS OF LABOUR) Working-class** municipal bodies in inter-war Italy – eventually destroyed by the Fascists.

**CAMP OF NATIONAL UNITY (OZON):** Polish movement on which **Pilsudski**'s authoritarian single-party dictatorship was based.

**CANDOUR** Weekly newspaper of the British **League of Empire Loyalists**.

**CAPITALISM** Socio-economic system based on private capital. Its relationship with fascism is a source of much controversy. For Marxian writers, fascism was either the highest stage of capitalism or a 'dictatorship of the bourgeoisie' under 'organised capitalism'. According to this view, fascist policies were driven by an alliance of capital and the military. A more flexible Marxian interpretation posits an alliance of convenience among like-minded but distinct actors. For non-Marxists, the relationship is more problematic: fascism is seen as a form of state control of the economy without comprehensive state ownership. In this view, capitalists often collaborated with fascists in order to survive or as a means of controlling union power, while still hoping to control and moderate the emerging regimes; yet, they were alarmed at the tendency toward permanent revolution and **violence**, the incoherence of fascist ideology and its persistent anti-capitalist undercurrents. The fascists operated a system of crony capitalism, i.e. one that gave preference to national corporations and pro-fascist businesses; in general they also opposed liberal economic policies and transnational capital, especially if it had Jewish connections. There were internal tensions between the radically anti-capitalist tendencies inherited from **socialism** and syndico-anarchism, and the pragmatic need for party finance and centres of national economic power like the arms and steel industries. Post-war far-right movements, like the Italian *Movimento Sociale Italiano* (MSI) and the French *Front National* (FN), have dabbled in free-market **liberalism** but in a rather unconvincing way.

**CAPORETTO, BATTLE OF** Humiliating defeat for Italy's military forces in November 1917. **Mussolini** exploited the shame of this experience for good political effect in subsequent years.

**CARINTHIA** Austrian province that is now the power base of *Freiheitliche Partei Österreichs* (FPÖ) leader, Jörg **Haider**.

**CARNARO, CHARTER OF** 'Pre-Fascist' document drawn up by de **Ambris** in association with **D'Annunzio** in September 1920. It mixed syndicalist, corporatist and nationalist ideas, and anticipated the main drift of **Mussolini**'s thinking in a variety of ways. It acted as the 'Constitution of **Fiume**' when D'Annunzio and his followers took over the Adriatic port in their 'dress rehearsal' of a fascist takeover.

**CARTEL OF THE PRODUCTIVE ESTATES** German coalition movement that brought together the main bodies on the pre-1914 extra-parliamentary right: namely, the **Agrarian League**, the Central Association of German Industrialists and the Imperial German Middle Class League. The Cartel was established in 1913.

**CATHOLICISM** Principal religion in Southern and much of East Central Europe. Catholic social teaching, the Church's staunch anti-Communism and Papal encyclicals on economic issues were broadly compatible with important themes in fascist and far-right party programmes in inter-war Europe. However, the Church, both in Germany and Italy, was also critical of fascist violence and excesses, and Catholic youth organisations found themselves in competition with those established by fascists. While **Mussolini** had to compromise with the Vatican, some far-right regimes, notably those of **Pétain** in France and **Franco** in Spain, were more genuinely Catholic in orientation.

**CAUSA** Name of 'Rev' Sun Myung **Moon**'s political operation. CAUSA gained a significant base in North America, acquired anti-Communist contacts in several South American countries and also attracted some support in Western Europe.

**CD-ACTUEEL** Journal of the modern Dutch *Centrum Democraten*.

**CD-INFO** Newsletter of the modern Dutch *Centrum Democraten*.

**CENTRAL AGENCIES OF THE REICH** Body involved in centralised economic planning in Nazi Germany.

**CENTRE NATIONAL DES INDÉPENDANTS ET DES PAYSANS (NATIONAL CENTRE OF INDEPENDENTS AND PEASANTS) (CNIP)** Post-war French movement whose discourse was a mixture of mainstream-right and far-right themes.

**CENTRO ACADÉMICO DE DEMOCRACIA CRISTA** Portuguese student association that supported the right-wing dictatorship and stood for French-style 'integral nationalism'.

**CENTRUM DEMOCRATEN (CENTRE DEMOCRATS) (CD)** Small Dutch anti-immigrant party founded in 1984. Although hostile to the liberal-democratic system, it has won seats in both the Second Chamber and local elections.

**CENTRUM PARTIJ (CENTRE PARTY) (CP)** Dutch far-right party that won one seat in the 1984 parliamentary elections. Set up by ex-*Nationale Centrum Partij* (NCP) members, it folded in the mid-1980s.

**CENTRUM PARTIJ '86 (CENTRE PARTY '86) (CP'86)** Successor to the bankrupt Dutch far-right *Centrum Partij*. It was formed in 1986 – hence the movement's title.

**CENTRUMSTROMING** Dutch term denoting the *Centrum Partij* and its successor movements.

**CERCLE PROUDHON** Nationalist-syndicalist study group established in France in the early twentieth century.

**ČETNIKS (CHETNIKS)** Paramilitary arm of the ultra-nationalist Serbian Radical Party and the only movement banned from contesting the 1990 Yugoslav elections. During the **Second World War** the 'Chetniks' were the main Serb **resistance** fighters. The term is also used as a loose description of any Serb paramilitary organisation in the former Yugoslavia.

**CHACO WAR** Conflict between Bolivia and Paraguay fought over territorial claims to the Chaco desert (1929–35, and, at its most intense, from 1932). The war further militarised both societies but also fostered modernising and populist tendencies within subsequent dictatorships (such as the 'military socialist' regime of Major German **Busch** in Bolivia, 1936–9). Over 80,000 soldiers died in the conflict. Though Bolivia started the war expecting huge gains, Paraguay ultimately won control of most of the Chaco.

**CHAMBER OF FASCES AND CORPORATIONS** Corporative body that replaced the Chamber of Deputies in 1938 as part of **Mussolini**'s move towards dictatorship in Italy.

**CHILEAN ACTION** Newspaper of the inter-war *Movimiento Nacional Socialista de Chile* (MNS).

**CHRISTIAN CRUSADE** Radical right-wing movement in post-war America. It was especially active in anti-Communist campaigns in the 1950s and 1960s.

**CHRISTIAN DEMOCRACY** Centrist political tendency associated with either Catholic or multi-denominational Christian parties in Europe and Latin America. Christian Democracy typically combines social and cultural **conservatism** on **family** issues, anti-Communism and a moderately reformist welfare state agenda, and is generally hostile to the politics of class conflict. In the inter-war years Christian Democratic movements were classed by fascists as 'bourgeois' or 'plutocratic' parties and were suspected of links with traditional élites and outspoken anti-fascist elements in the churches. Influential in Catholic Action and the *Partito Populare Italiano* (PPI) in Italy, and the *Mouvement Républicain Populaire* (MRP) in France, some Christian Democrats veered to the right, others to the left. In Latin America (e.g. Chile) some endorsed military rule, citing what they saw as the greater danger of Communism.

**CHRISTIAN DEMOCRATS** Inter-war Chilean movement (originally known as the *Falange*) that stood for a radical brand of populist **Catholicism**. The modern Christian Democrats are organised as a centre-right party along West European lines. Although they gave tentative support to **Pinochet**'s coup in 1973, they have been a moderating influence in Chilean politics since the restoration of **democracy**.

**CHRISTIAN FUNDAMENTALISM** Literally, a form of **Christianity** that reverts to the fundamentals of the faith and its doctrinal source (principally, the Bible). The term can be used to refer to social and cultural **conservatism** in the major Christian denominations, including **Catholicism**. It is also used to refer to numerous small Bible-centred and right-wing Protestant sects that have emerged in the US since the 1980s. Some of the more extreme groups use Biblical interpretation to understand, explain or predict current events in ways that justify racial superiority, **Aryan race** doctrines, **anti-Semitism** and violent rebellion against the US government in preparation for a war of Armageddon in Israel and conflict with a satanic 'World Government'. However, the majority of fundamentalists, while exhibiting very conservative attitudes on **gender**, the **family** and **patriotism** (by European standards), do not adhere to these extreme positions. In many respects, aspects of fundamentalism have been mainstreamed in key US denominations and in the Republican Party.

**CHRISTIAN IDENTITY** Far-right US movement whose ideology is a mix of **white supremacism** and **anti-Semitism**. The key figure in the organisation is ex-**Ku Klux Klan** member Wesley Swift.

**CHRISTIAN NATIONALISM** Ideology of the *Afrikaner Weerstandsbeweging* (AWB) and other pro-**Apartheid** South African groups. The ultimate aim of these movements is a 'Christian National' state. Christian Nationalism is related to **Christian Socialism**.

**CHRISTIAN PATRIOT'S DEFENCE LEAGUE (CPDL)** US paramilitary group founded in 1977. It argues that its extremist doctrine is based on Christian foundations.

**CHRISTIAN RIGHT** Socially conservative far-right tendency in the contemporary US.

**CHRISTIAN SOCIALISM** White supremacist ideology championed by pro-**Apartheid** groups in South Africa. Christian Socialism is related to **Christian Nationalism**.

**CHRISTIANITY** Has a complex relationship with fascism and the far right. Devout and socially conservative right-wingers often genuinely endorsed religious tradition and sought Church legitimation for their regimes. In addition, conservative Christians often endorsed far-right regimes as the lesser of two evils, especially when confronted with militant atheism in the USSR. However, Nazis and more militant fascists saw Christian compassion as a debilitating feature of the Judeo-Christian tradition that had weakened great empires like Rome. They also resented powerful religious institutions like the Catholic Church, which retained considerable independence from their projected totalitarian state institutions. The Nazis' effort to create a new German national church was a failure.

**CHRISTLICH-SOZIALE PARTEI (CHRISTIAN SOCIAL PARTY) (CSP)** Political movement that was a key element in the phenomenon of **'Austrofascism'**. Its ideology was a mixture of **conservatism**, clericalism and **corporatism**. Led by Karl **Lueger**, the anti-leftist CSP shifted rightwards during the inter-war period; so far that it took on authoritarian, fascist traits itself and supported the *Heimwehr*.

**CHRISTUS REX (CHRIST THE KING)** Journal of the far-right *Rex* movement in Belgium.

**CHRYSSI AVGHI (GOLDEN DAWN)** Tiny Greek neo-fascist group of the 1990s.

**CIRCULO ESPAÑOL DE AMIGOS DE EUROPA (SPANISH CIRCLE OF FRIENDS OF EUROPE) (CEDADE)** Europe-wide neo-Nazi movement founded in 1965 by Spanish, German and Italian activists. It specialised in **propaganda.**

**CIRCULOS DE ESTUDOS SOCIAIS VECTOR (SOCIAL STUDIES CIRCLES VECTOR)** Pro-**Salazar** organisation that was formed in the aftermath of the dictator's exit from power.

**CIRCULOS DOCTRINALES JOSÉ ANTONIO (JOSÉ ANTONIO DOCTRINAL CIRCLES)** Nostalgic far-right movement active in late 1970s Spain.

**CIVIC RELIGION** Phenomenon whereby a political ideology acquires the character of an official **religion**. Fascist and Communist regimes emphasised ideological orthodoxy and a messianic approach to politics. They used symbolism, education and ritual to consolidate their hold on power. The Fascist 'Dodecalogue', in imitation of the Ten Commandments, was one illustration of this tendency in the Italian regime.

**CIVIL RIGHTS MOVEMENT** Broad-ranging US protest coalition that was able to destabilise the **Ku Klux Klan** in the 1960s, particularly in the southern states. It played a leading role in campaigning against racial prejudice and, as such, it emerged as the prime enemy of the far right in the post-war US.

**CIVILISATION** A major current of values, art and human endeavor stretching over a substantial period of history. **Hitler**'s concept of a 'One Thousand Year Reich' and Mussolini's notion of a new Roman Empire suggested that fascism was more than a programme for government and was, in fact, a blueprint for civilisation; hence the many grandiose terms employed by fascist movements and regimes: *Uomo Fascista* (Fascist Man), 'New Age', 'New Man', 'New Woman'. Fascist hopes of creating a new civilisation were always illusory.

**CLARENDON CLUB** Right-wing study group associated with controversial revisionist historian, David Irving.

**CLARION** National-socialist newspaper of the **British Fascists**.

**CLASSIC FASCISM** Term associated with the 'model' regimes of **Mussolini** and **Hitler**.

**CLERICO-FASCISM** Controversial term attached by historians to **Hlinka**'s conservative–nationalist People's Party in 1930s Slovakia and the Christian–Corporate State of **Dollfuss** and **Schuschnigg** in 1930s Austria.

**CLUB DE L'HORLOGE** Think-tank of the French *Nouvelle Droite*. In several key areas its discourse – a blend of anti-**egalitarianism** and *laissez-faire* economics – overlaps with that of the *Front National* (FN). However, the *Club* does not endorse **Le Pen**'s organisation in either electoral or political terms.

**CODE DE LA NATIONALITÉ (NATIONALITY CODE)** Piece of French legislation that has become a battleground for the *Front National* (FN) and its political opponents. While **Le Pen** and some mainstream political figures would like nationality laws to be tightened, the contemporary left has, on the whole, advertised its belief in a 'liberal', 'welcoming' nation.

**COLD WAR** Period of intense ideological struggle and limited peripheral wars spearheaded by the US and the Soviet Union in various phases between 1947 and 1989. Neo-Nazis and fascists shared the zealous anti-Communism of the US and its allies, as well as European conservative parties. The East German and Soviet regimes also used the Nazi legacy in their **propaganda** campaigns, especially in efforts to blacken West Germany with the tar of Nazi and 'revanchist' policies. Far-right dictatorships in Latin America also benefited from US opposition to Communism, which the US saw as a worse evil than rightist dictatorship.

**COLLABORATION** Co-operation with the leading fascist powers, especially with the German and Italian armies of occupation. Its significance lies in the fact that many countries did not come to terms with collaboration for decades after the end of the war. This resulted in a succession of revelations, scandals and controversies, most notably in France, Italy, the Baltic states and Switzerland.

**COLLABORATIONISM** Variation on the theme of **collaboration**. In France collaborationism came to denote the phenomenon of 'ideological' rather than 'governmental' or 'everyday' collaboration. The French Nazis – figures such as **Brasillach**, **Drieu la Rochelle** and **Doriot** – were based in Paris during the Occupation and were at the cutting edge of collaborationism: expounding Hitlerite doctrine, aping Nazi ritual and openly declaring their love for Germany. Collaborationists hoped that the Allies would be defeated and thereafter they themselves would play a prominent role in Hitler's 'New Europe'. On the whole they were small in number and viewed as irrelevant by both the Nazis and the **Vichy** regime. However, as a concept, collaborationism was hugely important: it signified 'voluntary' rather than 'involuntary' collaboration with the Nazis.

**COLLECTIVE SECURITY** International system based on shared responsibility for global security. In such a scenario, aggression is identified and acted upon by the international community as a whole and it is the community of states, rather than a balance of power, which guarantees the peace. International institutions, international law, political will and a consensus on international norms are important factors in a collective security regime. The **League of Nations** and the **United Nations** were heavily influenced by this approach to international security. Fascist regimes rejected collective security structures because they saw them as serving the interests of the dominant powers and the status quo.

**COLLECTIVISM** Key element in both fascist and Communist ideology. It emphasises the inability to achieve 'true freedom' without immersion in a collective group represented by the state or the ruling party. For the left, the collective entity was a class-based one; for fascists, it was the nation. Collectivist ideologies see **individualism** as selfish and counterproductive.

**COLONELS, THE** Nickname given to the group of Greek military figures that came to power via a 1967 coup. Although they claimed to be 'non-political', their ideological agenda contained fascist traits.

**COLONIALISM** Territorial expansionism usually associated with the unrestricted exploitation of resources and/or the settlement of colonists in conquered land. It was seen as symbolic of Great-Power Status in the late nineteenth century. Italy, Germany and Japan felt cheated of colonial empires in the early years of the twentieth century and this became a theme in fascist **propaganda** in these countries.

**COLUMN 88** Conspiratorial group wielding much influence on the modern British far-right. It was named after an underground Nazi group in 1930s Austria.

COMBAT Newspaper of the **National Labour Party** (NLP) in the late 1950s. It became the newspaper of the **British National Party** (BNP), with John Bean as editor.

COMBAT 18 Extremist organisation on the modern British far right. In the 1990s it emerged as a shady movement that employed direct-action tactics.

COMBAT EUROPÉEN Post-war neo-Nazi publication associated with the *Nouvel Ordre Européen* (NOE).

COMBATTENTISMO Literally, 'spirit of the trenches' (from the Italian). It was this 'spirit' that **Mussolini** traded upon in the years immediately following the First World War. **Veterans** were particularly attracted to *Il Duce*'s strong sense of **patriotism** and determination to end the 'impotence' associated with the liberal era in Italy.

COMINTERN (COMMUNIST INTERNATIONAL) An alliance of far-left parties spearheaded by the Soviet Bolsheviks, and, later, the Soviet Communist Party (1919–43). The aim was to promote revolution on the Bolshevik model. The existence of key Comintern documents, including Lenin's *Twenty-One Points* of 1920, was cited by fascists as evidence of a Jewish–Bolshevik conspiracy against Germany and the nations of Europe. The Comintern was dissolved in 1943 but Soviet control of Eastern Europe facilitated similar ventures after the war. Though initially geared to revolution, the Comintern was essentially a tool of the national interests of the USSR, even under Lenin and especially under Stalin.

COMISSOES DE TRABALHADORES Bodies that co-ordinated the anti-rightist purges in Portugal after 1974.

COMITATI D'AZIONE PER L'UNIVERSALITÀ DI ROMA (CAUR) Evangelical fascist organisation active in inter-war Italy.

COMITATO CORPORATIVO CENTRALE (CENTRAL CORPORATIVE COMMITTEE) Body established by **Mussolini** in 1938 to co-ordinate state economic policy.

COMITATO DI LIBERAZIONE NAZIONALE (COMMITTEE FOR NATIONAL LIBERATION) (CLN) Body that steered Italy into the post-**Mussolini** era – and also came into conflict with the embryonic *Movimento Sociale Italiano* (MSI).

COMITATO INTERMINISTERIALE PER L'AUTARCHIA (INTERMINISTERIAL COMMITTEE ON AUTARCHY) Body established by **Mussolini** in 1939 to co-ordinate Italian economic policy in readiness for war.

COMITÉ D'ACTION ET DE DÉFENSE DES BELGES D'AFRIQUE (CADBA) Post-war Belgian movement with a zealous pro-colonial agenda. It evolved into the *Mouvement d'Action Civique* (MAC).

COMITÉ DES FORGES French trade union suppressed by **Vichy** decree of November 1940.

COMITÉ DES HOUILLÈRES French trade union suppressed by **Vichy** decree of November 1940.

COMITÉ SECRET D'ACTION RÉVOLUTIONNAIRE (SECRET COMMITTEE FOR REVOLUTIONARY ACTION) (CSAR) Sinister French far-right group responsible for a failed coup attempt against the Third Republic in 1937. The *Cagoulards* or 'Hooded Men' (as they were known) were led by Eugène **Deloncle** and were famed for their conspiratorial methods and fanatical anti-Communist ideology.

**COMITÉS D'ORGANISATION** Administrative bodies set up by the **Vichy** regime in August 1940 as agents of French economic planning.

**COMITÉS SOCIAUX (SOCIAL COMMITTEES)** Bodies set up to arbitrate on wages and related issues as part of **Vichy**'s corporate economic structure.

**COMMITTEE FOR TRUTH IN HISTORY** Revisionist body set up to enquire further into the 'reality' of the **Holocaust**.

**COMMUNIÓN TRADICIONALISTA (TRADITIONALIST COMMUNION) (CT)** Arch-conservative movement born in nineteenth-century Spain (also known as Carlism). Strongly Catholic and counter-revolutionary, the Carlists are viewed by some as the first Spanish fascists. During the 1936–9 Civil War, they offered massive support to the Nationalists and in April 1937 **Franco** oversaw the merger of Carlism and Falangism, thus creating the *Movimiento Nacional*. Carlism lost its independence but through Franco was able to achieve many of its long-standing ideological goals.

**COMMUNISM** Totalitarian Marxist dictatorship, such as that established in the Soviet Union. The term can also refer to a utopian egalitarian society following a period of 'socialist construction'. Fascists identified Communist parties as the primary enemy in world politics. Communism was also a focus for rivalry and competition, since it offered an alternative model of radical social engineering using totalitarian structures and modern technologies.

**CONCENTRATION CAMPS** Used by the Nazis as prisons for opponents and enemies of the regime – Jews, Communists, homosexuals, **gypsies** and anti-**Hitler** agitators. Camps were built at Dachau, Ravensbruck, Sachsenhausen, Oranienburg, Belsen and Buchenwald, and also in Austria, Czechoslovakia, Holland and Poland. They were all under *Schutzstaffel* (SS) control. Some prisoners were exploited as slave labour; others were used as guinea pigs in medical experiments. Concentration camps were designed as 'way stations' on the road to extermination centres, but during the war many camps were turned into the latter.

**CONCORDAT** Compromise agreement between the Italian state and Catholic Church, as heralded by the 1929 Lateran Treaty.

**CONFEDERACIÓN ESPAÑOLA DE DERECHAS AUTÓNOMAS (SPANISH CONFEDERATION OF AUTONOMOUS RIGHTIST GROUPS) (CEDA)** Founded in March 1933 and led by **Gil Robles**, CEDA was a right-wing movement embodying both radical and reactionary positions. At heart it was Catholic, nationalist, anti-liberal and anti-Communist; significantly, it was also supportive of corporative ideas. However, it saw itself not as a fascist group but as a rival to emerging fascist movements.

**CONFÉDÉRATION FRANÇAISE DES TRAVAILLEURS CHRÉTIENS** French trade union suppressed by **Vichy** decree of November 1940.

**CONFÉDÉRATION GÉNÉRALE DU PATRONAT** French employers' organisation suppressed by **Vichy** decree of November 1940.

**CONFÉDÉRATION GÉNÉRALE DU TRAVAIL** French trade union suppressed by **Vichy** decree of November 1940.

**CONFEDERATION OF CIVIL WAR VETERANS** Spanish organisation that has become associated with the far right.

**CONFEDERATION OF INDEPENDENT PO-LAND (KPN)** Movement of the mainstream right that has taken inter-war dictator **Pilsudski** as its role model.

**CONFEDERAZIONE GENERAL DEL LAVORO (GENERAL CONFEDERATION OF LABOUR)** Italian trade union organisation founded in 1904. **Mussolini**'s Fascists reached an agreement with it in 1921.

**CONFEDERAZIONE GENERALE DELLE CORPORAZIONI FASCISTE** Early Italian corporatist body that was dissolved in 1928.

**CONFEDERAZIONE ITALIANA SINDACATI NAZIONALI LAVORATORI (ITALIAN CONFEDERATION OF NATIONAL WORKERS' UNIONS) (CISNAL)** Body affiliated to the Italian *Movimento Sociale Italiano* (MSI).

**CONFINDUSTRIA** High-profile and influential association of businessmen in **Mussolini**'s Italy.

**CONQUISTA DEL ESTADO, LA** Movement assumed by some to be the first example of Spanish fascism in action.

**CONSERVATISM** A political orientation that emphasises the preservation of things of value from the past. As such, it has been associated with the right and centre-right. However, the concept has specific meanings in different countries and time periods, depending on local political culture. Conservatives usually support the capitalist system, but often disagree on the relative importance of the state and community. AngloAmerican conservatives have inherited elements of economic liberalism or libertarianism (or in some cases both) from the **New Right** in the US. European conservative parties remain more centrist and statist. Their opposition to violent and revolutionary upheavals and to the wholesale overturning of social institutions pitted conservatives against ra-

dical fascism. On the other hand, appeals to anti-Communism, **nationalism** and some elements of tradition attracted many **middle-class** conservatives to far-right parties, both in the inter-war years and in post-**Cold War** Europe.

**CONSERVATIVE PHILOSOPHY GROUP** Controversial cell within the British Conservative Party.

**CONSERVATIVE REVOLUTION** Ambiguous slogan used by various far-right movements and regimes to sum up their political and economic agenda (e.g. the French *Action Française* (AF)). More generally, the concept of Conservative Revolution has its origins in the writings of German theorists, **Jung** and **Jünger**, and others.

**CONSIGLIO DELLE CORPORAZIONI FASCISTE** Official title of the Minister of Corporations in Fascist Italy.

**CONSORZIO SOVVENZIONI VALORI INDUSTRIALI (CSVI)** Italian organisation that gave significant financial assistance to industry and banks during the Fascist period.

**CONTINENTALISM** Current of thought in early twentieth-century Japanese foreign policy that saw expansion into China and North-East Asia as essential to national security. It was especially prominent after the 1905 Russo-Japanese War and was also a key motivating force behind expansionism in **Manchuria** and southern China in the 1930s. Continentalism was partly a response to the increased activity of European powers, Russia and the US in East Asia after 1890.

**CONTRAS** A loose coalition of armed right-wing groups fighting the left-wing Sandinista regime in Nicaragua during the 1980s. Some genuinely feared that the Sandinistas wanted to establish a Cuban-style dictatorship and envisaged a democratic future; others were merely the agents of the old authoritarian regime toppled by the Sandinistas. Several Contra factions committed serious human rights violations in the civil war. The Contras were largely funded by the US through covert CIA operations. They were gradually disbanded following the electoral defeat of the Sandinistas in 1990.

**CORPORATISM** The collective management of the economy by employers, workers' representatives and state officials using formal mechanisms at national level. As an idea it originated in medieval **Catholicism** and the guild system, and was heavily influenced by Catholic social teaching and strengthened by Papal encyclicals, specifically *Quadragessimo Anno* in 1931; it was also viewed as a counter to the class conflict encouraged by Marxist and socialist parties. In the fascist conception, the Corporate State was designed to bring employers, employees and party officials together to control and arbitrate upon the economic life of the nation. All the key fascist regimes made varying efforts in this area; in practice, however, participation in, and conduct of, the resulting corporations was imposed on the parties, with unions having less autonomy than the employers. It usually served as a smokescreen behind which employers and party representatives could clamp down on independent trade unions to their own advantage. A more voluntary form of corporatism, commonly referred to as **neocorporatism**, influenced the 1937 Irish constitution and the Christian Democrat parties in Europe before and after the war.

**COSMOPOLITANISM** Belief in the search for universal and shared norms or values, as opposed to emphasising the importance of local or national values. Cosmopolitan historians like Friedrich Meinecke were persecuted by the Nazis for questioning

national priorities and ideologies. Given their stress on racial, ethnic or national chauvinism, most far-right movements oppose cosmopolitanism. In modern-day France, for instance, the **Front National** (FN) contrasts its own ultra-nationalist agenda with the 'subversive', 'cosmopolitan' outlook of the mainstream parties on policy matters such as **immigration**, education and nationality code reform.

**COUNTER-REVOLUTION** A backlash against a social or political revolution. If revolutionaries and revolutionary forces are assumed to be of the left, then counter-revolutionaries are assumed to be of the right. Hostility to the Revolution of 1789 played an important part in the construction of far-right politics in France during the nineteenth century and early twentieth century. In a different sense, many Marxists equate fascism to the emergence of 'counter-revolutionary forces'; and as such the term has graduated into a term of abuse.

**COUP D'ÉTAT** A military seizure of power. Coups have constituted the principal mechanism by which right-wing authoritarian regimes have come to power in Latin America.

**CRISTEROS** Reactionary mass grouping in inter-war Mexico. In 1937 it evolved into the **Unión Nacional Sinarquista**.

**CRITICA FASCISTA** Inter-war Italian journal edited by Fascist moderniser, Giuseppe **Bottai**.

**CROATIAN NATIONAL COMMITTEE** Ultra-nationalist organisation of the 1990s that merged into the NDZ.

**CROATIAN PARTY OF RIGHTS YOUTH GROUP** Ultra-nationalist movement of the 1990s. Youth wing of Paraga's movement.

**CROIX DE FEU (CF)** Inter-war French fascist movement founded in 1928 and led by Colonel de la **Rocque**. By the mid-1930s it had become the largest extra-parliamentary *ligue* in France and by 1936 had evolved into a political party – the *Mouvement Social Français*/*Parti Social Français* (MSF/PSF). Paramilitary in style and tone, the organisation was conceived as a giant ex-servicemen's association. It demanded a stronger Republic and in its approach to politics emphasised notions of discipline, **patriotism** and courage. At one point in the mid-1930s it claimed to have over 2 million members. It was feared by the left.

**CROIX GAMMÉE** French phrase for **Swastika**.

**CRYPTO-FASCISM** Label pinned on post-war ultra-nationalist movements that on the one hand commit themselves to the 'respectable' liberal–democratic process, but on the other harbour a 'hidden' fascist agenda and style. It could be argued that the NDP in Germany and the *Front National* (FN) in France are both archetypal crypto-fascist movements.

**CULTURAL NATIONALISM** Form of **nationalism** in which the nation is defined in terms of culture, **language**, **race** and history; it is more exclusive than civic or political nationalism. Cultural ideas were especially important in the history of German nationalism in the nineteenth and twentieth centuries.

**CULTURAL PESSIMISM** Socio-political determinant of fascism's impact. It equates to 'despair' with traditional political solutions and, in fascist eyes, heralds the dawn of a new 'brighter' era (the fascist epoch).

**CYCLICAL CONCEPTION OF HISTORY** The assumption that historical trends repeat themselves over time. This contrasts with the liberal and socialist view of history as a linear process. Fascist interpretations of history are only partly cyclical, in that they assume the rebirth of all old civilisations, as in the idea of a new Roman Empire. However, they also imply that the next manifestation of the culture in question will be better than the previous one. In the context of fascism Griffin has referred to this combination of rebirth and progression as 'palingenetic nationalism'.

# D

**DANISH PEOPLE'S PARTY (DPP)** Breakaway movement from, and successor to, the Danish **Progress Party**. Formed in 1995, the DPP won more than 7 per cent of the national vote in the 1998 elections. Its political programme is a blend of anti-Europeanism and anti-multi-culturalism, but the movement has been described as 'populist' rather than 'extreme'.

**DANMARKS NATIONALSOCIALISTISKE ARBEIDER PARTI (DANISH NATIONAL SOCIALIST WORKERS' PARTY) (DNSAP)** Movement founded in 1930 and led by Frits **Clausen**, the 'Danish **Führer**'. The DNSAP had minimal electoral impact, but gained 2.1 per cent of the vote in 1943 (and thus two deputies). It aped **Hitler**'s Nazi Party but always remained an insignificant force, even during the wartime German occupation.

**DANSK SAMLING** Small radical right-wing movement active in inter-war Denmark.

**DANZIG** Polish city, now Gdansk, which became a 'free' or 'international' city under the terms of the **Versailles** settlement. It was located in the 'Polish Corridor', an area between Germany proper and East Prussia that gave Poland access to the Baltic. **Hitler** accused Poland of oppressing Germans in the city and he increased pressure on the Polish government in an effort to regain control over it. Nazi demands and Polish rejection of them formed the backdrop to Hitler's invasion of Poland in September 1939.

**DAWES PLAN** Scheme designed to schedule German reparation payments in the wake of the First World War and balance the need for German solvency with her obligation to make reparations. Implementation proved difficult and was resisted by many Germans who saw it as discriminatory and intrusive. It was replaced by the more conciliatory **Young Plan** later in the decade.

**DECADENCE** Phenomenon of moral decline condemned by social and cultural conservatives. For those on the fascist right, it has denoted unbounded **materialism**, sexual permissiveness and even licentious musical forms like jazz. For fascists, moral decline took on a particular meaning and was allegedly exacerbated by selfish **middle class** and Jewish élites who avoided hard work, sacrifice and the cleansing struggle of **war**.

**DECEMBER PROGRAMME** Initiative for German remilitarisation, designed to enable it to fight a war on several fronts (1933).

**DECOLONISATION** After the **Second World War**, far-right political groups opposed European decolonisation on the grounds that it symbolised national humiliation. In France the far right used the issue to influence the Army to undermine the stability of the Fourth Republic.

**DÉFENSE DE L'OCCIDENT** French neofascist journal edited after 1953 by Maurice **Bardèche**. It defended **collaboration** and was an early vehicle for the ideas of Alain de **Benoist**.

**DEMOCRACY** Literally, rule of the people, often understood as majority rule. Fascists had an ambivalent attitude to democracy: they believed that the people could not lead but needed to be led by an élite party; however, they also claimed that, since their ruling parties represented the whole nation, fascist dictatorships were actually a novel form of democracy. Fascists dismissed existing liberal democratic systems as mere 'plutocracies' dominated by wealthy Jews and unrepresentative élites.

**DEMOCRAZIA NAZIONALE (NATIONAL DE-MOCRACY) (DN)** Breakaway party from the Italian *Movimento Sociale Italiano* (MSI). DN wanted to cultivate a more 'respectable' image than its parent movement.

**DEMO-LIBERALISM** Term used by fascists to denote their two main enemies: 'democratic proletarian socialism' and 'bourgeois liberalism'.

**DENAZIFICATION** The process of purging Nazi sympathisers from positions of power and influence in post-war Germany. The exercise was controversial because it was not implemented in an even-handed way, with some Nazis, notably prominent scientists, being drawn into US and British military research schemes.

**DERZHAVA (GREAT POWER)** Russian political bloc dating from 1995 comprising ex-Communist and nationalist forces associated with Alexander **Rutskoi**. The term also refers to the cult of Russia as a great power under both the Tsars and Stalin.

**DÉSAPARECIDOS (THE DISAPPEARED)** Victims of right-wing military dictatorship in Latin America – most notably in Chile, Uruguay and Argentina – who were presumed kidnapped by military death squads in the 1970s and 1980s but whose remains have not been found.

**DEUS PATRIA FAMILIA (GOD, COUNTRY, FAMILY)** Newspaper of the Portuguese *Frente Académica Patriotica* (FAP) movement in the 1940s.

**DEUTSCHE ADELSGENOSSENSCHAFT (DAG)** Aristocratic movement that dabbled in **anti-Semitism** in the 1920s and offered support to **Hitler** in the 1930s.

**DEUTSCHE AKTIONS GRUPPEN (GERMAN ACTION GROUP)** Anti-immigrant movement operational in West Germany during the 1980s.

**DEUTSCHE ALTERNATIVE (DA)** Small German neo-Nazi movement formed by **Kühnen** in 1989.

**DEUTSCHE ARBEITERPARTEI (GERMAN WORKERS' PARTY) (DAP)** (1) German movement led by Anton **Drexler**. Founded in 1918, it pre-dated Nazism in its political ideas, and its racist, anti-capitalist programme attracted the support of many *Völkisch* groups. **Hitler** spent his formative political years as a member of the party. It was relaunched as the *Nationalsozialistische Deutsche Arbeiterpartei* (NSDAP) in 1920. (2) Movement formed in 1904 that acted as a vehicle for early nationalsocialist ideas in Austria. It evolved into the **DNSAP** in 1918.

**DEUTSCHE ARBEITS FRONT (GERMAN LABOUR FRONT) (DAF)** State corporatist body set up by **Hitler** in 1933 and headed by Robert **Ley**. The DAF aimed to bring employers and employees together and re-volutionise many other aspects of the German economic system. In practice, however, it did very little except smash the trade union movement; it had little independence and simply became a vehicle for Nazi **propaganda**. Membership figures were impressive, but only because attachment to the DAF was compulsory.

**DEUTSCHE AUFBAU PARTEI (GERMAN CONSTRUCTION PARTY) (DAP)** Constituent element of the far-right *Deutsche Rechtspartei* (DReP) coalition movement established in 1946.

**DEUTSCHE BANK** Organisation that, in a financial sense, benefited enormously from **Hitler's autarchy** policy.

**DEUTSCHE BAUERN- UND LANDVOLK-PARTEI (GERMAN FARMERS' AND PEASANTS' PARTY) (DB-LP)** Constituent element of the far-right *Deutsche Rechtspartei* (DReP) coalition movement established in 1946.

**DEUTSCHE BÜRGER INITIATIVE (GERMAN CITIZENS' INITIATIVE) (DBI)** Militant grouping led by Manfred Roeder that supported neo-Nazi activity in West Germany in the 1980s.

**DEUTSCHE FRAUEN FRONT (GERMAN WOMEN'S FRONT) (DFF)** Small neo-Nazi women's group led by Ursula Müller.

**DEUTSCHE KONSERVATIVE PARTEI (GERMAN CONSERVATIVE PARTY) (DKP)** Founded in 1946 and heir to the *Deutsche National Volks Partei* (DNVP). Its manifesto bore the odd trace of Nazism, and some ex-*Nationalsozialistische Deutsche Arbeiterpartei* (NSDAP) members did support the movement. The DKP was part of the 1946 *Deutsche Rechtspartei* (DReP) coalition and in 1950 merged to form the German Reich Party.

**DEUTSCHE LIGA FÜR VOLK UND HEIMAT (DLVH)** Founded in 1991, an offshoot of the German *Republikaner* movement.

**DEUTSCHE NATIONAL VOLKS PARTEI (GERMAN NATIONAL PEOPLE'S PARTY) (DNVP)** Conservative–authoritarian movement founded in 1919. Throughout the 1920s it was at the forefront of anti-Weimar politics and won almost one hundred parliamentary seats in 1924. Its **nationalism** was both *Völkisch* and anti-Semitic in character; but as a party it was devoid of the radical cutting edge and mass appeal that characterised genuine fascism. In the 1930s, under the leadership of **Hugenberg**, the DNVP supported the Nazi Party.

**DEUTSCHE NATIONAL ZEITUNG** Newspaper of the German *Deutsche Volks Union* (DVU).

**DEUTSCHE NATIONALISTEN (DN)** German movement founded in 1993 that called for the compulsory repatriation of foreigners. Its leader was Michael Petri.

**DEUTSCHE RECHTSPARTEI (GERMAN RIGHTS PARTY) (DReP)** First significant attempt at a post-war Nazi-style movement. Founded in 1946, it was a coming together of the *Deutsche Konservative Partei* (DKP), *Deutsche Aufbau Partei* (DAP) and *Deutsche Bauern- und Landvolk-Partei* (DB-Lp), and found reasonable favour in northern Germany. Advancing a nationalist–monarchist programme, it won five Bundestag seats in the late 1940s.

**DEUTSCHE REICHSPARTEI (GERMAN REICH PARTY) (DRP)** Neo-Nazi movement formed in the aftermath of the **Second World War**. It took its name from a late nineteenth-century political movement and – even when it was a dangerous/illegal strategy – publicly expounded its admiration for certain aspects of Nazism (and boasted many ex-Nazis in its ranks). It won the odd local election seat but never scored more than 1.1 per cent in national polls. The successor movement to the *Deutsche Konservative Partei* (DKP) and *Deutsche Rechtspartei* (DReP), it even-

tually disbanded in 1964 and split into the DRP and *Sozialistische Reichspartei* (SRP).

**DEUTSCH-RUSSISCHES GEMEINSCHAFTS-WERK-FÖRDERVEREIN NORD-OSTPREUS-SEN (DRGW-FNOP)** Far-right support group that aims to help ethnic Germans resident in the ex-USSR.

**DEUTSCHE STIMME** Influential *National Demokratische Partei Deutschlands* (NPD) journal of the 1980s.

**DEUTSCHE VÖLKISCHE PARTEI** Anti-Semitic movement active in pre-1914 Germany.

**DEUTSCHE VÖLKISCHER SCHUTZ- UND TRUTZBUND** Pan-German League programme of 1919: highly nationalistic, anti-leftist and 'anti-system'.

**DEUTSCHE VOLKS UNION (GERMAN PEOPLES' UNION) (DVU)** Arguably the most important far-right group in post-war Germany. At times it has claimed to have more then 20,000 members. Fiercely anti-immigrant, the DVU was founded as an association in 1971 by Dr Gerhard **Frey** and in 1987 evolved into an overtly electoral force – *Deutsche Volks Union/Liste D*. As such it is viewed by some as a good example of '**crypto-fascism**'. It has a fraught relationship with the *Republikaner* movement.

**DEUTSCHE WOCHEN-ZEITUNG** Weekly paper of **Frey**'s *Deutsche Volks Union* (DVU).

**DEUTSCHER KAMERADSCHAFTSBUND (DKB)** Small xenophobic movement founded in Germany in 1991.

**DEUTSCHES JUNGVOLK (DJ)** Nazi organisation for boys aged 10–14.

**DEVENIR EUROPÉEN** Post-war Euro-fascist group based in France.

**DICTATORSHIP** Rule by an unelected or unaccountable person or institution that can dictate terms to society according to its arbitrary preferences. Fascist movements traditionally extolled the virtues of dictatorship and the weaknesses or inadequacies of democracy. However, neo-fascist and post-fascist movements have tried to distance themselves from a preoccupation with dictatorship.

**DIETSLAND-EUROPA** Journal associated with the post-war Flemish nationalist movement, **Were Di**.

**DIFFERENTIALISM** Modern term used to denote the anti-egalitarian philosophy favoured by fascists and neo-fascists.

**DIORAMA LETTERARIO** Italian **New Right** publication – with *Movimento Sociale Italiano* (MSI) connections.

**DIREKTE AKTION/MITTEL DEUTSCHLAND (DA/MD)** Far-right German group established in 1993.

**DIRIGISME** Detailed and intrusive state direction of the economy and/or society. Dirigisme was central to both fascist and Communist systems. However, in the case of fascism, there was no requirement for outright state ownership of the means of production, so long as the economy could be harnessed to serve what fascists deemed to be the 'national interest'.

**DIVENIRE SOCIALE, IL** Neo-syndicalist periodical published in Italy prior to 1914.

**DNSAP** Party founded in 1918 (formerly the DAP). It was in effect the 'Austrian Nazi Party'. The DNSAP was beset by internal quarrels and lacked a charismatic leader. In 1926 it became the *National-sozialistische Deutsche Arbeiterpartei* (NSDAP).

**DORADOS (GOLDSHIRTS)** Nickname of Mexican movement, *Acción Revolucionaria Mexicana*.

**DRANCY** Paris suburb where German occupation forces and their agents constructed what became their most notorious concentration and transit camp in France during the **Second World War**.

**DREUX** Unremarkable town 30 miles west of Paris where **Le Pen's** *Front National* (FN) made its political breakthrough in 1983 – and where Marie-France **Stirbois** won a parliamentary by-election for the party in 1989. Both events sent shockwaves through the French political establishment.

**DREYFUS AFFAIR** High-level political scandal that tore France in two in the 1890s and helped to catalyse far-right activity in many spheres. Most notably, it led directly to the founding of the *Action Française* (AF) – arguably an example of early French fascism.

**DUCISMO Leadership cult** – hence *Il Duce*, **Mussolini**'s nickname. Both terms originate from the Latin *dux*.

# E

**EAST ASIAN CO-PROSPERITY SPHERE** Term used by Japanese militarists (mainly during the **Second World War**) to describe their would-be sphere of influence in East Asia. It was designed to appeal to Asian solidarity against European 'imperialists'; in practice, it referred to the projected area of Japanese political, economic and military hegemony in the Far East and the western Pacific. It was a concept derived from imperialist thought and was not specifically fascist.

**ECO-FASCISM** Alternative name for **Green fascism**.

**ECONOMIC NATIONALISM** Umbrella term that, for fascists, denotes a range of economic approaches including one or several of the following: **protectionism**, **autarchy** and **corporatism**.

**ECONOMIC SELF-SUFFICIENCY** The aim of many fascist states and movements, particularly in the context of preparing for a war situation. Also referred to as **autarchy**.

**EDELWEISS PIRATES** Opposition group to **Hitler**. It catered for young people – mostly of a Communist or **working-class** background – and caused some embarrassment to the regime. It was not particularly well organised but was still viewed as 'deviant' by the Nazi authorities, and many of its members were consequently executed.

**EE (UNION OF NATIONALLY MINDED)** Reactionary anti-Communist movement active in 1940s Greece.

**EESTI VABADUSSÕJALASTE LIIT (ESTONIAN WAR OF INDEPENDENCE VETERANS' LEAGUE) (EVL)** Fascist group that emerged out of Estonia's 1918–20 independence war against Russia. It was founded officially in 1929.

**EGALITARIANISM** Belief in the essential equality of all human beings and the need for policies to promote equality of opportunity and/or equality of outcome. It is a feature of many strands of philosophical, sociological and religious thought, notably **socialism**, feminism and some variants of **liberalism**, and also a key theme in the discourse of the French and Russian revo-

lutions. It is generally opposed by fascists and far-right groups who view **élitism**, racial superiority or the hegemony of the strongest as higher values. Modern neoconservatives and some liberals acknowledge the equal dignity of all human beings but are sceptical of policies designed to privilege the systematic and coercive pursuit of equality over other values like personal freedom.

**ELECTORAL FASCISM** Label pinned on modern 'fascist' movements that minimise their 'revolutionary' attacks on liberal democracy. The *Movimento Sociale Italiano* (MSI) in Italy and *Front National* (FN) in France are good examples.

**ELEFTEROFRONOI (FREE BELIEVERS) (EL)** Party of Greek General, Ionnis Metaxas. EL subtly aped **Hitler** and **Mussolini** – it believed in censorship, terror and **authoritarianism** – and also bore some resemblance to integral nationalist movements of the same era in other countries. Its ultimate aim was a totalitarian system. In 1932 the EL won two seats in the national parliament.

**ELEMENTI** Italian **New Right** journal promoting the notion of cultural and national renaissance.

**ELÉMENTS** Journal of the *Groupement de Recherche et d'Étude pour la Civilisation Européennes* (GRECE) movement in post-war France.

**ÉLITISM** (1) A belief in the desirability of rule by élites, as opposed to the masses. Élites can be selected on the basis of competences or qualities that make them fit to rule, or by criteria such as class, **race** or **religion**. (2) A sociological theory that predicts the emergence of élites (i.e. groups of people holding a concentration of power, whatever the intentions of social planners or constitutional lawyers). This approach does not necessarily endorse élite rule, although Vilfredo **Pareto**, one of its most important theorists, did. Fascists were influenced by both concepts. Indeed, they used, or misused, the sociological theories to make a case for hierarchical and racist political structures, believing themselves to be eminently fit to rule over others. Moreover, in **Hitler**'s case, **eugenics** and indoctrination were used in a most systematic way to reproduce and allegedly improve the 'quality' and 'purity' of the élite 'Master Race' and its leadership cadres.

**ELLINIKO ETHNIK KOMMA (GREEK NATIONAL SOCIALIST PARTY) (EEK)** Small 1930s fascist movement led by ex-royalist George Merkouris.

**ELLINIKOS KOSMOS (GREEK WORLD)** Newspaper of the *Ethniki Politiki Enosis* (EPEN) movement in 1980s Greece.

**EMANCIPATION NATIONALE, L'** Newspaper of **Doriot**'s *Parti Populaire Français* (PPF).

**ENABLING ACT** Law that consolidated the Nazis' hold on power. Passed in March 1933, it created a situation in which **Hitler** was no longer accountable to the Reichstag, and thus marked the transition from democracy to dictatorship. Within months the Nazi Party was the only legal political movement in Germany.

**ENCICLOPEDIA ITALIANA** The 1932 version of this publication included **Gentile**'s celebrated definition of Italian Fascism.

**ENDLÖSUNG (FINAL SOLUTION)** Phrase used by the Nazis to describe the **Holocaust**.

**ENGLISH NATIONALIST MOVEMENT** Contemporary 'Third Positionist' organisation.

**ENLIGHTENMENT** Historical period, culminating in the late eighteenth century, during which rational and scientific methods replaced **religion** as the basis of knowledge, and the values of individual liberty, equality and elements of democracy came to prominence in Western thought. Associated with the ideals of the French and American revolutions, its principles were questioned by nineteenth-century cultural conservatives and thinkers in the Romantic movement. It was fiercely criticised by fascists and the far right, who saw it as the source of problems linked to radicalism, sexual permissiveness and the collapse of social order in the twentieth century.

**ENOMENO ETHNIKO KINEMA (UNITED NATIONALIST MOVEMENT) (ENEK)** Greek national-socialist grouping founded in 1979. It polled less than 0.25 per cent at both the 1984 and 1989 European elections.

**ENOSIS NEON AXIOMATIKON (UNION OF JUNIOR OFFICERS) (ENA)** Ultra-royalist movement in 1940s Greece.

**ENTE NAZIONALE DI ASSISTENZA (NATIONAL WELFARE ASSOCIATION) (ENAS)** Affiliate body of the Italian *Movimento Sociale Italiano* (MSI).

**ENTE NAZIONALE IDROCARBURI (ENI)** Giant state oil company established by **Mussolini**.

**ERGÄNZUNGSGEBIETE** Term used by **Hitler** to sum up the notion of client states in Eastern Europe.

**ERSATZ FASCISM** Alternative term to substitute-, bogus-, or **pseudo-fascism**.

**ESTABLISHMENT** Concept used by radical theorists to describe an assumed power élite in a given society. The nature, existence or power of a cohesive establishment is contested by writers from other perspectives. Fascists portrayed the establishment as consisting of liberal, socialist and, in some cases, Jewish élites whose interests were incompatible with those of 'ordinary people' and the nation. Many Marxians assume a convergence of interests between fascists and the capitalist élite that constitutes the establishment in their paradigm. Institutionalist approaches to politics define the civil service, the **armed forces** and monarchies as the core of the establishment. Traditional élites in Germany, Italy, Hungary and Romania frequently collaborated with fascists to counter socialist opposition forces or in the belief that they could co-opt and tame them.

**ESTADO NOVO (NEW STATE) (EN)** (1) Corporate structure established by **Salazar** in Portugal in 1934. Its title suggested radicalism, but in reality the EN was exactly the opposite: conservative, backward and devoid of modern ambition. Influenced by **Maurras** and the *Action Française* (AF), it was both un-fascist and anti-fascist, and ultimately tried to destroy the authentically fascist *Nacional Sindicalismo* (NS) **Blueshirts**; (2) Corporate structure established by **Vargas** as Brazilian President during the period 1937–45.

**ESTAT CATALÀ** Semi-fascist separatist movement active in inter-war Catalonia.

**ETELKÖZ ASSOCIATION (EKSZ)** Ultra-patriotic Hungarian secret society that liaised with **Hitler** in an effort to overthrow inter-war leader, **Horthy**. It was founded in Hungary in 1919.

**ETHNIC CLEANSING** Systematic displacement of large numbers of people of one ethnic group to make way for another, usually through destruction of property, mass terror and atrocities. The term is primarily linked to regional inter-ethnic conflicts in the 1990s, but arguably the phenomenon has a longer history and could be applied to instances of displacement, terror and **colonialism** associated with some fascist and far-right regimes.

**ETHNIC NATIONALISM** An ideology that defines a nation as a community bound together by a shared ethnic or racial identity. It is similar to **cultural nationalism** but not as inclusive as civic or political nationalism.

**ETHNIC TRANSFERS** Inevitable product of post-1945 territorial change in Europe. Ethnic transfers helped to fuel the growth of **ultra-nationalism** and armed conflict in the decades following the ending of the war.

**ETHNICITY** Membership of, or association with, a particular racial or tribal group. Racist and fascist groups may use it as a basis for processes of inclusion, exclusion or discrimination.

**ETHNIKI DEMOKRATIKI ENOSIS (NATIONAL DEMOCRATIC UNION) (EDE)** Far-right monarchist party that just broke through the 1 per cent barrier in the 1974 Greek elections. Led by Petros **Garoufalias**, it had military connections but existed only briefly.

**ETHNIKI NEMESIS (NATIONAL NEMESIS) (EN)** Pro-fascist movement active in 1940s Greece.

**ETHNIKI ORGANOSSIS NEOLAIAS (NATIONAL YOUTH ORGANISATION) (EON)** Fascist youth movement set up by Greek leader General **Metaxas** in the late 1930s.

**ETHNIKI PARATAXIS (NATIONAL ALIGNMENT) (EP)** Ultra-royalist Greek movement founded in 1977 and led by ex-Prime Minister, Stephanos **Stephanopoulos**. It displayed nostalgia for the former military **junta** and a dislike for **democracy**, even though it won five out of 300 seats in the 1977 elections.

**ETHNIKI PARATAXIS ERGAZOMENOU LAOU (NATIONAL ALIGNMENT OF THE WORKING PEOPLE) (EPEL)** Greek far-right movement that scored almost 2 per cent in the 1950 elections.

**ETHNIKI POLITIKI ENOSIS (NATIONAL PO-LITICAL UNION) (EPEN)** Greek far-right movement formed in the mid-1980s. It had little time for parliament and looked back on the 1967 military coup with favour. Anti-Communist and anti-Semitic, it gained one MEP in the 1984 elections.

**ETHNIKISTIKI ENOSIS ELLADOS (NATIO-NAL UNION OF GREECE) (EEE)** Small militaristic and anti-Semitic movement formed in 1927 and based in Macedonia. It disappeared in 1933 only to re-emerge in 1940 after the German invasion. Although it had *c.* 7,000 members (1931), it performed abysmally in the January 1936 elections.

**ETHNIKO AGROTIKO KOMMA HITON (NATIONAL AGRARIAN X PARTY)** Greek extreme-right organisation that polled just under 1 per cent in the 1950 elections.

**ETHNIKO KINIMA NEON EPISTIMONON (NATIONAL MOVEMENT OF YOUNG SCIEN-TISTS) (EKNE)** Para-state organ formed by the Greek military **junta** in the mid-1970s.

**ETHNIKO KOMMA (NATIONAL PARTY) (EK)** Extreme-right coalition that scored 0.1 per cent in the 1990 Greek elections. Its political programme was a blend of economic liberalism and anti-Muslim **ultra-nationalism**.

**ETHNIKOSOCIALISTIKO KOMMA MAKE-DONIAS KAI THRAKIS (NATIONAL SOCIA-LIST PARTY OF MACEDONIA AND** **THRACE) (EKM)** Greek far-right movement of the 1930s.

**ETHNOCENTRISM** Insensitivity to the concerns, histories or identities of other cultural or ethnic groups. It is a term frequently invoked by radical, feminist and post-modernist critiques of Western history and social science.

**ETHNOCRATIC STATE** A racial state devoted to the advancement of one ethnic or racial group at the expense of others. In such states race policies, including legislation in support of **eugenics**, discrimination or hate **propaganda**, hold a central place and take precedence over all other considerations. In recent times, the concept has been appropriated as an important theme in the discourse of the Greater Romania Party.

**EUGENICS** Scientific approach to reproduction of stronger people by selective breeding. It was popular, albeit for different reasons, among both European social democratic reformers and racial theorists of the 1920s and 1930s. The Nazis practised eugenics for the purpose of purifying and consolidating a so-called 'Master Race' of **Aryan** and German stock.

**EUROFASCISM** Brand of fascism that emerged in 1951 at the pan-European **Malmö Congress**. Eurofascist doctrine was based around anti-Communism, **anti-Semitism** and belief in a regenerated Europe.

**EUROPAE** Official publication of the *Nouvel Ordre Européen* (NOE).

**EUROPE-ACTION** Short-lived French neo-fascist group led by Dominique Venner. It emerged out of *Jeune Nation* in 1960 and originally took the form of a monthly journal. It was anti-Communist and gradually moved from violent **nationalism** to a more legal Europeanism.

**EUROPE DES PATRIES (EUROPE OF NATIONS)** The non-federal dream of many far-right and neo-fascist groups, including **Le Pen**'s *Front National* (FN).

**EUROPE RÉELLE, L'** Brussels-based publication of the *Nouvel Ordre Européen* (NOE).

**EUROPEAN, THE** Journal associated with **British Union of Fascists** (BUF) leader, Oswald **Mosley**.

**EUROPEAN ELITE** Journal of post-war French movement, *Ordre Nouveau*.

**EUROPEAN NOTEBOOKS** Post-war French far-right publication.

**EUROPEAN PARLIAMENT (EP)** Legislature of the European Union. In recent decades it has been home to a significant far-right grouping. At the same time it has also published a range of 'warning' studies on the rise of **neo-fascism** in contemporary Europe (including the *Ford Report* and the *Evrigenis Report*).

**EUROPEAN SOCIAL MOVEMENT** Alternative name for the Eurofascist 'International' established at Malmö in 1951.

**EUROPESE SOCIALE BEWEGING (ESB)** Pan-European far-right movement founded in 1951.

**EUTHANASIA** Medical intervention designed to kill ageing or terminally ill people. It was used by the Nazis to eliminate physically and mentally handicapped people so as to ensure a strong and healthy stock of Germans for reproductive purposes.

**EVERYTHING FOR THE COUNTRY PARTY** Political organisation associated with the Legion and Iron Guard in 1930s Romania.

**EXÉRCITO DE LIBERTAÇÃO NACIONAL (PORTUGUESE LIBERATION ARMY) (ELP)** Anti-Communist terror group associated with Spinola's *Movimento Democrático de Libertação Nacional* (MDLP) in the mid-1970s. It displayed some nostalgia for the former authoritarian dictatorship.

**EXHIBITION OF THE FASCIST REVOLUTION** Event held in Italy to mark the tenth anniversary of the **March on Rome**.

**EXTERMINATION CAMPS** The Nazis' enemies were initially housed in **concentration camps**, then moved into extermination centres. Estimates suggest that over 6 million people were killed in them overall.

# F

**FAIRE FRONT** Extreme-right (but anti-**Le Pen**) movement that emerged out of *Ordre Nouveau* in France in 1973.

**FAISCEAU, LE** French movement active between 1925 and 1927, and hailed as the first non-Italian fascist organisation. It was founded by *Action Française* (AF) dissident Georges **Valois**, and espoused an original mix of syndicalist, nationalist and corporatist ideas. The group – which idolised **Mussolini** and attracted many ex-AF members – also boasted a powerful paramilitary arm.

**FAISCEAUX NATIONAUX ET EUROPÉENS (FNE)** French movement of the 1970s which attempted to resurrect the spirit of 1930s-style fascism. It was formerly known as the *Féderation d'Action Natio-nale et Européenne* (FANE).

**FALANGE** (1) Long-standing right-wing party and **militia** movement of the Lebanese Christian community. It was a powerful force in Lebanese politics, especially in the 1970s and 1980s. Opponents charge that the Falangists were key players in the massacre of Palestinians by Christian militia forces at the refugee camps of Chabra and Chatilla in 1982, as a reprisal for the assassination of the Falangist leader, Bashir Gemayel. (2) Chilean movement formed in 1938 – far more liberal and moderate than the Spanish *Falange*.

**FALANGE ESPAÑOLA (SPANISH PHALANX) (FE)** The FE was born in 1933 and in 1934 merged with *Juntas de Ofensiva Nacional-Sindicalista* (JONS) to form *FE de las JONS*. It gained 0.7 per cent of the vote in the 1936 elections and in its early years was led by José Antonio **Primo de Rivera** and Manuel **Hedilla**. Under General **Franco** it supported the military revolt of 1936 against the Second Republic and became the major force on the Nationalist right during the Civil War. It believed in **corporatism** and traditional **nationalism** (but not **anti-Semitism**) and went on to take part in **Fascist International** meetings. In 1937 Franco fused the *FE de las JONS* with the Carlist movement to create the organisation viewed thereafter as Franco's main support base or 'Spain's official fascist party'.

**FALANGE ESPAÑOLA (AUTÉNTICA) (AUTHENTIC SPANISH PHALANX) (FEA)** Far-right organisation active in 1970s Spain that laid claim to being the 'true' successor to **Franco**'s political movement.

**FALANGE ESPAÑOLA (INDEPENDIENTE) (INDEPENDENT SPANISH PHALANX) (FEI)** Spanish far-right group of the 1970s that

took part in the 1977 *Junta Coordinadora Nacional Sindicalista* (JCNS) coalition.

**FALANGE ESPAÑOLA DE LAS JUNTAS DE OFENSIVA NACIONAL-SINDICALISTA (FE DE LAS JONS)** Far-right Spanish organisation formed in 1934 after the merger of the *Falange Española* (FE) and the *Juntas de Ofensiva Nacional-Sindicalista* (JONS).

**FALANGE ESPAÑOLA TRADICIONALISTA (FET)** Francoist movement set up by Spanish ex-pats in 1930s Mexico.

**FALANGE ESPAÑOLA TRADICIONALISTA Y DE LAS JUNTAS DE OFENSIVA NACIONAL-SINDICALISTA (SPANISH TRADITIONALIST PHALANX OF COMMITTEES FOR NATIONAL SYNDICALIST ATTACK) (FET Y DE LAS JONS)** Far-right Spanish group formed in 1937 after the merger of the *FE de las JONS* and the Carlist movement. Under **Franco** it developed into the official state party but had no real power or independence, and gradually lost influence. 'Falangism' emerged as a unique brand of authoritarian **conservatism** and was used strategically by Franco to give his regime a modern, radical image. Thus, Franco's dictatorship was only para-fascist at best.

**FALANGE SOCIALISTA BOLIVIANA (FSB)** Bolivian movement founded in 1935 and led by de la Vega. It aimed to establish a national-syndicalist state along Spanish lines but gradually recoiled into the moderate centre.

**FAMILY** Viewed by social and cultural conservatives as the primary unit in society, and normally defined in terms of nuclear family with husband, wife and children. Fascists competed with social conservative and Christian parties in advocacy of policies to sustain the traditional family but also invested it with the function of reproducing the nation, both in terms of babies and in the transmission of nationalist ideology.

**FAMILY IMPERIALISM** Theory that stresses the 'father-like' **authoritarianism** of fascism.

**FASCES** The symbol of Italian Fascism – an axe bound in rods. This image originated in Ancient Rome and was not only appropriated by **Mussolini**, but **Pétain** in France as well. *Fascio* equates to 'bundle' in Italian; hence the plural *fasci*.

**FASCI DI AZIONE RIVOLUZIONARIA (FAR)** Network of neo-syndicalist associations active in the years prior to **Mussolini**'s seizure of power. Commentators view them as proto-Fascist in nature.

**FASCI DI COMBATTIMENTO** Name of **Mussolini**'s first political grouping – established in March 1919. Its early political agenda included commitments to abolish the monarchy and introduce a maximum eight-hour day for workers. The movement also boasted a violent paramilitary arm. By 1920 it claimed to have more than 200,000 members and in 1921 evolved into the *Partito Nazionale Fascista* (PNF).

**FASCI GIOVANILI** Youth organisations set up by **Mussolini**'s Fascist movement.

**FASCISANT** Alternative to 'para-fascist'.

**FASCISMO** 'Spirit' of early twentieth-century Italian Fascism.

**FASCIST GAZETTE** Newspaper of the **National Fascists** in 1920s Britain.

**FASCIST GRAND COUNCIL** Hugely important co-ordinating body established in Italy in 1922. Six years later **Mussolini** deemed it to be the highest ranking organisation within his regime.

**FASCIST INTERNATIONAL** Worldwide organisation established at the **Malmö Congress** in 1951.

**FASCIST MINIMUM** Term used in the context of defining and explaining fascism as a concept. It denotes the core elements of the ideology.

**FASCISTI** (1) Shorthand name for **Mussolini**'s Fascist organisation. (2) Early title of the **British Fascists**.

**FASCISTISATION** Term used to denote the spread of Fascist ideology throughout Italian society via agitation and **propaganda** in primary social organisations like youth clubs, schools and workplace groups. These were to be gradually affiliated to party-related institutions and used as a conduit for ideological propaganda (and used more generally).

**FATHERLAND** Emotive term used by fascists to describe the 'spiritual' nation.

**FE** Falangist journal in inter-war Spain.

**FEBRERISTAS** Inter-war Paraguayan movement that mixed corporatist, Catholic and nationalist ideas, and attempted a seizure of power in 1936. It lacked genuine fascist credentials and evolved into a left-wing party.

**FÉDÉRATION D'ACTION NATIONALE ET EUROPÉENNE (FEDERATION OF NATIONAL AND EUROPEAN ACTION) (FANE)** French neo-fascist group active in the 1970s and led by Marc Frédériksen. It evolved into the *Faisceaux Nationaux et Européens* (FNE).

**FÉDÉRATION DES ETUDIANTS NATIONA-LISTES (FEDERATION OF NATIONALIST STUDENTS) (FEN)** French far-right grouping that supported **Tixier-Vignancourt**'s bid for the presidency in 1965. Guru of the *Nouvelle Droite*, Alain de **Benoist**, was a member of the movement.

**FÉDÉRATION NATIONALE DES JAUNES DE FRANCE** Established in 1904, this grouping was anti-Marxist, anti-Semitic and wished to attract working people away from **socialism**.

**FÉDÉRATION OUEST-EUROPÉENNE (WEST EUROPEAN FEDERATION) (FOE)** Pro-**Hitler** movement formed in 1963. FOE was part of the **World Union of National Socialists** (WUNS) coalition.

**FEDRELANDSLAGET (PATRIOTIC LEAGUE)** Semi-fascist Norwegian movement founded in 1925. Nationalist and fiercely anti-Communist, it lost support towards the end of the 1930s.

**FÊTE BLEU-BLANC-ROUGE** Annual Paris gathering of the French *Front National* (FN). The festival is designed along exactly the same lines as the Communist *Fête d'Humanité*.

**FIGARO MAGAZINE, LE** French publication in which the ideas of the *Nouvelle Droite* began to circulate in the 1980s.

**FIN DE SIÈCLE** Literally, 'end-of-century'. In the history of Europe the 1880s and 1890s, plus the first decade of the twentieth century, are associated with a revolt against **liberalism** that ultimately led to fascism. As such, the phrase *fin de siècle* has come to denote a spirit of rebellion.

**FINE GAEL** Second largest party and main opposition movement in the Republic of Ireland. It is centre-right, Christian Democrat in orientation, although it has an active social democratic and liberal left wing. At its foundation in 1932, it incorporated elements of the National Guard **'Blueshirts'**, as well as the pro-Anglo-Irish Treaty *Cumann na nGaedhal* and Centre parties. Blueshirt leader, Eoin **O'Duffy**, was official leader of *Fine Gael* until 1934, but he was seen as ineffectual and the fascist element remained subordinate to the conservative and pro-British *Cumann na nGaedhal* faction. By 1939, the party had endorsed a strategy of neutrality. From the late 1960s onwards, the left wing of the party came to prominence.

**FINNIFICATION** Ultra-nationalist aim of the Finnish *Isänmaallinen Kansanliike* (IKL) movement in the 1930s.

**FINSIDER** Giant financial body set up in Italy in 1937. It remained in operation until 1943.

**FIUME** Adriatic port – now known as Rijeka – that witnessed **D'Annunzio**'s year-long 'dress rehearsal' for fascism. This episode commenced in September 1919 and paved the way for **Mussolini**'s entrance into Italian politics.

**FLAG, THE** British **National Front** (NF) newspaper around which a significant internal party faction developed.

**FOCAL POINT** Journal of the revisionist **Focus Policy Group**.

**FOCUS POLICY GROUP** Contemporary movement associated with historian David Irving.

**FOITITIKO SOMATIO (ALL STUDENT UNION) (FS)** Greek national-socialist movement of the 1930s – fervently anti-Communist and particularly strong in Athens University.

**FOLK** Post-war far-right US publication.

**FORÇA NATIONAL-NOVA MONARQUIA (NATIONAL FORCE-NEW MONARCHY PARTY) (FN-NM)** Small Portuguese far-right youth coalition born in 1989.

**FORCES NOUVELLES** Previous name of post-war Belgian movement *Parti des Forces Nouvelles.*

**FÖRDERWERK MITTELDEUTSCHE JUGEND (SUPPORT GROUP OF CENTRAL GERMAN YOUTH) (FMJ)** Small neo-Nazi support group active in modern Germany.

**FORZA ITALIA (GO FOR IT, ITALY) (FI)** Mainstream populist Berlusconi-led alliance that befriended the *Alleanza Nazionale* (AN) in the 1990s.

**FOSTERLÄNDSKA FØRBUNDET (FATHERLAND ASSOCIATION)** Small radical right-wing movement active in inter-war Sweden.

**FOUR YEAR PLAN FOR INDUSTRY Göring**-masterminded initiative of 1936 that aimed to control all aspects of Nazi economic policy.

**FRANCISTES** Inter-war French fascist party founded by **Bucard**. Hostile to the left and all aspects of liberal democracy, it looked to **Mussolini**'s Italy rather than **Hitler**'s Germany as its guiding light (and did not absorb **anti-Semitism** into its discourse). On the whole the movement's political agenda was negative rather than positive and attracted only a small following. After 1940 the collaborationist right incorporated many *Francistes.*

**FRANCISQUE** Axe-like agricultural implement used by the ancient Gauls. The **Vichy** administration co-opted this image – symbolising strength and traditional values – as its main motif. It also awarded the *Francisque* medal to distinguished servants of the regime.

**FRANCO-PRUSSIAN WAR** Conflict of 1870–1 that helped create burning resentments among political leaders and ordinary people in France. Prussia annexed Alsace and Lorraine in 1871, a territorial adjustment that inflamed opinion and was instrumental in the birth of a new 'revolutionary', 'pre-fascist' right. Political figures such as **Boulanger** and **Barrès** based their whole nationalist outlook on issues that emerged out of the war.

**FRANKFURT SCHOOL OF CRITICAL THEORY** Academic group comprising political theorists, sociologists and social psychologists – many of a Marxist or Freudian persuasion – that was at the forefront of efforts to understand, rationalise and explain the rise of fascism in the 1930s and later. Members offered a variety of critiques, many of which are still highly influential. The group relocated to the US following **Hitler**'s seizure of power. Key Frankfurt theorists included Horkheimer, Adorno and Neumann.

**FRANQUISM (FRANCOISM)** Name given to the doctrine of Spanish conservative-fascist, General **Franco**. His ideology was a unique mixture of **authoritarianism**, **Catholicism** and state **corporatism**. *Franquism* was never totalitarian enough to be genuinely fascist, but it incorporated many fascist-style traits.

**FREE BRITAIN** Journal of the British **National Workers' Party** in the immediate post-war period.

**FREEDOM COUNCIL** German neo-Nazi support group of the 1970s, led by **Frey**.

**FREEDOM FESTIVAL** Regular event organised by the **Christian Patriot's Defence League** in modern-day America.

**FREEMASONRY** A controversial and secretive international fraternity. Members claim that it is chiefly a means of social interaction and is devoted to charity and mutual aid. In Spain, tension between Freemasonry and the Catholic Church, arising from its oaths, rituals and alleged anti-**Catholicism**, was a factor in **Franco**'s hostility to the movement. Right-wing and socially conservative Catholic parties or dictatorships have often referred to the existence of Masonic conspiracies in league with international **Communism**.

**FREIHEITLICHE DEUTSCHE ARBEITER-PARTEI (FREE GERMAN WORKERS' PARTY) (FAP)** Small modern German neo-Nazi group. Anti-foreigner and anti-democracy, the movement has contested elections but its political strategy is based primarily on violence. It has a large appeal among the German skinhead community.

**FREIHEITLICHE PARTEI ÖSTERREICHS (FREEDOM PARTY OF AUSTRIA) (FPÖ)** Austrian movement that has evolved into one of the most controversial political groupings in contemporary Europe. Founded in 1956, it has always associated itself with pan-German ideas but it was only in the mid-1980s that Jörg **Haider**'s unique brand of radical right-wing **populism** gained the ascendancy. In the 1990 federal elections, the FPÖ broke through the 15 per cent barrier for the first time; in the 1994 parliamentary poll it won 22 per cent; and in 1999 it scored 23 per cent in European elections. Although Haider has attracted notoriety for his ambivalence about the Nazi period – and the movement is shunned by important sections of opinion at home and abroad – the FPÖ has entered government at a national le-

vel. Its doctrine is now a radical blend of free-market **liberalism** and hardline anti-foreigner sentiment.

**FREIHEITLICHEN THESEN** Highly significant *Freiheitliche Partei Österreichs* (FPÖ) document published in 1993 that highlighted **Haider**'s ultra-nationalist agenda.

**FREIKORPS (FREE CORPS)** Counter-revolutionary paramilitary units that emerged in Germany in the immediate aftermath of 1918. They were manned by ex-Army officers, mercenaries and right-wing extremists; and, quite significantly, used the **Swastika** as their main symbol. The *Freikorps* helped put down the Spartakist Rising of 1919 and specialised in anarchic murder raids on left-wing targets. They also supported right-wing plots against the **Weimar Republic**.

**FRELIMO** Marxist and nationalist guerilla movement that fought Portuguese rule in Mozambique, ultimately establishing a one-party Marxist state. Frelimo was fiercely opposed by the far right.

**FRENCH REVOLUTION** Watershed political event (1789–99) inspired by *philosophes* such as Rousseau. It is an episode that far-right spokesmen – particularly in France – have been unable to ignore. While some on the extreme right 'accepted' the Revolution (**Boulanger** and **Barrès**, for example), others (like **Maurras** and **Pétain**) spent much of their political careers inveighing against it. In broader terms, the Revolution gave birth to a range of political ideas that have been rejected by many on the far right (liberty and equality, for example). There is also a school of thought that says fascist ideology has its deepest origins in the intransigent, anti-**Enlightenment** writings of counter-revolutionary theorist Joseph de Maistre.

**FRENTE** Newspaper of the Portuguese *Frente Nacional Revolucionária* (FNR).

**FRENTE ACADÉMICA PATRIOTICA (PATRI-OTIC ACADEMIC FRONT) (FAP)** Pro-**Salazar** organisation active in Portugal in the 1940s.

**FRENTE DE ESTUDANTES NACIONALISTAS (FEN)** Portuguese neo-fascist movement based in the student sector. It was active in the 1960s and published a newspaper of the same name.

**FRENTE NACIONAL (NATIONAL FRONT) (FN)** Spanish far-right movement founded in 1986 by Blas **Piñar** as successor to *Fuerza Nueva*. It tried to update and tone down Falangist–Francoist ideology but did not win any seats in the 1987 and 1989 elections.

**FRENTE NACIONAL ESPAÑOL (SPANISH NATIONAL FRONT) (FNE)** Nostalgic pro-*Falange* group of the 1970s. In 1976 it was allowed to call itself *FE de las JONS*.

**FRENTE NACIONAL REVOLUCIONÁRIA (NATIONAL REVOLUTIONARY FRONT)(FNR)** Portuguese neo-fascist grouping founded in 1966.

**FRENTE SINDICALISTA NACIONAL** Trade union body connected to the Spanish *Frente Nacional*.

**FREUNDESKREIS FREIHEIT FÜR DEUTSCH-LAND (FRIENDSHIP CIRCLE FOR FREE-DOM OF GERMANY) (FFD)** Neo-Nazi grouping founded in 1989 and banned in 1993.

**FREUNDESKREIS UNABHÄNGIGE NACHRI-CHTEN (FRIENDSHIP CIRCLE FOR INDE-PENDENT INTELLIGENCE) (FUN)** German neo-Nazi movement founded in 1969.

**FRISINNEDE FOLKEPARTI (LIBERAL PEO-PLE'S PARTY)** Norwegian conservative grouping (previously known as *Frisinnede Venstre*) that supported **Quisling**'s *Nasjonal Samling* (NS) party after 1933. It ultimately became semi-fascist in political orientation.

**FRONT DE LA JEUNESSE (FJ)** Anti-immigrant, anti-leftist movement active in French-speaking Belgium. Its paramilitary arm was outlawed in 1981.

**FRONT DE LIBÉRATION NATIONALE (FLN)** Terroristic Algerian independence organisation that confronted the ultra-nationalist *Algérie Française* movement in the 1950s and 1960s. Although the FLN was an organisation of the left, some commentators detect a populist, national-socialist edge to the movement that reminds them of fascism.

**FRONT NATIONAL (FN)** Party of the French ultra-right founded in 1972 and personified by leader Jean-Marie **Le Pen**. Powerfully anti-immigrant and anti-leftist, the movement's doctrine is summed up by the slogan 'France for the French'. The FN's breakthrough came in a 1983 by-election and in 1984 its emergence was confirmed when it polled 10 per cent in the European elections. It gained thirty-five parliamentary seats in 1986 – thereby causing all sorts of problems for the mainstream right – and in 1995 Le Pen won 15 per cent of the vote in the presidential election. His party also triumphed in four significant mayoral contests in the mid-1990s (**Toulon**, **Marignane**, **Orange** and **Vitrolles**), giving it 'real power' for the first time. In 1999 the movement split in two after the desertion of Le Pen's deputy Bruno **Mégret** to form the *Front National-Mouvement National* (renamed the MNR). The rump

FN scored only 5.7 per cent in the 1999 European elections.

**FRONT NATIONAL JEUNESSE (NATIONAL YOUTH MOVEMENT) (FNJ)** Youth wing of **Le Pen**'s *Front National* (FN).

**FRONT NATIONAL-MOUVEMENT NATIONAL (FN-MN)** Breakaway movement from the *Front National* (FN). The FN-MN was founded in 1999 as a result of deep schism within **Le Pen**'s party. Led by neo-conservative Bruno **Mégret**, it scored 3.5 per cent in the 1999 European elections. It was later renamed the MNR.

**FRONT NATIONAL-NATIONAAL FRONT (FN-NF)** Anti-foreigner, anti-leftist Belgian movement led by Daniel **Féret**. Founded in 1985, it is particularly strong in Brussels and won one seat in the 1988 local elections. It is modelled on the French *Front National* (FN) and rebuts allegations that it is fascist in any sense.

**FRONT NOUVEAU DE BELGIQUE/FRONT NIEUWE BELGIË** Modern Belgian far-right movement.

**FRONT PARTIJ (FRONT PARTY) (FP)** Early Flemish nationalist movement founded in the aftermath of the First World War. It grew significantly during the inter-war period.

**FRONT PAYSAN** French coalition movement founded by Henri **Dorgères** in 1934. A boisterous advocate of 'peasant fascism', it campaigned on a pro-farm, pro-village agenda and specialised in violent direct-action tactics. Dorgères's creation also boasted a green-shirted youth movement.

**FRONTBEWEGING (FRONT MOVEMENT) (FB)** Early Flemish nationalist movement born in the aftermath of the First World War.

**FRONTE DELLA GIOVENTÙ** Youth organisation of the Italian *Movimento Sociale Italiano* (MSI).

**FRONTE NAZIONALE (NATIONAL FRONT)** *Movimento Sociale Italiano* (MSI) offshoot movement founded in the early 1960s by **Borghese**.

**FRONTE UNIVERSITARIO DI AZIONE NAZIONALE (UNIVERSITY FRONT FOR NATIONAL ACTION) (FUAN)** Rome-based student organisation attached to the Italian *Movimento Sociale Italiano* (MSI).

**FRONTKÄMPFER ASSOCIATION** *Völkisch* movement – embodying an **Aryan** and anti-Communist ideology – active in 1920s Austria.

**FUERZA JOVEN** Youth wing of the Spanish *Fuerza Nueva*.

**FUERZA NUEVA (NEW FORCE) (FN)** Spanish far-right grouping active between 1976 and 1982. Led by Blas **Piñar**, it failed to pass the 1 per cent barrier in any national election.

**FUERZA NUEVA DEL TRABAJO (FNT)** Trade union body affiliated to the Spanish *Fuerza Nueva*.

**FUERZA POPULAR (POPULAR FORCE)** Formed in 1947 – successor to the Mexican movement, *Unión Nacional Sinarquista*.

**FÜHRER** Official title adopted by **Hitler** after 1931. He consolidated his position still further in 1934 after the death of President **Hindenburg**. The *Führerprinzip* (leadership principle) stated that all organisations within Germany required a charismatic and authoritative leader, and, in line with this, **Himmler** (for example) became *Schutzstaffel* (SS) Führer. Each

Führer was given unrestricted power and deemed to be above the law.

**FUNDAMENTALISM** A return to the perceived fundamentals of a given religious or political creed. The term is frequently used with reference to **Christianity** and **Islam**, and often in a pejorative sense. Fundamentalists are likely to employ literal interpretations of key texts and to insist on strict adherence to core norms and values. Religious fundamentalists also question the ability to distinguish between the public and private spheres, and between faith and the practice of everyday life. They are generally socially conservative, favouring traditional **family** structures and **gender** roles. Some US Christian fundamentalists also claim biblical justification for white supremacist or violent anti-government actions.

**FUTURISM** Noted tendency in Italian art and public discourse dating from 1909, especially associated with Filippo **Marinetti**, many of whose ideas were incorporated into the ideology of Fascism. Futurists extolled the virtues of youth, action, speed and emerging technology (like that of the automobile). They urged a violent rejection of the past, which they associated with the 'self-satisfied', 'smug' **middle-class** society of late nineteenth-century Italy. Offending middle-class sensibilities was a virtue to them: they urged people to be offensive to women, to close universities and to abolish museums, the Church and the monarchy. They brought a brash, youthful arrogance and a streak of rebellion to the right-wing nationalist movements that they influenced.

**FUTURO PRESENTE (PRESENT FUTURE) (FP)** Modern Portuguese neo-fascist movement that publishes a newspaper of the same name.

**GARDA DE FIER (IRON GUARD)** The organisational base of the **Legion of the Archangel Michael** – founded in 1930 and a prime example of fascism in inter-war Romania. Zealously nationalistic, and spurred on by chief ideologue Corneliu **Codreanu**, the Iron Guard pinpointed Jews and Communists as the chief antinational threats. It gained 478,000 votes (and sixty-six seats) in the 1937 elections and became the third largest movement in the country. Iron Guard personnel joined the **Antonescu** government at the beginning of the war, but were not compatible with the **Hitler**-backed regime. The *Garda de Fier* was crushed in 1941.

**GAULEITERS** Hitler's henchmen in provincial Germany. Over time they became an important source of support for the **Führer**.

**GAULLISM** Political doctrine that surrounded, and outlived, General de Gaulle – a figure reviled on all sections of the French far right. His **resistance** forces opposed **Vichy** and Marshal **Pétain** during the Occupation and two decades later he alienated *Algérie Française* supporters when as French President he granted Algeria its independence. For these reasons and others there is little love lost between modern-day Gaullists and **Le Pen's** *Front National* (FN).

**GEMEINSCHAFT UNABHÄNGIGER DEUTSCHER (FELLOWSHIP OF INDEPENDENT GERMANS) (GUD)** German pro-Nazi movement founded in 1949 by Dr Fritz Dorls.

**GENDER** A person's sense of sexual identity, as opposed to his/her biological sex. Fascists share with social conservatives a traditionalist view of gender roles and the functional division of labour between the sexes. Thus, men were intended to be strong, assertive and protective; women were to represent the caring, compassionate and nurturing side of human society. Men would be breadwinners and soldiers; women would be home-makers. In Italy and Germany, instruments of totalitarian mobilisation, like state-run women's or youth movements, were used to reinforce these values. Gender and **family** relationships were geared to reproduction in the context of marriage. Whether influenced by religious teaching (as in **Vichy** France or **Franco**'s Spain) or by violent machismo doctrines (as in Germany), fascists penalised those who deviated from these norms.

**GENERAL DUTCH FASCIST UNION** Dutch fascist front – founded in 1932. In the 1937 elections the Union scored less than 0.5 per cent.

**GENERIC FASCISM** Imperfect 'model' employed by historians and political scientists to enhance their understanding of fascist ideology. The term carries the implicit assumption that in whatever context it emerges, fascism possesses a range of common features – a mistaken assumption perhaps, but, even so, one that can help overall comprehension. It is taken as read that generic fascism can never be a total reality.

**GERMAN ETHNIC FREEDOM PARTY (DVPF)** Radical right-wing alliance active in 1920s Germany.

**GERMAN FAITH MOVEMENT** Pagan 'religion' established by the Nazis as a retort to orthodox **Christianity**.

**GERMAN FATHERLAND PARTY** Proto-fascist group founded in September 1917. Although it was fiercely anti-Semitic, the movement was devoid of a mass base and

a radical agenda – hence its characterisation as 'proto-fascist'.

**GERMAN PEACE UNION** Modern German far-right grouping led by Gerhard **Frey**.

**GERMAN REVOLUTION** Term used by the Nazis to describe their own conquest of power.

**GERMAN SOCIALIST PARTY (DSP)** Extreme right-wing movement led by Julius **Streicher** that voluntarily fused with the *Nationalsozialistische Deutsche Arbeiterpartei* (NSDAP) in 1922.

**GERMAN VÖLKISCH DEFENSIVE AND OFFENSIVE LEAGUE (DVSUTB)** Authoritarian right-wing movement that claimed to have more than 150,000 members in the early 1920s. Intensely anti-Weimar and ultra-nationalistic, the organisation never really evolved into a mass party. It was banned in 1922.

**GERMANY FIRST** Name of the *Deutsche Volks Union*'s post-1987 electoral list.

**GERSTEIN DOCUMENT** Historical text at the centre of revisionist controversy (Kurt Gerstein was a *Schutzstaffel* (SS) officer involved in the gassing of Jews).

**GESINNUNGSGEMEINSCHAFT DER NEUEN FRONT (GDNF)** Modern German national-socialist organisation – successor movement to the *Aktionsfront Nationaler Sozialisten/Nationale Aktivisten* (ANS/NA).

**GESTAPO (GEHEIME STAATSPOLIZEI)** Nazi secret police organisation created in 1933 by **Göring**. Part of the *Schutzstaffel* (SS), the Gestapo aimed to rid Germany of **Hitler**'s enemies: primarily, Jews, Communists and socialists. **Himmler** became its leader in 1934; five years later the Gestapo merged with the **Heydrich**-led *Sicherheitsdienst* (SD) security service. Estimates suggest that around 40,000 people worked for the unit; it also relied on thousands of agents and informers. During the war it managed all the Nazis' concentration camps and **extermination camps**. Historians have debated the level of Gestapo efficiency, but there is no doubt that the organisation terrified ordinary people.

**GIOLITTIAN PERIOD** Period of Italian political history between 1892 and 1921 dominated by the Liberals under Giovanni Giolitti. Giolitti pursued some right-wing policies (e.g. an expansionist campaign in Africa) but was also willing to compromise with unions during the post-1918 *Biennio Rosso* years characterised by strikes and demonstrations. Fascists painted Giolitti as weak in the face of Communist and anarchist violence but exploited his desire for pragmatic accommodation in order to gain ground for themselves.

**GIOVENTÙ FASCISTA (FASCIST YOUTH)** Inter-war Italian fascist publication.

**GIOVENTÙ ITALIANA DEL LITTORIO (GIL)** Organisation founded in 1937 that grouped together all fascist youth movements in **Mussolini**'s Italy. It replaced the *Opera Nazionale Balilla* (ONB). Membership of GIL became compulsory in 1939.

**GLEICHSCHALTUNG** Literally, 'co-ordination'. The word is used to describe the process by which the Nazis established and consolidated their dictatorship in the years following 1933.

**GNR** National-revolutionary cell associated with the French *Front National* (FN).

**GOBINEAU SOCIETY** German movement founded in 1893 that promoted racial ideas.

**GOLDSHIRTS** Nickname of Mexican movement *Acción Revolucionaria Mexicana*.

**GØTEBORGS STIFTSIDNING** Newspaper of the Swedish *Kyrkliga Folkpartiet* movement.

**GOTHIC RIPPLES** British anti-Semitic publication.

**GREAT CROATIA** Separatist dream of *Ustasha* nationalists – inspired by Tomislav's Croatia of the Middle Ages.

**GREAT DEPRESSION** Watershed period of economic downturn that most historians agree was fundamental to the rise of fascism, and in particular German Nazism. The term refers specifically to the years 1929–34.

**GREATER ALBANIA** Aim of Albanian ultra-nationalists in **Kosovo**, Macedonia and Albania itself. The concept would also embrace Albanian-populated regions in southern Serbia. Although the Albanian government is cool on the idea, it is especially popular among the bands of young Albanian militants in rural Macedonia and Kosovo radicalised by the Kosovo war of 1999.

**GREATER BRITAIN, THE** Keynote **British Union of Fascists** (BUF) policy statement of 1932.

**GREATER BRITAIN MOVEMENT (GBM)** Neo-Nazi group of the 1960s that emerged out of the **National Socialist Movement**. The organisation was led by **Tyndall** and **Webster**, and in 1967 merged into the newly created **National Front** (NF).

**GREATER FINLAND** Ultra-nationalist dream of inter-war Finnish fascist group, **Academic Karelia Society** (AKS).

**GREATER HOLLAND** Ultimate aim of ultra-nationalist Flemish separatists in Belgium.

**GREATER HUNGARY** Ultra-nationalist dream of inter-war Hungarian fascists.

**GREATER SERBIA** Dream of modern Serbian ultra-nationalists, as outlined by Slobodan Milošević in his 1986 **SANU Memorandum**.

**GREEN FASCISM** Phrase used to describe the coming-together of ecology and **ultra-nationalism**. In Germany, Italy and France, among other countries, fascist and neo-fascist movements have chosen to interpret ecology as a right-wing rather than left-wing concern. Utilising the argument that the earth is the land and the land is the **nation**, ultra-nationalists have claimed conservation and environmentalism for themselves. Hence the notion of 'blood and soil' – used frequently in fascist and neo-fascist discourse.

**GREENSHIRTS** (1) Nickname of the **National Corporate Party** in inter-war Ireland. (2) Movement created by Yugoslav leader Stojadinović as part of his '**fascistisation**' efforts in the mid-1930s. (3) Nickname of **Dorgères**'s *Front Paysan* in 1930s France. (4) Alternative name for **Salazar**'s youth organisation, *Mocidade Portuguesa*.

**GREY WOLVES** Modern Turkish group with links to European neo-Nazi movements.

**GREYSHIRTS** Inter-war South African movement that tried to ape **Hitler**- and **Mussolini**-style fascism. After 1945 it merged with the **National Party**.

**GROSSDEUTSCHE VOLKSGEMEINSCHAFT Rosenberg**'s organisation that championed national-socialist ideas in inter-war Germany.

**GROSSRAUMWIRTSCHAFT** Name given to the Nazis' plan for the reconstruction of Europe.

**GROUP OF THE EUROPEAN RIGHT** Far-right coalition in the European Parliament born in the 1980s. The alliance incorporated neo-fascist and ultra-nationalist deputies from a variety of member states (including France, Germany, Italy and Greece).

**GROUPE UNION DÉFENSE (GUD)** Fascist student group founded in Paris in the 1960s. Its activists specialised in urban violence – and the *Front National* (FN) denied all links with the movement.

**GROUPEMENT DE RECHERCHE ET D' ÉTUDE POUR LA CIVILISATION EUROPÉENNES (RESEARCH AND STUDY GROUP FOR EUROPEAN CIVILISATION) (GRECE)** The main face of the French *Nouvelle Droite*. GRECE is a right-wing think-tank that has impacted upon the thinking of far-right groups in France and Europe. Its agenda is distinctive – covering politics, society, economics, culture and **aesthetics** – and its discourse is highly original, blending together anti-**egalitarianism**, anti-leftism, elitism and paganism. It glorifies European **civilisation** and seeks a '**Third Way**' between **liberalism** and **Communism**.

**GROUPUSCULE** French term denoting a small extreme-right (or extreme-left) grouping.

**GRUNWALD** Anti-Semitic cell that existed inside the Polish Communist Party in the 1970s and 1980s.

**GRUPO DE OFICIALES UNIDOS** Argentine military grouping that surrounded Juan **Perón** in the mid-twentieth century.

**GRUPOS REVOLUCIONARIOS DE ACCIÓN INTERNACIONAL (INTERNATIONAL REVOLUTIONARY ACTION GROUPS) (GRAI)** Modern Spanish far-right terrorist movement.

**GRUPPI UNIVERSITARI FASCISTI** Fascist students' union in inter-war Italy.

**GUERRILLEROS DE CRISTO REY (WAR-RIORS OF CHRIST THE KING)** Shady Spanish far-right group of the 1970s.

**GUOMINDANG** Alternative name for the Chinese **Kuomintang** (KMT).

**GYPSIES** Social group often viewed as 'un-integrated' and 'anti-national' by far-right and fascist groups. Ultra-nationalists in Romania, Serbia and France, for instance, have all stigmatised gypsies.

H

**HAMMER PRESS** Influential anti-Semitic publishing house in Nazi Germany.

**HEGELIANISM** Doctrine that influenced fascism's conception of the state, though frequently through misapplication. Hegel believed that the state was the highest form of social organisation and that both individual and collective rights find their highest expression in it. Though much of his writing suggests that Hegel himself admired liberal constitutions, the Nazis seized on this apparent state-wor-ship to justify their policies. Hegel's view that the obligation to defend one's state binds the citizenry together is accepted in a general way by most non-pacifists. The Nazis used Hegel's **patriotism** to jus-tify the idea of an obligation to obedi-ence and loyalty unto death, and the glorification of blood sacrifice. Finally, Hegel's dialectical method, where contra-dictory processes combine to produce more powerful driving forces for history, was used by both Communist and Nazi propagandists in their claim that through

absolute submission to an all-powerful state, the individual could somehow find 'true' freedom.

**HEIMATTREUE VEREINIGUNG DEUTSCH-LANDS (HOMELAND LOVING UNION)** Small German neo-Nazi movement based in Baden-Württemberg. It was founded in December 1988.

**HEIMWEHR (HOME DEFENCE LEAGUES)** Austrian paramilitary organisation that is regarded as proto-fascist or semi-fascist in nature. It was formed in the aftermath of 1918 and consisted mainly of National Guards and war **veterans**. In terms of ideology, *Heimwehren* mixed virulent anti-socialism with national **corporatism**. After a period of radicalisation in the late 1920s – and a failed coup attempt in 1931 – the organisation was neutralised by **Schuschnigg**, Austria's para-fascist leader after **Dollfuss**. Following this, some disen-chanted *Heimwehr* members threw in their lot with German Nazism.

**HELLENISATION** Literally, the policy of enhancing and imposing Greek culture – as favoured by those on the far right in contemporary Greece.

**HERD INSTINCT** Psychological theory that has been advanced to explain the way in which ordinary people became devoted followers of **Hitler** in the 1930s. The thesis implies that Germans willingly submitted themselves to **authoritarianism**.

**HERRENVOLK** Neo-spiritual concept em-braced by **Hitler** that implied Germany was the 'chosen race'.

**HETEROPHOBIA** The fear of difference. This has been displayed by many fascist movements and regimes in the delineation of 'enemies of the nation' (immigrants, socialists, homosexuals and the like).

**HETERONOMIC THEORY** In the context of Marxist theorising, the notion that fascism was *determined* by, and was *a function of*, modern **capitalism**.

**HIERARCHY** Polar opposite of an egalitarian social or political order. The concept of hierarchy is explicitly favoured by most fascist movements; other far-right groups are sometimes more egalitarian or democratic. Nazis and Fascists believed that power structures in social and political institutions should take the shape of a pyramid, with a leader on top and with each person of lower rank knowing his or her place in the structure. Like **élitism**, hierarchy was seen as both inevitable and desirable. For the Nazis, hierarchies were everywhere: Nazi racial theories, for instance, assumed a 'natural' hierarchy of races. The notion of hierarchy is central to leadership cults like the Nazi *Führerprinzip*.

**HILFSORGANISATION AUF GEGENSEITIGKEIT DER WAFFEN-SS (HIAG)** *Schutzstaffel* (SS) **veterans** association.

**HILFSORGANISATION FÜR NATIONALE POLITISCHE GEFANGENE UND DEREN ANGEHÖRIGE (ORGANISATION FOR THE ASSISTANCE OF NATIONAL POLITICAL PRISONERS) (HNG)** German neo-Nazi support group led by Christa Goerth. Its specific remit is to campaign on behalf of far-right political prisoners.

**HINDU FUNDAMENTALISM** Current of thought in Indian politics that defines the nation in narrow religious and cultural terms, specifically as Hindu rather than Muslim. This tendency runs counter to the secular and democratic socialist Indian establishment represented by the Congress Party. It found early expression in rivals to Congress and more recently in the *Bharatiya Janata* Party (BJP). After Hindu nationalists had attacked a Muslim religious shrine at Ayodhya in 1992, the BJP made an electoral breakthrough in 1998 and led one of the few non-Congress governments in Indian history. In power, under the leadership of Atal Behal Vajpayee, the BJP has pursued moderate policies, it has not stoked militant Hinduism and has gone even further than Congress in co-operation with Western countries. Critics still fear the influence of a more militant sister organisation, the *Rashtriya Swayamsevak Sangh* (RSS), whose assertive and military-style parades are reminiscent of far-right behaviour in other countries.

**HISPANIDAD** Name given to the regenerative vision put forward by the Spanish far right in the 1930s. This vision also implied the strengthening of ties with South America.

**HISTORICAL REVIEW PRESS** Historical revisionist publishing house.

**HISTORICAL REVISIONISM** A specific form of **revisionism** that underplays or actually denies Nazi crimes, particularly the **Holocaust**. The sophistication of revisionists can vary from the crude to the pseudo-academic.

**HISTORIKERSTREIT (HISTORIANS' DEBATE)** High-level re-examination of Nazism and the **Holocaust** involving German scholars in the mid-1980s.

**HITLER-CENTRISM** Alternative term to 'Hitlerism'.

**HITLER JUGEND (HITLER YOUTH) (HJ)** Nazi movement founded in 1926 that was compulsory for all German boys aged between fourteen and eighteen. It put the emphasis on physical rather than intellectual training and as a consequence its 'syllabus' was a mixture of outdoor pursuits and semi-military exercises. It claimed to have almost 8 million members and, not unexpectedly, came into serious conflict with the German school system.

**HITLERISM** Notion that implies the Nazi period can be 'explained away' by reference to one 'crazed' leader. Some scholars view 'Hitlerism' as a totally inadequate way of theorising about the German experience in the 1930s.

**HLINKA GUARD** Separatist Slovak paramilitary organisation of the 1930s with its own youth section – Hlinka Youth. The doctrine of the Hlinka Guard was a mix of **corporatism**, **Catholicism** and **anti-Semitism**, and it only acquired genuine fascist credentials after the setting up of the Slovak **puppet state** in 1939. Some would argue that even then it was more para-fascist than fascist. It was also known as Hlinka's People's Party/Slovak People's Party.

**HOARE—LAVAL PACT** A December 1935 agreement brokered by Samuel Hoare (UK) and Pierre **Laval** (France) that confirmed **Mussolini**'s gains in Abyssinia by specifically partitioning the African territory between Italy and the **League of Nations**. The agreement was disowned by the cabinet in London but, in line with the policy of appeasement, Italy got away with its aggression and there was no concerted international military action against her.

**HOHENZOLLERN** Dynasty that collapsed in 1918 – a development that paved the way for the establishment of the **Weimar Republic**. Some historians have located continuities between the Second Reich of the Hohenzollerns and the **Third Reich** of **Hitler**.

**HOLOCAUST** Systematic policy of genocide launched by the Nazis against the Jews during the **Second World War**. **Heydrich** and the *Schutzstaffel* (SS) were responsible for strategy, and the Nuremberg Laws (1935) and *Kristallnacht* (1938) were key landmarks on the road to the 'Final Solution'. There is some debate over whether the Holocaust was always a Nazi goal or whether it was a more extreme version of the established policy of harassment and persecution of Jews, pushed to its limits in the course of the war because of **Hitler**'s growing frustration with the tide of events. The tone of Hitler's writings, especially *Mein Kampf,* suggests a long-term and over-arching goal but the timing of the main anti-Jewish measures lends some credence to the latter explanation. Estimates say that more than 6 million Jews died.

**HOLOCAUST DENIAL** School of thought that intentionally denies or minimises the historical fact of the **Holocaust** and/or Nazi culpability for it.

**HOMOSEXUALITY** Fascist attacks on libertarian and secular values in the early twentieth century pinpointed homosexuality as a key form of deviance. Fascists shared the opinion of the Catholic Church, of social conservatives and of much of inter-war society, that homosexual lifestyles were morally wrong and should not be explicitly validated by the state. As such, they supported campaigns of violence and murder against homosexuals. **Hitler** sent many homosexuals to the labour camps and they were treated as a blemish on the 'purity' of the race. The revelation that Ernst **Röhm**, *Sturm Abteilung* (SA) leader, was a homosexual was a factor in his demise and in the suppression of the movement in 1934. Many modern far-right movements are also explicitly hostile to homosexuality.

**HOSSBACH** Conference and Protocol of 1937 that made plain **Hitler**'s desire to expand territorially in line with *Lebensraum.*

**HOYERSWERDA** German town that was the scene of a notorious racist attack in September 1991.

**HRANAO** Inter-war Croatian terror group modelled on Nazi lines.

**HRVATSKA ČISTA STRANKA PRAVA (CROATIAN PARTY OF PURE RIGHTS) (HCSP)** Ultra-nationalist Croatian movement founded by Ivan Gabelica and Nedeljko Gabelica.

**HRVATSKA DEMOKRATSKA STRANKA PRAVA (CROATIAN DEMOCRATIC PARTY OF RIGHTS) (HDSP)** Croatian extreme-right movement of the 1990s led by Krešimir Pavelić.

**HRVATSKA DEMOKRATSKA ZAJEDNICA (CROATIAN DEMOCRATIC UNION) (HDZ)** Franjo **Tudjman**'s political organisation. Formed in 1989, the movement contains both ultra-nationalist and neo-fascist factions.

**HRVATSKA STRANKA PRAVA (CROATIAN PARTY OF RIGHTS) (HSP)** Far-right Croatian organisation led by **Paraga**. Its doctrine is a blend of **ultra-nationalism** and free-market economics. It has also demonstrated its nostalgia for the wartime *Ustasha*. HSP support and membership grew during the 1990s.

**HRVATSKE OBRAMBENE SNAGE (CROATIAN DEFENCE FORCE) (HOS)** Paramilitary force of the Croatian *Hrvatska Stranka Prava* (HSP). It utilised the *Ustasha* slogan, 'Ready for the Homeland', in the 1990s and displayed intense anti-Serb and anti-Communist attitudes.

**HUMANISM** Belief in the potential of human beings for self-awareness and self-improvement, and of the central role of human beings in the natural and social worlds. The concept is frequently associated with rationalist, liberal, socialist and atheist beliefs, and is fiercely opposed by fascist movements, as well as by many traditionalist, Romantic and socially conservative thinkers, especially those influenced by religious and mystical concepts of the **nation**.

**HUMANITARIANISM** A liberal and compassionate approach to social problems and to international relations. It is castigated by the far right as symptomatic of weakness and, as such, a distraction from the pursuit of the national interest.

**HUMANITY** A term used to emphasise the features shared by all members of the human race, much favoured by liberals and humanitarians. Fascists stressed differences among peoples and sought to create a 'New Man' that would be above the common humanity described by others. This rejection of traditional conceptions of humanity was partly related to racial theories and partly to the fascists' claim to be constructing not only a new government but a new **civilisation**.

**HUNGARIAN DEMOCRATIC FORUM (MDF)** Party of government in the early 1990s. Its internal unity was shattered in 1993 when one of its leading figures, Istvan **Csurka**, was accused of **anti-Semitism**. However, the party itself is more socially conservative than neo-fascist.

**HUNGARIAN HITLERITE MOVEMENT** Green-shirted proto-fascist group founded by **Meskó** in 1932.

**HUNGARIAN JUSTICE PARTY** Modern ultra-nationalist movement.

**HUNGARIAN NATIONAL SOCIALIST PARTY** Inter-war proto-fascist movement led by Count **Festetics**.

**HUNGARISM** Ultra-nationalist creed advanced by Hungarian fascist movements.

**IDEA NAZIONALE, L'** Rome-based journal of the *Associazione Nazionale Italiana* (ANI). In the 1920s it evolved into a Fascist publication.

**IDEAL TYPE** Theory employed by historians, political scientists and sociologists to explain and somehow 'measure' the fascist credentials of specific movements. The model, developed by Weber, assumes that each and every generic concept (such as fascism) has common-denominator characteristics. Ideal-type theory can never hope to be totally accurate, but it can help students of fascism to understand the phenomenon better.

**IDENTITÉ** Title of the French *Front National*'s former theoretical review.

**IDENTITY** Key issue for all far-right movements whose most important badges of identity are ethnic, national or cultural, rather than class or **gender**-based.

**IDENTITY CHURCHES** Phenomenon of the modern-day US far right. Identity Churches are home to extreme Christian fundamentalists who blend notions of **white supremacism** with **anti-Semitism**.

**IDEOLOGY** A coherent system of beliefs that justifies or is a motivation for political action. Contrary to widespread belief, an ideology need not be based on false beliefs: what matters is its relationship to action. Fascists' anti-intellectual streak meant they were more interested in ideol-

ogy as a pointer to action than in any abstract philosophy of fascism.

**IEROS SYNDESMOS ELLINON AXIOMATI-KON (SACRED BOND OF GREEK OFFICERS)** Royalist and anti-Communist movement active in 1940s Greece.

**IMMIGRATION** Major issue for far-right parties, especially in the 1990s. Immigration is seen as a threat to the purity of the national racial stock and as a competitive pressure on the economy under conditions of **unemployment**. Far-right parties therefore favour restrictions on immigration and oppose liberal regimes for asylum seekers. They have co-operated across Europe to promote restrictive legislation, supported discriminatory national policies and have often been associated with violent attacks on foreigners.

**IMPERIAL FASCIST LEAGUE (IFL)** Small black-shirted British fascist movement formed in 1928 by ex-Britons Society member Arnold **Leese**. Fervently anti-Semitic and anti-socialist, the IFL was extremely unsuccessful but spread fear among the Jewish population through its rabid pamphlet campaigns and **propaganda**.

**IMPERIAL RULE ASSISTANCE ASSOCIATION** Para-fascist 'single-party' organisation established in Japan in 1940. It was set up with the aim of mobilising public support for the government. Because of its emphasis on the imperial throne, and on Japanese tradition, it quickly attracted the wrath of authentic fascists.

**IMPERIALISM** Literally, empire-building. For non-Marxists, this involves direct and overt conquest by states. Neo-Marxists also view the preponderance of **capitalism** and relationships of economic dependency as symptomatic of imperialism. Fascist regimes believed in imperialism – **Mussolini**, for example, saw expansionism as an antidote to the alleged second-class status of Italy. However, like the Communists during the **Cold War**, fascists routinely attacked the imperialism of the 'plutocratic' Western powers. This anti-imperialism was a particularly effective tool of Italian **propaganda** in the Middle East.

**IMPERO** Rome-based fascist newspaper in the 1920s.

**INDEPENDENT PARTY** Danish far-right movement of the 1950s and 1960s that never scored more than 3 per cent in national elections.

**INDIVIDUALISM** Belief in the centrality of the individual and individual rights as against the prerogatives of the state or the collective. It is a principal strand in Anglo-American liberal philosophy and economics, and is seen by fascists as a challenge to the collective power of the nation and the state, as well as a pretext for the greed of big business (in the Nazi view, Jewish financial circles). It was also denounced as a cover for the alleged licentiousness, **decadence** and permissiveness of what they characterised as 'smug bourgeois society'.

**INDO-EUROPEAN** Alternative term to **Aryan**.

**INITIATIVE VOLKSWILLE (INITIATIVE FOR THE POPULAR WILL) (IV)** Movement founded by **Kühnen** in West Germany in the late 1980s. It superseded the banned NS.

**INSECURITÉ** Word used by **Le Pen** and the *Front National* (FN) to denote what they see as the negative economic and political effects of post-war North African **immigration** into France. The term has now passed into common usage.

**INSTITUT D'ACTION FRANÇAISE** Pseudo-academic arm of the *Action Française* (AF).

**INTEGRAL CORPORATISM** Brand of corporatism advocated by Italian philosopher Ugo Spirito. He envisaged a situation in which producers rather than shareholders took on the ownership role in society – and hence was attacked as a 'Communist'.

**INTEGRAL NATIONALISM** Ideology that emphasises the 'integral' whole of the nation and its constituent parts. Many fascist and semi-fascist movements are loyal to integral nationalism.

**INTEGRALISM Ideology** of extreme Catholic **nationalism** as championed by the *Ação Integralista Brasileira* (AIB) in Brazil, the *Action Française* (AF) in France, elements of the reactionary right in Portugal and many other movements.

**INTEGRALISMO LUSITANO (LUSITANIAN INTEGRALISM)** Portuguese creed of conservative **nationalism** that was particularly influential in the early twentieth century. It was the Portuguese equivalent of the *Action Française*'s **integral nationalism**, as practised by **Maurras**. It had the same enemies as fascism – e.g. **liberalism** – but it did not aim at any kind of mass revolt against the regime *in situ*.

**INTERESSEN GEMEINSCHAFT FARBEN-INDUSTRIE (IG FARBEN)** Massive chemicals conglomerate that came to be associated with many of the worst aspects of the Nazi regime. Following a 1933 agreement, IG became a leading player in Hitler's economic planning and drive towards **autarchy**. The company was a partner in the Nazis' campaign of anti-Semitic terror – Jews were killed by an IG gas, Zyklon-B – and actually benefited from it financially.

**INTERHAMWE** Hutu-dominated **militia** in Rwanda that was charged with the killing of half a million Tutsis at the height of Rwanda's civil war in 1994. The militia preached a doctrine of **élitism** and hatred.

**INTERNAL MACEDONIAN REVOLUTION- ARY ORGANISATION (IMRO)** Fascist-style hit-squad that operated in inter-war Macedonia.

**INTERNATIONAL CENTRE OF FASCIST STUDIES (CINEF)** Swiss-based organisation that espoused the 'revisionist' creed of **Universal Fascism** in the 1930s.

**INTERNATIONAL FASCISM** Alternative term to **Universal Fascism**.

**INTERNATIONAL MONETARY FUND** Global organisation that Russian neo-fascist **Zhirinovsky** claims is to blame for many of his country's modern ills.

**INTERNATIONAL THIRD POSITION (ITP)** Small British Strasserite grouping with European links. Nick **Griffin** is a former leader.

**INTERNATIONALES HILFSKOMITEE FÜR NATIONALE POLITISCHE VERFOLGTE UND DEREN ANGEHÖRIGE (INTERNA- TIONAL COMMITTEE FOR THE ASSIS- TANCE OF THOSE PERSECUTED FOR NATIONAL POLITICAL REASONS AND THEIR DEPENDANTS) (IHV)** Small German neo-Nazi support group founded by Ernst Tag in 1987.

**INTERNATIONALISM** A belief in co-operating with like-minded movements across national frontiers. It is more prominent among socialists than on the right – in part because of the cosmopolitan strains in left-wing ideology – but is now a feature of post-war **neo-fascism**. Ironically, national prejudices can be a potential obstacle to reaching the full potential of far-right internationalism.

**INTERVENTIONISM** In the Italian context, the desire for full-scale military intervention in the First World War. In time, the half-hearted nature of liberal governments' intervention plans led to the rise of **Mussolini** – a man who promised great things in the sphere of foreign policy.

**INVISIBLE EMPIRE** US paramilitary group. Alabama-based and led by James Farrands, it collapsed in 1987.

**IRREDENTISM** The desire to regain national territory that has been, or is deemed to be, lost to other states. Italian Fascists' campaigns to regain territory lost after the First World War and the interest of the Hungarian far right in regaining **Transylvania** were symptomatic of irredentism. The issue of irredentist claims is further complicated by disputed interpretations of international treaties or historical record. Irredentism exacerbates international tension and also serves to cultivate a **myth** of 'nation as victim' – a useful **propaganda** tool for extremist movements.

**IRISH NATIONAL SOCIALIST PARTY** Modern far-right grouping.

**ISÄNMAALLINEN KANSANLIIKE (PEO- PLE'S PATRIOTIC MOVEMENT) (IKL)** Finnish fascist movement that was founded in April 1932, banned (unsuccessfully) in 1938 and then folded in 1944. Heir to the **Lapua** movement, its revolutionary ideology was based around **corporatism** and anti-Communism, and its **nationalism** was both anti-Swede and anti-Russian. It won 8 per cent of the vote in the 1936 elections, but thereafter moved towards extra-parliamentary activity. The IKL was led by Vihtori **Kosola** and collaborated with the Nazis between 1941 and 1943.

**ISLAM Religion** founded by Muhammad and involving 'submission' to God (Allah) and obedience to his teaching, as enunciated in Muhammad's holy book, the Qu'ran (or Koran). European far-right movements are hostile to Islamic political activism and to the recognition of Islamic identity among immigrants, portraying Islam as an external threat to the Christian heritage of Europe. On the other hand, some liberal and feminist critics characterise Islamic policies as extreme-right in nature. Most Muslims are socially conservative on **family**, **gender** and sexual norms. This is based on a fusion of the worlds of faith and material life. Hence, religion is fundamentally political. However, traditional Muslims focus on the living of the spiritual life and are relatively passive in political terms. In contrast, a younger generation of Islamic revivalists (also called fundamentalists) combines radical anti-Americanism with militant social **conservatism** and an endorsement of violence to produce a more potent political Islam. The latter, much influenced by the Iranian Revolution and the cult of martyrdom in Shia Islam, contains a combination of left and right themes that is not dissimilar to European fascism.

**ISRAELI RIGHT** The right-wing end of the Israeli political spectrum is dominated by religious parties and representatives of the 200,000 West Bank settlers. They constitute a 'nationalist bloc' in the Knesset and frequently align themselves with Likud. Though some pursue Orthodox Jewish concerns, they are mostly preoccupied with encouraging a tough security policy towards Palestinian violence and opposing

the 'land for peace' strategy at the heart of the Arab–Israeli peace process since the 1990s. Some settlers go further and use violence against local Palestinians or even against the Israeli political élite, as for instance in the case of the assassination of Israeli Prime Minister Yitzhak Rabin in 1995.

**ISTITUTO DI RICONSTRUZIONE INDUS-TRIALE (INDUSTRIAL RECONSTRUCTION INSTITUTE) (IRI)** Italian body established by **Mussolini**'s fascist regime in 1933 and led by Beneduce. It was designed to supply credit to big business in the absence of help from the banking sector, and by the late 1930s controlled most of Italian heavy industry.

**ISTITUTO MOBILIARE ITALIANO (IMI)** Finance organisation founded in November 1931 by **Mussolini**. It supplied capital to depression-hit companies.

**ITALIAN ACADEMY** Establishment founded by **Mussolini** in 1929 to placate and impress Italy's intellectual community.

**JÄGER** Finnish hunters who were particularly attracted to the ideas of the proto-fascist **Academic Karelia Society** (AKS).

**JAPANISM** Vague ultra-nationalist creed prominent in 1930s Japan.

**JE SUIS PARTOUT** Extreme anti-Semitic publication that became notorious in 1930s France. During the war it became a vehicle for collaborationist writing.

**JEUNE DROITE** French study group of the 1930s. Its members were mainly pro-*Action Française* (AF) writers and intellectuals – and many went on to become collaborationists during the German occupation.

**JEUNE EUROPE** Pan-European movement that organises reunion events for Nazi **veterans**.

**JEUNE NATION** Subversive French fascist group of the 1950s led by Pierre **Sidos**. Overtly anti-democratic, it espoused a revolutionary doctrine based on **militarism** and **corporatism**. It was outlawed in 1958.

**JEUNESSES PATRIOTES (JP)** French far-right group founded in 1924 as a response to the election of a left-wing government (the *Cartel des Gauches*). Heir to the *Ligue des Patriotes*, the JP stood for Catholicism, anti-Communism and a fierce Bonapartist-style **nationalism**. Although Pierre **Taittinger**, its leader, dallied between anti-regime and pro-regime stances, it claimed to have over 100,000 members at one point. JP activists wore blue berets and had two idols: **Mussolini** and **Joan of Arc**. The organisation had genuine fascist credentials but some observers view it merely as a paternalistic ex-servicemen's association.

**JOACHIM OF FLORA** Twelfth-century figure who figures prominently in millenarian discourses of some fascists.

**JOAN OF ARC** Heroine of many groups on the French far right on account of her 'super-patriotic' deeds in the fifteenth century. However, most neutral observers would argue that **Pétain** and **Le Pen** (and others) have thoroughly misrepresented the political motivation of the teenage warrior.

**JOHN BIRCH SOCIETY** Conspiratorial US movement founded in 1958 and named after an American soldier killed by Chinese Communists in the immediate post-war period. Led by Robert H.W. **Welch**, the organisation was paranoid about the spread of left-wing ideas and genuinely believed that there were undercover Communists at the heart of the US government.

**JOURNAL OF HISTORICAL REVIEW** Revisionist publication of the IHR.

**JULY PLOT** Alternative name for the **Stauffenberg Plot** of July 1944.

**JUNGE FRONT (YOUNG FRONT) (JF)** Youth movement of the German neo-Nazi *Volkssozialistische Bewegung Deutschlands/Partei der Arbeit* (VSBD/PdA).

**JUNGMÄDELBUND (JM)** Nazi organisation for girls aged 10–14.

**JUNI-KLUB** Radical German nationalist group founded in 1919. It was particularly frustrated by the **Versailles** settlement.

**JUNTA** From the Spanish for 'meeting' or 'gathering'. It denotes a military regime with strong representation from various factions, rather than a unitary dictatorship. Juntas usually imply a provisional military government, though many have stayed in power for years or legitimated themselves in the form of more institutionalised dictatorships. Many Argentine military regimes, for instance, constituted coalitions in which the heads of the Army, the Air Force and the Navy played a prominent part.

**JUNTA COORDINADORA DE FUERZAS NACIONALES (CO-ORDINATING COMMITTEE OF NATIONAL FORCES)** Secretive Spanish far-right coalition movement founded in 1985.

**JUNTA COORDINADORA NACIONAL SINDICALISTA (NATIONAL SYNDICALIST CO-ORDINATING COMMITTEE) (JCNS)** Modern

Spanish far-right grouping that tried to claim the **Franco** legacy for itself.

**JUNTAS DE OFENSIVA NACIONAL-SINDI-CALISTA (COMMITTEES FOR NATIONAL SYNDICALIST ATTACK) (JONS)** Small Spanish far-right movement founded in 1931 by **Ramos** and **Redondo**. Although it put forward a corporatist vision, it was anti-*Falange*. However, by 1934 it had merged with *Falange Española* to form *FE de las JONS*.

**JUNTA DE SALVACÃO NACIONAL (NATIONAL SALVATION COMMITTEE) (JSN)** Organisational body that emerged after the demise of the Portuguese dictatorship. Led by General Spinola, it helped to co-ordinate an anti-dictatorship purge.

**JUNTAS ESPAÑOLAS (SPANISH COMMITTEES) (JJ.EE)** Far-right movement established in the mid-1980s. Madrid-based, it specialised in **propaganda** and aimed to federate the extreme right.

**JUSTICIALISMO** Argentine brand of **corporatism**.

**JUVENTADES DE FRENTE NACIONAL (JFN)** Movement for young people (aged between twenty and thirty) established by the Spanish *Frente Nacional* in 1987. It deliberately tried to divest itself of *Falange*-style ritual and paramilitary violence.

**JUVENTUD DE ACCIÓN POPULAR (POPULAR ACTION YOUTH) (JAP)** Far-right youth movement in inter-war Spain.

K

**KAMPFVERLAG** Left-wing publishing house suppressed by **Hitler**.

**KANSALLINEN KOKOOMUS (NATIONAL COALITION PARTY)** Conservative allies of the Finnish *Isänmaallinen Kansanliike* (IKL) movement *c.* 1933.

**KANSANKOKONAISUUS** Finnish term meaning 'rejuvenated national community' – the ultimate dream of fascists in inter-war Finland.

**KAPP PUTSCH** Early right-wing attempt to overthrow the **Weimar Republic**. The March 1920 revolt was led by Wolfgang **Kapp** – founder of the far-right Fatherland Party – and General von Lüttwitz. Significantly, the symbol of von Lüttwitz's Erhardt Brigade was the **Swastika**. The rebels were unhappy at the **Versailles** settlement and Weimar's general weakness. The coup effort failed because the Army, on the whole, stayed loyal to the Republic.

**KATHEDER SOZIALISTEN** School of Historical Economists influential in 1860s Germany. Implicit in its national-socialist doctrine was belief in **autarchy** and territorial expansion.

**KEMALISTS** Inter-war grouping of pro-Western Turkish nationalists. The Kemalists were led by Kemal Atatürk and critics argue that his authoritarian regime exhibited some semi-fascist traits.

**KHMER ROUGE** Extreme Communist movement led by Pol **Pot** that ruled Cambodia from 1975–9. It forced the educated middle classes to work in the countryside and killed 2 million people deemed enemies of the regime. It represented an extreme form of **Communism**, abolishing money and many other institutions of modern society. The comparison with fascism is mostly based on its use of mass killing and terror, as well as its claim that *Khmer Rouge* **socialism** was a national phenomenon peculiar to Cambodia, echoing Ceauşescu's claims for 'National'

301

Communism in Romania. It was driven from power by the pro-Soviet Vietnamese in 1979. It participated in guerrilla campaigns and opposition coalition movements until a peace process and national reconciliation began in the 1990s.

**KOMMA ARHON IONNOU METAXA (PARTY OF JOHN METAXAS PRINCIPLES)** Small extreme-right movement that won 0.1 per cent of the vote in the Greek elections of 1956.

**KOMMA HITON ETHNIKIS ANTISTASEOS (X PARTY OF NATIONAL RESISTANCE)** Greek far-right grouping that won 0.2 per cent in the 1946 elections.

**KOMMA PROODEFTIKON (PROGRESSIVE PARTY) (KP)** Greek ultra-right movement founded in 1979.

**KOMMA TIS 4 AVGOUSTOU (4TH AUGUST PARTY) (K4A)** Insignificant national-socialist group in post-war Greece. The movement idolised the military regime of **Metaxas**; its name commemorates the date in 1936 when the General arrived in power.

**KONSERVATIVE STUDENTFORENING (CONSERVATIVE STUDENT ASSOCIATION)** Inter-war Norwegian group that was slightly influenced by fascist ideas.

**KONSERVATIVE UNGDOM (DANISH CONSERVATIVE YOUTH MOVEMENT)** Organisation heavily influenced by the German Nazis in the 1930s – particularly in terms of ritual and ideas.

**KORNEUBURG OATH** Political statement of the Austrian *Heimwehr* published in 1930. Its tone was strongly anti-parliamentary.

**KOSOVO** Region in southern Serbia that has symbolic resonances for Serbian na-

tionalists on account of the Battle of Kosovo Polje (1389), where Christian Serbs made a stand against invading Turkish armies. As a result, Serbs oppose ceding control of Kosovo to its Albanian population. This caused ongoing conflict, **ethnic cleansing** and NATO intervention in 1998 and 1999. The symbolism of Kosovo was a major factor in the tendency of neo-Communists like Slobodan Milošević to adopt radical nationalist positions.

**KRAFT DURCH FREUDE (STRENGTH THROUGH JOY)** Nazi social movement that attempted to control the leisure time of German workers.

**KRATOS (THE STATE)** Newspaper of the 1930s Greek movement, **Organisation of the National Sovereign State**.

**KRISTALLNACHT (CRYSTAL NIGHT/NIGHT OF BROKEN GLASS)** Name given to the Nazis' anti-Jewish **pogrom** of the 9–10 November 1938. Thousands of Jews were arrested, synagogues were set alight and Jewish shops were looted – all on a spurious pretext (the murder of a German officer by a Jew). Although the Nazi leadership was not impressed by the orderliness of *Kristallnacht*, it did act as a spur to further anti-Jewish persecution.

**KRUMPENDORF** Austrian town in which **Haider**, *Freiheitliche Partei Österreichs* (FPÖ) leader, made an infamous speech praising *Schutzstaffel* (SS) **veterans** (1995).

**KU KLUX KLAN (KKK)** Bigoted US organisation particularly strong in the Deep South. Formed in 1866, the KKK became notorious for its white supremacist ideology and fear of 'decadence' and 'decay'. It developed a distinctive ritual: members wore white hoods and victims (primarily black Americans and Jews) were either flogged or burnt. The movement was banned in 1871, but reformed in 1915. Its activity peaked in the 1920s and it still exists today.

**KUOMINTANG (NATIONAL PEOPLE'S PARTY OF CHINA) (KMT)** Non-fascist Chinese nationalist party founded by Sun Yat Sen, and subsequently led by Chiang Kai-Shek, which has been associated with both democracy and dictatorship in twentieth-century China. It originated in the 1911 liberal and moderately left-wing nationalist rebellion against foreign domination in Imperial China, and it led the 1912 Revolution. The movement governed mainland China between 1928 and 1949. Under Sun, it aligned itself with the Communists and was also influenced by the Russians. Under Chiang, it became more right wing, focusing its energies on opposing Japanese occupation and Mao Zedong's Communist insurgency. The latter struggle became extremely bitter towards the end of the **Second World War** and the KMT grew more ruthless and intolerant of opponents. The party fled to Taiwan and created the Republic of China following the Communist victory on the mainland in 1949. The KMT became the ruling party in a one-party authoritarian dictatorship. Its official policy was anti-Communist and sought the reunification of China under non-Communist rule. The Republic was abandoned by most other states but underwent internal democratisation in the late 1980s and granted free elections in 1996. The KMT modernised its structures and policies but still favours Chinese reunification. It opposes outright independence for Taiwan.

**KWANTUNG** Japan's savage army in **Manchuria** during the 1930s and 1940s. It was a law unto itself and wanted to quicken the pace of Japanese expansionism in Asia. Some commentators argue that the *Kwantung* outdid the German *Schutzstaffel* (SS) in terms of murderous brutality.

**KYRKLIGA FOLKPARTIET (RELIGIOUS PEOPLE'S PARTY)** Small Swedish movement established in 1930 and led by priest Ivar Rhedin. A confirmed admirer of **Hitler**, Rhedin wanted a new authoritarian state structure.

# L

**LABOUR, CHARTER OF** Nazi initiative of 1934 that dealt with all aspects of workers' lives, including conditions of employment, remuneration and holidays. Most commentators see it as being biased against the worker.

**LABOUR FRONT** Nazi organisation that filled the void left by trade unions after they had been dissolved.

**LACERBA** Radical Italian newspaper that came under the influence of neo-syndicalists in the first years of the twentieth century.

**LAISSEZ-FAIRE** Liberal, free-market philosophy rejected by most brands of fascism. It is seen as serving plutocratic capitalist (and, allegedly, Jewish) élites. However, since the 1980s, some far-right movements have supported neo-liberal free-market policies, primarily in order to compete with mainstream conservative parties. The American far right is an exception. It has generally supported free-market policies at home, while frequently favouring a protectionist policy on international trade.

**LANDVOLKBEWEGUNG** Name given to the wave of peasant unrest in Germany at the end of the 1930s. The Nazis were able to exploit this discontent along with other circumstantial factors.

**LANGUAGE** Key variable in **cultural nationalism**. Nineteenth-century linguistics, the Romantic movement and Darwinian science encouraged a search for the roots of national or racial groups. In the twentieth century, fascist movements stressed the unity and uniqueness of national languages. Far-right parties in the former Soviet Union, especially in the Baltic states, have favoured using language tests as a basis for discrimination against the Russian minority.

**LAPUA** Influential cross-sectional movement that embodied radical inter-war Finnish **nationalism**. It was formed in 1929, moved towards a fascist agenda the year after and was banned in 1932. There was a strong indigenous element to its manifesto, even though leader Vihtori **Kosola** was a **Mussolini** clone. At its most extreme, *Lapua* was a violent anti-Communist terror group.

**LAPUAN PÄIVÄKÄSKY (THE LAPUA DAILY ORDER)** Newspaper of the Finnish *Lapua* movement.

**LATERAN ACCORDS** Mussolini's pact with the Catholic Church, signed in February 1929, that re-established Vatican State sovereignty for the first time since Italian reunification in 1870. The Church's role in politics was curbed. Church-supported organisations were permitted but were to confine themselves to spiritual guidance. **Catholicism** became the official religion of the state. Historians generally regard the Lateran Accords as a masterstroke in the art of political compromise.

**LATVIAN INDEPENDENCE PARTY (LNKK)** Ultra-nationalist organisation that won

13 per cent of the vote in the 1993 elections.

**LATVIS** Newspaper of the Latvian *Pērkonkrusts*.

**LAUSANNE, TREATY OF** Agreement of 1923 arising out of the **Versailles** Conference that divided the spoils of the defeated Ottoman Empire. It granted Dodecanese to Italy but gave Syria, Lebanon, Iraq and Jordan to France and Britain. It was criticised by fascists for favouring traditional colonial powers.

**LAVORO, CARTA DEL (CHARTER OF LABOUR)** Keynote proclamation of the **Mussolini** regime in April 1927. In lessening trade union power, the Charter placated Italian industrialists.

**LEADERSHIP CULT** Personality cults surrounded leaders of many fascist (and Communist) regimes. German **patriotism** was equated with absolute loyalty to the person of Adolf **Hitler** under the *Führerprinzip*. Similarly, **Mussolini** took on the title of *Il Duce*. Leadership cults were a key feature of fascist **propaganda**, with exaggerated or outright false claims about the strength, virtue, modest social background or intelligence of the leader.

**LEAGUE OF EMPIRE LOYALISTS (LEL)** Formed in 1954 and influenced heavily by the pro-Empire, anti-Semitic doctrines of A.K. **Chesterton**. It was more conservative than radical, specialised in bizarre non-violent publicity stunts and boasted a membership of *c.* 2,500 in 1967 – the year it was subsumed by the **National Front** (NF).

**LEAGUE OF NATIONS** Universal **collective security** organisation set up after the First World War as a result of the Treaty of **Versailles**. It was originally intended to act against aggression. However, it failed to respond to Japan's invasion of **Manchuria** and Italian aggression in Abyssinia. The League's effectiveness was further weakened by a requirement for consensus decision-making among the key members of its Council and by the absence of major powers from its organs at critical points in the inter-war period. Japan characterised it as racist while **Hitler** showed contempt for it, not least because of its association with Versailles. The USSR was also expelled over its aggression against Finland following the **Nazi–Soviet Pact** of 1939. Despite President Woodrow Wilson's support, the isolationist US was never a member. The League faded into obscurity as war approached and was wound up by the Allies in 1946.

**LEAGUE OF ST GEORGE (LSG)** British far-right group established by ex-Mosleyites in the mid-1970s.

**LEAGUE OF YOUTH** Movement in which Eoin **O'Duffy** – Ireland's most famous fascist – began his political career.

**LEBENSRAUM** Literally, 'living space'. The term was coined in the 1870s but assumed huge significance in the 1930s when it became a key plank of Hitler's Nazi ideology. It is a reference to territory to be held by Germany beyond the confines of Greater Germany, e.g. most of Eastern Europe. In a more extreme form, it would have involved the 'Germanisation' of large areas of European Russia as well. Hitler believed that *Lebensraum* would help solve Germany's over-population problem.

**LEFT FASCISM** Brand of fascism associated with the **Strasser** brothers during the Nazi period in Germany. 'Left fascism', or **Strasserism**, survived the war and has impacted on many neo-fascist movements.

**LEGA NORD (NORTHERN LEAGUE)** Populist Italian movement born in the early 1980s. The League's green-shirted activists campaign for a federal Italy and emphasise the innate superiority of the northern regions. The organisation, led by Umberto **Bossi**, is hostile to **immigration**, multi-culturalism and state interference in the economy. Some on the left see it as neo-fascist in political orientation.

**LEGIÃO PORTUGUESA (PORTUGUESE LEGION) (LP)** Paramilitary force of **Salazar**'s *Estado Novo*. It sent men to fight for **Franco** during the **Spanish Civil War**.

**LÉGION NATIONALE** Maurrasian movement that emerged in inter-war Belgium. Led by Hoornaert, its doctrine was an amalgam of **corporatism** and monarchism.

**LEGION/LEAGUE OF THE ARCHANGEL GABRIEL** Romanian far-right movement of the 1930s whose most famous sub-unit was the Iron Guard.

**LEGION OF THE ARCHANGEL MICHAEL** Terrorist gang formed by Romanian fascist **Codreanu** in 1927.

**LENINISM** Variant of **Marxism**, also known as Marxism–Leninism or Marxist-Leninism, associated with Vladimir Lenin, founder of the Soviet Union. The doctrine emphasised the difficulty of achieving spontaneous socialist revolution, arguing instead for a revolution led by a disciplined vanguard party. The resulting 'dictatorship of the proletariat' would build **socialism** pending the future emergence of a communist utopia. Leninism was the basis for Communist Party dictatorship in the Soviet Union. Many features of that system were copied by the German and Italian fascists but they rejected outright **state** ownership of all economic assets and were bitterly opposed to the Marxian roots of Leninism.

**LEONARDO, IL** Ultra-nationalist Italian newspaper founded in 1903. It anticipated many key fascist themes.

**LEPÉNISME** Body of nationalist ideas associated with Jean-Marie **Le Pen**, founder and leader of the *Front National* (FN) in France.

**LEUCHTER REPORT** Document published in 1988 by gas chamber expert Fred Leuchter. Its conclusion – that the chambers could not have been used for mass gassings – has been cited as important evidence by Historical Revisionist spokesmen.

**LEVA FASCISTA** Process whereby members of Italian fascist youth movements 'graduated' into full party membership at the age of twenty-one.

**LIBERAL INTERNATIONAL** Global network of liberal political movements. The Austrian *Freiheitliche Partei Österreichs* (FPÖ) joined it in 1979 but had to resign from it with the onset of **Haider**'s right-wing populist leadership.

**LIBERALISM** Term used to describe a wide range of ideological positions. All liberalisms share a dislike of dictatorship and violence. Nineteenth-century economic liberalism and post-**Second World War** Continental European liberalism were free market-oriented and individualist but twentieth-century US liberalism was interventionist and mildly social-democratic. Other liberal movements have been reformist. Social liberals are libertarian and secularist on Church–state issues and sexual morality. Far-right movements have opposed most or all of these strands of liberalism and have thus seen liberalism

itself as a symptom of weakness and **decadence** in the state.

**LIBERALNO-DEMOKRATICHESKAYA PARTIYA ROSSII (RUSSIAN LIBERAL DEMOCRATIC PARTY) (LDPR)** Far-right party with a misleading name, headed by archnationalist, Vladimir **Zhirinovsky**. It is hostile to the centre-right political élite that has governed Russia since the collapse of **Communism** and is preoccupied with the loss of Russian power, expounding an irredentist policy aimed at regaining territory from former republics of the USSR. Party support peaked during the Yeltsin years. The more assertive, nationalist and partially authoritarian agenda of Vladimir Putin stole the thunder of the 'Liberal Democrats' and of other far-right groups at the start of the twenty-first century.

**LIBERTAD** Weekly paper associated with Spanish Falangist **Redondo**.

**LIBERTATE (LIBERTY)** Newspaper of the **Legion of the Archangel Michael** in 1930s Romania.

**LIBERTY BELL PUBLICATIONS** Far-right publishing house in post-war America.

**LIBERTY LOBBY** Far-right faction in post-war America.

**LIBRO E MOSCHETTO (THE BOOK AND THE RIFLE)** Weekly journal published for students by **Mussolini**'s Fascist Party.

**LIGUE DES PATRIOTES** French pressure group of the 1880s that was part of the 'new right' phenomenon which emerged out of military defeat in 1871 and the loss of Alsace–Lorraine. Led by Paul **Déroulède**, the movement campaigned vociferously for 'revenge' against the new Germany and was particularly interested in the 'racial' dimension to France's defeat.

As such it saw France's salvation in physical fitness and restored military greatness. Some historians view the *Ligue* as a significant element in French **'pre-fascism'**.

**LIGUES** Name given to the thuggish extra-parliamentary groups that sprung up in 1920s and 1930s France. There were hundreds and thousands of *ligues*, but probably the most famous were the *Jeunesses Patriotes* (JP), *Croix de Feu* (CF) and the *Parti Populaire Français* (PPF). The *ligues* appeared to be more interested in provocative urban agitation than in actually gaining power.

**LIJST PIM FORTUYN** Organisation formed in 2002 as a vehicle for the personal ambitions of maverick politician Pim **Fortuyn**. After Fortuyn's assassination in May 2002, the Lijst Pim Fortuyn came second in the Dutch parliamentary elections, sending shockwaves through the Netherlands and European politics more generally. The movement is hardline on issues of asylum and immigration but liberal on social issues.

**LION, THE** Newspaper of the **British Fascists** (BF).

**LISTE AUSLÄNDER RAUS/NATIONALE SAMMLUNG (FOREIGNERS OUT LIST/NATIONAL ASSEMBLY)** Proposed title for the 1989 NS election list – before the West German movement was outlawed.

**LISTE AUSLÄNDERSTOPP** West German far-right group that emerged in the early 1980s and scored 3 per cent in regional elections.

**LITTLE ENTENTE** A 1922 pact among three East European states, Czechoslovakia, Yugoslavia and Romania, aimed at countering ultra-nationalist Hungarian revisionism.

**LOCARNO, TREATY OF** Agreement between France, Germany and Belgium, signed in 1925. Locarno aimed to ease international tension by guaranteeing European borders fixed at **Versailles** and demilitarising the Rhineland. In March 1936 **Hitler** – quite intentionally – violated the treaty by sending German troops into the Rhineland. In retrospect, this action can be seen as a landmark in the lead-up to the outbreak of world war.

**LUPA, LA** Early twentieth-century Italian newspaper of the national-syndicalist right.

**MAFIA** Secret criminal organisation whose influence **Mussolini** was successful in curbing during the 1920s and 1930s. After the fall of *Il Duce* in 1943, Mafiosi were generally regarded as bona fide anti-Fascists.

**MALMÖ CONGRESS** Pan-European fascist event staged in 1951. Representatives from fourteen countries attended the gathering and, though they split into 'hardline' and 'moderate' camps, their legacy was the birth of **Eurofascism** and the establishment of the Malmö International.

**MANCHUKUO** Japanese **puppet state** in **Manchuria**. Manchuria and Korea had been coveted by the traditional right in Japan for some time before the Japanese occupation in the 1930s.

**MANCHURIA** Region of north-east China that was the subject of competition among Far Eastern powers, notably the Soviet Union, China and Japan, in the early twentieth century. It was occupied by Japan in 1931 and became the **puppet state** of **Manchukuo**. It was briefly held by the

USSR at the end of the war before reversion to China.

**MANIFESTE, LE** Modern French antifascist publication.

**MANIFESTO OF THE COUNTRY** Keynote 1993 policy statement issued by the Romanian *Partidul Dreapta Naţională* (PDN).

**MÄNTSÄLÄ AFFAIR** Name given to Finnish fascists' unsuccessful coup attempt in 1932.

**MARCH ON ROME** Key landmark in **Mussolini**'s rise to power. It took place on the 27 and 28 October 1922, and led ultimately to the Italian King asking Mussolini to enter government.

**MARIGNANE** Airport suburb of Marseilles where the *Front National*'s Daniel Simonpieri won municipal power in 1995.

**MARONITE CHRISTIANS** Lebanese religious and cultural community with links to France and the Catholic Church. A privileged élite during and after French colonial rule, the Maronites found themselves increasingly outnumbered by Muslims and threatened by radical left-wing militias in the 1970s. In the long civil war (1975–88), they divided into many factions, some of which modelled themselves on the Spanish *Falange*. Some far-right groups became involved in unrestrained terrorist warfare with Palestinians, the radical left and Shi'ite **militia**. Major Sa'ad Haddad ruled an Israeli-defended enclave in south Lebanon with an iron fist for most of the 1980s. Christian militias were implicated in the massacre of up to 2,000 Palestinian refugees at Chabra and Chatilla camps, Beirut, in 1984. The Maronite cause attracts the sympathy of conservative Catholic, Jewish, French and anti-Islamic groups in Europe.

**MARXISM** Body of thought derived from the writings of Karl Marx and Friedrich Engels. It described the historical transition from feudalism to **capitalism**, **socialism** and a utopian **Communism**, and offered an egalitarian and revolution-oriented critique of capitalism that linked economic and political systems to underlying material forces and class formations. Variants, including neo-Marxism, have attempted to update the ideology in the light of change. Marxism–**Leninism**, the official ideology of the USSR, emphasised the vanguard role of a ruling party and justified a totalitarian **dictatorship** on the way to utopian Communism. Fascists were especially hostile to the Marxist appeal to workers across frontiers, since this put class before **nation**. This explains the stress on national forms of socialism in fascist ideology. Marx's Jewish background is also relevant to fascist hostility, especially in Germany.

**MASS SOCIETY** An unstructured society associated with **modernity**, urbanisation and mass culture. It is best understood if contrasted with traditional society in which everyone knew their place in a **hierarchy**. Mass society was a theme in interwar sociology and philosophy, with stress being laid on the isolation and alienation of individuals uprooted by migration, **unemployment** and **war**. Mass society was believed to be prone to extremist movements and demagogues who would offer to restore meaning and cohesion to the social order.

**MATERIALISM** Belief system or way of life that attaches supreme importance to material factors like wealth, as opposed to ideas, values or spiritual things. In political philosophy, it refers to paradigms that explain history in terms of the distribution of wealth and military resources or the configuration of the forces of production. Though fascists sought power in material terms, fascist ideology claimed to be driven by higher things, especially a spiritual concept of the **nation**. Much fascist discourse echoed religious attacks on the materialism of **capitalism** (greed) and the materialist philosophy behind the Marxist theory of history.

**MCCARTHYISM** Phenomenon associated with the vehement anti-Communist campaign in the US from 1950–4. It took its name from Senator Joseph **McCarthy**, whose Congress committee sought to remove Communists and Communist sympathisers from key areas of public life, including the movie industry, the professions and the Federal Government. Though there was some **Cold War** Communist subversion and espionage, McCarthy exaggerated the scale of this activity and often targeted innocent people of moderately left-wing persuasion. His campaign collapsed when he began to attack the US Army, and he eventually lost the support of mainstream conservatives and the Republican Party. McCarthyism is now used as a pejorative description of any ideologically motivated witch-hunt, whatever its orientation.

**MEIJI RESTORATION** The termination of closed-society shogun and samurai rule in Japan in 1868 through the restoration of the Emperor. It was undertaken by modernising élites in response to Western pressure to open Japan to the outside world. Western-style bureaucracy, military organisation and industrialisation increased the country's self-confidence and facilitated expansionism from the 1890s. Modernisers sought to learn from the West in order to compete with it, a doctrine taken to extremes by the militarists of the 1930s and 1940s.

**MEIN KAMPF (MY STRUGGLE)** **Hitler**'s political testimony, written while in Landsberg prison in 1925. It put forward an élitist, totalitarian vision and was dominated by crude anti-Semitic and national-socialist ideas.

**METOPO ETHNIKISTIKIS NEOLAIAS (NATIONALIST YOUTH FRONT) (MEN)** Tiny Greek far-right party founded in 1989.

**MIDDLE CLASS** [In Marxian sociological discourse, broadly synonymous with the 'bourgeoisie'.] The middle classes had an ambiguous relationship with fascism. They shared its anti-Communist instincts and desire for order but feared the violent and brutalising aspects of fascist rule. Fascists despised the 'bourgeois respectability' of middle-class lifestyle, although fascist leaders indulged in it when they themselves reached the pinnacle of power. Fascists drew heavily on middle-class support when centre-right parties appeared to falter during the inter-war crisis, and also used their association with middle-class parties and institutions to enhance their respectability. Fascist **propaganda** distinguished between the middle class on the one hand, and, allegedly Jewish-led high financial and banking circles on the other, but the relationship was still tense and uneasy.

**MIGUELISM** Portuguese doctrine of the early twentieth century that blended **corporatism**, **Catholicism** and **authoritarianism**, and as such anticipated early fascist ideas.

**MILAN CONFERENCE** Event hosted by **Mussolini** in 1919 at which he reflected on Italy's involvement in the First World War and put forward his blueprint for her future.

**MILICE** Paramilitary police organisation established by the **Vichy** administration in 1943. It was headed first by **Laval** and then by **Darnand**, and became a key symbol of Franco-German **collaboration**. It played a significant role in the mass round-up of Jews in France.

**MILITARISM** Ambiguous term used to describe the exaltation of war and military power. It conflates **bellicism**, a belief in the value of war in itself, with pessimistic variants of realism that see war as undesirable but often necessary or unavoidable. Fascist movements have generally been overtly bellicist, since they portray international politics and the relationship among races as a Darwinian struggle in which only the fittest survive. The totalitarian projects of Nazism and Italian Fascism largely involved deliberate mobilisation for war. In other far-right regimes, such as **Franco's dictatorship** in Spain or **Pinochet**'s Chile, militarism was directed at internal enemies and was based on a cult of the **armed forces**. Fascist militarism is reflected in a discourse and symbolism of combat, struggle and discipline, leading inevitably to a rejection of pacifism and **collective security**.

**MILITIA** Type of irregular military grouping associated with far-right formations. In modern-day America, in particular, such paramilitary organisations are commonly viewed as the most sinister face of the far right. All militias share a powerful belief in **individualism** and the right to bear arms. The most extreme militias have launched armed attacks on federal government; the more moderate organisations have simply advertised their hostility to 'excessive' federal power.

**MILIZIA VOLONTARIA PER LA SICUREZZA NAZIONALE (VOLUNTARY MILITIA FOR NATIONAL SECURITY) (MVSN)** Successor to the Fascist *squadristi* – Mussolini's new regular **militia**. The MVSN was founded in 1923.

**MILLWALL** District of London that has, in relative terms, become a stronghold for the **British National Party** (BNP).

**MINIMUM VITAL** The 'living wage' prescribed by **Vichy**'s 1941 Labour Charter.

**MINISTRY FOR ARMS AND MUNITIONS** Government department involved in centralised economic planning under **Hitler**.

**MINISTRY OF CORPORATIONS** Government department set up by **Mussolini** in September 1926 to help establish the Corporate State.

**MIŞCAREA** Journal of the modern-day **Movement for Romania** (MPR).

**MOCIDADE PORTUGUESA (PORTUGUESE YOUTH) (MP)** Compulsory youth movement established by **Salazar**'s *Estado Novo* in 1936.

**MODERNISATION** A much-disputed term denoting any combination of mechanisation, industrialisation, mass education, urbanisation, secularisation and the development of mass society. Influenced by the Futurists, Italian Fascists saw modern industry, technology, social organisation and communications media as valuable instruments of state power. On the other hand, they feared the potential disorder, social reform and challenge to nationhood associated with some modernising philosophies, especially **socialism**. They also sought alliances with conservative groups who were sometimes antimodern. Thus, Fascism – and fascism – was selective and ambiguous in its response to these processes.

**MODERNITY** Controversial concept in sociology, history and philosophy. It can refer to the post-Renaissance world built around a belief in science, technology and rationality, or, more narrowly, to the products of technological and social change in the past two centuries. There is a debate over whether fascism is a modernising or an anti-modern force. Its **mysticism** and frequent rejection of rationality, together with its **ruralism** and focus on roots and tradition, suggest it is anti-modern. On the other hand, its use of mass mobilisation, totalitarian mechanisms and orchestration and mechanisation of society for racial purity or war are seen as extreme manifestations of modernity. One of the strongest modernist influences on Italian Fascism was the Futurist movement.

**MONARCHIST PARTY** Italian group that forged a short-lived electoral alliance with the *Movimento Sociale Italiano* (MSI) in 1950.

**MONDAY CLUB** Notorious grouping on the fringes of the British Conservative Party.

**MONTECATINI** Italian chemical firm that had a monopoly on the production of fertilisers under **Mussolini**. It benefited directly from his **autarchy** policy.

**MONTREUX CONFERENCE** International fascist gathering held in 1934.

**MOON ORGANISATION** Front movement for 'Rev' Sun Myung **Moon**. The body has a political and religious agenda: it is associated with the South Korean **Unification Church** and also has strong links with the **World Anti-Communist League**.

**MOSLEY MANIFESTO** 1930 memorandum – focusing mainly on economic issues – which paved the way for the formation of Oswald **Mosley**'s **New Party**.

**MOTHERLAND PARTY (ANAP)** Leading Turkish conservative political party that, according to critics, has been infiltrated by '**Grey Wolves**' and **Nationalist Action**

**Party** (MHP) sympathisers in the post-war period.

**MOUVEMENT D'ACTION CIVIQUE (MAC)** Far-right Belgian movement formed in 1960. It specialised in terrorist violence and pro-imperial nostalgia.

**MOUVEMENT NATIONAL RÉPUBLICAIN (NATIONAL REPUBLICAN MOVEMENT)** *Front National* (FN) offshoot organisation led by Bruno **Mégret**. It was previously known as the *Front National-Mouvement National* (FN-MN).

**MOUVEMENT NATIONAL ROYALISTE (NATIONAL ROYALIST MOVEMENT) (MNR)** Post-war Belgian movement that was home to many ex-collaborators.

**MOUVEMENT NATIONALISTE DE PROGRÈS** French far-right movement of the 1970s. It was led by Pierre **Bousquet** and expounded a '**Third Way**' doctrine.

**MOUVEMENT NATIONALISTE WALLON (MNW)** Regionalist extreme-right movement in post-war Belgium.

**MOUVEMENT SOCIAL BELGE (BELGIAN SOCIAL MOVEMENT) (MSB)** Small Belgian neo-fascist party founded in 1950. It was home to various ex-collaborators and ex-*Rex* activists.

**MOUVEMENT SOCIAL NATIONALISTE** Tiny Nazi group in post-war Belgium.

**MOUVEMENT SOCIALISTE D'UNITÉ (MSUF)** Anti-Communist and anti-immigrant French organisation founded in 1948 by René **Binet**. Its symbol was the Celtic cross – a clear indicator of its neo-fascist character.

**MOVEMENT FOR ROMANIA (MPR)** Ultra-nationalist grouping founded in 1991 that sees itself as heir to the Iron Guard of the 1930s.

**MOVIMENTO DE AÇÃO NACIONAL (MAN)** Short-lived skinhead group active on the Portuguese far right in the early 1990s.

**MOVIMENTO DEMOCRÁTICO DE LIBERTA-ÇÃO NACIONAL (DEMOCRATIC MOVE-MENT FOR THE LIBERATION OF PORTUGAL) (MDLP)** Rightist group of the 1970s founded by General Spinola. The organisation was dominated by military figures.

**MOVIMENTO DES FORÇAS ARMADAS (ARMED FORCES MOVEMENT) (MFA)** Body responsible for the coup that brought down the Portuguese dictatorship in the mid-1970s.

**MOVIMENTO DI AZIONE RIVOLUZIO-NARIA (REVOLUTIONARY ACTION MOVE-MENT) (MAR)** Radical Italian nationalist grouping of the 1970s founded by Carlo Fumagalli.

**MOVIMENTO INDEPENDENTE PARA A RE-CONSTRUCÃO NACIONAL (INDEPENDENT MOVEMENT OF NATIONAL RECONSTRUC-TION) (MIRN)** Pro-colonial organisation established in Portugal in 1977. It was founded by General **Kaúlza de Arriaga** and later evolved into the *Partido de Dir-eita Portuguesa* (PDP). It stood for an authoritarian solution to the country's problems and recruited its leaders from extreme-right circles.

**MOVIMENTO JOVEM PORTUGAL (YOUNG PORTUGAL MOVEMENT) (MJP)** Neo-fascist movement of the 1960s based in the university sector.

**MOVIMENTO NACIONALISTA PORTUGUÊS (PORTUGUESE NATIONALIST MOVEMENT) (MNP)** Neo-fascist movement of the 1970s.

**MOVIMENTO SOCIALE ITALIANO (ITA-LIAN SOCIAL MOVEMENT) (MSI)** Arguably the most high-profile neo-fascist move-ment in post-war Europe. Founded in De-cember 1946, most of its early members were radical ex-Fascists who had been as-sociated with the **Salò Republic**. Giorgio **Almirante** emerged as the organisation's first leader. MSI doctrine was an amalgam of **nationalism**, **corporatism** and anti-Communism; it also wanted a strong ex-ecutive president and the regular use of referenda. In 1972 the MSI won 9 per cent of the national vote. In March 1994, the right-wing *Alleanza Nazionale* alliance, of which it was a part, registered 14 per cent, and a month later entered government when it was awarded five cabinet positions in the administration headed by Silvio Berlusconi. The AN has exerted consider-able influence and now considers itself to be 'post-fascist' in political orientation. The old MSI elements remain as an in-formal tendency within the AN.

**MOVIMIENTO NACIONAL (NATIONAL MOVEMENT)** Semi-fascist grouping that emerged in Spain towards the end of the **Franco** regime.

**MOVIMIENTO NACIONAL SOCIALISTA DE CHILE (MNS)** Imitation Nazi organisation founded in 1932 by Jorge Gonzales von Mareés. It believed in **corporatism**, strong executive authority and viewed Chile as fundamentally 'European'. The *Nacis* won a 4 per cent share of the vote in pre-war elections, but were also attracted to violent tactics. Their 1938 coup attempt, however, was a complete failure.

**MOVIMIENTO NACIONALISTA DE CHILE (MNCH)** Far-right movement – heavily in-fluenced by corporatist ideas – that took up where the *Movimiento Nacional Socia-lista de Chile* (MNS) left off. It was foun-ded in 1940.

**MOVIMIENTO NACIONALISTA REVOLU-CIONARIO (MNR)** Radical cross-sectional Bolivian group that was influenced by Nazism. The organisation was active around the time of the 1952 Revolution.

**MUKDEN INCIDENT** Bombing on a strategic rail line in **Manchuria** that led to the Japanese occupation of Shenyang, then Mukden. The incident was the pretext for the full Japanese occupation of Manchuria. The actions of Japan led to the Lytton Report.

**MUNICH CONFERENCE** International summit held in September 1938 at which Chamberlain and other 'appeasers' granted Hitler the **Sudetenland**.

**MUNICH PUTSCH** Alternative name for the **Beer Hall Putsch**.

**MYSTICISM** An approach to life in which the transcendental is more important than the material. It infects some fascist thinking about **nation** and nationality. The belief is that **blood**, soil, **identity** and **language** are imbued with qualities that cannot be understood in purely rational terms. It is a very strong factor in East European far-right thinking, especially in Russia and Romania. It stands in sharp contrast to the materialist understanding of history at the heart of **Marxism**.

**MYTH** A simplified and abstract idea designed to galvanise the masses into action. As used by fascists, the concept originates in the writings of French syndicalist theoretician, Georges **Sorel**. This type of myth can look forward to an apocalyptical event or backward to an idealised past state. Sorelian thought had a significant impact on fascist **propaganda** techniques and the cult of action.

**NACIONAL SINDICALISMO (NATIONAL SYNDICALISM/BLUESHIRTS) (NS)** Portuguese movement formed in 1932, led by Rolão **Preto**, and outlawed in 1934. It was a genuinely radical fascist alternative to **Salazar**'s para-fascist *União Nacional*. In ideological terms it was ultra-nationalist, fervently Catholic and convinced that a mixture of **syndicalism** and **corporatism** could solve the economic and social problems that liberal-democracy could not (in this respect it was much influenced by **Maurras** and the *Action Française* (AF) in France). NS boasted its own youth movement and gained most support from the young urban middle classes. Estimates put its membership at *c.* 50,000. It executed a failed coup attempt in 1935.

**NACIONALNA DEMOKRATSKA LIGA (LEAGUE OF DEMOCRACY) (NDL)** Small Croatian nationalist movement of the 1990s led by Ivan **Vekić**.

**NACISMO** Name given to the political creed of the Chilean *Movimiento Nacional Socialista de Chile* (MNS) in the 1930s.

**NARODNA RADIKALNA (PEOPLE'S RADICAL PARTY)** Mainstream Serb party founded in the 1870s. Today it stands for territorial aggrandisement and a powerful brand of **ethnic nationalism**.

**NARODOWA DEMOKRACJA (NATIONAL DEMOCRATIC MOVEMENT) (ND)** Inter-war Polish movement. Many ND dissidents moved towards the semi-fascist **Pilsudski**.

**NASJONAL SAMLING (NATIONAL UNITY PARTY) (NS)** Norwegian party founded by **Quisling** in 1933. Its doctrine was a unique mix of **corporatism**, **Christianity** and anti-Communism, and incorporated a passionate belief in 'Nordic supremacy'. During the 1930s it failed to pass the 3 per cent barrier in national elections, but following occupation in 1940 it became the only legal party. Quisling became Head of State and his movement formed a 'puppet' government. By 1942 the NS was completely Nazified.

NATION A group of people who define themselves as distinct by virtue of a shared history or culture. They usually seek some level of political autonomy and, in many cases, sovereign statehood. The culture can be based on language, race, ethnicity or alternatively on loyalty to political institutions or ideologies. Fascists stressed the collective character of the nation as a community, and, thus, the absolute subordination of individual rights to the national interest. They also preferred the cultural interpretation of nation, defined in terms of ethnicity, as opposed to the civic or political concept.

NATION EUROPA German-speaking fascist forum created in 1950 by ex-*Schutzstaffel* (SS) member Arthur Erhardt.

NATIONAAL SOCIALISTISCHE BEWEGING (NATIONAL SOCIALIST MOVEMENT) (NSB) Dutch fascist movement that ended up collaborating with the Nazi occupiers in 1940. It was founded in 1931 and led by Anton **Mussert**. It peaked in 1935 when it scored almost 8 per cent in elections and boasted a membership of *c*. 60,000. However, by 1937 its share of the national vote had halved. Its value system was based on **corporatism** and a secular **conservatism**. As the 1930s wore on, the NSB became more anti-Semitic, and by 1940 Mussert was *de facto* Head of State under Nazi auspices.

NATIONAL ALLIANCE Splinter group of the American NSWPP active in the 1970s. It was led by William **Pierce**.

NATIONAL ASSOCIATION FOR THE ADVANCEMENT OF WHITE PEOPLE (NAAWP) Supremacist movement established by David **Duke** in 1980.

NATIONAL BOLSHEVISM Current of fascist thinking associated with **Niekisch**. It held that German Nazism was a perversion of 'real' fascism and, thus, that aspiring fascists and fascisms should look towards the USSR, rather than **Hitler**, for inspiration. It is self-evident that the **Führer** did not approve of National Bolshevism.

NATIONAL CHRISTIAN DEFENCE LEAGUE (LANC) Romanian far-right group – forerunner to the Iron Guard – established by Corneliu **Codreanu** and Alexandru **Cuza** in 1924. Codreanu quit in the late 1920s because, in his view, the movement was insufficiently radical.

NATIONAL CHRISTIAN PARTY Romanian movement born in 1935 out of a fusion of **Cuza**'s **National Christian Defence League** and **Goga**'s ultra-nationalist agrarian group. It failed to cross the 10 per cent barrier in the 1937 elections but held power temporarily in 1937–8 before the commencement of King **Carol**'s dictatorship.

NATIONAL COMMUNISM Term used to describe Nicolae Ceauşescu's 'Romanian' brand of relatively independent foreign and domestic policy in the Soviet bloc. Ceauşescu stressed national culture and won the approval of some post-Communist far-right movements like the *Partidul România Mare* (PRM).

NATIONAL CONFEDERATION Pro-Nazi Czech Protectorate administration set up in March 1939 under the leadership of **Beran**.

NATIONAL CORPORATE PARTY O'Duffy's final effort to create an Irish fascist movement. This grouping had a short-lived and unsuccessful existence in the mid-1930s.

**NATIONAL DEMOCRAT** Early 1980s British far-right journal. In time it was renamed *Scorpion*.

**NATIONAL DEMOCRATIC** Type of fascism akin to '**Third Positionism**'.

**NATIONAL DEMOCRATIC PARTY** Neo-fascist grouping in post-war Austria.

**NATIONAL DEMOKRATISCHE PARTEI DEUTSCHLANDS (NATIONAL DEMOCRATIC PARTY OF GERMANY) (NPD)** Neo-Nazi movement founded in 1964 and led in its early days by Friedrich Thielen and Adolf von **Thadden**. Strongly anti-immigrant, the party was heir to the *Deutsche Reichspartei* (DRP) and BHE, and put forward a '**Third Way**' policy agenda. It thrived on protest politics, appealing in particular to the '**small man**' in German society. Although it exhibited nostalgia for the Nazi era and engaged in acts of violence, it contested elections and came close on occasions to passing the 10 per cent barrier. It was the most significant neo-Nazi party to emerge after 1945.

**NATIONAL ECONOMIC CHAMBER** German body that extended state control to all economic and industrial areas.

**NATIONAL EUROPESE SOCIALE BEWEGING (NATIONAL EUROPEAN SOCIALIST MOVEMENT) (NESB)** Dutch far-right movement founded in 1953 and banned in 1955. It looked nostalgically upon the *Nationaal Socialistische Beweging* (NSB).

**NATIONAL FASCIST COMMUNITY** Czechoslovakia's only genuine fascist movement in the inter-war period. It was led by General Radola **Gajda** and polled 8 per cent in the 1935 elections. It was banned by **Beran**'s pro-Nazi **National Confederation** ad-

ministration at the start of the **Second World War**.

**NATIONAL FASCISTS** Tiny British group founded in 1925. Anti-Communist and anti-Semitic, it was more militant than the **British Fascists** movement it emerged out of. Members wore black shirts and engaged in acts of vandalism.

**NATIONAL FRONT (NF)** British party founded in 1967. Labelled variously as 'neo-Nazi', 'Strasserite' and 'Third Positionist', the movement put heavy emphasis on **nationalism**, **race** and anti-immigration policy. Its first chairman was A.K. **Chesterton**. In the 1970s it tried to make itself attractive to both **working-class** voters and Conservative Party dissidents. It had occasional electoral successes but in the 1979 elections – when it fielded over 300 candidates – it could not attain more than a 1.5 per cent share of the national vote.

**NATIONAL FRONT NEWS** Publication of the modern-day British **National Front**, around which a significant internal faction developed.

**NATIONAL GUARD** Alternative name for **O'Duffy**'s Blueshirt movement in 1930s Ireland.

**NATIONAL LABOUR PARTY (NLP)** British neo-Nazi party formed in 1958 by John Bean and John **Tyndall**. It was nostalgic for Empire and overt in its anti-immigrant **racism**. It merged to form the **British National Party** in 1960.

**NATIONAL LABOUR STATUTE** **Salazar**'s 1933 decree that banned workers' strikes.

**NATIONAL LEGIONARY STATE** Creation of Romanian leader General **Antonescu** that incorporated members of the fascist Iron Guard.

**NATIONAL OFFENSIVE (NO)** Small off-shoot movement from the German *Freiheitliche Deutsche Arbeiterpartei* (FAP).

**NATIONAL PARTY** (1) Political movement that created the system of **Apartheid** in South Africa, which established the country's reputation as a pariah in the international community. It held power continuously between 1949 and the early 1990s. (2) Short-lived British movement of the radical right – formed in 1917. (3) **National Front** (NF) breakaway movement founded in 1975 and dominated by Strasserites. Less extreme than the **Tyndall/Webster**-led NF, the NP won two local election seats in mid-Lancashire in 1976.

**NATIONAL-POPULISM** Label pinned on many far-right groups on account of their self-identification with concepts of 'nation' and 'people'. In France **Boulangism** and *Lepénisme* have both attracted this label.

**NATIONAL PREFERENCE** Policy idea put forward by the French *Front National* (FN) which puts a premium on differentiating between 'nationals' and 'non-nationals' in the granting of welfare and other rights.

**NATIONAL-RADIKALA SAMLINGSPARTIET (NATIONAL RADICAL UNITY PARTY)** Radical right-wing movement in inter-war Sweden – led by C.S. Dahlin.

**NATIONAL REVIEW** British far-right journal of the mid-1980s.

**NATIONAL REVOLUTION** Name given to the **Vichy** regime's ultra-traditionalist policy agenda, fundamental to which was a pro-**family** crusade, a 'back to the land' programme and – perhaps ironically – a strong technocratic drive. Although Germany occupied northern France in 1940, Vichy was given some leeway to govern in the south.

**NATIONAL REVOLUTIONARY** Brand of fascism associated with German writer, Ernst **Jünger**. It stressed soldierly solidarity and the need for a new heroic élite.

**NATIONAL SALVATION FRONT (NSF)** Anti-Yeltsin movement active in Russia in the early 1990s. It mixed **ultra-nationalism** with a staunch extra-parliamentary position.

**NATIONAL-SOCIALISM** Term used as a synonym for many brands of fascism – especially those represented by **Hitler**, **Mosley** and **Barrès**. It was used in many countries to denote the specific combination of '**nationalism**' and '**socialism**' that stood as the essence of fascist ideology in the economic sphere.

**NATIONAL SOCIALIST ACTION GROUP (NSAG)** Small far-right grouping active in Britain in the 1980s.

**NATIONAL SOCIALIST ALLIANCE British National Party** (BNP) splinter group of the 1990s.

**NATIONAL SOCIALIST FREEDOM PARTY (NSFP)** Radical right-wing group active in 1920s Germany; Gregor **Strasser** and Erich **Ludendorff** were key members of the movement.

**NATIONAL SOCIALIST LEAGUE** Minute pro-**Hitler** group founded by sacked **British Union of Fascists** (BUF) officials William **Joyce** and John **Beckett**. It existed between 1937 and 1939.

**NATIONAL SOCIALIST MOVEMENT (NSM)** British far-right movement founded in 1962.

**NATIONAL SOCIALIST PARTY** (1) Populist Czech organisation of the 1930s. (2) Short-lived French movement founded in 1903 by Pierre **Biétry**.

**NATIONAL SOCIALIST POLITICAL ORGANISATION (ESPO)** Small early-1940s Greek fascist group that sprung up after the Axis invasion. Pro-German and anti-Jew, ESPO upheld the national tradition. It had a couple of thousand members and was led by Dr Speros Sterodemas.

**NATIONAL SOCIALIST WHITE PEOPLE'S PARTY (NSWPP)** US neo-Nazi group that was founded in 1968 and collapsed in the 1970s.

**NATIONAL SOCIALIST WORLD** Journal of WUNS.

**NATIONAL-SOCIALISTE, LE** Pro-Hitler *Fédération Ouest-Européene* (FOE) publication banned in 1964.

**NATIONAL SOZIALISTISCHE DEUTSCHE ARBEITERPARTEI – AUSLANDS UND AUFBAUORGANISATION (NATIONAL SOCIALIST GERMAN WORKERS' PARTY – OVERSEAS BUILD-UP ORGANISATION)** Modern German neo-Nazi organisation.

**NATIONAL SYNDICALISM** Italian movement closely aligned to **Mussolini**'s Fascist Party.

**NATIONAL UNITY PARTY** Romanian movement of the 1990s particularly noted for its strident anti-Hungarian discourse. In addition to Hungarians, it has singled out Jews and **gypsies** as 'anti-national' dangers. The organisation is led by Gheorghe **Funar** and has won seats in both the Senate and Romanian parliament.

**NATIONAL WORKERS' PARTY** Small-scale British fascist movement that emerged in the immediate post-war period. It was an offshoot of the Britons Society.

**NATIONALE CENTRUM PARTIJ (NCP)** Dutch movement that anticipated the emergence of the *Centrum Partij* (CP). It was founded in 1980 but was soon dissolved.

**NATIONALE JONG-STUDENTEN VERENIGING (NATIONALIST YOUNG STUDENTS ASSOCIATION) (NJSV)** Ultra-nationalist Flemish movement founded in 1982.

**NATIONALE LIST** German neo-Nazi movement founded in 1989 and active throughout the 1990s. Based in Hamburg, it was led by Thomas Wulff and Christian Worch, and operated on the fringes of legality.

**NATIONALE SAMMLUNG (NATIONAL ASSEMBLY) (NS)** German neo-Nazi group founded in 1988, outlawed in 1989 and led by **Kühnen**.

**NATIONALE STUDENTENVERENIGING (NATIONALIST STUDENT CONFEDERATION) (NSV)** Belgian extreme-right movement active between 1976 and 1982.

**NATIONALE VOLKSPARTIJ/CP'86** New Dutch political formation arising from a far-right merger – 1995.

**NATIONALER BLOC (NATIONAL BLOCK) (NB)** German neo-Nazi movement founded in 1991 and proscribed in 1993. It was based in Bavaria.

**NATIONALISM** Doctrine that seeks to advance the political, economic and cultural interests of a given **nation**. Nations are peoples that consider themselves distinct by virtue of a common history and value system, and are usually associated with a specific place (country). Many seek to create nation-states, i.e. states that are co-terminous with the boundaries of national populations. Though the term was used in a loose sense for several centuries, modern nationalism originated with the French Revolution in which the French people were declared sovereign rulers of France. In civic or political nationalism, the people are defined by citizenship and by loyalty to national political values (e.g. in the US). Cultural nationalism, strongest in the nineteenth century, defines peoples in terms of race, ethnicity and language, and it was this which appealed to fascists. They sought the aggrandisement and glorification of the nation through war and expansionism. Nationalism serves the same purpose in rightist totalitarianism as Marxian class theories do in that of the left, as a unifying force and the focus of obligatory solidarity.

**NATIONALISM TODAY** Newspaper of the British **National Front** (NF) in the 1980s.

**NATIONALIST ACTION PARTY (MHP)** Neofascist Turkish movement that has been home to far-right 'Grey Wolves'. The MHP was led by militarist Alparslan **Turkes** during the 1980s and expounds a powerful belief in Turkish **nationalism**.

**NATIONALIST ALIGNMENT** Greek extreme-right grouping that scored less than 0.05 per cent in the 1990 parliamentary elections.

**NATIONALIST ALLIANCE** North American organisation associated with Dr William **Pierce**. It has links with various far-right movements.

**NATIONALIST MOVEMENT (MN)** Portuguese grouping of the late 1970s that looked back nostalgically on the **Salazar** dictatorship.

**NATIONALIST RIGHT, THE** Modern-day Romanian far-right newspaper.

**NATIONALISTISCHE FRONT (NATIONALIST FRONT) (NF)** Strasserite movement active in 1980s West Germany.

**NATIONALISTISCHE FRONT-BUND SOZIALREVOLUTIONÄRER NATIONALISTEN (NATIONALIST FRONT-LEAGUE OF SOCIAL REVOLUTIONARY NATIONALISTS) (NF-BSN)** West German Strasserite coalition formed in 1982.

**NATIONALITY ACT** Piece of legislation enacted by Mrs Thatcher's administration in Britain. It is argued by some observers that this 1981 act was so hardline that it helped to marginalise the **National Front** (NF).

**NATIONALREVOLUTIONÄRE ARBEITERFRONT (NATIONAL REVOLUTIONARY WORKERS' FRONT) (NRAF)** Bremen-based neo-Nazi group of the mid-1980s.

**NATIONALSOCIALISTISKA ARBETARPARTIET (NATIONAL SOCIALIST WORKERS' PARTY) (NSWP)** Small Swedish fascist movement that, in alliance with *Sveriges-National-Socialistiska Partiet*, scored less than 1 per cent in the 1936 elections. In 1938 it became *Svensk Socialistisk Samling*.

**NATIONALSOZIALISTISCHE BETRIEBSZELLENORGANISATION (NSBO)** Nazi trade union movement that embodied the hopes of leftist followers of **Hitler**. In 1934 the organisation was crushed by the **Führer** himself.

**NATIONALSOZIALISTISCHE DEUTSCHE ARBEITERPARTEI (NATIONAL SOCIALIST GERMAN WORKERS' PARTY) (NSDAP)** (1) German mass movement of the 1930s and 1940s. It was originally known as the German Workers' Party. **Hitler** joined the movement in 1919 and the title, National Socialist German Workers' Party, was adopted a year later. Hitler became leader in 1921 and its early political programme was socialist in tone. Following the **Beer Hall Putsch** of 1923 the NSDAP was banned, but reformed in 1925. Although the organisation boasted its own paramilitary arm – the *Sturm Abteilung* (SA) – it was determined to gain power democratically. In 1930 it won 107 seats and gradually emerged as a mass party. In 1932 it gained 37 per cent of the vote, and, in 1933, 43 per cent. After Hitler had been made Chancellor, the Nazi Party was deemed to be the only legal party; and through the *Schutzstaffel* (SS) and Hitler Youth, as well as many other bodies, it came to exert totalitarian control over Germany until the end of the **Second World War**. It disappeared in 1945 after Hitler's death – and was legally forbidden from reappearing. (2) Austrian sister party to the German NSDAP formed in 1926, outlawed in July 1934 and formerly known as the DAP/DNSAP. It never acquired the size or importance of the German Nazi movement and was constantly outwitted by Austria's para-fascist leader, **Dollfuss**, with whom it refused to collude. Dollfuss was eventually ousted by Hitler's *Anschluss*, not the efforts of the Austrian NSDAP. (3) Neo-Nazi movement of the 1980s with its headquarters in Lincoln, US.

**NATIONALSOZIALISTISCHE FREIHEITS-PARTEI (NATIONAL SOCIALIST FREEDOM PARTY)** Early incarnation of the Nazi Party. It took part in the 1924 elections under this name.

**NAZI–SOVIET PACT** August 1939 agreement between Germany and the Soviet Union that committed each state not to go to war against the other. It effectively rendered the USSR neutral once war began in September 1939. Under secret protocols, Poland was partitioned and the Baltic states were treated as part of the Soviet sphere of influence. The agreement demonstrated the importance of **pragma-**tism and *realpolitik*, even for two dictators whose rhetoric suggested an intense mutual hatred. The treaty was a taboo subject in the Soviet Union until the rise of the Baltic independence movements under Mikhail Gorbachev in the late 1980s.

**NAZIFICATION** The process whereby a political organisation evolves, radicalises and tries to ape German Nazism. The *Rex* movement *c.* 1937–40 in Belgium is a good example.

**NEA TAKSI (NEW ORDER) (NT)** Greek far-right movement that emerged out of military **dictatorship**. It was active between 1974 and 1977, and had links with neo-fascist groups in Italy

**NEDERLANDS BLOK (DUTCH BLOCK) (NB)** Offshoot of the far-right *Centrum Democraten*.

**NEDERLANDSE OPPOSITIE UNIE (NOU)** Post-war Dutch far-right movement that was more open than most in engaging with the democratic process.

**NEDERLANDSE VOLKSUNIE (NVU)** Dutch neo-Nazi group founded in 1971 that stood on the fringes of legality, championing an openly racist programme. It scored 0.1 per cent in the 1981 elections and disappeared soon after.

**NEO-CORPORATISM** A modification of corporatist ideas to take account of changing circumstances. It is used to refer to a voluntary form of **corporatism** practised by centrist political parties in post-war Western Europe and it involves national planning and wage agreements negotiated by a combination of government, unions, employers' organisations and farmers' groups. Neo-corporatism has been popular in strands of **Christian Democracy**, among Social Democrats and, arguably, on the left of the British Conservative Party in the 1970s. Modern neo-corporatists stress the voluntary and negotiated nature of this notion rather than any fascism-related connections it might have.

**NEO-FASCISM** Label pinned on post-war movements of the ultra-right that have links to **'classic fascism'**, but set their sights on the democratic road to power. In relation to movements of the inter-war period, neo-fascist parties have a newness and **modernity** about their **ideology** and political style.

**NEOLAIAS (EON)** Cross-class youth movement set up by General **Metaxas**'s *Elefterofronoi* (EL) party in 1930s Greece. It was a mixture of boy-scoutism and **paramilitarism**.

**NEO-LIBERALISM** Label pinned on modern Scandinavian far-right parties to denote their progressive attitudes to welfarism and the economy. Not to be confused with Anglo-Saxon free market neo-liberalism.

**NEO-NAZISM** Label pinned on post-war movements of the ultra-right that aim specifically to resurrect the **ideology** and style of the German Nazi Party.

**NEO-SOCIALISM** Political creed of many pro-Nazi French fascists in the 1930s and 1940s, especially **Déat**.

**NEO-SYNDICALISM** A modification of **syndicalism** to take account of changing circumstances. Syndicalism was a radical left-wing and anarchist philosophy advocating direct action by workers and unions to oppose and frustrate the operation of **capitalism**. Fascists liked some of its anti-capitalist rhetoric and its direct-action approach but sought to distance themselves from some of its more left-wing tendencies.

**NEUE KRONEN ZEITUNG** Austrian newspaper with some noticeable sympathy for Haider's *Freiheitliche Partei Österreichs* (FPÖ) movement.

**NEW AGE** Name of *Le Faisceau*'s newspaper in inter-war France.

**NEW ECONOMIC ORDER** Term used by Nazi officials to denote their pan-European economic blueprint.

**NEW ECONOMIC STRUCTURE** The ultimate aim of the Japanese fascist–military government; National Policy Companies contributed towards this high-profile objective.

**NEW EUROPEAN ORDER** Similar to 'New Order' but applied to Europe. It denoted the Nazi vision of a restructured Europe, rid of Jews and other 'inferior races', and dominated by Germany and Italy. While pro-fascist states or quiescent neutrals would survive in France, Iberia and South-Eastern Europe, Poland and vast areas of Russia would constitute a virtual slave labour camp and *Lebensraum* for Germany; Italy would control the Mediterranean and an isolated Britain would be forced to accept this fascist hegemony.

**NEW NATIONAL FRONT (NNF)** British movement founded by John **Tyndall** in 1982.

**NEW ORDER** (1) Term used by all three Axis regimes to describe the 'ideal', 'would-be' rearrangement of European and East Asian politics under their respective hegemonies. (2) Splinter group of the neo-Nazi American NSWPP, led by Matt Koehl. (3) Small Neo-Nazi movement active in Portugal between 1980 and 1982. (4) Small fascist group active in inter-war South Africa.

**NEW PARTY** Sir Oswald **Mosley**'s first attempt at creating a political movement after resigning from the Labour Government in 1930. Its programme was dominated by economic concerns.

**NEW RIGHT** In conventional political discourse, a term that refers to the neoliberal and anti-statist strand in Anglo-American **conservatism** in the 1980s and 1990s. New Right policies favour a rolling back of the state and a radical critique of social democracy, and are much less nostalgic and racist than earlier strands of conservatism. New Right spokesmen in Britain and the US are divided on social and **gender** issues. Some favour a recasting of social conservatism in utilitarian terms, while others embrace libertarianism. The far right has responded in two ways: by describing its own racist and extremist philosophy as 'New Right' or '*Nouvelle Droite*', or, by mixing themes from this approach with some of the anti-government rhetoric of the Anglo-American New Right. The strategy leads to considerable confusion, not unlike that resulting from Vladimir **Zhirinovsky**'s decision to name his illiberal party the 'Liberal Democratic Party'.

**NEW WORLD ORDER** Vision of an international order regulated by a consensus among the major powers and action against aggression set out by US President George Bush in the context of the Gulf War in 1991. Tensions among the powers ever since and the lack of will to act against human rights violations in the Balkans and Rwanda have somewhat tarnished the concept. The European far right, notably the French *Front National* (FN), as well as the European left, derided the idea as self-serving and hypocritical on the part of the US. Nonetheless, academics like Francis Fukuyama have defended the existence of a tenuous new consensus around **democracy**, international norms and free-market **capitalism**.

**NEZAVISMA DRŽAVA HRVATSKA (INDEPENDENT STATE OF CROATIA) (NDH)** Formal title of the *Ustasha* regime that ruled Croatia between 1941 and 1945. Elements of the modern Croatian right look upon the NDH with nostalgia.

**NIEUWE KRACHTEN** Flemish name of Belgian movement *Parti des Forces Nouvelles* (PFN).

**NIGHT OF THE LONG KNIVES** Name given to **Hitler**'s **putsch** of 1934. It removed key rivals from within the Nazi Party, including *Sturm Abteilung* (SA) leader, Ernst **Röhm**.

**NIHILISM** Belief in nothingness and a rejection of all past knowledge, partly indebted to the work of Friedrich **Nietzsche**. It has a paradoxical relationship with fascism. Whereas fascists believed very strongly in the **nation** or the strong **state**, they did require their followers to reject their previous socialisation into 'smug' bourgeois notions of civilised behaviour and society. Nihilism and relativism were often the first steps on the way to fascism. Nietzsche's rejection of God was a useful starting point in the brutalisation of the mind. Only someone who had cleared their mind of compassion or moral scruples, for instance, could uncritically follow a leader like **Hitler** or rejoice in the **Holocaust**. The nihilistic strand was especially evident in the flirtation with anarchism that was a feature of '**prefascism**' in the late nineteenth and early twentieth centuries. However, it is important to realise that mature fascism merely used nihilism as a device for smashing pre-existing moral sensitivities. Unlike true nihilists, however, it posited an alternative belief system to replace the nihilism and alienation of modern society.

**NOONTIDE PRESS** US publishing house that deals in racist material.

**NORDIC THINKING** Ideological approach adopted by inter-war Norwegian fascists, stressing the primacy of Norwegian values and heritage. Hence the 'Nordic Principle', the basis of European **civilisation** according to inter-war Norwegian fascists.

**NORDIC WORLD FEDERATION/MOVEMENT** The ultimate aim of Norwegian fascist, Vidkun **Quisling** – basically, a coming together of all Nordic peoples in an anti-Jewish and anti-Marxist coalition.

**NORDISK FOLKREISNING (NORDIC FOLK AWAKENING)** Regenerationist organisation founded by Norwegian fascist, **Quisling**, in 1931.

**NORMAL FASCISM** Phrase used by Nolte to describe one particular 'level' of fascism. He argues that 'normal fascism' equates to the **Mussolini** system in Italy.

**NORTHERN LEAGUE** (1) Regionalist and anti-immigrant movement active in modern Italy – see entry for *Lega Nord*. (2) Trans-national organisation founded in 1958 to promote Teutonic solidarity among Nazi sympathisers and create links between the radical right and conservative right. Roger **Pearson** was its first leader.

**NORTHERN WORLD** Publication associated with the trans-national **Northern League**.

**NOTRE EUROPE** Publication of the *Faisceaux Nationaux et Européens* (FNE)/*Fédération d'Action Nationale et Européenne* (FANE).

**NOUA DREAPTĂ** Modern Romanian far-right newspaper.

**NOUVEL EUROPE MAGAZINE (NEM)** Far-right Belgian magazine founded in 1944.

It was edited by Emile Lecerf and in time spawned 'NEM-clubs'. *Nouvel Europe Magazine* was '**Third Way**' in political orientation and also had **New Right** connections.

**NOUVEL ORDRE EUROPÉEN (NEW EUROPEAN ORDER) (NOE)** Franco-Swiss organisation that emerged out of the 1951 international fascist congress in Malmö. It was global in both character and scope.

**NOUVELLE DROITE (NEW RIGHT) (ND)** Umbrella term used to denote the various flowerings of radical right-wing thinking in France from the 1970s onwards. In organisational terms the phenomenon of the *Nouvelle Droite* encompasses the *Groupement de Recherche et d'Étude pour la Civilisation Européennes* (GRECE), the *Club de l'Horloge*, *Nouvelle École* and other 'new' right-wing cells and study groups. In ideological terms, it synthesises a unique series of attitudes: most notably, the belief in science and élites, and the rejection of **egalitarianism**, multi-culturalism and anti-**racism**. It is also hostile to **Christianity** and **Marxism**, to the US and the values represented by the former USSR. Alain de **Benoist** has become the leading spokesman for the *Nouvelle Droite*; **Nietzsche** and Julius **Evola** rank among the most significant influences on its thinking. There is some interplay with the *Front National* (FN). **Le Pen**'s movement has certainly been influenced by its ideas but, understandably perhaps, the *Nouvelle Droite* is not keen to be associated with such a controversial political figure. Even so, some commentators view the *Nouvelle Droite* as the embodiment of a new type of modern '**Third Way**' fascism.

**NOUVELLE ÉCOLE** Post-war French journal that championed the ideas of the *Nouvelle Droite*.

**NOVECENTO** Inter-war cultural movement that viewed Italian Fascism as a positive, enlightened force. The philosophy of *Novecentismo* also spawned a journal called *Novecento*.

**NOVISMO** Literally 'newism', a key ideological current that infiltrated the Italian Fascist movement in the 1920s. **Mussolini**'s son was a leading 'novist'. He and others argued that *Il Duce* personified a new epoch in Western **civilisation** and that Fascists should rid themselves of 'dated' ideas and conservative allies.

**NS KAMPFRUG (NATIONAL-SOCIALIST BATTLE CRY)** German neo-Nazi publication associated with Gary Lex Lauck.

**NUCLEI ARMATI RIVOLUZIONARI (NAR)** Military wing of the Italian *Movimento Sociale Italiano* (MSI).

**NUEVA ACRÓPOLIS (NEW ACROPOLIS)** Pro-Nazi Spanish organisation of the 1980s.

**NUOVA DESTRA (NEW RIGHT) (ND)** Italian movement founded in the late 1970s. It sought to break with the past and rethink the whole nature and meaning of political combat. It shared much in common with the French *Nouvelle Droite*.

**NUREMBERG TRIALS** An attempt to bring Nazism to justice after the horrors of the **Second World War** and the **Holocaust**. The trials began in November 1945 and passed sentence on those Nazis who had not already escaped Germany or committed suicide. **Frick**, **Keitel**, **Ribbentrop** and **Rosenberg** were hanged; **Speer** and **Hess** were given long prison terms; others were acquitted. Nuremberg was a poignant setting for these set-piece events because of **Hitler**'s many rallies in the city. However, in the sense that the trials did not evaluate the guilt of Russia, they were not entirely satisfactory.

**NY DEMOKRATI (NEW DEMOCRACY)** Militant right-wing Swedish party formed in 1991 by Bert **Karlsson** and Ian **Wachmeister**. By the end of the 1990s it had become an almost non-existent electoral force.

**NYILASKERESZTES PÁRTOT (ARROW CROSS PARTY-HUNGARIST MOVEMENT)** Fascist organisation – with a strong **working-class** following – that polled around 30 per cent in national elections towards the end of the 1930s. The party was marginalised by the superficial '**Nazification**' of the **Horthy** regime, but in 1944 took over the running of the country in association with the Nazis. Hungary under the Arrow Cross became the ultimate in puppet states and was particularly efficient in aiding the Nazis' anti-Jewish **pogrom**. The organisation, led by Ferenc **Szálasi**, was previously known as the **Party of National Will**. The new title was adopted in 1937.

# O

**OBÓŹ NARODOWO-RADYKALNY (CAMP OF RADICAL NATIONALISM) (ONR)** Polish ultra-nationalist movement of the 1930s. Its discourse was dominated by **anti-Semitism** and the need for a strong state.

**OBÓŹ ZJEDNOCZENIA (OZN)** Polish movement founded by General Śmigly-Rydz in 1937. It looked back nostalgically on the **Pilsudski** era and also sought an alliance with the far-right *Falanga* movement.

**OCCIDENT** French neo-fascist group founded in 1964 by Pierre **Sidos**. Fiercely anti-leftist, it had a strong following among students and operated on the fringes of legality. It was eventually banned in 1968.

**ODAL RING** Paramilitary terror group in post-war Belgium.

**ODESSA** Organisational network that helped key figures in the Nazi Party, particularly members of the *Schutzstaffel* (SS), to flee Germany after 1945.

**ŒUVRE, L'** French fascist journal of the 1930s and 1940s.

**ŒUVRE FRANÇAISE** Neo-fascist movement formed in the late 1960s and led by Pierre **Sidos**. It was the successor movement to *Jeune Nation*.

**OFFICE CENTRAL DE RÉPARTITION DES PRODUITS INDUSTRIELS** Government agency responsible for French economic policy during the **Vichy** period.

**OJCZYZNA (THE FATHERLAND)** Ultra-nationalist newspaper in 1990s Poland.

**OKLAHOMA BOMBING** Terrorist crime in 1995 associated with far-right US extremists.

**OKTOBERFEST** Munich festival that was the scene of a massive neo-Nazi bombing incident in 1980. Thirteen people were killed.

**OLYMPIA RALLY** Notorious public event in the history of the **British Union of Fascists** (BUF) – 1934.

**ONR-FALANGA** Fascist movement active in inter-war Poland. It stood for a particularly virulent brand of Catholic **anti-Semitism**.

**OPERA NAZIONALE BALILLA (NATIONAL BALILLA AGENCY) (ONB)** Body established by **Mussolini** in 1926 to promote Fascist ideology among the young. Affiliation to the ONB ultimately became the only route to survival for previously autonomous youth clubs and sporting organisations. It had to compete with many and various Catholic youth groups.

**OPERA NAZIONALE DOPOLAVORO (NATIONAL AFTER-WORK LEISURE ORGANISATION) (OND)** Formed in 1925, this body regulated all aspects of 'leisure time' in **Mussolini**'s Italy. It was interested in popular culture, sport, rural life, working conditions; in sum, the moral and economic well-being of individual Italians.

**ORANGE** Southern French town where Jacques Bompard gained municipal power for the *Front National* (FN) in 1995.

**ORDENSBURGEN (ORDER CASTLES)** Schools established by the Nazis for the training of future national-socialist leaders. *Ordensburgen* were the first to be founded – in 1933.

**ORDER, THE** Militant right-wing American movement with **Ku Klux Klan** links, founded in 1983.

**ORDINE NUOVO (NEW ORDER) (ON)** Radical *Movimento Sociale Italiano* (MSI) splinter group founded in 1956 by Elio **Massagrande**. It operated on the fringes of Italian politics.

**ORDRE NOUVEAU (NEW ORDER) (ON)** Neo-fascist group, founded in 1969, which attempted to become the 'French *Movimento Sociale Italiano*'. It failed – but helped to give birth to **Le Pen**'s *Front National* in 1972.

**ORGANIC CONCEPTION OF SOCIETY** Belief that society is like a living organism that evolves from nature over time, as something that is deep-rooted and natural rather than artificial. It is a key feature of cultural and social **conservatism**, as well as **cultural nationalism**. Those who believe in the organic conception of society argue that radical experimentation with 'the natural order of things' is undesirable. For fascist leaders, the **'nation'** or the 'people', or the '*Volk*' extolled by **Hitler**, had the same organic character.

**ORGANISATION DE L'ARMÉE SECRÈTE (SECRET ARMY ORGANISATION) (OAS)** In 1961, as the reality of Algerian independence from France drew closer, the OAS was born. It comprised mainly ultra-nationalistic ex-Army personnel. The movement's hardline *Algérie Française* vision resulted in a sustained campaign of anti-republican terror, including bombings and assassinations.

**ORGANISATION OF THE NATIONAL SOVEREIGN STATE** Far-right Greek movement of the 1930s led by Theodore Skilakakis – who became Interior Minister under General **Metaxas** in 1936. It was based in Thessaloniki.

**ORTHODOX CHURCH** Organisation that in Russia and Serbia, in the late twentieth and early twenty-first centuries, has frequently been linked to far-right extremism.

**OSSEWA BRANDWAG/OSSEWABRANDWAG (OX-WAGON SENTINEL) (OB)** South African ultra-nationalist movement of the inter-war years. It championed Afrikaner culture and displayed noticeable sympathy for the Nazis.

**OSTPOLITIK** Literally, 'eastern policy'. Term used to describe Germany's relations with Communist Eastern Europe, especially its efforts at *détente* with East Germany under Chancellor Willy Brandt, during the late 1960s and 1970s. This policy was opposed by the far right and by many conservatives as well. The term can also be used more loosely to cover German policy towards countries in the 'buf-

fer zone' between Germany and Russia throughout the twentieth century. **Hitler** saw expansion here, and into Russia itself, as a guarantee of *Lebensraum* or 'living space' for Germany.

**OSTRAUM** German term for satellite states not directly administered by Berlin and not incorporated into the Reich.

**OUR NATION (ON)** Far-right British movement active mainly in the 1980s and associated with Martin **Webster**.

# P

**PAGEANTRY** Fascist and far-right movements use the symbolism of flags, parades, military drills, uniforms, emblems and salutes for purposes of self-glorification and to make very public statements about their presence in the public sphere. The orchestration and mobilisation of large numbers of participants conveys a sense of discipline and power, as exemplified in the torch-lit processions and massed ranks of adulating crowds seen at Hitler's Nuremberg rallies.

**PAISLEYISM** Strand of Ulster Unionism associated with the Reverend Ian Paisley's Democratic Unionist Party in Northern Ireland and encapsulated in the slogan 'No Surrender'. It embraces ultra-loyalism, fear of treachery by the British Government and a fundamentalist Biblical Protestantism that is often harshly critical of what it disparagingly calls 'the Church of Rome'. Hardcore supporters of Paisleyism are associated with Paisley's own Free Presbyterian Church. Though opposed to **terrorism**, the movement is not averse to hinting at violence, as, for instance, when Dr Paisley's supporters marched against the Anglo-Irish Agreement in the early 1980s carrying firearms licenses.

**PALAZZO CHIGI AGREEMENT** Important pact signed in December 1923 by **Mussolini** and Italian industrialists.

**PALAZZO VIDONI AGREEMENT** Pact signed in October 1925 by **Mussolini** and Italian industrialists.

**PAMYAT (NATIONAL PATRIOTIC FRONT)** Far-right nationalist and anti-Semitic movement in post-Communist Russia. Operating under the slogan of 'God, Tsar, Nation', its programme combines conservative Slavophile doctrines with support for other far-right parties in Europe. It advocates restoration of an autocratic monarchy, economic nationalism, a ruralist economy, anti-Westernism and a central role for the Russian Orthodox Church. Always on the fringe, it has been further marginalised by Vladimir Putin's nationalist policies, but is still capable of noisy and symbolic protest.

**PANELLINIO ETHNIKO METOPO (PANHELLENIC NATIONAL FRONT) (PEM)** National-socialist movement that emerged in 1930s Athens, employing terror tactics against local Communists.

**PAN-NATIONALISM** Form of **nationalism** that attempts to unite peoples of the same cultural or ethnic family under one roof, with or without a single state. Hitler and most German nationalists wanted to bring the Germans of Austria and the Czech **Sudetenland** into one country; *Pamyat* and modern Russian cultural nationalists want to bring Russians, Ukrainians and Belorussians together under the banner of pan-Slavism; while pan-Turkism emphasises commonalities among the peoples of Turkey, Central Asia and western China. For inter-war fascists, 'pan-nationalisms'

offered a basis for aggressive expansionism and/or **irredentism**.

**PARA-FASCISM** Label pinned on right-wing authoritarian governments that, for pragmatic political purposes, wish to give off the impression that they are populist and dynamic fascist-type regimes, while at the same time resisting any genuine moves in a radical direction. Para-fascist regimes do not have a popular revolutionary base and usually view 'authentic' fascism as a threat they have to neutralise. The inter-war regimes headed by **Salazar** in Portugal and **Dollfuss** in Austria are generally viewed as the best examples of para-fascism in action. Para-fascism is also referred to as 'fascism from above' and 'cosmetic fascistisation'.

**PARAMILITARISM** Phenomenon associated with fascist and radical left-wing groups that involves the mobilisation of private armies alongside or behind political parties. Examples include the *squadristi* in Fascist Italy, the Nazi Storm Troopers and the Falangist militia in modern Lebanon. These organisations could be highly disciplined, especially when the movement as a whole was in power, but they also provided street-fighters and a thuggish element that menaced and harassed political opponents. Fascist and far-right **propaganda** emphasises the heroic, violent and combative spirit of their paramilitary groups.

**PARLIAMENTARY DEMOCRACY** Political system in which executive power is dependent on a democratically elected and party-dominated legislature. Fascists viewed parliamentary systems as talking shops and abhorred the multiplicity of parties that often arose in them. On the other hand, they were often adept at using parliamentary procedures and coalition politics to their advantage, as they gave smaller parties a platform from which to play a disproportionately influential role in national politics.

**PARTEI DER ARBEIT (PDA)** Small German far-right movement of the 1980s that evolved into the *Volkssozialistische Bewegung Deutschlands/Partei der Arbeit* (VSBD/PdA).

**PARTI DES FORCES NOUVELLES (PARTY OF THE NEW FORCES) (PFN):** (1) Belgian movement founded in 1975. Xenophobic and illiberal, it scored just over 1 per cent in 1989 elections. (2) Small French movement of the extreme right. It was formed in 1974 after the dissolution of *Ordre Nouveau* and won just over 1 per cent of votes in the 1979 European elections. It disappeared in the early 1980s.

**PARTI NATIONAL BELGE (PNB)** Post-war Belgian movement that advanced a strongly pro-colonial discourse and was influenced heavily by the **integral nationalism** of the *Action Française*. It gained 0.1 per cent of the vote in the 1961 parliamentary elections and disappeared in 1972.

**PARTI NATIONALISTE FRANÇAIS (PNF)** Extreme-right organisation that emerged out of the journal, *Militant*, in the 1970s.

**PARTI NATIONALISTE FRANÇAIS EUROPÉEN (PNFE)** Small anti-immigrant group active in 1980s France.

**PARTI PATRIOTIQUE RÉVOLUTIONNAIRE (PPR)** French fascist movement founded by Biaggi in 1954. Based in Algeria, its main constituency was students and military **veterans**.

**PARTI POPULAIRE FRANÇAIS (PPF)** Raucous anti-Communist movement founded by ex-Communist Jacques **Doriot** in 1936. It stood for a powerful, authoritarian brand of **nationalism** and utilised **Joan of Arc** as its main patriotic symbol (this, however, did not stop it from adopting a pro-German stance in the late 1930s). Estimates put PPF membership at anything between 50,000 and 300,000 – predominantly young, disenchanted **working-class** males. It has been argued that the party's discourse was more overtly fascist during the German occupation than it was prior to it.

**PARTI RÉPUBLICAIN ET SOCIAL** Successor movement to the French *Jeunesses Patriotes* (JP).

**PARTI SOCIAL FRANÇAIS (PSF)** Successor movement to the *Croix de Feu* (CF). The PSF was a political movement in a way that the CF was not. Led by Colonel de la **Rocque**, it was more moderate in its nationalist and anti-Communist discourse, and attracted a slightly more respectable clientele. In the late-1930s it claimed to have between 1 and 3 million members, but the dislocation of war put an end to its influence.

**PARTI SOCIALISTE DESTOURIEN** Post-war Tunisian movement based on national-socialist foundations.

**PARTIAL FASCISM** Alternative term to **semi-fascism**.

**PARTIDO DE DEMOCRACIA CRISTA (CHRISTIAN DEMOCRATIC PARTY) (PDC)** Small pro-colonial group on the radical right of Portuguese politics in the 1970s. It made alliances with the *Movimento Independente para a Reconstrucão Nacional* (MIRN) and the *Partido de Direita Portuguesa* (PDP) but never received more than 2 per cent of votes in national elections.

**PARTIDO DE DIREITA PORTUGUESA (PARTY OF THE PORTUGUESE RIGHT) (PDP)** Successor movement to the far-right *Movimento Independente para a Reconstru-*

*cão Nacional* (MIRN). Staunchly anti-Communist, it believed that authoritarian solutions were required to solve the nation's problems. It had very limited electoral success.

**PARTIDO DE PROGRESSO (PROGRESS PARTY) (PP)** Portuguese far-right movement born in the mid-1970s after the fall of the **dictatorship**.

**PARTIDO FORÇA NATIONAL** 1990s successor movement to the Portuguese *Força National-Nova Monarquia* (FN-NM).

**PARTIDO LIBERAL (LIBERAL PARTY) (PL)** Portuguese neo-fascist movement that emerged in the mid-1970s after the demise of the right-wing dictatorship.

**PARTIDO NACIONALISTA ESPAÑOL (SPANISH NATIONALIST PARTY) (PNE)** Small proto-fascist movement founded by Dr José María **Albiñana y Sanz** in 1930. The PNE is regarded by historians as one of the first flowerings of Spanish fascism.

**PARTIDO REVOLUCIONARIO INSTITUTIONAL (PRI)** Inter-war Mexican movement that gained power on a populist agenda that was both rightist and leftist in origin. The PRI had a hegemonic position in the Mexican political system until liberalisation in the late 1990s.

**PARTIDUL DREAPTA NAŢIONALĂ (PARTY OF THE NATIONAL RIGHT) (PDN)** Romanian extreme-right movement founded in 1992 that has had almost non-existent electoral success. Nostalgic for the inter-war Iron Guard movement, the PDN believes in an ethnocratic state and is hostile to all immigrants and national minorities, especially Hungarians. The party is led by Radu **Sorescu** and boasts its own green and black uniform.

**PARTIDUL ROMÂNIA MARE (GREATER ROMANIA PARTY) (PRM)** Modern political movement that mixes **ultra-nationalism** and nostalgia for the Ceauşescu regime. It is particularly hostile to Jews, Hungarians and **gypsies**.

**PARTIDUL UNITATI NATIONALE ROMÂNE (ROMANIAN NATIONAL UNITY PARTY) (PUNR)** Zealous anti-Hungarian movement active in modern-day Romania. Led by **Funar**, it is part of the Romanian Cradle organisation and has polled around 8 per cent in national elections.

**PARTITO DEMOCRATICO DI UNITÀ MONARCHIA (DEMOCRATIC PARTY OF MONARCHIST UNITY) (PDUM)** Later name of the Italian *Partito Popolare Monarchico* (PPM).

**PARTITO FASCISTA REPUBBLICANO (FASCIST REPUBLICAN PARTY) (PFR)** **Mussolini**'s revamped movement, formed in 1943. The PFR's political programme had much in common with early Italian Fascism, but it was slightly more socialist and anti-Semitic (and its formal title indicated its break with monarchism). *Il Duce*'s new organisation dominated the short-lived **Salò Republic** and, in the aftermath of war, was to inspire the creation and discourse of the *Movimento Sociale Italiano* (MSI).

**PARTITO NAZIONALE FASCISTA (NATIONAL FASCIST PARTY) (PNF)** Founded in November 1921, this movement supplied **Mussolini** with his political base for the duration of his premiership. The PNF was heir to the *Fasci di Combattimento* and absorbed the *Associazione Nazionale Italiana* (ANI). Its programme was based on the twin pillars of **nationalism** and **corporatism**. The PNF wavered between legal and illegal political tactics.

**PARTITO NAZIONALE MONARCHIO (NATIONAL MONARCHIST PARTY) (PNM)** Far-right monarchist group active in post-war Italy and led by Achille Lauro.

**PARTITO POPOLARE MONARCHICO (PPM)** Far-right Italian monarchist group that was able to pass the 10 per cent barrier in early post-war elections.

**PARTITO POPULARE ITALIANO (ITALIAN POPULAR PARTY) (PPI)** Christian Democrat-style movement active in inter-war Italy. Led by Sturzo, it was influential in Catholic circles but detested by **Mussolini**'s Fascists – who regarded it as significant competition, particularly in the north.

**PARTY OF HUNGARIAN REVIVAL** Ultra-nationalist movement of the 1930s and 1940s led by Béla **Imrédy**. It boasted a respectable, middle- and upper-class membership.

**PARTY OF NATIONAL WILL** Hungarian fascist movement founded by Ferenc **Szálasi** in 1935. It was later renamed the Arrow Cross Party.

**PARTY OF RACIAL DEFENCE** Inter-war ethnic Hungarian movement supported by the **Awakening Hungarians** and *Etelköz Association* (EKSZ). **Gömbös** was its leading spokesman.

**PARTY OF ROMANIAN NATIONAL UNITY (PRNU)** Modern far-right party that has supported post-Ceauşescu administrations.

**PARTY OF WELL-BEING** Splinter group of the Danish **Progress Party**, formed in 1990.

**PASSATISMO (PASTISM)** The main enemy of society, according to Italian Futurists, who had a major influence on early Fascism.

**PATRIE** Emotive French word denoting 'fatherland'. It is often employed by fas-cists or neo-fascists to describe the abstract entity at the crux of their nationalist discourse.

**PATRIOT MOVEMENT** Loose grouping of right-wing activist groups in the US since 1980. Patriot groups are generally pro-gun, anti-tax and conservative. Some have clearly racist agendas and some have been linked to terrorist violence.

**PATRIOTIKO KINEMA (PATRIOTIC MOVEMENT)** Greek neo-fascist organisation.

**PATRIOTISM** Love of country. It is distinguishable from **nationalism** in the sense that the latter links love of country to the agenda of the nation-state. Conservatives, nationalists, fascists and traditionalists often draw on patriotic sentiment, though their critics on the left challenge their claim of a monopoly on patriotism. Fascist parties generally attempt to equate patriotism with support for their movements or leaders.

**PAX** Polish Catholic movement that existed, with government approval, in the post-war period. Its head was ex-*Falanga* leader, Boleslaw **Piasecki**.

**PAYS RÉEL, LE** Newspaper of the *Rex* movement in Belgium.

**PEARL HARBOR** US naval base in the Hawaiian Islands attacked by Japan in December 1941. The raids propelled the US into the **Second World War** after years of procrastination and isolationism. Japan aimed to neutralise the US Navy to give herself a free hand in the western Pacific but the humiliation merely strengthened US resolve.

**PEASANT UNION** Latvian movement that ended democracy in 1934 and then established its own fascist rule.

**PEASANTRY** Poor landholders, frequently the bastion of traditional and conservative thinking, especially on family issues and social policy. Idealised by fascist movements who extolled their roots in the land, their hard work and their connection with the soil of the 'fatherland'. Peasant life was contrasted with the rootlessness, chaos, radicalism and **materialism** of urban society. Fascist appeals to the peasantry were an attempt to tap into traditional **conservatism** but, apart from Nazi efforts at fixing agricultural prices, fascist policies did little to help the rural poor in practice. However, East European fascist movements, like the Romanian Iron Guard, were more genuinely ruralist in this sense than their Western counterparts.

**PĒRKONKRUST (THUNDER CROSS)** Fascist movement in inter-war Latvia (formerly *Ugunkrust*). They published a newspaper of the same name.

**PERÓNISM** Movement associated with Argentine General Juan **Perón** and his followers. It stood as a coalition of non-Communist trade unions, populist sections of the **armed forces** and conservative élites in an autocratic military regime that copied some fascist traits. In power, Perón gradually abandoned much of his left-wing **populism** and the dictatorship evolved into a classic Latin American military system. Modern-day *Perónistas*, notably under the leadership of Carlos Menem in the 1990s, reconciled themselves to liberal democracy and adopted a free-market economic agenda.

**PERUVIANISATION** Nationalist dream of the Peruvian **APRA** movement.

**PESARO** Scene of **Mussolini**'s famous August 1926 speech in which a policy of deflation was announced.

**PHILO-NAZI** Label pinned on the most obsessive mimics of, or collaborators with, Nazism: for example, **Beran** in Czechoslovakia and van **Tonningen** in the Netherlands.

**PHINEAS PRIESTHOOD** Modern US phenomenon of 'leaderless resistance', whereby individual armed terrorists take it upon themselves to shoot down 'anti-national' enemies such as Jews, blacks, left-wing radicals and homosexuals. The Priesthood claims biblical authority.

**PILSUDSKI REGIME** Ruled Poland in the inter-war years. Nolte views it as an archetypal example of 'early fascism'.

**PLAN** The ultimate product of organised **capitalism** and fascism's alliance with big business. Hitler and Mussolini both tried to control the economy via Four-Year Plans.

**PLATONIC PHILOSOPHY** Thought of the Greek philosopher, Plato, which emphasised the distinction between crude public opinion and 'true' knowledge. Plato's *Republic* appeared to argue for rule by a knowledgeable and virtuous élite that could bring justice to society. Subsequent collectivist, utopian and totalitarian blueprints can be traced, at least in part, to this world view. This negative influence of Plato has been a key theme for writers like Karl Popper. Marxist theorists, on the other hand, contest the linkage among these philosophies and their indebtedness to Plato.

**PLEBISCITE** A referendum on a single issue in public policy. A favourite instrument of dictators like **Hitler** in Germany and **Dollfuss** in Austria. The Nazis used plebiscites to legitimate Hitler's seizure of power and the *Anschluss* or 'Union' of Austria and Germany. This was to counter charges that they were undemocratic, but it was also part of a totalitarian strategy of mobilising the masses behind the regime. Nazi plebiscites often produced exaggerated positive votes due to the use of fraud and/or intimidation.

PLUTOCRACY Rule by the wealthy. Derogatory term for capitalist liberal democracy much favoured by Nazi and Fascist propagandists. Referred to the alleged power of an élite based around banking and financial interests, especially Jewish magnates like the Rothschilds.

PNEUMATIKI ANANEOTIKI ORMI (INTELLECTUAL RENOVATING MOVEMENT) (PAO) Greek neo-fascist movement of the 1970s, led by Dakoglou.

POGROM From Russian, 'gromit', to destroy – the systematic massacre of a large number of people, especially those of the same ethnic or religious background. Anti-Semitic pogroms were a feature of East European and Russian history. The Europe-wide persecution of Jews under Nazi rule constituted an extended pogrom.

POLICE STATE A political system in which a state police force exercises wide-ranging powers to suppress political dissent using methods that include arbitrary arrest, detention, torture, intrusive surveillance and intimidation. The Soviet Cheka (and, later, KGB), the German **Gestapo** and Communist Romania's *Securitate* have all been central players in the machinery of their respective dictatorships. A police state was a feature of the classic Communist and fascist regimes, though both post-Communist and post-fascist parties now appear to reject it as essential to their philosophies.

POLICIA DE VIGILANCIA E DEFESA DO ESTADO (PVDE) **Salazar**'s original secret police force.

POLICIA INTERNACIONAL E DE DEFESA DO ESTADO (PIDE) **Salazar**'s post-*Policia de Vigilancia e Defesa do Estado* (PVDE) secret police force.

POLITICA Portuguese neo-fascist journal founded in 1969.

POLITICAL SOLDIER Variant of the Third Position strategy, calling for a new fighting élite to take responsibility for the future. This brand of fascism is particularly associated with Julius **Evola**'s writings.

POLITIKI ANEXARTITOS PARATAXIS (POLITICALLY INDEPENDENT ALIGNMENT) (PAP) Extreme-right movement and home to **Metaxas** loyalists who fought the 1950 Greek elections.

POLITIKI ANOIXI (POLITICAL SPRING) Strongly nationalistic Greek movement of the 1990s led by Antonis Samaras.

POLSKA WSPÓLNOTA NARODOWA-POLSKIE STRONNICTWO NARODOWE (POLISH NATIONALIST UNION - THE POLISH NATIONALIST PARTY) (PWN-PSN) Anti-Semitic and anti-Catholic movement that emerged in the 1990s. A negligible electoral force, it blames the Jews for all of Poland's misfortunes.

POPOLO D'ITALIA, IL Early fascist newspaper and mouthpiece for **Mussolini**.

POPULAR FRONT Name given to the organised left in situations where it has united to oppose fascism. France and Spain both gave birth to 'anti-fascist' ententes between socialists and Communists in the inter-war period.

POPULAR PARTY Anti-immigration and anti-abortion. Paulo **Portas**'s modern far-right movement is now stronger than the

Portuguese Communist party in electoral terms.

**POPULAR SOCIALIST VANGUARD** Successor movement to the Chilean *Movimiento Nacional Socialista de Chile* (MNS), established in 1941.

**POPULISM** An approach to politics that appeals to the 'man or woman in the street' and casts them in a favourable light relative to wealthy, educated or influential élites. Fascist leaders liked to represent themselves as people from humble origins who were sympathetic to the people. Similarly, they sought public approval and adulation for their policies, in spite of the fact that men like **Mussolini** and **Hitler** were not typical of other Italians and Germans, and enjoyed power and élite status. Though conservative populist movements can be genuine, fascist populism was often merely a matter of tactics and style. Mussolini's experience with **socialism** and Hitler's hostility to **democracy** made both men contemptuous of the masses from an early stage.

**POPULIST PARTY** American far-right organisation founded in 1984, associated with Willis **Carto**, and linked to the **Liberty Lobby**.

**POSSE COMITATUS (POWER OF THE COUNTRY)** US white revolutionary group formed in 1969. Anti-Semitic and anti-tax, it believes that government should be organised at county level. It is also loyal to the notion of vigilante justice.

**POST-FASCISM** Label pinned on modern far-right movements, such as the *Alleanza Nazionale* (AN) in Italy, which have not only adapted to the demands of liberal democracy but have actively tried to disassociate themselves from the history of inter-war fascism.

**POUJADISM** Label pinned on the Pierre **Poujade**-led *Union de Défense des Commerçants et Artisans* (UDCA) in 1950s France.

**POWELLISM** Name given to the controversial brand of political ideas espoused by British Conservative MP Enoch **Powell** in the late 1960s and early 1970s. Powell not only predicted racial violence, but expressed a distaste for non-white **immigration** into Britain. Powell left the Conservative Party in 1974.

**PRAGMATISM** A strategy based on non-adherence to rigid ideological positions. For the inter-war fascists, pragmatism amounted to short-term compromise aimed at consolidating long-term objectives. Examples include **Hitler**'s apparent concessions to the German centre-right in order to build a coalition before his accession to power, **Mussolini**'s acceptance of business funding despite his earlier anti-capitalist campaigns, Hitler's alliance with the Soviet Union in order to win time in the early phases of the **Second World War** and the ability of neo-fascists in post-war Europe to blend in with nationalist, free-market, regionalist and mainstream conservatives in order to gain respectability. Pragmatism and policy ambiguity allow fascist and far-right groups to appeal to a wide spectrum of opinion depending on time and circumstances.

**PRE-FASCISM** Disputed label pinned retrospectively on the 'embryonic' fascism that emerged in the period *c.*1880–1914. Historians have detected 'pre-fascism' mainly in France, Italy and Germany. **Barrès, Gobineau** and **Sorel**, for example, are commonly viewed as 'pre-fascist' theoreticians, while the *Associazione Nazionale Italiana* (ANI) and the *Deutsche National Volks Partei* (DNVP) are regarded by some as archetypal 'pre-fascist' organisations.

**PRÉSENT** Reactionary French far-right newspaper, close to Catholic fundamentalist integralist thinking and the political value system of the *Front National* (FN).

**PRIMATO** Pro-**Mussolini** cultural review edited by Giuseppe **Bottai**.

**PROGRESS PARTY** (1) Norwegian 'anti-system' movement that has thrived on issues of **immigration** and welfare. Since the early 1970s its political strength has wavered but it has never gone beyond the 15 per cent it scored in 1997. (2) Anti-immigrant movement in modern Denmark. It specialised in anti-tax rhetoric and acts of civil disobedience, and polled a highly respectable 16 per cent in the 1973 elections.

**PROPAGANDA** The propagation of ideas to serve political or ideological purposes. The term comes from the *Congregatio de Propaganda Fides*, a seventeenth-century Catholic Church agency charged with the 'propagation' of the faith. Contrary to popular opinion, propaganda can be truthful: it is defined by its purpose rather than by its style or content. However, much of the odium attached to the concept can be attributed to Joseph **Göbbels**'s style of propaganda that depended on half-truths, exaggeration, scapegoating and the manipulation of emotions like fear and hatred. Nazi propaganda was relatively successful among Germans outside the Reich but less so among non-Germans. Italian Fascist propaganda was sometimes a target of ridicule and was less virulent. Both regimes made significant use of radio and the cinema, and placed enormous emphasis on propaganda techniques.

**PROPAGANDA DUE (P2)** Post-war European network that provided cover for extreme-right sympathisers.

**PROPORTIONAL REPRESENTATION (PR)** An electoral system that ensures proportionality in the conversion of votes cast for a party into seats held by the party in an elected assembly. It is generally seen as advantageous to small parties and fringe movements. Plurality systems, like those in Britain or the US, are aimed at providing a clear winning party rather than ensuring local representation. Some countries with PR, like Germany, have percentage thresholds that parties must breach to win any seats. This was designed to prevent the election of small Communist or neo-Nazi parties. Despite its democratic credentials, PR can have unrepresentative outcomes when small parties hold the balance of power and dictate the composition of governments.

**PROTECTIONISM** The protection of powerful national industries by means of import bans, tariffs and subsidies. A popular strategy among economic nationalists of all persuasions and especially among statists in many countries during the inter-war years. It was a feature of fascist economic policy and matched the fascist belief in **autarchy**. Ironically, it was both a cause and an after-effect of the world economic crisis of the 1920s and 1930s.

**PROTO-FASCISM** Contentious label pinned on political movements that display signs of fascism, but lack the radicalism and **populism** usually associated with full-blown fascism. In whatever country they appear, proto-fascist movements invariably antedate, and often usher in, genuine fascist organisations. In literal terms, proto-fascism means 'primitive fascism'.

**PROTOCOLS OF THE ELDERS OF ZION** Document circulated in nineteenth-century Russia that suggested the existence of an international Jewish conspiracy to 'take over the world'. It was cited as evidence to justify anti-Semitic policies in both Tsarist and Communist Russia, as well as in Nazi Germany. It is a centrepiece of *Pamyat*'s anti-Semitic campaigns in modern Russia.

**PSD (SOCIAL DEMOCRATIC PARTY)** Peasant movement set up by **Vargas** as part of his new Corporate State structure in inter-war Brazil.

**PSEUDO-FASCISM** Alternative term to **crypto-fascism**.

**PSYCHO-HISTORY** Name given to the academic discipline that seeks to explain historical phenomena – including fascism – in psychological terms.

**PTB (BRAZILIAN LABOUR PARTY)** Urban movement set up by **Vargas** as part of his new Corporate State structure in the 1930s.

**PUBLIC ORDER ACT** 1936 law that prohibited both marches and political uniforms, thus sealing the demise of **Mosley's British Union of Fascists** (BUF).

**PUPPET STATE** A state that is nominally independent but whose leaders are under the control of, or slavishly serve, another state. It differs slightly from a **satellite state** in that the latter is more autonomous in some policy areas. **Manchuria**, then named **Manchukuo**, was a Japanese puppet state in north-eastern China during the **Second World War**. The Japanese set up the last of the Chinese Manchu Emperors, Pu Yi, as its leader but his role was only a nominal one: Japan pulled the strings.

**PUTSCH** From the German for 'striking a blow'. In essence, a violent seizure of power. Though similar to a revolutionary takeover or military coup, the word has negative connotations. Putschists are usually shady characters with little popular support and plotters who have no respect for legalities. **Hitler's** involvement in the 1923 '**Beer Hall Putsch**', an attempt to

upstage a right-wing nationalist plot against the **Weimar Republic**, backfired and resulted in his imprisonment. It also convinced him of the need for allies within the **establishment** and a respectable political strategy to go alongside his penchant for violent stunts. A sudden and violent seizure of power appealed to both Italian and German fascists because it constituted powerful **propaganda** written in actions rather than words.

**QUOTA NOVANTA** Term used in connection with the revaluation of the lira under Mussolini. The set 'quota' (of 90 lira equating to £1 sterling) was achieved in December 1927.

**RACE** A key theme in the discourse of many, though not all, fascist movements. It is most prominent in German Nazism, and in South African and US white supremacist doctrines. For **Hitler**, the **Aryan** races, especially the Germanic strands, were superior to others. He placed the Jewish and Slavic peoples at the bottom of his **hierarchy**, reserving a particular hatred for the former. These theories found expression in, among other things, the gassing of Jews in the **Holocaust**, systematic violence, discrimination and media abuse directed at minorities, legislation against sexual intercourse and intermarriage among races, and eugenic and medical experimentation on members of racial minorities. **Mussolini**, **Pétain** and other fascist or far-right leaders were less preoccupied with race but pursued policies of **cultural nationalism** and discrimination. They sometimes facilitated some of the Nazis' more extreme racial policies in order to impress Hitler.

**RACIAL PRESERVATION SOCIETY (RPS)** Post-war British movement, elements of which merged with other groups to form the **National Front** (NF) in 1967.

**RACISM** Prejudice and/or discrimination against others on the grounds of **race**. It was particularly prominent in inter-war Europe, **Apartheid** South Africa, the southern US until the late 1960s and some West European communities with high levels of **immigration**. There is general agreement on its association with overt prejudice and discrimination, but social conservatives and liberals disagree on the significance of, or responses to, more indirect or unintended manifestations, such as the concept of 'institutionalised racism'.

**RADICAL CONTINUITY** Label pinned on 'National Communist' movements active in post-**Cold War** Eastern Europe that still advertise the 'achievements' of ex-socialist rulers. Such organisations have grafted **ultra-nationalism** on to their traditional left-wing dogma.

**RADICAL FASCISM** Phrase used by Nolte to describe one particular 'level' of fascism. He argues that 'radical fascism' equates to the **Hitler** regime in Germany.

**RADICAL RETURN** Label pinned on far-right and neo-fascist movements active in post-**Cold War** Eastern Europe that still use inter-war fascist organisations as their political 'model'.

**RADICAL RIGHT** Loose term used to describe right-wing trends that go beyond mainstream **conservatism** and imply a de-

sire for far-reaching change. Since what constitutes the mainstream may vary over time, and may be contested at any stage, the boundaries of the radical right are hard to pin down. Some factions within established conservative parties may be radical relative to their peers; however, when looking at the political spectrum as a whole, the radical right is largely synonymous with the far right but excludes hardline traditionalists or conservatives who simply want to maintain the status quo.

**RAHVUSRIIK** Estonian term for the strong national state desired by inter-war fascists in that country.

**RAHVUSRIIK TERVIK** Estonian term denoting an 'integral national community'.

**RAPALLO, TREATIES OF** Agreements of 1920 and 1922 under which Italy recognised the boundaries of the state of Yugoslavia after the First World War. **Fiume**, now Rijeka, became an internationalised free city. Italian nationalists under **D'Annunzio**, as well as **Mussolini**, wanted revisions to the treaty. The 1922 document settled financial claims between Russia and Germany after the First World War and facilitated Soviet training of the German Army, despite the demilitarisation clauses in the Treaty of **Versailles**.

**RAPE OF NANKING** Japanese assault on the Chinese city of Nanking in 1937 – an attack marked by massive human rights violations and the death of up to 300,000 civilians.

**RASHTRIYA SWAYAMSEVAK SANGH (NATIONAL VOLUNTEER FORCE) (RSS)** Secretive and militant Hindu nationalist organisation in India, dating from the 1920s. It idolises a specifically Hindu Indian nation or *rashtra*. It is associated with the *Bharatiya Janata* Party (BJP), though the BJP itself is much more moderate. With a discourse that emphasises the significance of warrior gods and military drill for young members, it is reminiscent of far-right organisations in inter-war Europe. Since the BJP's rise to a party of government in the 1990s, it has distanced itself from the RSS.

**RASSEMBLEMENT NATIONAL POPULAIRE (RNP)** Pro-German movement formed by Marcel **Déat** in 1941. Its leaders wanted it to be the single party around which the new 'Nazi' France would be built, but it quickly lost members and coherency. In the end it became something of an irrelevance.

**REACTIONARY RIGHT** Contested and pejorative term used by left-wing historians to describe conservative and traditionalist political forces resisting change, as opposed to those using right-wing ideas to advance radical change. It has degenerated into a term of abuse and assumes a linear view of history, with forward-looking 'progress' being met by backward-looking 'reaction'. In the inter-war period the 'reactionary right' wanted to restore traditional authority but feared the potentially radical consequences of hardcore fascism. Nonetheless, it frequently co-operated with fascists because of a shared dislike of **liberalism** and **socialism**.

**REICH ECONOMIC CHAMBER** Body at the heart of centralised economic planning in Nazi Germany.

**REICH FOOD ESTATE** Unit into which German farmers were organised under **Hitler**.

**REICHSARBEITSDIENST (REICHS LABOUR FRONT)** Labour service that operated under **Hitler**. All males aged between eighteen and twenty-five were forced to work

for a six-month period in some sector of the economy – a system that had the effect of lowering the overall **unemployment** total.

**REICHSJUGENDFÜHRER** Title given by the Nazis to the party official with overall responsibility for youth organisations.

**REICHSMARK** German trading bloc under **Hitler**.

**REICHSTAND DER DEUTSCHEN INDUSTRIE (ASSOCIATION OF GERMAN INDUSTRIALISTS)** Nazi organisation in which both **Krupp** and **Thyssen** played a leading role.

**REICHSWEHR** Name of the German army, 1920–35. **Hitler** was Commander in Chief between 1933 and 1935.

**REICHSWERKE HERMANN GÖRING (HERMANN GÖRING IRONWORKS)** State organisation that supplied the Nazi administration with cut-price domestic ore. It played a major part in **Hitler**'s Four Year **Plan**.

**REINHARDT PLAN** Nazi plan for building motorways that had its origins in Weimar Germany.

**RELIGION** Inter-war fascists appealed to conventional **Christianity** where religious institutions were powerful or in order to consolidate alliances with traditional conservatives. The Nazis also wanted to supplant Christianity with a religion that would validate their own agenda. More conservative far-right movements like Francoism in Spain valued religion for its own sake and associated themselves with Church institutions and traditions. The belief in social order and the traditional **family**, as well as a commitment to anti-**Communism**, made religious movements attractive to the far right. More recently, some of the more exotic Christian Fundamentalist groups in the US have preached anti-democratic, conspiratorial, racist and messianic political doctrines shared with far-right groups.

**RENAMO (MOZAMBIQUE NATIONAL RESISTANCE)** Anti-Communist guerrillas who fought the one-party Marxist dictatorship in Mozambique during the 1970s and 1980s. The group focused on economic sabotage and committed human rights violations. Critics charged that it was merely an instrument of the South African security services. However, it converted itself into a legitimate political party in 1992 and contested, but lost, free elections in 1994.

**RENOVACIÓN ESPAÑOLA** Radical Alfonsine monarchist group founded in 1933 and influenced heavily by the Maurrasian *Action Française* (AF). It was nationalist, authoritarian, violent, counter-revolutionary, but fascist only if a broad definition is being used.

**REPUBBLICA SOCIALE ITALIANA (ITALIAN SOCIAL REPUBLIC) (RSI)** Short-lived political arrangement that emerged following the armistice in 1943. Also known as the **Salò Republic** on account of the town on Lake Garda that hosted the regime's **propaganda** ministry. After being rescued by the Nazis, **Mussolini** became the nominal head of the RSI, and many ex-Fascists rallied to it, including **Gentile**, **Marinetti** and **Starace**. Its doctrine harked back to early 'radical' Fascism, but its ideology was merely superficial given the extent of German dominance in Italy. The RSI died with Mussolini.

**REPUBLICAN NATIONAL GUARD** Blackshirted **militia** of the 1943 **Salò Republic**.

**REPUBLICAN PARTY** Extreme-right movement active in the modern Czech Republic. It was hostile to the Havel administration.

**REPUBLIKANER PARTEI (REPUBLICAN PARTY) (REP)** Crypto-fascist German party. Led by Franz **Schönhuber**, the movement gained 7.1 per cent of the national vote and six MEPs in 1989 but thereafter declined in electoral popularity. Although it steers clear of pro-**Hitler** rhetoric, it is fiercely anti-foreigner, favours some kind of authoritarian regime and does harbour its own pro-Nazi wing. It also campaigned for German Reunification in the late 1980s. The REP has forged alliances on a German level (with the *Deutsche Volks Union* (DVU)) and the European level (with the *Front National* (FN) and other far-right groupings).

**REQUETÉS** Carlist paramilitary force – a component part of the pro-Nationalist **armed forces** during the **Spanish Civil War**.

**RESISTANCE** Name given both to internal dissent directed against the Nazi and fascist regimes of wartime Europe and to the organisations that planned or conducted these operations. Communists played a disproportionate role in these activities in Italy, France and Yugoslavia. Debates about the scale of resistance, and who should get the credit for it, have raged across Europe since 1945. There was also a disjuncture between resistance fighters on the ground and their public leaders operating at a distance in Britain or North Africa.

**RESISTÊNCIA** Journal of the post-war radical right in Portugal.

**REVANCHE (REVENGE)** Political issue and idea that emerged in the aftermath of the **Franco-Prussian War** of 1870–1 and dominated French politics up until 1914. It helped to galvanise a new type of right – radical, revolutionary, nationalist and, in some historians' eyes, 'pre-fascist' or 'proto-fascist'. This '**New Right**' was dominated by the desire to gain '*revanche*' against Germany for the provinces annexed in 1871 – Alsace and Lorraine. Unfortunately for figures like **Boulanger** and **Barrès**, the new Third Republic was not interested in revenge.

**REVISIONISM** The revision of history in the light of subsequent findings. In the context of the Holocaust and the study of fascism, it can also be an alternative for Historical Revisionism.

**REVOLUCÃO NACIONAL** Newspaper of the *Nacional Sindicalismo* (NS) fascist movement in 1930s Portugal – edited by **Preto**.

**REVOLUTIONARY LEAGUE (FASCIO) FOR INTERNATIONAL ACTION** Syndicalist pressure group established in October 1914 to campaign for Italian involvement in the First World War. It also provided **Mussolini**'s Fascist movement with many key theorists. This body was renamed Leagues (*Fasci*) of Revolutionary Action.

**REVOLUTIONARY NATIONALISM** Variant of fascism associated with **Jünger**. Revolutionary nationalists prefer the notion of a '**Third Way**' to the political strategies pursued by **Hitler** and **Mussolini**. In essence, revolutionary nationalism equates to **Strasserism**.

**REVOLUTIONARY RIGHT** 'Revolution' implies turning society upside down, often through violent upheaval, coupled with radical social, political and/or economic transformation. Fascists portrayed themselves as revolutionaries in so far as their model political systems would topple **liberalism** and its value system, and fundamentally reorder European international relations. **Hitler**'s racial state would also have been revolutionary in this sense. The appeal to revolution made fascism seem

forward looking and a viable rival to **Communism**. However, fascist co-operation with the old élites, and the mismatch between their ambitions and power, meant their performance in power was less far-reaching than expected. More traditionalist regimes, like **Franco**'s Spain, were ultimately more conservative than revolutionary.

**REX** From *Christus Rex* (Christ the King). *Rex* was a proto-fascist conservative–Catholic Belgian movement influenced heavily by the *Action Française* (AF) in France. *Rex* was both anti-Communist and anti-capitalist. Its main symbol was a broom – indicating its desire to 'clean up' Belgian politics. The Rexists gained almost 12 per cent in the 1936 elections but thereafter evolved in an anti-democratic, paramilitary direction. By 1940 the movement's leader, **Degrelle**, was collaborating with the **Gestapo**. Nevertheless, *Rex* and its charismatic supremo survived into the post-war period. Its monthly newspaper was also called *Rex*.

**RHINELAND** Area of Germany occupied by France in 1923. **Hitler** used this event to justify his own violations of the post-1918 settlement. Hitler remilitarised the Rhineland in March 1936; Britain and France did not react to this development.

**RIGHT** General shorthand for 'conservatives', as opposed to the forces of change. It is often used to refer to anti-socialist parties, though the roles can be reversed, as they were for a while during the collapse of **Communism** in the Soviet Union, when advocates of capitalist liberal democracy were promoting change and the Communists were resisting it. Since the end of the **Cold War**, the terms 'left' and 'right' have been difficult to apply with ease or consistency and can be quite misleading. Ultra-right-wing forces are extreme right-wing groups that resort to illegal or violent action in the pursuit of their aims.

**RIGHT CLUB** Anti-Semitic cell associated with Conservative MP William Maule **Ramsay** and active during the **Second World War**.

**RIGHTS OF MAN** Liberal, egalitarian creed derived from the 1789 *Declaration of the Rights of Man and the Citizen* – a creed cherished by many on the contemporary left, especially in France. For fascists and neo-fascists the notion of the rights of man is anathema. **Vichy** banned the *Declaration* in 1940 and **Le Pen**'s *Front National* (FN) has continually poured scorn on it. In many ways the rise of the radical right can be seen as a reaction to it.

**RIKSFØRBUNDET LANDSBYGDENS FOLK (SWEDISH NATIONAL RURAL UNION)** Organisation with minor national-socialist connections – founded in 1929.

**RISORGIMENTO** The process whereby Italy was unified in the mid-nineteenth century. Italian Fascists were undecided about whether to view the **Mussolini** era as a continuation of the nationalist *Risorgimento* tradition or a break with it.

**ROCK AGAINST RACISM (RAR)** 1980s music-inspired anti-fascist movement.

**RÖHM PURGE** Name given to the *Schutzstaffel* (SS) purge of *Sturm Abteilung* (SA) officials in June 1934. On Hitler's instructions, more than eighty 'traitors to the Reich' were killed in cold blood, including SA leader Ernst **Röhm**.

**ROMANISATION** Policy pursued by Nicolae Ceaușescu's Communist regime in the 1970s, under which Romanians from other parts of the country were introduced into the mixed but predominantly Hungarian

region of **Transylvania**. This caused new tensions between the pre-existing Romanian and Hungarian populations – which was exploited by extreme right-wing groups in both Hungary and Romania after the fall of **Communism**.

**ROMANITÀ** The cult of Ancient Rome, exploited consistently, and with much bravado, by **Mussolini**.

**ROMANTICISM** Movement in European, and especially German, philosophy and culture during the nineteenth century that sought to reaffirm cultural identity through a search for the roots of nations, languages and cultural forms. Romanticism was partly a rejection of rationalism and the **Enlightenment**. It facilitated the study of linguistics (in search of **language** roots) and the questioning of **modernity** that fed into '**pre-fascism**' at a later date.

**ROME CONGRESS** 1921 event at which **Mussolini** outlined Fascism's attachment to the collective (**nation** and **state**) over and above the individual.

**ROME–BERLIN–TOKYO AXIS** Alliance of Italy, Germany and Japan. It became a reality from 1937 when Italy joined the **Anti-Comintern Pact** against the Soviet Union.

**ROSA DEI VENTI (WIND ROSE)** Italian neo-fascist organisation led by Amos Spiazzi.

**ROSSIISKOE YEDINSTVO (RUSSIAN UNITY)** Anti-Yeltsin coalition of the 1990s that has been accused of incorporating 'fascist elements'.

**ROSTOCK** German town that was the scene of a notorious and fatal racist arson attack in August 1992. The episode came to symbolise the upsurge in **neo-fascism** in the newly unified Germany.

**ROYALISM** Belief in the virtues of monarchy, often reflected in the desire to restore monarchies after war or republican revolution. In the particular case of France it became a metaphor for conservative opposition to left-wing and revolutionary ideas after the 1789 Revolution. Though some monarchies, notably those in Romania and Bulgaria, dabbled in proto-fascist ideas, royalism has generally been a traditionalist and conservative phenomenon, rather than a manifestation of fascism.

**RURAL FASCISM** Type of fascism associated with **Grandi** in Italy and **Dorgères** in France during the inter-war years. 'Rural fascism' simply emphasised the 'neglected' concerns of agricultural workers.

**RURALISM** A belief in the virtues of the countryside or an agrarian society. It was a key feature of conservative and populist ideology in Ireland and Continental Europe during the 1920s and 1930s, and is partly a reaction against **modernity**, urbanisation and industrialisation. Fascists adopted ruralist slogans to attract support away from traditional agrarian populist parties but also because the link with the soil fitted their work ethic and their concept of nations and races as entities with deep and permanent roots in the past.

**RUSSIAN NATIONAL UNION** Small neo-Nazi movement that is hostile to **Communism**, **democracy** and ethnic minorities (including Jews). Led by Alexander **Barkashov**, it has been active since the fall of Communism.

**RUSSIAN REVOLUTION** Usually refers to the Bolshevik seizure of power in Russia in October 1917, though it may be loosely applied to the overthrow of the Tsar earlier in the same year as well. Its consequences were far reaching and included: a Bolshevik peace with Germany and active cultivation of the Social Democrat governments of the **Weimar Republic**, thus providing fuel for Nazi **propaganda**; the totalitarian Soviet state, especially under Stalin, which served both as a partial model and a focus for rivalry with the fascist regimes; a fear of spontaneous socialist revolution or subversion across Europe that dented the progress of socialist parties and provided pretexts for right-wing **dictatorship** and **violence**; and revolutions in Hungary and Bavaria, in the immediate aftermath of the war, which seemed to confirm these fears and aided the emergence of far-right groups in both countries.

**SABATO FASCISTA** Name given to the Saturday-afternoon pageants that members of Italian fascist youth groups had to attend.

**SAKURAKAI** (Society of the Cherry): Small, conspiratorial Japanese movement founded in 1930. It consisted of Army and Navy personnel, and its main aim was military **dictatorship** Society members were in favour of full-scale Japanese expansionism.

**SALÒ REPUBLIC** Alternative name for the 1943 Italian Social Republic.

**SAMFUNNSPARTIET (COMMONWEALTH PARTY)** Inter-war Norwegian movement with some fascist traits. Its leader, Brochman, was ultimately accused of **collaboration** with the Nazis.

**SAMMLUNG** German term denoting 'national unification', as utilised by a variety of far-right movements.

**SAN SEPOLCRO PIAZZA** Milan venue at which **Mussolini** held his first Fascist meeting on 23 March 1919.

**SANEAMENTO** Name given to the process by which Portugal tried to 'defascistise' itself at the end of the **Salazar** regime.

**SANU MEMORANDUM** 1986 document released by Slobodan Milošević that outlined his aim of a **Greater Serbia**.

**SATELLITE STATE** A state whose formal sovereignty is internationally recognised but is under the effective control of another, e.g. the East European Communist states under the control of the Soviet Union during the **Cold War**. Fear of outright subjugation made **Vichy** France a satellite state of Nazi Germany; Slovakia, following the dismemberment of Czechoslovakia, was too weak to be anything but a satellite of Germany.

**SCAPEGOAT THEORY** Notion of the 'enemy within' – a common element in all fascist systems. Jews, immigrants, leftists, homosexuals and **gypsies** have borne the brunt of fascist and neo-fascist scapegoating.

**SCHENGEN AGREEMENT** Landmark in the history of European economic unity – and violently opposed by far-right groups such as the *Front National* (FN) in France.

**SCHUTZSTAFFEL (SS)** Élite Guard of the Nazi Party. Originally part of the *Sturm Abteilung* (SA), the SS was formed in 1925 and evolved into one of the most important institutions of the **Third Reich**. **Himmler** became SS chief in 1929, and under his leadership the organisation set up the first **concentration camps** and carried out the infamous anti-SA purge of June 1934. The SS was conceived as a

vanguard movement but by 1934 had over 100,000 officials.

**SCORPION** Modern British far-right journal.

**SCYTHE CROSS** Hungarian fascist movement of the 1930s. Led by **Böszörmény**, the party aimed to attract peasant support in particular. It led a futile Budapest demonstration in 1936.

**SEARCHLIGHT** British anti-fascist magazine.

**SECOND WORLD WAR** Global conflict (1939–45) involving Axis Powers (Germany, Italy and Japan) and an alliance of states led by Britain, and, later, the Soviet Union and the United States. It was caused by German expansionism in Central Europe and Japanese expansion in the Asia–Pacific. One of the most destructive wars in history and the bloodiest in modern times, it was also the only one in which atomic weapons were used. The conflict was marked by a Nazi campaign of genocide against the Jews. The war resulted in the weakening of the European colonial powers and a shift of power away from Central Europe to the USSR and US, as well as extensive Soviet territorial gains and the partitioning of Europe. War was envisaged by **Hitler** but anticipated to happen several years later.

**SECRETARIADO DE PROPAGANDA NACIO- NAL (SECRETARIAT FOR NATIONAL PRO- PAGANDA)** Key state organisation under the **Salazar** regime.

**SECULARISM** Belief in the neutrality of the state in religious matters and its non-affiliation with religious institutions. It finds expression in the Western liberal norm of the 'separation of Church and state'. In its more militant form, it can be perceived as anti-religious or anti-clerical. Secularism is viewed by fascists and many social conservatives as hostile to religious traditions and morality, and, in the educational sphere, as a cover for indoctrination of the young in 'progressive' ideology.

**SECURITATE** Romanian secret-police body under Communist rule. After the fall of the Ceauşescu regime, some former members drifted into pro-fascist nostalgia.

**SECURITÉ ET LIBERTÉ** Militant French right-wing group set up in 1979 under the auspices of the Gaullist movement.

**SELVAGGIO, IL (THE PRIMITIVE)** Early twentieth-century Italian cultural journal. It was particularly interested in the anti-modern creed, *Strapaese*, which came to impact upon Italian Fascism.

**SEMI-FASCISM** Label pinned on movements/regimes that possess a limited amount of fascist traits or credentials. 'Semi-fascism' is a stepping-stone on the road to **'total fascism'** and is probably best illustrated by the profusion of far-right groupings in inter-war France; most of which possessed some fascist traits, but not enough to be regarded as examples of genuine fascism.

**SEMPRE PRONTI** Paramilitary arm of the *Associazione Nazionale Italiana* (ANI).

**SERVICE DU TRAVAIL OBLIGATOIRE (STO)** Wartime scheme concocted by Nazi officials and **Laval** that organised the transfer of French workers to Germany, so as to oil **Hitler**'s war machine.

**SICHERHEITSDIENST (SECURITY SERVICE) (SD)** Secret-police organ of the Nazi Party.

**SIEMENS** Electronics company in Nazi Germany that supplied the **Hitler** regime with arms.

**SILVER SHIRTS Ku Klux Klan** paramilitary organisation founded in 1933 by William Dudley Pelley. The aim of the movement was to ape Nazism.

**SINARQUISTAS** Nickname of the Mexican *Unión Nacional Sinarquista* (UNS), active in the 1930s and 1940s.

**SIX LAWS OF THE LEGION** Principles of the Romanian **Legion/League of the Archangel Gabriel**: discipline, hard work, silence, education, mutual help and honour.

**SIXTH OF FEBRUARY 1934** Evocative date in French political history when, according to left-wing observers, the fascist right was on the verge of executing a coup against the Third Republic.

**SKINHEADS** Aggressive and politicised young people, with a distinctive hair style, who have become an important vehicle for the spread of fascist and neo-fascist ideas in the post-war period, particularly in **working-class** circles. Hence the phrases 'Nazi-skin' and 'skinhead fascism'.

**SKREWDRIVER National Front**-supporting rock band led by Ian Stuart **Donaldson**.

**SLAVS** Ethnic groups affiliated to the Russians. They are divided into Western Slavs (e.g. Poles and Czechs) and Eastern Slavs (e.g. Ukrainians and Russians). **Hitler** viewed the Slavs, especially the Russians, as one of the lower races worthy of particular hatred. This attitude, together with his anti-Communism, explained the more barbarous human rights violations and war crimes committed by the Germans on the Russian front in the second half of the **Second World War**.

**SMALL MAN** Phrase used to describe the type of artisan that Nazism and other far-right movements – like the *Union de Défense des Commerçants et Artisans* (UDCA) and *Front National* (FN) in France – have glorified in their rhetoric. Individuals like **Hitler**, **Poujade** and **Le Pen** have viewed themselves as spokesmen for the 'downtrodden' and 'disenfranchised'. In France '*les petits contre les gros*' is a theme that underpins large sections of extreme-right discourse.

**SNIA VISCOSA** Italian chemical firm that benefited particularly from **Mussolini**'s drive towards self-sufficiency.

**SOCIAL ACTION INITIATIVE** Neo-Nazi group based in the Republic of Ireland. It was active during the 1980s.

**SOCIAL DARWINISM** A doctrine that emphasises the survival of the fittest in competition for resources, power or cultural survival. It is based on an analogy with Charles Darwin's theory of natural selection and has been influential in economics, politics, sociology and international relations. It has been applied to the evolution and survival of racial groups by many writers, and was particularly favoured by **Hitler**. The theory was misused to construct a myth of German superiority and racial purity, and to justify even more extreme racial policies. Social Darwinian logic was also applied to the survival of the German **nation** through trial and victory in war.

**SOCIAL FASCISM** Communist theory – associated with Manuilsky and the **Third International** – which stated that social democracy was in alliance with fascism.

**SOCIALISM** An **ideology** originally urging the creation of a just and egalitarian society by means of the collective or **working-class** ownership of the means of production, distribution and exchange. It originated in early nineteenth-century writings but was crystallised in the work of Karl Marx and Friedrich Engels. Subsequent development led in different directions, including **Communism, Marxism,** socialist anarchism, democratic socialism and social democracy. Twentieth-century socialists reconciled themselves to reforming **capitalism** in the direction of greater **egalitarianism** but often disagreed about the centrality and scope of public ownership and state planning. Socialism tended to be internationalist and stressed the importance of class rather than **nation**. Early fascists shared the socialist critique of capitalist élites and **middle-class** values but saw their ideology as a type of socialism compatible with the 'nation'. Thus, **Mussolini** was originally a socialist and **Hitler** styled his philosophy 'national-socialism'.

**SOCIALIST LABOUR PARTY** Extreme-right movement in modern Romania.

**SOCIALIST PEOPLE'S LIBYAN ARAB JAMA-HIRIYA** Modern political movement that blends **populism** with **national-socialism**.

**SOCIETÀ FINANZIARIA ITALIANA** Finance organisation that aimed to prevent damaging bank collapses during the **Mussolini** era.

**SOCIÉTÉ D'ÉTUDES ET DE RELATIONS PUBLIQUES (SERP)** French company that FN leader Jean-Marie **Le Pen** was associated with during the 1960s. SERP specialised in historical songs and speeches and acquired notoriety for its Nazi-era interests.

**SOCIJALISTIČKA PARTIJA SRBIJE (SOCIA-LIST PARTY OF SERBIA) (SPS)** The former governing party of Milošević in Serbia – home to many ultra-nationalists.

**SOKOLI ZHIRINOVSKOGO (ZHIRINOVSKI FALCONS)** Nickname of the *Liberalno-Demokraticheskaya Partiya Rossii* (LDPR) faction in the modern Russian parliament.

**SOLDIERLY NATIONALISM** German brand of **'National Revolutionary'** fascism.

**SOLIDARIDAD ESPAÑOLA** Tiny Spanish extreme-right group active in the 1980s and led by Tejero.

**SOLIDARITÉ FRANÇAISE** Inter-war French fascist movement founded by perfume tycoon François Coty. Its blue-shirted activists were at the forefront of the extra-parliamentary riots of 6 February 1934.

**SOLINGEN** German town that was the scene of a neo-Nazi arson attack in 1993. Five Turkish people were killed in the incident.

**SONDERMELDUNG** A trumpeted announcement of victory that could interrupt a broadcast at a moment's notice. The phenomenon reflected the dramatic and bombastic style of **propaganda** in German radio broadcasts under the Nazis.

**SONS OF GLYNDWR** Extremist Welsh nationalist group.

**SOS RACISME** French anti-racist movement particularly hostile to **Le Pen**'s *Front National* (FN).

**SOUTH AFRICAN CONSERVATIVE PARTY** Right-wing competitor to the **National Party** in the 1980s. It was even more hardline than the National Party, opposing all concessions to the ANC or the dismantling of white minority rule.

**SOZIALISTISCHE REICHSPARTEI (SOCIALIST REICHS PARTY) (SRP)** Extreme right-wing 'anti-system' party that won twenty-two seats in the West German parliament in the early 1950s.

**SPANISH CIVIL WAR** Long-running military conflict in the late 1930s that gave birth to many variants of fascism, including Falangism and Francoism.

**SPEARHEAD** Modern British far-right magazine.

**SPECIAL TRIBUNAL FOR THE DEFENCE OF THE STATE** Illiberal body set up by **Mussolini** in 1926 to administer justice to suspected anti-Fascists.

**SPOTLIGHT, THE** Far-right publication in modern-day America.

**SQUADRISTI** Fascist hit-squads born in the early 1920s. They emerged as the paramilitary arm of **Mussolini**'s movement and carried on their irregular 'law enforcement' work throughout the rest of the decade. *Squadrismo* was an important aspect of early Italian Fascism.

**SRONAO** Nazi-style separatist movement active in inter-war Serbia.

**SRPSKA PARTIJA JEDINSTVA (SERBIAN UNITY PARTY) (SPJ)** Ultra-nationalist movement of the far right led by Arkan (Željko Ražnjatović).

**SRPSKA RADIKALNA STRANKA (SERBIAN RADICAL PARTY) (SRS)** Contemporary ultra-nationalist movement whose ultimate aim is the creation of a **Greater Serbia**. The SRS boasts its own paramilitary arm and is led by Vojislav **Šešelj**.

**STALINGRAD (NOW VOLGOGRAD), BATTLE OF** City where the Soviet Red Army scored a decisive victory over the Germans after a prolonged siege in 1942–3. The battle marked the turning of the tide on the Russian front, halted the German advance and initiated the retreat that culminated in the defeat of the **Third Reich**. Casualties were in the millions

**STALINISM** Form of totalitarian Communist dictatorship in the Soviet Union under Joseph Stalin and, more broadly, in the Communist states under Soviet control after the **Second World War**. The modified and less extreme form after 1956 was termed neo-Stalinism. At its height, it involved mass terror, the use of **concentration camps**, purges and assassinations within the ruling party, a police state, ideological orthodoxy and a cult of personality around the party leader. Though condemned by fascists, it provided a model for **totalitarianism** and one-party rule, as well as a focus for competition.

**STÄNDESTAAT (STATE OF ESTATES)** Corporate State structure established by **Dollfuss** in Austria in 1934. To some it equated to a 'clerical dictatorship'; to others a semi-fascist infrastructure based on ultra-nationalist **'Austrian ideology'**. Whatever the verdict, the *Ständestaat* entailed the abolition of parliament and ascendancy of Christian-Socialist doctrine.

**STATE** A political and administrative entity exercising a monopoly on the legitimate and effective use of force in a given territory. German philosophy, especially that of Hegel, put great emphasis on the state as the embodiment of the community. This concept was central to the autocratic Prussian state and to **Hitler**'s Reich. The centrality of the state was also a key element in French and Russian political culture. Anglo-American tradition, in contrast, has tended to view state power as a negative factor and has been more individualist in orientation. Most fascist regimes emphasised the importance of absolute state power.

**STATE CAPITALISM** Phrase used to describe the economic policy of many fascist regimes – essentially a mixture of state-imposed regulations and private industry.

**STATE OF NATIONAL RENAISSANCE** Name given by King **Carol** II of Romania to his para-fascist royal dictatorship in 1938.

**STAUFFENBERG PLOT** Unsuccessful anti-**Hitler** coup led by Count von **Stauffenberg** in July 1944. In the aftermath of the episode, 150 conspirators were executed.

**STICHTING OUD POLITICKE DELINQUEN-TEN (SOPD)** The first far-right group to emerge in the Netherlands after the **Second World War**. It attempted to make political capital out of the **collaboration** issue, and evolved into the *National Europese Sociale Beweging* (NESB) in 1953.

**STORM FALCONS** Paramilitary force of the South African *Afrikaner Weerstandsbeweging* (AWB).

**STORMJAERS** Storm Troopers of the South African *Ossewa Brandwag/Ossewabrandwag* (OB) during the inter-war period.

**STRACITTÀ (HYPER-CITY)** Futurist-style movement that fed into Italian Fascism.

**STRAJERI (WATCH)** Youth movement of King **Carol** II's **State of National Renaissance**.

**STRAPAESE (HYPER-VILLAGE)** Anti-modern theory that acquired significant influence in inter-war Italy. It played on the intrinsic importance of rural life and regional customs, and impacted upon the political outlook of the **Mussolini** regime.

**STRASSERISM** 'Third Way' theory based on the political ideas of German brothers Gregor and Otto **Strasser** – both members of the Nazi Party. Strasserites (or revolutionary nationalists) believe in a political solution that by-passes both **Communism** and **liberalism**. Strasserism has influenced many post-war movements on the far right.

**STRONNICTWO NARODOWE (SN)** Modern Polish nationalist movement that views both Germans and Jews as 'anti-national' threats. In economic matters it pursues a '**Third Way**' philosophy.

**STURM ABTEILUNG (STORM TROOPERS) (SA)** Nazi paramilitary organisation founded in 1921. **Hitler** gave it a very specific role: to disrupt opponents' political meetings and spread Nazi **propaganda**. It had a military structure and many members were former soldiers. The SA played a major role in bringing Hitler to power but was subsequently disappointed by the direction taken by the Nazi regime. On 30 June 1934 – 'the **Night of the Long Knives**' – Hitler's *Schutzstaffel* (SS) purged the SA. Thereafter the SA had only minimal power and significance.

**SUDETEN GERMAN PARTY** Czech movement founded in 1933 that developed a deeply anti-Czech, pro-German outlook. Led by **Henlein**, it yearned for the assimilation of the **Sudetenland** into Germany – a goal it achieved through **Hitler**.

**SUDETENLAND** German-speaking part of Czechoslovakia that was at the centre of diplomatic controversy in the late 1930s. The Munich Conference of September 1938 transferred the Sudetenland to Germany; **Hitler**'s troops occupied the territory in October 1938 – a key event in the lead-up to war.

**SUPREMACISM** Doctrine akin to chauvinism that stresses the superiority of one group over others. It manifested itself in racial theories such as 'white supremacy' in South Africa and the southern US.

**SURVIVAL OF THE FITTEST** The result of a process of natural selection in which fitter organisms survive, while weaker ones die or are killed by their 'fitter' neighbours. It says that a stronger organism takes the form it does because its essential features were more conducive to its survival than those of its rivals. The theory came to prominence in Charles Darwin's work on natural selection. Fascists applied it to the survival of 'pure' and allegedly superior racial groups, as well as to the survival of nations in war.

**SURVIVALISTS** Name given to key movements and individuals on the modern US white revolutionary right. They believe that the US is heading for a **race**-dominated civil war.

**SUUR-SUOMI (GREATER FINLAND)** Ultra-nationalist dream of Finnish inter-war fascist group, **Academic Karelia Society** (AKS).

**SVENSK SOCIALISTISK SAMLING** Tiny Swedish national-socialist movement founded out of the ashes of the *National-socialistiska Arbetarpartiet* (NSWP) in 1938. It scored less than 2 per cent in the 1944 elections. The party was dissolved in 1945.

**SVENSKA FOLKPARTIET (SWEDISH PEOPLE'S PARTY)** Small inter-war movement of the radical right. It was led by Captain Ebbe Almqvist.

**SVENSKA NATIONALSOCIALISTIKA FRIHETSFØRBUNDET (SWEDISH NATIONAL SOCIALIST FREEDOM LEAGUE)** Small fascist movement formed in 1924.

**SVERIGES NATIONALSOCIALISTISKA PARTIET (SWEDISH NATIONAL SOCIALIST**

PARTY) (SNSP) Small movement that, in alliance with *Nationalsocialistiska Arbetarpartiet*, scored less than 1 per cent in the 1936 elections.

SWASTIKA Ancient religious symbol co-opted first by anti-Semites, then by army groups and then by Nazis. **Hitler** used the hooked cross motif against a red and white background – with red symbolising Nazi blood and white racial purity. The symbol became part of the German flag in 1935.

SWEDISH OPPOSITION Small semi-fascist movement of the 1930s.

SWING YOUTH Opposition movement to **Hitler** that associated itself with 'deviant' sub-cultures such as jazz. The organisation caused the Nazi regime some embarrassment.

SWISS NAZI PARTY Post-war political grouping.

SYNDESMOS AXIOMATIKON NEON (SAN) Greek far-right grouping active in the 1940s.

SYNDICALISM Revolutionary socialist theory that inspired the corporatist ideology of **Mussolini**. As an ex-socialist, the Italian Fascist leader was fully acquainted with the essential features of **syndicalism**, such as self-governing unions and occupation-based economic organisation. In the end Italian Fascism incorporated many syndicalist ideas.

TACUARA Extreme Argentine terror group whose mid-twentieth-century programme was based around **Catholicism** and **anti-Semitism**.

TAG, DER German newspaper that advanced a pro-Nazi/nationalist line in the inter-war years.

TAGMATA ASFALEIAS (SECURITY BATTALIONS) (TA) Greek movement that collaborated with the Germans in their war against resisters after 1941.

TAGMATA ERGASSIAS (LABOUR BATTALIONS) (TE) Compulsory youth movement established by General **Metaxas**'s *Elefterofronoi* (EL) party in 1930s Greece. At one point over half a million young people were enrolled in the TE.

TARGET Publication of the British **League of St George**.

TECOS Post-war Mexican movement that was expelled from the **World Anti-Communist League** on account of its rabid **anti-Semitism**.

TEMPO PRESENTE Neo-fascist Portuguese review.

TENENTISMO Name given to the mentality of radical protest in 1920s Brazil that helped to fuel fascist-style movements.

TERNI STEELWORKS Significant economic achievement of **Mussolini**'s Fascist regime.

TERRORISM Usually defined as the use of illegal **violence** against civil society to achieve political objectives, especially by targeting civilians. As a term it is partially subjective and controversial because of the negative connotations attached to the object of the concept by the user – others may characterise the actions as 'revolutionary violence'. Far-right movements in post-war Europe, and, latterly, in the US, have used assassinations and car bombings to spread a climate of fear. Some rightist violence is unprovoked and some occurs in the form of competition with far-left or anarchist terrorism.

**TERZA POSIZIONE (THIRD POSITION) (TP)** Violent Italian neo-fascist movement.

**TEUTONIC RACE** Alternative term for the Germanic peoples, especially those originating in northern Germany and southern Scandinavia in ancient times. It was fundamental to **Hitler**'s notion of a pure German **race** stretching back to antiquity.

**THE COVENANT, THE SWORD AND THE ARM OF THE LORD (CSA)** Paramilitary white supremacist movement active in post-war America.

**THIRD HELLENIC CIVILISATION** Totalitarian dream of the *Elefterofronoi* (EL) party in 1930s Greece.

**THIRD INTERNATIONAL** Inter-war Communist forum that delineated fascism as the 'agent' of monopoly **capitalism**. It also identified the phenomenon of **'social fascism'**.

**THIRD POSITION** Small modern British grouping on the extreme right.

**THIRD POSITIONISM** Umbrella term that denotes a modern brand of '**Third Way**' fascism. Third Positionists steer a course between '**classic fascism**' and **neo-Nazism**, and engage in combat that can be both intellectual and paramilitary.

**THIRD REICH** Key piece of Nazi nomenclature. The phrase originated in the writings of Arthur **Moeller van den Bruck**, a key theorist of **Conservative Revolution**. Hitler saw his regime as successor to the Second Reich of the **Hohenzollern**s.

**THIRD WAY** (1) Term used by fascist governments and movements to denote the ultimate objective of economic policy: in effect, to steer a middle course between capitalism and socialism. In doing this, many fascist officials saw themselves as pursuing an extremely progressive, enlightened and even 'revolutionary' policy. The notion of a 'Third Way' sounded good on paper, but in reality it was a fairly hollow idea. It was useful in propaganda terms, but over time most fascist regimes settled for a pragmatic alliance with the forces of big business. (2) Small modern British far-right movement.

**THIRD WORLD** Term popularly used to refer to poorer or industrialising non-Western countries, and partly based on categorisation by Argentine economist, Raul Prebisch. However, it is increasingly misleading due to the complex stratification of power among non-Western states, but is still used as a badge of solidarity by non-Western states. Far-right movements share with many conservatives a critical view of liberal and socialist solidarity with Third World revolutionary movements and view Third World states as a source of threats and instability. Far-right racists also see the Third World as a source of immigrants who could bring 'impurities' into the national racial stock. However, there is no uniform response to Third World issues. Far-right groups can often express solidarity with chauvinist or anti-American regimes in the Middle East or Asia, while white supremacists in South Africa and military dictators in Latin America can find support among some sections of the far right in Europe and the US.

**THOMAS HOBBES STICHTING** Scientific bureau of the *Centrum Democraten*, named after the favourite philosopher of Hans **Janmaat**, the leading figure on the Dutch extreme right during the 1980s.

**THULE SEMINAR** New-rightist German movement founded in 1980 that believes in 'European rebirth'.

**THULE SOCIETY** German political association of the inter-war years that had significant links with the Nazi Party.

**THYSSEN** German steel corporation that developed strong links with **Hitler**'s Nazi Party.

**TIERGARTENSTRASSE 4 (T4 PROGRAMME)** Campaign to kill the old and infirm as part of the Nazis' efforts at racial purification. It was named after a district of Berlin.

**TODT** Organisation involved in centralised economic planning during the Nazi period in Germany.

**TŌHŌKAI (SOCIETY OF THE EAST)** Interwar Japanese movement of the radical right. Led by Nakano **Seigō**, it imitated European fascism and demanded revolutionary change. Its members wore black shirts.

**TOTAL FASCISM** Phrase used to describe the ideology of fascist regimes when they have moved on from **'partial fascism'**.

**TOTALITARIANISM** A political system aiming at total state control of society, or a fusion of state and civil society, for the purposes of large-scale social engineering based on the precepts of an official **ideology**. Totalitarian systems differ from autocracies in the wider range of issue-areas under control and in their preoccupation with organised mass participation in politics. Totalitarians are more interested in structuring and marshalling public opinion than in the mere suppression of dissent. The classical totalitarian systems, represented by **Stalinism** and Nazism at the height of their power, were also characterised by police states, leadership cults, arbitrary terror and hypnotic **propaganda**. Nonetheless, despite their aspirations, even the Italian Fascists failed to control civil society effectively, though Hitler's **Third Reich** came close. Other far-right regimes were more authoritarian than totalitarian in character. As used by US political scientists like Carl Friedrich and Zbigniew Brzezinski, the concept tended to bracket Communists and fascists together, leading critics on the left to dismiss it as a **Cold War** rhetorical device. The debate over its validity continues.

**TOTUL PENTRU TARA (ALL FOR THE FATHERLAND)** Later name of the Romanian Iron Guard.

**TOULON** French city where Jean-Marie Le Chevallier gained municipal power for **Le Pen**'s *Front National* in 1995.

**TRABALHISMO** Name given to **Vargas**'s pro-worker **populism** in 1930s Brazil.

**TRADITIONALISM** Loose term referring to adherence to traditional beliefs or practices. Many far-right movements are traditionalist, wishing to return to a golden past or a rural idyll marked by social conservatism and **family** values. Hardcore fascism, on the other hand, appeals to the past in a different way, suggesting that if elements of past values are restored, they will be radically transformed as well. While traditionalist voters may have been attracted to fascism, the fascists themselves often had a contempt for nostalgic or romantic traditionalism on its own. The most extreme opponents of traditionalism on the far right were the Italian Futurists in the pre-Fascist period.

**TRANSYLVANIA** Region in north-west Romania populated by ethnic Magyars (Hungarians). The area was lost to Hungary following the 1920 Treaty of Trianon, which penalised Austria–Hungary for its role in the First World War. Though the Communists stressed socialist solidarity in place of **nationalism**, Nicolae Ceauşescu's form of 'national Communism' led to discrimination and persecution of the Hungarians. The post-Communist far right in Hungary emphasise this loss of national territory and play up the issue, but the far right in Romania are equally adamant that Transylvania will be forever Romanian. Mainstream parties in both countries argue the case but have been careful to avoid the risk of violent confrontation.

**TRINCERISMO** Literally, 'spirit of the trenches' – an important influence on Italian Fascism in the years following 1918.

**TROPAS NACISTAS DE ASALTO (TNA)** Paramilitary arm of the Chilean *Movimiento Nacional Socialista de Chile* (MNS).

**UFA WOCHENSCHAU** Weekly newsreel that pursued a pro-Nazi/Nationalist line during the inter-war period in Germany.

**UGUNKRUST (FIRE CROSS)** Latvian fascist movement of the inter-war period. Its powerful *Völkisch* discourse meant it was particularly intolerant of minority nationalities. It had a strong following among students but was eventually outwitted by Latvia's para-fascist leader, **Ulmanis**.

**ULSTER DEFENCE ASSOCIATION (UDA)** Loyalist paramilitary organisation in Northern Ireland.

**ULSTER FREEDOM FIGHTERS (UFF)** Loyalist paramilitary organisation in Northern Ireland.

**ULSTER VOLUNTEER FORCE (UVF)** Loyalist paramilitary organisation in Northern Ireland.

**ULTRA-NATIONALISM** Extreme form of nationalism that is far beyond the mainstream and may involve recourse to violent and illegal actions. Ultra-nationalists usually feel betrayed by mainstream conservative and nationalist parties. Fascist and far-right oppositional violence is often motivated by ultra-nationalism.

**ULTRAS** Nickname pinned on various extreme extreme-right activists – for instance, the most radical of the *Algérie Française* activists in the 1950s and early 1960s. In this context, the phrase 'Ultra Ultras' also emerged.

**UNEMPLOYMENT** Seen by many as an economic condition conducive to the rise of fascist and other anti-system parties in capitalist liberal democracies. It is said to foster alienation, discontent and powerlessness, as well as envy towards immigrants and minority groups among poorer sections of the majority. Conservative critics of this thesis deny a direct causal relationship between deprivation and fascism, and warn against the dangers of explaining away or excusing indefensible violence and extremism, while minimising individual responsibility for one's actions.

**UNGE HØIRE (YOUNG CONSERVATIVES)** Inter-war Norwegian group that was slightly influenced by fascist ideas.

**UNIÃO NACIONAL (NATIONAL UNION) (UN)** (1) Single party created in 1930 by Portugal's para-fascist leader, **Salazar**. It tried to pose as a mass movement, but failed visibly, and simply became part of the state structure. In time it was outflanked by the ultra-radical *Nacional Sindicalismo* (NS) **Blueshirts**. It was on its last legs by the early-1940s; (2) Title of the NS newspaper in inter-war Portugal.

**UNIFICATION CHURCH** Body set up by **Moon** in Korea. It has engaged in a range of anti-Communist campaigns around the world (particularly in the 1980s) and has strong links with the **World Anti-Communist League**.

**UNION DE DÉFENSE DES COMMERÇANTS ET ARTISANS (UDCA)** Flash-in-the-pan movement that campaigned for the protection of French artisans and shop-keepers during the mid-1950s economic downturn. Led by Pierre **Poujade**, the UDCA was a pressure group that developed a protest-based political programme. **Poujadism** was anti-tax, anti-big business and anti-Paris. Its nationalist instincts meant that it targeted Jewish capitalists for special abuse and also supported the cause of *Algerie Française*. Enemies dubbed the UDCA fascist on account of its direct-action tactics and the Hitler-esque rhetoric employed by its leader. The UDCA eventually evolved into a political party, *Unité et Fraternité Française* (UFF), so that it could contest the parliamentary elections of 1956.

**UNION DÉMOCRATIQUE POUR LE RE-SPECT DU TRAVAIL (UDRT)** Far-right Belgian protest movement formed in 1978 and led by Robert Hendrickx.

**UNION FRANÇAISE POUR L'EURO-DROITE DES PATRIES** Title of the French far-right list in the 1979 European Elections.

**UNIÓN MONÁRQUICA ESPAÑOLA (UME)** Authoritarian royalist movement active in inter-war Spain. José Antonio **Primo de Rivera** was a leading light in the UME before moving over to the *Falange*.

**UNION MOVEMENT** Oswald **Mosley**'s pro-European unity movement founded in 1948. It had little electoral success and eventually merged into the **National Front** (NF) in 1966.

**UNIÓN NACIONAL (NATIONAL UNION) (UN)** Spanish far-right coalition grouping that won 2 per cent of the vote in the 1979 elections.

**UNIÓN NACIONAL SINARQUISTA (UNS)** Successor movement to the Mexican *Cristero* movement. The UNS was founded in 1937 and mixed a pro-Hispanic, ultra-nationalist creed with **corporatism** and **Catholicism**. It portrayed itself as a low-level mass party but has been branded both reactionary and quasi-fascist. It died away after 1945, was banned in 1948 and eventually metamorphosised into *Fuerza Popular*.

**UNION OF NATIONAL AND INDEPENDENT REPUBLICANS (UNIR)** The first neo-fascist movement to appear in post-war France. It was founded by Maurice **Bardèche** in 1951 and won four seats in the National Assembly. The UNIR based its programme on **race** and the desirability of a new pan-European **civilisation**.

**UNIÓN PATRIOTICA** 'Single party' created by General Miguel **Primo de Rivera** to help establish his 1923–30 **dictatorship** in Spain. He was influenced significantly by **Mussolini**, but his regime never acquired a popular base. *Unión Patriotica* was an artificial creation and ultimately a failure.

**UNION OF RUSSIAN PEOPLE (URP)** Early twentieth-century movement that some regard as the first example of Russian fascism.

**UNION POUR UNE NOUVELLE DÉMOCRA-TIE (UND)** Precursor to the Belgian FN–NF.

**UNITÉ ET FRATERNITÉ FRANÇAISE (FRENCH UNION AND FRATERNITY) (UFF)** When Pierre **Poujade**'s *Union de Défense des Commerçants et Artisans* (UDCA) pressure group decided to contest the 1956 parliamentary elections, it was forced to do so under different colours. Hence the birth of the UFF: ultra-nationalist, anti-Semitic and champion of all small traders in France. The new party won a staggering fifty-two seats in the poll – a development that sent shockwaves through the French political **establishment**. However, following an economic upturn in the late 1950s, the UFF and its demagogic leader disappeared into obscurity.

**UNITÉ NATIONALE DES INDÉPENDANTS RÉPUBLICAINS (UNIR)** Post-war French movement that sought to rehabilitate Marshal **Pétain**. It also had links with the young Jean-Marie **Le Pen**.

**UNITED FRONT** 'Anti-fascist' theory put forward by Trotsky, who argued that socialists and Communists should ignore their differences and unite against fascism – especially in Germany.

**UNITED FRONT FROM BELOW** School of thought that said Communists should reject alliances with other political groupings in the war against fascism in the inter-war period, and use the 'masses' instead.

**UNITED IRISHMAN** Pro-*Cumann na nGaedhal* newspaper that frequently published Blueshirt and pro-**Mussolini** propaganda in 1930s Ireland.

**UNITED NATIONS (UN)** Inter-governmental organisation arising out of dialogue among the major powers towards the end of the **Second World War**. The term was also used by the countries allied against the Axis Powers in a 1942 declaration of intent. In addition to promoting peace and security, the UN has shown a strong interest in opposing genocide and racial discrimination. The wartime legacy was also evident in the exclusion of Francoist Spain from the organisation at its founda-

tion. While US conservatives since the 1970s have roundly criticised the UN for alleged profligacy and left-wing ideological bias, the more extreme right-wing 'militia' and 'patriot' movements of the 1990s charged it with secretly planning the establishment of a World Government and of involvement in a lurid and complex conspiracy against US sovereignty.

**UNIVERSAL FASCISM** School of thinking prominent in the 1930s that emphasised fascism's international applications and also seemed to imply that fascism was a generic phenomenon. **Mussolini** was the chief apostle of Universal Fascism.

**UNIVERSAL NAZISM** Variant of **Universal Fascism** that emerged after 1945.

**UNIVERSALITÀ FASCISTA** Italian Fascist periodical of the 1930s.

**UNIVERSITY REFORM** Argentine movement founded in 1918 that anticipated **Perónism** in its political discourse.

**UOMO QUALUNQUE (MAN IN THE STREET) (UQ)** Italian neo-fascist party led by Guglielmo **Giannini**. It broke through the 5 per cent barrier in the 1946 poll and also achieved some significant local election success. It published a political journal of the same name.

**USTAŠA-HRVATSKA REVOLUCIONARNA ORGANIZACIJA (CROATIAN REVOLUTIONARY *USTASHA*) (UHRO)** Savage authoritarian movement that, with Nazi support, ruled Croatia between 1941 and 1945. Its ideology was based on separatist, anti-Serb **nationalism**, **corporatism** and violent **anti-Semitism**. The *Ustasha* **militia** was responsible for the death of around 700,000 Serbs and thousands of Jews. Although the *Ustasha* had links with Italian Fascism, its negative, secessionist creed meant that it was more proto-fascist than fascist.

The movement was founded by **Pavelić** in 1932.

**USTASHA YOUTH** Croatian neo-fascist organisation of the 1990s.

**UTOPIA** Newspaper established by **Mussolini** in his pre-Fascist days.

**VABADASSÒ JALASTE LIIT (CENTRAL LEAGUE OF THE VETERANS OF THE WAR OF INDEPENDENCE) (EVL)** Proto-fascist Estonian group founded in 1929 as a response to political and economic crisis. Paramilitary in style, it was influenced by both German and Finnish fascism. It was outlawed in 1934 as para-fascist Estonian head of state, **Päts**, moved his own administration to the right. The movement executed a failed coup attempt in 1935.

**VATERLÄNDISCHE FRONT (FATHERLAND FRONT)** Political party created by **Dollfuss** in inter-war Austria – a 'front' designed to give the impression that **'Austrofascism'** had a mass following. It had paramilitary and corporatist traits but is generally regarded as conservative rather than fascist.

**VATERLANDSPARTEI (FATHERLAND PARTY)** Pre-fascist German movement led by Anton **Drexler**. Conservative and nationalist, it acted as a radical right-wing lobby group.

**VATRA ROMÂNEASCĂ (ROMANIAN CRADLE)** Fanatical anti-Hungarian movement established in 1990 with links to Ceauşescu's ex-Communist regime and, also, to 1930s fascism. The *Partidul Unitati Nationale Romane* (PUNR) is its political embodiment.

**VERBOND VAN DIETSE NATIONAAL-SOLIDARISTEN (LEAGUE OF NETHERLAND-NATIONAL SOLIDARISTS) (VERDINASO)** Authoritarian far-right movement active in inter-war Flanders. Led by van **Severen**, it espoused a powerful brand of pro-Flemish separatism. Its politics were conservative–corporatist and over time the party became increasingly anti-Semitic.

**VEREINIGUNG DER VERFOLGTEN DES NAZI-REGIMES (ASSOCIATION OF VICTIMS OF THE NAZI REGIME) (VVN)** German anti-fascist group founded in 1970.

**VERONA, CHARTER OF** Political programme of the Italian **Partito Fascista Repubblicano** (PFR), as outlined in 1943.

**VERSAILLES DIKTAT** Pejorative Nazi description of the Treaty of **Versailles**. The Treaty incorporated the Covenant of the **League of Nations**, restricted the size of the German Army, redrew the boundaries of the Kaiser's Reich in favour of France and Germany's neighbours, and imposed heavy reparations and financial penalties on Germany for its role in the First World War.

**VERSAILLES, TREATY OF** Settlement reached at the end of the First World War that incorporated the Covenant of the **League of Nations**. It restricted the size of the German Army, demilitarised the Rhineland, imposed financial penalties on Germany and blamed her leaders for the war itself. As such, it was a target of attack for right-wing groups in Germany and throughout Europe. **Hitler**'s initial acts of aggression were designed to revise the territorial settlement arising from the treaties. However, once his expansion went further than the German-populated areas of Austria and the **Sudetenland**, Europeans realised that his ambitions exceeded the mere revision of Versailles.

**VERZET** Modern Belgian anti-fascist journal.

**VETERANS** The social dislocation caused by the First World War left many relatively young ex-servicemen feeling bitter and disappointed. They returned to face economic hardship and anti-war sentiment. Many blamed the **establishment** parties or the left for betraying their military leaders and capitulating to the Allies. Hardened by war but angered by the peace treaties, they formed an important component of the street-fighting Storm Troopers and *squadristi* in Germany and Italy. War and army camaraderie had a similar effect on the core group of military leaders around **Franco** in Spain.

**VICHY** French regime led by Marshal **Pétain** that collaborated with Nazi Germany between 1940 and 1944. Following military defeat in June 1940, the Third Republic voted itself out of existence and Pétain swiftly acceded to the position of head of state. He signed the Franco-German Armistice that split the country in two: Germany occupied the north and western coastal areas, while Pétain led a notionally independent administration in the south. From the central town of Vichy – the capital of the Unoccupied Zone – the Marshal led a revivalist government that, through the **National Revolution**, sought to return France to her ancient roots (particularly in the spheres of agricultural and social policy). Some commentators, aware of **collaboration** and **Hitler's** covert influence, have portrayed Pétain's political agenda as fascist, but in reality Vichy's priorities matched Hitler's only after the German invasion of the Southern Zone in 1942. While the aged Marshal tried to play up Vichy's patriotic credentials – a difficult task – **Laval** masterminded the administration's diplomatic relationship with Nazi Germany.

**VIOLENCE** An important feature of fascist and many far-right movements. Its importance arises from activists' conception of themselves as people who value action over words. Street violence, intimidation, thuggery and paramilitary drill were a feature of Brownshirt and Blackshirt activity during the fascist rise to power in Germany and Italy. Themes of combat and struggle only heighten the cult of violence. However, many far-right and neo-fascist groups conceal or even abandon violence in order to gain **middle-class** votes or cast a respectable image.

**VIT ARISKT MOSTÅND (WHITE ARYAN RESISTANCE) (VAM)** Modern Swedish organisation.

**VITALISM** The belief that living organisms, especially human beings, are infused with a non-material life force or spirit. German *Völkisch* **nationalism** applied this to a whole **race** or **nation**, implying that it was given life by a spirit of community or nationhood. The idea is also implicit in the concept of the nation used by the extremist *Rashtriya Swayamsevak Sangh* (RSS) group in India.

**VITROLLES** Marseilles suburb where Catherine **Mégret** won municipal power for the *Front National* (FN) in 1997.

**VITTORIO VENETO** First World War battle (1918) in which Italian forces roundly defeated Austria–Hungary and drove their forces from Italian soil, following earlier losses for the Italian side. The victory hastened the demise of the Habsburg Empire and was loudly celebrated by Italian nationalists for decades afterwards.

**VLAAMS BLOC (FLEMISH BLOC) (VB)** The modern face of Flemish **ultra-nationalism**. Founded by Karel **Dillen**, it began life in 1978 as a temporary electoral coalition but has evolved into one of the most significant far-right movements in Western Europe. It scored consistently well throughout the 1980s and 1990s – particularly in its Antwerp stronghold – and broke through the 20 per cent barrier in the mid-1990s. Its policy agenda is dominated by the demand for an independent Flanders, with Brussels as capital. It is also hostile to **immigration**, abortion and **homosexuality**.

**VLAAMS BLOC JONGEREN (VBJ)** Youth movement of the Belgian *Vlaams Bloc* (VB).

**VLAAMS-NATIONALE PARTIJ (VNP)** Pre-**Vlaams Bloc** vehicle for extreme Flemish **nationalism** – founded in 1977 by Karel **Dillen**.

**VLAAMS-NATIONALE RAAD (VNR)** Extreme Flemish nationalist movement founded in 1973 and led by Karel **Dillen**.

**VLAAMSCH NATIONAAL VERBOND (FLEMISH NATIONAL FEDERATION) (VNV)** Small inter-war Belgian group with Nazi traits led by Staf de **Clerq**. The VNV was a vehicle for Flemish **nationalism**, **anti-Semitism** and authoritarian ideas.

**VLAAMSE CONCENTRATIE (VC)** Shady and short-lived Flemish nationalist movement founded in 1949. It was both anti-leftist and sympathetic to wartime collaborators.

**VLAAMSE LIBERALEN EN DEMOCRATEN (FLEMISH LIBERALS AND DEMOCRATS) (VLD)** Modern Belgian movement that has embraced some *Vlaams Bloc* (VB) ideas on **immigration**.

**VLAAMSE MILITANTEN ORDE (VMO)** Racist neo-Nazi terror group founded *c.* 1950. Anti-democratic and anti-leftist, it was a vehicle for extreme Flemish **nationalism**. Its private **militia** was outlawed.

**VLAAMSE MILITANTENORGANISATIE** Later name of the Flemish *Vlaamse Militanten Orde* (VMO).

**VLAAMSE NIEUWE ORDE (VNO)** Later name of Flemish *Vlaamse Militanten Orde* (VMO).

**VLAAMSE VOLKSPARTIJ (VVP)** Extreme Flemish nationalist movement founded by Lode **Claes** in 1977.

**VOCE, LA** Ultra-nationalist, interventionist publication that had significant influence in Italy prior to 1914.

**VITLUS (STRUGGLE)** Newspaper of the Estonian *Vabadassò Jalaste Liit* (EVL).

**VOLK** German word for people or **race** – seen by the Nazis as an organic, almost spiritual community with deep roots in the past. *Völkisch* thinking was common among fringe nationalist and racist groups in Munich and Vienna in the early years of the twentieth century and these undercurrents had a significant influence on **Hitler**'s racial thinking.

**VOLK DER MITTE (PEOPLE OF THE MIDDLE)** Myth (or assumption) associated with the *Völkisch* movement of the early twentieth century – namely, that European **civilisation** revolved around Germany.

**VOLKSBEGEHREN INITIATIVE** **Haider**'s highly controversial demand that the Austrian government adopt tough **immigration** legislation.

**VÖLKISCHER BEOBACHTER (PEOPLE'S OBSERVER)** Nazi newspaper.

**VOLKSGEMEINSCHAFT** Phrase used by the Nazis to denote 'community of the people'.

**VOLKSSEELE** Norwegian term for 'national soul', as used by **Quisling**.

**VOLKSSOZIALISTISCHE BEWEGUNG DEUTSCHLANDS/PARTEI DER ARBEIT (POPULAR SOCIALIST MOVEMENT OF GERMANY/LABOUR PARTY) (VSBD/PDA)** Pro-Nazi Strasserite movement outlawed in 1982.

**VOLKSUNIE (VU)** Flemish nationalist movement founded in 1954. Karel **Dillen** was a high-profile youth activist and the movement became home to many ex-collaborators.

**VOORPOST (ADVANCE POSITION)** Belgian far-right movement boasting its own **militia**. It was founded in 1976.

**WALLOON LEGION** Pro-Nazi group of Belgian volunteers that fought for **Hitler** on the Eastern Front.

**WANDERVOGEL** German *Völkisch* youth movement founded in 1903.

**WANNSEE CONFERENCE** Event at which the Nazi leadership first discussed the notion of a 'Final Solution' – January 1942.

**WAR** Violent conflict, normally between sovereign states, for the achievement of political purposes. The Nazis relied to a considerable extent on **Ludendorff**'s interpretation of von **Clausewitz**'s concept of 'total war', namely, that war was a struggle of maximum exertion fought to the bitter end. However, von Clausewitz also argued that real war was constrained and dictated by politics. Fascists also saw war as a testing ground for the **survival of the**

**fittest**. In their glorification of war, they showed themselves to be bellicists.

**WAR CRIMES** Violations of the international laws of war, especially the 1924 Geneva Convention (which protected civilians and provided for the humane treatment of prisoners of war).

**WEHRMACHT** Name given to the combined forces of Army, Air Force and Navy under the **Third Reich**.

**WEHRSPORTGRUPPE HOFFMANN (WAR SPORT GROUP HOFFMANN)** Right-wing terror organisation active in West Germany and banned in 1980. It was led by Karl-Heinz **Hoffmann**.

**WEIMAR REPUBLIC** German regime born in 1919. It was ridiculed, and then overthrown, by **Hitler**'s Nazi Party.

**WELTPOLITIK (GLOBAL POLICY)** The declared foreign-policy doctrine of Kaiser Wilhelm II of Germany after the dismissal of Chancellor Otto von Bismarck in 1890. It implied a world role for Germany, a dominant role in Europe and military parity with Britain. Critics, then and since, charged that it was as much about verbal bluster as a viable policy. **Hitler**'s assertive position and his demands on the international community in the 1930s sounded similar, but he had a greater resolve and military preparedness for its implementation, at least in the European theatre.

**WERE DI (DEFEND YOURSELF)** Far-right Flemish group founded in 1961. Its leader was Karel **Dillen** and it gained notoriety for its pro-**Apartheid** stance.

**WERE DI VERBOND VAN NEDERLANDSE WERK-GEMEENSCHAPPEN (WD, VNW)** Pre-*Vlaams Bloc* vehicle for Flemish **ultra-**

nationalism. Formed in 1962, its first leader was **Dillen**.

**WESTERN DESTINY** Post-war far-right US publication.

**WESTLAND NEW POST** Subversive Belgian neo-Nazi organisation active in the 1970s and 1980s. It tried to infiltrate the Belgian Army.

**WHITE DEFENCE LEAGUE** British far-right movement founded in 1958 and associated with Colin **Jordan**. In 1960 it merged with the **National Labour Party** (NLP) to form the **British National Party.**

**WHITE ROSE** Anti-Nazi group active in Munich in 1942 and 1943.

**WHITE SUPREMACISM** Belief that the white races are inherently superior to Africans, Asians or Native American peoples. It is sometimes backed up with claims of divine justification or a mandate to structure society along hierarchical lines. White supremacist ideas are prominent in Nazi racial thought, as well as in South Africa and the southern US.

**WIJNINCKX COMMISSION** Special Senate enquiry into far-right politics in post-war Belgium.

**WIKING-JUGEND** Modern German pro-Nazi group.

**WILL** Volition or spirit of a group. Following Rousseau's conception of a 'General Will' that was more than the aggregate of individual wills or desires, extreme cultural nationalists and fascists suggested that their actions reflected the collective will of the 'nation'. This too could not be reduced to individual choices on the part of particular citizens but had a mysterious quality only known to the leader or the movement. The concept also suggested that the 'nation' was capable of anything if it could generate sufficient collective will to achieve it.

**WILL TO POWER** Concept in the philosophy of Friedrich **Nietzsche**. In essence 'will to power' was deemed to be the driving force behind human competition and creativity. The idea was linked by fascists to the Social Darwinian notion of the **'survival of the fittest'**, so as to justify the cult of action and war. Nietzsche's sister, Elisabeth, was associated with right-wing thinking in early twentieth-century Germany; she helped to interpret his ideas, especially the will to power in ways that suited the fascist cause.

**WISSEN, DAS** Nationalist newspaper in early twentieth-century Germany that anticipated many key Nazi themes.

**WNP** Polish neo-Nazi movement led by Boleslaw Tejkowski.

**WOCHE, DIE** Weekly Nazi newspaper.

**WORKING CLASS** Term usually applied to industrial workers, although social change in the twentieth century has caused considerable ambiguity about precise boundaries among class groups. Workers are traditionally assumed to support parties of the left. Far-right parties appeal to the social conservatism of many working-class voters, as well as to those who are envious of the success of foreigners, immigrants or minority groups.

**WORLD ANTI-COMMUNIST LEAGUE (WACL)** Organisation that boasted almost one hundred national branches in the 1960s and 1970s. It attracted the support of many anti-Communist, far-right and authoritarian figures, including Sun Myung **Moon** and right-wing dictators in Taiwan and South Korea.

**WORLD UNION OF NATIONAL SOCIALISTS (WUNS)** Neo-Nazi group based in the US.

**XENOPHOBIA** Fear or hatred of foreigners. Such emotions are frequently stirred up by racist far-right parties in an effort to promote national chauvinism or hostility to immigrants.

**YASUKUNI** Japanese shrine near Tokyo devoted to the victims of war. The shrine dates from the mid-nineteenth century but the Japanese secretly added the names of wartime leaders, including **Tōjō**, to the roll of honour at the shrine some time before 1979. A proposed visit by Japanese Prime Minister, Yunichiro Koizumi, caused tension with neighbouring Asian countries in 2001 but delighted some **veterans** and far-right nationalists.

**YOUNG NATIONAL FRONT (YNF)** Youth movement of the British **National Front (NF)**.

**YOUNG PLAN** Scheme put forward in 1929 to ease the burden on Germany arising from its war reparations. It succeeded the **Dawes Plan** of 1924, which had similar aims. Neither initiative went far enough for the nationalist right, which organised a campaign of protest and agitation against them. **Hitler** used this issue to boost his nationalist credentials and facilitate a broad right-wing and anti-Weimar front. The campaign aligned the Nazis

with **Hugenburg,** and gave them unexpected access to his press and publishing empire.

**YOUTH MOVEMENTS** Organised mass groupings of young people. In the context of fascist (and Communist) systems, their function was to mobilise youth and socialise them into the **ideology** and structures of the ruling party. They also served as a vehicle for social control, averting 'idleness' and curbing 'anti-social activities'. The attempt to create a party or state monopoly on youth movements, especially in Italy and Germany, was aimed at countering and smashing rival Church or voluntary organisations.

**YUZONSHA (SOCIETY FOR THE PRESERVATION OF THE NATIONAL ESSENCE)** Ultra-nationalist Japanese movement founded in 1921 by Kita **Ikki** and Okawa **Shumei**.

**Z-PLAN Hitler**'s blueprint for German naval supremacy – January 1939.

**ZBOR (NATIONAL YUGOSLAV MOVEMENT)** Proto-fascist Serb movement founded in 1935 and led by **Ljotić**. Anti-Semitic, anti-Communist and anti-federal, its value system was dominated by Christianity and **corporatism**. It scored approximately 1 per cent in both the 1935 and 1938 elections. *Zbor* was banned in 1940 but played a part in the German administration of Serbia after 1941.

**ZIONISM** Israeli **nationalism**, especially as expressed in terms of the return of all the Israeli people to a Jewish homeland in Israel. It dates from the late nineteenth century to the present day and refers to both the movements for Israeli nationhood and the philosophy behind it. Zionism also featured in a nineteenth-century Russian **propaganda** campaign, which was later taken up by the Nazis; it postulated the existence of a series of documents, under the heading of the '**Protocols of the Elders of Zion**', which amounted to a conspiratorial agenda for Jewish domination of the world. Zionism ultimately benefited from the **Second World War** in so far as guilt over the fate of the Jews facilitated Western support for the establishment of the State of Israel. Zionism is used as a pejorative term by Arab commentators and critics of Israel, who say it has become justification for Israeli oppression of the Palestinians. In the 1970s, a pro-Arab majority in the **United Nations** General Assembly adopted resolutions equating Zionism with **racism**, thus linking Israel with **Apartheid** South Africa. However, these were rescinded in the 1990s and most observers now acknowledge that it comes in many forms, some more tolerant and inclusive than others. Zionism has also given birth to the World Zionist Organisation.

# GUIDE TO
# SECONDARY READING

**NOTES**

- There is a vast amount of literature on fascism, so this survey has to be selective.
- It is confined to a cross-section of important and accessible English-language secondary sources (books and articles). It is not just a survey of recent literature on fascism and the far right, but includes studies written from the 1920s right through to 2000.
- It is divided into thematic sections. The headings are intended to aid the reader but they are not set in stone. A book on Nazi economic policy will probably be located in the Germany section. A book on European fascisms – containing a specialist chapter on France – will be placed under the 'International fascisms' heading rather than 'France'. These are rules of thumb and no more.
- Many general national histories and many general books about nationalism and right-wing politics will also shed light on fascism and the far right. For the most part, these titles are not included in the survey, but they would obviously give the reader even more context and background on the subject of fascism and the far right.
- Some secondary surveys that also include a collection of extracts are included in the guide to primary sources.

**GENERAL AND INTRODUCTORY TEXTS**

The richness of fascism as an ideology is explored in a range of survey studies. R. Griffin, *Fascism* (Oxford, Oxford University Press, 1995) and *The Nature of Fascism* (London, Routledge, 1994) are the most topical and best-crafted introductions to the subject. The former is an anthology of primary texts, but the commentary that puts the documents into context is helpful and highly authoritative; the latter is a more standard account that examines 'pre-fascism', 'classic fascism' and neo-fascism in a thorough and incisive manner. See also Griffin's article, 'Revolution from the right: Fascism' in D. Parker (ed.), *Revolutions and Revolutionary Tradition in the West 1560–1989* (London, Routledge, 1999).

R. Eatwell, *Fascism: A History* (London, Vintage, 1996) explores four national traditions (Italy, Germany, France and Britain). H.R. Kedward, *Fascism in Western Europe 1900–45* (London, Blackie, 1969) mixes survey-style analysis of national fascisms with a more theoretical approach. J.D. Forman, *Fascism: The Meaning and Experience of Reactionary Revolution* (New York, New Viewpoints, 1974) is a general survey that includes a very useful chapter on the US experience, and O.-E. Schüddekopf, *Fascism* (London, Weidenfeld & Nicolson, 1973) is a fairly standard profile that tries to unpick the main threads of fascist ideology (and also includes a collection of illustrations). See also N. O'Sullivan, *Fascism* (London, J.M. Dent, 1983), R. Tames, *Fascism* (London, Hodder, 2000) and G. Allardyce, 'What fascism is not: Thoughts on the deflation of a concept', *The American History Review* 84(2), a highly significant contribution to the debate about fascism.

Three book chapters are also worthy of note. R. Eccleshall, V. Geoghegan, R. Jay and R. Wilford, *Political Ideologies: An Introduction* (London, Hutchinson, 1986), A. Heywood, *Political Ideologies: An Introduction* (London, Macmillan, 1992), and R. Eatwell and A. Wright (eds), *Contemporary Political Ideologies* (London, Pinter, 1994) all contain excellent sections on fascism as an 'ism'.

On a more theoretical level M. Neocleous, *Fascism* (Buckinghamshire, Oxford University Press, 1997) is a provocative and original study, and S.J. Woolf (ed.), *The Nature of Fascism* (London, Weidenfeld & Nicolson, 1968) is an interesting collection of essays on social, economic and political themes. See also R. Eatwell, 'Towards a new model of generic fascism', *Journal of Theoretical Politics* 4 (1992).

Fascism, by necessity, is also touched upon in two broader survey studies. H. Rogger and E. Weber (eds), *The European Right: A Historical Profile* (Berkeley, CA, University of California Press, 1966) is particularly helpful in the way it examines the right on a country-by-country basis; and R. Eatwell and N. O'Sullivan, *The Nature of the Right: American and European Politics and Political Thought since 1789* (London, Pinter, 1992) is essential reading for those who wish to understand the theoretical background to right-wing politics.

With regard to general reference works, J.M. Roberts (ed.), *Purnell History of the Twentieth Century* (London, Purnell, 1968), is highly authoritative. See also D. Miller (ed.), *The Blackwell Encyclopedia of Political Thought* (Oxford, Basil Blackwell, 1987) and P. Rees, *Fascism and Pre-fascism in Europe 1890–1945: A Bibliography of the Extreme Right*, 2 vols (Sussex, Harvester Press, 1985). Finally, R. Thurlow, *Fascism* (Cambridge, Cambridge University Press, 1999) is a short, neat introduction that is particularly strong on topicality and accessibility.

## INTERNATIONAL 'FASCISMS'

A number of studies act as 'guided tours' to fascism around the world. S. Larsen, B. Hatgvet and J. Myklebust (eds), *Who Were the Fascists?* (Oslo, Universitetsforlaget, 1980) is a gigantic study and covers both inter-war and post-war fascisms (many quite obscure). A. Del Boca and M. Giovana,

*Fascism Today: A World Survey* (New York, Pantheon, 1969) is a broad-ranging guide and contains useful chapters on African and Latin American variants. S.J. Woolf (ed.), *European Fascism* (London, Methuen, 1981) is a collection of specialist articles and is extremely comprehensive. F. Carsten, *The Rise of Fascism* (London, Batsford, 1967) deals with Italy, Germany, Finland, Hungary, Romania, Spain, Flanders, Belgium, Britain and Austria, as well as offering a helpful synopsis of the (extremely important) pre-1914 period. G.L. Mosse (ed.), *International Fascism* (London, Sage, 1979) takes a similar approach, and contains specific articles on Italy, Germany, France, Belgium, Romania and Spain.

A.J. De Grand offers a comparative examination of the two 'classic' regimes in *Fascist Italy and Nazi Germany: The 'Fascist' Style* (London, Routledge, 1995). See also S. Payne, *Fascism: Comparison and Definition* (Madison, University of Wisconsin Press, 1980) and W. Laqueur and G.L. Mosse, *International Fascism* (New York, Harper & Row, 1966). The volume edited by W. Laqueur, *Fascism: A Reader's Guide* (London, Penguin, 1982), remains an excellent introduction not just to the various national brands of fascism but to the literature that has accumulated on the subject (in English and native languages).

## THEORY AND INTERPRETATIONS

A.J. Gregor, *Theories of Fascism* (Morristown, NJ, General Learning Press, 1974), is an excellent introduction to competing interpretations. R. de Felice, *Interpretations of Fascism* (Cambridge, MA, Harvard University Press, 1977), is a very helpful book and examines a range of 'classic' perspectives on fascism, focusing particularly on the Italian experience. See also R. De Felice and M. Ledeen, *Fascism: An Informal Introduction to its Theory and Practice* (New Brunswick, NJ, Transaction, 1976). R. Griffin's reader, *International Fascism* (London, Arnold, 1998), demonstrates the variety of theoretical interpretations on offer. H.A. Turner (ed.), *Reappraisals of Fascism* (New York, New Viewpoints, 1975) contains six essays on theory, starting with Nolte and moving on to economic and 'totalitarian' theses. The *Journal of Contemporary History* 1(4), 'Special Issue' (October 1976) is also a useful resource and features eleven essays on leftist, Bonapartist and Trotskyist interpretations, among others.

The volume edited by Larsen, Hagtvet and Myklebust contains two excellent theoretical overviews – one by Payne, the other by Hagtvet and Kühnl. R. Thurlow's general survey contains a useful summary, and R.A.H. Robinson, *Fascism in Europe* (London, Historical Association, 1981) is a neat 34-page study that also summarises the chief perspectives.

From a left-wing viewpoint, M. Kitchen, *Fascism* (London, Macmillan, 1976) assesses an array of rival interpretations. D. Renton, *Fascism: Theory and Practice* (London, Pluto, 1999) is a more up-to-date guide to the historiography of fascism and is particularly strong on the various left-wing strands. And D. Beetham (ed.), *Marxists in Face of Fascism* (Manchester, Manchester

University Press, 1983) is a superb anthology of Marxist writings (of various hues) on fascism *c.* 1921–38.

To understand the Orthodox Marxist approach to fascism, see R. Palme Dutt, *Fascism and Social Revolution* (London, Lawrence & Wishart, 1934), an emotive but disciplined *cri de coeur*. See also G. Dimitrov, *Against Fascism and War* (Sofia, Sofia Press, 1979) and P. Togliatti, *Lectures on Fascism* (London, Lawrence & Wishart, 1976) – a collection of themed discourses.

For an insight into the world of non-Orthodox Marxists, and their interpretation of fascism, see for example M. Vajda, *Fascism as a Mass Movement* (London, Allison & Busby, 1976), and N. Poulantzas, *Fascism and Dictatorship* (London, Verso, 1979) – a classic synthesis of Marxist ideas. Here see also J. Caplan, 'Theories of fascism: Nicos Poulantzas as historian', *History Workshop Journal* 3 (1977).

Trotsky's key works include *The Struggle against Fascism in Germany* (London, Pathfinder, 1971), *Fascism, Stalinism and the United Front* (London, Bookmarks, 1989) and *On France* (New York, Monad Press, 1979), a very interesting angle on the events of 1934 and other issues. In this context, see also R.S. Wistrich, 'Leon Trotsky's theory of fascism', *Journal of Contemporary History* 11(4) (1976), and M. Kitchen, 'Trotsky's theory of fascism', *Social Praxis* 2(1–2) (1974). On Thalheimer, another key dissident, refer to the analyses of J. Düllfer, 'Bonapartism, fascism and national socialism', *Journal of Contemporary History* 11(2) (1976), and M. Kitchen, 'August Thalheimer's theory of fascism', *Journal of the History of Ideas* 34(1) (1973).

The classic psychological accounts are T.W. Adorno *et al.*, *The Authoritarian Personality* (New York, Norton, 1950); W. Reich, *The Mass Psychology of Fascism* (New York, Farrar, Straus & Giroux, 1946) – a book that was banned by the Nazis; and E. Fromm, *Fear of Freedom* (London, Routledge & Kegan Paul, 1986). See also Fromm's work, *The Sane Society* (London, Routledge & Kegan Paul, 1963).

Leaving explicitly leftist accounts to one side, the most important socioeconomic interpretations are B. Moore Jnr, *The Social Origins of Dictatorship and Democracy* (London, Allen Lane, 1967) and S.M. Lipset, *Political Man* (London, Heinemann, 1960).

The classic 'totalitarian' interpretations emerge in H. Arendt, *The Origins of Totalitarianism* (London, André Deutsch, 1986), C.J. Friedrich, *Totalitarianism* (New York, 1964), C.J. Friedrich and Z. Brzezinski, *Totalitarian Dictatorship and Autocracy* (New York, Praeger, 1967), and C.J. Friedrich, M. Curtis and B.R. Barber, *Totalitarianism in Perspective* (New York, Praeger, 1969).

E. Nolte, in *Three Faces of Fascism* (New York, Holt, Rhinehart & Winston, 1965), puts forward his own 'theory of fascism' and also acts as a guide to competing theoretical interpretations.

## NEO-FASCISM AND THE EXTREME RIGHT IN THE POST-WAR PERIOD

P. Hainsworth (ed.), *The Politics of the Extreme Right* (London, Pinter, 2000) is the most topical survey – comprehensive, highly analytical and particularly strong on the blossoming of far-right ideas in post-Soviet Eastern Europe. His other study, *The Extreme Right in Europe and the USA* (London, Pinter, 1994) is equally authoritative. L. Cheles, R. Ferguson and M. Vaughan (eds), *Neo-Fascism in Europe* (London, Longman, 1991) is a detailed country-by-country guide to right-wing extremism in the post-war world and boasts a helpful chapter on the phenomenon of Historical Revisionism. The second edition of the book, *The Far Right in Western and Eastern Europe* (London, Longman, 1995), includes extra chapters on East European and lesser-known West European variants. P. Hockenos, *Free to Hate* (London, Routledge, 1993) concentrates on the post-Communist right in Eastern Europe. K. von Beyme (ed.), *Right-Wing Extremism in Post-War Europe* (London, Cass, 1988 – WEP Special Edition, 11(2)) offers the reader a very thorough dissection of right-wing extremism in Italy, West Germany, France, Britain and Spain, as well as two provocative overview articles. And there are two topical essays at the end of Griffin's reader, *International Fascism*.

P. Wilkinson, *The New Fascists* (London, Grant McIntyre, 1981) is an exploration of the fascist 'comeback' and is particularly interested in the terroristic ultra-right and the relationship between far-right extremism in the 1930s and 1970s.

G. Harris, *The Dark Side of Europe: The Extreme Right Today* (Edinburgh, Edinburgh University Press, 1990/1994) is a thorough but 'involved' analysis of the contemporary far-right, as is G. Ford, *Fascist Europe: The Rise of Racism and Xenophobia in Europe* (London, Pluto, 1992), a country-by-country guide to the neo-fascist danger (and originally published as an official European Parliament report in 1991). In this context, see also R. Genn and A. Lerman, *Fascism and Racism in Europe: The Report of the European Parliament's Committee of Inquiry*, Patterns of Prejudice, 20(2), pp. 13–25. H. Jaeger, *The Reappearance of the Swastika* (London, Gamma, 1960), is a slightly strange 'amateur' survey of neo-Nazisms.

Other literature on the post-war extreme right includes S. Larsen *et al.* (eds), *Modern Europe after Fascism* (Princeton, NJ, Princeton University Press, 1995); C.T. Husbands, 'Contemporary right-wing extremism in Western-European democracies', *European Journal of Political Research* IX (1981), pp. 75–99; *The Extreme Right in Europe and the United States* (Anne Frank Stichting, Amsterdam, 1984); R. Hill and A. Bell, *The Other Side of Terror: Inside Europe's Neo-Nazi Network* (London, Grafton, 1988). See also the two Hainsworth volumes and the Cheles *et al.* edited collection for helpful country-by-country reading lists.

With regard to reference, see F. Müller-Rommel and G. Pridham, *Small Parties in Western Europe* (London, Sage, 1991) for a helpful guide to a plethora of modern far-right movements. C. Ó'Maoláin, *The Radical Right: A*

*World Directory* (London, Longman, 1987) is the ultimate compendium and contains a vast amount of descriptive information on contemporary far-right movements. And M. Riff (ed.), *Dictionary of Modern Political Ideologies* (Manchester, Manchester University Press, 1987) is also very useful.


## INTER-WAR HISTORIES

S.J. Lee, *European Dictatorships 1918–1945* (London, Routledge, 2000), deals with Italian, German and Spanish regimes in an effective and incisive manner and brings to life the historiography of the period. M. Kitchen, *Europe between the Wars* (London, Longman, 1993) is an effective survey of national political histories. M. Blinkhorn (ed.), *Fascists and Conservatives* (London, Unwin Hyman, 1990) is an excellent country-by-country guide to the relationship between radical and reactionary rights. Finally, for another angle on the period, see S.M. Cullen, 'Leaders and martyrs: Codreanu, Mosley and José Antonio', *History* 71 (1986).


## ROOTS OF FASCISM

On the intellectual pre-history of fascism, P. Hayes, *Fascism* (London, Allen & Unwin, 1973) delves into the nineteenth century to locate the many and varying origins of the ideology. See also G.L. Mosse, 'The genesis of fascism', *Journal of Contemporary History* 1(1) (1966).

On Gobineau, refer to M. Biddiss, *Father of Racist Ideology: The Social and Political Thought of Count Gobineau* (London, Weidenfeld & Nicolson, 1970), an in-depth intellectual biography that debates the lineage and legacy of the Frenchman's ideas.

On Sorel, see J. Jennings, *Syndicalism in France* (Basingstoke, Macmillan, 1990); J. Roth, 'Revolution and morale in modern French thought: Sorel, and the Sorelians', *FHS* 3(2) (1963), and *The Cult of Violence: Sorel and the Sorelians* (Berkeley, University of California Press, 1980).

On Nietzsche, see William Bluhm, *The Freedom of the Over-Man: Nietzsche, Nazism and Humanist Existentialism. Theories of the Political Systems* (Englewood Cliffs, Prentice-Hall, 1978).


## FASCIST IDEOLOGY

Z. Sternhell, 'Fascist ideology', in Laqueur's reader is an excellent introduction to the topic, and A.J. Gregor, *The Ideology of Fascism: The Rationale of Totalitarianism* (New York, Free Press, 1969) chronicles the evolution of fascist ideology, placing significant emphasis on the phenomenon of proto-fascism. A. Hamilton, *The Appeal of Fascism* (London, Blond, 1971) is a clearly structured guide to the most significant fascist intellectuals in inter-war Europe. See also Z. Sternhell, M. Sznajder and M. Ashéri, *The Foundations of Fascist Ideology*

(Princeton, Princeton University Press, 1993) and A.C. Pinto, 'Fascist ideology revisited: Zeev Sternhell and his critics', *European History Quarterly* 16. On the right and New Right, see R. Levitas, *The Ideology of the New Right* (Cambridge, Polity Press, 1986) and D. Green, *The New Right* (Brighton, Wheatsheaf Books, 1987).

## SOCIETY AND ECONOMY

Here there are a plethora of studies: D. Mühlberger (ed.), *The Social Basis of European Fascist Movements* (London, Croom Helm, 1987); G. Germani, 'Political socialization of youth in fascist regimes: Italy and Spain', in S.P. Huntingdon and C.H. Moore (eds), *Authoritarian Politics in Modern Society*, (New York, 1970); and D.J. Saposs, 'The role of the middle class in social development: Fascism, populism, Communism, socialism', in *Economic Essays in Honor of Wesley Clair Mitchell* (New York, 1935). See also M. Durham, *Women and Fascism* (London, Routledge, 1998).

Refer also to G. Eley, 'What produces fascism: Preindustrial traditions or a crisis of the capitalist state?', *Politics and Society* 12(1) (1983); D. Guérin, *Fascism and Big Business* (London, Pathfinder, 1974) – an anarchist perspective; C. Haidar, *Capital and Labour under Fascism* (New York, 1930); H.A. Turner Jnr, 'Fascism and modernization' in H.A. Turner Jnr (ed.), *Reappraisals of Fascism* (New York, New Viewpoints, 1975); W.G. Welk, *Fascist Economic Policy* (Cambridge, MA, 1938), and any of the many works by A. Milward, for example: *The Fascist Economy in Norway* (Oxford, Clarendon, 1972); *The German Economy at War* (London, Athlone, 1965); *The New Order and the French Economy* (Aldershot, Gregg Revivals, 1993); *The Reconstruction of Western Europe, 1945–51* (London, Methuen, 1984); *War, Economy and Society, 1939–1945* (London, Allen Lane, 1977).

## DIPLOMACY AND INTERNATIONAL RELATIONS

On German thinking in the 1930s, see K. Haushofer, 'Defence of German geopolitics' in E. Walsh, *Total Power: A Footnote to History* (New York, Doubleday, 1948) and E. Wiskemann, *The Rome–Berlin Axis* (London, Collins, 1966). More generally, see Chapter 6 of P. Kennedy, *The Rise and Fall of the Great Powers: Economic Change and Military Conflict from 1500 to 2000* (London, Fontana, 1988) and also A. Iriye, *Japan and the Wider World: From the Mid-Nineteenth Century to the Present* (London, Longman, 1997). For a Spanish angle, consult I. Saz, 'Foreign policy under the dictatorship of Primo de Rivera', in S. Balfour and P. Preston (eds), *Spain and the Great Powers in the Twentieth Century* (London, Routledge, 1999). See also the helpful section in Eatwell and Wright.

## ANTI-FASCISM

This is a big subject but, for a taster, refer to J. Strachey, *The Menace of Fascism* (London, Gollancz, 1933) and D. Renton, *Fascism and Anti-Fascism* (Basingstoke, Macmillan, 2000). For a 1990s perspective, see C. Bambery, *Killing the Nazi Menace: How to Stop the Fascists* (London, Bookmarks, 1992); for a 1980s view, see C. Sparks, *Never Again! The Hows and Whys of Stopping Fascism* (London, Bookmarks, 1980); for a 1970s approach, see T. Grant, *The Menace of Fascism: What it is and How to Fight it* (London, Militant, 1978); and for a 1960s viewpoint, see Q. Hoare, 'What is fascism?', *New Left Review* 20 (1963).

## ITALY

As regards general surveys of the Mussolini era, R.J.B. Bosworth, *The Italian Dictatorship: Problems and Perspectives in the Interpretation of Mussolini and Fascism* (London, Hodder, 1998) is strong on the post-war historiography of Fascism. J. Whittam, *Fascist Italy* (Manchester, Manchester University Press, 1995) is an incisive and non-polemical guide to the Mussolini era, and also includes a range of documents. P. Morgan, *Italian Fascism 1919–45* (Basingstoke, Macmillan, 1995) is a concise and accessible survey. A. Lyttelton, *The Seizure of Power: Fascism in Italy 1919–1929* (London, Weidenfeld & Nicolson, 1987) explains how the Mussolini regime consolidated itself. E. Wiskemann, *Fascism in Italy* (London, Macmillan, 1969), is a short overview, as is G. Carocci, *Italian Fascism* (London, Penguin, 1975). In terms of reference, see P.V. Cannistraro (ed.), *A Historical Dictionary of Fascist Italy* (Westport CT, Greenwood Press, 1982).

See also A.J. Gregor's two histories – *The Ideology of Fascism* (London, Collier-Macmillan, 1969) and *Italian Fascism and Developmental Dictatorship* (New Jersey, Princeton University Press, 1979) – and also F. Chabod, *A History of Italian Fascism* (London, 1963), H. Finer, *Mussolini's Italy* (London, Grosset & Dunlap, 1964) and D.L. Germino, *The Italian Fascist Party in Power* (Minneapolis, 1960).

The most significant contemporary accounts were written by G. Salvemini, *The Fascist Dictatorship in Italy* (London, 1928), *Under the Axe of Fascism* (London, 1936) and *Italian Fascism* (London, Gollancz, 1938). See A. Tasca/A. Rossi, *The Rise of Italian Fascism, 1918–1922* (London, Methuen, 1938) – a leftist view – and also H.W. Schneider, *Making the Fascist State* (New York, 1928) and L. Villari, *The Fascist Experiment* (London, 1926).

In terms of broader histories, D. Mack Smith, *Italy* (Ann Arbor, 1969) traces the history of Italy from the 1860s to the 1960s. C. Seton-Watson, *Italy from Liberalism to Fascism* (London, Methuen, 1967) is a general survey history that includes separate bibliographies of work in Italian and English. A.W. Salomone (ed.), *Italy from the Risorgimento to Fascism* (Newton Abbot, David & Charles, 1970) explores a range of perspectives on the origins of Fascism and includes an extended narrative chronology. M. Clark, *Modern Italy 1871–1982* (London, Longman, 1995) situates the Fascist era within 200 years of national history. M. Robson, *Italy: Liberalism and Fascism 1870–1945* (London, Hodder & Stoughton, 2000) is an updated guide for students.

On the origins of Italian Fascism, refer to: G. Salvemini, *The Origins of Fascism in Italy* (New York, Harper & Row, 1973 [1961]), who argues that it was war rather than the political situation prior to 1914 that gave birth to Fascism; J.A. Thayer, *Italy and the Great War. Politics and Culture 1870–1915* (University of Wisconsin Press, 1964); and Z. Sternhell, M. Sznajder and M. Ashéri, *The Birth of Fascist Ideology* (Princeton, NJ, Princeton University Press, 1994).

For other angles on origins, see A.J. Gregor, *The Young Mussolini and the Intellectual Origins of Fascism* (Berkeley, University of California Press, 1979); A.J. De Grand, *The Italian Nationalist Association and the Rise of Fascism in Italy* (London, University of Nebraska Press, 1978); F. Borkenau, *Pareto* (London, Chapman & Hall, 1946); M.A. Ledeen, *The First Duce: D'Annunzio at Fiume* (Baltimore, John Hopkins University Press, 1977). On the Liberal period that Mussolini attacked so violently, see A.W. Salomone, *Italy in the Giolittian Era* (Philadelphia, University of Pennsylvania Press, 1960), which includes an introductory essay by Salvemini.

There is a range of Mussolini biographies. D. Mack Smith, *Mussolini* (London, Paladin, 1983) is a highly accessible study. L. Fermi, *Mussolini* (Chicago, Chicago University Press, 1961) devotes considerable space to his childhood and 'socialist phase'. The 1960s spawned Sir I. Kirkpatrick, *Mussolini* (London, Odhams, 1964) and C. Hibbert, *Benito Mussolini* (London, 1962), and the 1930s G. Megaro, *Mussolini in the Making* (London, 1938).

On other key Fascist figures see H.S. Harris, *The Social Philosophy of Giovanni Gentile* (University of Illinois Press, 1960).

On the corporate state, see C.T. Schmidt, *The Corporative State in Action: Italy under Fascism* (New York, 1939). On an adjacent subject, see D.D. Roberts, *The Syndicalist Tradition in Italian Fascism* (Manchester, Manchester University Press, 1979). On the vexed question of Mussolini's relationship with the country's industrialists, see R. Sarti, *Fascism and the Industrial Leadership in Italy, 1919–1940* (London, 1971), and 'Mussolini and the industrial leadership in the Battle of the Lira 1925–1927', *Past and Present* (May 1970), pp. 97–112. See also F. Adler, 'Italian industrialists and radical fascism', *Telos* 30 (1976–7).

On some interesting social issues, see V. De Grazia, *How Fascism Ruled Women* (Berkeley, University of California Press, 1994), T. Koon, *Believe, Obey, Fight: Political Socialisation of Youth in Fascist Italy 1922–43* (Chapel Hill, NC, University of North California Press, 1985), and M. Michaelis, *Mussolini and the Jews* (Oxford, Clarendon, 1978). Chapters 4 and 5 of D. Mack Smith, *Italy and its Monarchy* (London, Yale University Press, 1989) cast interesting light on Mussolini's relationship with the King.

On culture, a good general guide is E.R. Tannenbaum, *Fascism in Italy: Society and Culture 1922–1945* (London, Allen Lane, 1973). See also W.L. Anderson, 'Fascism and culture: Avant-gardes and secular religion in the Italian case', *Journal of Contemporary History* 24 (1989) and P.V. Cannistraro, 'Mussolini's cultural revolution: Fascist or nationalist?', *Journal of Contemporary History* 7(3–4) (1972). On the complex issue that was Church–state relations, see D.A. Binchy, *Church and State in Fascist Italy* (Oxford, 1970) and D. Moore, *Church and State in Italy 1850–1960* (Oxford, 1960).

On foreign policy, see A. Cassels, *Mussolini's Early Diplomacy* (Princeton, 1970). On the Axis relationship, see F.W. Deakin, *The Brutal Friendship: Mussolini, Hitler and the Fall of Italian Fascism* (London, Penguin, 1966), and, on Abyssinia, G.W. Baer, *The Coming of the Italian–Ethiopian War* (Cambridge, MA, 1967) and A. Sbacchi, *Ethiopia under Mussolini* (London, Zed Books, 1989).

On other important aspects of Fascist Italy, see M. Ledeen, *Universal Fascism: the Theory and Practice of the Fascist International, 1928–1936* (New York, Howard Fertig, 1972) and M. Stone, 'Staging fascism: The exhibition of the fascist revolution', *Journal of Contemporary History* 28 (1993).

As regards regional studies, refer to: P. Corner, *Fascism in Ferrara 1915–1925* (Oxford, Clarendon, 1976); A. Kelikian, *Town and Country under Fascism: The Transformation of Brescia, 1915–1926* (Oxford, Oxford University Press, 1986); F. Snowden, *The Fascist Revolution in Tuscany* (Cambridge, Cambridge University Press, 1989); W.L. Anderson, *Avant-Garde Florence: From Fascism to Modernism* (Cambridge, MA, Harvard University Press, 1993); and A.L. Cardoza, *Agrarian Elites and Italian Fascism: The Province of Bologna, 1901–1926* (Princeton, NJ, Princeton University Press, 1982).

On post-Mussolini Italy, see L.B. Weinberg, *After Mussolini: Italian Neo-Fascism and the Nature of Fascism* (Washington, DC, University Press of America, 1979), and two studies by F. Ferraresi: *The Post-War Italian Radical Right* (Cambridge, Polity, 1993), and 'The radical right in postwar Italy', *Politics and Society* XVI (1988), pp. 71–119. See also R.H. Drake, 'Julius Evola and the ideological origins of the radical right in contemporary Italy', in P.H. Merke (ed.), *Political Violence and Terror, Motifs and Motivations* (Los Angeles, University of California Press, 1986), pp. 161–89. In addition, S. Gundle and S. Parker (eds), *The New Italian Republic* (London, Routledge, 1996) puts the *Movimento Sociale Italiano* (MSI) and *Alleanza Nazionale* (AN) in helpful context.

## GERMANY

In terms of general studies I. Kershaw, *The Nazi Dictatorship, Problems and Perspectives of Interpretation* (London, Arnold, 2000) is an excellent analytical study. C. Fischer, *The Rise of the Nazis* (Manchester, Manchester University Press, 1995) focuses on the ideology and class-based constituencies of the party, and includes selected documents and a helpful thematic bibliography. K.D. Bracher, *The German Dictatorship* (London, Penguin, 1973) is a thorough examination of all aspects of the Nazi regime. R.A. Brady, *The Spirit and Structure of German Fascism* (New York, Howard Fertig, 1969) examines the institutions of Nazism. M. Broszat, *The Hitler State* (London, Longman, 1981) offers an in-depth interpretation. More topically, see also M. Burleigh, *The Third Reich – a New History* (London, Macmillan, 2000).

J. Hiden and J. Farquharson, *Exploring Hitler's Germany* (London, Batsford, 1983) is strong on historiographical insights, as is P. Ayçoberry, *The Nazi Question* (London, Routledge, 1979). H.A. Turner, *Nazism and the Third Reich* (New York, Quadrangle, 1972) contains nine themed essays including contributions from Messrs Bullock, Mason and Mommsen. G.L. Mosse, *Nazism: A Historical and Comparative Analysis of National Socialism* (Oxford, Blackwell, 1978) is a very personal 'interview-style' assessment of Hitler's regime. R. Geary, *Hitler and Nazism* (London, Routledge, 1994) is a concise survey in the Lancaster Pamphlet series. J. Noakes, *Government, Party and People in Nazi Germany* (Exeter, University of Exeter, 1980) is a small but useful overview. Finally, H.Vogt, *The Burden of Guilt: A Short History of Germany 1914–1945* (London, Oxford University Press, 1965) is, as the title implies, a slightly emotive study written by a German who lived through the aftermath of Nazism.

See also J.M. Rhodes, *The Hitler Movement* (Stanford, Hoover International Press, 1980), R. Heberle, *From Democracy to Nazism* (New York, Grosset & Dunlap, 1970), D. Orlow, *History of the Nazi Party, 1933–45* (Pittsburgh, University of Pittsburgh Press, 1973), S. Taylor, *Germany 1918–1933: Revolution, Counter-Revolution and the Rise of Hitler* (London, Duckworth, 1986), R. Brady, *The Spirit and Structure of German Fascism* (New York, Fertig, 1969 [1937]) and D. Guérin, *The Brown Plague: Travels in Late Weimar and Early Nazi Germany* (London, Duke Press, 1994).

For important contemporary perspectives, refer to F. Neumann, *Behemoth: The Structure and Practice of National Socialism* (New York, Octagon Books, 1944) – a classic; R.M. Brickner, *Is Germany Incurable?* (Philadelphia, 1943); and R.T. Clark, *The Fall of the German Republic* (London, 1935).

The issue of origins is well covered. H. Glaser, *The Cultural Roots of National Socialism* (London, Croom Helm, 1978) sees Nazism as a response to a decaying provincial culture. D. Gasman, *The Scientific Origins of National Socialism* (London, Macdonald, 1971) explores the influence of monism on the Nazis' *Völkisch* ideas. And F. Stern (ed.), *The Path to Dictatorship 1918–1933* (London, Praeger, 1967) incorporates ten scholarly essays on a variety of political themes. See also G.L. Mosse, *The Crisis of German Ideology: Intellectual Origins of the Third Reich* (New York, Grosset & Dunlap, 1964) and R.D.O. Butler, *The Roots of National Socialism, 1783–1933* (London, 1941).

On the Weimar Republic there are a number of solid studies. The most recent surveys include: P. Bookbinder, *Weimar Germany: The Republic of the Reasonable* (Manchester, Manchester University Press, 1996), which explores political and social themes, and includes a range of documents and a helpful biblio-graphical essay; E.J. Feuchtwanger, *From Weimar to Hitler: Germany 1918–33* (London, Macmillan, 1995), which argues that Weimar was more progressive than some observers would have it; H. Heiber, *The Weimar Republic* (Oxford, Basil Blackwell, 1995), which combines narrative and analysis; M. Broszat, *Hitler and the Collapse of Weimar Germany* (Oxford, Berg, 1993), which explores the complex relationship between the two; A.J. Nicholls, *Weimar and the Rise of Hitler* (London, Macmillan, 1991), a very readable introduction; D.J.K. Peukert, *The Weimar Republic* (London, Penguin, 1991), an original slant on the subject; J.W. Hiden, *The Weimar Republic* (Longman, London, 1991), an accessible account augmented by selected documents; E. Kolb, *The Weimar Republic* (London, Routledge, 1990), a useful profile; and G. Scheele, *The Weimar Republic* (Connecticut, Greenwood, 1975), whose sub-title, 'Over-ture to the Third Reich', is instantly provocative. This is all in addition to E. Eyck's comprehensive two-volume work, *A History of the Weimar Republic* (London, Oxford University Press, 1962/3).

On the historical continuities in modern German history, see two studies by G. Eley: *Reshaping the German Right: Radical Nationalism and Political Change after Bismarck* (New Haven, Yale University Press, 1980) and *From Unification to Nazism* (Boston, Allen & Unwin, 1990). On the theoretical level, see W. Sauer, 'National socialism: Totalitarianism or fascism?', *American Historical Review* 73 (1967).

On Hitler there are a range of biographies: I. Kershaw, *Hitler* (London, Allen Lane, 1998/2000) is a giant two-volume work. Kershaw's other studies are also impressive: *The Hitler Myth* (Oxford, Oxford University Press, 1987) and *Hitler* (London, Longman, 1991). A.L.C. Bullock, *Hitler: A Study in Tyranny* (London, 1964) is probably the most famous biography, and argues that Nazism can only be understood through the personality of the man. W. Carr, *Hitler* (London, Arnold, 1978) assesses his career as 'politician', 'dictator' and 'military commander'. On Hitler's early days – family back-ground and school life – see F. Jetzinger, *Hitler's Youth* (Connecticut, Green-wood, 1976). See also H. Lasswell, 'The psychology of Hitlerism', *Political Quarterly* 4 (1933).

M. Burleigh and W. Wippermann, *The Racial State: Germany, 1933–45* (Cambridge, Cambridge University Press, 1991) examines the ideas and poli-cies that lay behind the emergence of a new type of political structure and explains how women, homosexuals and other groups fared under the Nazi system. See also G.L. Mosse, *Towards the Final Solution* (New York, Howard Fertig, 1978) and P.G.J. Pulzer, *The Rise of Political Anti-Semitism in Germany and Austria* (New York, 1964).

W. Carr, *Arms, Autarchy and Aggression* (London, Arnold, 1972) is an in-depth examination of German foreign policy between 1933 and 1939. J.W. Hiden, *Germany and Europe 1919–39* (Longman, London, 1993) is a good general survey and contains useful maps and tables. K. Hildebrand, *The*

*Foreign Policy of the Third Reich* (London, Batsford, 1973), is also a good synopsis. And *The Sudeten Question* (Munich, Sudeten German Council, 1984) is a neat educational guide to one of the most significant foreign-policy issues.

On the military, see F.L. Carsten, *The Reichswehr and Politics 1918–1933* (Oxford, Clarendon, 1966), a study that traces the relationship between the Army and the German establishment. On the centrality of terror, see R. Bessel, *Political Violence and the Rise of Nazism: The Storm Troopers in Eastern Germany 1925–1934* (London, Yale University Press, 1984), a book that focuses on the political strategy pursued by rank-and-file *Sturm Abteilung* (SA) officials, and is at the same time a regional study of note.

On society, see D.F. Crew, *Nazism and German Society 1933–1945* (London, Routledge, 1994), an impressive collection of essays on social themes. R Grunberger, *A Social History of the Third Reich* (London, Weidenfeld & Nicolson, 1971) is an in-depth survey, focusing on thirty different subjects. R.F. Hamilton, *Who Voted for Hitler?* (New Jersey, Princeton University Press, 1982) is an incisive guide to the electoral geography of Nazism; on this issue, see also K.O. Lessker, 'Who voted for Hitler? A new look at the class basis of Nazism', *American Journal of Sociology* 74 (1968). T. Mason, *Nazis, Fascism and the Working Class* (Cambridge, Cambridge University Press, 1995) incorporates a series of authoritative essays on social and labour history, and F.L. Carsten, *The German Workers and the Nazis* (Aldershot, Scolar, 1995) delves into the ordinary lives of people and their opposition to the Hitler regime. See also D. Schoenbaum, *Hitler's Social Revolution* (New York, 1966), R. Dahrendorf, *Society and Democracy in Germany* (New York, 1967), and P. Baldwin, 'Social interpretations of Nazism: Renewing a tradition', *Journal of Contemporary History* 25(1) (1990).

On economic issues, see A.A. Schweizer, *Big Business in the Third Reich* (Indiana, 1964), and H.A. Turner, 'Big business and the rise of Hitler', *American Historical Review* 75 (1969). See also B.H. Klein, *Germany's Economic Preparations for War* (Harvard, 1959) and R. Bowen, *German Theories of the Corporative State* (New York, 1947).

On Nazism and youth, see P.D. Stachura, *The German Youth Movement 1900–1945* (London, Macmillan, 1981), a book that looks at the phenomenon of political organisations for the young in broader terms and across five decades. See also P. Lowenberg, 'The psychohistorical origins of the Nazi Youth cohort', *American Historical Review* 76(5) (December 1971).

On religion and mysticism in the Nazi era, see N. Goodrick-Clarke, *The Occult Roots of Nazism* (Wellingborough, The Aquarian Press, 1985), an exploration of the not insignificant relationship between Aryan cults and Hitler's ideology, and this book includes some helpful illustrations. The same author has also written *Hitler's Priestess*, a provocative assessment of the influence of Savitri Devi on Nazi ideology. See also J.H. Brennan, *Occult Reich*

(London, Futura, 1974) and R.A. Pois, *National Socialism and the Religion of Nature* (London, Croom Helm, 1986).

On opposition to the Nazis, see H. Graml, H. Mommsen, H.-J. Reichardt and E. Wolf, *The German Resistance to Hitler* (London, Batsford, 1970) – a good overview. See also A. Merson, *Communist Resistance in Nazi Germany* (London, Lawrence & Wishart, 1985).

Other important topics also have their historians. On Hitler's rallies, see T. Burden, *The Nuremberg Party Rallies, 1923–39* (London, Pall Mall Press, 1967); on the post-war trials see J.J. Heydecker and J. Leeb, *The Nuremberg Trial* (Connecticut, Greenwood, 1962). See also Z.A.B. Zeman, *Nazi Propaganda* (Oxford, 1964); M. Quinn, *The Swastika* (London, Routledge, 1995); J. Cornwell, *Hitler's Pope: The Secret History of Pius XII* (London, Viking Press, 1999); P. Lowenberg, 'The unsuccessful adolescence of Heinrich Himmler', *American Historical Review* 76(3) (June 1971). R. Harris, *Selling Hitler* (London, Faber & Faber, 1991) is the bizarre story of the faked Hitler Diaries. And for another perspective on the whole era, see J. Heartfield, *Photomontages of the Nazi Period* (London, Universe Books, 1977).

As regards local studies the best to consult are J. Noakes, *The Nazi Party in Lower Saxony 1921–1933* (London, Oxford University Press, 1971), G. Pridham, *Hitler's Rise to Power: The Nazi Movement in Bavaria 1923–33* (London, Granada, 1973) – which is particularly interesting because of the Munich Putsch – and W.S. Allen, *The Nazi Seizure of Power. The Experience of a Single German Town. 1922–1935* (London, Penguin, 1989), which brings to light the case of Northeim.

On the post-war era, see R. Stöss, 'The problem of right-wing extremism in West Germany', in von Beyme's edited volume. See also W. Wippermann, 'The post-war German left and fascism', *Journal of Contemporary History* 11(4) (1976).

## FRANCE

France has a long tradition of right-wing politics and this is reflected in the field of literature. A number of survey studies of the right have been published and each helps us to put French fascism in its proper context. M. Winock's recently translated volume, *Nationalism, Anti-Semitism and Fascism in France* (Stanford, Stanford University Press, 1998) is a provocative examination of 'nation-centred' discourse and concludes that France has been a fertile breeding ground for fascist ideas. Rémond's *The Right Wing in France* (Pennsylvania, University of Philadelphia Press, 1971) is a classic study but he is sceptical about the notion of an indigenous French fascist tradition. M. Anderson pays significant attention to the *ligues* tradition in *Conservative Politics in France* (London, Allen & Unwin, 1974), and E.J. Arnold's edited collection of essays, *The Development of the Radical Right in France: From Boulanger to Le Pen* (London, Macmillan, 2000), is topical, broad-ranging and places particular emphasis on the defensive style of nationalism associated with the concept of 'anti-France'.

There are a range of other good overview studies. P.M. Rutkoff, *Revanche and Revision* (Athens, OH, Ohio University Press, 1981) examines the importance of the defeat in 1871 as a spur to radical right-wing activity; P. Mazgaj, 'The origins of the French radical right: A historiographical essay', *French Historical Studies* (autumn 1987) assesses how historians have dealt with this issue; B. Jenkins, *Nationalism in France* (London, Routledge, 1990) explores the growth of a new right-wing nationalism in the period after 1880; R. Tombs, (ed.), *Nationhood and Nationalism in France: From Boulangism to the Great War 1889–1918* (London, HarperCollins, 1991) presents a selection of specialist essays on the same topic; and H. Tint, *The Decline of French Patriotism, 1870–1940* (London, 1964) sheds interesting light on the political ideas of Barrès and Maurras, two men innately connected with the rise of 'pre-fascist' and 'early fascist' ideas in France.

On the *Ligue des Patriotes*, a key 'pre-fascist' organisation, see P.M. Rutkoff, 'The *Ligue des Patriotes*: The nature of the radical right and the Dreyfus Affair', *French Historical Studies* 8(4) (autumn 1974) and Z. Sternhell, 'Paul Déroulède and the origins of modern French nationalism', *Journal of Contemporary History* VI (1971).

The central debate about French fascism – illusion or reality? – is best illustrated by the wealth of studies on the inter-war period. R. Soucy and Z. Sternhell identify the emergence of a new 'revolutionary right' in the late nineteenth and early twentieth centuries. Soucy puts particular emphasis on the role of Barrès. See *French Fascism: The Case of Maurice Barrès* (Berkeley, University of California Press, 1972) and 'Barrès and fascism', *French Historical Studies* (spring 1967). On Barrès, see also G.F. Putnam, 'The meaning of *Barrèsisme*', *Western Political Quarterly* VII (June 1954) and C. Stewart Doty, *From Cultural Rebellion to Counterrevolution: The Politics of Maurice Barrès* (Ohio, Ohio University Press).

On Boulangism, which can help unlock a lot of doors as regards the origins of French fascism, see two studies by W.D. Irvine: *The Boulanger Affair Reconsidered* (New York, Oxford University Press, 1989) – a good interpretative study – and 'French royalists and Boulangism', *French Historical Studies* (1988). See also F.H. Seagar, *The Boulanger Affair: Political Crossroad of France 1886–1889* (New York, Cornell University Press, 1969) – a straight political history – and two helpful articles: B. Fulton, 'The Boulanger affair revisited: The preservation of the Third Republic, 1889', *French Historical Studies* 17(2) (fall 1991) and C. Stewart Doty, 'Parliamentary Boulangism after 1889', *The Historian* 32 (February 1970).

On the Dreyfus Affair – a key landmark in the history of French anti-Semitism – see J.-D. Bredin, *The Affair* (London, Sidgwick & Jackson, 1987) and R. Kedward, *The Dreyfus Affair* (London, Longman, 1965). On anti-Semitism more generally in this period, see S. Wilson, *Ideology and Experience:*

*Antisemitism in France at the Time at the Dreyfus Affair* (London, Associated University Press, 1982) and S. Wilson, 'The antisemitic riots of 1898 in France', *The Historical Journal* XVI(4) (1973). On this theme, and anticipating developments in the twentieth century, see also R. Wistrich, *Anti-Semitism: The Longest Hatred* (London, Mandarin, 1992) and P.J. Kingston, *Anti-Semitism in France during the 1930s: Origins, Personalities and Propaganda* (Hull, University of Hull, 1983).

On the 1920s political context, see Soucy's *Fascism in France: The First Wave, 1924–1933* (New Haven, Yale University Press, 1986), and, on the 1930s, *French Fascism: The Second Wave 1933–1939* (London, Yale University Press, 1995). Soucy's keynote article, 'The nature of fascism in France', *Journal of Contemporary History* 1 (1966), examines the issue on a broader level and also brings the Vichy regime into the argument. Z. Sternhell takes a similar tack to Soucy. In 'National socialism and anti-Semitism: The case of Maurice Barrès', *Journal of Contemporary History* 8(4) and *Neither Right nor Left* (Berkeley, University of California Press, 1986), he depicts French fascism as a unique ideological synthesis.

On the *Action Française*, see E. Weber, *Action Française* (Stanford, Stanford University Press, 1962), E.R. Tannenbaum, *The Action Française* (New York, Wiley, 1962), and two articles by S. Wilson, 'History and traditionalism: Maurras and the *Action Française*', *Journal of the History of Ideas* 28 (1968) and 'The *Action Française* in French intellectual life', *The Historical Journal* XII(2) (1969). On another interesting inter-war movement, refer to R.O. Paxton, *French Peasant Fascism: Henry Dorgères's Greenshirts and the Crises of French Agriculture, 1929–1939* (Oxford, Oxford University Press, 1997).

On the key fascist personalities, see G. Allardyce, 'The political transition of Jacques Doriot', *Journal of Contemporary History* 1(1) (1966), R.J. Soucy, 'Drieu la Rochelle and the modernist anti-modernism in French fascism', *Modern Language Notes* 95(4) (1980) and W.R. Tucker, 'Politics and aesthetics: The Fascism of Robert Brasillach', *Western Political Quarterly* 15(4) (December 1962).

On fascist agitation in the 1930s, see A. Werth, *France in Ferment* (London, 1934), M. Beloff, 'The sixth of February', in J. Joll (ed.), *The Decline of the Third Republic* (St Antony's Papers No. 5) (London, 1959), and two articles by G. Warner: 'The Stavisky affair and the riots of February 6th 1934', *History Today* (June 1958) and 'The Cagoulard conspiracy', *History Today* (July 1960).

On Vichy there is an array of studies. On Pétain, see N. Atkin, *Pétain* (London, Longman, 1998) – a highly accessible biography – and on Pétain's trial, J. Roy, *The Trial of Marshal Pétain* (London, Faber & Faber, 1968). The best guides to the Vichy regime – and its unique policy agenda – are: R. Aron, *The Vichy Regime* (Putnam, 1958), a classic study; R.O. Paxton, *Vichy France: Old Guard and New Order 1940–1944* (New York, Columbia University Press, 1982), an excellent overview; and P. Farmer, *Vichy Political Dilemma* (London, Octagon, 1977), which is very strong on the National Revolution. In addition,

J. Sweets, *Choices in Vichy France* (New York, Oxford University Press, 1994) is a provocative study that raises a number of significant questions about France and French people under the Vichy administration.

On Vichy and society, see two excellent works by W.D. Halls: *The Youth of Vichy France* (Oxford, Clarendon, 1981) and *Politics, Society and Christianity in Vichy France* (Oxford, Berg, 1995). On the economy, see A.S. Milward, *The New Order and the French Economy* (Oxford, 1970).

On Laval and collaboration, see D. Thomson, *Two Frenchmen: Pierre Laval and Charles de Gaulle* (London, Cresset, 1951), which includes a superbly nuanced political biography of Laval; and also G. Warner, *Pierre Laval and the Eclipse of France*, (London, Eyre & Spottiswoode, 1968), M. Dank, *The French against the French: Collaboration and Resistance* (Philadelphia, Lippincott, 1974) and D. Johnson, 'A question of guilt: Pierre Laval and the Vichy regime', *History Today* 38 (January 1988). See also C. Micaud, *The French Right and Nazi Germany 1933–1939* (Duke University Press, 1943), a study that looks at the French right in the context of the international situation.

On France and the Holocaust, see M.R. Marrus and R.O. Paxton, *Vichy France and the Jews* (Stanford, Stanford University Press, 1995) – an excellent study – and P. Webster, *Pétain's Crime* (London, Papermac, 1992), a more journalistic work. On the phenomenon of collaborationism, see R. Cobb, *French and Germans, Germans and French* (Hanover, NH, Brandeis University Press, 1983), a very helpful depiction of the varying types of Franco-German relationship.

H. Rousso, *The Vichy Syndrome: History and Memory in France since 1944* (London, Harvard University Press, 1994) is a hugely original enquiry into the legacy of Vichy; A. Werth, *France 1940–55* (Holt, Rinehart & Winston, New York, 1956) is a useful political history, and S. Fishman, L.L. Downs, I. Sinanoglou, L.V. Smith, and R. Zaretsky (eds), *France at War: Vichy and the Historians* (Oxford, Berg, 2000) is a highly topical review of Vichy historiography.

R. Gildea, *France since 1945* (Oxford, Oxford University Press, 1996) is an incisive guide to the post-war period and covers lots of interesting ground. On Poujadism, see Eatwell's article in P.G. Cerny (ed.), *Social Movements and Protest in Modern France* (London, Pinter, 1982). Two excellent histories of the Algerian War help us to understand the *Algérie Française* phenomenon: A. Horne, *A Savage War of Peace* (London, Penguin, 1985) and E. Behr, *The Algerian Problem* (London, Penguin, 1961). For a broader perspective, refer to R.F. Betts, *France and Decolonisation 1900–1960* (London, Macmillan, 1991) and A. Clayton, *The Wars of French Decolonization* (London, Longman, 1994).

Four books have been recently published about the *Front National* (FN). J. Marcus's readable profile, *The National Front and French Politics* (London, Macmillan, 1995), H.G. Simmons's in-depth dissection of the movement, *The French National Front: The Extremist Challenge to Democracy* (Oxford, Westview, 1996), P. Davies's analysis of FN political ideas and the party's record 'in power' at a local level, *The National Front in France: Ideology, Discourse and*

*Power* (London, Routledge, 1999) and E.G. Declair's, *Politics on the Fringe: The People, Policies, and Organisation of the French National Front* (London, Duke University Press, 1999), an excellent general profile of the movement. See also P. Fysh and J. Wolfreys, *The Politics of Racism in France* (Basingstoke, Macmillan, 1998).

For a left-wing view, see G. Jenkins, 'The threat of Le Pen', *Socialist Review* (June 1988). Refer also to P. Fysh and J. Wolfreys, 'Le Pen, the National Front and the extreme right in France', *Parliamentary Affairs* (1992).


## SPAIN AND PORTUGAL

### Spain

There are many general histories of the Civil War period that contain excellent analyses of early Spanish fascism, the *Falange* and Franco's regime. The best to consult is H. Thomas, *The Spanish Civil War* (London, 1961) – an epic account. Two studies by R. Carr put the Civil War into context: *Spain 1808– 1939* (Oxford, Oxford University Press, 1966) and the edited volume, *The Republic and the Civil War in Spain* (London, 1971). See also G. Brenan, *The Spanish Labyrinth* (Cambridge, Cambridge University Press, 1943) – an early study.

On the phenomenon that was Spanish fascism, see S. Ben-Ami, *Fascism from Above* (Oxford, Clarendon, 1983), an interpretative study of the Primo de Rivera dictatorship. On the *Falange*, see S. Payne, *Falange: A History of Spanish Fascism* (Stanford, Stanford University Press, 1961/2) – the standard work – and S. Ellwood, *Spanish Fascism in the Franco Era: Falange Española de las JONS 1936–1986* (London, Macmillan, 1987), a three-phase history of the movement. P. Preston, *The Politics of Revenge: Fascism and the Military in Twentieth Century Spain* (London, Routledge, 1990) puts the conflict between fascist militarism and democracy into context; refer also to articles by the same author in Woolf's collection of articles about European fascism and Blinkhorn's edited volume on the radical right and conservative right in inter-war Europe.

On Franco the man, see P. Preston, *Franco: A Biography* (London, Harper-Collins, 1993), an enormous and highly authoritative piece of work. See also A. Lloyd, *Franco* (London, Longman, 1969) – Chapter 6 in particular. There are several helpful surveys of the regime. S. Payne, *The Franco Regime* (London, Phoenix, 2000) is a giant 641-page portrayal; E. de Blaye, *Franco and the Politics of Spain* (London, Penguin, 1976), pays particular attention to the doctrine of *Franquism* ; J. Grugel and T. Rees, *Franco's Spain* (London, Arnold, 1997) analyses the politics and policies of the regime; and M. Richards, *A Time of Silence* (Cambridge, Cambridge University Press, 1998) concentrates on the undoubted illiberalism of the early years.

And to bring the subject of Spanish fascism closer to home, refer to

H. Francis, *Miners against Fascism* (London, Lawrence & Wishart, 1984), the story of Welsh miners who joined the military struggle in the 1930s.

## Portugal

On Salazar, the most helpful studies are A.C. Pinto, *Salazar's Dictatorship and European Fascism* (New York, Columbia University Press, 1995), a modern comparative interpretation of the regime, and D.L. Raby, *Fascism and Resistance in Portugal 1941–74* (Manchester, Manchester University Press, 1988), a guide to the range of leftist, liberal and military opposition to Salazar. See also T. Gallagher, 'From hegemony to opposition: The ultra right before and after 1974', in L.S. Graham and D.L. Wheeler (eds), *In Search of Modern Portugal: The Revolution and its Consequences* (Madison, University of Wisconsin Press, 1983), and the chapter by the same author in Blinkhorn's inter-war survey.

## GREAT BRITAIN AND IRELAND

### Great Britain

The best general history of British fascism is R.C. Thurlow, *Fascism in Modern Britain* (Stroud, Sutton, 2000). This is a thorough, topical and highly accessible survey study. *British Fascism* (London, Croom Helm, 1980), edited by K. Lunn and R.C. Thurlow, is not able to account for developments in the 1980s and 1990s, but the essays included in the volume are provocative and the British Union of Fascists (BUF) is particularly well covered.

On a broader level T. Kushner and K. Lunn (eds), *Traditions of Intolerance: Historical Perspectives on Fascism and Race Discourse in Britain* (Manchester, Manchester University Press, 1989), explore the various forms of racism in modern British society and the different types of fascism 'in action'. The collection of essays they have edited point to a variety of interesting and perhaps under-studied social currents. In another anthology of articles, *The Failure of British Fascism* (Basingstoke, Macmillan, 1996), M. Cronin takes a different tack, assessing the factors that have inhibited the many and various expressions of far-right protest.

On the BUF and the 1930s, see D.S. Lewis, *Illusions of Grandeur* (Manchester, Manchester University Press, 1987), which focuses on the ideology of the movement and opposition to it; C. Cross, *The Fascists in Britain* (London, Barrie & Rockliff, 1961), a good general account that also features eight pages of evocative photos; R. Benewick, *The Fascist Movement in Britain* (London, Penguin, 1972), an investigation into the rise and fall of the BUF and other far-right strands (this book was previously published as *Political Violence and Public Order* [London, Penguin, 1969]); and G.C. Lebzelter, *Political Anti-Semitism in England 1918–1939* (London, Macmillan, 1978), contains very useful sections on the BUF and other far-right organisations of the inter-war period.

For a good local angle on the party, see J.D. Brewer, *Mosley's Men* (Aldershot, Gower, 1984), an intricate dissection of the Birmingham branch, and particularly strong on organisational details and membership figures. As regards contemporary profiles, refer to F. Mullally, *Fascism inside England* (London, Morris, 1946), a post-BUF survey (complete with illustrations), and J. Drennan, *BUF: Oswald Mosley and British Fascism* (Murray, 1934).

The National Front (NF) – the best known modern movement of the far right – has come under much scrutiny. N. Fielding, *The National Front* (London, Routledge, 1981), is an in-depth profile that focuses primarily on the racial ideology of the movement. See also M. Walter, *The National Front* (London, Fontana, 1987), S. Taylor, *The National Front and English Politics* (London, Macmillan, 1982) and M. Billig, *Fascists: A Social-Psychological View of the National Front* (London, Harcourt Brace Jovanovich, 1978).

On opposition to fascism in Britain, see N. Copsey, *Anti-Fascism in Britain* (Basingstoke, Palgrave, 2000), a comprehensive guide that covers the whole of the twentieth century: the failure of British fascism, the far right and the fight for political recognition. See also *Searchlight* publications.

### Ireland

M. Manning, *The Blueshirts* (Dublin, Macmillan, 1970) is a comprehensive history of Ireland's most significant fascist movement and includes many insights into the character of its leader, O'Duffy. Further material comes in the shape of M. Cronin, 'The Blueshirt movement 1932–5: Ireland's fascists?', *JCH* 30(2) and Chapter 2 of P.S. Stanfield, *Yeats and Politics in the 1930s* (London, Macmillan, 1988), which details W.B. Yeats's involvement with O'Duffy's Blueshirts.

### AUSTRIA

F.L. Carsten, *Fascist Movements in Austria from Schönerer to Hitler* (London, Saga, 1977), is a general survey that covers all possible variants. On 'early fascism', see A.G. Whiteside, *Austrian National Socialism before 1918* (The Hague, 1962). On the inter-war experience, see E. Bukey, *Hitler's Austria* (Chapel Hill, University of North Carolina Press, 2000) – a fascinating exploration of Austria's reaction to Hitler and Nazism. See also L. Jedlicka, 'The Austrian Heimwehr', *Journal of Contemporary History* 1(1) (1966) and P.R. Sweet, 'Mussolini and Dollfuss, an episode in fascist diplomacy', in J. Braunthal, *The Tragedy of Austria* (London, 1948). On theory, see G. Botz, 'Austro-Marxist interpretations of fascism', *Journal of Contemporary History* 11(4), and on more recent high-level controversy, B. Cohen and L. Rosenzweig, *Waldheim* (London, Robson, 1988).

## BELGIUM AND THE NETHERLANDS

### Belgium

M. Conway, *Collaboration in Belgium: Léon Degrelle and the Rexist Movement 1940–1944* (Newhaven–London, Yale, 1993), is the key study and paints a vivid picture of *Rex* and its leader. See also the chapter by J. Stengers in Rogger and Weber.

### The Netherlands

There is very little on Dutch fascism, so the best place to start is R.B. Andeweg and G.A. Irwin, *Dutch Government and Politics* (London, Macmillan, 1993), which introduces the modern far right and puts it in a helpful context.

### GREECE

On a general level, see R. Clogg, *Parties and Elections in Greece* (London, Hurst & Co., 1988). For more specific analysis, see R. Clogg and L. Yanna-poulos (eds), *Greece under Military Rule* (London, Secker & Warburg, 1972), a collection of articles that helps to shed light on all aspects of the Colonels' coup. Likewise, C. Woodhouse, *The Rise and Fall of the Greek Colonels* (St Albans, Granada, 1985) profiles the background to the coup, the reality of it and the legacy. See also two helpful chapters on the Greek far right – in Blinkhorn's edited collection and Hayes's book. There is also a useful section on the modern-day Greek far right in Hainsworth's volume published in 1994.

### SCANDINAVIA

### Norway

See O. Hoidal, *Quisling. A Study in Treason* (Oxford University Press, Oxford, 1989) and A.S. Milward, *The Fascist Economy in Norway* (Oxford, 1972).

### Finland

D. Arter, *Politics and Policy-Making in Finland* (Brighton, Wheatsheaf, 1987), introduces the modern *Lapua* movement and helps to contextualise it. See also M. Rintala, *Three Generations: The Extreme Right in Finnish Politics* (Bloomington, 1982) and L. Karvonen, 'From white to blue-and-black. Finnish fascism in the inter-war period', *Commentationes Scientarum Socialium* 36 (1988).

## Sweden

See the volume edited by S. Larsen, B. Hagtvet and J. Myklebust for a variety of insights, and the chapter on Scandinavia in Hainsworth's volume published in 2000.

## Denmark

There is very little on the Danish far right, but J. Fitzmaurice, *Politics in Denmark* (London, Hurst, 1981), introduces the modern-day Progress Party and places it in its proper context. See also the chapter in Hainsworth's volume published in 1994.

## EASTERN EUROPE

For excellent general background, see R.J. Crampton, *Eastern Europe in the Twentieth Century* (London, Routledge, 1991) and C.A. Macartney and A.W. Palmer, *Independent Eastern Europe – A History* (London, 1962). Three works by H. Seton-Watson also help to set the scene: *Eastern Europe between the Wars* (Cambridge, 1946), *The East European Revolution* (London, 1950), and 'Fascism: Right and left', *Journal of Contemporary History* 1 (1966). See also P.F. Sugar (ed.), *Native Fascism in the Successor States, 1918–1945* (California, 1971) and N.M. Nagy-Talavera, *The Green Shirts and the Others: A History of Fascism in Hungary and Rumania* (Stanford, 1970).

## Czechoslovakia

See V. Mastny, *The Czechs under Nazi Rule* (New York, Columbia University Press, 1971), which deals with the reality of occupation and resistance between 1939 and 1942. Refer to Y. Jelinek, 'Slovakia's internal policy and the Third Reich, August 1940–February 1941', *Central European History* (September 1971) and 'Bohemia–Moravia, Slovakia and the Third Reich during the Second World War', *East European Quarterly* 2 (1969). See also 'Storm-troopers in Slovakia: the Rodobrana and the Hlinka-Guard', *Journal of Contemporary History* 3 (1971).

## Estonia

See A. Kasekamp, 'The Estonian Veterans' League: A fascist movement?', *Journal of Baltic Studies* 24(3).

## Hungary

See C.A. Macartney, *October Fifteenth – A History of Modern Hungary 1929–1945*, 2 vols (Edinburgh, Edinburgh University Press, 1969), for general background. Refer also to G. Magos, 'The role of the British and American imperialists in the stabilisation of Horthy Fascism', *Acta Historica* II (1954) and I. Deák, 'Hungary', in the volume edited by Weber and Rogger, for a more in-depth analysis of the Magyar right.


## Poland

H. Roos, *A History of Modern Poland 1916–1945* (London, Eyre & Spottiswoode, 1966), helps to contextualise the Polish experience during the inter-war years.


## Romania

See M. Sturdza, *The Suicide of Europe* (Belmost, MA, 1968) and E. Weber, 'The men of the Archangel', *Journal of Contemporary History* 1 (1966). See also Weber's article in the volume edited by Weber and Rogger.


## Russia

See J.J. Stephen, *The Russian Fascists* (London, Hamish Hamilton, 1978), for the bizarre story of the *émigré* Russian Fascist Union (1925–45), and H. Rogger, 'Was there a Russian fascism?', *Journal of Modern History* (1964).


## ASIA AND AUSTRALASIA


## Japan

See O. Tanin and E. Yohan, *Militarism and Fascism in Japan* (Connecticut, Greenwood, 1975), an in-depth study of that country's complex 'military–fascist' tradition. See also G.J. Kasza, 'Fascism from below? A comparative perspective on the Japanese right 1931–1936', *Journal of Contemporary History* 19(4); B.-A. Ami Shillony, *Politics and Culture in Wartime Japan* (Oxford, Clarendon Press, 1981); and T. Najita, 'Nakano Seigō and the spirit of the Meiji Restoration in Twentieth-Century Japan', in J.W. Morley (ed.), *Dilemmas of Growth in Prewar Japan* (Princeton, NJ, Princeton University Press, 1971).


## New Zealand

P. Spoonley, *The Politics of Nostalgia* (Palmerston North, Dunmore, 1987), is a specialist study on the New Zealand far right – its history and contemporary flowerings.

# AFRICA

## South Africa

On Apartheid, see C. Bloomberg, *Christian-Nationalism and the Rise of Afrikaner Broederbond in South Africa 1918–48* (New York, Macmillan, 1981) and P.J. Furlong, *Between Crown and Swastika. The Impact of the Radical Right on the Afrikaner Nationalist Movement in the Fascist Era* (London, Wesleyan University Press, 1992).

## Uganda

On the nature of the Amin dictatorship, see M. Mamdani, *Imperialism and Fascism in Uganda* (London, Heinemann, 1983) and A. Omara-Otunnu, *Politics and the Military in Uganda, 1890–1985* (Oxford, Macmillan, 1987).

## Zaire

On Mobuto, see C. Young and T. Turner, *The Rise and Decline of the Zairian State* (London, University of Wisconsin Press, 1985), a thorough history.

# AMERICAS

## US

On the imitation Nazism of the German–American community in the 1930s, see S.A. Diamond, *The Nazi Movement in the United States 1924–1941* (London, Cornell University Press, 1974). On the Ku Klux Klan, see W.P. Randel, *The Ku Klux Klan* (London, Hamish Hamilton, 1965), for a good general survey and a helpful thematic bibliography. For more on the modern US battleground, see S. Carmichael and C.V. Hamilton, *Black Power* (London, Penguin, 1971), a concise survey. See also W.T. Martin Riches, *The Civil Rights Movement* (London, Macmillan, 1997), a book that covers the Clinton era and includes a useful glossary; and K. Verney, *Black Civil Rights in America* (London, Routledge, 2000), a clear and incisive summary. On the modern far right, see L. Zeskind, *The 'Christian Identity Movement'* (Atlanta, Center for Democratic Renewal, 1986) and M. Durham, 'Preparing for Armageddon: Citizen militias, the Patriot Movement and the Oklahoma City bombing', *Terrorism and Political Violence* (spring 1996).

By way of introduction to the specific political culture of South America, see R.J. Alexander, *Latin American Political Parties* (New York, Praeger, 1973) and A.E. van Niekerk, *Populism and Political Development in Latin America* (Rotterdam, University of Rotterdam Press, 1974). Refer also to the extremely helpful chapter in Laqueur's reader.

## Argentina

See D. Rock, *Argentina in the Twentieth Century* (London, 1975), for general context. On Perónism, see R.J. Alexander, *The Perón Era* (New York, 1951), G.I. Blanksten, *Perón's Argentina* (New York, 1953) and J. Kirkpatrick, *Leader and Vanguard in Mass Society: A Study of Peronist Argentina* (Cambridge, MA, 1971). On more specific issues, see two studies by P.H. Smith: 'The social base of Peronism', *Hispanic American Historical Review* 52(1) (February 1972) and 'Social mobilisation, political participation and the rise of Juan Perón', *Political Science Quarterly* LXXXIV (March 1969). Refer also to W. Little, 'Electoral aspects of Peronism, 1945–55', *Journal of Inter-American Studies* 53 (August 1973) and F. Hoffman, 'Perón and After', *Hispanic American Historical Review* 36(4) (November 1956). On another key aspect of the Argentina experience, see E.T. Glauert, 'Ricardo Rojas and the emergence of Argentine cultural nationalism', *Hispanic American Historical Review* 43(3) (August 1963).

## Bolivia

See H. Klein, *Parties and Political Change in Bolivia, 1880–1952* (London, Cambridge University Press, 1969).

## Brazil

On Vargas, see two studies by R. Levine, *The Vargas Regime: The Critical Years, 1934–38* (New York, Columbia University Press, 1970) and 'Brazil's Jews during the Vargas regime and after', *Luso-Brazilian Review* V(1) (June 1968), plus J.W.F. Dulles, *Vargas of Brazil: A Political Biography* (Austin, TX, University of Texas Press, 1967), R. Bourne, *Getulio Vargas of Brazil, 1883–1995* (London, 1974) and K. Loewenstein, *Brazil under Vargas* (New York, 1942). On other aspects of the Brazilian experience, see S. Hilton, '*Acção Integralista Brasileira*: Fascism in Brazil, 1932–1938', *Luso-Brazilian Review* IX(2) (December 1972), F.D. McCann, 'Vargas and the destruction of the Brazilian *Integralista* and Nazi Parties', *The Americas* (July 1969) and R.J. Alexander, 'Brazilian *Tenentismo*', *Hispanic American Historical Review* 36 (1956).

## Chile

See M. Sznajder, 'A case of non-European fascism. Chilean national socialism in the 1930s', *Journal of Contemporary History* 28(2) and M.H. Spooner, *Soldiers in a Narrow Land* (London, University of California Press, 1999), an in-depth profile of the Pinochet regime. For a recent study, see H. O'Shaughnessy, *Pinochet, the Politics of Torture* (New York, New York University Press, 2000).

**Mexico**

See A. Michaels, 'Fascism and *Sinarquismo*: Popular nationalisms against the Mexican Revolution', *The Journal of Church and State* VIII(2) (1966).

**Peru**

See R.J. Alexander, *Aprismo* (Kent, Ohio, 1973) and H. Kantor, *The Ideology and Programme of the Aprista Movement* (Berkeley, 1964).

## HISTORICAL REVISIONISM AND HOLOCAUST DENIAL

See R. Eatwell, 'The Holocaust Denial: A study in propaganda technique', in Cheles *et al.* (1991) for a very helpful overview. See also D. Lipstadt, *The Holocaust Denial* (New York, Free Press, 1993) and G. Seidel, *The Holocaust Denial* (Leeds, Beyond the Pale, 1986).

## USEFUL WEBSITES

- http://www.pagesz.net/stevek/europe/duce.html: The History Guide lectures, 2000.
- http://www.brookes.ac.uk/schools/humanities/Roger/roghome.htm: Roger Griffin's Links Pages, offering access to many of his own papers and book chapters.
- http://www.yale.edu/lawweb/avalon: Avalon library.
- http://www.holocaust-trc.org/wmp16.htm: the Holocaust Education Program Resource Guide.

# NOTES

## INTRODUCTION

1 Francis Fukuyama characterised world history as one of great ideological struggles but suggested that the relative consensus around liberal democracy and capitalism since 1990 means that international politics is now about short-term national interests. See F. Fukuyama, 'The end of history', *The National Interest* 16 (summer 1989), pp. 3–16.
2 Z. Sternhell, *Neither Right nor Left: Fascist Ideology in France*, Chichester, Princeton University Press, 1986.
3 R. Bosworth, *The Italian Dictatorship: Problems and Perspectives in the Interpretation of Mussolini and Fascism*, London, Hodder, 1998, p. 38.
4 R. Griffin, *The Nature of Fascism*, London, Routledge, 1991, p. 121.
5 Griffin, *The Nature of Fascism*, Chapter 5.
6 This refers to the former East German Communists, formerly the 'Socialist Unity Party of Germany' (SED). Strictly speaking, the SED also included former Social Democrats who were forced to align themselves with the Communists.
7 For a clear but simple illustration of these ways of interpreting the political spectrum, see A. Heywood, *Politics*, Macmillan Foundations Series, London, Macmillan, 1997, pp. 234–5.
8 We use the term 'Marxian' to refer to broadly Marxist approaches and those derived from Marxism.
9 Sternhell, *Neither Right nor Left*, pp. 17–19.
10 This is a theme in Karl Dietrich Bracher's account of the German nationalist right and its motives for early collaboration with Hitler. See K. Bracher, *The German Dictatorship: The Origins, Structure and Consequences of National Socialism*, London, Penguin, 1973, Chapters 1–5.

## HISTORIOGRAPHY

1 A.J. Gregor, *Interpretations of Fascism*, New Jersey, General Learning Press, 1974, p. 2.
2 S. Payne, 'The concept of fascism', in S. Larsen, B. Hagtvet and J. Myklebust (eds), *Who Were the Fascists*, Oslo, Universitetsforlaget, 1980, pp. 14–25.
3 Gregor, *Interpretations*, p. 27.
4 E. Nolte, 'The problem of fascism in recent scholarship', in H.A. Turner, *Reappraisals of Fascism*, New York, New Viewpoints, 1975, pp. 26–42.
5 H. Arendt, *The Origins of Totalitarianism*, London, André Deutsch, 1986 [1951].
6 Nolte, 'Scholarship'.
7 Take, for example, the two books cited above and W. Laqueur (ed.), *Fascism: A Reader's Guide*, London, Penguin, 1976. Note in particular his words on pp. 7–8.
8 See R. Griffin (ed.), *Fascism*, Oxford, Oxford University Press, 1995, pp. 1–12.
9 See G. Allardyce, 'What fascism is not: Thoughts on the deflation of a concept', taken from Griffin, *Fascism*, pp. 301–2.
10 Payne, 'Concept'.

11 B. Hagtvet and S. Larsen, 'Contemporary approaches to fascism: A survey of paradigms', in Larsen *et al.* (eds), *Fascists*, pp. 26–51.
12 R. de Felice, *Interpretations of Fascism*, Cambridge, MA, Harvard University Press, 1977, pp. 1–106.
13 R. Thurlow, *Fascism*, Cambridge, Cambridge University Press, 1999, pp. 3–6.
14 Hagtvet and Larsen, 'Approaches'.
15 Gregor, *Interpretations*, p. 28.
16 Gregor, *Interpretations*, p. 28, pp. 38–42 and p. 44.
17 Gregor, *Interpretations*, pp. 30–3.
18 P. Drucker, *The End of Economic Man*, taken from Griffin, *Fascism*, p. 271.
19 Gregor, *Interpretations*, p. 33 and p. 44.
20 Gregor, *Interpretations*, pp. 42–5 and pp. 243–5.
21 See Gregor, *Interpretations*, pp. 50–77; see also M. Kitchen, *Fascism*, London, Macmillan, 1982, pp. 18–19 – 'psychological' theories are also linked to 'totalitarian' theories.
22 H.R. Kedward, *Fascism in Western Europe 1900–45*, London, Blackie, 1969, p. 182.
23 Kedward, *Europe*, p. 182.
24 Kitchen, *Fascism*, p. 12.
25 F.L. Carsten, 'Interpretations of fascism', in Laqueur, *Fascism*, pp. 457–87.
26 T.W. Adorno, E. Frenkel-Brunswik, D. Levinson and R. Nevitt Sanford, *The Authoritarian Personality*, taken from Griffin, *Fascism*, p. 289; the quote comes from Kitchen, *Fascism*, pp. 20–1.
27 E. Fromm, *The Fear of Freedom*, taken from Griffin, *Fascism*, pp. 275–6. See Kedward, *Europe*, p. 193.
28 Kedward, *Europe*, pp. 193–4.
29 Fromm, *Freedom*; see also Kitchen, *Fascism*, p. 15.
30 See Kedward, *Europe*, pp. 184–5 and p. 192; G.M. Platt, 'Thoughts on a theory of collective action: Language effect, and ideology in revolution', taken from Griffin, *Fascism*, pp. 290–2; K. Theweleit, *Male Fantasies*, taken from Griffin, op. cit., pp. 292–3.
31 Kitchen, *Fascism*, p. 17 and p. 19; Gregor, *Interpretations*, pp. 78–85.
32 Payne, 'Concept'; see Gregor, *Interpretations*, p. 54 and p. 247.
33 S. Lipset, *Political Man*, taken from Griffin, *Fascism*, pp. 285–6.
34 Kitchen, *Fascism*, p. 64; K. Epstein, 'A new study of fascism', in Turner, *Reappraisals*, pp. 2–25.
35 Gregor, *Interpretations*, p. 129 and p. 131. See also Griffin, *Fascism*, p. 260.
36 Kitchen, *Fascism*, p. x.
37 See Gregor, *Interpretations*, Chapter 4.
38 See Gregor, *Interpretations*, p. 89.
39 Kitchen, *Fascism*, p. 61.
40 H. Turner, 'Fascism and modernisation', in Turner, *Reappraisals*, pp. 117–40.
41 A. Cassels, 'Janus: The two faces of fascism', in Turner, *Reappraisals*, pp. 69–92; see also R. Griffin (ed.), *International Fascism*, London, Arnold, 1998, pp. 101–24.
42 Gregor, *Interpretations*, pp. 202–7.
43 Griffin, *Fascism*, p. 281
44 Payne, 'Concept'.
45 P. Drucker, taken from Kedward, *Europe*, p. 217.
46 Drucker, *Economic Man*.
47 G.L. Mosse, 'Toward a general theory of fascism', taken from Griffin, *Fascism*, pp. 303–4.
48 See Z. Sternhell, *Neither Right nor Left*, Berkeley, University of California Press, 1986.
49 R. Eatwell, *Fascism: A History*, London, Vintage, 1996, p. ix.

50 R. Eatwell, 'Fascism', in R. Eatwell and A. Wright (eds), *Contemporary Political Ideologies*, London, Pinter, 1994.

51 Comintern Sixth Annual Congress (1928), taken from Griffin, *Fascism*, pp. 261–2.

52 Comintern Plenum on Fascism (1923), taken from Griffin, *Fascism*, pp. 260–1.

53 See Carsten, 'Interpretations'.

54 Carsten, 'Interpretations'.

55 Kitchen, *Fascism*, pp. 31–2.

56 See Kitchen, *Fascism*, p. 30.

57 Kitchen's summary, *Fascism*, p. 27.

58 Kitchen, *Fascism*, p. 35.

59 Gregor, *Interpretations*, p. 234.

60 Kitchen, *Fascism*, p. 35.

61 Kitchen, *Fascism*, p. 43.

62 E. Nolte, *Three Faces of Fascism*, London, Weidenfeld & Nicolson, 1965, p. 3.

63 The description comes courtesy of A. Heywood, *Political Ideologies*, London, Macmillan, 1992, p. 214.

64 Nolte, *Faces*, Parts 2, 3 and 4.

65 Kitchen, *Fascism*, p. 44.

66 See D. Renton, *Fascism: Theory and Practice*, London, Pluto, 1999, p. 18. There is, in addition, a very fine distinction between Marxist 'historians', 'activists' and 'polemicists'. The best collections of Marxist writings are D. Beetham (ed.), *Marxists in the Face of Fascism*, Manchester, Manchester University Press, 1983, and Griffin, *International*, pp. 59–97.

67 Renton, *Fascism*, pp. 3–4.

68 Comintern Plenum on Fascism (1933), taken from Griffin, *Fascism*, pp. 262–3.

69 *ABC of Political Terms: A Short Guide* (a Soviet dictionary), taken from Griffin, *Fascism*, pp. 282–3.

70 R. Griffin, *The Nature of Fascism*, London, Routledge, 1994, p. 3.

71 See Kitchen, *Fascism*, p. 73, although at times Marxists didn't want to assume that the capitalism–fascism 'transformation' was inevitable.

72 See Griffin, *Fascism*, p. 260.

73 Comintern Sixth Annual Congress (1928), taken from Griffin, *Fascism*, p. 262.

74 Kitchen, *Fascism*, p. 46.

75 Turner, *Reappraisals*, p. xi.

76 See Griffin, *Fascism*, p. 279; see also *ABC* and Griffin, *Nature*, p. 3.

77 See Griffin, *Nature*, p. 3. Stalin said social democracy and fascism were 'twins' – see Griffin, *Fascism*, p. 261 and p. 263. In 1928 the Comintern announced: 'Alongside social-democracy, which helps the bourgeoisie to oppress the working class and blunt its proletarian vigilance, stands fascism' (taken from Griffin, *Fascism*, p. 261); in time, however, Social Democrats came to be regarded as allies.

78 Griffin, *Nature*, p. 3.

79 See P. Togliatti, *Lectures on Fascism*, London, Lawrence & Wishart, 1976, pp. 1–10. See also Griffin, *Fascism*, p. 272.

80 Gregor, *Interpretations*, p. 157; Griffin, *Nature*, p. 2; see also B. Hagtvet and S. Larsen, 'Approaches'.

81 Payne, 'Concept'.

82 See G.L. Mosse, *Nazism: A Historical and Comparative Analysis of National Socialism*, Oxford, Blackwell, 1978, p. 18; Nolte, 'Scholarship'; see also Comintern Sixth Annual Congress (1928), taken from Griffin, *Fascism*, p. 261.

83 Traces of these explanations can be seen in the Orthodox Marxist view – all dealt with earlier.

84 See Griffin, *Fascism*, p. 283.

85 See Griffin, *Nature*, p. 3. However, the Orthodox view has never died out and was still prevalent in Eastern Europe up until the Fall of Communism. See Renton, *Fascism*, p. 4. Fascism, of course, has undergone the same evolution – hence the various strands of neo-fascism.

86 See A–Z of Historians for more on each of these thinkers.

87 Gregor, *Interpretations*, p. 167.

88 Kitchen, *Fascism*, pp. 88–91; Gregor, *Interpretations*, pp. 168–9.

89 Griffin, *Fascism*, p. 279.

90 Griffin, *Nature*, p. 4.

91 Gregor, *Interpretations*, pp. 167–8; even though Renton, writing in 1999, still sees fascism as a 'specific form of reactionary mass movement', *Fascism*, p. 3.

92 Griffin, *Nature*, p. 3.

93 See Renton especially, *Fascism*.

94 Renton, *Fascism*, p. 3.

95 J. Petzold, *The Demagogy of Hitler-Fascism*, taken from Griffin, *Fascism*, pp. 283–4.

96 Kitchen, *Fascism*, p. ix; Nolte, *Faces*, op. cit., p. 19.

97 Kitchen, *Fascism*, p. x.

98 Kitchen, *Fascism*, p. ix; see also Nolte, *Faces*, p. 18.

99 Nolte, *Faces*, p. 19.

100 Griffin, *Fascism*, p. 248.

101 Griffin, *Fascism*, p. 247.

102 See L. Salvatorelli, *Nazionalfascismo*, Turin, Einaudi, 1923, and G. Borgese, *Goliath: The March of Fascism*, London, Victor Gollancz, 1938.

103 Griffin, *Fascism*, p. 279.

104 Gregor, *Interpretations*, p. 204. At certain junctures liberal thinking does overlap with Marxist thinking.

105 Mosse, *Nazism*, p. 18.

106 Nolte, *Faces*, p. 249.

107 P. Vita-Finzi, 'Italian Fascism and the intellectuals', in S.J. Woolf (ed.), *The Nature of Fascism*, London, Wiedenfeld & Nicolson, 1968, pp. 226–44; Kitchen, *Fascism*, p. 60; Salvatorelli is quoted in Gregor, *Interpretations*, p. 200.

108 G. Germani, 'Fascism and class', in Woolf, *Nature*, p. 66; G. Borgese, 'The intellectual origins of Fascism', taken from Griffin, *Fascism*, pp. 256–7.

109 Renton, *Fascism*, p. 24.

110 D. Irving, *Hitler's War*, taken from Griffin, *Fascism*, pp. 335–7.

111 R. Eatwell, 'The Holocaust denial: A study in propaganda technique', in L. Cheles, R. Ferguson and M.Vaughan (eds), *Neo-Fascism in Europe*, London, Longman, 1991, pp. 127–34.

112 Griffin, *Nature*, pp. 168–9.

113 Hagtvet and Larsen, 'Approaches'.


## ROOTS AND ORIGINS OF FASCISM

1 See P. Hayes, *Fascism*, London, Allen & Unwin, 1973, p. 17.

2 M. Kitchen, *Fascism*, London, Macmillan, 1976, pp. vii–viii; see also H.A. Turner, *Reappraisals of Fascism*, New York, New Viewpoints, 1975, p. x; E. Nolte, 'The problem of fascism in recent scholarship', in Turner, *Reappraisals*, pp. 26–42; and R. Eatwell, 'Fascism', in R. Eatwell and A. Wright (eds), *Contemporary Political Ideologies*, London, Pinter, 1994, pp. 212–37.

3 Hayes, *Fascism*, p. 17 and p. 19.

4 R. Eatwell, 'Fascism'.

5 Z. Sternhell, 'Fascist ideology', in W. Laqueur (ed.), *Fascism: A Reader's Guide*, London, Penguin, 1982, pp. 325–406.

6 See R. Soucy, *French Fascism: The Case of Maurice Barrès*, Berkeley, University of California Press, 1972; Sternhell, 'Ideology'.

7 See, for example, R. Magraw, *France 1815–1914*, London, Fontana, 1983, pp. 260–84.

8 Sternhell, 'Ideology'.

9 A. Heywood, *Political Ideologies*, London, Macmillan, 1998, pp. 228–9.

10 Sternhell, 'Ideology'.

11 R. Griffin, *Fascism*, Oxford, Oxford University Press, 1995, pp. 29–30.

12 Griffin, *Fascism*, p. 23.

13 Heywood, *Ideologies*, p. 216.

14 See K. Epstein, 'A new study of fascism' in Turner, *Reappraisals*, pp. 2–25; see also Eatwell, 'Fascism'.

15 R. Wilford, 'Fascism', in R. Eccleshall, V. Geoghegan, R. Jay and R. Wilford, *Political Ideologies*, London, Hutchinson, 1986, pp. 217–50.

16 See Heywood, *Ideologies*, pp. 216–29.

17 M. Barrès, 'Scènes et doctrines du nationalisme', taken from J.S. McClelland (ed.), *The French Right*, London, Jonathan Cape, 1971, pp. 163–4.

18 J. Weiss, *Conservatism in Europe 1770–1945*, London, Thomas & Hudson, 1977, p. 105.

19 G.F. Putnam, 'The meaning of *Barrèsisme*', *Western Political Quarterly* VII (June 1954), pp. 161–82; see also Soucy, *Barrès*.

20 'Essay on inequality among human races'.

21 Hayes, *Fascism*, p. 22; Wilford, 'Fascism'; Epstein, 'Fascism'.

22 Hayes, *Fascism*, p. 21.

23 Wilford, 'Fascism'; R. Griffin, *The Nature of Fascism*, London, Routledge, 1994, p. 86.

24 See Chapters 3 and 4 in Griffin, *Nature*.

25 Griffin, *Nature*, p. 89.

26 R. Eatwell, *Fascism: A History,* London, Vintage, 1996, p. 13.

27 See Chapter 2 of Eatwell, *History*.

28 Epstein, 'Fascism', p. 6.

29 Eatwell, *History*, pp. 39–40; W.S. Allen, 'The appeal of fascism and the problem of national disintegration', in Turner, *Reappraisals*, pp. 44–68 (quote from p. 49).

30 Griffin, *Nature*, pp. 63–4; Eatwell, *History*, p. 26.

31 See Mussolini quoted in Griffin, *Fascism*, pp. 28–9; see also Allen, 'Disintegration', p. 49.

32 Epstein, 'Fascism', pp. 6–7.

33 Eatwell, *History*, p. 29.

34 Allen, 'Disintegration'.

35 Eatwell, *History*, p. 47.

36 A. Lyttelton, 'Italian Fascism', in Laqueur, *Fascism*, pp. 81–114.

## EVOLUTION OF IDEOLOGY

1 B. Evans, 'Political ideology in Britain', in L. Robins (ed.), *Updating British Politics*, London, Politics Association, 1984, pp. 125–41; M. Seliger, *Ideology and Politics*, London, Allen & Unwin, 1976.

2 A. Gramsci, *Selections from the Prison Notebooks*, eds Q. Hoare and G. Smith, New York, International Publishers, pp. 169–71; cited by R. Cox, 'Social forces, states and world order: Beyond international relations theory', *Millennium* 10(2) (1981), pp. 126–55.

3 A. Hitler, *Mein Kampf*, Chapter 6. Reprinted online at www.stormfront.org (far-right site).

4 T. Burden, *The Nuremberg Party Rallies, 1923–39*, London, Pall-Mall Press, 1967, p. 18.

5 R. Griffin, *The Nature of Fascism*, London, Routledge, 1991, p. 32.

6 R. Griffin, *Fascism*, Oxford Reader series, London, Oxford University Press, 1995, p. 3.

7 B. Mussolini, 'Fascism's myth: The nation', Address to Fascist Congress, 24 October 1922; reprinted in Griffin, *Fascism*, pp. 43–4.

8 N. Goodrick-Clarke, *Hitler's Priestess: Savitri Devi, the Hindu-Aryan Myth and Neo-Nazism*, London, New York University Press, 1998, pp. 43–63.

9 S. Huntington, 'The clash of civilisations', *Foreign Affairs* 72 (summer 1993), pp. 22–49. For an account of competing Chinese traditions, many of which also influenced Japan, see R. Dawson, *The Chinese Experience*, London, Phoenix, 1978, pp. 69–133.

10 O. Dietrich, 'The press and world politics', in J. von Ribbentrop (ed.) *Germany Speaks*, London, Thornton & Butterworth, 1938, p. 345.

11 B. Mussolini, 'What is Fascism?'.

12 This was the main theme running through their seminal work. See C. Friedrich and Z. Brzezinski, *Totalitarian Dictatorship and Autocracy*, Cambridge, MA, Harvard University Press, 1956.

13 In a speech on 3 January 1925, Mussolini made specific reference to 'totalitarian' controls he was planning to impose on Italian society. See J. Whittam, *Fascist Italy*, Manchester, Manchester University Press, 1995, p. 82.

14 G. Gentile, 'The origins and doctrine of Fascism' (1934), in A. Lyttelton, *Italian Fascisms: From Pareto to Gentile*, London, Jonathan Cape, 1973, pp. 301–15.

15 In the writings of Maurice Barrès, in particular.

16 R. Wagner, 'The Diary of Richard Wagner 1865–1882: The brown book', 1980, p. 73. Taken from the Richard Wagner Archive website. Available online at http://users.utu.fi/hansalmi/spirit.html [accessed 20 August 2001].

17 H. Arendt, *The Origins of Totalitarianism*, London, Allen & Unwin, 1967, pp. 231–2.

18 B. Glanville, 'Sport in the thirties', in M. Gilbert and A.J.P. Taylor (eds), *Purnell History of the Twentieth Century*, London, BPC Publishing, Vol. 4, 1968, pp. 1507–12; M. Burleigh and W. Wippermann, *The Racial State*, p. 84.

19 For a sense of the tone of Futurism, see F. Marinetti, 'The Futurist manifesto', reprinted in A. Lyttelton (ed.) *Italian Fascisms: From Pareto to Gentile*, London, Jonathan Cape, 1973, pp. 219–25.

20 *Lapua*, 'The battle for a new Finland', editorial in *Lapuan Päiväkäsky*, 1931; reprinted in Griffin, *Fascism*, p. 213. Originally quoted in *Juha Siltala Lapuan liike Ja Kyyditykset 1930*, Helsinki, Otava, 1985.

21 Sternhell provides an excellent account, albeit with a French focus. See Z. Sternhell, *Neither Left nor Right: Fascist Ideology in France*, Chichester, Princeton University Press, 1986, pp. 4–89.

22 For an example of this kind of fare, see the merchandise traded by the US-based far-right group, Stormfront. Online at http://www.stormfront.org/.

23 Other neo-conservatives have flirted with libertarianism.

24 For a sampling, see Griffin, *Fascism*, pp. 346–51, and Griffin's commentary, p. 315 and p. 346.

25 F. Fukuyama, 'The end of history', *The National Interest* 16 (summer 1989), pp. 3–16.

## NATION AND RACE

1 Z. Sternhell, 'Fascist Ideology', in W. Laqueur (ed.), *Fascism: A Reader's Guide*, London, Penguin, 1982, pp. 325–406.
2 P. Hayes, *Fascism*, London, George Allen & Unwin, 1973, p. 23; R. Wilford, 'Fascism', in R. Eccleshall, V. Geoghegan, R. Jay and R. Wilford (eds), *Political Ideologies*, London, Hutchinson, 1986, pp. 217–50.
3 Hayes cites this in *Fascism*, p. 24.
4 R. Eatwell, 'Fascism', in R .Eatwell and A. Wright, *Contemporary Political Ideologies*, London, Pinter, 1994, p. 173.
5 See Sternhell, 'Ideology'.
6 Sternhell, 'Ideology'.
7 J. Krejčí, 'Introduction: Concepts of left and right', in L. Cheles, R. Ferguson and M. Vaughan (eds), *Neo-Fascism in Europe*, London, Longman, 1991, pp. 1–18.
8 Hayes, *Fascism*, p. 51 and R. Griffin, *The Nature of Fascism*, London, Routledge, 1994, p. 38, echoed by Krejčí, 'Introduction', and G. Gable, 'The far right in contemporary Britain', in Cheles *et al.*, *Neo-Fascism*, pp. 245–64.
9 Griffin, *Nature*, p. 41.
10 Eatwell, 'Fascism', p. 176.
11 Hayes, *Fascism*, pp. 20–1.
12 Wilford, 'Fascism', p. 220.
13 M. Barrès, 'Scènes et doctrines du nationalisme', taken from J.S. McClelland (ed.), *The French Right*, London, Jonathan Cape, 1971, pp. 189–92.
14 Wilford, 'Fascism', p. 219. Griffin, *Nature*, p. 48.
15 R. Griffin, *Fascism*, Oxford, Oxford University Press, 1995, p. 3.
16 See Griffin, *Fascism*, pp. 231–6.
17 Leaflets carrying this message were being distributed by the party in the early 1990s.
18 See Griffin, *Fascism*, p. 32 and p. 368. 'Midwife' is a term used by the Italian, Farinacci.
19 'Are you more French than he is?'
20 A.C. Pinto, 'The radical right in contemporary Portugal', in Cheles *et al.*, *Neo-Fascism*, pp. 167–91; see also Griffin, *Fascism*, pp. 223–6.
21 See E. Nolte, *Three Faces of Fascism*, London, Weidenfeld & Nicolson, 1965; see also J.S. McClelland, 'The reactionary right: The French Revolution, Charles Maurras and the *Action Française*', in R. Eatwell and N. O'Sullivan, *The Nature of the Right*, London, Pinter, 1992, pp. 79–98.
22 W.S. Allen, 'The appeal of fascism and the problem of national disintegration', in H.A. Turner, *Reappraisals of Fascism*, New York, New Viewpoints, 1975, pp. 44–68; see also M. Kitchen, *Fascism*, London, Macmillan, 1976, p. 27.
23 D. Childs, 'The far right in Germany since 1945', in Cheles *et al.*, *Neo-Fascism*, pp. 66–85.
24 Pinto, 'Portugal', p. 174.
25 Wilford, 'Fascism', p. 232.
26 Hayes, *Fascism*, p. 21; Wilford, 'Fascism'. See R. Eatwell, 'The Holocaust denial: A study in propaganda technique', in Cheles *et al.*, *Neo-Fascism*, pp. 120–46.
27 S. Ellwood, 'The extreme right in Spain: A dying species?', in Cheles *et al.*, *Neo-Fascism*, pp. 147–66.
28 Griffin, *Nature*, p. 49.
29 Cited in Hayes, *Fascism*, p. 21.
30 Sternhell, 'Ideology', p. 338.
31 Sternhell, 'Ideology', p. 337.
32 Hayes, *Fascism*, p. 23; Sternhell, 'Ideology', p. 335.
33 Ellwood, 'Spain'.

34 Griffin, *Fascism*, p. 8.
35 J. Linz, 'Some notes towards a comparative study of fascism in sociological historical perspective', in Laqueur, *Fascism*, pp. 13–114.
36 Hayes, *Fascism*, p. 20.

## CIVIL SOCIETY

1  R. Griffin, 'Revolution from the right: Fascism', in R. Griffin and D. Parker (eds) *Revolutions and Revolutionary Tradition in the West, 1560–1989*, London, Routledge, 1999. Available online at http://www.brookes.ac.uk/schools/humanities/Roger/fascrev.htm [accessed 15 August 2001].
2 For a general account of Nazi policies towards homosexuals, see M. Burleigh and W. Wippermann, *The Racial State: Germany 1933–1945*, Cambridge, Cambridge University Press, 1991, pp. 184–91.
3 J. Whittam, *Fascist Italy*, Manchester, Manchester University Press, 1995, p. 71.
4 P. Davies, *The National Front in France*, London, Routledge, 1999, pp. 223–4.
5 On the cult of Joan of Arc, see Davies, *The National Front in France*, pp. 112–16.
6 See A. von Saldern, 'Victims or perpetrators: Controversies about the role of women in the Nazi state', in D. Crew (ed.) *Nazism and German Society, 1933–45*, London, Routledge, 1994, pp. 141–65.
7 Whittam, *Fascist Italy*, pp. 73–5.
8 German policy on women is described by R. Brady, *The Spirit and Structure of German Fascism*, New York, Fertig, 1969, pp. 199–231.
9 On Nazi 'biological purification' programmes, see U. Gerhardt, *Ideas about Illness: An Intellectual and Political History of Medical Sociology*, London, Macmillan, 1989, pp. 345–6.
10 See H. Rose, 'Screening awakens spectres of the past', *UNESCO Courier* (September 1999). Available online at http://www.unesco.org/courier/1999_09/uk/dossier/intro.htm [accessed 20 August 2001); L. Hall, 'Women, feminism and eugenics', in R. Peel (ed.) *Essays in the History of Eugenics*, London, Galton Institute, 1998, pp 36–51; A. Drouard, 'Eugenics in France and Scandinavia: Two case studies', in R. Peel (ed.) *Essays in the History of Eugenics*, pp. 173–207.
11 Burleigh and Wippermann, *The Racial State*, pp. 136–51.
12 P. Preston, *Franco: A Biography*, London, HarperCollins, 1993, p. 619.
13 Preston, *Franco*, pp. 350–1.
14 M. Deas, 'Latin America: Unrest and dictatorship', in J.M. Roberts and A.J.P. Taylor (eds) *Purnell History of the Twentieth Century*, London, BPC, Vol. 4, 1968, pp. 1478–84.
15 H. Thomas, 'The Spanish Civil War', in Roberts and Taylor (eds) *Purnell History of the Twentieth Century*, Vol. 4, pp. 1598–1603.
16 Davies, *The National Front in France*, pp. 28–30.
17 It is true that the Church has given the Tridentines some space in order to avoid a worsening confrontation, yet any claim of 'devoutness' would be open to question if the claimant endorsed what is in effect a schism.
18 Mussolini, *Doctrine of Fascism* (1932).
19 D. Orlow, *History of the Nazi Party, 1933–45*, Pittsburgh, University of Pittsburgh Press, 1973, pp. 229–30.
20 J. Cornwell, *Hitler's Pope: The Secret History of Pius XII*, London, Viking Press, 1999.
21 *Uomini*, Milan, December 1935. Mazoni Pamphlet Collection, Duke University, 1996. Available online at http://scriptorium.lib.duke.edu/mazzoni/exhibit/earlyfascism/A90.html [accessed May 2001].
22 'The Fascist Decalogue', reprinted in S. Kreis, 'Europe Lecture 9 – The Age of

Anxiety: Europe in the 1920s', in *The History Guide*, Lectures (2000). Available online at http://www.pagesz.net/ stevek/europe/duce.html [accessed 17 August 2001].

23 S. Vasiliev, 'Either us or them! The national idea against Zionism', *Pamyat* website, undated but online on 1 April 2001. Available at http://www.pamyat.org/about.html.

24 On occult influences in the Thule Society, an organisation which, in turn, shaped the attitudes of the early Nazis, see K. Bracher, *The German Dictatorship: The Origins, Structure and Nature of National Socialism*, London, Penguin, 1970, p. 109.

25 N. Goodrick-Clarke, *Hitler's Priestess: Savitri Devi, the Hindu-Aryan Myth and Neo-Nazism*, London, New York University Press, 1998.

26 Bracher, *The German Dictatorship*, pp. 289–98.

## THE ECONOMY

1 S.J. Woolf, 'Did a Fascist economic system exist?', in S.J. Woolf (ed.) *The Nature of Fascism*, London, Weidenfeld & Nicolson, 1968, p. 119; see also D. Childs, 'The far right in Germany since 1945', in L. Cheles, R. Ferguson and M. Vaughan (eds), *Neo-Fascism in Europe*, London, Longman, 1991, p. 66.

2 Childs, 'The far right in Germany since 1945', p. 66.

3 D. Renton, *Fascism: Theory and Practice*, London, Pluto, 1999, p. 33.

4 Childs, 'The far right in Germany since 1945', p. 79. See also C.T. Husbands, 'Militant neo-Nazism in the Federal Republic of Germany in the 1980s', in Cheles *et al.*, *Neo-Fascism in Europe*, p. 93.

5 Woolf, 'Did a Fascist economic system exist?'; R. Chiarini, 'The *Movimento Sociale Italiano*: A historical profile' in Cheles *et al.*, *Neo-Fascism in Europe*, p. 22.

6 J. Whittam, *Fascist Italy*, Manchester, Manchester University Press, 1995, p. 61, p. 62 and p. 93.

7 See A.S. Milward, 'Fascism and the economy', in W. Laqueur (ed.), *Fascism: A Reader's Guide*, London, Penguin, 1982, p. 420.

8 Woolf, 'Did a Fascist economic system exist?', p. 143.

9 R. Eatwell, 'Fascism', in R. Eatwell and A. Wright, *Contemporary Political Ideologies*, London, Pinter, 1994, p. 178.

10 M. Kitchen, *Fascism*, London, Macmillan, 1982, p. 51.

11 Eatwell, 'Fascism', p. 179.

12 J. Krejčí, 'Introduction: Concepts of left and right', in Cheles *et al.*, *Neo-Fascism in Europe*, pp. 2–5.

13 P. Hayes, *Fascism*, London, Allen & Unwin, 1973, Chapter 8.

14 Milward, 'Fascism and the economy', p. 417 and p. 428.

15 Kitchen, *Fascism*, p. 49.

16 Hayes, *Fascism*, p. 105.

17 Woolf, 'Did a Fascist economic system exist?', p. 137.

18 Eatwell, 'Fascism', p. 180. See also Whittam, *Fascist Italy*, p. 23, p. 29, and p. 51.

19 Eatwell, 'Fascism', p. 171.

20 Woolf, 'Did a Fascist economic system exist?', pp. 127–8.

21 See H.A. Turner (ed.), *Reappraisals of Fascism*, New York, New Viewpoints, 1975, pp. 117–40.

22 A. Schweitzer, quoted and discussed in Milward, 'Fascism and the economy', p. 415.

23 For more on Trotsky's thinking, see *The Struggle against Fascism in Germany*, London, Pathfinder, 1971; *Fascism, Stalinism and the United Front*, London, Bookmarks, 1989; and *On France*, New York, Monad Press, 1979.

24 Kitchen, *Fascism*, pp. 46–7.

25 Nonetheless, in the 1980s the FN was a movement that glorified free trade and 'Reaganomics'.

26 Eatwell, 'Fascism', pp. 179–80.

27 Chiarini, 'The *Movimento Sociale Italiano*', p. 27.
28 Whittam, *Fascist Italy*, p. 65; Hayes, *Fascism*, p. 101.
29 Gramsci quoted by Kitchen, *Fascism*, p. 51.
30 Hayes, *Fascism*, p. 101; Milward, 'Fascism and the economy', p. 424.
31 See Eatwell, 'Fascism', p. 179.

## DIPLOMACY AND INTERNATIONAL RELATIONS

1 A. Hitler, 'Eastern orientation or eastern policy?', extract from *Mein Kampf*, Boston, Houghton-Mifflin, 1942. Reprinted in G. Ó Tuathail, S. Dalby and P. Routledge (eds), *The Geopolitics Reader*, London, Routledge, 1998, pp. 36–9.
2 C. von Clausewitz, *On War*, London, Wordsworth, Book I, 1997, pp. 1, 3 and 7.
3 Von Clausewitz, *On War*, Book I, pp. 1, 22–4 and 24–8.
4 G. Gentile and B. Mussolini, 'The Doctrine of Fascism', from *Enciclopedia Italiana* (1932), reprinted at the Racial Nationalism Library (far-right) site. Available online at http://netjunk.com/users/library/fascism.htm [accessed 22 August 2001].
5 W. Deist, 'The road to ideological war: Germany, 1918–1945', in W. Murray, M. Knox and A. Berstein (eds), *The Making of Strategy: Rulers, States and War*, Cambridge, Cambridge University Press, 1994, pp. 352–92.
6 P. Morgan, *Italian Fascism, 1919–1945*, London, Macmillan, 1995, p. 143.
7 A. Iriye, *Japan and the Wider World, from the Mid-Nineteenth Century to the Present*, London, Longman, 1997, pp. 86–7.
8 J. Whittam, *Fascist Italy*, Manchester, Manchester University Press, p. 109.
9 N. Rich, *Hitler's War Aims: Ideology, the Nazi State and the Course of Expansion*, London, André Deutsch, 1973, pp. 180–203.
10 A.J.P. Taylor, *The Origins of the Second World War*, Harmondsworth, Penguin, 1961.
11 S. Cohen, 'Geopolitics', in L. Freedman (ed), *War*, Oxford Reader series, Oxford, Oxford University Press, 1994, pp. 81–5.
12 M. O'Driscoll, 'Inter-war Irish–German diplomacy: Continuity, ambiguity and appeasement in Irish foreign policy', in M. Kennedy and J. Morrison Skelly (eds), *Irish Foreign Policy: From Independence to Internationalism, 1919–66*, Dublin, Four Courts Press, 2000, pp. 74–95.
13 H. Kissinger, *Diplomacy*, London, Simon & Schuster, 1994, p. 283.
14 N. Rich, *Hitler's War Aims*, p. 157.
15 R. Crampton, *Eastern Europe in the Twentieth Century*, London, Routledge, 1994, pp. 84–5.
16 J. Göbbels, *Diaries: Excerpts, 1942–43*, Part 2, Nizkor.org site. Entry for 8 May 1943, p. 357. Available online at http://www.nizkor.org/hweb/people/g/goebbels-joseph/goebbels-1948-excerpts-02.html.
17 S. Balfour, 'Spain and the great powers in the aftermath of the disaster of 1898', in S. Balfour and P. Preston (eds), *Spain and the Great Powers in the Twentieth Century*, London, Routledge, 1999, pp. 13–31.
18 P. Preston, *Franco: A Biography*, London, HarperCollins, 1993, p. 21.
19 B. Loveman, *For La Patria: Politics and the Armed Forces in Latin America*, Wilmington, Scholarly Resources, 1999, pp. 105–8.
20 *Rossiya* 27(86) (July 1992), p. 3; cited by R. Sakwa, *Russian Politics and Society*, London, Routledge, 1993, p. 15.
21 J. Whittam, *Fascist Italy*, Manchester, Manchester University Press, 1995, p. 105.
22 M. Robson, *Italy, Liberalism and Fascism, 1870–1945*, London, Hodder & Stoughton, 1992, p. 126.
23 Mussolini, statement on foreign policy presented to the Fascist Grand Council, 4–5 February 1939; from R. de Felice, *Mussolini il Duce ii*, Turin, Guilio Einaudi Editore, 1981; reprinted in J. Whittam, *Fascist Italy*, pp. 164–5.

24 Robson, *Italy, Liberalism and Fascism, 1870–1945*, p. 116.
25 G. Salvemini, *The Origins of Fascism in Italy*, London, Harper & Row, 1973, p. 13 and pp. 16–17.
26 B. Liddell-Hart, *History of the Second World War*, London, Macmillan, 1997, p. 13.
27 Robson, *Italy: Liberalism and Fascism, 1870–1945*, p. 121.
28 B. Sullivan, 'The strategy of the decisive weight: Italy, 1882–1922', in W. Murray, M. Knox and A. Berstein (eds), *The Making of Strategy*, Cambridge, Cambridge University Press, 1994, pp. 307–51.
29 Sullivan, 'The strategy of the decisive weight'.
30 On Le Pen's ambivalent or pro-Iraqi stance in the Gulf War of 1991, see P. Davies, *The National Front in France*, London, Routledge, 1999, pp. 83–4.

## THE PRACTICE OF POLITICS IN GOVERNMENT AND OPPOSITION

1 L. Cheles, 'Nostalgia *dell'avvenire*: The new propaganda of the MSI, between tradition and innovation', in L. Cheles, R. Ferguson and M. Vaughan (eds), *Neo-Fascism in Europe*, London, Longman, pp. 43–65.
2 G. Sorel, *Reflections on Violence*, New York, The Free Press/Macmillan, 1950, pp. 122–6.
3 P. Morgan, *Italian Fascism, 1919–1945*, London, Macmillan, 1995, p. 12.
4 Morgan, *Italian Fascism*, p. 77.
5 K. Bracher, *The German Dictatorship: The Origins, Structure and Consequences of National Socialism*, London, Penguin, 1973, pp. 122–9.
6 M. Broszat, *The Hitler State: The Foundation and Development of the Internal Structure of the Third Reich*, London, Longman, 1981, pp. 204–8.
7 P. Preston, *Franco: A Biography*, London, HarperCollins, 1993, pp. 259–61 and pp. 446–7.
8 Much of Bosworth's work on Italian Fascism is an attack on de Felice's 'anti-anti-Fascism'. See R. Bosworth, *The Italian Dictatorship: Problems and Perspectives in the Interpretation of Mussolini and Fascism*, London, Hodder, 1998.
9 Morgan, *Italian Fascism*, p. 11.
10 A. Lyttelton, 'The Fascist takeover', in M. Gilbert and A.J.P. Taylor (eds), *Purnell History of the Twentieth Century*, London, BPC Publishing, Vol. 3, 1968, pp. 1073–6.
11 A. Aquarone, 'Mussolini's Italy' in Gilbert and Taylor, *Purnell History*, Vol. 3, pp. 1081–9.
12 G. Smith, *Democracy in Western Germany: Parties and Politics in the Federal Republic*, London, Heinemann, 1979, p. 30.
13 For an excellent but concise analysis of the *Reichstag* manœuvres, see Smith, *Democracy in Western Germany*, pp. 19–31.
14 Broszat, *The Hitler State*, pp. 57–95.
15 P. Preston, *Franco: A Biography*, London, HarperCollins, 1993, pp. 259–61 and pp. 446–7.
16 J. Whittam, *Fascist Italy*, Manchester, Manchester University Press, 1995, pp. 128–34.
17 D. Condradt, *The German Polity*, White Plains, Longman, 1996, pp. 106–7.
18 In its report on the risk of domestic terrorism for 2000 and beyond, under the auspices of Project Megiddo, the FBI notes that the majority of militia groups may have bizarre ideas about, for example, a UN conspiracy against the US, but are essentially non-violent. See FBI (undated) 'Project Megiddo'. Available online at http://www.google.com/search?q=cache:2EZ82_dESTcC:permanent.access.gpo.gov/lps3578/www.fbi.gov/library/megiddo/megiddo.pdf+%22Megiddo%22&hl=en [accessed 7 January 2002].
19 For a sample of this, listen to WWCR short-wave radio on 12160 kHz in the evening hours (Europe and North America).

20 For an account of these regimes, see M. Deas, 'Latin America: Unrest and dictatorship', in J.M. Roberts and A.J.P. Taylor (eds), *Purnell History of the Twentieth Century*, London, BPC Publishing, Vol. 4, 1968, pp. 1478–84.
21 See J. King Fairbank and M. Goldman, *China: A New History*, London, Harvard University Press, 1998, p. 291.
22 Bracher, *The German Dictatorship*, pp. 590–602.
23 Preston, *Franco*, p. 780
24 P. Davies, *The National Front in France*, London, Routledge, 1999, pp. 166–220.

# BIBLIOGRAPHY

This bibliography covers sources for the seven sections in Part II.

Allen, W.S., 'The appeal of fascism and the problem of national disintegration', in H.A. Turner (ed.) *Reappraisals of Fascism*, New York, New Viewpoints, 1975, pp. 44–68.

Anderson, E., *An Atlas of World Political Flashpoints: A Sourcebook of Geopolitical Crisis*, London: Pinter, 1993.

Aquarone, A., 'Mussolini's Italy' in J.M. Roberts and A.J.P. Taylor (eds) *Purnell History of the Twentieth Century*, Vol. 3, London, BPC Publishing, 1968, pp. 1081–9.

Arendt, H., *The Origins of Totalitarianism*, 3rd edn, London, Allen & Unwin, 1967, pp. 231–2.

Avalon Project, Yale Law School. Available online at http://www.yale.edu/lawweb/avalon/avalon.htm [accessed 1 August 2001].

Balfour, S., 'Spain and the great powers in the aftermath of the disaster of 1898', in S. Balfour and P. Preston (eds), *Spain and the Great Powers in the Twentieth Century*, London, Routledge, 1999, pp. 13–31.

Barrès, M., 'Scènes et doctrines du nationalisme', in J.S. McClelland (ed.) *The French Right*, London, Jonathan Cape, 1971, pp. 189–92.

Behr, Edward, *Hirohito: Behind the Myth*, New York, Villard, 1989.

Bix, H., *Hirohito and the Making of Modern Japan*, London, Duckworth, 2001.

Blinkhorn, M. (ed.) *Fascists and Conservatives: The Radical Right and the Establishment in Twentieth-Century Europe*, London, Unwin-Hyman, 1990.

Bluhm, W., *The Freedom of the Over-Man: Nietzsche, Nazism and Humanist Existentialism*, Theories of the Political Systems series, Englewood Cliffs, Prentice-Hall, 1978.

Bookbinder, P., *Weimar Germany: The Republic of the Reasonable*, Manchester, Manchester University Press, 1996.

Bosworth, R., *The Italian Dictatorship: Problems and Perspectives in the Interpretation of Mussolini and Fascism*, London, Hodder/Arnold, 1998.

Bracher, K., *The German Dictatorship: The Origins, Structure and Nature of National Socialism*, trans. J. Steinberg, London, Penguin, 1970.

Brady, R., *The Spirit and Structure of German Fascism*, New York, Fertig, 1969 [1937].

Broszat, M. *The Hitler State: The Foundation and Development of the Internal Structure of the Third Reich*, trans. J. Hiden, London, Longman, 1981.

Burden, T., *The Nuremberg Party Rallies, 1923–39*, London, Pall-Mall Press, 1967.

Burleigh, M. and Wippermann, W., *The Racial State: Germany 1933–1945*, Cambridge, Cambridge University Press, 1991.

Carocci, G., *Italian Fascism*, London, Penguin, 1975.

Cheles, L., '*Nostalgia dell'avvenire*: The new propaganda of the MSI, between tradition and innovation', in L. Cheles, R. Ferguson and M. Vaughan (eds) *Neo-Fascism in Europe*, London, Longman, 1991, pp. 43–65.

Cheles, L., Ferguson, R. and Vaughan, M. (eds) *Neo-Fascism in Europe*, London, Longman, 1991.

——, *The Far Right in Western and Eastern Europe*, London, Longman, 1995.

Chiarini, R., 'The Movimento Sociale Italiano: A historical profile', in L. Cheles, R. Ferguson and M. Vaughan (eds) *Neo-Fascism in Europe*, London, Longman, 1991, pp. 19–42.

Childs, D., 'The far right in Germany since 1945', in L. Cheles, R. Ferguson and M. Vaughan (eds) *Neo-Fascism in Europe*, London, Longman, 1991, pp. 66–85.

Von Clausewitz, C. *On War*, trans. J. Graham, London, Wordsworth, 1997.

Cohen, S., 'Geopolitics', in L. Freedman (ed.) *War*, Oxford Reader series, Oxford, Oxford University Press, 1994, pp. 81–5.

Condradt, D., *The German Polity*, 6th edn, White Plains, Longman, 1996.

Cook, C. and Paxton, J. (eds) *European Political Facts, 1918–1973*, London, Macmillan, 1975.

Cornwell, J., *Hitler's Pope: The Secret History of Pius XII*, London, Viking Press, 1999.

Crampton, R., *Eastern Europe in the Twentieth Century*, London, Routledge, 1994.

Davies, P., *France and the Second World War: Occupation, Collaboration and Resistance*, London, Routledge, 2001.

——, *The National Front in France*, London, Routledge, 1999.

Dawson, R., *The Chinese Experience*, History of Civilisation series, London, Weidenfeld & Nicolson, 1978.

Deas, M., 'Latin America: Unrest and dictatorship', in J.M. Roberts and A.J.P. Taylor (eds) *Purnell History of the Twentieth Century*, Vol. 4, London, BPC Publishing, 1968, pp. 1478–84.

Deist, W., 'The road to ideological war: Germany, 1918–1945', in W. Murray, M. Knox and A. Berstein (eds) *The Making of Strategy: Rulers, States and War*, Cambridge, Cambridge University Press, 1994, pp. 352–92.

Dietrich, O., 'The press and world politics', in J. von Ribbentrop (ed.) *Germany Speaks*, London, Thornton & Butterworth, 1938.

Douhet, G., 'The command of the air', in L. Freedman (ed.) *War*, Oxford Reader series, London, Oxford University Press, 1994, pp. 228–31.

Dower, J., *Embracing Defeat: Japan in the Aftermath of World War II*, New York, W.W. Norton, 2000.

Drouard, A., 'Eugenics in France and Scandinavia: Two case studies', in R. Peel (ed.) *Essays in the History of Eugenics*, London, Galton Institute, 1998, pp. 173–207.

Dyker, D.A. and Vejvoda, I., *Yugoslavia and After: A Study in Fragmentation, Despair and Rebirth*, Harlow: Addison Wesley-Longman, 1996.

Eatwell, R., 'Fascism', in R. Eatwell and A. Wright (eds) *Contemporary Political Ideologies*, London, Pinter, 1994, pp. 212–37.

Eatwell, R. and Wright, A. (eds) *Contemporary Political Ideologies*, London, Pinter, 1994.

Eccleshall, R., Geoghegan, V., Jay, R. and Wilford, R., *Political Ideologies: An Introduction*, London, Hutchinson, 1986.

Evans, B., 'Political ideology in Britain', in L. Robins (ed.) *Updating British Politics*, London, Politics Association, 1984, pp. 125–41.

Fachot, M., 'Counteracting hate radio', Radio Netherlands, Media Network Dossier (Revision 2). Available online at http://www.rnw.nl/realradio/dossiers/html [accessed 1 January 2001].

Fairbank, J. King and Goldman M., *China: A New History*, London, Harvard University Press, 1998.

Fichte, J., 'Love of fatherland entails a willingness to fight for it', in E. Luard (ed.) *Basic Texts in International Relations: The Evolution of Ideas about International Society*, London, Macmillan, 1992, pp. 61–4.

Freedman, L., *War*, Oxford Readers series, Oxford, Oxford University Press, 1994.

Friedrich, C. and Brzezinski, Z., *Totalitarian Dictatorship and Autocracy*, Cambridge. MA, Harvard University Press, 1956.

Front National (France) Home Page (English): party publicity, 20 August 2001. Available online at http://www.front-national.com/.

Fry, W., Tedeschi, J. and Tortorice, J. (eds) (1998) 'Italian Life under Fascism' (University of Wisconsin Madison). Available online at http://www.library.wisc.edu/libraries/dpf/fascism/home.html [accessed 21 March 2002).

Fukuyama, F., 'The end of history', *The National Interest* 16 (summer 1989), pp. 3–16.

Gable, G., 'The far right in contemporary Britain', in L. Cheles, R. Ferguson and M. Vaughan (eds) *Neo-Fascism in Europe*, London, Longman, 1991, pp. 245–64.

Gentile, G., 'The origins and doctrine of Fascism' [1934] in A. Lyttelton, *Italian Fascisms: From Pareto to Gentile*, London, Jonathan Cape, 1973, pp. 301–15.

Gentile, G. and Mussolini, B., 'The doctrine of Fascism', from *Enciclopedia Italiana* (1932). Reprinted at the *Racial Nationalism Library* (far-right) site. Available online at http://netjunk.com/users/library/fascism.htm [accessed 22 August 2001].

Gerhart, U., *Ideas about Illness: An Intellectual and Political History of Medical Sociology*, London, Macmillan, 1989.

Gilpin, R., *The Political Economy of International Relations*, Oxford, Princeton University Press, 1987.

Glanville, B., 'Sport in the thirties', in J.M. Roberts and A.J.P. Taylor (eds) *Purnell History of the Twentieth Century*, Vol. 4, London, BPC, 1968, pp. 1507–12.

Glenny, M., *The Rebirth of History: Eastern Europe in the Age of Democracy*, London, Penguin, 1993.

Goebbels, J., *Diaries*, excerpts, 1942–3, Part 2, Nizkor.org site. Entry for 8 May 1943, p. 357. Available online at http://www.nizkor.org/hweb/people/g/goebbels-joseph/goebbels-1948-excerpts-02. html.

——, *The Goebbels Diaries*, ed. H. Trevor-Roper, London: Martin, Secker & Warburg, 1978.

Goodrick-Clarke, N., *Hitler's Priestess: Savitri Devi, the Hindu-Aryan Myth, and Neo-Nazism*, London, New York University Press, 1998.

Gramsci, A., *Selections from the Prison Notebooks*, eds Q. Hoare and G. Smith, New York, International Publishers, 1971, pp. 169–71; cited by R. Cox, 'Social forces, states and world order: Beyond international relations theory', *Millennium* 10(2) (1981), pp. 126–55.

Griffin, R., 'Revolution from the right: Fascism', in R. Griffin and David Parker (eds) *Revolutions and Revolutionary Tradition in the West, 1560–1989*, London, Routledge, 1999. Available online at http://www.brookes.ac.uk/schools/humanities/Roger/fascrev.htm [accessed 15 August 2001].

——, *Fascism*, Oxford Reader Series, London, Oxford University Press, 1995.

——, *The Nature of Fascism*, London. Routledge, 1994 [1991].

Hainsworth, P. (ed.) *The Politics of the Extreme Right*, London, Pinter, 2000.

Hainsworth, P. (ed.) *The Extreme Right in Europe and the USA*, London, Pinter, 1982.

Hall, L., 'Women, feminism and eugenics', in R. Peel (ed.) *Essays in the History of Eugenics*, London, Galton Institute, 1998.

Haushofer, K., 'Defence of German geopolitics', in E. Walsh, *Total Power: A Footnote to History*, New York, Doubleday, 1948; reprinted in G. Ó Tuathail, S. Dalby and P. Routledge (eds) *The Geopolitics Reader*, London, Routledge, 1998, pp. 40–3.

Hayes, P., *Fascism*, London, Allen & Unwin, 1973.

Hegel, G.W.F. *The Philosophy of Right*, ed. T.M. Knox, Oxford, Oxford University Press, 1967 [1952].

Heiber, H., *The Weimar Republic*, London, Blackwell, 1993.

Heywood, A., *Political Ideologies*, London, Macmillan, 1998.

——, *Politics*, Macmillan Foundations series, London, Macmillan, 1997.

The History Place: World War II. Available online at http://www.historyplace.com/worldwar2 [accessed 1 May 2001].

Hitler, A., *Mein Kampf*, Boston, Houghton-Mifflin, 1942; and on Stormfront.org (far-right site). Available online at http://www.stormfront.org.

——, 'Eastern orientation or eastern policy?' – extracted from Mein Kampf, Boston, Houghton-Mifflin, 1942; reprinted in G. Ó Tuathail, S. Dalby and P. Routledge (eds) *The Geopolitics Reader*, London, Routledge, 1994, pp. 36–9.

Hutchinson, J. and Smith, A.D. (eds) *Nationalism*, Oxford Reader series, Oxford, Oxford University Press, 1994.

*Hutchinson Almanac*, London, Helicom, Annual, 1999 and 2000.

Internet Modern History Sourcebook. Available online at http://www.fordham.edu.

Iriye, A., *Japan and the Wider World: From the Mid-Nineteenth Century to the Present*, London, Longman, 1997.

Jaffrelot, C., *The Hindu Nationalist Movement and Indian Politics*, London, Hurst, 1996.

Kavanagh, D., *Dictionary of Political Biography*, Oxford, Oxford University Press, 1998.

Kennedy, P., *The Rise and Fall of the Great Powers: Economic Change and Military Conflict from 1500 to 2000*, London Fontana/HarperCollins, 1988.

Kissinger, H., *Diplomacy*, London, Simon & Schuster, 1994.

Kitchen, M., *Fascism*, London, Macmillan, 1982.

Kochan, L., *The Making of Modern Russia*, Harmondsworth, Penguin, 1962.

Kreis, Stephen, 'Europe', Lecture 9, 'The age of anxiety: Europe in the 1920s', in *The History Guide* lectures (2000). Available online at http://www.pagesz.net/stevek/europe/duce.html [accessed 17 August 2001].

Krejčí, J., 'Introduction: Concepts of left and right', in L. Cheles, R. Ferguson and M. Vaughan (eds) *Neo-Fascism in Europe*, London, Longman, 1991, pp. 2–5.

Laqueur, W. (ed.) *Fascism: A Reader's Guide*, London, Penguin, 1982.

Liddell-Hart, B., *History of the Second World War*, London, Macmillan, 1997.

Linz, J., 'Some notes towards a comparative study of fascism in sociological historical perspective', in W. Laqueur, *Fascism, A Reader's Guide*, London, Penguin, 1982, pp. 13–114.

Loveman, B., *For La Patria: Politics and the Armed Forces in Latin America*, Wilmington, Scholarly Resources, 1999.

Lyttelton, A. (ed.) *Italian Fascisms: From Pareto to Gentile*, London, Jonathan Cape, 1973.

——, 'The Fascist takeover', in J.M. Roberts and A.J.P. Taylor (eds) *Purnell History of the Twentieth Century*, Vol. 3, London, BPC Publishing, 1968, pp. 1073–6.

McClelland, J.S., 'The reactionary right: The French Revolution, Charles Maurras and the *Action Française*', in R. Eatwell and N. O'Sullivan (eds) *The Nature of the Right*, London, Pinter, 1992, pp. 79–98.

Magnusson, D., *Chambers Biographical Dictionary*, Edinburgh, Chambers, 1990.

Magraw, R., *France 1815–1914*, London, Fontana, 1983.

Mann, G., *The History of Germany since 1789*, London, Penguin, 1985.

Marinetti, F., 'The Futurist manifesto', in A. Lyttelton (ed.) *Italian Fascisms: From Pareto to Gentile*, London, Jonathan Cape, 1973, pp. 215–19.

Mitchell, B.R., *European Historical Statistics, 1750–1970*, London, Macmillan, 1975.

Morgan, P., *Italian Fascism, 1919–1945*, London, Macmillan, 1995.

Morton, L., 'The Japanese decision for war', *US Naval Institute Proceedings*, Vol. 80, 1954, pp. 1325–35. Available online at http://www.army.mil/cmh-pg/books/70–7_04.htm.

Mussolini, B., 'Fascism's myth: The nation', address to Fascist Congress, 24 October 1922; reprinted in R. Griffin (ed.) *Fascism*, Oxford Reader Series, Oxford, Oxford University Press, 1995, pp. 43–4.

Mussolini, B. and Gentile, G., 'Doctrine of Fascism', *Enciclopedia Italiana* (1932); extracts in Stephen Kreis (ed.) *The History Guide: Lectures on Twentieth Century – Europe*. Available online at http://www.pagesz. net/ stevek/europe/duce.html.

——, 'What is Fascism?', *Enciclopedia Italiana* (1932); reprinted in *Internet Modern History Sourcebook*, Fordham University, 1997. Available online at http://www.ford-ham.edu/halsall/mod/mussolini-fascism.html [accessed 17 August 2001].

Noakes, J. and Pridham, G. (eds) *Documents on Nazism, 1919–45*, London, Jonathan Cape, 1974.

Nolte, E., *Three Faces of Fascism*, London, Weidenfeld & Nicolson, 1965.

O'Driscoll, M., 'Inter-war Irish–German diplomacy: Continuity, ambiguity and appeasement in Irish foreign policy', in M. Kennedy and J. Morrison Skelly (eds) *Irish Foreign Policy, 1919–1966: From Independence to Internationalism*, Dublin, Four Courts Press, 2000.

Orlow, D., *History of the Nazi Party, 1933–45*, Pittsburgh, University of Pittsburgh Press, 1973.

Oxford University Press, *Oxford Dictionary of World History*, Oxford, Oxford University Press, 2000.

Palmer, A., *Dictionary of Twentieth Century History*, London, Penguin, 1999.

Pinto, A.C., 'The radical right in contemporary Portugal', in L. Cheles, R. Ferguson and M. Vaughan (eds) *Neo-Fascism in Europe*, London, Longman, 1991, pp. 167–91.

Preston, P., *Franco: A Biography*, London, HarperCollins, 1993.

Putnam, G.F., 'The meaning of *Barrèsisme*', *Western Political Quarterly* 7 (June 1954), pp. 161–82.

Renton, D., *Fascism: Theory and Practice*, London, Pluto, 1999.

Rich, N., *Hitler's War Aims: Ideology, the Nazi State and the Course of Expansion*, London, André Deutsch, 1973.

Richard Wagner Archive site. Available online at http://users.utu.fi/hansalmi/spirit.html.

Roberts, J.M. and Taylor, A.J.P. (eds) *Purnell History of the Twentieth Century*, London, BPC Publishing, 1968.

Robertson, D., *Penguin Dictionary of Politics*, 2nd edn, London, Penguin, 1993.

Robson, M., *Italy, Liberalism and Fascism, 1870–1945*, London, Hodder & Stoughton, 1992.

Rose, H., 'Screening awakens spectres of the past', *UNESCO Courier* (September 1999). Available online at http://www.unesco.org/courier/1999_09/uk/dossier/intro.htm [accessed 20 August 2001].

Rosenberg, A., *Selected Writings*, ed. R. Pois, London, Jonathan Cape, 1970.

Routledge, *Concise Routledge Encyclopedia of Philosophy*, London, Routledge, 2000.

RSS website (Indian far-right). Available online at http://www.rss.org [accessed 20 August 2001].

Sakwa, R., *Russian Politics and Society*, London, Routledge, 1993.

Von Saldern, A., 'Victims or perpetrators? Controversies about the role of women in the Nazi state', in D. Crew, *Nazism and German Society, 1933–45*, London, Routledge, 1994, pp. 141–65.

Salvemini, G., *The Origins of Fascism in Italy*, London, Harper-Row, 1973.

Saz, I., 'Foreign Policy under the dictatorship of Primo de Rivera', in S. Balfour and P. Preston (eds) *Spain and the Great Powers in the Twentieth Century*, London: Routledge, 1994, pp. 13–31.

Seliger, M., *Ideology and Politics*, London, Allen & Unwin, 1976.

Shillony, B., *Politics and Culture in Wartime Japan*, Oxford, Clarendon Press, 1981.

Simon Wiesenthal Centre web gallery. Available online at http://motlc.wiesenthal.com/gallery/pg42/pg8/pg42824.html.

Smith, G., *Democracy in Western Germany: Parties and Politics in the Federal Republic*, London, Heinemann, 1979.

Snyder, L., *Encyclopedia of the Third Reich*, Ware, Wordsworth, 1998.

Sorel, G., *Reflections on Violence*, New York: The Free Press/Macmillan, 1950.

Soucy, R., *French Fascism: The Case of Maurice Barrès*, Berkeley, University of California Press, 1972.

Sternhell, Z., *Neither Right nor Left: Fascist Ideology in France*, Chichester, Princeton University Press, 1986.

Sullivan, B., 'The strategy of the decisive weight: Italy, 1882–1922', in W. Murray, M. Knox and A. Berstein (eds) *The Making of Strategy: Rulers, States and War*, Cambridge, Cambridge University Press, 1994, pp. 307–51.

Tabata, M., 'Japan: The triumphant overture', in J.M. Roberts and A.J.P. Taylor (eds) *Purnell History of the Twentieth Century*, Vol. 5, London, BPC, 1968, pp. 1837–40.

Taylor, A.J.P., *The Origins of the Second Word War*, Harmondsworth, Penguin, 1961.

Thomas, H., 'The Spanish Civil War', in J.M. Roberts and A.J.P. Taylor (eds) *Purnell History of the Twentieth Century*, Vol. 4, London: BPC, 1968, pp. 1598–1602.

Townson, D., *Dictionary of Modern History, 1789–1945*, London, Penguin, 1995.

Turner Jnr, H.A. (ed.) *Reappraisals of Fascism*, New York, New Viewpoints, 1975.

*Uomini*, Milan, December 1935. Mazzoni Pamphlet Collection, Duke University, 1996. Available online at http://scriptorium.lib.duke.edu/mazzoni/exhibit/earlyfascism/A90.html [accessed 15 May 2001].

Vasiliev, S., 'Either us or them! The national idea against Zionism', *Pamyat* website, undated but online on 1 April 2001. Available online at http://www.pamyat.org/about.html.

Weiss, J., *Conservatism in Europe 1770–1945*, London, Thomas & Hudson, 1977.

Whittam, J., *Fascist Italy*, Manchester, Manchester University Press, 1995.

Wilford, R., 'Fascism', in R. Eccleshall, V. Geoghegan, R. Jay and R. Wilford, *Political Ideologies*, London, Hutchinson, 1986, pp. 217–50.

Woolf, S.J. (ed.) *The Nature of Fascism*, London, Weidenfeld & Nicolson, 1968.

# INDEX

404